DIGITAL DESIGN

THIRD EDITION

M. Morris Mano
CALIFORNIA STATE UNIVERSITY, LOS ANGELES

Prentice Hall
Upper Saddle River, NJ 07458

Library of Congress Cataloging-in-Publication Data
CIP Data on file.

Vice President and Editorial Director, ECS: *Marcia J. Horton*
Publisher: *Tom Robbins*
Acquisitions Editor: *Eric Frank*
Editorial Assistant: *Jessica Romeo*
Vice President and Director of Production and Manufacturing, ESM: *David W. Riccardi*
Executive Managing Editor: *Vince O'Brien*
Managing Editor: *David A. George*
Production Editor: *Lakshmi Balasubramanian*
Director of Creative Services: *Paul Belfanti*
Creative Director: *Carole Anson*
Art Director and Cover Designer: *Jonathan Boylan*
Art Editor: *Adam Velthaus*
Manufacturing Manager: *Trudy Pisciotti*
Manufacturing Buyer: *Lisa McDowell*
Marketing Manager: *Holly Stark*
Marketing Assistant: *Karen Moon*

© 2002, 1991, 1984 by Prentice-Hall, Inc.
Pearson Education
Upper Saddle River, New Jersey 07458

Verilogger Pro and SynaptiCAD are trademarks of SynaptiCAD, Inc., Blacksburg, VA 24062–0608.

Printed in the United States of America

Reprinted with corrections September, 2002.

10   9   8   7   6   5   4

ISBN 0-13-062121-8

Prentice-Hall International (UK) Limited, *London*
Prentice-Hall of Australia Pty. Limited, *Sydney*
Prentice-Hall of Canada, Inc., *Toronto*
Prentice-Hall Hispanoamericana, S. A., *Mexico City*
Prentice-Hall of India Private Limited, *New Delhi*
Prentice-Hall of Japan, Inc., *Tokyo*
Pearson Asia Pte. Ltd., *Singapore*
Editora Prentice-Hall do Brasil, Ltda., *Rio de Janeiro*

To My Wife, Children, and Grandchildren

CONTENTS

PREFACE

Digital design is concerned with the design of digital electronic circuits. Digital circuits are employed in the design and construction of systems such as digital computers, data communication, digital recording, and many other applications that require digital hardware. This book presents the basic tools for the design of digital circuits and provides the fundamental concepts used in the design of digital systems. It is suitable for use as a textbook in an introductory course in an electrical engineering, computer engineering, or computer science curriculum.

Many of the features in this third edition remain the same as those of the previous editions except for rearrangement of the material or changes in emphasis due to changes in the technology. Combinational circuits are covered in one chapter instead of two, as in the previous edition. The sequential circuit chapter emphasizes design with *D* flip-flops instead of *JK* and *SR* flip-flops. The material on memory and programmable logic are combined in one chapter. Chapter 8 has been revised to include register transfer level (RTL) design procedures.

The main revision in the third edition is the inclusion of sections on Verilog Hardware Description Language (HDL). The HDL material is inserted in separate sections so it can be covered or skipped as desired. The presentation is at a suitable level for beginning students that are learning digital circuits and a hardware description language at the same time.

- Digital circuits are introduced in Chapters 1 through 3 with an introduction to Verilog HDL in Section 3-9.
- Further discussion of HDL occurs in Section 4-11 following the study of combinational circuits.
- Sequential circuits are covered in Chapters 5 and 6 with corresponding HDL examples in Sections 5-5 and 6-6.
- The HDL description of memory is presented in Section 7-2.

- The RTL symbols used in Verilog HDL are introduced in Sections 8-2.
- Examples of HDL descriptions in the RTL and structural level are provided in Sections 8-5 and 8-8.
- Section 10-10 covers switch-level modeling corresponding to CMOS circuits.
- Section 11-19 supplements the hardware experiments of Chapter 11 with HDL experiments. Now the circuits designed in the laboratory can be checked by means of hardware components and/or by HDL simulation.

The CD-ROM in the back of the book contains the Verilog HDL source code files for the examples in the book and two simulators provided by SynaptiCAD. The first simulator is Ver-iLogger Pro, a traditional Verilog simulator that can be used to simulate the HDL examples in the book and to verify the solutions of HDL problems. The second is a new type of simulation technology, called an Interactive Simulator. This simulator allows engineers to simulate and analyze design ideas before a complete simulation model or schematic is available. This technology is particularly useful for students, because they can quickly enter Boolean and D flip-flop or latch input equations to check equivalency or to experiment with flip-flops and latch designs. Tutorials are available as HTML files in the CD-ROM Flash display and as MS Word files in the SynaptiCAD installed directory under Book Tutorials.

Additional resources are available in a companion Website at http//www. prenhall.com/mano. It includes all the Verilog HDL examples from the book for downloading, all of the figures and tables in the book in PDF format, tutorials on the use of the Verilog software in the CD-ROM, and more.

The following is a brief description of the topics that are covered in each chapter with emphasis on the revisions that were made for the third edition.

Chapter 1 presents the various binary systems suitable for representing information in digital systems. The binary number system is explained and binary codes are illustrated. Examples are given for addition and subtraction of signed binary numbers and decimal numbers in BCD.

Chapter 2 introduces the basic postulates of Boolean algebra and shows the correlation between Boolean expressions and their corresponding logic diagrams. All possible logic operations for two variables are investigated and from that, the most useful logic gates used in the design of digital systems are determined. The characteristics of integrated circuit gates are mentioned in this chapter but a more detailed analysis of the electronic circuits of the gates is done in Chapter 10.

Chapter 3 covers the map method for simplifying Boolean expressions. The map method is also used to simplify digital circuits constructed with AND-OR, NAND, or NOR gates. All other possible two-level gate circuits are considered and their method of implementation is explained. Verilog HDL is introduced together with simple gate-level modeling examples.

Chapter 4 outlines the formal procedures for the analysis and design of combinational circuits. Some basic components used in the design of digital systems, such as adders and code converters, are introduced as design examples. Frequently used digital logic functions such as parallel adder and subtractor, decoders, encoders, and multiplexers are explained, and their use in the design of combinational circuits is illustrated. HDL examples are given in the gate-level, dataflow, and behavioral modeling to show the alternative ways available for describing combinational circuits in Verilog HDL. The procedure for writing a simple test bench to provide stimulus to an HDL design is presented.

Chapter 5 outlines the formal procedures for the analysis and design of clocked synchronous sequential circuits. The gate structure of several types of flip-flops is presented together with a discussion on the difference between level and edge triggering. Specific examples are used to show the derivation of the state table and state diagram when analyzing a sequential circuit. A number of design examples are presented with emphasis on sequential circuits that use D-type flip-flops. Behavioral modeling in Verilog HDL for sequential circuits is explained. HDL Examples are given to illustrate Mealy and Moore models of sequential circuits.

Chapter 6 deals with various sequential circuits components such as registers, shift registers, and counters. These digital components are the basic building blocks from which more complex digital systems are constructed. HDL descriptions of shift registers and counter are presented.

Chapter 7 deals with random access memory (RAM) and programmable logic devices. Memory decoding and error correction schemes are discussed. Combinational and sequential programmable devices are presented such as ROM, PAL, CPLD, and FPGA.

Chapter 8 deals with the register transfer level (RTL) representation of digital systems. The algorithmic state machine (ASM) chart is introduced. A number of examples demonstrate the use of the ASM chart, RTL representation, and HDL description in the design of digital systems. This chapter is the most important chapter in the book as it prepares the student for more advanced design projects.

Chapter 9 presents formal procedures for the analysis and design of asynchronous sequential circuits. Methods are outlined to show how an asynchronous sequential circuit can be implemented as a combinational circuit with feedback. An alternate implementation is also described that uses SR latches as the storage elements in asynchronous sequential circuits.

Chapter 10 presents the most common integrated circuit digital logic families. The electronic circuits of the common gate in each family is analyzed using electrical circuit theory. A basic knowledge of electronic circuits is necessary to fully understand the material in this chapter. Examples of Verilog switch-level descriptions demonstrate the ability to simulate circuits constructed with MOS and CMOS transistors.

Chapter 11 outlines experiments that can be performed in the laboratory with hardware that is readily available commercially. The operation of the integrated circuits used in the experiments is explained by referring to diagrams of similar components introduced in previous chapters. Each experiment is presented informally and the student is expected to produce the circuit diagram and formulate a procedure for checking the operation of the circuit in the laboratory. The last section supplements the experiments with corresponding HDL experiments. Instead of, or in addition to, the hardware construction, the student can use the Verilog HDL software provided on the CD-ROM to simulate and check the design.

Chapter 12 presents the standard graphic symbols for logic functions recommended by an ANSI/IEEE standard. These graphic symbols have been developed for SSI and MSI components so that the user can recognize each function from the unique graphic symbol assigned. The chapter shows the standard graphic symbols of the integrated circuits used in the laboratory experiments. The various digital components that are represented throughout the book are similar to commercial integrated circuits. However, the text does not mention specific integrated circuits except in Chapters 11 and 12. The practical application of digital design will be enhanced by doing the suggested experiments in Chapter 11 while studying the theory presented in the text.

Each chapter has a list of references and a set of problems. Answers to selected problems appear in at the end of the book to aid the student and to help the independent reader. A solutions manual is available for the instructor from the publisher.

I would like to thank Charles Kime for introducing me to Verilog. My greatest thanks go to Jack Levine for guiding me and checking the sections, examples, and problem solutions to all Verilog HDL material. Thanks go to Tom Robbins for helping me decide to write the third edition and my editor Eric Frank for his patience throughout the revision. Appreciation goes to Gary Covington and Donna Mitchell for providing the CD-ROM from SynaptiCad. Thanks also to those who reviewed the third edition: Thomas G. Johnson, *California State University*; Umit Uyar, *City University of New York*; Thomas L. Drake, *Clemson University*; and Richard Molyet, *University of Toledo*. Finally, I am grateful to my wife Sandra for encouraging me to pursue this project.

M. MORRIS MANO

1 Binary Systems

1-1 DIGITAL SYSTEMS

Digital systems have such a prominent role in everyday life that we refer to the present technological period as the digital age. Digital systems are used in communication, business transactions, traffic control, space guidance, medical treatment, weather monitoring, the Internet, and many other commercial, industrial, and scientific enterprises. We have digital telephones, digital television, digital versatile discs, digital cameras, and of course, digital computers. The most striking property of the digital computer is its generality. It can follow a sequence of instructions, called a program, that operates on given data. The user can specify and change the program or the data according to the specific need. Because of this flexibility, general-purpose digital computers can perform a variety of information processing tasks that range over a wide spectrum of applications.

One characteristic of digital systems is their ability to manipulate discrete elements of information. Any set that is restricted to a finite number of elements contains discrete information. Examples of discrete sets are the 10 decimal digits, the 26 letters of the alphabet, the 52 playing cards, and the 64 squares of a chessboard. Early digital computers were used for numeric computations. In this case, the discrete elements used were the digits. From this application, the term *digital* computer emerged. Discrete elements of information are represented in a digital system by physical quantities called signals. Electrical signals such as voltages and currents are the most common. Electronic devices called transistors predominate in the circuitry that implements these signals. The signals in most present-day electronic digital systems use just two discrete values and are therefore said to be *binary*. A binary digit, called a *bit*, has two values: 0 and 1. Discrete elements of information are represented with groups of bits called *binary codes*. For example, the decimal digits 0 through 9 are represented in a digital system with a code of four bits. By using various techniques, groups of bits can be made

1

to represent discrete symbols, which are then used to develop the system in a digital format. Thus, a digital system is a system that manipulates discrete elements of information that is represented internally in binary form.

Discrete quantities of information either emerge from the nature of the data being processed or may be quantized from a continuous process. For example, a payroll schedule is an inherently discrete process that contains employee names, social security numbers, weekly salaries, income taxes, and so on. An employee's paycheck is processed using discrete data values such as letters of the alphabet (names), digits (salary), and special symbols (such as $). On the other hand, a research scientist may observe a continuous process, but record only specific quantities in tabular form. The scientist is thus quantizing his continuous data, making each number in his table a discrete quantity. In many cases, the quantization of a process can be performed automatically by an analog-to-digital converter.

The general-purpose digital computer is the best-known example of a digital system. The major parts of a computer are a memory unit, a central processing unit, and input-output units. The memory unit stores programs as well as input, output, and intermediate data. The central processing unit performs arithmetic and other data processing operations as specified by the program. The program and data prepared by a user are transferred into memory by means of an input device such as a keyboard. An output device, such as a printer, receives the results of the computations and the printed results are presented to the user. A digital computer can accommodate many input and output devices. One very useful device is a communication unit that provides interaction with other users through the Internet. A digital computer is a powerful instrument and can perform not only arithmetic computations, but also logical operations. In addition, it can be programmed to make decisions based on internal and external conditions.

There are fundamental reasons why commercial products are made with digital circuits. Like a digital computer, most digital devices are programmable. By changing the program in a programmable device, the same underlying hardware can be used for many different applications. Dramatic cost reductions in digital devices have come about because of the advances in digital integrated circuit technology. As the number of transistors that can be put on a piece of silicon increases to produce complex functions, the cost per unit decreases and digital devices can be bought at an increasingly reduced price. Equipment built with digital integrated circuits can perform at a speed of hundreds of millions of operations per second. Digital systems can be made to operate with extreme reliability by using error-correcting codes. An example of this is the digital versatile disk (DVD) in which digital information representing video, audio, and other data is recorded without a loss of a single item. Digital information on a DVD is recorded in such a way that by examining the code in each digital sample before it is played back, any error can be automatically identified and corrected.

A digital system is an interconnection of digital modules. To understand the operation of each digital module, it is necessary to have a basic knowledge of digital circuits and their logical function. The first seven chapters of this book present the basic tools of digital design such as logic gate structures, combinational and sequential circuits, and programmable logic devices. Chapter 8 introduces digital design at the register transfer level (RTL). Chapters 9 and 10 deal with asynchronous sequential circuits and the various integrated digital logic families. Chapters 11 and 12 introduce commercial integrated circuits and show how they can be connected in the laboratory to perform experiments with digital circuits.

An important trend in digital design is the use of hardware description language (HDL). HDL resembles a programming language and is suitable for describing digital circuits in textual form. It is used to simulate a digital system to verify its operation before hardware is built in. It is also used in conjunction with logic synthesis tools to automate the design. HDL descriptions of digital circuits are presented throughout the book.

As previously stated, digital systems manipulate discrete quantities of information that are represented in binary form. Operands used for calculations may be expressed in the binary number system. Other discrete elements, including the decimal digits, are represented in binary codes. Data processing is carried out by means of binary logic elements using binary signals. Quantities are stored in binary storage elements. The purpose of this chapter is to introduce the various binary concepts as a frame of reference for further study in the succeeding chapters.

1-2 BINARY NUMBERS

A decimal number such as 7,392 represents a quantity equal to 7 thousands plus 3 hundreds, plus 9 tens, plus 2 units. The thousands, hundreds, etc. are powers of 10 implied by the position of the coefficients. To be more exact, 7,392 should be written as

$$7 \times 10^3 + 3 \times 10^2 + 9 \times 10^1 + 2 \times 10^0$$

However, the convention is to write only the coefficients and from their position deduce the necessary powers of 10. In general, a number with a decimal point is represented by a series of coefficients as follows:

$$a_5 a_4 a_3 a_2 a_1 a_0 \cdot a_{-1} a_{-2} a_{-3}$$

The a_j coefficients are any of the 10 digits $(0, 1, 2, \ldots, 9)$, and the subscript value j gives the place value and, hence, the power of 10 by which the coefficient must be multiplied. This can be expressed as

$$10^5 a_5 + 10^4 a_4 + 10^3 a_3 + 10^2 a_2 + 10^1 a_1 + 10^0 a_0 + 10^{-1} a_{-1} + 10^{-2} a_{-2} + 10^{-3} a_{-3}$$

The decimal number system is said to be of *base,* or *radix,* 10 because it uses 10 digits and the coefficients are multiplied by powers of 10. The *binary* system is a different number system. The coefficients of the binary numbers system have only two possible values: 0 or 1. Each coefficient a_j is multiplied by 2^j. For example, the decimal equivalent of the binary number 11010.11 is 26.75, as shown from the multiplication of the coefficients by powers of 2:

$$1 \times 2^4 + 1 \times 2^3 + 0 \times 2^2 + 1 \times 2^1 + 0 \times 2^0 + 1 \times 2^{-1} + 1 \times 2^{-2} = 26.75$$

In general, a number expressed in a base-r system has coefficients multiplied by powers of r:

$$a_n \cdot r^n + a_{n-1} \cdot r^{n-1} + \ldots + a_2 \cdot r^2 + a_1 \cdot r + a_0 + a_{-1} \cdot r^{-1} + a_{-2} \cdot r^{-2} + \ldots + a_{-m} \cdot r^{-m}$$

The coefficients a_j range in value from 0 to $r - 1$. To distinguish between numbers of different bases, we enclose the coefficients in parentheses and write a subscript equal to the base used (except sometimes for decimal numbers, where the content makes it obvious that it is decimal). An example of a base-5 number is

$$(4021.2)_5 = 4 \times 5^3 + 0 \times 5^2 + 2 \times 5^1 + 1 \times 5^0 + 2 \times 5^{-1} = (511.4)_{10}$$

The coefficient values for base 5 can be only 0, 1, 2, 3, and 4. The octal number system is a base-8 system that has eight digits: 0, 1, 2, 3, 4, 5, 6, 7. An example of an octal number is 127.4. To determine its equivalent decimal value, we expand the number in a power series with a base of 8:

$$(127.4)_8 = 1 \times 8^2 + 2 \times 8^1 + 7 \times 8^0 + 4 \times 8^{-1} = (87.5)_{10}$$

Note that the digits 8 and 9 cannot appear in an octal number.

It is customary to borrow the needed r digits for the coefficients from the decimal system when the base of the number is less than 10. The letters of the alphabet are used to supplement the 10 decimal digits when the base of the number is greater than 10. For example, in the *hexadecimal* (base 16) number system, the first ten digits are borrowed from the decimal system. The letters A, B, C, D, E, and F are used for digits 10, 11, 12, 13, 14, and 15, respectively. An example of a hexadecimal number is

$$(B65F)_{16} = 11 \times 16^3 + 6 \times 16^2 + 5 \times 16^1 + 15 \times 16^0 = (46,687)_{10}$$

As noted before, the digits in a binary number are called *bits*. When a bit is equal to 0, it does not contribute to the sum during the conversion. Therefore, the conversion from binary to decimal can be obtained by adding the numbers with powers of two corresponding to the bits that are equal to 1. For example,

$$(110101)_2 = 32 + 16 + 4 + 1 = (53)_{10}$$

There are four 1's in the binary number. The corresponding decimal number is the sum of the four powers of two numbers. The first 24 numbers obtained from 2 to the power of n are listed in Table 1-1. In computer work, 2^{10} is referred to as K(kilo), 2^{20} as M(mega), 2^{30} as G(giga), and 2^{40} as T(tera). Thus $4K = 2^{12} = 4096$ and $16M = 2^{24} = 16,777,216$. Computer capacity is usually given in bytes. A *byte* is equal to eight bits and can accommodate one keyboard character. A computer hard disk with 4 gigabytes of storage has a capacity of $4G = 2^{32}$ bytes (approximately 4 billion bytes).

Arithmetic operations with numbers in base r follow the same rules as for decimal numbers. When a base other than the familiar base 10 is used, one must be careful to use only the

Table 1-1
Powers of Two

n	2^n	n	2^n	n	2^n
0	1	8	256	16	65,536
1	2	9	512	17	131,072
2	4	10	1,024	18	262,144
3	8	11	2,048	19	524,288
4	16	12	4,096	20	1,048,576
5	32	13	8,192	21	2,097,152
6	64	14	16,384	22	4,194,304
7	128	15	32,768	23	8,388,608

r-allowable digits. Examples of addition, subtraction, and multiplication of two binary numbers are as follows:

augend:	101101	minuend:	101101	multiplicand:	1011
addend:	+100111	subtrahend:	−100111	multiplier:	× 101
sum:	1010100	difference:	000110		1011
					0000
					1011
				product:	110111

The sum of two binary numbers is calculated by the same rules as in decimal, except that the digits of the sum in any significant position can be only 0 or 1. Any carry obtained in a given significant position is used by the pair of digits one significant position higher. The subtraction is slightly more complicated. The rules are still the same as in decimal, except that the borrow in a given significant position adds 2 to a minuend digit. (A borrow in the decimal system adds 10 to a minuend digit.) Multiplication is very simple. The multiplier digits are always 1 or 0. Therefore, the partial products are equal either to the multiplicand or to 0.

1-3   NUMBER BASE CONVERSIONS

The conversion of a number in base *r* to decimal is done by expanding the number in a power series and adding all the terms as shown previously. We now present a general procedure for the reverse operation of converting a decimal number to a number in base *r*. If the number includes a radix point, it is necessary to separate the number into an integer part and a fraction part, since each part must be converted differently. The conversion of a decimal integer to a number in base *r* is done by dividing the number and all successive quotients by *r* and accumulating the remainders. This procedure is best illustrated by example.

EXAMPLE 1-1

Convert decimal 41 to binary. First, 41 is divided by 2 to give an integer quotient of 20 and a remainder of $\frac{1}{2}$. The quotient is again divided by 2 to give a new quotient and remainder. This process is continued until the integer quotient becomes 0. The *coefficients* of the desired binary number are obtained from the *remainders* as follows:

	Integer Quotient		Remainder	Coefficient
$41/2 =$	20	+	$\frac{1}{2}$	$a_0 = 1$
$20/2 =$	10	+	0	$a_1 = 0$
$10/2 =$	5	+	0	$a_2 = 0$
$5/2 =$	2	+	$\frac{1}{2}$	$a_3 = 1$
$2/2 =$	1	+	0	$a_4 = 0$
$1/2 =$	0	+	$\frac{1}{2}$	$a_5 = 1$

Therefore, the answer is $(41)_{10} = (a_5 a_4 a_3 a_2 a_1 a_0)_2 = (101001)_2$

The arithmetic process can be manipulated more conveniently as follows:

Integer	Remainder
41	
20	1
10	0
5	0
2	1
1	0
0	1

101001 = answer

The conversion from decimal integers to any base-r system is similar to the example, except that division is done by r instead of 2.

■

EXAMPLE 1-2

Convert decimal 153 to octal. The required base r is 8. First, 153 is divided by 8 to give an integer quotient of 19 and a remainder of 1. Then 19 is divided by 8 to give an integer quotient of 2 and a remainder of 3. Finally, 2 is divided by 8 to give a quotient of 0 and a remainder of 2. This process can be conveniently manipulated as follows:

153	
19	1
2	3
0	2

$= (231)_8$

The conversion of a decimal *fraction* to binary is accomplished by a method similar to that used for integers. However, multiplication is used instead of division, and integers are accumulated instead of remainders. Again, the method is best explained by example.

■

EXAMPLE 1-3

Convert $(0.6875)_{10}$ to binary. First, 0.6875 is multiplied by 2 to give an integer and a fraction. The new fraction is multiplied by 2 to give a new integer and a new fraction. This process is continued until the fraction becomes 0 or until the number of digits have sufficient accuracy. The coefficients of the binary number are obtained from the integers as follows:

	Integer		Fraction	Coefficient
$0.6875 \times 2 =$	1	+	0.3750	$a_{-1} = 1$
$0.3750 \times 2 =$	0	+	0.7500	$a_{-2} = 0$
$0.7500 \times 2 =$	1	+	0.5000	$a_{-3} = 1$
$0.5000 \times 2 =$	1	+	0.0000	$a_{-4} = 1$

Therefore, the answer is $(0.6875)_{10} = \left(0.a_{-1} a_{-2} a_{-3} a_{-4}\right)_2 = (0.1011)_2$

To convert a decimal fraction to a number expressed in base r, a similar procedure is used. Multiplication is by r instead of 2, and the coefficients found from the integers may range in value from 0 to $r - 1$ instead of 0 and 1.

■

EXAMPLE 1-4

Convert $(0.513)_{10}$ to octal.

$$0.513 \times 8 = 4.104$$
$$0.104 \times 8 = 0.832$$
$$0.832 \times 8 = 6.656$$
$$0.656 \times 8 = 5.248$$
$$0.248 \times 8 = 1.984$$
$$0.984 \times 8 = 7.872$$

The answer, to seven significant figures, is obtained from the integer part of the products

$$(0.513)_{10} = (0.406517\ldots)_8$$

The conversion of decimal numbers with both integer and fraction parts is done by converting the integer and the fraction separately and then combining the two answers. Using the results of Examples 1-1 and 1-3, we obtain

$$(41.6875)_{10} = (101001.1011)_2$$

From Examples 1-2 and 1-4, we have

$$(153.513)_{10} = (231.406517)_8$$

■

1-4 OCTAL AND HEXADECIMAL NUMBERS

The conversion from and to binary, octal, and hexadecimal plays an important role in digital computers. Since $2^3 = 8$ and $2^4 = 16$, each octal digit corresponds to three binary digits and each hexadecimal digit corresponds to four binary digits. The first 16 numbers in the decimal, binary, octal, and hexadecimal number systems are listed in Table 1-2.

The conversion from binary to octal is easily accomplished by partitioning the binary number into groups of three digits each, starting from the binary point and proceeding to the left and to the right. The corresponding octal digit is then assigned to each group. The following example illustrates the procedure:

$$(\underset{2}{10}\ \ \underset{6}{110}\ \ \underset{1}{001}\ \ \underset{5}{101}\ \ \underset{3}{011}\ \cdot\ \underset{7}{111}\ \ \underset{4}{100}\ \ \underset{0}{000}\ \ \underset{6}{110})_2 = (26153.7406)_8$$

Table 1-2
Numbers with Different Bases

Decimal (base 10)	Binary (base 2)	Octal (base 8)	Hexadecimal (base 16)
00	0000	00	0
01	0001	01	1
02	0010	02	2
03	0011	03	3
04	0100	04	4
05	0101	05	5
06	0110	06	6
07	0111	07	7
08	1000	10	8
09	1001	11	9
10	1010	12	A
11	1011	13	B
12	1100	14	C
13	1101	15	D
14	1110	16	E
15	1111	17	F

Conversion from binary to hexadecimal is similar, except that the binary number is divided into groups of four digits:

$$(\underset{2}{10} \quad \underset{C}{1100} \quad \underset{6}{0110} \quad \underset{B}{1011} \cdot \underset{F}{1111} \quad \underset{2}{0010})_2 = (2C6B.F2)_{16}$$

The corresponding hexadecimal (or octal) digit for each group of binary digits is easily remembered after studying the values listed in Table 1-2.

Conversion from octal or hexadecimal to binary is done by reversing the preceding procedure. Each octal digit is converted to its three-digit binary equivalent. Similarly, each hexadecimal digit is converted to its four-digit binary equivalent. This is illustrated in the following examples:

$$(673.124)_8 = (\underset{6}{110} \quad \underset{7}{111} \quad \underset{3}{011} \cdot \underset{1}{001} \quad \underset{2}{010} \quad \underset{4}{100})_2$$

and

$$(306.D)_{16} = (\underset{3}{0011} \quad \underset{0}{0000} \quad \underset{6}{0110} \cdot \underset{D}{1101})_2$$

Binary numbers are difficult to work with because they require three or four times as many digits as their decimal equivalent. For example, the binary number 111111111111 is equivalent to decimal 4095. However, digital computers use binary numbers and it is sometimes necessary for the human operator or user to communicate directly with the machine by means of binary numbers. One scheme that retains the binary system in the computer, but reduces the number of digits the human must consider, utilizes the relationship between the binary number system and the octal or hexadecimal system. By this method, the human thinks in terms of octal or hexadecimal numbers and performs the required conversion by inspection when direct communication with the machine is necessary. Thus the binary number 111111111111 has 12 digits and is expressed in octal as 7777 (four digits) or in hexadecimal as FFF (three digits). During communication between people (about binary numbers in the computer), the octal or hexadecimal representation is more desirable because it can be expressed more compactly with a third or a quarter of the number of digits required for the equivalent binary number. Thus, most computer manuals use either octal or hexadecimal numbers to specify binary quantities. The choice between them is arbitrary, although hexadecimal tends to win out, since it can represent a byte with two digits.

1-5 COMPLEMENTS

Complements are used in digital computers for simplifying the subtraction operation and for logical manipulation. There are two types of complements for each base-r system: the radix complement and the diminished radix complement. The first is referred to as the r's complement and the second as the $(r-1)$'s complement. When the value of the base r is substituted in the name, the two types are referred to as the 2's complement and 1's complement for binary numbers, and the 10's complement and 9's complement for decimal numbers.

Diminished Radix Complement

Given a number N in base r having n digits, the $(r-1)$'s complement of N is defined as $(r^n - 1) - N$. For decimal numbers, $r = 10$ and $r - 1 = 9$, so the 9's complement of N is $(10^n - 1) - N$. In this case, 10^n represents a number that consists of a single 1 followed by n 0s. $10^n - 1$ is a number represented by n 9s. For example, if $n = 4$, we have $10^4 = 10,000$ and $10^4 - 1 = 9999$. It follows that the 9's complement of a decimal number is obtained by subtracting each digit from 9. Some numerical examples follow:

The 9's complement of 546700 is $999999 - 546700 = 453299$.

The 9's complement of 012398 is $999999 - 012398 = 987601$.

For binary numbers, $r = 2$ and $r - 1 = 1$, so the 1's complement of N is $(2^n - 1) - N$. Again, 2^n is represented by a binary number that consists of a 1 followed by n 0s. $2^n - 1$ is a binary number represented by n 1's. For example, if $n = 4$, we have $2^4 = (10000)_2$ and $2^4 - 1 = (1111)_2$. Thus the 1's complement of a binary number is obtained by subtracting each digit from 1. However, when subtracting binary digits from 1, we can have either $1 - 0 = 1$ or $1 - 1 = 0$, which causes the bit to change from 0 to 1 or from 1 to 0. Therefore, the 1's complement of a binary number is formed by changing 1's to 0's and 0's to 1's. The following are some numerical examples:

The 1's complement of 1011000 is 0100111.

The 1's complement of 0101101 is 1010010.

The $(r - 1)$'s complement of octal or hexadecimal numbers is obtained by subtracting each digit from 7 or F (decimal 15), respectively.

Radix Complement

The r's complement of an n-digit number N in base r is defined as $r^n - N$, for $N \neq 0$ and 0 for $N = 0$. Comparing with the $(r - 1)$'s complement, we note that the r's complement is obtained by adding 1 to the $(r - 1)$'s complement since $r^n - N = [(r^n - 1) - N] + 1$. Thus, the 10's complement of decimal 2389 is $7610 + 1 = 7611$ and is obtained by adding 1 to the 9's-complement value. The 2's complement of binary 101100 is $010011 + 1 = 010100$ and is obtained by adding 1 to the 1's-complement value.

Since 10^n is a number represented by a 1 followed by n 0's, $10^n - N$, which is the 10's complement of N, can be formed also by leaving all least significant 0's unchanged, subtracting the first nonzero least significant digit from 10, and subtracting all higher significant digits from 9.

The 10's complement of 012398 is 987602.

The 10's complement of 246700 is 753300.

The 10's complement of the first number is obtained by subtracting 8 from 10 in the least significant position and subtracting all other digits from 9. The 10's complement of the second number is obtained by leaving the two least significant 0's unchanged, subtracting 7 from 10, and subtracting the other three digits from 9.

Similarly, the 2's complement can be formed by leaving all least significant 0's and the first 1 unchanged, and replacing 1's with 0's and 0's with 1's in all other higher significant digits.

The 2's complement of 1101100 is 0010100.

The 2's complement of 0110111 is 1001001.

The 2's complement of the first number is obtained by leaving the two least significant 0's and the first 1 unchanged, and then replacing 1's with 0's and 0's with 1's in the other four most-significant digits. The 2's complement of the second number is obtained by leaving the least significant 1 unchanged and complementing all other digits.

In the previous definitions, it was assumed that the numbers did not have a radix point. If the original number N contains a radix point, the point should be removed temporarily in order to form the r's or $(r - 1)$'s complement. The radix point is then restored to the complemented number in the same relative position. It is also worth mentioning that the complement of the complement restores the number to its original value. The r's complement of N is $r^n - N$. The complement of the complement is $r^n - (r^n - N) = N$, and is equal to the original number.

Subtraction with Complements

The direct method of subtraction taught in elementary schools uses the borrow concept. In this method, we borrow a 1 from a higher significant position when the minuend digit is smaller than the subtrahend digit. The method works well when people perform subtraction with paper and pencil. However, when subtraction is implemented with digital hardware, the method is less efficient than the method that uses complements.

The subtraction of two n-digit unsigned numbers $M - N$ in base r can be done as follows:

1. Add the minuend, M, to the r's complement of the subtrahend, N. This performs $M + (r^n - N) = M - N + r^n$.

2. If $M \geq N$, the sum will produce an end carry, r^n, which can be discarded; what is left is the result $M - N$.

3. If $M < N$, the sum does not produce an end carry and is equal to $r^n - (N - M)$, which is the r's complement of $(N - M)$. To obtain the answer in a familiar form, take the r's complement of the sum and place a negative sign in front.

The following examples illustrate the procedure:

EXAMPLE 1-5

Using 10's complement, subtract $72532 - 3250$.

$$
\begin{aligned}
M &= 72532 \\
\text{10's complement of } N &= +\ \underline{96750} \\
\text{Sum} &= 169282 \\
\text{Discard end carry } 10^5 &= -\underline{100000} \\
Answer &= 69282
\end{aligned}
$$

■

Note that M has 5 digits and N has only 4 digits. Both numbers must have the same number of digits, so we write N as 03250. Taking the 10's complement of N produces a 9 in the most significant position. The occurrence of the end carry signifies that $M \geq N$ and that the result is positive.

EXAMPLE 1-6

Using 10's complement, subtract $3250 - 72532$.

$$
\begin{aligned}
M &= 03250 \\
\text{10's complement of } N &= +\ \underline{27468} \\
\text{Sum} &= 30718
\end{aligned}
$$

There is no end carry.
Therefore, the answer is $-$(10's complement of 30718) $= -69282$

■

Note that since $3250 < 72532$, the result is negative. Since we are dealing with unsigned numbers, there is really no way to get an unsigned result for this case. When subtracting with complements, the negative answer is recognized from the absence of the end carry and the complemented result. When working with paper and pencil, we can change the answer to a signed negative number in order to put it in a familiar form.

Subtraction with complements is done with binary numbers in a similar manner using the procedure outlined previously.

EXAMPLE 1-7

Given the two binary numbers $X = 1010100$ and $Y = 1000011$, perform the subtraction (a) $X - Y$ and (b) $Y - X$ using 2's complements.

$$
\begin{array}{rr}
\textbf{(a)} \qquad\qquad X = & 1010100 \\
\text{2's complement of } Y = & +\ \underline{0111101} \\
\text{Sum} = & 10010001 \\
\text{Discard end carry } 2^7 = & -\underline{10000000} \\
\textit{Answer: } X - Y = & 0010001 \\
\end{array}
$$

$$
\begin{array}{rr}
\textbf{(b)} \qquad\qquad Y = & 1000011 \\
\text{2's complement of } X = & +\ \underline{0101100} \\
\text{Sum} = & 1101111 \\
\end{array}
$$

There is no end carry.
Therefore, the answer is $Y - X = -(2\text{'s complement of } 1101111) = -0010001$

■

Subtraction of unsigned numbers can also be done by means of the $(r - 1)$'s complement. Remember that the $(r - 1)$'s complement is one less than the r's complement. Because of this, the result of adding the minuend to the complement of the subtrahend produces a sum that is 1 less than the correct difference when an end carry occurs. Removing the end carry and adding 1 to the sum is referred to as an *end-around carry*.

EXAMPLE 1-8

Repeat Example 1-7 using 1's complement.

(a) $X - Y = 1010100 - 1000011$

$$
\begin{array}{rr}
X = & 1010100 \\
\text{1's complement of } Y = & +\ \underline{0111100} \\
\text{Sum} = & 10010000 \\
\text{End-around carry} = & +\ \underline{\qquad\quad 1} \\
\textit{Answer: } X - Y = & 0010001 \\
\end{array}
$$

(b) $Y - X = 1000011 - 1010100$

$$
\begin{array}{rr}
Y = & 1000011 \\
\text{1's complement of } X = & +\ \underline{0101011} \\
\text{Sum} = & 1101110 \\
\end{array}
$$

There is no end carry.
Therefore, the answer is $Y - X = -(1\text{'s complement of } 1101110) = -0010001$

■

Note that the negative result is obtained by taking the 1's complement of the sum since this is the type of complement used. The procedure with end-around carry is also applicable for subtracting unsigned decimal numbers with 9's complement.

1-6   SIGNED BINARY NUMBERS

Positive integers (including zero) can be represented as unsigned numbers. However, to represent negative integers, we need a notation for negative values. In ordinary arithmetic, a negative number is indicated by a minus sign and a positive number by a plus sign. Because of hardware limitations, computers must represent everything with binary digits. It is customary to represent the sign with a bit placed in the leftmost position of the number. The convention is to make the sign bit 0 for positive and 1 for negative.

It is important to realize that both signed and unsigned binary numbers consist of a string of bits when represented in a computer. The user determines whether the number is signed or unsigned. If the binary number is signed, then the leftmost bit represents the sign and the rest of the bits represent the number. If the binary number is assumed to be unsigned, then the leftmost bit is the most significant bit of the number. For example, the string of bits 01001 can be considered as 9 (unsigned binary) or as +9 (signed binary) because the leftmost bit is 0. The string of bits 11001 represent the binary equivalent of 25 when considered as an unsigned number or as −9 when considered as a signed number. This is because the 1 that is in the leftmost position designates a negative and the other four bits represent binary 9. Usually, there is no confusion in identifying the bits if the type of representation for the number is known in advance.

The representation of the signed numbers in the last example is referred to as the *signed-magnitude* convention. In this notation, the number consists of a magnitude and a symbol (+ or −) or a bit (0 or 1) indicating the sign. This is the representation of signed numbers used in ordinary arithmetic. When arithmetic operations are implemented in a computer, it is more convenient to use a different system for representing negative numbers, referred to as the *signed-complement* system. In this system, a negative number is indicated by its complement. Whereas the signed-magnitude system negates a number by changing its sign, the signed-complement system negates a number by taking its complement. Since positive numbers always start with 0 (plus) in the left-most position, the complement will always start with a 1, indicating a negative number. The signed-complement system can use either the 1's or the 2's complement, but the 2's complement is the most common.

As an example, consider the number 9 represented in binary with eight bits. +9 is represented with a sign bit of 0 in the leftmost position, followed by the binary equivalent of 9, which gives 00001001. Note that all eight bits must have a value and, therefore, 0s are inserted following the sign bit up to the first 1. Although there is only one way to represent +9, there are three different ways to represent −9 with eight bits:

signed-magnitude representation:	10001001
signed-1's-complement representation:	11110110
signed-2's-complement representation:	11110111

In signed-magnitude, −9 is obtained from +9 by changing the sign bit in the leftmost position from 0 to 1. In signed-1's complement, −9 is obtained by complementing all the bits of

Table 1-3
Signed Binary Numbers

Decimal	Signed-2's complement	Signed-1's complement	Signed magnitude
+7	0111	0111	0111
+6	0110	0110	0110
+5	0101	0101	0101
+4	0100	0100	0100
+3	0011	0011	0011
+2	0010	0010	0010
+1	0001	0001	0001
+0	0000	0000	0000
−0	—	1111	1000
−1	1111	1110	1001
−2	1110	1101	1010
−3	1101	1100	1011
−4	1100	1011	1100
−5	1011	1010	1101
−6	1010	1001	1110
−7	1001	1000	1111
−8	1000	—	—

+9, including the sign bit. The signed-2's-complement representation of −9 is obtained by taking the 2's complement of the positive number, including the sign bit.

Table 1-3 lists all possible 4-bit signed binary numbers in the three representations. The equivalent decimal number is also shown for reference. Note that the positive numbers in all three representations are identical and have 0 in the leftmost position. The signed-2's complement system has only one representation for 0, which is always positive. The other two systems have either a positive 0 or a negative 0, which is something not encountered in ordinary arithmetic. Note that all negative numbers have a 1 in the leftmost bit position; this is the way we distinguish them from the positive numbers. With four bits, we can represent 16 binary numbers. In the signed-magnitude and the 1's complement representations, there are eight positive numbers and eight negative numbers, including two zeros. In the 2's complement representation, there are eight positive numbers, including one zero and eight negative numbers.

The signed-magnitude system is used in ordinary arithmetic, but is awkward when employed in computer arithmetic because of the separate handling of the sign and the magnitude. Therefore, the signed-complement is normally used. The 1's complement imposes some difficulties and is seldom used for arithmetic operations. It is useful as a logical operation since the change of 1 to 0 or 0 to 1 is equivalent to a logical complement operation, as will be shown in the next chapter. The following discussion of signed binary arithmetic deals exclusively with the signed-2's-complement representation of negative numbers. The same procedures can be applied to the signed-1's-complement system by including the end-around carry as done with unsigned numbers.

Arithmetic Addition

The addition of two numbers in the signed-magnitude system follows the rules of ordinary arithmetic. If the signs are the same, we add the two magnitudes and give the sum the common sign. If the signs are different, we subtract the smaller magnitude from the larger and give the result the sign of the larger magnitude. For example, $(+25) + (-37) = -(37 - 25) = -12$ and is done by subtracting the smaller magnitude 25 from the larger magnitude 37 and using the sign of 37 for the sign of the result. This is a process that requires the comparison of the signs and the magnitudes and then performing either addition or subtraction. The same procedure applies to binary numbers in signed-magnitude representation. In contrast, the rule for adding numbers in the signed-complement system does not require a comparison or subtraction, but only addition. The procedure is very simple and can be stated as follows for binary numbers:

The addition of two signed binary numbers with negative numbers represented in signed-2's-complement form is obtained from the addition of the two numbers, including their sign bits. A carry out of the sign-bit position is discarded.

Numerical examples for addition follow:

+ 6	00000110		− 6	11111010
+13	00001101		+13	00001101
+19	00010011		+ 7	00000111
+ 6	00000110		−6	11111010
−13	11110011		−13	11110011
− 7	11111001		−19	11101101

Note that negative numbers must be initially in 2's complement and that if the sum obtained after the addition is negative, it is in 2's-complement form.

In each of the four cases, the operation performed is addition with the sign bit included. Any carry out of the sign-bit position is discarded, and negative results are automatically in 2's-complement form.

In order to obtain a correct answer, we must ensure that the result has a sufficient number of bits to accommodate the sum. If we start with two n-bit numbers and the sum occupies $n + 1$ bits, we say that an overflow occurs. When one performs the addition with paper and pencil, an overflow is not a problem, because we are not limited by the width of the page. We just add another 0 to a positive number or another 1 to a negative number in the most-significant position to extend them to $n + 1$ bits and then perform the addition. Overflow is a problem in computers because the number of bits that hold a number is finite, and a result that exceeds the finite value by 1 cannot be accommodated.

The complement form of representing negative numbers is unfamiliar to those used to the signed-magnitude system. To determine the value of a negative number when in signed-2's complement, it is necessary to convert it to a positive number to place it in a more familiar form. For example, the signed binary number 11111001 is negative because the leftmost bit is 1. Its 2's complement is 00000111, which is the binary equivalent of +7. We therefore recognize the original negative number to be equal to −7.

Arithmetic Subtraction

Subtraction of two signed binary numbers when negative numbers are in 2's-complement form is very simple and can be stated as follows:

Take the 2's complement of the subtrahend (including the sign bit) and add it to the minuend (including the sign bit). A carry out of the sign-bit position is discarded.

This procedure occurs because a subtraction operation can be changed to an addition operation if the sign of the subtrahend is changed. This is demonstrated by the following relationship:

$$(\pm A) - (+B) = (\pm A) + (-B);$$
$$(\pm A) - (-B) = (\pm A) + (+B).$$

But changing a positive number to a negative number is easily done by taking its 2's complement. The reverse is also true because the complement of a negative number in complement form produces the equivalent positive number. Consider the subtraction of $(-6) - (-13) = +7$. In binary with eight bits, this is written as $(11111010 - 11110011)$. The subtraction is changed to addition by taking the 2's complement of the subtrahend (-13) to give $(+13)$. In binary, this is $11111010 + 00001101 = 100000111$. Removing the end carry, we obtain the correct answer: $00000111(+7)$.

It is worth noting that binary numbers in the signed-complement system are added and subtracted by the same basic addition and subtraction rules as unsigned numbers. Therefore, computers need only one common hardware circuit to handle both types of arithmetic. The user or programmer must interpret the results of such addition or subtraction differently, depending on whether it is assumed that the numbers are signed or unsigned.

1-7   BINARY CODES

Digital systems use signals that have two distinct values and circuit elements that have two stable states. There is a direct analogy among binary signals, binary circuit elements, and binary digits. A binary number of n digits, for example, may be represented by n binary circuit elements, each having an output signal equivalent to 0 or 1. Digital systems represent and manipulate not only binary numbers, but also many other discrete elements of information. Any discrete element of information distinct among a group of quantities can be represented with a binary code. The codes must be in binary because computers can only hold 1's and 0's. It must be realized that binary codes merely change the symbols, not the meaning of the elements of information that they represent. If we inspect the bits of a computer at random, we will find that most of the time they represent some type of coded information rather than binary numbers.

An n-bit binary code is a group of n bits that assume up to 2^n distinct combinations of 1's and 0's, with each combination representing one element of the set that is being coded. A set of four elements can be coded with two bits, with each element assigned one of the following bit combinations: 00, 01, 10, 11. A set of eight elements requires a 3-bit code and a set of 16 elements requires a 4-bit code. The bit combination of an n-bit code is determined from the count in binary from 0 to $2^n - 1$. Each element must be assigned a unique binary bit combination and no two elements can have the same value; otherwise, the code assignment will be ambiguous.

Although the *minimum* number of bits required to code 2^n distinct quantities is n, there is no *maximum* number of bits that may be used for a binary code. For example, the 10 decimal digits can be coded with 10 bits, and each decimal digit can be assigned a bit combination of nine 0's and a 1. In this particular binary code, the digit 6 is assigned the bit combination 0001000000.

BCD Code

Although the binary number system is the most natural system for a computer, most people are more accustomed to the decimal system. One way to resolve this difference is to convert the decimal numbers to binary, perform all arithmetic calculations in binary, and then convert the binary results back to decimal. This method requires that we store the decimal numbers in the computer so they can be converted to binary. Since the computer can accept only binary values, we must represent the decimal digits by means of a code that contains 1's and 0's. It is also possible to perform the arithmetic operations directly with decimal numbers when they are stored in the computer in coded form.

A binary code will have some unassigned bit combinations if the number of elements in the set is not a multiple power of 2. The 10 decimal digits form such a set. A binary code that distinguishes among 10 elements must contain at least four bits, but 6 out of the 16 possible combinations remain unassigned. Different binary codes can be obtained by arranging four bits in 10 distinct combinations. The code most commonly used for the decimal digits is the straight binary assignment as listed in Table 1-4. This is called binary coded decimal and is commonly referred to as BCD. Other decimal codes are possible and a few of them are presented later in this section.

Table 1-4 gives the 4-bit code for one decimal digit. A number with k decimal digits will require $4k$ bits in BCD. Decimal 396 is represented in BCD with 12 bits as 0011 1001 0110, with each group of 4 bits representing one decimal digit. A decimal number in BCD is the same as its equivalent binary number only when the number is between 0 and 9. A BCD number

Table 1-4
Binary Coded Decimal (BCD)

Decimal symbol	BCD digit
0	0000
1	0001
2	0010
3	0011
4	0100
5	0101
6	0110
7	0111
8	1000
9	1001

greater than 10 looks different than its equivalent binary number, even though both contain 1's and 0's. Moreover, the binary combinations 1010 through 1111 are not used and have no meaning in the BCD code. Consider decimal 185 and its corresponding value in BCD and binary:

$$(185)_{10} = (0001\ 1000\ 0101)_{BCD} = (10111001)_2$$

The BCD value has 12 bits, but the equivalent binary number needs only 8 bits. It is obvious that a BCD number needs more bits than its equivalent binary value. However, there is an advantage in the use of decimal numbers because computer input and output data are generated by people that use the decimal system.

It is important to realize that BCD numbers are decimal numbers and not binary numbers, although they use bits in their representation. The only difference between a decimal number and BCD is that decimals are written with the symbols $0, 1, 2, \ldots, 9$ and BCD numbers use the binary code $0000, 0001, 0010, \ldots, 1001$. The decimal value is exactly the same. Decimal 10 is represented in BCD with eight bits as 0001 0000 and decimal 15 as 0001 0101. The corresponding binary values are 1010 and 1111 and have only four bits.

BCD Addition

Consider the addition of two decimal digits in BCD, together with a possible carry from a previous less significant pair of digits. Since each digit does not exceed 9, the sum cannot be greater than $9 + 9 + 1 = 19$, with the 1 in the sum being a previous carry. Suppose we add the BCD digits as if they were binary numbers. The binary sum will produce a result in the range from 0 to 19. In binary, this will be from 0000 to 10011, but in BCD, it is from 0000 to 1 1001; the first 1 being a carry and the next four bits being the BCD digit sum. When the binary sum is equal to or less than 1001 (without a carry), the corresponding BCD digit is correct. However, when the binary sum is greater than or equal to 1010, the result is an invalid BCD digit. The addition of $6 = (0110)_2$ to the binary sum converts it to the correct digit and also produces a carry as required. This is because the difference between a carry in the most significant bit position of the binary sum and a decimal carry differ by $16 - 10 = 6$. Consider the following three BCD additions:

4	0100	4	0100	8	1000
+5	+0101	+8	+1000	+9	1001
9	1001	12	1100	17	10001
			+0110		+0110
			10010		10111

In each case, the two BCD digits are added as if they were two binary numbers. If the binary sum is greater or equal to 1010, we add 0110 to obtain the correct BCD digit sum and a carry. In the first example, the sum is equal to 9 and is the correct BCD digit sum. In the second example, the binary sum produces an invalid BCD digit. The addition of 0110 produces the correct BCD digit sum 0010 (2) and a carry. In the third example, the binary sum produces a carry.

This condition occurs when the sum is greater than or equal to 16. Although the other four bits are less than 1001, the binary sum requires a correction because of the carry. Adding 0110, we obtain the required BCD digit sum 0111 (7) and a BCD carry.

The addition of two n-digit unsigned BCD numbers follows the same procedure. Consider the addition of $184 + 576 = 760$ in BCD:

BCD carry	1	1		
	0001	1000	0100	184
	+0101	0111	0110	+576
Binary sum	0111	10000	1010	
Add 6		0110	0110	
BCD sum	0111	0110	0000	760

The first, least significant pair of BCD digits produces a BCD digit sum of 0000 and a carry for the next pair of digits. The second pair of BCD digits plus a previous carry produces a digit sum of 0110 and a carry for the next pair of digits. The third pair of digits plus a carry produces a binary sum of 0111 and does not require a correction.

Decimal Arithmetic

The representation of signed decimal numbers in BCD is similar to the representation of signed numbers in binary. We can use either the familiar sign and magnitude system or the signed-complement system. The sign of a decimal number is usually represented with four bits to conform to the 4-bit code of the decimal digits. It is customary to designate a plus with four 0's and a minus with the BCD equivalent of 9, which is 1001.

The signed-magnitude system is seldom used in computers. The signed-complement system can be either the 9's or the 10's complement, but the 10's complement is the one most often used. To obtain the 10's complement of a BCD number, we first take the 9's complement and then add one to the least significant digit. The 9's complement is calculated from the subtraction of each digit from 9.

The procedures developed for the signed-2's complement system in the previous section apply also to the signed-10's complement system for decimal numbers. Addition is done by adding all digits, including the sign digit, and discarding the end carry. This assumes that all negative numbers are in 10's complement form. Consider the addition $(+375) + (-240) = +135$ done in the signed-complement system.

$$
\begin{array}{r}
0\ 375 \\
+9\ 760 \\
\hline
0\ 135
\end{array}
$$

The 9 in the leftmost position of the second number represents a minus and 9760 is the 10's complement of 0240. The two numbers are added and the end carry is discarded to obtain

+135. Of course, the decimal numbers inside the computer must be in BCD, including the sign digits. The addition is done with BCD digits as described previously.

The subtraction of decimal numbers either unsigned or in the signed-10's complement system is the same as in the binary case. Take the 10's complement of the subtrahend and add it to the minuend. Many computers have special hardware to perform arithmetic calculations directly with decimal numbers in BCD. The user of the computer can specify by programmed instructions to perform the arithmetic operation with decimal numbers directly without having to convert them to binary.

Other Decimal Codes

Binary codes for decimal digits require a minimum of four bits per digit. Many different codes can be formulated by arranging four bits in 10 distinct possible combinations. The BCD and three other representative codes are shown in Table 1-5. Each code uses only 10 bit combinations out of possible 16 combinations that can be arranged with four bits. The other six unused combinations in each case have no meaning and should be avoided.

The BCD and the 2421 codes are examples of weighted codes. In a weighted code, each bit position is assigned a weighting factor in such a way that each digit can be evaluated by adding the weights of all the 1's in the coded combination. The BCD code has weights of 8, 4, 2, and 1, which correspond to the power of two values of each bit. The bit assignment 0110 for example, is interpreted by the weights to represent decimal 6 because $8 \times 0 + 4 \times 1 + 2 \times 1 + 1 \times 0 = 6$. The bit combination 1101 when weighted by the respective digits 2421 gives

Table 1-5
Four Different Binary Codes for the Decimal Digits

Decimal digit	BCD 8421	2421	Excess-3	8 4-2-1
0	0000	0000	0011	0 0 0 0
1	0001	0001	0100	0 1 1 1
2	0010	0010	0101	0 1 1 0
3	0011	0011	0110	0 1 0 1
4	0100	0100	0111	0 1 0 0
5	0101	1011	1000	1 0 1 1
6	0110	1100	1001	1 0 1 0
7	0111	1101	1010	1 0 0 1
8	1000	1110	1011	1 0 0 0
9	1001	1111	1100	1 1 1 1
	1010	0101	0000	0 0 0 1
Unused	1011	0110	0001	0 0 1 0
bit	1100	0111	0010	0 0 1 1
combi-	1101	1000	1101	1 1 0 0
nations	1110	1001	1110	1 1 0 1
	1111	1010	1111	1 1 1 0

the decimal equivalent of $2 \times 1 + 4 \times 1 + 2 \times 0 + 1 \times 1 = 7$. Note that some digits can be coded in two possible ways in the 2421 code. Decimal 4 can be assigned to bit combinations 0100 or 1010 since both combinations add up to a total weight of four.

The 2421 and the excess-3 codes are examples of self-complementing codes. Such codes have the property that the 9's complement of a decimal number is obtained directly by changing 1's to 0's and 0's to 1's in the code. For example, decimal 395 is represented in the excess-3 code as 0110 1100 1000. The 9's complement 604 is represented as 1001 0011 0111, which is simply obtained by complementing each bit of the code (as with the 1's complement of binary numbers).

The excess-3 code has been used in some older computers because of its self-complementing property. This is an unweighted code where each coded combination is obtained from the corresponding binary value plus 3. Note that the BCD code is not self-complementing.

The $8, 4, -2, -1$ code is an example of assigning both positive and negative weights to a decimal code. In this case, the bit combination 0110 is interpreted as a decimal 2 and is calculated from $8 \times 0 + 4 \times 1 + (-2) \times 1 + (-1) \times 0 = 2$.

Gray Code

The output data of many physical systems produce quantities that are continuous. These data must be converted into digital form before they are applied to a digital system. Continuous or analog information is converted into digital form by means of an analog-to-digital converter. It is sometimes convenient to use the Gray code shown in Table 1-6 to represent the digital data when it is converted from analog data. The advantage of the Gray code over the straight

Table 1-6
Gray Code

Gray code	Decimal equivalent
0000	0
0001	1
0011	2
0010	3
0110	4
0111	5
0101	6
0100	7
1100	8
1101	9
1111	10
1110	11
1010	12
1011	13
1001	14
1000	15

binary number sequence is that only one bit in the code group changes when going from one number to the next. For example, in going from 7 to 8, the Gray code changes from 0100 to 1100. Only the first bit changes from 0 to 1; the other three bits remain the same. When comparing this with binary numbers, the change from 7 to 8 will be from 0111 to 1000, which causes all four bits to change values.

The Gray code is used in applications where the normal sequence of binary numbers may produce an error or ambiguity during the transition from one number to the next. If binary numbers are used, a change from 0111 to 1000 may produce an intermediate erroneous number 1001 if the rightmost bit takes longer to change in value than the other three bits. The Gray code eliminates this problem since only one bit changes in value during any transition between two numbers.

A typical application of the Gray code occurs when analog data are represented by continuous change of a shaft position. The shaft is partitioned into segments, and each segment is assigned a number. If adjacent segments are made to correspond with the Gray-code sequence, ambiguity is eliminated when detection is sensed in the line that separates any two segments.

ASCII Character Code

Many applications of digital computers require the handling of data not only of numbers, but also of letters. For instance, an insurance company with thousands of policy holders will use a computer to process its files. To represent the names and other pertinent information, it is necessary to formulate a binary code for the letters of the alphabet. In addition, the same binary code must represent numerals and special characters (such as $). An alphanumeric character set is a set of elements that includes the 10 decimal digits, the 26 letters of the alphabet, and a number of special characters. Such a set contains between 36 and 64 elements if only capital letters are included, or between 64 and 128 elements if both uppercase and lowercase letters are included. In the first case, we need a binary code of six bits, and in the second, we need a binary code of seven bits.

The standard binary code for the alphanumeric characters is ASCII (American Standard Code for Information Interchange). It uses seven bits to code 128 characters, as shown in Table 1-7. The seven bits of the code are designated by b_1 through b_7, with b_7 being the most-significant bit. The letter A, for example, is represented in ASCII as 1000001 (column 100, row 0001). The ASCII code contains 94 graphic characters that can be printed and 34 non-printing characters used for various control functions. The graphic characters consist of the 26 uppercase letters (A through Z), the 26 lowercase letters (a through z), the 10 numerals (0 through 9), and 32 special printable characters such as %, *, and $.

The 34 control characters are designated in the ASCII table with abbreviated names. They are listed again below the table with their functional names. The control characters are used for routing data and arranging the printed text into a prescribed format. There are three types of control characters: format effectors, information separators, and communication-control characters. Format effectors are characters that control the layout of printing. They include the familiar typewriter controls such as backspace (BS), horizontal tabulation (HT), and carriage return (CR). Information separators are used to separate the data into divisions such as paragraphs and pages. They include characters such as record separator (RS) and file separator (FS). The communication-control characters are useful during the transmission of text between remote ter-

Table 1-7
American Standard Code for Information Interchange (ASCII)

$b_4 b_3 b_2 b_1$	$b_7 b_6 b_5$							
	000	**001**	**010**	**011**	**100**	**101**	**110**	**111**
0000	NUL	DLE	SP	0	@	P	`	p
0001	SOH	DC1	!	1	A	Q	a	q
0010	STX	DC2	"	2	B	R	b	r
0011	ETX	DC3	#	3	C	S	c	s
0100	EOT	DC4	$	4	D	T	d	t
0101	ENQ	NAK	%	5	E	U	e	u
0110	ACK	SYN	&	6	F	V	f	v
0111	BEL	ETB	'	7	G	W	g	w
1000	BS	CAN	(	8	H	X	h	x
1001	HT	EM	)	9	I	Y	i	y
1010	LF	SUB	*	:	J	Z	j	z
1011	VT	ESC	+	;	K	[	k	{
1100	FF	FS	,	<	L	\	l	|
1101	CR	GS	–	=	M	]	m	}
1110	SO	RS	.	>	N	∧	n	~
1111	SI	US	/	?	O	–	o	DEL

Control characters

NUL	Null	DLE	Data-link escape
SOH	Start of heading	DC1	Device control 1
STX	Start of text	DC2	Device control 2
ETX	End of text	DC3	Device control 3
EOT	End of transmission	DC4	Device control 4
ENQ	Enquiry	NAK	Negative acknowledge
ACK	Acknowledge	SYN	Synchronous idle
BEL	Bell	ETB	End-of-transmission block
BS	Backspace	CAN	Cancel
HT	Horizontal tab	EM	End of medium
LF	Line feed	SUB	Substitute
VT	Vertical tab	ESC	Escape
FF	Form feed	FS	File separator
CR	Carriage return	GS	Group separator
SO	Shift out	RS	Record separator
SI	Shift in	US	Unit separator
SP	Space	DEL	Delete

minals. Examples of communication-control characters are STX (start of text) and ETX (end of text), which are used to frame a text message when transmitted through telephone wires.

ASCII is a 7-bit code, but most computers manipulate an 8-bit quantity as a single unit called a *byte.* Therefore, ASCII characters most often are stored one per byte. The extra bit is sometimes used for other purposes, depending on the application. For example, some printers recognize 8-bit ASCII characters with the most-significant bit set to 0. Additional 128 8-bit characters with the most-significant bit set to 1 are used for other symbols such as the Greek alphabet or italic type font.

Error-Detecting Code

To detect errors in data communication and processing, an eighth bit is sometimes added to the ASCII character to indicate its parity. A *parity bit* is an extra bit included with a message to make the total number of 1's either even or odd. Consider the following two characters and their even and odd parity:

	With even parity	With odd parity
ASCII A = 1000001	01000001	11000001
ASCII T = 1010100	11010100	01010100

In each case, we insert an extra bit in the leftmost position of the code to produce an even number of 1's in the character for even parity or an odd number of 1's in the character for odd parity. In general, one or the other parity is adopted, with even parity being more common.

The parity bit is helpful in detecting errors during the transmission of information from one location to another. This is handled by generating an even parity bit in the sending end for each character. The 8-bit characters that include parity bits are transmitted to their destination. The parity of each character is then checked in the receiving end. If the parity of the received character is not even, it means that at least one bit has changed value during the transmission. This method detects one, three, or any odd combination of errors in each character that is transmitted. An even combination of errors is undetected. Additional error detection codes may be needed to take care of an even combination of errors.

What is done after an error is detected depends on the particular application. One possibility is to request retransmission of the message on the assumption that the error was random and will not occur again. Thus, if the receiver detects a parity error, it sends back the ASCII NAK (negative acknowledge) control character consisting of an even parity eight bits 10010101. If no error is detected, the receiver sends back an ACK (acknowledge) control character, 00000110. The sending end will respond to an NAK by transmitting the message again until the correct parity is received. If, after a number of attempts, the transmission is still in error, a message can be sent to the operator to check for malfunctions in the transmission path.

1-8   BINARY STORAGE AND REGISTERS

The binary information in a digital computer must have a physical existence in some information-storage medium for storing individual bits. A *binary cell* is a device that possesses two stable states and is capable of storing one bit of information. The input to the cell receives excitation signals that set it to one of the two states. The output of the cell is a physical quantity that distinguishes between the two states. The information stored in a cell is 1 when it is in one stable state and 0 when in the other stable state.

Registers

A *register* is a group of binary cells. A register with n cells can store any discrete quantity of information that contains n bits. The state of a register is an n-tuple number of 1's and 0's, with each bit designating the state of one cell in the register. The content of a register is a function of the interpretation given to the information stored in it. Consider, for example, a 16-bit register with the following content:

$$1100001111001001$$

A register with 16 cells can be in one of 2^{16} possible states. If one assumes that the content of the register represents a binary integer, then the register can store any binary number from 0 to $2^{16} - 1$. For the particular example shown, the content of the register is the binary equivalent of the decimal number 50121. If it is assumed that the register stores alphanumeric characters of an eight-bit code, the content of the register is any two meaningful characters. For the ASCII code with an even parity placed in the eighth most-significant bit position, the register contains the two characters C (left eight bits) and I (right eight bits). On the other hand, if one interprets the content of the register to be four decimal digits represented by a four-bit code, the content of the register is a four-digit decimal number. In the excess-3 code, the register holds the decimal number 9096. The content of the register is meaningless in BCD because the bit combination 1100 is not assigned to any decimal digit. From this example, it is clear that a register can store discrete elements of information and that the same bit configuration may be interpreted differently for different types of data.

Register Transfer

A digital system is characterized by its registers and the components that perform data processing. A *register transfer* operation is a basic operation in digital systems. It consists of a transfer of binary information from one set of registers into another set of registers. The transfer may be direct from one register to another, or may pass through data processing circuits to perform an operation. Figure 1-1 illustrates the transfer of the information among registers and demonstrates pictorially the transfer of binary information from a keyboard into a register in the memory unit. The input unit is assumed to have a keyboard, a control circuit, and an input register. Each time a key is struck, the control enters an equivalent eight-bit alphanumeric character code into the input register. We shall assume that the code used is the ASCII code with an odd-parity bit. The information from the input register is transferred into the eight least significant cells of a processor register. After every transfer, the input register is cleared to enable the control to insert a new eight-bit code when the keyboard is struck again. Each eight-bit character transferred to the processor register is preceded by a shift of the previous character to the next eight cells on its left. When a transfer of four characters is completed, the processor register is full, and its contents are transferred into a memory register. The content stored in the memory register shown in Fig. 1-1 came from the transfer of the characters "J," "O," "H," and "N" after the four appropriate keys were struck.

To process discrete quantities of information in binary form, a computer must be provided with devices that hold the data to be processed and circuit elements that manipulate individual bits of information. The device most commonly used for holding data is a register.

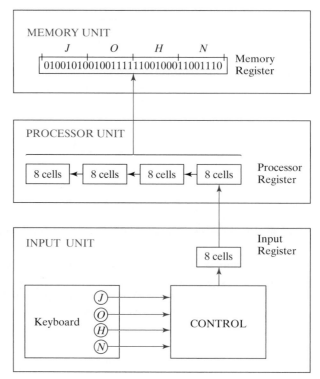

FIGURE 1-1
Transfer of information with registers

Manipulation of binary variables is done by means of digital logic circuits. Figure 1-2 illustrates the process of adding two 10-bit binary numbers. The memory unit, which normally consists of millions of registers, is shown in the diagram with only three of its registers. The part of the processor unit shown consists of three registers—$R1$, $R2$, and $R3$—together with digital logic circuits that manipulate the bits of $R1$ and $R2$ and transfer into $R3$ a binary number equal to their arithmetic sum. Memory registers store information and are incapable of processing the two operands. However, the information stored in memory can be transferred to processor registers. Results obtained in processor registers can be transferred back into a memory register for storage until needed again. The diagram shows the contents of two operands transferred from two memory registers into $R1$ and $R2$. The digital logic circuits produce the sum, which is transferred to register $R3$. The contents of $R3$ can now be transferred back to one of the memory registers.

The last two examples demonstrated the information-flow capabilities of a digital system in a very simple manner. The registers of the system are the basic elements for storing and holding the binary information. Digital logic circuits process the binary information stored in the registers. Digital logic circuits and registers are covered in Chapters 2 through 6. The memory unit is explained in Chapter 7. The register transfer level for describing and designing digital systems is covered in Chapter 8.

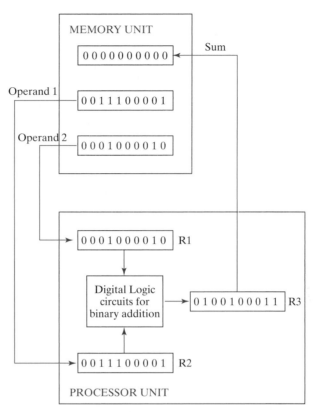

FIGURE 1-2
Example of binary information processing

1-9   BINARY LOGIC

Binary logic deals with variables that take on two discrete values and operations that assume logical meaning. The two values the variables take may be called by different names (*true* and *false, yes* and *no,* etc.), but for our purpose, it is convenient to think in terms of bits and assign the values of 1 and 0. The binary logic introduced in this section is equivalent to an algebra called Boolean algebra. The formal presentation of Boolean algebra is covered in more detail in Chapter 2. The purpose of this section is to introduce Boolean algebra in a heuristic manner and relate it to digital logic circuits and binary signals.

Definition of Binary Logic

Binary logic consists of binary variables and logical operations. The variables are designated by letters of the alphabet such as *A, B, C, x, y, z,* etc., with each variable having two and only two distinct possible values: 1 and 0. There are three basic logical operations: AND, OR, and NOT.

1. **AND:** This operation is represented by a dot or by the absence of an operator. For example, $x \cdot y = z$ or $xy = z$ is read "x AND y is equal to z." The logical operation AND is interpreted to mean that $z = 1$ if and only if $x = 1$ and $y = 1$; otherwise $z = 0$. (Remember that x, y, and z are binary variables and can be equal either to 1 or 0, and nothing else.)

2. **OR:** This operation is represented by a plus sign. For example, $x + y = z$ is read "x OR y is equal to z," meaning that $z = 1$ if $x = 1$ or if $y = 1$ or if both $x = 1$ and $y = 1$. If both $x = 0$ and $y = 0$, then $z = 0$.

3. **NOT:** This operation is represented by a prime (sometimes by an overbar). For example, $x' = z$ (or $\bar{x} = z$) is read "not x is equal to z," meaning that z is what x is not. In other words, if $x = 1$, then $z = 0$; but if $x = 0$, then $z = 1$. The NOT operation is also referred to as the complement operation, since it changes a 1 to 0 and a 0 to 1.

Binary logic resembles binary arithmetic, and the operations AND and OR have similarities to multiplication and addition, respectively. In fact, the symbols used for AND and OR are the same as those used for multiplication and addition. However, binary logic should not be confused with binary arithmetic. One should realize that an arithmetic variable designates a number that may consist of many digits. A logic variable is always either 1 or 0. For example, in binary arithmetic, we have $1 + 1 = 10$ (read: "one plus one is equal to 2"), whereas in binary logic, we have $1 + 1 = 1$ (read: "one OR one is equal to one").

For each combination of the values of x and y, there is a value of z specified by the definition of the logical operation. These definitions may be listed in a compact form using *truth tables*. A truth table is a table of all possible combinations of the variables showing the relation between the values that the variables may take and the result of the operation. The truth tables for the operations AND and OR with variables x and y are obtained by listing all possible values that the variables may have when combined in pairs. The result of the operation for each combination is then listed in a separate row. The truth tables for AND, OR, and NOT are listed in Table 1-8. These tables clearly demonstrate the definition of the operations.

Logic Gates

Logic gates are electronic circuits that operate on one or more input signals to produce an output signal. Electrical signals such as voltages or currents exist throughout a digital system in

Table 1-8
Truth Tables of Logical Operations

AND			OR			NOT	
x	y	$x \cdot y$	x	y	$x + y$	x	x'
0	0	0	0	0	0	0	1
0	1	0	0	1	1	1	0
1	0	0	1	0	1		
1	1	1	1	1	1		

either of two recognizable values. Voltage-operated circuits respond to two separate voltage levels that represent a binary variable equal to logic 1 or logic 0. For example, a particular digital system may define logic 0 as a signal equal to 0 volt and logic 1 as a signal equal to 4 volts. In practice, each voltage level has an acceptable range as shown in Fig. 1-3. The input terminals of digital circuits accept binary signals within the allowable range and respond at the output terminals with binary signals that fall within the specified range. The intermediate region between the allowed regions is crossed only during state transition. Any desired information for computing or control can be operated on by passing binary signals through various combinations of logic gates with each signal representing a particular binary variable.

The graphic symbols used to designate the three types of gates are shown in Fig. 1-4. The gates are blocks of hardware that produce the equivalent of logic 1 or logic 0 output signals if input logic requirements are satisfied. The input signals x and y in the AND and OR gates may exist in one of four possible states: 00, 10, 11, or 01. These input signals are shown in Fig. 1-5 together with the corresponding output signal for each gate. The timing diagrams illustrate the response of each gate to the four input signal combinations. The horizontal axis of the timing

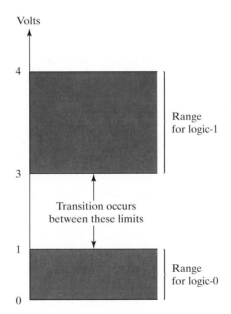

FIGURE 1-3
Example of binary signals

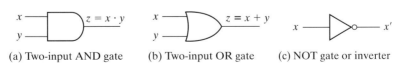

(a) Two-input AND gate   (b) Two-input OR gate   (c) NOT gate or inverter

FIGURE 1-4
Symbols for digital logic circuits

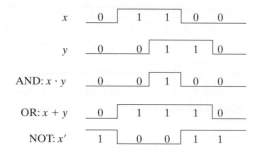

FIGURE 1-5
Input-output signals for gates

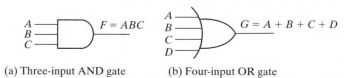

(a) Three-input AND gate   (b) Four-input OR gate

FIGURE 1-6
Gates with multiple inputs

diagram represents time and the vertical axis shows the signal as it changes between the two possible voltage levels. The low level represents logic 0 and the high level represents logic 1. The AND gate responds with a logic 1 output signal when both input signals are logic 1. The OR gate responds with logic 1 output signal if any input signal is logic 1. The NOT gate is commonly referred to as an inverter. The reason for this name is apparent from the signal response in the timing diagram, where it is shown that the output signal inverts the logic sense of the input signal.

AND and OR gates may have more than two inputs. An AND gate with three inputs and an OR gate with four inputs are shown in Fig. 1-6. The three-input AND gate responds with logic 1 output if all three inputs are logic 1. The output produces logic 0 if any input is logic 0. The four-input OR gate responds with logic 1 if any input is logic 1; its output becomes logic 0 only when all inputs are logic 0.

PROBLEMS

1-1 List the octal and hexadecimal numbers from 16 to 32. Using A and B for the last two digits, list the numbers from 10 to 26 in base 12.

1-2 What is the exact number of bytes in a system that contains (a) 32K byte, (b) 64M bytes, and (c) 6.4G byte?

1-3 What is the largest binary number that can be expressed with 12 bits? What is the equivalent decimal and hexadecimal?

1-4 Convert the following numbers with the indicated bases to decimal: $(4310)_5$, and $(198)_{12}$.

1-5 Determine the base of the numbers in each case for the following operations to be correct: (a) $14/2 = 5$; (b) $54/4 = 13$, (c) $24 + 17 = 40$.

1-6 The solution to the quadratic equation $x^2 - 11x + 22 = 0$ is $x = 3$ and $x = 6$. What is the base of the numbers?

1-7 Express the following numbers in decimal: $(10110.0101)_2$, $(16.5)_{16}$, and $(26.24)_8$.

1-8 Convert the following binary numbers to hexadecimal and to decimal: (a) 1.11010, (b) 1110.10. Explain why the decimal answer in (b) is 8 times that of (a).

1-9 Convert the hexadecimal number 68BE to binary and then from binary convert it to octal.

1-10 Convert the decimal number 345 to binary in two ways: (a) convert directly to binary; (b) convert first to hexadecimal, then from hexadecimal to binary. Which method is faster?

1-11 Do the following conversion problems:
(a) Convert decimal 34.4375 to binary.
(b) Calculate the binary equivalent of $1/3$ out to 8 places. Then convert from binary to decimal. How close is the result to $1/3$?
(c) Convert the binary result in (b) into hexadecimal. Then convert the result to decimal. Is the answer the same?

1-12 Add and multiply the following numbers without converting them to decimal.
(a) Binary numbers 1011 and 101.
(b) Hexadecimal numbers 2E and 34.

1-13 Perform the following division in binary: $1011111 \div 101$.

1-14 Find the 9's- and the 10's-complement of the following decimal numbers:
(a) 98127634   (b) 72049900   (c) 10000000   (d) 00000000.

1-15 (a) Find the 16's-complement of AF3B.
(b) Convert AF3B to binary.
(c) Find the 2's-complement of the result in (b).
(d) Convert the answer in (c) to hexadecimal and compare with the answer in (a).

1-16 Obtain the 1's and 2's complements of the following binary numbers:
(a) 11101010   (b) 01111110   (c) 00000001   (d) 10000000   (e) 00000000.

1-17 Perform subtraction on the following unsigned numbers using the 10's-complement of the subtrahend. Where the result should be negative, 10's complement it and affix a minus sign. Verify your answers.
(a) $7188 - 3049$ (b) $150 - 2100$ (c) $2997 - 7992$ (d) $1321 - 375$

1-18 Perform subtraction on the following unsigned binary numbers using the 2's-complement of the subtrahend. Where the result should be negative, 2's complement it and affix a minus sign.
(a) $11011 - 11001$ (b) $110100 - 10101$ (c) $1011 - 110000$ (d) $101010 - 101011$

1-19 The following decimal numbers are shown in sign-magnitude form: +9826 and +801. Convert them to signed 10's-complement form and perform the following operations: (Note that the sum is +10627 and requires six digits).
(a) $(+9826) + (+801)$ (b) $(+9826) + (-801)$
(c) $(-9826) + (+801)$ (d) $(-9826) + (-801)$

1-20 Convert decimal +61 and +27 to binary using the signed-2's complement representation and enough digits to accomodate the numbers. Then perform the binary equivalent of $(+27) + (-61)$, $(-27) + (+61)$ and $(-27) + (-61)$. Convert the answers back to decimal and verify that they are correct.

1-21 Convert decimal 9126 to both BCD and ASCII codes. For ASCII, an odd parity bit is to be appended at the left.

1-22 Represent the unsigned decimal numbers 965 and 672 in BCD and then show the steps necessary to form their sum.

1-23 Formulate a weighted binary code for the decimal digits using weights 6,3,1,1.

1-24 Represent decimal number 6027 in (a) BCD, (b) excess-3 code, and (c) 2421 code.

1-25 Find the 9's complement of 6027 and express it in 2421 code. Show that the result is the 1's complement of the answer to (c) in Problem 1-24. This demonstrates that the 2421 code is self-complementing.

1-26 Assign a binary code in some orderly manner to the 52 playing cards. Use the minimum number of bits.

1-27 Write the expression "G. Boole" in ASCII using an eight-bit code. Include the period and the space. Treat the leftmost bit of each character as a parity bit. Each 8-bit code should have even parity. (George Boole was a 19th century mathematician. Boolean algebra, introduced in the next chapter, bears his name.)

1-28 Decode the following ASCII code: 1001010 1100001 1101110 1100101 0100000 1000100 1101111 1100101.

1-29 The following is a string of ASCII characters whose bit patterns have been converted into hexadecimal for compactness: 4A EF 68 6E 20 C4 EF E5. Of the 8 bits in each pair of digits, the leftmost is a parity bit. The remaining bits are the ASCII code.
(a) Convert to bit form and decode the ASCII.
(b) Determine the parity used: odd or even.

1-30 How many printing characters are there in ASCII? How many of them are special characters (not letters or numerals)?

1-31 What bit must be complemented to change an ASCII letter from capital to lowercase, and vice versa?

1-32 The state of a 12-bit register is 100010010111. What is its content if it represents
(a) three decimal digits in BCD?   (b) three decimal digits in the excess-3 code?
(c) three decimal digits in the 84-2-1 code?   (d) a binary number?

1-33 List the ASCII code for the 10 decimal digits with an even parity bit in the leftmost position.

1-34 Assume a 3-input AND gate with output F and a 3-input OR gate with output G. Inputs are A, B, and C. Show the signals (by means of a timing diagram similar to Fig. 1-5) of the outputs F and G as functions of the three inputs ABC. Use all 8 possible combinations of ABC.

REFERENCES

1.   CAVANAGH, J. J. 1984. *Digital Computer Arithmetic*. New York: McGraw-Hill.

2.   SCHMID, H. 1974. *Decimal Computation*. New York: John Wiley.

3.   MANO, M. M. 1988. *Computer Engineering: Hardware Design*. Englewood Cliffs, NJ: Prentice-Hall.

4.   NELSON, V. P., H. T. NAGLE, J. D. IRWIN, and B. D. CARROLL 1997. *Digital Logic Circuit Analysis and Design*. Upper Saddle River, NJ: Prentice Hall.

2 Boolean Algebra and Logic Gates

2-1 BASIC DEFINITIONS

Boolean algebra, like any other deductive mathematical system, may be defined with a set of elements, a set of operators, and a number of unproved axioms or postulates. A *set* of elements is any collection of objects having a common property. If S is a set, and x and y are certain objects, then $x \in S$ denotes that x is a member of the set, S, and $y \notin S$ denotes that y is not an element of S. A set with a denumerable number of elements is specified by braces: $A = \{1, 2, 3, 4\}$, i.e., the elements of set A are the numbers 1, 2, 3, and 4. A *binary operator* defined on a set S of elements is a rule that assigns to each pair of elements from S a unique element from S. As an example, consider the relation $a * b = c$. We say that $*$ is a binary operator if it specifies a rule for finding c from the pair (a, b) and also if $a, b, c \in S$. However, $*$ is not a binary operator if $a, b \in S$, when the rule finds $c \notin S$.

The postulates of a mathematical system form the basic assumptions from which it is possible to deduce the rules, theorems, and properties of the system. The most common postulates used to formulate various algebraic structures are:

1. *Closure*. A set S is closed with respect to a binary operator if, for every pair of elements of S, the binary operator specifies a rule for obtaining a unique element of S. For example, the set of natural numbers $N = \{1, 2, 3, 4, \dots \}$ is closed with respect to the binary operator plus $(+)$ by the rules of arithmetic addition, since for any $a, b \in N$ we obtain a unique $c \in N$ by the operation $a + b = c$. The set of natural numbers is not closed with respect to the binary operator minus $(-)$ by the rules of arithmetic subtraction because $2 - 3 = -1$ and $2, 3 \in N$, while $(-1) \notin N$.

2. *Associative law*. A binary operator $*$ on a set S is said to be associative whenever

$$(x * y) * z = x * (y * z) \text{ for all } x, y, z, \in S$$

33

3. *Commutative law*. A binary operator $*$ on a set S is said to be commutative whenever

$$x * y = y * x \text{ for all } x, y \in S$$

4. *Identity element*. A set S is said to have an identity element with respect to a binary operation $*$ on S if there exists an element $e \in S$ with the property

$$e * x = x * e = x \text{ for every } x \in S$$

Example: The element 0 is an identity element with respect to the operation $+$ on the set of integers $I = \{ \ldots, -3, -2, -1, 0, 1, 2, 3, \ldots \}$, since

$$x + 0 = 0 + x = x \text{ for any } x \in I$$

The set of natural numbers, N, has no identity element since 0 is excluded from the set.

5. *Inverse*. A set S having the identity element e with respect to a binary operator $*$ is said to have an inverse whenever, for every $x \in S$, there exists an element $y \in S$ such that

$$x * y = e$$

Example: In the set of integers, I, with $e = 0$, the inverse of an element a is $(-a)$ since $a + (-a) = 0$.

6. *Distributive law*. If $*$ and $\cdot$ are two binary operators on a set S, $*$ is said to be distributive over $\cdot$ whenever

$$x * (y \cdot z) = (x * y) \cdot (x * z)$$

An example of an algebraic structure is a *field*. A field is a set of elements, together with two binary operators, each having properties 1 through 5, and both operators combined to give property 6. The set of real numbers, together with the binary operators $+$ and $\cdot$, form the field of real numbers. The field of real numbers is the basis for arithmetic and ordinary algebra. The operators and postulates have the following meanings:

The binary operator $+$ defines addition.

The additive identity is 0.

The additive inverse defines subtraction.

The binary operator $\cdot$ defines multiplication.

The multiplicative identity is 1.

The multiplicative inverse of $a = 1/a$ defines division, i.e., $a \cdot 1/a = 1$.

The only distributive law applicable is that of $\cdot$ over $+$:

$$a \cdot (b + c) = (a \cdot b) + (a \cdot c)$$

2-2   AXIOMATIC DEFINITION OF BOOLEAN ALGEBRA

In 1854 George Boole introduced a systematic treatment of logic and developed for this purpose an algebraic system now called *Boolean algebra*. In 1938 C. E. Shannon introduced a two-valued Boolean algebra called *switching algebra*, in which he demonstrated that the properties of bistable electrical switching circuits can be represented by this algebra. For the formal definition of Boolean algebra, we shall employ the postulates formulated by E. V. Huntington in 1904.

Boolean algebra is an algebraic structure defined by a set of elements, B, together with two binary operators, $+$ and $\cdot$, provided that the following (Huntington) postulates are satisfied:

1. **(a)** Closure with respect to the operator $+$.
   (b) Closure with respect to the operator $\cdot$.

2. **(a)** An identity element with respect to $+$, designated by 0: $x + 0 = 0 + x = x$.
   (b) An identity element with respect to $\cdot$, designated by 1: $x \cdot 1 = 1 \cdot x = x$.

3. **(a)** Commutative with respect to $+$: $x + y = y + x$.
   (b) Commutative with respect to $\cdot$: $x \cdot y = y \cdot x$.

4. **(a)** $\cdot$ is distributive over $+$: $x \cdot (y + z) = (x \cdot y) + (x \cdot z)$.
   (b) $+$ is distributive over $\cdot$: $x + (y \cdot z) = (x + y) \cdot (x + z)$.

5. For every element $x \in B$, there exists an element $x' \in B$ (called the complement of x) such that (a) $x + x' = 1$ and (b) $x \cdot x' = 0$.

6. There exists at least two elements $x, y \in B$ such that $x \neq y$.

Comparing Boolean algebra with arithmetic and ordinary algebra (the field of real numbers), we note the following differences:

1. Huntington postulates do not include the associative law. However, this law holds for Boolean algebra and can be derived (for both operators) from the other postulates.

2. The distributive law of $+$ over $\cdot$, i.e., $x + (y \cdot z) = (x + y) \cdot (x + z)$, is valid for Boolean algebra, but not for ordinary algebra.

3. Boolean algebra does not have additive or multiplicative inverses; therefore, there are no subtraction or division operations.

4. Postulate 5 defines an operator called *complement* that is not available in ordinary algebra.

5. Ordinary algebra deals with the real numbers, which consitute an infinite set of elements. Boolean algebra deals with the as yet undefined set of elements, B, but in the two-valued Boolean algebra defined next (and of interest in our subsequent use of this algebra), B is defined as a set with only two elements, 0 and 1.

Boolean algebra resembles ordinary algebra in some respects. The choice of symbols $+$ and $\cdot$ is intentional to facilitate Boolean algebraic manipulations by persons already familiar with ordinary algebra. Although one can use some knowledge from ordinary algebra to deal with Boolean algebra, the beginner must be careful not to substitute the rules of ordinary algebra where they are not applicable.

It is important to distinguish between the elements of the set of an algebraic structure and the variables of an algebraic system. For example, the elements of the field of real numbers are numbers, whereas variables such as a, b, c, etc., used in ordinary algebra, are symbols that stand for real numbers. Similarly, in Boolean algebra, one defines the elements of the set B, and variables such as x, y, and z are merely symbols that represent the elements. At this point, it is important to realize that in order to have a Boolean algebra, one must show:

1. the elements of the set B,

2. the rules of operation for the two binary operators, and

3. that the set of elements, B, together with the two operators, satisfies the six Huntington postulates.

One can formulate many Boolean algebras, depending on the choice of elements of B and the rules of operation. In our subsequent work, we deal only with a two-valued Boolean algebra, i.e., one with only two elements. Two-valued Boolean algebra has applications in set theory (the algebra of classes) and in propositional logic. Our interest here is with the application of Boolean algebra to gate-type circuits.

Two-Valued Boolean Algebra

A two-valued Boolean algebra is defined on a set of two elements, $B = \{0, 1\}$, with rules for the two binary operators $+$ and $\cdot$ as shown in the following operator tables (the rule for the complement operator is for verification of postulate 5):

x	y	$x \cdot y$
0	0	0
0	1	0
1	0	0
1	1	1

x	y	$x + y$
0	0	0
0	1	1
1	0	1
1	1	1

x	x'
0	1
1	0

These rules are exactly the same as the AND, OR, and NOT operations, respectively, defined in Table 1-8. We must now show that the Huntington postulates are valid for the set $B = \{0, 1\}$ and the two binary operators defined before.

1. *Closure* is obvious from the tables since the result of each operation is either 1 or 0 and $1, 0 \in B$.

2. From the tables, we see that
   (a) $0 + 0 = 0$ $0 + 1 = 1 + 0 = 1$;
   (b) $1 \cdot 1 = 1$ $1 \cdot 0 = 0 \cdot 1 = 0$.
   This establishes the two *identity elements*, 0 for $+$ and 1 for $\cdot$, as defined by postulate 2.

3. The *commutative* laws are obvious from the symmetry of the binary operator tables.

4. (a) The *distributive* law $x \cdot (y + z) = (x \cdot y) + (x \cdot z)$ can be shown to hold true from the operator tables by forming a truth table of all possible values of x, y, and z. For each combination, we derive $x \cdot (y + z)$ and show that the value is the same as $(x \cdot y) + (x \cdot z)$.

x	y	z	y + z	x · (y + z)	x · y	x · z	(x · y) + (x · z)
0	0	0	0	0	0	0	0
0	0	1	1	0	0	0	0
0	1	0	1	0	0	0	0
0	1	1	1	0	0	0	0
1	0	0	0	0	0	0	0
1	0	1	1	1	0	1	1
1	1	0	1	1	1	0	1
1	1	1	1	1	1	1	1

(b) The *distributive* law of + over · can be shown to hold true by means of a truth table similar to the one above.

5. From the complement table, it is easily shown that
   (a) $x + x' = 1$, since $0 + 0' = 0 + 1 = 1$ and $1 + 1' = 1 + 0 = 1$.
   (b) $x \cdot x' = 0$, since $0 \cdot 0' = 0 \cdot 1 = 0$ and $1 \cdot 1' = 1 \cdot 0 = 0$, which verifies postulate 5.

6. Postulate 6 is satisfied because the two-valued Boolean algebra has two distinct elements, 1 and 0, with $1 \neq 0$.

We have just established a two-valued Boolean algebra having a set of two elements, 1 and 0, two binary operators with operation rules equivalent to the AND and OR operations, and a complement operator equivalent to the NOT operator. Thus, Boolean algebra has been defined in a formal mathematical manner and has been shown to be equivalent to the binary logic presented heuristically in Section 1-9. The heuristic presentation is helpful in understanding the application of Boolean algebra to gate-type circuits. The formal presentation is necessary for developing the theorems and properties of the algebraic system. The two-valued Boolean algebra defined in this section is also called "switching algebra" by engineers. To emphasize the similarities between two-valued Boolean algebra and other binary systems, this algebra was called "binary logic" in Section 1-9. From here on, we shall drop the adjective "two-valued" from Boolean algebra in subsequent discussions.

2-3   BASIC THEOREMS AND PROPERTIES OF BOOLEAN ALGEBRA

Duality

The Huntington postulates have been listed in pairs and designated by part (a) and part (b). One part may be obtained from the other if the binary operators and the identity elements are interchanged. This important property of Boolean algebra is called the *duality principle*. It states that every algebraic expression deducible from the postulates of Boolean algebra remains valid if the operators and identity elements are interchanged. In a two-valued Boolean algebra, the identity elements and the elements of the set, B, are the same: 1 and 0. The duality principle has many applications. If the *dual* of an algebraic expression is desired, we simply interchange OR and AND operators and replace 1's by 0's and 0's by 1's.

Basic Theorems

Table 2-1 lists six theorems of Boolean algebra and four of its postulates. The notation is simplified by omitting the binary operator whenever this does not lead to confusion. The theorems and postulates listed are the most basic relationships in Boolean algebra. The theorems, like the postulates, are listed in pairs; each relation is the dual of the one paired with it. The postulates are basic axioms of the algebraic structure and need no proof. The theorems must be proven from the postulates. The proofs of the theorems with one variable are presented below. At the right is listed the number of the postulate that justifies each step of the proof.

THEOREM 1(a): $x + x = x$.

$$
\begin{aligned}
x + x &= (x + x) \cdot 1 &&\text{by postulate:} && 2(\text{b}) \\
&= (x + x)(x + x') &&&& 5(\text{a}) \\
&= x + xx' &&&& 4(\text{b}) \\
&= x + 0 &&&& 5(\text{b}) \\
&= x &&&& 2(\text{a})
\end{aligned}
$$

THEOREM 1(b): $x \cdot x = x$.

$$
\begin{aligned}
x \cdot x &= xx + 0 &&\text{by postulate:} && 2(\text{a}) \\
&= xx + xx' &&&& 5(\text{b}) \\
&= x(x + x') &&&& 4(\text{a}) \\
&= x \cdot 1 &&&& 5(\text{a}) \\
&= x &&&& 2(\text{b})
\end{aligned}
$$

Table 2-1
Postulates and Theorems of Boolean Algebra

Postulate 2	(a)	$x + 0 = x$	(b)	$x \cdot 1 = x$
Postulate 5	(a)	$x + x' = 1$	(b)	$x \cdot x' = 0$
Theorem 1	(a)	$x + x = x$	(b)	$x \cdot x = x$
Theorem 2	(a)	$x + 1 = 1$	(b)	$x \cdot 0 = 0$
Theorem 3, involution		$(x')' = x$		
Postulate 3, commutative	(a)	$x + y = y + x$	(b)	$xy = yx$
Theorem 4, associative	(a) $x + (y + z) = (x + y) + z$		(b)	$x(yz) = (xy)z$
Postulate 4, distributive	(a)	$x(y + z) = xy + xz$	(b)	$x + yz = (x + y)(x + z)$
Theorem 5, DeMorgan	(a)	$(x + y)' = x'y'$	(b)	$(xy)' = x' + y'$
Theorem 6, absorption	(a)	$x + xy = x$	(b) $x(x + y) = x$	

Note that theorem 1(b) is the dual of theorem 1(a) and that each step of the proof in part (b) is the dual of part (a). Any dual theorem can be similarly derived from the proof of its corresponding pair.

THEOREM 2(a): $x + 1 = 1$.

$$\begin{aligned}
x + 1 &= 1 \cdot (x + 1) && \text{by postulate:} & 2\text{(b)} \\
&= (x + x')(x + 1) && & 5\text{(a)} \\
&= x + x' \cdot 1 && & 4\text{(b)} \\
&= x + x' && & 2\text{(b)} \\
&= 1 && & 5\text{(a)}
\end{aligned}$$

THEOREM 2(b): $x \cdot 0 = 0$ by duality.

THEOREM 3: $(x')' = x$. From postulate 5, we have $x + x' = 1$ and $x \cdot x' = 0$, which defines the complement of x. The complement of x' is x and is also $(x')'$. Therefore, since the complement is unique, we have that $(x')' = x$.

The theorems involving two or three variables may be proven algebraically from the postulates and the theorems that have already been proven. Take, for example, the absorption theorem.

THEOREM 6(a): $x + xy = x$.

$$\begin{aligned}
x + xy &= x \cdot 1 + xy && \text{by postulate:} & 2\text{(b)} \\
&= x(1 + y) && & 4\text{(a)} \\
&= x(y + 1) && & 3\text{(a)} \\
&= x \cdot 1 && & 2\text{(a)} \\
&= x && & 2\text{(b)}
\end{aligned}$$

THEOREM 6(b): $x(x + y) = x$ by duality.

The theorems of Boolean algebra can be shown to hold true by means of truth tables. In truth tables, both sides of the relation are checked to yield identical results for all possible combinations of variables involved. The following truth table verifies the first absorption theorem.

x	y		xy	x + xy
0	0		0	0
0	1		0	0
1	0		0	1
1	1		1	1

The algebraic proofs of the associative law and DeMorgan's theorem are long and will not be shown here. However, their validity is easily shown with truth tables. For example, the truth table for the first DeMorgan's theorem $(x + y)' = x'y'$ is shown below.

x	y	$x + y$	$(x + y)'$		x'	y'	$x'y'$
0	0	0	1		1	1	1
0	1	1	0		1	0	0
1	0	1	0		0	1	0
1	1	1	0		0	0	0

Operator Precedence

The operator precedence for evaluating Boolean expressions is (1) parentheses, (2) NOT, (3) AND, and (4) OR. In other words, the expression inside the parentheses must be evaluated before all other operations. The next operation that holds precedence is the complement, then follows the AND, and finally the OR. As an example, consider the truth table for DeMorgan's theorem. The left side of the expression is $(x + y)'$. Therefore, the expression inside the parentheses is evaluated first and the result then complemented. The right side of the expression is $x'y'$. Therefore, the complement of x and the complement of y are both evaluated first and the result is then ANDed. Note that in ordinary arithmetic, the same precedence holds (except for the complement) when multiplication and addition are replaced by AND and OR, respectively.

2-4   BOOLEAN FUNCTIONS

Boolean algebra is an algebra that deals with binary variables and logic operations. A Boolean function described by an algebraic expression consists of binary variables, the constants 0 and 1, and the logic operation symbols. For a given value of the binary variables, the function can be equal to either 1 or 0. Consider as an example the following Boolean function:

$$F_1 = x + y'z$$

The function F_1 is equal to 1 if x is equal to 1 or if both y' and z are equal to 1. F_1 is equal to 0 otherwise. The complement operation dictates that when $y' = 1$ then $y = 0$. Therefore, we can say that $F_1 = 1$ if $x = 1$ or if $y = 0$ and $z = 1$. A Boolean function expresses the logical relationship between binary variables. It is evaluated by determining the binary value of the expression for all possible values of the variables.

A Boolean function can be represented in a truth table. A truth table is a list of combinations of 1's and 0's assigned to the binary variables and a column that shows the value of the function for each binary combination. The number of rows in the truth table is 2^n, where n is the number of variables in the function. The binary combinations for the truth table are obtained from the binary numbers by counting from 0 through $2^n - 1$. Table 2-2 shows the truth table for the function F_1. There are eight possible binary combinations for assigning bits to the three variables x, y, and z. The column labeled F_1 contains either 0 or 1 for each of these combina-

Table 2-2
Truth Tables for F_1 and F_2

x	y	z	F_1	F_2
0	0	0	0	0
0	0	1	1	1
0	1	0	0	0
0	1	1	0	1
1	0	0	1	1
1	0	1	1	1
1	1	0	1	0
1	1	1	1	0

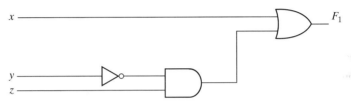

FIGURE 2-1
Gate implementation of $F_1 = x + y'z$

tions. The table shows that the function is equal to 1 when $x = 1$ or when $yz = 01$. It is equal to 0 otherwise.

A Boolean function can be transformed from an algebraic expression into a circuit diagram composed of logic gates. The logic-circuit diagram for F_1 is shown in Fig. 2-1. There is an inverter for input y to generate the complement. There is an AND gate for the term $y'z$ and an OR gate that combines the two terms. In logic-circuit diagrams, the variables of the function are taken as the inputs of the circuit and the binary variable F_1 is taken as the output of the circuit.

There is only one way that a Boolean function can be represented in a truth table. However, when the function is in algebraic form, it can be expressed in a variety of ways. The particular expression used to designate the function will also dictate the interconnection of gates in the logic circuit diagram. By manipulating a Boolean expression according to Boolean algebra rules, it is sometimes possible to obtain a simpler expression for the same function and thus reduce the number of gates in the circuit and the number of inputs to the gate. Consider for example the following Boolean function:

$$F_2 = x'y'z + x'yz + xy'$$

The implementation of this function with logic gates is shown in Fig. 2-2(a). Input variables x and y are complemented with inverters to obtain x' and y'. The three terms in the expression are implemented with three AND gates. The OR gate forms the logical OR of the three terms. The truth table for F_2 is listed in Table 2-2. The function is equal to 1 when $xyz = 001$ or 011

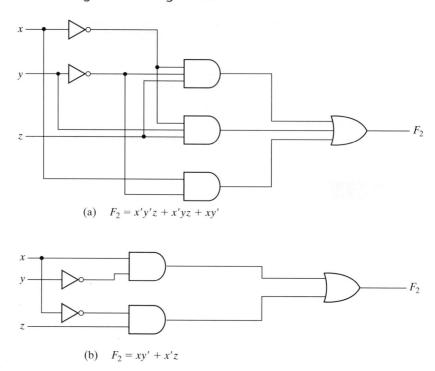

(a) $F_2 = x'y'z + x'yz + xy'$

(b) $F_2 = xy' + x'z$

FIGURE 2-2
Implementation of Boolean function F_2 with gates

or when $xy = 10$ (irrespective of the value of z); it is equal to 0 otherwise. This produces four 1's and four 0's for F_2.

Now consider the possible simplification of the function by applying some of the identities of Boolean algebra:

$$F_2 = x'y'z + x'yz + xy' = x'z(y' + y) + xy' = x'z + xy'$$

The function is reduced to only two terms and can be implemented with gates as shown in Fig. 2-2(b). It is obvious that the circuit in (b) is simpler than the one in (a), yet both implement the same function. It is possible to verify by means of a truth table that the two expressions are equivalent. The simplified expression is equal to 1 when $xz = 01$ or when $xy = 10$. This produces the same four 1's in the truth table. Since both expression produce the same truth table, they are said to be equivalent. Therefore, the two circuits have the same outputs for all possible input binary combinations of the three variables. Each implement the same identical function but the one with fewer gates and less inputs to gates would be preferable because it requires less wires and components.

Algebraic Manipulation

When a Boolean expression is implemented with logic gates, each term requires a gate and each variable within the term designates an input to the gate. We define a *literal* to be a single variable within a term that may be complemented or not. The function of Fig. 2-2(a) has three terms and eight literals, the one in Fig. 2-2(b) has two terms and four literals. By reducing the number of terms, the number of literals, or both in a Boolean expression, it is often possible to obtain a simpler circuit. The manipulation of Boolean algebra consists mostly of reducing an expression for the purpose of obtaining a simpler circuit. Functions of up to five variables can be simplified by the map method described in the next chapter. For complex Boolean functions, digital designers use computer minimization programs. The only manual method available is a cut–and–try procedure employing the basic relations and other manipulations techniques that become familiar with use. The following examples illustrate the algebraic manipulation of Boolean algebra.

EXAMPLE 2-1

Simplify the following Boolean functions to a minimum number of literals.

1. $x(x' + y) = xx' + xy = 0 + xy = xy.$
2. $x + x'y = (x + x')(x + y) = 1(x + y) = x + y.$
3. $(x + y)(x + y') = x + xy + xy' + yy' = x(1 + y + y') = x.$
4. $xy + x'z + yz = xy + x'z + yz(x + x')$
$$= xy + x'z + xyz + x'yz$$
$$= xy(1 + z) + x'z(1 + y)$$
$$= xy + x'z.$$
5. $(x + y)(x' + z)(y + z) = (x + y)(x' + z)$ by duality from function 4.

∎

Functions 1 and 2 are the dual of each other and use dual expressions in corresponding steps. An easier way to simplify function 3 is by means of postulate 4(b) from Table 2-1: $(x + y)(x + y') = x + yy' = x.$ The fourth function illustrates the fact that an increase in the number of literals sometimes leads to a final simpler expression. Function 5 is not minimized directly, but can be derived from the dual of the steps used to derive function 4. Functions 4 and 5 are known as the *consensus theorem*.

Complement of a Function

The complement of a function F is F' and is obtained from an interchange of 0's for 1's and 1's for 0's in the value of F. The complement of a function may be derived algebraically through DeMorgan's theorem. This pair of theorems is listed in Table 2-1 for two variables. DeMorgan's theorems can be extended to three or more variables. The three-variable form of the first DeMorgan's theorem is derived as follows, using postulates and theorems listed in Table 2-1:

$(A + B + C)' = (A + x)'$	let $B + C = x$
$= A'x'$	by theorem 5(a) (DeMorgan)
$= A'(B + C)'$	substitute $B + C = x$
$= A'(B'C')$	by theorem 5(a) (DeMorgan)
$= A'B'C'$	by theorem 4(b) (associative)

DeMorgan's theorems for any number of variables resemble in form the two-variable case and can be derived by successive substitutions similar to the method used in the preceding derivation. These theorems can be generalized as follows:

$$(A + B + C + D + \ldots + F)' = A'B'C'D' \ldots F'$$
$$(ABCD \ldots F)' = A' + B' + C' + D' + \ldots + F'$$

The generalized form of DeMorgan's theorem states that the complement of a function is obtained by interchanging AND and OR operators and complementing each literal.

EXAMPLE 2-2

Find the complement of the functions $F_1 = x'yz' + x'y'z$ and $F_2 = x(y'z' + yz)$. By applying DeMorgan's theorem as many times as necessary, the complements are obtained as follows:

$$F_1' = (x'yz' + x'y'z)' = (x'yz')'(x'y'z)' = (x + y' + z)(x + y + z')$$
$$F_2' = [x(y'z' + yz)]' = x' + (y'z' + yz)' = x' + (y'z')'(yz)'$$
$$= x' + (y + z)(y' + z')$$

A simpler procedure for deriving the complement of a function is to take the dual of the function and complement each literal. This method follows from the generalized DeMorgan's theorem. Remember that the dual of a function is obtained from the interchange of AND and OR operators and 1's and 0's.

EXAMPLE 2-3

Find the complement of the functions F_1 and F_2 of Example 2-2 by taking their duals and complementing each literal.

1. $F_1 = x'yz' + x'y'z$.
   The dual of F_1 is $(x' + y + z')(x' + y' + z)$.
   Complement each literal: $(x + y' + z)(x + y + z') = F_1'$.

2. $F_2 = x(y'z' + yz)$.
   The dual of F_2 is $x + (y' + z')(y + z)$.
   Complement each literal: $x' + (y + z)(y' + z') = F_2'$.

2-5   CANONICAL AND STANDARD FORMS

Minterms and Maxterms

A binary variable may appear either in its normal form (x) or in its complement form (x'). Now consider two binary variabes x and y combined with an AND operation. Since each variable may appear in either form, there are four possible combinations: $x'y'$, $x'y$, xy', and xy. Each of these

Table 2-3
Minterms and Maxterms for Three Binary Variables

x	y	z	Minterms		Maxterms	
			Term	Designation	Term	Designation
0	0	0	$x'y'z'$	m_0	$x + y + z$	M_0
0	0	1	$x'y'z$	m_1	$x + y + z'$	M_1
0	1	0	$x'yz'$	m_2	$x + y' + z$	M_2
0	1	1	$x'yz$	m_3	$x + y' + z'$	M_3
1	0	0	$xy'z'$	m_4	$x' + y + z$	M_4
1	0	1	$xy'z$	m_5	$x' + y + z'$	M_5
1	1	0	xyz'	m_6	$x' + y' + z$	M_6
1	1	1	xyz	m_7	$x' + y' + z'$	M_7

four AND terms is called a *minterm*, or a *standard product*. In a similar manner, n variables can be combined to form 2^n minterms. The 2^n different minterms may be determined by a method similar to the one shown in Table 2-3 for three variables. The binary numbers from 0 to $2^n - 1$ are listed under the n variables. Each minterm is obtained from an AND term of the n variables, with each variable being primed if the corresponding bit of the binary number is a 0 and un-primed if a 1. A symbol for each minterm is also shown in the table and is of the form m_j, where j denotes the decimal equivalent of the binary number of the minterm designated.

In a similar fashion, n variables forming an OR term, with each variable being primed or un-primed, provide 2^n possible combinations, called *maxterms*, or *standard sums*. The eight max-terms for three variables, together with their symbolic designation, are listed in Table 2-3. Any 2^n maxterms for n variables may be determined similarly. Each maxterm is obtained from an OR term of the n variables, with each variable being unprimed if the corresponding bit is a 0 and primed if a 1. Note that each maxterm is the complement of its corresponding minterm, and vice versa.

A Boolean function can be expressed algebraically from a given truth table by forming a minterm for each combination of the variables that produces a 1 in the function, and then tak-ing the OR of all those terms. For example, the function f_1 in Table 2-4 is determined by ex-

Table 2-4
Functions of Three Variables

x	y	z	Function f_1	Function f_2
0	0	0	0	0
0	0	1	1	0
0	1	0	0	0
0	1	1	0	1
1	0	0	1	0
1	0	1	0	1
1	1	0	0	1
1	1	1	1	1

pressing the combinations 001, 100, and 111 as $x'y'z$, $xy'z'$, and xyz, respectively. Since each one of these minterms results in $f_1 = 1$, we have

$$f_1 = x'y'z + xy'z' + xyz = m_1 + m_4 + m_7$$

Similarly, it may be easily verified that

$$f_2 = x'yz + xy'z + xyz' + xyz = m_3 + m_5 + m_6 + m_7$$

These examples demonstrate an important property of Boolean algebra: Any Boolean function can be expressed as a sum of minterms (with "sum" meaning the ORing of terms).

Now consider the complement of a Boolean function. It may be read from the truth table by forming a minterm for each combination that produces a 0 in the function and then ORing those terms. The complement of f_1 is read as

$$f_1' = x'y'z' + x'yz' + x'yz + xy'z + xyz'$$

If we take the complement of f_1', we obtain the function f_1:

$$f_1 = (x + y + z)(x + y' + z)(x' + y + z')(x' + y' + z)$$
$$= M_0 \cdot M_2 \cdot M_3 \cdot M_5 \cdot M_6$$

Similarly, it is possible to read the expression for f_2 from the table:

$$f_2 = (x + y + z)(x + y + z')(x + y' + z)(x' + y + z)$$
$$= M_0 M_1 M_2 M_4$$

These examples demonstrate a second property of Boolean algebra: Any Boolean function can be expressed as a product of maxterms (with "product" meaning the ANDing of terms). The procedure for obtaining the product of maxterms directly from the truth table is as follows. Form a maxterm for each combination of the variables that produces a 0 in the function, and then form the AND of all those maxterms. Boolean functions expressed as a sum of minterms or product of maxterms are said to be in *canonical form*.

Sum of Minterms

It was previously stated that for n binary variables, one can obtain 2^n distinct minterms, and that any Boolean function can be expressed as a sum of minterms. The minterms whose sum defines the Boolean function are those that give the 1's of the function in a truth table. Since the function can be either 1 or 0 for each minterm, and since there are 2^n minterms, one can calculate the possible functions that can be formed with n variables to be 2^{2^n}. It is sometimes convenient to express the Boolean function in its sum of minterms form. If not in this form, it can be made so by first expanding the expression into a sum of AND terms. Each term is then inspected to see if it contains all the variables. If it misses one or more variables, it is ANDed with an expression such as $x + x'$, where x is one of the missing variables. The following example clarifies this procedure.

EXAMPLE 2-4

Express the Boolean function $F = A + B'C$ in a sum of minterms. The function has three variables, A, B, and C. The first term A is missing two variables; therefore:

$$A = A(B + B') = AB + AB'$$

This function is still missing one variable:

$$A = AB(C + C') + AB'(C + C')$$
$$= ABC + ABC' + AB'C + AB'C'$$

The second term $B'C$ is missing one variable:

$$B'C = B'C(A + A') = AB'C + A'B'C$$

Combining all terms, we have

$$F = A + B'C$$
$$= ABC + ABC' + AB'C + AB'C' + A'B'C$$

But $AB'C$ appears twice, and according to theorem 1 $(x + x = x)$, it is possible to remove one of them. Rearranging the minterms in ascending order, we finally obtain

$$F = A'B'C + AB'C + AB'C + ABC' + ABC$$
$$= m_1 + m_4 + m_5 + m_6 + m_7$$

■

It is sometimes convenient to express the Boolean function, when in its sum of minterms, in the following short notation:

$$F(A, B, C) = \Sigma(1, 4, 5, 6, 7)$$

The summation symbol Σ stands for the ORing of terms; the numbers following it are the minterms of the function. The letters in parentheses following F form a list of the variables in the order taken when the minterm is converted to an AND term.

An alternate procedure for deriving the minterms of a Boolean function is to obtain the truth table of the function directly from the algebraic expression and then read the minterms from the truth table. Consider the Boolean function given in Example 2-4:

$$F = A + B'C$$

The truth table shown in Table 2-5 can be derived directly from the algebraic expression by listing the eight binary combinations under variables A, B, and C and inserting 1's under F for those

Table 2-5
Truth Table for F = A + B′C

A	B	C	F
0	0	0	0
0	0	1	1
0	1	0	0
0	1	1	0
1	0	0	1
1	0	1	1
1	1	0	1
1	1	1	1

combinations where $A = 1$, and $BC = 01$. From the truth table, we can then read the five minterms of the function to be 1, 4, 5, 6, and 7.

Product of Maxterms

Each of the 2^{2^n} functions of n binary variables can be also expressed as a product of maxterms. To express the Boolean function as a product of maxterms, it must first be brought into a form of OR terms. This may be done by using the distributive law, $x + yz = (x + y)(x + z)$. Then any missing variable x in each OR term is ORed with xx'. This procedure is clarified by the following example.

EXAMPLE 2-5

Express the Boolean function $F = xy + x'z$ in a product of maxterm form. First, convert the function into OR terms using the distributive law:

$$F = xy + x'z = (xy + x')(xy + z)$$
$$= (x + x')(y + x')(x + z)(y + z)$$
$$= (x' + y)(x + z)(y + z)$$

The function has three variables: x, y, and z. Each OR term is missing one variable; therefore:

$$x' + y = x' + y + zz' = (x' + y + z)(x' + y + z')$$
$$x + z = x + z + yy' = (x + y + z)(x + y' + z)$$
$$y + z = y + z + xx' = (x + y + z)(x' + y + z)$$

Combining all the terms and removing those that appear more than once, we finally obtain:

$$F = (x + y + z)(x + y' + z)(x' + y + z)(x' + y + z')$$
$$= M_0 M_2 M_4 M_5$$

A convenient way to express this function is as follows:

$$F(x, y, z) = \Pi(0, 2, 4, 5)$$

The product symbol, Π, denotes the ANDing of maxterms; the numbers are the maxterms of the function.

■

Conversion between Canonical Forms

The complement of a function expressed as the sum of minterms equals the sum of minterms missing from the original function. This is because the original function is expressed by those minterms that make the function equal to 1, whereas its complement is a 1 for those minterms that the function is a 0. As an example, consider the function

$$F(A, B, C) = \Sigma(1, 4, 5, 6, 7)$$

This has a complement that can be expressed as

$$F'(A, B, C) = \Sigma(0, 2, 3) = m_0 + m_2 + m_3$$

Now, if we take the complement of F' by DeMorgan's theorem, we obtain F in a different form:

$$F = (m_0 + m_2 + m_3)' = m_0' \cdot m_2' \cdot m_3' = M_0 M_2 M_3 = \prod(0, 2, 3)$$

The last conversion follows from the definition of minterms and maxterms as shown in Table 2-3. From the table, it is clear that the following relation holds true:

$$m_j' = M_j$$

That is, the maxterm with subscript j is a complement of the minterm with the same subscript j, and vice versa.

The last example demonstrates the conversion between a function expressed in sum of minterms and its equivalent in product of maxterms. A similar argument will show that the conversion between the product of maxterms and the sum of minterms is similar. We now state a general conversion procedure. To convert from one canonical form to another, interchange the symbols Σ and $\prod$ and list those numbers missing from the original form. In order to find the missing terms, one must realize that the total number of minterms or maxterms is 2^n, where n is the number of binary variables in the function.

A Boolean function can be converted from an algebraic expression to a product of maxterms by using a truth table and the canonical conversion procedure. Consider, for example, the Boolean expression

$$F = xy + x'z$$

First, we derive the truth table of the function, as shown in Table 2-6. The 1's under F in the table are determined from the combination of the variable where $xy = 11$ or $xz = 01$. The minterms of the function are read from the truth table to be 1, 3, 6 and 7. The function expressed in sum of minterms is

$$F(x, y, z) = \Sigma(1, 3, 6, 7)$$

Since there are a total of eight minterms or maxterms in a function of three variable, we determine the missing terms to be 0, 2, 4, and 5. The function expressed in product of maxterm is

$$F(x, y, z) = \prod(0, 2, 4, 5)$$

This is the same answer obtained in Example 2-5.

Table 2-6
Truth Table for F = xy + x'z

x	y	z	F
0	0	0	0
0	0	1	1
0	1	0	0
0	1	1	1
1	0	0	0
1	0	1	0
1	1	0	1
1	1	1	1

Standard Forms

The two canonical forms of Boolean algebra are basic forms that one obtains from reading a function from the truth table. These forms are very seldom the ones with the least number of literals, because each minterm or maxterm must contain, by definition, *all* the variables either complemented or uncomplemented.

Another way to express Boolean functions is in *standard* form. In this configuration, the terms that form the function may contain one, two, or any number of literals. There are two types of standard forms: the sum of products and products of sums.

The *sum of products* is a Boolean expression containing AND terms, called *product terms*, of one or more literals each. The *sum* denotes the ORing of these terms. An example of a function expressed in sum of products is

$$F_1 = y' + xy + x'yz'$$

The expression has three product terms of one, two, and three literals. Their sum is in effect an OR operation.

The logic diagram of a sum-of-products expression consists of a group of AND gates followed by a single OR gate. This configuration pattern is shown in Fig. 2-3(a). Each product term requires an AND gate except for a term with a single literal. The logic sum is formed with an OR gate whose inputs are the outputs of the AND gates and the single literal. It is assumed that the input variables are directly available in their complement, so inverters are not included in the diagram. This circuit configuration is referred to as a two-level implementation.

A *product of sums* is a Boolean expression containing OR terms, called *sum terms*. Each term may have any number of literals. The *product* denotes the ANDing of these terms. An example of a function expressed in product of sums is

$$F_2 = x(y' + z)(x' + y + z')$$

This expression has three sum terms of one, two, and three literals. The product is an AND operation. The use of the words *product* and *sum* stems from the similarity of the AND operation to the arithmetic product (multiplication) and the similarity of the OR operation to the arithmetic sum (addition). The gate structure of the product of sums expression consists of a group

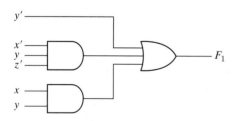

(a) Sum of Products

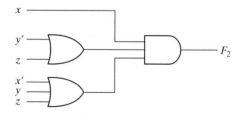

(b) Product of Sums

FIGURE 2-3
Two-level implementation

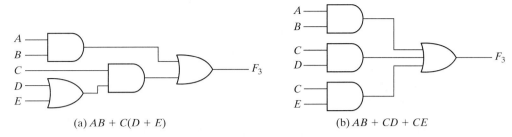

(a) $AB + C(D + E)$ (b) $AB + CD + CE$

FIGURE 2-4
Three- and Two-Level implementation

of OR gates for the sum terms (except for a single literal) followed by an AND gate. This is shown in Fig. 2-3(b). This standard type of expression results in a two-level gating structure.

A Boolean function may be expressed in a nonstandard form. For example, the function

$$F_3 = AB + C(D + E)$$

is neither in sum of products nor in product of sums. The implementation of this expression is shown in Fig. 2-4(a). This requires two AND gates and two OR gates. There are three levels of gating in this circuit. It can be changed to a standard form by using the distributive law to remove the parentheses:

$$F_3 = AB + C(D + E) = AB + CD + CE$$

The sum-of-products expression is implemented in Fig. 2-4(b). In general, a two-level implementation is preferred because it produces the least amount of delay through the gates when the signal propagates from the inputs to the output.

2-6   OTHER LOGIC OPERATIONS

When the binary operators AND and OR are placed between two variables, x and y, they form two Boolean functions, $x \cdot y$ and $x + y$, respectively. It was stated previously that there are 2^{2n} functions for n binary variables. For two variables, $n = 2$, and the number of possible Boolean functions is 16. Therefore, the AND and OR functions are only two of a total of 16 possible functions formed with two binary variables. It would be instructive to find the other 14 functions and investigate their properties.

The truth tables for the 16 functions formed with two binary variables, x and y, are listed in Table 2-7. Each of the 16 columns, F_0 to F_{15}, represents a truth table of one possible function for the two variables, x and y. Note that the functions are determined from the 16 binary combinations that can be assigned to F. The 16 functions can be expressed algebraically by means of Boolean functions. This is shown in the first column of Table 2-8. The Boolean expressions listed are simplified to their minimum number of literals.

Although each function can be expressed in terms of the Boolean operators AND, OR, and NOT, there is no reason one cannot assign special operator symbols for expressing the other

Table 2-7
Truth Tables for the 16 Functions of Two Binary Variables

x	y	F_0	F_1	F_2	F_3	F_4	F_5	F_6	F_7	F_8	F_9	F_{10}	F_{11}	F_{12}	F_{13}	F_{14}	F_{15}
0	0	0	0	0	0	0	0	0	0	1	1	1	1	1	1	1	1
0	1	0	0	0	0	1	1	1	1	0	0	0	0	1	1	1	1
1	0	0	0	1	1	0	0	1	1	0	0	1	1	0	0	1	1
1	1	0	1	0	1	0	1	0	1	0	1	0	1	0	1	0	1

functions. Such operator symbols are listed in the second column of Table 2-8. However, all the new symbols shown, except for the exclusive-OR symbol, $\oplus$, are not in common use by digital designers.

Each of the functions in Table 2-8 is listed with an accompanying name and a comment that explains the function in some way. The 16 functions listed can be subdivided into three categories:

1. Two functions that produce a constant 0 or 1.

2. Four functions with unary operations: complement and transfer.

3. Ten functions with binary operators that define eight different operations: AND, OR, NAND, NOR, exclusive-OR, equivalence, inhibition, and implication.

Table 2-8
Boolean Expressions for the 16 Functions of Two Variables

Boolean functions	Operator symbol	Name	Comments
$F_0 = 0$		Null	Binary constant 0
$F_1 = xy$	$x \cdot y$	AND	x and y
$F_2 = xy'$	x/y	Inhibition	x, but not y
$F_3 = x$		Transfer	x
$F_4 = x'y$	y/x	Inhibition	y, but not x
$F_5 = y$		Transfer	y
$F_6 = xy' + x'y$	$x \oplus y$	Exclusive-OR	x or y, but not both
$F_7 = x + y$	$x + y$	OR	x or y
$F_8 = (x + y)'$	$x \downarrow y$	NOR	Not-OR
$F_9 = xy + x'y'$	$(x \oplus y)'$	Equivalence	x equals y
$F_{10} = y'$	y'	Complement	Not y
$F_{11} = x + y'$	$x \subset y$	Implication	If y, then x
$F_{12} = x'$	x'	Complement	Not x
$F_{13} = x' + y$	$x \supset y$	Implication	If x, then y
$F_{14} = (xy)'$	$x \uparrow y$	NAND	Not-AND
$F_{15} = 1$		Identity	Binary constant 1

Constants for binary functions can be equal to only 1 or 0. The complement function produces the complement of each of the binary variables. A function that is equal to an input variable has been given the name *transfer*, because the variable x or y is transferred through the gate that forms the function without changing its value. Of the eight binary operators, two (inhibition and implication) are used by logicians but are seldom used in computer logic. The AND and OR operators have been mentioned in conjunction with Boolean algebra. The other four functions are extensively used in the design of digital systems.

The NOR function is the complement of the OR function and its name is an abbreviation of *not-OR*. Similarly, NAND is the complement of AND and is an abbreviation of *not-AND*. The exclusive-OR, abbreviated XOR, is similar to OR, but excludes the combination of *both* x and y being equal to 1. The equivalence is a function that is 1 when the two binary variables are equal, i.e., when both are 0 or both are 1. The exclusive-OR and equivalence functions are the complements of each other. This can be easily verified by inspecting Table 2-7. The truth table for the exclusive-OR is F_6 and for the equivalence is F_9, and these two functions are the complements of each other. For this reason, the equivalence function is called exclusive-NOR, abbreviated XNOR.

Boolean algebra, as defined in Section 2-2, has two binary operators, which we have called AND and OR, and a unary operator, NOT (complement). From the definitions, we have deduced a number of properties of these operators and now have defined other binary operators in terms of them. There is nothing unique about this procedure. We could have just as well started with the operator NOR ($\downarrow$), for example, and later define AND, OR, and NOT in terms of it. There are, nevertheless, good reasons for introducing Boolean algebra in the way it has been introduced. The concepts of "and," "or," and "not" are familiar and are used by people to express everyday logical ideas. Moreover, the Huntington postulates reflect the dual nature of the algebra, emphasizing the symmetry of $+$ and $\cdot$ with respect to each other.

2-7 DIGITAL LOGIC GATES

Since Boolean functions are expressed in terms of AND, OR, and NOT operations, it is easier to implement a Boolean function with these type of gates. The possibility of constructing gates for the other logic operations is of practical interest. Factors to be weighed when considering the construction of other types of logic gates are (1) the feasibility and economy of producing the gate with physical components, (2) the possibility of extending the gate to more than two inputs, (3) the basic properties of the binary operator, such as commutativity and associativity, and (4) the ability of the gate to implement Boolean functions alone or in conjunction with other gates.

Of the 16 functions defined in Table 2-8, two are equal to a constant and four are repeated twice. There are only ten functions left to be considered as candidates for logic gates. Two—inhibition and implication—are not commutative or associative and thus are impractical to use as standard logic gates. The other eight: complement, transfer, AND, OR, NAND, NOR, exclusive-OR, and equivalence, are used as standard gates in digital design.

The graphic symbols and truth tables of the eight gates are shown in Fig. 2-5. Each gate has one or two binary input variables designated by x and y and one binary output variable

Name	Graphic symbol	Algebraic function	Truth table

| AND | | $F = xy$ | <table><tr><td>x</td><td>y</td><td>F</td></tr><tr><td>0</td><td>0</td><td>0</td></tr><tr><td>0</td><td>1</td><td>0</td></tr><tr><td>1</td><td>0</td><td>0</td></tr><tr><td>1</td><td>1</td><td>1</td></tr></table> |

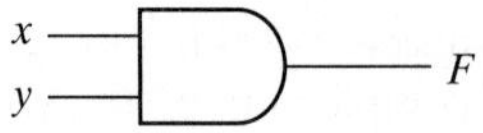

AND — $F = xy$

x	y	F
0	0	0
0	1	0
1	0	0
1	1	1

OR — $F = x + y$

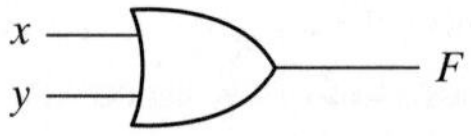

x	y	F
0	0	0
0	1	1
1	0	1
1	1	1

Inverter — $F = x'$

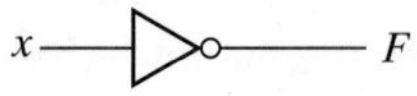

x	F
0	1
1	0

Buffer — $F = x$

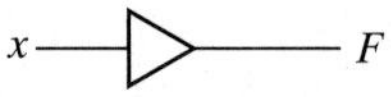

x	F
0	0
1	1

NAND — $F = (xy)'$

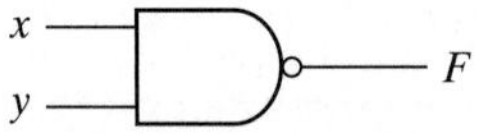

x	y	F
0	0	1
0	1	1
1	0	1
1	1	0

NOR — $F = (x + y)'$

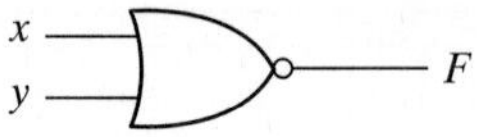

x	y	F
0	0	1
0	1	0
1	0	0
1	1	0

Exclusive-OR (XOR) — $F = xy' + x'y = x \oplus y$

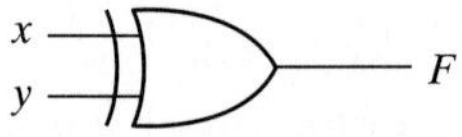

x	y	F
0	0	0
0	1	1
1	0	1
1	1	0

Exclusive-NOR or equivalence — $F = xy + x'y' = (x \oplus y)'$

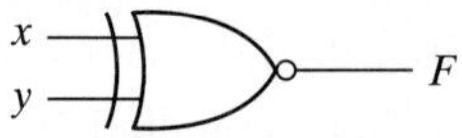

x	y	F
0	0	1
0	1	0
1	0	0
1	1	1

FIGURE 2-5
Digital logic gates

designated by F. The AND, OR, and inverter circuits were defined in Fig. 1-6. The inverter circuit inverts the logic sense of a binary variable. It produces the NOT, or complement, function. The small circle in the output of the graphic symbol of an inverter (referred to as a *bubble*) designates the logic complement. The triangle symbol by itself designates a buffer circuit. A buffer produces the *transfer* function, but does not produce a logic operation, since the binary value of the output is equal to the binary value of the input. This circuit is used for power amplification of the signal and is equivalent to two inverters connected in cascade.

The NAND function is the complement of the AND function, as indicated by a graphic symbol that consists of an AND graphic symbol followed by a small circle. The NOR function is the complement of the OR function and uses an OR graphic symbol followed by a small circle. The NAND and NOR gates are extensively used as standard logic gates and are in fact far more popular than the AND and OR gates. This is because NAND and NOR gates are easily constructed with transistor circuits and because digital circuits can be easily implemented with them.

The exclusive-OR gate has a graphic symbol similar to that of the OR gate, except for the additional curved line on the input side. The equivalence, or exclusive-NOR, gate is the complement of the exclusive-OR, as indicated by the small circle on the output side of the graphic symbol.

Extension to Multiple Inputs

The gates shown in Fig. 2-5—except for the inverter and buffer—can be extended to have more than two inputs. A gate can be extended to have multiple inputs if the binary operation it represents is commutative and associative. The AND and OR operations, defined in Boolean algebra, possess these two properties. For the OR function, we have

$$x + y = y + x \qquad \text{(commutative)}$$

and

$$(x + y) + z = x + (y + z) = x + y + z \qquad \text{(associative),}$$

which indicates that the gate inputs can be interchanged and that the OR function can be extended to three or more variables.

The NAND and NOR functions are commutative, and their gates can be extended to have more than two inputs, provided that the definition of the operation is slightly modified. The difficulty is that the NAND and NOR operators are not associative [i.e., $(x \downarrow y) \downarrow z \neq x \downarrow (y \downarrow z)$], as shown in Fig. 2-6 and the following equations:

$$(x \downarrow y) \downarrow z = \left[(x + y)' + z\right]' = (x + y)z' = xz' + yz'$$
$$x \downarrow (y \downarrow z) = \left[x + (y + z)'\right]' = x'(y + z) = x'y + x'z$$

To overcome this difficulty, we define the multiple NOR (or NAND) gate as a complemented OR (or AND) gate. Thus, by definition, we have

$$x \downarrow y \downarrow z = (x + y + z)'$$
$$x \uparrow y \uparrow z = (xyz)'$$

The graphic symbols for the 3-input gates are shown in Fig. 2-7. In writing cascaded NOR and NAND operations, one must use the correct parentheses to signify the proper sequence of the

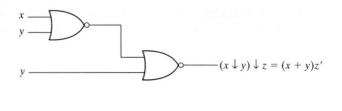

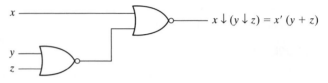

FIGURE 2-6
Demonstrating the nonassociativity of the NOR operator; $(x \downarrow y) \downarrow z \neq x \downarrow (y \downarrow z)$

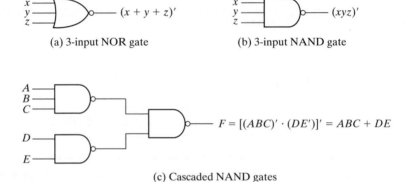

(a) 3-input NOR gate   (b) 3-input NAND gate

(c) Cascaded NAND gates

FIGURE 2-7
Multiple-input and cascated NOR and NAND gates

gates. To demonstrate this, consider the circuit of Fig. 2-7(c). The Boolean function for the circuit must be written as

$$F = \left[(ABC)'(DE)'\right]' = ABC + DE$$

The second expression is obtained from DeMorgan's theorem. It also shows that an expression in sum of products can be implemented with NAND gates. Further discussion of NAND and NOR gates can be found in Section 3-6.

The exclusive-OR and equivalence gates are both commutative and associative and can be extended to more than two inputs. However, multiple-input exclusive-OR gates are uncommon from the hardware standpoint. In fact, even a 2-input function is usually constructed with other types of gates. Moreover, the definition of the function must be modified when extended to more than two variables. The exclusive-OR is an *odd* function, i.e., it is equal to 1 if the

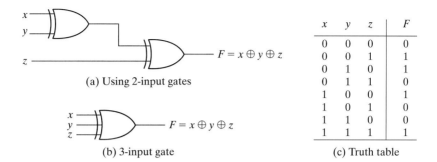

(a) Using 2-input gates

(b) 3-input gate

x	y	z	F
0	0	0	0
0	0	1	1
0	1	0	1
0	1	1	0
1	0	0	1
1	0	1	0
1	1	0	0
1	1	1	1

(c) Truth table

FIGURE 2-8
3-input exclusive-OR gate

input variables have an odd number of 1's. The construction of a 3-input exclusive-OR function is shown in Fig. 2-8. It is normally implemented by cascading 2-input gates, as shown in (a). Graphically, it can be represented with a single 3-input gate, as shown in (b). The truth table in (c) clearly indicates that the output F is equal to 1 if only one input is equal to 1 or if all three inputs are equal to 1, i.e., when the total number of 1's in the input variables is *odd*. Further discussion of exclusive-OR can be found in Section 3-8.

Positive and Negative Logic

The binary signal at the inputs and outputs of any gate has one of two values, except during transition. One signal value represents logic-1 and the other logic-0. Since two signal values are assigned to two logic values, there exist two different assignments of signal level to logic value, as shown in Fig. 2-9. The higher signal level is designated by H and the lower signal level by L. Choosing the high-level H to represent logic-1 defines a positive logic system. Choosing the low-level L to represent logic-1 defines a negative logic system. The terms positive and negative are somewhat misleading since both signals may be positive or both may be negative. It is not the actual signal values that determine the type of logic, but rather the assignment of logic values to the relative amplitudes of the two signal levels.

Hardware digital gates are defined in terms of signal values such as H and L. It is up to the user to decide on a positive or negative logic polarity. Consider, for example, the electronic gate

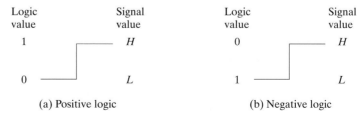

(a) Positive logic

(b) Negative logic

FIGURE 2-9
Signal assignment and logic polarity

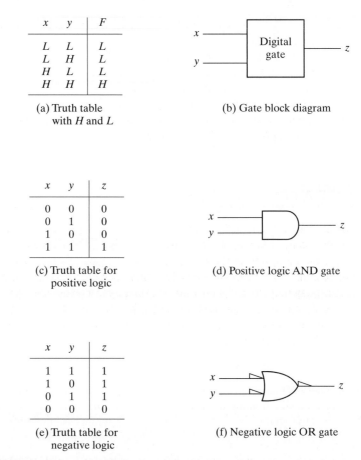

x	y	F
L	L	L
L	H	L
H	L	L
H	H	H

(a) Truth table
with H and L

(b) Gate block diagram

x	y	z
0	0	0
0	1	0
1	0	0
1	1	1

(c) Truth table for
positive logic

(d) Positive logic AND gate

x	y	z
1	1	1
1	0	1
0	1	1
0	0	0

(e) Truth table for
negative logic

(f) Negative logic OR gate

FIGURE 2-10
Demonstration of positive and negative logic

shown in Fig. 2-10(b). The truth table for this gate is listed in Fig. 2-10(a). It specifies the physical behavior of the gate when H is 3 volts and L is 0 volts. The truth table of Fig. 2-10(c) assumes positive logic assignment, with $H = 1$ and $L = 0$. This truth table is the same as the one for the AND operation. The graphic symbol for a positive logic AND gate is shown in Fig. 2-10(d).

Now consider the negative logic assignment for the same physical gate with $L = 1$ and $H = 0$. The result is the truth table of Fig. 2-10(e). This table represents the OR operation even though the entries are reversed. The graphic symbol for the negative logic OR gate is shown in Fig. 2-10(f). The small triangles in the inputs and output designate a *polarity indicator*. The presence of this polarity indicator along a terminal signifies that negative logic is assumed for the signal. Thus, the same physical gate can operate either as a positive logic AND gate or as a negative logic OR gate.

The conversion from positive logic to negative logic, and vice versa, is essentially an operation that changes 1's to 0's and 0's to 1's in both the inputs and the output of a gate. Since this operation produces the dual of a function, the change of all terminals from one polarity to the other results in taking the dual of the function. The result of this conversion is that all AND operations are converted to OR operations (or graphic symbols) and vice versa. In addition, one must not forget to include the polarity-indicator triangle in the graphic symbols when negative logic is assumed. In this book, we will not use negative logic gates and will assume that all gates operate with a positive logic assignment.

2-8   INTEGRATED CIRCUITS

An integrated circuit (abbreviated IC) is a silicon semiconductor crystal, called a *chip*, containing the electronic components for constructing digital gates. The various gates are interconnected inside the chip to form the required circuit. The chip is mounted in a ceramic or plastic container, and connections are welded to external pins to form the integrated circuit. The number of pins may range from 14 on a small IC package to several thousands on a larger package. Each IC has a numeric designation printed on the surface of the package for identification. Vendors provide data books, catalogs, and Internet websites that contain descriptions and information about the ICs that they manufacture.

Levels of Integration

Digital ICs are often categorized according to their circuit complexity as measured by the number of logic gates in a single package. The differentiation between those chips that have a few internal gates and those having hundreds of thousands of gates is made by a customary reference to a package as being either a small-, medium-, large-, or very large-scale integration device.

Small-scale integration (SSI) devices contain several independent gates in a single package. The inputs and outputs of the gates are connected directly to the pins in the package. The number of gates is usually fewer than 10 and is limited by the number of pins available in the IC.

Medium-scale integration (MSI) devices have a complexity of approximately 10 to 1,000 gates in a single package. They usually perform specific elementary digital operations. MSI digital functions are introduced in Chapter 4 as decoders, adders, and multiplexers and in Chapter 6 as registers and counters.

Large-scale integration (LSI) devices contain thousands of gates in a single package. They include digital systems such as processors, memory chips, and programmable logic devices. Some LSI components are presented in Chapter 7.

Very large-scale integration (VLSI) devices contain hundred of thousands of gates within a single package. Examples are large memory arrays and complex microcomputer chips. Because of their small size and low cost, VLSI devices have revolutionized the computer system design technology, giving the designer the capability to create structures that were previously uneconomical to build.

Digital Logic Families

Digital integrated circuits are classified not only by their complexity or logical operation, but also by the specific circuit technology to which they belong. The circuit technology is referred to as a digital logic family. Each logic family has its own basic electronic circuit upon which more complex digital circuits and components are developed. The basic circuit in each technology is a NAND, NOR, or inverter gate. The electronic components employed in the construction of the basic circuit are usually used to name the technology. Many different logic families of digital integrated circuits have been introduced commercially. The following are the most popular:

TTL	transistor-transistor logic;
ECL	emitter-coupled logic;
MOS	metal-oxide semiconductor;
CMOS	complementary metal-oxide semiconductor.

TTL is a logic family that has been in operation for a long time and is considered as standard. ECL has an advantage in systems requiring high-speed operation. MOS is suitable for circuits that need high component density, and CMOS is preferable in systems requiring low power consumption. Low power consumption is essential for VLSI design, and therefore, CMOS has become the dominant logic family, while TTL and ECL are declining in use. The analysis of the basic electronic digital gate circuit in each logic family is presented in Chapter 10.

The characteristics of digital logic families are usually compared by analyzing the circuit of the basic gate in each family. The most important parameters that are evaluated and compared are discussed in Section 10-2. They are listed here for reference.

Fan-out specifies the number of standard loads that the output of a typical gate can drive without impairing its normal operation. A standard load is usually defined as the amount of current needed by an input of another similar gate of the same family.

Fan-in is the number of inputs available in a gate.

Power dissipation is the power consumed by the gate that must be available from the power supply.

Propagation delay is the average transition delay time for the signal to propagate from input to output. The operating speed is inversely proportional to the propagation delay.

Noise margin is the maximum external noise voltage added to an input signal that does not cause an undesirable change in the circuit output.

Computer-Aided Design (CAD)

The design of digital systems with VLSI circuits containing millions of transistors is a formidable task. Systems of this complexity are usually impossible to develop and verify without the assistance of computer-aided design tools. CAD tools consist of software programs that support computer-based representation and aid in the development of digital hardware by automating the design process. Electronic design automation covers all phases of the design of integrated circuits. A typical design flow for creating VLSI circuits consists of a sequence of steps beginning with design entry and culminating with the generation of the database that contains the photomask used to fabricate the IC. There are a variety of options available for creating the physical realization of a digital circuit in silicon. The designer can choose between an application-specific integrated circuit (ASIC), a field-programmable gate array (FPGA), a programmable logic device (PLD), or a full-custom IC. With each of these devices comes a set of CAD tools that provide the necessary software to facilitate the hardware fabrication of the unit.

Some CAD systems include an editing program for creating and modifying schematic diagrams on a computer screen. This process is called *schematic capture* or schematic entry. With the aid of menus, keyboard commands, and the mouse, a schematic editor can draw circuit diagrams of digital circuits in the computer screen. Components can be placed on the screen from a list in an internal library and can then be connected with lines that represent wires. The schematic entry software creates and manages a database containing the information created with the schematic. Primitive gates and functional blocks have associated models that allow the behavior and timing of the circuit to be verified. This verification is performed by applying inputs to the circuit and using a logic simulator to determine the outputs.

An important development in the design of digital systems is the use of a hardware description language (HDL). HDL resembles a programming language, but is specifically oriented to describe digital hardware. It represents logic diagrams and other digital information in textual form. It is used to simulate the system before its construction to check the functionality and verify its operation before it is submitted to fabrication. An important application is its logic synthesis software, which automates the design of digital systems. HDL has become very important in recent years and is the best method available for the design of complex digital systems. HDL is introduced in Sec 3-9 and because of its importance, we include HDL descriptions of digital circuits, components, and design procedures throughout the entire book.

PROBLEMS

2-1   Demonstrate by means of truth tables the validity of the following identities:

(a)   DeMorgan's theorem for three variables: $(x + y + z)' = x'y'z'$ and $(xyz)' = x' + y' + z'$

(b)   The distributive law: $x + yz = (x + y)(x + z)$

2-2   Simplify the following Boolean expressions to a minimum number of literals:

(a) $xy + xy'$ (b) $(x + y)(x + y')$

(c) $xyz + x'y + xyz'$ (d) $(A + B)'(A' + B')'$

2-3   Simplify the following Boolean expressions to a minimum number of literals:

(a) $ABC + A'B + ABC'$ (b) $x'yz + xz$

(c) $(x + y)'(x' + y')$ (d) $xy + x(wz + wz')$

(e) $(BC' + A'D)(AB' + CD')$

2-4   Reduce the following Boolean expressions to the indicated number of literals:

(a) $A'C' + ABC + AC'$ to three literals

(b) $(x'y' + z)' + z + xy + wz$ to three literals

(c) $A'B(D' + C'D) + B(A + A'CD)$ to one literal

(d) $(A' + C)(A' + C')(A + B + C'D)$ to four literals

2-5 Find the complement of $F = x + yz$; then show that $FF' = 0$ and $F + F' = 1$.

2-6 Find the complement of the following expressions:
(a) $xy' + x'y$ (b) $(AB' + C)D' + E$
(c) $(x + y' + z)(x' + z')(x + y)$

2-7 Given the Boolean functions F_1 and F_2.
(a) Show that the Boolean function $E = F_1 + F_2$ contains the sum of the minterms of F_1 and F_2.
(b) Show that the Boolean function $G = F_1 F_2$ contains only the minterms that are common to F_1 and F_2.

2-8 List the truth table of the function:

$$F = xy + xy' + y'z$$

2-9 Logical operations can be performed on strings of bits by considering each pair of corresponding bits separately (this is called bitwise operation). Given two 8-bit strings $A = 10101101$ and $B = 10001110$, evaluate the 8-bit result after the following logical operations: (a) AND, (b) OR, (c) XOR, (d) NOT A, (e) NOT B.

2-10 Draw the logic diagrams for the following Boolean expressions:
(a) $Y = A'B' + B(A + C)$ (b) $Y = BC + AC'$
(c) $Y = A + CD$ (d) $Y = (A + B)(C' + D)$

2-11 Given the Boolean function:

$$F = xy + x'y' + y'z$$

(a) implement it with AND, OR, and inverter gates,
(b) implement it with OR and inverter gates, and
(c) implement it with AND and inverter gates.

2-12 Simplify the Boolean function T_1 and T_2 to a minimum number of literals.

A	B	C	T_1	T_2
0	0	0	1	0
0	0	1	1	0
0	1	0	1	0
0	1	1	0	1
1	0	0	0	1
1	0	1	0	1
1	1	0	0	1
1	1	1	0	1

2-13 The logical sum of all minterms of a Boolean function of n variables is 1.
(a) Prove the previous statement for $n = 3$.
(b) Suggest a procedure for a general proof.

2-14 Obtain the truth table of the following functions and express each function in sum of minterms and product of maxterms:
(a) $(xy + z)(y + xz)$ (b) $(A' + B)(B' + C)$
(c) $y'z + wxy' + wxz' + w'x'z$

2-15 Given the Boolean function

$$F = xy'z + x'y'z + w'xy + wx'y + wxy$$

(a) Obtain the truth table of the function.
(b) Draw the logic diagram using the original Boolean expression.
(c) Simplify the function to a minimum number of literals using Boolean algebra.
(d) Obtain the truth table of the function from the simplified expression and show that it is the same as the one in part (a).
(e) Draw the logic diagram from the simplified expression and compare the total number of gates with the diagram of part (b).

2-16 Express the following function in sum of minterms and product of maxterms:

$$F(A, B, C, D) = B'D + A'D + BD$$

2-17 Express the complement of the following functions in sum of minterms:
(a) $F(A, B, C, D) = \Sigma(0, 2, 6, 11, 13, 14)$ (b) $F(x, y, z) = \Pi(0, 3, 6, 7)$

2-18 Convert the following to the other canonical form:
(a) $F(x, y, z) = \Sigma(1, 3, 7)$ (b) $F(A, B, C, D) = \Pi(0, 1, 2, 3, 4, 6, 12)$

2-19 Convert the following expressions into sum of products and product of sums:
(a) $(AB + C)(B + C'D)$ (b) $x' + x(x + y')(y + z')$

2-20 Draw the logic diagram corresponding to the following Boolean expressions without simplifying them:
(a) $BC' + AB + ACD$ (b) $(A + B)(C + D)(A' + B + D)$
(c) $(AB + A'B')(CD' + C'D)$

2-21 Show that the dual of the exclusive-OR is equal to its complement.

2-22 By substituting the Boolean expression equivalent of the binary operations as defined in Table 2-8, show the following:
(a) The inhibition operation is neither commutative nor associative.
(b) The exclusive-OR operation is commutative and associative.

2-23 Show that a positive logic NAND gate is a negative logic NOR gate and vice versa.

REFERENCES

1. BOOLE, G. 1854. *An Investigation of the Laws of Thought.* New York: Dover.

2. SHANNON, C. E. A symbolic analysis of relay and switching circuits. *Trans. AIEE* 57 (1938): 713-723.

3. HUNTINGTON, E. V. Sets of independent postulates for the algebra of logic. *Trans. Am. Math. Soc.,* **5** (1904): 288-309.

4. MANO, M. M. and C. R. Kime. 2000. *Logic and Computer Design Fundamentals,* 2nd ed. Upper Saddle River, NJ: Prentice Hall.

5. DIETMEYER, D. L. 1988. *Logic Design of Digital Systems,* 3rd ed. Boston: Allyn Bacon.

3

Gate-Level Minimization

3-1 THE MAP METHOD

The complexity of the digital logic gates that implement a Boolean function is directly related to the complexity of the algebraic expression from which the function is implemented. Although the truth table representation of a function is unique, when expressed algebraically, it can appear in many different forms. Boolean expressions may be simplified by algebraic means as discussed in Section 2-4. However, this procedure of minimization is awkward because it lacks specific rules to predict each succeeding step in the manipulative process. The map method provides a simple straightforward procedure for minimizing Boolean functions. This method may be regarded as a pictorial form of a truth table. The map method is also known as the Karnaugh map or K-map.

The map is a diagram made up of squares, with each square representing one minterm of the function. Since any Boolean function can be expressed as a sum of minterms, it follows that a Boolean function is recognized graphically in the map from the area enclosed by those squares whose minterms are included in the function. In fact, the map presents a visual diagram of all possible ways a function may be expressed in standard form. By recognizing various patterns, the user can derive alternative algebraic expressions for the same function, from which the simplest can be selected.

The simplified expressions produced by the map are always in one of the two standard forms: sum of products or product of sums. It will be assumed that the simplest algebraic expression is one with a minimum number of terms and with the fewest possible number of literals in each term. This produces a circuit diagram with a minimum number of gates and the minimum number of inputs to the gate. We will see subsequently that the simplest expression is not unique. It is sometimes possible to find two or more expressions that satisfy the minimization criteria. In that case, either solution would be satisfactory.

Two-Variable Map

The two-variable map is shown in Fig. 3-1(a). There are four minterms for two variables; hence, the map consists of four squares, one for each minterm. The map is redrawn in (b) to show the relationship between the squares and the two variables x and y. The 0 and 1 marked in each row and column designate the values of variables. Variable x appears primed in row 0 and unprimed in row 1. Similarly, y appears primed in column 0 and unprimed in column 1.

If we mark the squares whose minterms belong to a given function, the two-variable map becomes another useful way to represent any one of the 16 Boolean functions of two variables. As an example, the function xy is shown in Fig. 3-2(a). Since xy is equal to m_3, a 1 is placed inside the square that belongs to m_3. Similarly, the function $x + y$ is represented in the map of Fig. 3-2(b) by three squares marked with 1's. These squares are found from the minterms of the function:

$$m_1 + m_2 + m_3 = x'y + xy' + xy = x + y$$

The three squares could have also been determined from the intersection of variable x in the second row and variable y in the second column, which encloses the area belonging to x or y.

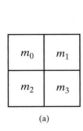

(a)   (b)

FIGURE 3-1
Two-variable Map

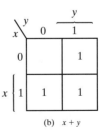

(a) xy (b) $x + y$

FIGURE 3-2
Representation of Functions in the Map

m_0	m_1	m_3	m_2
m_4	m_5	m_7	m_6

yz / x	0 0	0 1	$\overline{}$ y 11	10
0	$x'y'z'$	$x'y'z$	$x'yz$	$x'yz'$
x { 1	$xy'z'$	$xy'z$	xyz	xyz'

$\underline{}$ z

(a)   (b)

FIGURE 3-3
Three-variable Map

Three-Variable Map

A three-variable map is shown in Fig. 3-3. There are eight minterms for three binary variables. Therefore, the map consists of eight squares. Note that the minterms are not arranged in a binary sequence, but in a sequence similar to the Gray code (Table 1-6). The characteristic of this sequence is that only one bit changes in value from one adjacent column to the next. The map drawn in part (b) is marked with numbers in each row and each column to show the relationship between the squares and the three variables. For example, the square assigned to m_5 corresponds to row 1 and column 01. When these two numbers are concatenated, they give the binary number 101, whose decimal equivalent is 5. Another way of looking at square $m_5 = xy'z$ is to consider it to be in the row marked x and the column belonging to $y'z$ (column 01). Note that there are four squares where each variable is equal to 1 and four where each is equal to 0. The variable appears unprimed in those four squares where it is equal to 1 and primed in those squares where it is equal to 0. For convenience, we write the variable with its letter symbol under the four squares where it is unprimed.

To understand the usefulness of the map for simplifying Boolean functions, we must recognize the basic property possessed by adjacent squares. Any two adjacent squares in the map differ by only one variable, which is primed in one square and unprimed in the other. For example, m_5 and m_7 lie in two adjacent squares. Variable y is primed in m_5 and unprimed in m_7, whereas the other two variables are the same in both squares. From the postulates of Boolean algebra, it follows that the sum of two minterms in adjacent squares can be simplified to a single AND term consisting of only two literals. To clarify this, consider the sum of two adjacent squares such as m_5 and m_7:

$$m_5 + m_7 = xy'z + xyz = xz(y' + y) = xz$$

Here the two squares differ by the variable y, which can be removed when the sum of the two minterms is formed. Thus, any two minterms in adjacent squares that are ORed together will cause a removal of the different variable. The following examples explain the procedure for minimizing a Boolean function with a map.

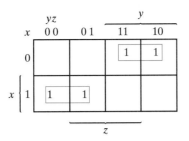

FIGURE 3-4
Map for Example 3-1; $F(x, y, z) = \Sigma(2, 3, 4, 5) = x'y + xy'$

EXAMPLE 3-1

Simplify the Boolean function

$$F(x, y, z) = \Sigma(2, 3, 4, 5)$$

First, a 1 is marked in each minterm that represents the function. This is shown in Fig. 3-4, where the squares for minterms 010, 011, 100, and 101 are marked with 1's. The next step is to find possible adjacent squares. These are indicated in the map by two rectangles, each enclosing two 1's. The upper right rectangle represents the area enclosed closed by $x'y$. This is determined by observing that the two-square area is in row 0, corresponding to x', and the last two columns, corresponding to y. Similarly, the lower left rectangle represents the product term xy'. (The second row represents x and the two left columns represent y'.) The logical sum of these two product terms gives the simplified expression:

$$F = x'y + xy'$$

■

There are cases where two squares in the map are considered to be adjacent even though they do not touch each other. In Fig. 3-3, m_0 is adjacent to m_2 and m_4 is adjacent to m_6 because the minterms differ by one variable. This can be readily verified algebraically:

$$m_0 + m_2 = x'y'z' + x'yz' = x'z'(y' + y) = x'z'$$
$$m_4 + m_6 = xy'z' + xyz' = xz' + (y' + y) = xz'$$

Consequently, we must modify the definition of adjacent squares to include this and other similar cases. This is done by considering the map as being drawn on a surface where the right and left edges touch each other to form adjacent squares.

EXAMPLE 3-2

Simplify the Boolean function

$$F(x, y, z) = \Sigma(3, 4, 6, 7)$$

The map for this function is shown in Fig. 3-5. There are four squares marked with 1's, one for each minterm of the function. Two adjacent squares are combined in the third column to give

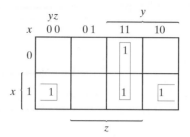

FIGURE 3-5
Map for Example 3-2; $F(x, y, z) = \Sigma(3, 4, 6, 7) = yz + xz'$

a two-literal term yz. The remaining two squares with 1's are also adjacent by the new definition and are shown in the diagram with their values enclosed in half rectangles. These two squares, when combined, give the two-literal term xz'. The simplified function becomes

$$F = yz + xz'$$

∎

Consider now any combination of four adjacent squares in the three-variable map. Any such combination represents the logical sum of four minterms and results in an expression of only one literal. As an example, the logical sum of the four adjacent minterms 0, 2, 4, and 6 reduces to a single literal term z':

$$\begin{aligned}
m_0 + m_2 + m_4 + m_6 &= x'y'z' + x'yz' + xy'z' + xyz' \\
&= x'z'(y' + y) + xz'(y' + y) \\
&= x'z' + xz' = z'(x' + x) = z'
\end{aligned}$$

The number of adjacent squares that may be combined must always represent a number that is a power of two such as 1, 2, 4, and 8. As a larger number of adjacent squares are combined, we obtain a product term with fewer literals.

One square represents one minterm, giving a term of three literals.

Two adjacent squares represent a term of two literals.

Four adjacent squares represent a term of one literal.

Eight adjacent squares encompass the entire map and produce a function that is always equal to 1.

EXAMPLE 3-3

Simplify the Boolean function

$$F(x, y, z) = \Sigma(0, 2, 4, 5, 6)$$

The map for F is shown in Fig. 3-6. First, we combine the four adjacent squares in the first and last columns to give the single literal term z'. The remaining single square representing minterm 5 is combined with an adjacent square that has already been used once. This is not only

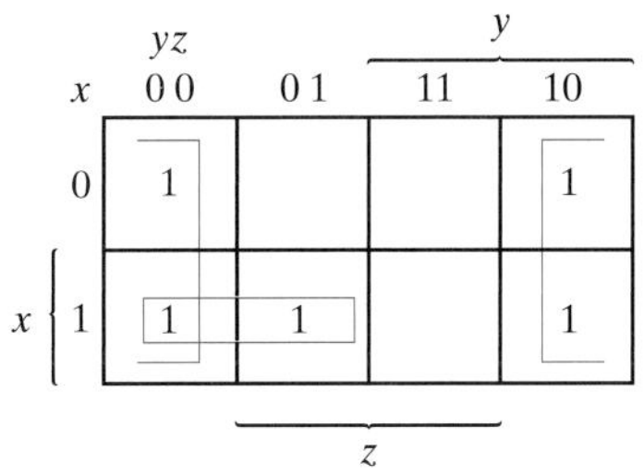

FIGURE 3-6
Map for Example 3-3; $F(x, y, z) = \Sigma(0, 2, 4, 5, 6) = z' + xy'$

permissible, but rather desirable, because the two adjacent squares give the two-literal term xy' and the single square represents the three-literal minterm $xy'z$. The simplified function is

$$F = z' + xy'$$

∎

If a function is not expressed in sum of minterms, it is possible to use the map to obtain the minterms of the function and then simplify the function to an expression with a minimum number of terms. It is necessary to make sure that the algebraic expression is in sum of products form. Each product term can be plotted in the map in one, two, or more squares. The minterms of the function are then read directly from the map.

EXAMPLE 3-4

Given the Boolean function

$$F = A'C + A'B + AB'C + BC$$

(a) express it in sum of minterms

(b) and find the minimal sum of products expression.

Three product terms in the expression have two literals and are represented in a three-variable map by two squares each. The two squares corresponding to the first term, $A'C$, are found in Fig. 3-7 from the coincidence of A' (first row) and C (two middle columns) to give squares 001

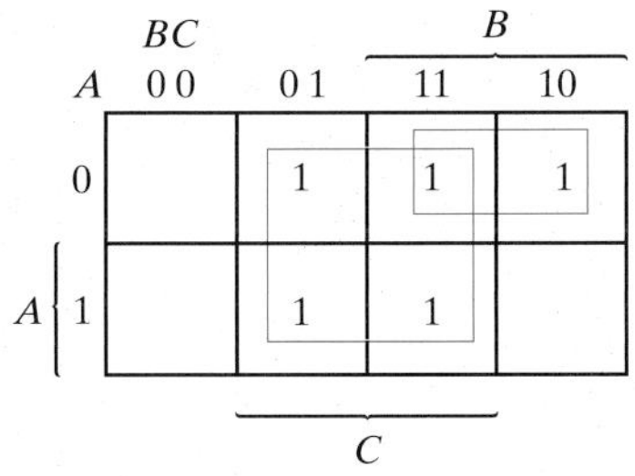

FIGURE 3-7
Map for Example 3-4; $A'C + A'B + AB'C + BC = C + A'B$

and 011. Note that when marking 1's in the squares, it is possible to find a 1 already placed there from a preceding term. This happens with the second term, $A'B$, which has 1's in squares 011 and 010. Square 011 is common with the first term, $A'C$, though, so only one 1 is marked in it. Continuing in this fashion, we determine that the term $AB'C$ belongs in square 101, corresponding to minterm 5, and the term BC has two 1's in squares 011 and 111. The function has a total of five minterms, as indicated by the five 1's in the map of Fig. 3-7. The minterms are read directly from the map to be 1, 2, 3, 5, and 7. The function can be expressed in sum of minterms form:

$$F(A, B, C) = \Sigma(1, 2, 3, 5, 7)$$

The sum of products expression as originally given has too many terms. It can be simplified, as shown in the map, to an expression with only two terms:

$$F = C + A'B$$

■

3-2   FOUR-VARIABLE MAP

The map for Boolean functions of four binary variables is shown in Fig. 3-8. In (a) are listed the 16 minterms and the squares assigned to each. In (b) the map is redrawn to show the relationship with the four variables. The rows and columns are numbered in a Gray code sequence, with only one digit changing value between two adjacent rows or columns. The minterm corresponding to each square can be obtained from the concatenation of the row number with the column number. For example, the numbers of the third row (11) and the second column (01), when concatenated, give the binary number 1101, the binary equivalent of decimal 13. Thus, the square in the third row and second column represents minterm m_{13}.

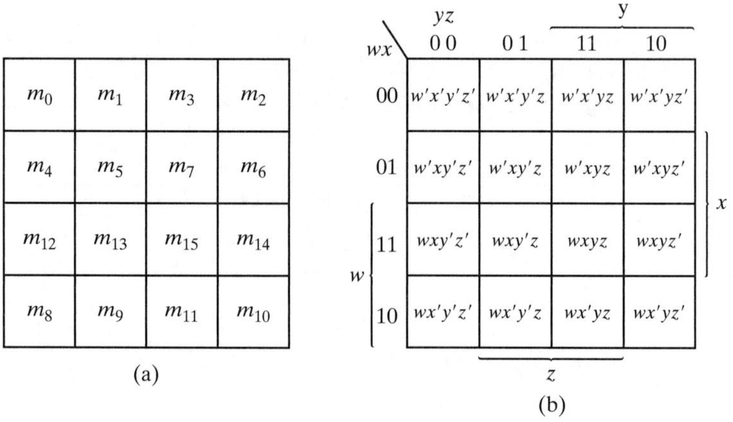

m_0	m_1	m_3	m_2
m_4	m_5	m_7	m_6
m_{12}	m_{13}	m_{15}	m_{14}
m_8	m_9	m_{11}	m_{10}

(a)

	yz		y	
wx	0 0	0 1	11	10
00	$w'x'y'z'$	$w'x'y'z$	$w'x'yz$	$w'x'yz'$
01	$w'xy'z'$	$w'xy'z$	$w'xyz$	$w'xyz'$
11	$wxy'z'$	$wxy'z$	$wxyz$	$wxyz'$
10	$wx'y'z'$	$wx'y'z$	$wx'yz$	$wx'yz'$

z

(b)

FIGURE 3-8
Four-variable Map

The map minimization of four-variable Boolean functions is similar to the method used to minimize three-variable functions. Adjacent squares are defined to be squares next to each other. In addition, the map is considered to lie on a surface with the top and bottom edges, as well as the right and left edges, touching each other to form adjacent squares. For example, m_0 and m_2 form adjacent squares, as do m_3 and m_{11}. The combination of adjacent squares that is useful during the simplification process is easily determined from inspection of the four-variable map:

> One square represents one minterm, giving a term of four literals.
>
> Two adjacent squares represent a term of three literals.
>
> Four adjacent squares represent a term of two literals.
>
> Eight adjacent squares represent a term of one literal.
>
> Sixteen adjacent squares represent the function equal to 1.

No other combination of squares can simplify the function. The following two examples show the procedure used to simplify four-variable Boolean functions.

EXAMPLE 3-5

Simplify the Boolean function

$$F(w, x, y, z) = \Sigma(0, 1, 2, 4, 5, 6, 8, 9, 12, 13, 14)$$

Since the function has four variables, a four-variable map must be used. The minterms listed in the sum are marked by 1's in the map of Fig. 3-9. Eight adjacent squares marked with 1's can be combined to form the one literal term y'. The remaining three 1's on the right cannot be combined to give a simplified term. They must be combined as two or four adjacent squares. The larger the number of squares combined, the smaller the number of literals in the term. In

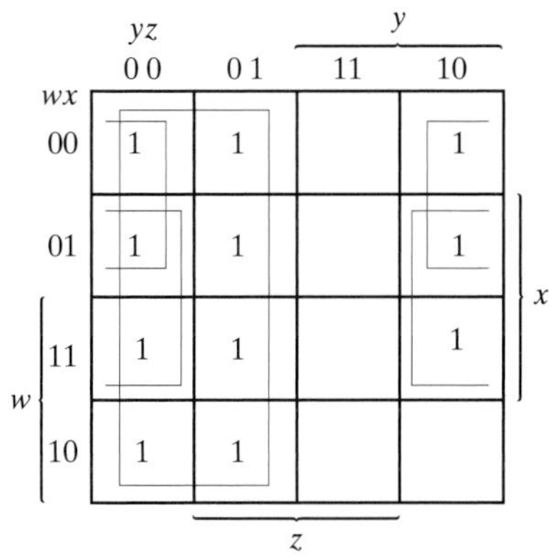

FIGURE 3-9
Map for Example 3-5; $F(w, x, y, z) = \Sigma(0, 1, 2, 4, 5, 6, 8, 9, 12, 13, 14)$
$= y' + w'z' + xz'$

this example, the top two 1's on the right are combined with the top two 1's on the left to give the term $w'z'$. Note that it is permissible to use the same square more than once. We are now left with a square marked by 1 in the third row and fourth column (square 1110). Instead of taking this square alone (which will give a term of four literals), we combine it with squares already used to form an area of four adjacent squares. These squares make up the two middle rows and the two end columns, giving the term xz'. The simplified function is

$$F = y' + w'z' + xz'$$

■

EXAMPLE 3-6

Simplify the Boolean function

$$F = A'B'C' + B'CD' + A'BCD' + AB'C'$$

The area in the map covered by this function consists of the squares marked with 1's in Fig. 3-10. This function has four variables and, as expressed, consists of three terms, each with three literals, and one term of four literals. Each term of three literals is represented in the map by two squares. For example, $A'B'C'$ is represented in squares 0000 and 0001. The function can be simplified in the map by taking the 1's in the four corners to give the term $B'D'$. This is possible because these four squares are adjacent when the map is drawn in a surface with top and bottom or left and right edges touching one another. The two left-hand 1's in the top row are combined with the two 1's in the bottom row to give the term $B'C'$. The remaining 1 may be combined in a two-square area to give the term $A'CD'$. The simplified function is

$$F = B'D' + B'C' + A'CD'$$

■

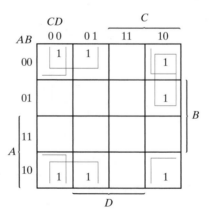

FIGURE 3-10
Map for Example 3-6; $A'B'C' + B'CD' + A'BCD' + AB'C' = B'D' + B'C' + A'CD'$

Prime Implicants

When choosing adjacent squares in a map, we must ensure that all the minterms of the function are covered when combining the squares. At the same time, it is necessary to minimize the number of terms in the expression and avoid any redundant terms whose minterms are already covered by other terms. Sometimes there may be two or more expressions that satisfy the simplification criteria. The procedure for combining squares in the map may be made more systematic if we understand the meaning of the terms referred to as prime implicant and essential prime implicant. A *prime implicant* is a product term obtained by combining the maximum possible number of adjacent squares in the map. If a minterm in a square is covered by only one prime implicant, that prime implicant is said to be *essential.*

The prime implicants of a function can be obtained from the map by combining all possible maximum numbers of squares. This means that a single 1 on a map represents a prime implicant if it is not adjacent to any other 1's. Two adjacent 1's form a prime implicant, provided that they are not within a group of four adjacent squares. Four adjacent 1's form a prime implicant if they are not within a group of eight adjacent squares, and so on. The essential prime implicants are found by looking at each square marked with a 1 and checking the number of prime implicants that cover it. The prime implicant is essential if it is the only prime implicant that covers the minterm.

Consider the following four-variable Boolean function:

$$F(A, B, C, D) = \Sigma(0, 2, 3, 5, 7, 8, 9, 10, 11, 13, 15)$$

The minterms of the function are marked with 1's in the maps of Fig. 3-11. Part (a) of the figure shows two essential prime implicants. One term is essential because there is only one way to include minterms m_0 within four adjacent squares. These four squares define the term $B'D'$. Similarly, there is only one way that minterm m_5 can be combined with four adjacent squares

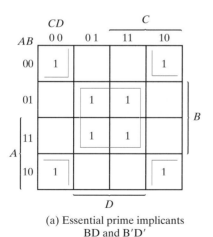

(a) Essential prime implicants
BD and B'D'

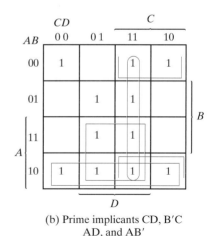

(b) Prime implicants CD, B'C
AD, and AB'

FIGURE 3-11
Simplification Using Prime Implicants

and this gives the second term BD. The two essential prime implicants cover eight minterms. The remaining three minterms, m_3, m_9, and m_{11}, must be considered next.

Figure 3-11(b) shows all possible ways that the three minterms can be covered with prime implicants. Minterm m_3 can be covered with either prime implicant CD or $B'C$. Minterm m_9 can be covered with either AD or AB'. Minterm m_{11} is covered with any one of the four prime implicants. The simplified expression is obtained from the logical sum of the two essential prime implicants and any two prime implicants that cover minterms m_3, m_9, and m_{11}. There are four possible ways that the function can be expressed with four product terms of two literals each:

$$
\begin{aligned}
F &= BD + B'D' + CD + AD \\
&= BD + B'D' + CD + AB' \\
&= BD + B'D' + B'C + AD \\
&= BD + B'D' + B'C + AB'
\end{aligned}
$$

The previous example has demonstrated that the identification of the prime implicants in the map helps in determining the alternatives that are available for obtaining a simplified expression.

The procedure for finding the simplified expression from the map requires that we first determine all the essential prime implicants. The simplified expression is obtained from the logical sum of all the essential prime implicants plus other prime implicants that may be needed to cover any remaining minterms not covered by the essential prime implicants. Occasionally, there may be more than one way of combining squares and each combination may produce an equally simplified expression.

3-3   FIVE-VARIABLE MAP

Maps for more than four variables are not as simple to use. A five-variable map needs 32 squares and a six-variable map needs 64 squares. When the number of variables becomes large, the number of squares becomes excessively large and the geometry for combining adjacent squares becomes more involved.

The five-variable map is shown in Fig. 3-12. It consists of 2 four-variable maps with variables A, B, C, D, and E. Variable A distinguishes between the two maps, as indicated on the top of the diagram. The left-hand four-variable map represents the 16 squares where $A = 0$, and the other four-variable map represents the squares where $A = 1$. Minterms 0 through 15 belong with $A = 0$ and minterms 16 through 31 with $A = 1$. Each four-variable map retains the previously defined adjacency when taken separately. In addition, each square in the $A = 0$ map is adjacent to the corresponding square in the $A = 1$ map. For example, minterm 4 is adjacent to minterm 20 and minterm 15 to 31. The best way to visualize this new rule for adjacent squares is to consider the two half maps as being one on top of the other. Any two squares that fall one over the other are considered adjacent.

By following the procedure used for the five-variable map, it is possible to construct a six-variable map with 4 four-variable maps to obtain the required 64 squares. Maps with six or more variables need too many squares and are impractical to use. The alternative is to employ

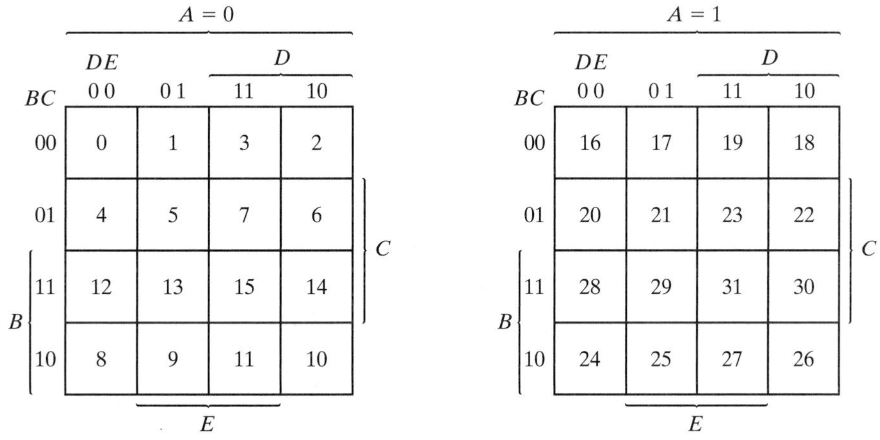

$A = 0$

BC \ DE	00	01	11	10
00	0	1	3	2
01	4	5	7	6
11	12	13	15	14
10	8	9	11	10

$A = 1$

BC \ DE	00	01	11	10
00	16	17	19	18
01	20	21	23	22
11	28	29	31	30
10	24	25	27	26

FIGURE 3-12
Five-variable Map

computer programs specifically written to facilitate the simplification of Boolean functions with a large number of variables.

From inspection, and taking into account the new definition of adjacent squares, it is possible to show that any 2^k adjacent squares, for $k = (0, 1, 2, \ldots, n)$ in an n-variable map, will represent an area that gives a term of $n - k$ literals. For the above statement to have any meaning, n must be larger than k. When $n = k$, the entire area of the map is combined to give the identity function. Table 3-1 shows the relationship between the number of adjacent squares and the number of literals in the term. For example, eight adjacent squares combine an area in the five-variable map to give a term of two literals.

Table 3-1
The Relationship Between the Number of Adjacent Squares and the Number of Literals In the Term

K	Number of Adjacent Squares 2^k	Number of Literals in a Term in an n-variable Map			
		$n = 2$	$n = 3$	$n = 4$	$n = 5$
0	1	2	3	4	5
1	2	1	2	3	4
2	4	0	1	2	3
3	8		0	1	2
4	16			0	1
5	32				0

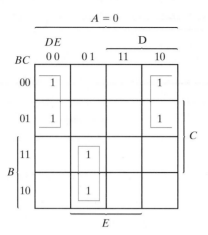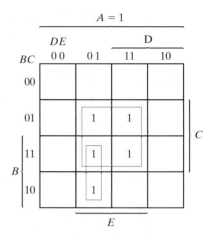

FIGURE 3-13
Map for Example 3-7; $F = A'B'E' + BD'E + ACE$

EXAMPLE 3-7

Simplify the Boolean function

$$F(A, B, C, D, E) = \Sigma (0, 2, 4, 6, 9, 13, 21, 23, 25, 29, 31)$$

The five-variable map for this function is shown in Fig. 3-13. There are six minterms from 0 to 15 that belong to the part of the map with $A = 0$. The other five minterms belong with $A = 1$. Four adjacent squares in the $A = 0$ map are combined to give the three-literal term $A'B'E'$. Note that it is necessary to include A' with the term because all the squares are associated with $A = 0$. The two squares in column 01 and the last two rows are common to both parts of the map. Therefore, they constitute four adjacent squares and give the three-literal term $BD'E$. Variable A is not included here because the adjacent squares belong to both $A = 0$ and $A = 1$. The term ACE is obtained from the four adjacent squares that are entirely within the $A = 1$ map. The simplified function is the logical sum of the three terms:

$$F = A B E + BD E + ACE$$

3-4   PRODUCT OF SUMS SIMPLIFICATION

The minimized Boolean functions derived from the map in all previous examples were expressed in the sum of products form. With a minor modification, the product of sums form can be obtained.

The procedure for obtaining a minimized function in product of sums follows from the basic properties of Boolean functions. The 1's placed in the squares of the map represent the minterms of the function. The minterms not included in the function denote the complement of the function. From this we see that the complement of a function is represented in the map by the squares not marked by 1's. If we mark the empty squares by 0's and combine them into valid adjacent squares, we obtain a simplified expression of the complement of the function, i.e., of F'. The complement of F' gives us back the function F. Because of the generalized DeMorgan's theorem, the function so obtained is automatically in the product of sums form. The best way to show this is by example.

EXAMPLE 3-8

Simplify the following Boolean function in (a) sum of products and (b) product of sums:

$$F(A, B, C, D) = \Sigma(0, 1, 2, 5, 8, 9, 10)$$

The 1's marked in the map of Fig. 3-14 represent all the minterms of the function. The squares marked with 0's represent the minterms not included in F and, therefore, denote the complement of F. Combining the squares with 1's gives the simplified function in sum of products:

(a) $F = B'D' + B'C' + A'C'D$

If the squares marked with 0's are combined, as shown in the diagram, we obtain the simplified complemented function:

$$F' = AB + CD + BD'$$

Applying DeMorgan's theorem (by taking the dual and complementing each literal as described in Section 2-4), we obtain the simplified function in product of sums:

(b) $F = (A' + B')(C' + D')(B' + D)$

■

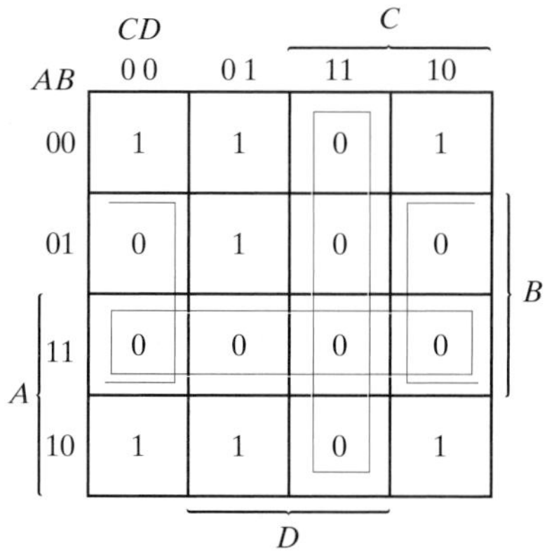

FIGURE 3-14
Map for Example 3-8; $F(A, B, C, D) = \Sigma(0, 1, 2, 5, 8, 9, 10)$
$= B'D' + B'C' + A'C'D = (A' + B')(C' + D')(B' + D)$

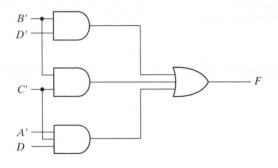

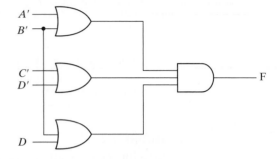

(a) $F = B'D' + B'C' + A'C'D$ (b) $F = (A' + B')(C' + D')(B' + D)$

FIGURE 3-15
Gate Implementation of the Function of Example 3-8

The implementation of the simplified expressions obtained in Example 3-8 is shown in Fig. 3-15. The sum of products expression is implemented in (a) with a group of AND gates, one for each AND term. The outputs of the AND gates are connected to the inputs of a single OR gate. The same function is implemented in (b) in its product of sums form with a group of OR gates, one for each OR term. The outputs of the OR gates are connected to the inputs of a single AND gate. In each case, it is assumed that the input variables are directly available in their complement, so inverters are not needed. The configuration pattern established in Fig. 3-15 is the general form by which any Boolean function is implemented when expressed in one of the standard forms. AND gates are connected to a single OR gate when in sum of products; OR gates are connected to a single AND gate when in product of sums. Either configuration forms two levels of gates. Thus, the implementation of a function in a standard form is said to be a two-level implementation.

Example 3-8 showed the procedure for obtaining the product of sums simplification when the function is originally expressed in the sum of minterms canonical form. The procedure is also valid when the function is originally expressed in the product of maxterms canonical form.

Table 3-2
Truth Table of Function F

x	y	z	F
0	0	0	0
0	0	1	1
0	1	0	0
0	1	1	1
1	0	0	1
1	0	1	0
1	1	0	1
1	1	1	0

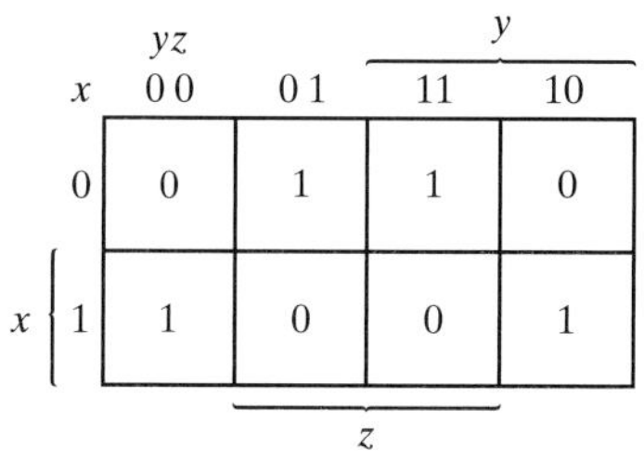

FIGURE 3-16
Map for the Function of Table 3-2

Consider, for example, the truth table that defines the function F in Table 3-2. In sum of minterms, this function is expressed as

$$F(x, y, z) = \Sigma(1, 3, 4, 6)$$

In product of maxterms, it is expressed as

$$F(x, y, z) = \Pi(0, 2, 5, 7)$$

In other words, the 1's of the function represent the minterms, and the 0's represent the maxterms. The map for this function is shown in Fig. 3-16. One can start simplifying this function by first marking the 1's for each minterm that the function is a 1. The remaining squares are marked by 0's. If, on the other hand, the product of maxterms is initially given, one can start marking 0's in those squares listed in the function; the remaining squares are then marked by 1's. Once the 1's and 0's are marked, the function can be simplified in either one of the standard forms. For the sum of products, we combine the 1's to obtain

$$F = x'z + xz'$$

For the product of sums, we combine the 0's to obtain the simplified complemented function

$$F' = xz + x'z'$$

which shows that the exclusive-OR function is the complement of the equivalence function (Section 2-6). Taking the complement of F', we obtain the simplified function in product of sums:

$$F = (x' + z')(x + z)$$

To enter a function expressed in product of sums in the map, take the complement of the function and from it find the squares to be marked by 0's. For example, the function

$$F = (A' + B' + C')(B + D)$$

can be entered in the map by first taking its complement,

$$F' = ABC + B'D'$$

and then marking 0's in the squares representing the minterms of F'. The remaining squares are marked with 1's.

3-5   DON'T-CARE CONDITIONS

The logical sum of the minterms associated with a Boolean function specifies the conditions under which the function is equal to 1. The function is equal to 0 for the rest of the minterms. This assumes that all the combinations of the values for the variables of the function are valid. In practice, there are some applications where the function is not specified for certain combinations of the variables. As an example, the four-bit binary code for the decimal digits has six combinations that are not used and consequently are considered as unspecified. Functions that have unspecified outputs for some input combinations are called incompletely specified functions. In most applications, we simply don't care what value is assumed by the function for the unspecified minterms. For this reason, it is customary to call the unspecified minterms of a function don't-care conditions. These don't-care conditions can be used on a map to provide further simplification of the Boolean expression.

It should be realized that a don't-care minterm is a combination of variables whose logical value is not specified. It cannot be marked with a 1 in the map because it would require that the function always be a 1 for such combination. Likewise, putting a 0 on the square requires the function to be 0. To distinguish the don't-care condition from 1's and 0's, an X is used. Thus, an X inside a square in the map indicates that we don't care whether the value of 0 or 1 is assigned to F for the particular minterm.

When choosing adjacent squares to simplify the function in a map, the don't-care minterms may be assumed to be either 0 or 1. When simplifying the function, we can choose to include each don't-care minterm with either the 1's or the 0's, depending on which combination gives the simplest expression.

EXAMPLE 3-9

Simplify the Boolean function

$$F(w, x, y, z) = \Sigma(1, 3, 7, 11, 15)$$

which has the don't-care conditions

$$d(w, x, y, z) = \Sigma(0, 2, 5)$$

The minterms of F are the variable combinations that make the function equal to 1. The minterms of d are the don't-care minterms that may be assigned either 0 or 1. The map simplification is shown in Fig. 3-17. The minterms of F are marked by 1's, those of d are marked by X's, and the remaining squares are filled with 0's. To get the simplified expression in sum of products, we must include all five 1's in the map, but we may or may not include any of the X's, depending on the way the function is simplified. The term yz covers the four minterms in the third column. The remaining minterm m_1 can be combined with minterm m_3 to give the three-literal term $w'x'z$. However, by including one or two adjacent X's we can combine four adjacent squares to give a two-literal term. In part (a) of the diagram, don't-care minterms 0 and 2 are included with the 1's, which results in the simplified function

$$F = yz + w'x'$$

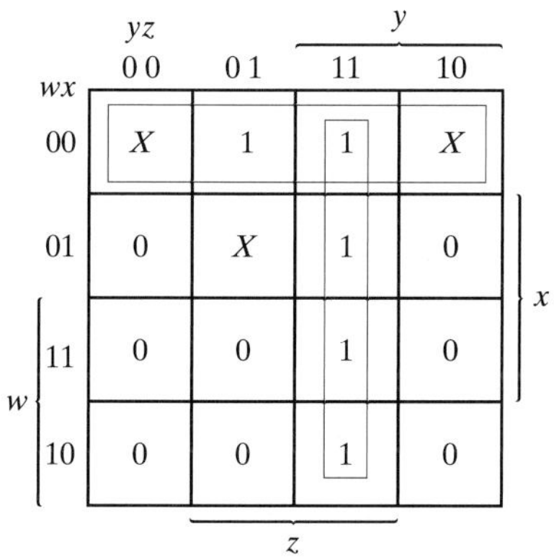

FIGURE 3-17
Example with don't-care Conditions

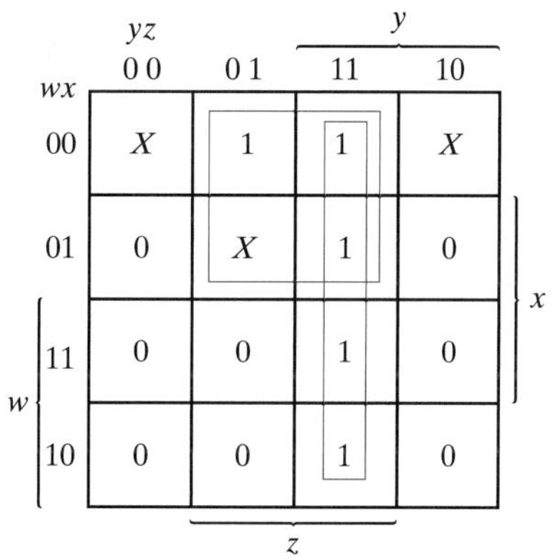

In part (b), don't-care minterm 5 is included with the 1's and the simplified function now is

$$F = yz + w'z$$

Either one of the preceding two expressions satisfies the conditions stated for this example.

■

The previous example has shown that the don't-care minterms in the map are initially marked with X's and are considered as being either 0 or 1. The choice between 0 and 1 is made depending on the way the incompletely specified function is simplified. Once the choice is made, the simplified function obtained will consist of a sum of minterms that includes those minterms that were initially unspecified and have been chosen to be included with the 1's. Consider the two simplified expressions obtained in Example 3-9:

$$F(w, x, y, z) = yz + w'x' = \Sigma(0, 1, 2, 3, 7, 11, 15)$$
$$F(w, x, y, z) = yz + w'z = \Sigma(1, 3, 5, 7, 11, 15)$$

Both expressions include minterms 1, 3, 7, 11, and 15 that make the function F equal to 1. The don't-care minterms 0, 2, and 5 are treated differently in each expression. The first expression includes minterms 0 and 2 with the 1's and leaves minterm 5 with the 0's. The second expression includes minterm 5 with the 1's and leaves minterms 0 and 2 with the 0's. The two expressions represent two functions that are algebraically unequal. Both cover the specified minterms of the function, but each covers different don't-care minterms. As far as the incompletely specified function is concerned, either expression is acceptable because the only difference is in the value of F for the don't-care minterms.

It is also possible to obtain a simplified product of sums expression for the function of Fig. 3-17. In this case, the only way to combine the 0's is to include don't-care minterms 0 and 2 with the 0's to give a simplified complemented function:

$$F' = z' + wy'$$

Taking the complement of F' gives the simplified expression in product of sums:

$$F(w, x, y, z) = z(w' + y) = \Sigma(1, 3, 5, 7, 11, 15)$$

For this case, we include minterms 0 and 2 with the 0's and minterm 5 with the 1's.

3-6   NAND AND NOR IMPLEMENTATION

Digital circuits are frequently constructed with NAND or NOR gates rather than with AND and OR gates. NAND and NOR gates are easier to fabricate with electronic components and are the basic gates used in all IC digital logic families. Because of the prominence of NAND and NOR gates in the design of digital circuits, rules and procedures have been developed for the conversion from Boolean functions given in terms of AND, OR, and NOT into equivalent NAND and NOR logic diagrams.

NAND Circuits

The NAND gate is said to be a universal gate because any digital system can be implemented with it. To show that any Boolean function can be implemented with NAND gates, we need only show that the logical operations of AND, OR, and complement can be obtained with NAND gates only. This is shown in Fig. 3-18. The complement operation is obtained from a one-input NAND gate that behaves exactly like an inverter. The AND operation requires two NAND gates. The first produces the NAND operation and the second inverts the logical sense of the signal. The OR operation is achieved through a NAND gate with additional inverters in each input.

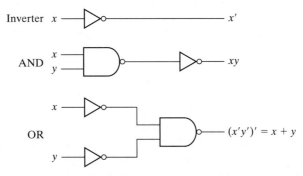

FIGURE 3-18
Logic Operations with NAND Gates

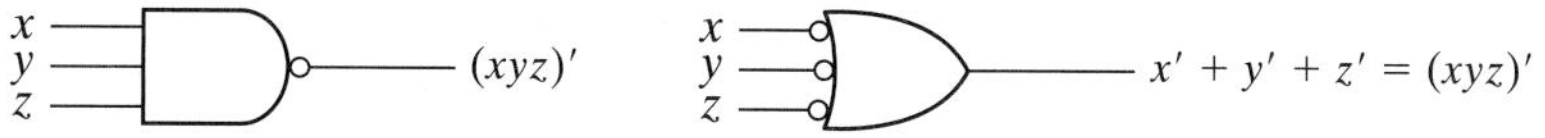

x
y
z
——— $(xyz)'$

x
y
z
——— $x' + y' + z' = (xyz)'$

(a) AND–invert

(b) Invert–OR

FIGURE 3-19
Two Graphic Symbols for NAND Gate

A convenient way to implement a Boolean function with NAND gates is to obtain the simplified Boolean function in terms of Boolean operators and then convert the function to NAND logic. The conversion of an algebraic expression from AND, OR, and complement to NAND can be done by simple circuit manipulation techniques that change AND-OR diagrams to NAND diagrams.

To facilitate the conversion to NAND logic, it is convenient to define an alternative graphic symbol for the gate. Two equivalent graphic symbols for the NAND gate are shown in Fig. 3-19. The AND-invert symbol has been defined previously and consists of an AND graphic symbol followed by a small circle negation indicator referred to as a bubble. Alternatively, it is possible to represent a NAND gate by an OR graphic symbol that is preceded by a bubble in each input. The invert-OR symbol for the NAND gate follows DeMorgan's theorem and the convention that the negation indicator denotes complementation. The two graphic symbols' representations are useful in the analysis and design of NAND circuits. When both symbols are mixed in the same diagram, the circuit is said to be in mixed notation.

Two-Level Implementation

The implementation of Boolean functions with NAND gates requires that the function be in sum of products form. To see the relationship between a sum of product expression and its equivalent NAND implementation, consider the logic diagrams drawn in Fig. 3-20. All three diagrams are equivalent and implement the function

$$F = AB + CD$$

The function is implemented in (a) with AND and OR gates. In (b), the AND gates are replaced by NAND gates and the OR gate is replaced by an NAND gate with an OR-invert graphic symbol. Remember that a bubble denotes complementation and two bubbles along the same

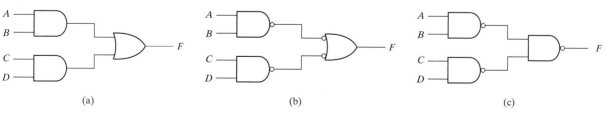

(a)   (b)   (c)

FIGURE 3-20
Three Ways to Implement $F = AB + CD$

line represent double complementation so both can be removed. Removing the bubbles on the gates of (b) produces the circuit of (a). Therefore, the two diagrams implement the same function and are equivalent.

In Fig. 3-20(c), the output NAND gate is redrawn with the AND-invert graphic symbol. When drawing NAND logic diagrams, the circuit shown in either (b) or (c) is acceptable. The one in (b) is in mixed notation and represents a more direct relationship with the Boolean expression it implements. The NAND implementation in Fig. 3-20(c) can be verified algebraically. The function it implements can be easily converted to a sum of products form by using DeMorgan's theorem:

$$F = \left((AB)'(CD)'\right)' = AB + CD$$

EXAMPLE 3-10

Implement the following Boolean function with NAND gates:

$$F(x, y, z) = (1, 2, 3, 4, 5, 7)$$

The first step is to simplify the function in sum of products. This is done by means of the map of Fig. 3-21(a) from which the simplified function is obtained:

$$F = xy' + x'y + z$$

The two-level NAND implementation is shown in Fig. 3-21(b) in mixed notation. Note that input z must have a one-input NAND gate (inverter) to compensate for the bubble in the second level

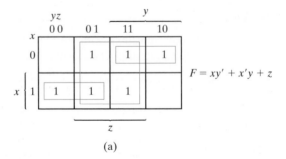

(a)

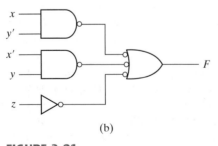

(b)

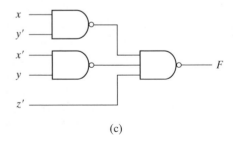

(c)

FIGURE 3-21
Solution to Example 3-10

gate. An alternative way of drawing the logic diagram is shown in Fig. 3-21(c). Here all the NAND gates are drawn with the same graphic symbol. The inverter with input z has been removed, but the input variable is complemented and denoted by z'.

The procedure described in the previous example indicates that a Boolean function can be implemented with two levels of NAND gates. The procedure for obtaining the logic diagram from a Boolean function is as follows:

1. Simplify the function and express it in sum of products.
2. Draw a NAND gate for each product term of the expression that has at least two literals. The inputs to each NAND gate are the literals of the term. This constitutes a group of first-level gates.
3. Draw a single gate using the AND-invert or the invert-OR graphic symbol in the second level, with inputs coming from outputs of first level gates.
4. A term with a single literal requires an inverter in the first level. However, if the single literal is complemented, it can be connected directly to an input of the second level NAND gate.

Multilevel NAND Circuits

The standard form of expressing Boolean functions results in a two-level implementation. There are occasions when the design of digital systems results in gating structures with three or more levels. The most common procedure in the design of multilevel circuits is to express the Boolean function in terms of AND, OR, and complement operations. The function can then be implemented with AND and OR gates. Then, if necessary, it can be converted into an all-NAND circuit. Consider for example the Boolean function:

$$F = A(CD + B) + BC'$$

Although it is possible to remove the parentheses and reduce the expression into a standard sum of products form, we choose to implement it as a multilevel circuit for illustration. The AND-OR implementation is shown in Fig. 3-22(a). There are four levels of gating in the circuit. The first level has two AND gates. The second level has an OR gate followed by an AND gate in the third level and an OR gate in the fourth level. A logic diagram with a pattern of alternate levels of AND and OR gates can be easily converted into a NAND circuit by using the mixed notation. This is shown in Fig. 3-22(b). The procedure is to change every AND gate to an AND-invert graphic symbol and every OR gate to an invert-OR graphic symbol. The NAND circuit performs the same logic as the AND-OR diagram as long as there are two bubbles along the same line. The bubble associated with input B causes an extra complementation, which must be compensated by changing the input literal to B'.

The general procedure for converting a multilevel AND-OR diagram into an all-NAND diagram using mixed notation is as follows:

1. Convert all AND gates to NAND gates with AND-invert graphic symbols.
2. Convert all OR gates to NAND gates with invert-OR graphic symbols.

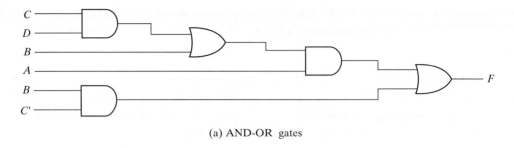

(a) AND-OR gates

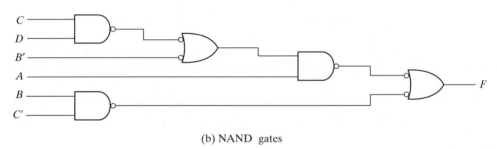

(b) NAND gates

FIGURE 3-22
Implementing $F = A(CD + B) + BC'$

3. Check all the bubbles in the diagram. For every bubble that is not compensated by another small circle along the same line, insert an inverter (one-input NAND gate) or complement the input literal.

As another example, consider the multilevel Boolean function

$$F = (AB' + A'B)(C + D')$$

The AND-OR implementation is shown in Fig. 3-23(a) with three levels of gating. The conversion into NAND with mixed notation is presented in part (b) of the diagram. The two additional bubbles associated with inputs C and D' cause these two literals to be complemented to C' and D. The bubble in the output NAND gate complements the output value, so we need to insert an inverter gate at the output in order to complement the signal again and get the original value.

NOR Implementation

The NOR operation is the dual of the NAND operation. Therefore, all procedures and rules for NOR logic are the dual of the corresponding procedures and rules developed for NAND logic. The NOR gate is another universal gate that can be used to implement any Boolean function. The implementation of the complement, OR, and AND operations with NOR gates is shown in Fig. 3-24. The complement operation is obtained from a one-input NOR gate that behaves

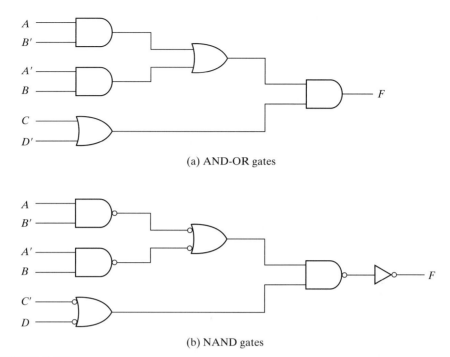

(a) AND-OR gates

(b) NAND gates

FIGURE 3-23
Implementing $F = (AB' + A'B)(C + D')$

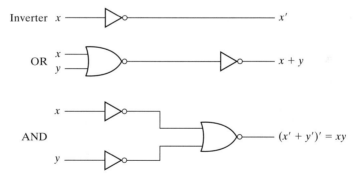

FIGURE 3-24
Logic Operations with NOR Gates

exactly like an inverter. The OR operation requires two NOR gates and the AND operation is obtained with a NOR gate that has inverters in each input.

The two graphic symbols for the mixed notation are shown in Fig. 3-25. The OR-invert symbol defines the NOR operation as an OR followed by a complement. The invert-AND symbol complements each input and then performs an AND operation. The two symbols designate the same NOR operation and are logically identical because of DeMorgan's theorem.

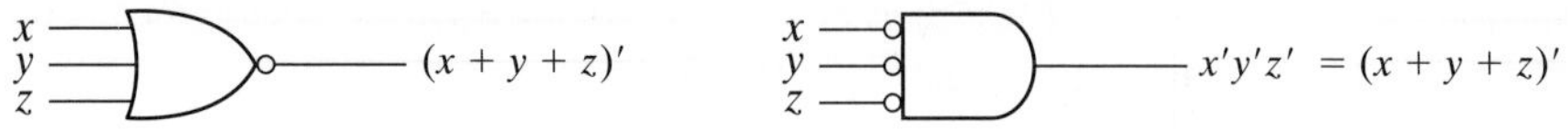

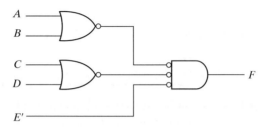

(a) OR–invert

(b) Invert–AND

FIGURE 3-25
Two Graphic Symbols for NOR Gate

FIGURE 3-26
Implementing $F = (A + B)(C + D)E$

A two-level implementation with NOR gates requires that the function be simplified in product of sums. Remember that the simplified product of sums expression is obtained from the map by combining the 0's and complementing. A product of sums expression is implemented with a first level of OR gates that produce the sum terms followed by a second level AND gate to produce the product. The transformation from the OR-AND diagram to a NOR diagram is achieved by changing the OR gates to NOR gates with OR-invert graphic symbols and the AND gate to a NOR gate with an invert-AND graphic symbol. A single literal term going into the second-level gate must be complemented. Fig. 3-26 shows the NOR implementation of a function expressed in product of sums:

$$F = (A + B)(C + D)E$$

The OR-AND pattern can be easily detected by the removal of the bubbles along the same line. Variable E is complemented to compensate for the third bubble at the input of the second-level gate.

The procedure for converting a multilevel AND-OR diagram to an all NOR diagram is similar to the one presented for NAND gates. For the NOR case, we must convert each OR gate to an OR- invert symbol and each AND gate to an invert-AND symbol. Any bubble that is not compensated by another bubble along the same line needs an inverter or the complementation of the input literal.

The transformation of the AND-OR diagram of Fig. 3-23(a) into a NOR diagram is shown in Fig. 3-27. The Boolean function for this circuit is

$$F = (AB' + A'B)(C + D')$$

The equivalent AND-OR diagram can be recognized from the NOR diagram by removing all the bubbles. To compensate for the bubbles in four inputs, it is necessary to complement the corresponding input literals.

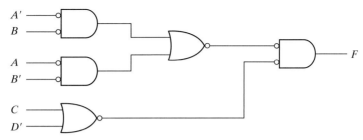

FIGURE 3-27
Implementing $F = (AB' + A'B)(C + D')$ with NOR Gates

3-7   OTHER TWO-LEVEL IMPLEMENTATIONS

The types of gates most often found in integrated circuits are NAND and NOR. For this reason, NAND and NOR logic implementations are the most important from a practical point of view. Some NAND or NOR gates (but not all) allow the possibility of a wire connection between the outputs of two gates to provide a specific logic function. This type of logic is called *wired logic*. For example, open-collector TTL NAND gates, when tied together, perform the wired-AND logic. (The open-collector TTL gate is shown in Chapter 10, Fig. 10-11.) The wired-AND logic performed with two NAND gates is depicted in Fig. 3-28(a). The AND gate is drawn with the lines going through the center of the gate to distinguish it from a conventional gate. The wired-AND gate is not a physical gate, but only a symbol to designate the function obtained from the indicated wired connection. The logic function implemented by the circuit of Fig. 3-28(a) is

$$F = (AB)' \cdot (CD)' = (AB + CD)'$$

and is called an AND-OR-INVERT function.

Similarly, the NOR output of ECL gates can be tied together to perform a wired-OR function. The logic function implemented by the circuit of Fig. 3-28(b) is

$$F = (A + B)' + (C + D)' = \left[(A + B)(C + D)\right]'$$

and is called an OR-AND-INVERT function.

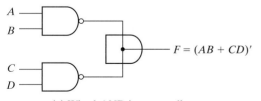

(a) Wired-AND in open-collector
   TTL NAND gates.

   (AND-OR-INVERT)

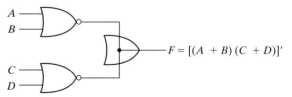

(b) Wired-OR in ECL gates

   (OR-AND-INVERT)

FIGURE 3-28
Wired Logic

A wired-logic gate does not produce a physical second-level gate since it is just a wire connection. Nevertheless, for discussion purposes, we will consider the circuits of Fig. 3-28 as two-level implementations. The first level consists of NAND (or NOR) gates and the second level has a single AND (or OR) gate. The wired connection in the graphic symbol will be omitted in subsequent discussions.

Nondegenerate Forms

It will be instructive from a theoretical point of view to find out how many two-level combinations of gates are possible. We consider four types of gates: AND, OR, NAND, and NOR. If we assign one type of gate for the first level and one type for the second level, we find that there are 16 possible combinations of two-level forms. (The same type of gate can be in the first and second levels, as in NAND-NAND implementation.) Eight of these combinations are said to be *degenerate* forms because they degenerate to a single operation. This can be seen from a circuit with AND gates in the first level and an AND gate in the second level. The output of the circuit is merely the AND function of all input variables. The other eight *nondegenerate* forms produce an implementation in sum of products or product of sums. The eight nondegenerate forms are as follows:

AND-OR	OR-AND
NAND-NAND	NOR-NOR
NOR-OR	NAND-AND
OR-NAND	AND-NOR

The first gate listed in each of the forms constitutes a first level in the implementation. The second gate listed is a single gate placed in the second level. Note that any two forms listed in the same line are the duals of each other.

The AND-OR and OR-AND forms are the basic two-level forms discussed in Section 3-4. The NAND-NAND and NOR-NOR forms were presented in Section 3-6. The remaining four forms are investigated in this section.

AND-OR-INVERT Implementation

The two forms NAND-AND and AND-NOR are equivalent forms and can be treated together. Both perform the AND-OR-INVERT function, as shown in Fig. 3-29. The AND-NOR form resembles the AND-OR form with an inversion done by the bubble in the output of the NOR gate. It implements the function

$$F = (AB + CD + E)'$$

By using the alternate graphic symbol for the NOR gate, we obtain the diagram of Fig. 3-29(b). Note that the single variable E is *not* complemented because the only change made is in the graphic symbol of the NOR gate. Now we move the bubble from the input terminal of the second-level gate to the output terminals of the first-level gates. An inverter is needed for the single variable to compensate for the bubble. Alternatively, the inverter can be

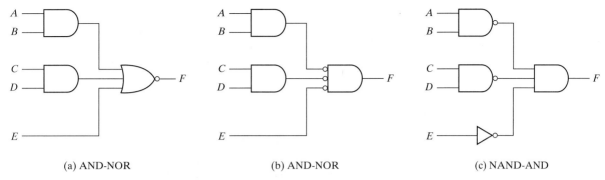

(a) AND-NOR   (b) AND-NOR   (c) NAND-AND

FIGURE 3-29
AND-OR-INVERT Circuits; $F = (AB + CD + E)'$

removed provided input E is complemented. The circuit of Fig. 3-29(c) is a NAND-AND form and was shown in Fig. 3-28 to implement the AND- OR-INVERT function.

An AND-OR implementation requires an expression in sum of products. The AND-OR-INVERT implementation is similar except for the inversion. Therefore, if the *complement* of the function is simplified in sum of products (by combining the 0's in the map), it will be possible to implement F' with the AND-OR part of the function. When F' passes through the always present output inversion (the INVERT part), it will generate the output F of the function. An example for the AND-OR-INVERT implementation will be shown subsequently.

OR-AND-INVERT Implementation

The OR-NAND and NOR-OR forms perform the OR-AND-INVERT function. This is shown in Fig. 3-30. The OR-NAND form resembles the OR-AND form, except for the inversion done by the bubble in the NAND gate. It implements the function

$$F = \left[(A + B)(C + D)E\right]'$$

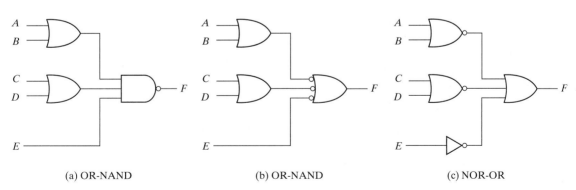

(a) OR-NAND   (b) OR-NAND   (c) NOR-OR

FIGURE 3-30
OR-AND-INVERT Circuits; $F = [(A + B)(C + D)E]'$

Table 3-3
Implementation with Other Two-Level Forms

Equivalent Nondegenerate Form		Implements the Function	Simplify F' in	To Get an Output of
(a)	**(b)***			
AND-NOR	NAND-AND	AND-OR-INVERT	Sum of products by combining 0's in the map	F
OR-NAND	NOR-OR	OR-AND-INVERT	Product of sums by combining 1's in the map and then complementing	F

*Form (b) requires an inverter for a single literal term.

By using the alternate graphic symbol for the NAND gate, we obtain the diagram of Fig. 3-30(b). The circuit in (c) is obtained by moving the small circles from the inputs of the second-level gate to the outputs of the first-level gates. The circuit of Fig. 3-30(c) is a NOR-OR form and was shown in Fig. 3-28 to implement the OR-AND-INVERT function.

The OR-AND-INVERT implementation requires an expression in product of sums. If the complement of the function is simplified in product of sums, we can implement F' with the OR-AND part of the function. When F' passes through the INVERT part, we obtain the complement of F', or F, in the output.

Tabular Summary and Example

Table 3-3 summarizes the procedures for implementing a Boolean function in any one of the four two-level forms. Because of the INVERT part in each case, it is convenient to use the simplification of F' (the complement) of the function. When F' is implemented in one of these forms, we obtain the complement of the function in the AND-OR or OR-AND form. The four two-level forms invert this function, giving an output that is the complement of F'. This is the normal output F.

EXAMPLE 3-11

Implement the function of Fig. 3-31(a) with the four two-level forms listed in Table 3-3. The complement of the function is simplified in sum of products by combining the 0's in the map:

$$F' = x'y + xy' + z$$

The normal output for this function can be expressed as

$$F = (x'y + xy' + z)'$$

which is in the AND-OR-INVERT form. The AND-NOR and NAND-AND implementations are shown in Fig. 3-31(b). Note that a one-input NAND or inverter gate is needed in the NAND-

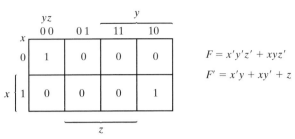

$$F = x'y'z' + xyz'$$
$$F' = x'y + xy' + z$$

(a) Map simplification in sum of products.

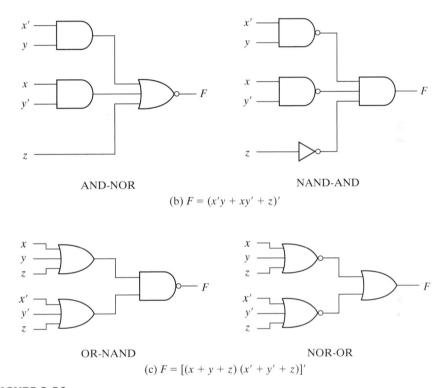

AND-NOR   NAND-AND

(b) $F = (x'y + xy' + z)'$

OR-NAND   NOR-OR

(c) $F = [(x + y + z)(x' + y' + z)]'$

FIGURE 3-31
Other Two-level Implementations

AND implementation, but not in the AND-NOR case. The inverter can be removed if we apply the input variable z' instead of z.

The OR-AND-INVERT forms require a simplified expression of the complement of the function in product of sums. To obtain this expression, we first combine the 1's in the map

$$F = x'y'z' + xyz'$$

Then we take the complement of the function

$$F' = (x + y + z)(x' + y' + z)$$

The normal output F can now be expressed in the form

$$F = \left[(x + y + z)(x' + y' + z)\right]'$$

which is in the OR-AND-INVERT form. From this expression, we can implement the function in the OR-NAND and NOR-OR forms, as shown in Fig. 3-31(c).

■

3-8   EXCLUSIVE-OR FUNCTION

The exclusive-OR (XOR), denoted by the symbol $\oplus$, is a logical operation that performs the following Boolean operation:

$$x \oplus y = xy' + x'y$$

It is equal to 1 if only x is equal to 1 or if only y is equal to 1, but not when both are equal to 1. The exclusive-NOR, also known as equivalence, performs the following Boolean operation:

$$(x \oplus y)' = xy + x'y'$$

It is equal to 1 if both x and y are equal to 1 or if both are equal to 0. The exclusive-NOR can be shown to be the complement of the exclusive-OR by means of a truth table or by algebraic manipulation:

$$(x \oplus y)' = (xy' + x'y)' = (x' + y)(x + y') = xy + x'y'$$

The following identities apply to the exclusive-OR operation:

$$x \oplus 0 = x$$
$$x \oplus 1 = x'$$
$$x \oplus x = 0$$
$$x \oplus x' = 1$$
$$x \oplus y' = x' \oplus y = (x \oplus y)'$$

Any of these identities can be proven by using a truth table or by replacing the $\oplus$ operation by its equivalent Boolean expression. It can be shown also that the exclusive-OR operation is both commutative and associative; that is,

$$A \oplus B = B \oplus A$$

and

$$(A \oplus B) \oplus C = A \oplus (B \oplus C) = A \oplus B \oplus C$$

This means that the two inputs to an exclusive-OR gate can be interchanged without affecting the operation. It also means that we can evaluate a three-variable exclusive-OR operation in any order and for this reason, three or more variables can be expressed without parentheses. This would imply the possibility of using exclusive-OR gates with three or more inputs. However, multiple-input exclusive-OR gates are difficult to fabricate with hardware. In fact, even a two-input function is usually constructed with other types of gates. A two-input exclusive-OR func-

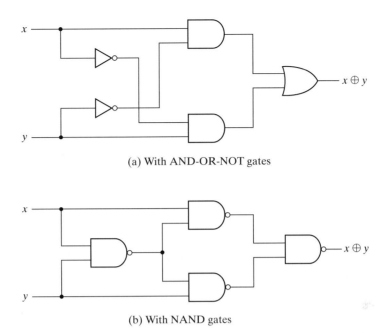

(a) With AND-OR-NOT gates

(b) With NAND gates

FIGURE 3-32
Exclusive-OR Implementations

tion is constructed with conventional gates using two inverters, two AND gates, and an OR gate, as shown in Fig. 3-32(a). Figure 3-32(b) shows the implementation of the exclusive-OR with four NAND gates. The first NAND gate performs the operation $(xy)' = (x' + y')$. The other two-level NAND circuit produces the sum of products of its inputs:

$$(x' + y')x + (x' + y')y = xy' + x'y = x \oplus y$$

Only a limited number of Boolean functions can be expressed in terms of exclusive-OR operations. Nevertheless, this function emerges quite often during the design of digital systems. It is particularly useful in arithmetic operations and error-detection and correction circuits.

Odd Function

The exclusive-OR operation with three or more variables can be converted into an ordinary Boolean function by replacing the $\oplus$ symbol with its equivalent Boolean expression. In particular, the three-variable case can be converted to a Boolean expression as follows:

$$A \oplus B \oplus C = (AB' + A'B)C' + (AB + A'B')C$$
$$= AB'C' + A'BC' + ABC + A'B'C$$
$$= \Sigma(1, 2, 4, 7)$$

The Boolean expression clearly indicates that the three-variable exclusive-OR function is equal to 1 if only one variable is equal to 1 or if all three variables are equal to 1. Contrary to the two-

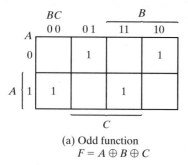

(a) Odd function
$F = A \oplus B \oplus C$

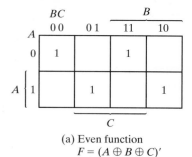

(a) Even function
$F = (A \oplus B \oplus C)'$

FIGURE 3-33
Map for a Three-variable Exclusive-OR Function

variable case, where only one variable must be equal to 1, in the three or more variable case, the requirement is that an odd number of variables be equal to 1. As a consequence, the multiple-variable exclusive-OR operation is defined as an *odd function*.

The Boolean function derived from the three-variable exclusive-OR operation is expressed as the logical sum of four minterms whose binary numerical values are 001, 010, 100, and 111. Each of these binary numbers has an odd number of 1's. The other four minterms not included in the function are 000, 011, 101, and 110, and they have an even number of 1's in their binary numerical values. In general, an *n*-variable exclusive-OR function is an odd function defined as the logical sum of the $2^n/2$ minterms whose binary numerical values have an odd number of 1's.

The definition of an odd function can be clarified by plotting it in a map. Figure 3-33(a) shows the map for the three-variable exclusive-OR function. The four minterms of the function are a unit distance apart from each other. The odd function is identified from the four minterms whose binary values have an odd number of 1's. The complement of an odd function is an even function. As shown in Fig. 3-33(b), the three-variable even function is equal to 1 when an even number of variables is equal to 1 (including the condition that none of the variables is equal to 1).

The 3-input odd function is implemented by means of 2-input exclusive-OR gates, as shown in Fig. 3-34(a). The complement of an odd function is obtained by replacing the output gate with an exclusive-NOR gate, as shown in Fig. 3-34(b).

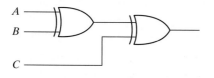

(a) 3-input odd function

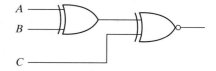

(b) 3-input even function

FIGURE 3-34
Logic Diagram of Odd and Even Functions

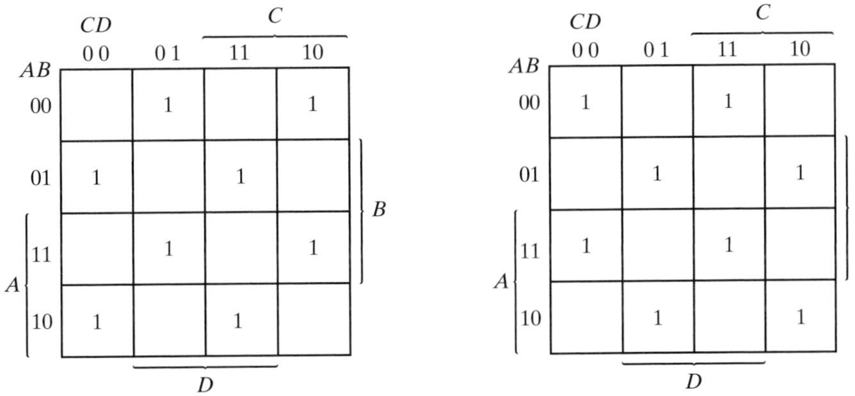

(a) Odd function
$F = A \oplus B \oplus C \oplus D$

(b) Even function
$F = (A \oplus B \oplus C \oplus D)'$

FIGURE 3-35
Map for a Four-variable Exclusive-OR Function

Consider now the the four-variable exclusive-OR operation. By algebraic manipulation, we can obtain the sum of minterms for this function:

$$A \oplus B \oplus C \oplus D = (AB' + A'B) \oplus (CD' + C'D)$$
$$= (AB' + A'B)(CD + C'D') + (AB + A'B')(CD' + C'D)$$
$$= \Sigma(1, 2, 4, 7, 8, 11, 13, 14)$$

There are 16 minterms for a four-variable Boolean function. Half of the minterms have binary numerical values with an odd number of 1's; the other half of the minterms have binary numerical values with an even number of 1's. When plotting the function in the map, the binary numerical value for a minterm is determined from the row and column numbers of the square that represents the minterm. The map of Fig. 3-35(a) is a plot of the four-variable exclusive-OR function. This is an odd function because the binary values of all the minterms have an odd number of 1's. The complement of an odd function is an even function. As shown in Fig. 3-35(b), the four-variable even function is equal to 1 when an even number of variables is equal to 1.

Parity Generation and Checking

Exclusive-OR functions are very useful in systems requiring error-detection and correction codes. As discussed in Section 1-7, a parity bit is used for the purpose of detecting errors during transmission of binary information. A parity bit is an extra bit included with a binary message to make the number of 1's either odd or even. The message, including the parity bit, is transmitted and then checked at the receiving end for errors. An error is detected if the checked parity does not correspond with the one transmitted. The circuit that generates the parity bit in the transmitter is called a *parity generator*. The circuit that checks the parity in the receiver is called a *parity checker*.

Table 3-4
Even-Parity-Generator Truth Table

Three-Bit Message			Parity Bit
x	y	z	P
0	0	0	0
0	0	1	1
0	1	0	1
0	1	1	0
1	0	0	1
1	0	1	0
1	1	0	0
1	1	1	1

As an example, consider a 3-bit message to be transmitted together with an even parity bit. Table 3-4 shows the truth table for the parity generator. The three bits—x, y, and z—constitute the message and are the inputs to the circuit. The parity bit P is the output. For even parity, the bit P must be generated to make the total number of 1's even (including P). From the truth table, we see that P constitutes an odd function because it is equal to 1 for those minterms whose numerical values have an odd number of 1's. Therefore, P can be expressed as a three-variable exclusive-OR function:

$$P = x \oplus y \oplus z$$

The logic diagram for the parity generator is shown in Fig. 3-36(a).

The three bits in the message, together with the parity bit, are transmitted to their destination, where they are applied to a parity-checker circuit to check for possible errors in the transmission. Since the information was transmitted with even parity, the four bits received must have an even number of 1's. An error occurs during the transmission if the four bits received have an odd number of 1's, indicating that one bit has changed in value during transmission. The output of the parity checker, denoted by C, will be equal to 1 if an error occurs, that is, if the four bits received have an odd number of 1's. Table 3-5 is the truth table for the even-parity checker. From it we see that the function C consists of the eight minterms with binary numerical

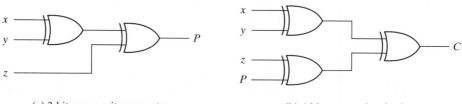

(a) 3-bit even parity generator   (b) 4-bit even parity checker

FIGURE 3-36
Logic Diagram of a Parity Generator and Checker

Table 3-5
Even-Parity-Checker Truth Table

Four Bits Received				Parity Error Check
x	y	z	P	C
0	0	0	0	0
0	0	0	1	1
0	0	1	0	1
0	0	1	1	0
0	1	0	0	1
0	1	0	1	0
0	1	1	0	0
0	1	1	1	1
1	0	0	0	1
1	0	0	1	0
1	0	1	0	0
1	0	1	1	1
1	1	0	0	0
1	1	0	1	1
1	1	1	0	1
1	1	1	1	0

values having an odd number of 1's. This corresponds to the map of Fig. 3-35(a), which represents an odd function. The parity checker can be implemented with exclusive-OR gates:

$$C = x \oplus y \oplus z \oplus P$$

The logic diagram of the parity checker is shown in Fig. 3-36(b).

It is worth nothing that the parity generator can be implemented with the circuit of Fig. 3-36(b) if the input P is connected to logic-0 and the output is marked with P. This is because $z \oplus 0 = z$, causing the value of z to pass through the gate unchanged. The advantage of this is that the same circuit can be used for both parity generation and checking.

It is obvious from the foregoing example that parity generation and checking circuits always have an output function that includes half of the minterms whose numerical values have either an odd or even number of 1's. As a consequence, they can be implemented with exclusive-OR gates. A function with an even number of 1's is the complement of an odd function. It is implemented with exclusive-OR gates, except that the gate associated with the output must be an exclusive-NOR to provide the required complementation.

3-9   HARDWARE DESCRIPTION LANGUAGE (HDL)

A hardware description language is a language that describes the hardware of digital systems in a textual form. It resembles a programming language, but is specifically oriented to describing hardware structures and behavior. It can be used to represent logic diagrams, Boolean expressions, and other more complex digital circuits. As a *documentation* language, HDL is used to represent and document digital systems in a form that can be read by both humans and computers and is suitable as an exchange language between designers. The language content can be stored and retrieved easily and processed by computer software in an efficient manner. There are two applications of HDL processing: simulation and synthesis.

Logic simulation is the representation of the structure and behavior of a digital logic system through the use of a computer. A simulator interprets the HDL description and produces readable output, such as a timing diagram, that predicts how the hardware will behave before it is actually fabricated. Simulation allows the detection of functional errors in a design without having to physically create the circuit. Errors that are detected during the simulation can be corrected by modifying the appropriate HDL statements. The stimulus that tests the functionality of the design is called a *test bench*. Thus, to simulate a digital system, the design is first described in HDL and then verified by simulating the design and checking it with a test bench, which is also written in HDL.

Logic synthesis is the process of deriving a list of components and their interconnections (called a *netlist*) from the model of a digital system described in HDL. The gate-level netlist can be used to fabricate an integrated circuit or to lay out a printed circuit board. Logic synthesis is similar to compiling a program in a conventional high-level language. The difference is that, instead of producing an object code, logic synthesis produces a database with instructions on how to fabricate a physical piece of digital hardware that implements the statements described by the HDL code. Logic synthesis is based on formal exact procedures that implement digital circuits and consists of that part of a digital design that can be automated with computer software.

There are many proprietary HDLs in industry developed by companies that design, or help in the design of integrated circuits. There are two standard HDLs that are supported by IEEE (Institute of Electrical and Electronics Engineers): VHDL and Verilog HDL. VHDL is a Department of Defense-mandated language. (The *V* in VHDL stands for the first letter in VHSIC, an acronym for Very High Speed Integrated Circuits.) Verilog began as a proprietary HDL promoted by a company called Cadence Data Systems, but Cadence transferred control of Verilog to a consortium of companies and universities known as Open Verilog International (OVI). VHDL is a harder language to learn than Verilog. Because Verilog is an easier language to learn and use, we have chosen it for this book. However, the Verilog HDL descriptions listed throughout the book are not just about Verilog, but rather to introduce the concept of computer-aided representation of digital systems by means of a typical hardware description language.

Module Representation

Verilog HDL has a syntax that describes precisely the legal constructs that can be used in the language. In particular, Verilog uses about 100 keywords—predefined, lowercase, identifiers that define the language constructs. Examples of keywords are module, endmodule, input, output, wire, and, or, not, etc. Any text between two slashes (//) and the end of the line is interpreted as a comment. Blank spaces are ignored and names are case sensitive, which means that uppercase and lowercase letters are distinguishable. A module is the building block in Verilog. It is declared by the keyword **module** and is always terminated by the keyword **endmodule.** We will show now a simple example to illustrate some aspects of the language.

The HDL description of the circuit of Fig. 3-37 is shown in HDL Example 3-1. The line with two slashes is a comment that explains the function of the circuit. The second line declares the module together with a name and a port list. The name (`smpl_circuit` in this case) is an identifier that is used to reference the module. Identifiers are names given to variables so that they can be referenced in the design. They are made up of alphanumeric characters and the underscore (_) and are case sensitive. Identifiers must start with an alphabetic character or an underscore. They cannot start with a number. The port list provides the interface by which the module communicates with the environment. In this example, the ports are the inputs and outputs of the circuit. The port list is enclosed in parentheses and commas are used to separate elements of a list. The statement is terminated with a semicolon (;). All keywords (which must be in lowercase) are printed in bold for clarity, but this is not a requirement of the language. Next, the **input** and **output** declarations define which of the ports are inputs and which are outputs. Internal connections are declared as wires. The circuit has one internal connection at terminal e and is declared with the keyword **wire.** The structure of the circuit is specified with the predefined primitive gates as keywords. Each gate declaration consists of an optional name (such as g1, g2, etc.) followed by the gate output and inputs separated with commas and enclosed in parentheses. The output is always listed first, followed by the inputs. For example, the OR gate is named g3, has output x, and inputs e and y. The module description ends with the keyword **endmodule.** Note that each statement is terminated with a semicolon, but there is no semicolon after **endmodule.**

HDL Example 3-1

```
//Description of simple circuit Fig. 3-37
module smpl_circuit(A,B,C,x,y);
    input A,B,C;
    output x,y;
    wire e;
    and g1(e,A,B);
    not g2(y, C);
    or g3(x,e,y);
endmodule
```

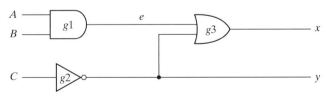

FIGURE 3-37
Circuit to Demonstrate HDL

Gate Delays

When HDL is used during simulation, it is sometimes necessary to specify the amount of delay from the input to the output of gates. In Verilog, the delay is specified in terms of *time units* and the symbol #. The association of a time unit with physical time is made using the `timescale compiler directive. (Compiler directives start with the ` (backquote) symbol.) Such a directive is specified before a module declaration. An example of a timescale directive is:

`timescale 1ns/100ps

The first number specifies the unit of measurement for time delays. The second number specifies the precision for which the delays are rounded off, in this case to 0.1 ns. If no timescale is specified, the simulator defaults to a certain time unit, usually 1 ns. (1 ns $= 10^{-9}$ sec). In this book, we will assume the default time unit.

HDL Example 3-2 repeats the description of the simple circuit with delays specified for each gate. The AND, OR, and NOT gates have a time delay of 30, 20, and 10 ns, respectively. If the circuit is simulated and the inputs change from 000 to 111, the outputs change as shown in Table 3-6. The output of the inverter at *y* changes from 1 to 0 after a 10 ns delay. The output of the AND gate at *e* changes from 0 to 1 after a 30 ns delay. The output of the OR gate at

HDL Example 3-2

```
//Description of circuit with delay
module circuit_with_delay (A,B,C,x,y);
    input A,B,C;
    output x,y;
    wire e;
    and #(30) g1(e,A,B);
    or #(20) g3(x,e,y);
    not #(10) g2(y,C);
endmodule
```

Table 3-6
Output of Gates After Delay

	Time Units (ns)	Input ABC	Output y e x
Initial	—	000	1 0 1
Change	—	111	1 0 1
	10	111	0 0 1
	20	111	0 0 1
	30	111	0 1 0
	40	111	0 1 0
	50	111	0 1 1

HDL Example 3-3

```
//Stimulus for simple circuit
module stimcrct;
reg A,B,C;
wire x,y;
circuit_with_delay cwd(A,B,C,x,y);
initial
    begin
        A = 1'b0; B = 1'b0; C = 1'b0;
      #100
        A = 1'b1; B = 1'b1; C = 1'b1;
      #100   $finish;
    end
endmodule

//Description of circuit with delay
module circuit_with_delay (A,B,C,x,y);
    input A,B,C;
    output x,y;
    wire e;
    and #(30) g1(e,A,B);
    or  #(20) g3(x,e,y);
    not #(10) g2(y,C);
endmodule
```

x changes from 1 to 0 at $t = 30$ ns, and then changes back to 1 at t = 50 ns. In both cases, the change in OR gate output results from a change in its inputs 20 ns earlier. It is clear from this result that although output x eventually returns to 1 after the input changes, the gate delays produce a 20 ns negative spike before that happens.

In order to simulate a circuit with HDL, it is necessary to apply inputs to the circuit for the simulator to generate an output response. An HDL description that provides the stimulus to a design is called a *test bench*. The writing of test benches is explained at the end of Section 4-11. Here we demonstrate the procedure with a simple example without dwelling on too many details. HDL Example 3-3 shows a test bench for simulating the circuit with delay. Two modules are included: a stimulus module and the circuit description module. The stimulus module stimcrct has no ports. The inputs to the circuit are declared with a **reg** keyword and the outputs with a **wire** keyword. The circuit_with_delay is instantiated with the name cwd. (The interaction between the stimulus module and the circuit module is demonstrated in Fig. 4-33.) The **initial** statement specifies the inputs between the keywords **begin** and **end.** Initially, $ABC = 000$. (A, B, and C are each set to 1'b0, which signifies one binary digit with a value of 0.) After 100 ns, the inputs change to $ABC = 111$. After another 100 ns, the simulation terminates. (**$finish** is a system task.) The timing diagram that results from the simulation is shown in Figure 3-38. The total simulation takes 200 ns. The inputs A, B, and C change from 0 to 1 after 100 ns. Output y is unknown for the first 10 ns, and output x is unknown for

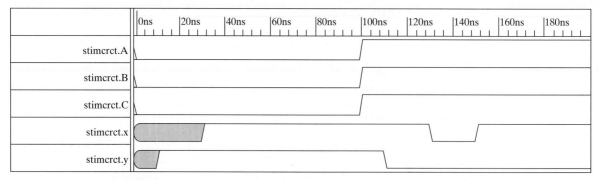

FIGURE 3-38
Simulation Output of HDL Example 3-3

the first 30 ns. Output *y* goes from 1 to 0 at 110 ns. Output *x* goes from 1 to 0 at 130 ns and back to 1 at 150 ns, just as we predicted in Table 3-6.

Boolean Expressions

Boolean expressions are specified in Verilog HDL with a continuous assignment statement consisting of the keyword **assign** followed by a Boolean expression. To distinguish the arithmetic plus from logical OR, Verilog HDL uses the symbols (&), (|), and (~) for AND, OR, and NOT (complement), respectively. Thus, to describe the simple circuit of Fig. 3-37 with a Boolean expression we use the statement

> **assign** x = (A & B) | ~C;

HDL Example 3-4 shows the description of a circuit that is specified with the following two Boolean expressions:

$$x = A + BC + B'D$$
$$y = B'C + BC'D'$$

HDL Example 3-4

```
//Circuit specified with Boolean expressions
module circuit_bln (x,y,A,B,C,D);
    input A,B,C,D;
    output x,y;
    assign x = A | (B & C) | (~B & D);
    assign y = (~B & C) | (B & ~C & ~D);
endmodule
```

The circuit has two outputs x and y and four inputs A, B, C, and D. The two **assign** statements describe the Boolean equations.

We have shown that a digital circuit can be described with HDL statements just as it can be drawn in a circuit diagram, or specified with a Boolean expression. The advantage of HDL is that it is suitable for processing with a computer.

User-Defined Primitives (UDP)

The logic gates used in HDL descriptions with keywords **and, or,** etc., are defined by the system and are referred to as *system primitives.* The user can create additional primitives by defining them in a tabular form. These types of circuits are referred to as user-defined primitives. One way of specifying a digital circuit in tabular form is by means of a truth table. UDP descriptions do not use the keyword **module.** Instead they are declared with the keyword **primitive.** The best way to demonstrate the primitive declarations is by means of an example.

HDL Example 3-5 defines a UDP with a truth table. It proceeds according to the following general rules:

- It is declared with the keyword **primitive** followed by a name and port list.
- There can be only one output and it must be listed first in the port list and declared with an **output** keyword.

HDL Example 3-5

```
//User defined primitive(UDP)
primitive crctp (x,A,B,C);
    output x;
    input A,B,C;
//Truth table for x(A,B,C) = Σ(0,2,4,6,7)
    table
//     A    B    C  :  x    (Note that this is only a comment)
       0    0    0  :  1;
       0    0    1  :  0;
       0    1    0  :  1;
       0    1    1  :  0;
       1    0    0  :  1;
       1    0    1  :  0;
       1    1    0  :  1;
       1    1    1  :  1;
    endtable
endprimitive

//Instantiate primitive
module declare_crctp;
    reg x,y,z;
    wire w;
    crctp (w,x,y,z);
endmodule
```

- There can be any number of inputs. The order in which they are listed in the **input** declaration must conform to the order in which they are given values in the table that follows.
- The truth table is enclosed within the keywords **table** and **endtable.**
- The values of the inputs are listed in order ending with a colon (:). The output is always the last entry in a row followed by a semicolon (;).
- It ends with the keyword **endprimitive.**

Note that the variables listed on top of the table are part of a comment and are shown only for clarity. The system recognizes the variables by the order that they are listed in the input declaration. A user-defined primitive can be employed in the construction of other digital circuits just as the system primitives are used. For example, the declaration

$$\text{crctp (w,x,y,z)}$$

will produce a circuit that implements

$$w\,(x, y, z) \;=\; \Sigma(0, 2, 4, 6, 7)$$

with inputs x, y, z and output w.

Although Verilog HDL uses this kind of description for UDPs only, other proprietary HDLs and computer-aided design (CAD) systems use other procedures to specify digital circuits in tabular form. The tables can be processed by CAD software to derive an efficient gate structure of the design.

In this section, we introduced HDL and presented simple examples of structural modeling. A more detailed presentation of Verilog HDL can be found in the next chapter. The reader familiar with combinational circuits can go directly to Sec. 4-11 to continue with this subject.

PROBLEMS

3-1 Simplify the following Boolean functions, using three-variable maps:
 (a) $F(x, y, z) = \Sigma\,(0, 2, 6, 7)$ (b) $F(A, B, C) = \Sigma(0, 2, 3, 4, 6)$
 (c) $F(a, b, c) = \Sigma\,(0, 1, 2, 3, 7)$ (d) $F(x, y, z) = \Sigma\,(3, 5, 6, 7)$

3-2 Simplify the following Boolean functions, using three-variable maps:
 (a) $F(x, y, z) = \Sigma\,(0, 1, 5, 7)$ (b) $F(x, y, z) = \Sigma(1, 2, 3, 6, 7)$

3-3 Simplify the following Boolean expressions, using three-variable maps:
 (a) $xy + x'y'z' + x'yz'$ (b) $x'y' + yz + x'yz'$
 (c) $A'B + BC' + B'C'$

3-4 Simplify the following Boolean functions, using x maps:
 (a) $F(x, y, z) = \Sigma\,(2, 3, 6, 7)$ (b) $F(A, B, C, D) = \Sigma(4, 6, 7, 15)$
 (c) $F(A, B, C, D) = \Sigma\,(3, 7, 11, 13, 14, 15)$ (d) $F(w, x, y, z) = \Sigma(2, 3, 12, 13, 14, 15)$

3-5 Simplify the following Boolean functions, using four-variable maps:
 (a) $F(w, x, y, z) = \Sigma(1, 4, 5, 6, 12, 14, 15)$
 (b) $F(A, B, C, D) = \Sigma(0, 1, 2, 4, 5, 7, 11, 15)$
 (c) $F(w, x, y, z) = \Sigma(2, 3, 10, 11, 12, 13, 14, 15)$
 (d) $F(A, B, C, D) = \Sigma(0, 2, 4, 5, 6, 7, 8, 10, 13, 15)$

3-6 Simplify the following Boolean expressions, using four-variable maps:
  (a) $A'B'C'D' + AC'D' + B'CD' + A'BCD + BC'D$
  (b) $x'z + w'xy' + w(x'y + xy')$

3-7 Simplify the following Boolean expressions, using four-variable maps:
  (a) $w'z + xz + x'y + wx'z$ (b) $B'D + A'BC' + AB'C + ABC'$
  (c) $AB'C + B'C'D' + BCD + ACD' + A'B'C + A'BC'D$
  (d) $wxy + yz + xy'z + x'y$

3-8 Find the minterms of the following Boolean expressions by first plotting each function in a map:
  (a) $xy + yz + xy'z$ (b) $C'D + ABC' + ABD' + A'B'D$
  (c) $wxy + x'z' + w'xz$

3-9 Find all the prime implicants for the following Boolean functions, and determine which are essential:
  (a) $F(w, x, y, z) = \Sigma(0, 2, 4, 5, 6, 7, 8, 10, 13, 15)$
  (b) $F(A, B, C, D) = \Sigma(0, 2, 3, 5, 7, 8, 10, 11, 14, 15)$
  (c) $F(A, B, C, D) = \Sigma(1, 3, 4, 5, 10, 11, 12, 13, 14, 15)$

3-10 Simplify the following Boolean functions by first finding the essential prime implicants:
  (a) $F(w, x, y, z) = \Sigma(0, 2, 4, 5, 6, 7, 8, 10, 13, 15)$
  (b) $F(A, B, C, D) = \Sigma(0, 2, 3, 5, 7, 8, 10, 11, 14, 15)$
  (c) $F(A, B, C, D) = \Sigma(1, 3, 4, 5, 10, 11, 12, 13, 14, 15)$

3-11 Simplify the following Boolean functions, using five-variable maps:
  (a) $F(A, B, C, D, E) = \Sigma(0, 1, 4, 5, 16, 17, 21, 25, 29)$
  (b) $F = A'B'CE' + A'B'C'D' + B'D'E' + B'CD' + CDE' + BDE'$

3-12 Simplify the following Boolean functions in product of sums:
  (a) $F(w, x, y, z) = \Sigma\ (0, 2, 5, 6, 7, 8, 10)$ (b) $F(A, B, C, D) = \Pi(1, 3, 5, 7, 13, 15)$

3-13 Simplify the following expressions in (1) sum of products and (2) products of sums:
  (a) $x'z' + y'z' + yz' + xy$ (b) $AC' + B'D + A'CD + ABCD$
  (c) $(A' + B' + D')(A + B' + C')(A' + B + D')(B + C' + D')$

3-14 Give three possible ways to express the following Boolean function with eight or fewer literals:

$$F = A'B'D' + AB'CD' + A'BD + ABC'D$$

3-15 Simplify the following Boolean function F, together with the don't-care conditions d, and then express the simplified function in sum of minterms:
  (a) $F(x, y, z) = \Sigma\ (0, 1, 2, 4, 5)$ (b) $F(A, B, C, D) = \Sigma(0, 6, 8, 13, 14)$
      $d(x, y, z) = \Sigma\ (3, 6, 7)$ $d(A, B, C, D) = \Sigma(2, 4, 10)$
  (c) $F(A, B, C, D) = \Sigma(1, 3, 5, 7, 9, 15)$
      $d(A, B, C, D) = \Sigma(4, 6, 12, 13)$

3-16 Simplify the following expressions, and implement them with two-level NAND gate circuits:
  (a) $AB' + ABD + ABD' + A'C'D' + A'BC'$
  (b) $BD + BCD' + AB'C'D'$

3-17 Draw a NAND logic diagram that implements the complement of the following function:

$$F(A, B, C, D) = \Sigma(0, 1, 2, 3, 4, 8, 9, 12)$$

3-18 Draw a logic diagram using only two-input NAND gates to implement the following expression:

$$(AB + A'B')(CD' + C'D)$$

3-19 Simplify the following functions, and implement them with two-level NOR gate circuits:
  (a) $F = wx' + y'z' + w'yz'$ (b) $F(w, x, y, z) = \Sigma(5, 6, 9, 10)$

3-20 Draw the multiple-level NAND circuit for the following expression:

$$(AB' + CD')E + BC(A + B)$$

3-21 Draw the multiple-level NOR circuit for the following expression:

$$w(x + y + z) + xyz$$

3-22 Convert the logic diagram of the circuit shown in Fig. 4-4 into a multiple-level NAND circuit.

3-23 Implement the following Boolean function F, together with the don't-care conditions d, using no more than two NOR gates:

$$F(A, B, C, D) = \Sigma(0, 1, 2, 9, 11)$$
$$d(A, B, C, D) = \Sigma(8, 10, 14, 15)$$

Assume that both the normal and complement inputs are available.

3-24 Implement the following Boolean function F, using the two-level forms (a) NAND-AND, (b) AND-NOR, (c) OR-NAND, and (d) NOR-OR:

$$F(A, B, C, D) = \Sigma(0, 1, 2, 3, 4, 8, 9, 12)$$

3-25 List the eight degenerate two-level forms and show that they reduce to a single operation. Explain how the degenerate two-level forms can be used to extend the number of inputs to a gate.

3-26 With the use of maps, find the simplest form in sum of products of the function $F = fg$, where f and g are, respectively,

$$f = wxy' + y'z + w'yz' + x'yz'$$

and

$$g = (w + x + y' + z')(x' + y' + z)(w' + y + z')$$

3-27 Show that the dual of the exclusive-OR is also its complement.

3-28 Derive the circuits for a three-bit parity generator and four-bit parity checker using odd parity bit.

3-29 Implement the following four Boolean expressions with three half adders

$$D = A \oplus B \oplus C$$
$$E = A'BC + AB'C$$
$$F = ABC' + (A' + B')C$$
$$G = ABC$$

3-30 Implement the following Boolean expression with exclusive-OR and AND gates:

$$F = AB'CD' + A'BCD' + AB'C'D + A'BC'D$$

3-31 Write the HDL gate structure description of the circuit of Fig. 3-22(a).

3-32 The exclusive-OR circuit of Fig. 3-32(a) has gates with delay of 10 ns for an inverter, 20 ns delay for an AND gate, and 30 ns delay for an OR gate. The input of the circuit goes from $xy = 00$ to $xy = 01$.
  (a) Determine the signals at the output of each gate from $t = 0$ to $t = 50$ ns.

(b) Write the HDL description of the circuit including the delays.

(c) Write a stimulus module (similar to HDL Example 3-3) and simulate the circuit to verify the answer in part (a).

3-33 Write the HDL description of the circuit of Fig. 3-37 using two Boolean expressions.

3-34 Write the HDL description of the circuit specified by the following Boolean functions:

$$x = A(CD + B) + BC'$$
$$y = (AB' + A'B)(C + D')$$
$$z = \left[(A + B)(C' + D'B)\right]'$$

Use continuous assignment statements.

3-35 Find the syntax errors in the following declarations (note that names for primitive gates are optional):

```
module Exmpl-3(A,B,C,D,F)
inputs A,B,C,
Output D,F;
and g1(A,B,D);
not (D,B,A);
OR (F,B,C);
endmodule;
```

3-36 Draw the logic diagram of the digital circuit specified by the following HDL description:

```
module circt (A,B,C,D,F);
input A,B,C,D;
output F;
wire w,x,y,z,a,d;
and (x,B,C,d);
and (y,a,C);
and (w,z,B);
or (z,y,A);
or (F,x,w);
not (a,A);
not (d,D);
endmodule
```

3-37 A majority logic function is a Boolean function that is equal to 1 if the majority of the variables are 1. The function is 0 otherwise. Write an HDL user-defined primitive for a 3-bit majority function.

REFERENCES

1.   BHASKER, J. 1997. *A Verilog HDL Primer.* Allentown, PA: Star Galaxy Press.

2.   HILL, F. J., and G. R. PETERSON. 1981. *Introduction to Switching Theory and Logical Design,* 3rd ed. New York: John Wiley.

3.   *IEEE Standard Hardware Description Language Based on the Verilog Hardware Description Language* (IEEE Std 1364–1995). 1995. New York: The Institute of Electrical and Electronics Engineers.

4.   KARNAUGH, M. A Map Method for Synthesis of Combinational Logic Circuits. *Transactions of AIEE, Communication and Electronics.* 72, part I (Nov. 1953): 593–99.

5.   KOHAVI, Z. 1978. *Switching and Automata Theory,* 2nd ed. New York: McGraw-Hill.

6.   MANO, M. M. and C. R. KIME. 2000. *Logic and Computer Design Fundamentals,* 2nd ed. Upper Saddle River, NJ: Prentice Hall.

7.   MCCLUSKEY, E. J. 1986. *Logic Design Principles.* Englewood Cliffs, NJ: Prentice-Hall.

8.   PALNITKAR, S. 1996. *Verilog HDL: A Guide to Digital Design and Synthesis.* SunSoft Press (A Prentice Hall Title).

Combinational Logic

4-1 COMBINATIONAL CIRCUITS

Logic circuits for digital systems may be combinational or sequential. A combinational circuit consists of logic gates whose outputs at any time are determined from the present combination of inputs. A combinational circuit performs an operation that can be specified logically by a set of Boolean functions. Sequential circuits employ storage elements in addition to logic gates. Their outputs are a function of the inputs and the state of the storage elements. The state of storage elements, in turn, is a function of previous inputs. As a consequence, the outputs of a sequential circuit depend not only on present values of inputs, but also on past inputs, and the circuit behavior must be specified by a time sequence of inputs and internal states. Sequential circuits are discussed in Chapter 5 and 9.

A combinational circuit consists of input variables, logic gates, and output variables. The logic gates accept signals from the inputs and generate signals to the outputs. This process transforms binary information from the given input data to a required output data. A block diagram of a combinational circuit is shown in Fig. 4-1. The n input binary variables come from an external source; the m output variables go to an external destination. Each input and

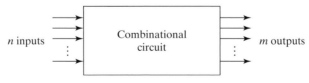

FIGURE 4-1
Block Diagram of Combinational Circuit

output variable exists physically as a binary signal that represents logic 1 and logic 0. In many applications, the source and destination are storage registers. If the registers are included with the combinational gates, then the total circuit must be considered as a sequential circuit.

For n input variables, there are 2^n possible binary input combinations. For each possible input combination, there is one possible output value. Thus, a combinational circuit can be specified with a truth table that lists the output values for each combination of input variables. A combinational circuit also can be described by m Boolean functions, one for each output variable. Each output function is expressed in terms of the n input variables.

In Chapter 1, we learned about binary numbers and binary codes that represent discrete quantities of information. The binary variables are represented physically by electric voltages or some other type of signal. The signals can be manipulated in digital logic gates to perform required functions. In Chapter 2, we introduced Boolean algebra as a way to express logic functions algebraically. In Chapter 3, we learned how to simplify Boolean functions to achieve economical gate implementations. The purpose of this chapter is to use the knowledge acquired in previous chapters and formulate systematic analysis and design procedures of combinational circuits. The solution of some typical examples will provide a useful catalog of elementary functions important for the understanding of digital systems.

There are several combinational circuits that are employed extensively in the design of digital systems. These circuits are available in integrated circuits and are classified as standard components. They perform specific digital functions commonly needed in the design of digital systems. In this chapter, we introduce the most important standard combinational circuits such as adders, subtractors, comparators, decoders, encoders, and multiplexers. These components are available in integrated circuits as MSI (medium scale integration) circuits. They are also used as *standard cells* in complex VLSI circuits such as application specific integrated circuits (ASIC). The standard cell functions are interconnected within the VLSI circuit in the same way as they are used in multiple-IC MSI design.

4-2   ANALYSIS PROCEDURE

The analysis of a combinational circuit requires that we determine the function that the circuit implements. This starts with a given logic diagram and culminates with a set of Boolean functions, a truth table, or a possible explanation of the circuit operation. If the logic diagram to be analyzed is accompanied by a function name or an explanation of what it is assumed to accomplish, then the analysis problem reduces to a verification of the stated function. The analysis can be performed manually by finding the Boolean functions or truth table, or by using a computer simulation program.

The first step in the analysis is to make sure that the given circuit is combinational and not sequential. The diagram of a combinational circuit has logic gates with no feedback paths or memory elements. A feedback path is a connection from the output of one gate to the input of a second gate that forms part of the input to the first gate. Feedback paths in a digital circuit define a sequential circuit and must be analyzed according to procedures outlined in Chapter 9.

Once the logic diagram is verified as a combinational circuit, one can proceed to obtain the output Boolean functions or the truth table. If the function of the circuit is under investigation, then it is necessary to interpret the operation of the circuit from the derived Boolean functions or truth table. The success of such investigation is enhanced if one has previous experience and familiarity with a wide variety of digital circuits.

To obtain the output Boolean functions from a logic diagram, proceed as follows:

1. Label all gate outputs that are a function of input variables with arbitrary symbols. Determine the Boolean functions for each gate output.

2. Label the gates that are a function of input variables and previously labeled gates with other arbitrary symbols. Find the Boolean functions for these gates.

3. Repeat the process outlined in step 2 until the outputs of the circuit are obtained.

4. By repeated substitution of previously defined functions, obtain the output Boolean functions in terms of input variables.

The analysis of the combinational circuit of Fig. 4-2 illustrates the proposed procedure. We note that the circuit has three binary inputs—A, B, and C—and two binary outputs—F_1 and F_2. The outputs of various gates are labeled with intermediate symbols. The outputs of gates that are a function of input variables only are T_1 and T_2. Output F_2 can be easily derived from the input variables. The Boolean functions for these three outputs are:

$$F_2 = AB + AC + BC$$
$$T_1 = A + B + C$$
$$T_2 = ABC$$

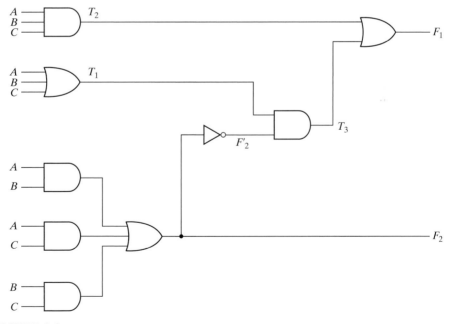

FIGURE 4-2
Logic Diagram for Analysis Example

Next, we consider outputs of gates that are a function of already defined symbols:

$$T_3 = F_2'T_1$$
$$F_1 = T_3 + T_2$$

To obtain F_1 as a function of A, B, and C, form a series of substitutions as follows:

$$F_1 = T_3 + T_2 = F_2'T_1 + ABC = (AB + AC + BC)'(A + B + C) + ABC$$
$$= (A' + B')(A' + C')(B' + C')(A + B + C) + ABC$$
$$= (A' + B'C')(AB' + AC' + BC' + B'C) + ABC$$
$$= A'BC' + A'B'C + AB'C' + ABC$$

If we want to pursue the investigation and determine the information-transformation task achieved by this circuit, we can draw the circuit from the derived Boolean expressions and try to recognize a familiar operation. The Boolean functions for F_1 and F_2 implement the circuit shown in Fig. 4-7 (Section 4-4) and is equivalent to a full adder circuit.

The derivation of the truth table for the circuit is a straightforward process once the output Boolean functions are known. To obtain the truth table directly from the logic diagram without going through the derivations of the Boolean functions, proceed as follows:

1. Determine the number of input variables in the circuit. For n inputs, form the 2^n possible input combinations and list the binary numbers from 0 to $2^n - 1$ in a table.

2. Label the outputs of selected gates with arbitrary symbols.

3. Obtain the truth table for the outputs of those gates that are a function of the input variables only.

4. Proceed to obtain the truth table for the outputs of those gates that are a function of previously defined values until the columns for all outputs are determined.

This process is illustrated using the circuit of Fig. 4-2. In Table 4-1, we form the eight possible combinations for the three input variables. The truth table for F_2 is determined directly

Table 4-1
Truth Table for the Logic Diagram of Fig. 4-2

A	B	C	F_2	F_2	T_1	T_2	T_3	F_1
0	0	0	0	1	0	0	0	0
0	0	1	0	1	1	0	1	1
0	1	0	0	1	1	0	1	1
0	1	1	1	0	1	0	0	0
1	0	0	0	1	1	0	1	1
1	0	1	1	0	1	0	0	0
1	1	0	1	0	1	0	0	0
1	1	1	1	0	1	1	0	1

from the values of A, B, and C, with F_2 equal to 1 for any combination that has two or three inputs equal to 1. The truth table for F'_2 is the complement of F_2. The truth tables for T_1 and T_2 are the OR and AND functions of the input variables, respectively. The values for T_3 are derived from T_1 and F'_2: T_3 is equal to 1 when both T_1 and F'_2 are equal to 1, and T_3 is equal to 0 otherwise. Finally, F_1 is equal to 1 for those combinations in which either T_2 or T_3 or both are equal to 1. Inspection of the truth table combinations for A, B, C, F_1, and F_2 shows that it is identical to the truth table of the full adder given in Section 4-4 for x, y, z, S, and C, respectively.

Another way of analyzing a combinational circuit is by means of logic simulation. In Sec. 4-11 we demonstrate the logic simulation and verification of the circuit of Fig. 4-2 using Verilog HDL. (See HDL Example 4-10.)

4-3   DESIGN PROCEDURE

The design of combinational circuits starts from the specification of the problem and culminates in a logic circuit diagram or a set of Boolean functions from which the logic diagram can be obtained. The procedure involves the following steps:

1. From the specifications of the circuit, determine the required number of inputs and outputs and assign a symbol to each.

2. Derive the truth table that defines the required relationship between inputs and outputs.

3. Obtain the simplified Boolean functions for each output as a function of the input variables.

4. Draw the logic diagram and verify the correctness of the design.

A truth table for a combinational circuit consists of input columns and output columns. The input columns are obtained from the 2^n binary numbers for the n input variables. The binary values for the outputs are determined from the stated specifications. The output functions specified in the truth table give the exact definition of the combinational circuit. It is important that the verbal specifications be interpreted correctly in the truth table. Word specifications are often incomplete and any wrong interpretation may result in an incorrect truth table.

The output binary functions listed in the truth table are simplified by any available method such as algebraic manipulation, the map method, or by means of computer-based simplification program. Frequently, there is a variety of simplified expressions from which to choose. In a particular application, certain criteria will serve as a guide in the process of choosing an implementation. A practical design must consider such constraints as the number of gates, number of inputs to a gate, propagation time of the signal through the gates, number of interconnections, limitations of the driving capability of each gate, and various other criteria that must be taken into consideration when designing with integrated circuits. Since the importance of each constraint is dictated by the particular application, it is difficult to make a general statement about what constitutes an acceptable implementation. In most cases the simplification begins by satisfying an elementary objective, such as producing the simplified Boolean functions in a standard form, and then proceed with further steps to meet other performance criteria.

Code Conversion Example

The availability of a large variety of codes for the same discrete elements of information results in the use of different codes by different digital systems. It is sometimes necessary to use the output of one system as the input to another. A conversion circuit must be inserted between the two systems if each uses different codes for the same information. Thus, a code converter is a circuit that makes the two systems compatible even though each uses a different binary code.

To convert from binary code A to binary code B, the input lines must supply the bit combination of elements as specified by code A and the output lines must generate the corresponding bit combination of code B. A combinational circuit performs this transformation by means of logic gates. The design procedure will be illustrated by an example that converts the binary coded decimal (BCD) to the excess-3 code for the decimal digits.

The bit combinations assigned to the BCD and excess-3 codes are listed in Table 1-5 (Section 1-7). Since each code uses four bits to represent a decimal digit, there must be four input variables and four output variables. Designate the four input binary variables by the symbols A, B, C, D, and the four output variables by w, x, y, and z. The truth table relating the input and output variables is shown in Table 4-2. The bit combinations for the inputs and their corresponding outputs are obtained directly from Section 1-7. Note that four binary variables may have 16 bit combinations, but only 10 are listed in the truth table. The 6 bit combinations not listed for the input variables are don't-care combinations. These values have no meaning in BCD and we assume that they will never occur. Therefore, we are at liberty to assign to the output variables either a 1 or a 0, whichever gives a simpler circuit.

The maps in Fig. 4-3 are plotted to obtain simplified Boolean functions for the outputs. Each one of the four maps represents one of the four outputs of the circuit as a function of the four input variables. The 1's marked inside the squares are obtained from the minterms that make

Table 4-2
Truth Table for Code-Conversion Example

Input BCD				Output Excess-3 Code			
A	B	C	D	w	x	y	z
0	0	0	0	0	0	1	1
0	0	0	1	0	1	0	0
0	0	1	0	0	1	0	1
0	0	1	1	0	1	1	0
0	1	0	0	0	1	1	1
0	1	0	1	1	0	0	0
0	1	1	0	1	0	0	1
0	1	1	1	1	0	1	0
1	0	0	0	1	0	1	1
1	0	0	1	1	1	0	0

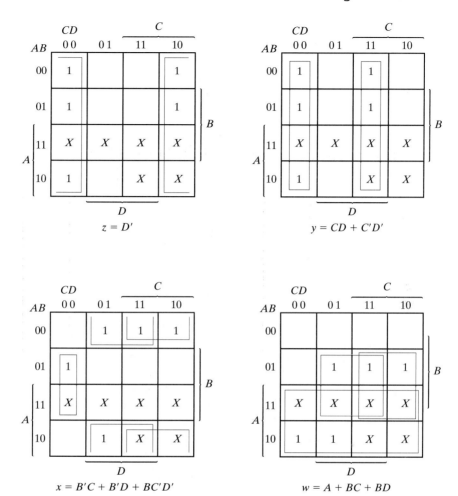

FIGURE 4-3
Maps for BCD to Excess-3 Code Converter

the output equal to 1. The 1's are obtained from the truth table by going over the output columns one at a time. For example, the column under output z has five 1's; therefore, the map for z has five 1's, each being in a square corresponding to the minterm that makes z equal to 1. The six don't-care minterms 10 through 15 are marked with an X. One possible way to simplify the functions in sum of products is listed under the map of each variable.

A two-level logic diagram may be obtained directly from the Boolean expressions derived by the maps. There are various other possibilities for a logic diagram that implements this circuit. The expressions obtained in Fig. 4-3 may be manipulated algebraically for the purpose of using common gates for two or more outputs. This manipulation, shown next, illustrates the flexibility obtained with multiple-output systems when implemented with three or more levels of gates:

$$z = D'$$
$$y = CD + C'D' = CD + (C + D)'$$
$$x = B'C + B'D + BC'D' = B'(C + D) + BC'D'$$
$$= B'(C + D) + B(C + D)'$$
$$w = A + BC + BD = A + B(C + D)$$

The logic diagram that implements these expressions is shown in Fig. 4-4. Note that the OR gate whose output is $C + D$ has been used to implement partially each of three outputs.

Not counting input inverters, the implementation in sum of products requires seven AND gates and three OR gates. The implementation of Fig. 4-4 requires four AND gates, four OR gates, and one inverter. If only the normal inputs are available, the first implementation will require inverters for variables B, C, and D, and the second implementation requires inverters for variables B and D.

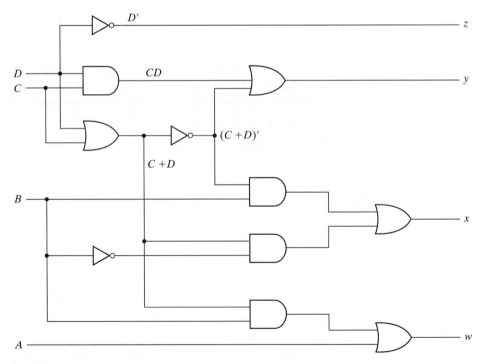

FIGURE 4-4
Logic Diagram for BCD to Excess-3 Code Converter

4-4   BINARY ADDER-SUBTRACTOR

Digital computers perform a variety of information processing tasks. Among the functions encountered are the various arithmetic operations. The most basic arithmetic operation is the addition of two binary digits. This simple addition consists of four possible elementary operations: $0 + 0 = 0, 0 + 1 = 1, 1 + 0 = 1$, and $1 + 1 = 10$. The first three operations produce a sum of one digit, but when both augend and addend bits are equal to 1, the binary sum consists of two digits. The higher significant bit of this result is called a *carry*. When the augend and addend numbers contain more significant digits, the carry obtained from the addition of two bits is added to the next higher order pair of significant bits. A combinational circuit that performs the addition of two bits is called a *half adder*. One that performs the addition of three bits (two significant bits and a previous carry) is a *full adder*. The names of the circuits stem from the fact that two half adders can be employed to implement a full adder.

A binary adder-subtractor is a combinational circuit that performs the arithmetic operations of addition and subtraction with binary numbers. We will develop this circuit by means of a hierarchical design. The half adder design is carried out first, from which we develop the full adder. Connecting n full adders in cascade produces a binary adder for two n-bit numbers. The subtraction circuit is included by providing a complementing circuit.

Half Adder

From the verbal explanation of a half adder, we find that this circuit needs two binary inputs and two binary outputs. The input variables designate the augend and addend bits; the output variables produce the sum and carry. We assign symbols x and y to the two inputs and S (for sum) and C (for carry) to the outputs. The truth table for the half adder is listed in Table 4-3. The C output is 1 only when both inputs are 1. The S output represents the least significant bit of the sum.

The simplified Boolean functions for the two outputs can be obtained directly from the truth table. The simplified sum of products expressions are

$$S = x'y + xy'$$
$$C = xy$$

The logic diagram of the half adder implemented in sum of products is shown in Fig. 4-5(a). It can be also implemented with an exclusive-OR and an AND gate as shown in Fig. 4-5(b). This form is used to show that two half adders can be used to construct a full adder.

Table 4-3
Half Adder

x	y	C	S
0	0	0	0
0	1	0	1
1	0	0	1
1	1	1	0

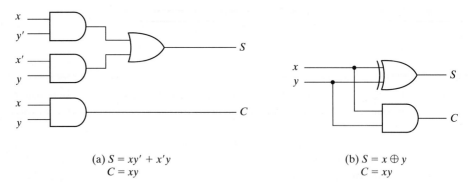

(a) $S = xy' + x'y$
$C = xy$

(b) $S = x \oplus y$
$C = xy$

FIGURE 4-5
Implementation of Half-Adder

Full-Adder

A full-adder is a combinational circuit that forms the arithmetic sum of three bits. It consists of three inputs and two outputs. Two of the input variables, denoted by x and y, represent the two significant bits to be added. The third input, z, represents the carry from the previous lower significant position. Two outputs are necessary because the arithmetic sum of three binary digits ranges in value from 0 to 3, and binary 2 or 3 needs two digits. The two outputs are designated by the symbols S for sum and C for carry. The binary variable S gives the value of the least significant bit of the sum. The binary variable C gives the output carry. The truth table of the full adder is listed in Table 4-4. The eight rows under the input variables designate all possible combinations of the three variables. The output variables are determined from the arithmetic sum of the input bits. When all input bits are 0, the output is 0. The S output is equal to 1 when only one input is equal to 1 or when all three inputs are equal to 1. The C output has a carry of 1 if two or three inputs are equal to 1.

The input and output bits of the combinational circuit have different interpretations at various stages of the problem. Physically, the binary signals of the inputs are considered binary digits to be added arithmetically to form a two-digit sum at the output. On the other hand, the same binary values are considered as variables of Boolean functions when expressed in the

Table 4-4
Full Adder

x	y	z	C	S
0	0	0	0	0
0	0	1	0	1
0	1	0	0	1
0	1	1	1	0
1	0	0	0	1
1	0	1	1	0
1	1	0	1	0
1	1	1	1	1

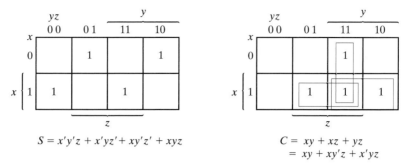

$$S = x'y'z + x'yz' + xy'z' + xyz$$

$$C = xy + xz + yz$$
$$= xy + xy'z + x'yz$$

FIGURE 4-6
Maps for Full Adder

truth table or when the circuit is implemented with logic gates. The maps for the outputs of the full adder are shown in Fig. 4-6. The simplified expressions are

$$S = x'y'z + x'yz' + xy'z' + xyz$$
$$C = xy + xz + yz$$

The logic diagram for the full adder implemented in sum of products is shown in Fig. 4-7. It can be also implemented with two half adders and one OR gate, as shown in Fig. 4-8. The S output from the second half adder is the exclusive-OR of z and the output of the first half adder, giving

$$\begin{aligned}
S &= z \oplus (x \oplus y) \\
&= z'(xy' + x'y) + z(xy' + x'y)' \\
&= z'(xy' + x'y) + z(xy + x'y') \\
&= xy'z' + x'yz' + xyz + x'y'z
\end{aligned}$$

The carry output is

$$C = z(xy' + x'y) + xy = xy'z + x'yz + xy$$

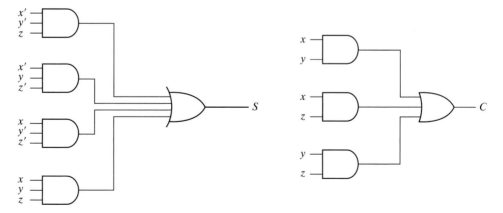

FIGURE 4-7
Implementation of Full Adder in Sum of Products

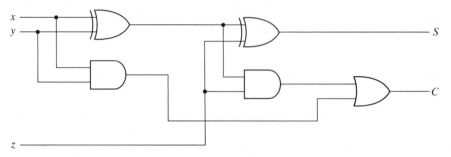

FIGURE 4-8
Implementation of Full Adder with Two Half Adders and an OR Gate

Binary Adder

A binary adder is a digital circuit that produces the arithmetic sum of two binary numbers. It can be constructed with full adders connected in cascade, with the output carry from each full adder connected to the input carry of the next full adder in the chain. Figure 4-9 shows the interconnection of four full adder (FA) circuits to provide a 4-bit binary ripple carry adder. The augend bits of A and the addend bits of B are designated by subscript numbers from right to left, with subscript 0 denoting the least significant bit. The carries are connected in a chain through the full adders. The input carry to the adder is C_0 and it ripples through the full adders to the output carry C_4. The S outputs generate the required sum bits. An n-bit adder requires n full adders with each output carry connected to the input carry of the next higher-order full adder.

To demonstrate with a specific example, consider the two binary numbers, $A = 1011$ and $B = 0011$. Their sum $S = 1110$ is formed with the four-bit adder as follows:

Subscript i:	3	2	1	0	
Input carry	0	1	1	0	C_i
Augend	1	0	1	1	A_i
Addend	0	0	1	1	B_i
Sum	1	1	1	0	S_i
Output carry	0	0	1	1	C_{i+1}

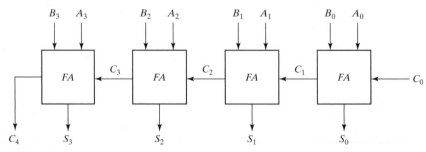

FIGURE 4-9
4-Bit Adder

The bits are added with full adders, starting from the least significant position (subscript 0), to form the sum bit and carry bit. The input carry C_0 in the least significant position must be 0. The value of C_{i+1} in a given significant position is the output carry of the full adder. This value is transferred into the input carry of the full adder that adds the bits one higher significant position to the left. The sum bits are thus generated starting from the rightmost position and are available as soon as the corresponding previous carry bit is generated. All the carries must be generated for the correct sum bits to appear at the outputs.

The 4-bit adder is a typical example of a standard component. It can be used in many applications involving arithmetic operations. Observe that the design of this circuit by the classical method would require a truth table with $2^9 = 512$ entries, since there are nine inputs to the circuit. By using an iterative method of cascading a standard function, it is possible to obtain a simple and straightforward implementation.

Carry Propagation

The addition of two binary numbers in parallel implies that all the bits of the augend and addend are available for computation at the same time. As in any combinational circuit, the signal must propagate through the gates before the correct output sum is available in the output terminals. The total propagation time is equal to the propagation delay of a typical gate times the number of gate levels in the circuit. The longest propagation delay time in an adder is the time it takes the carry to propagate through the full adders. Since each bit of the sum output depends on the value of the input carry, the value of S_i in any given stage in the adder will be in its steady state final value only after the input carry to that stage has been propagated. Consider output S_3 in Fig. 4-9. Inputs A_3 and B_3 are available as soon as input signals are applied to the adder. However, input carry C_3 does not settle to its final value until C_2 is available from the previous stage. Similarly, C_2 has to wait for C_1 and so on down to C_0. Thus, only after the carry propagates and ripples through all stages will the last output S_3 and carry C_4 settle to their final correct value.

The number of gate levels for the carry propagation can be found from the circuit of the full adder. The circuit is redrawn in Fig. 4-10 for convenience. The input and output variables use the subscript i to denote a typical stage in the adder. The signals at P_i and G_i settle to their

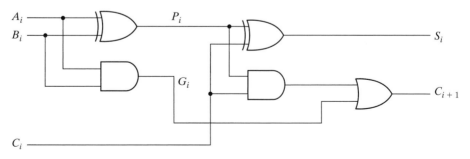

FIGURE 4-10
Full Adder with P and G Shown

steady state values after they propagate through their respective gates. These two signals are common to all full adders and depend only on the input augend and addend bits. The signal from the input carry C_i to the output carry C_{i+1}, propagates through an AND gate and an OR gate, which constitute two gate levels. If there are four full adders in the adder, the output carry C_4 would have $2 \times 4 = 8$ gate levels from C_0 to C_4. For an n-bit adder, there are $2n$ gate levels for the carry to propagate from input to output.

The carry propagation time is a limiting factor on the speed with which two numbers are added. Although the adder, or any combinational circuit, will always have some value at its output terminals, the outputs will not be correct unless the signals are given enough time to propagate through the gates connected from the inputs to the outputs. Since all other arithmetic operations are implemented by successive additions, the time consumed during the addition process is very critical. An obvious solution for reducing the carry propagation delay time is to employ faster gates with reduced delays. However, physical circuits have a limit to their capability. Another solution is to increase the equipment complexity in such a way that the carry delay time is reduced. There are several techniques for reducing the carry propagation time in a parallel adder. The most widely used technique employs the principle of *carry lookahead*.

Consider the circuit of the full adder shown in Fig. 4-10. If we define two new binary variables

$$P_i = A_i \oplus B_i$$
$$G_i = A_i B_i$$

the output sum and carry can be expressed as

$$S_i = P_i \oplus C_i$$
$$C_{i+1} = G_i + P_i C_i$$

G_i is called a *carry generate* and it produces a carry of 1 when both A_i and B_i are 1, regardless of the input carry C_i. P_i is called a *carry propagate* because it is the term associated with the propagation of the carry from C_i to C_{i+1}.

We now write the Boolean functions for the carry outputs of each stage and substitute for each C_i its value from the previous equations:

$$C_0 = \text{input carry}$$
$$C_1 = G_0 + P_0 C_0$$
$$C_2 = G_1 + P_1 C_1 = G_1 + P_1(G_0 + P_0 C_0) = G_1 + P_1 G_0 + P_1 P_0 C_0$$
$$C_3 = G_2 + P_2 C_2 = G_2 + P_2 G_1 + P_2 P_1 G_0 + P_2 P_1 P_0 C_0$$

Since the Boolean function for each output carry is expressed in sum of products, each function can be implemented with one level of AND gates followed by an OR gate (or by two-level NAND). The three Boolean functions for C_1, C_2, and C_3 are implemented in the carry looka-

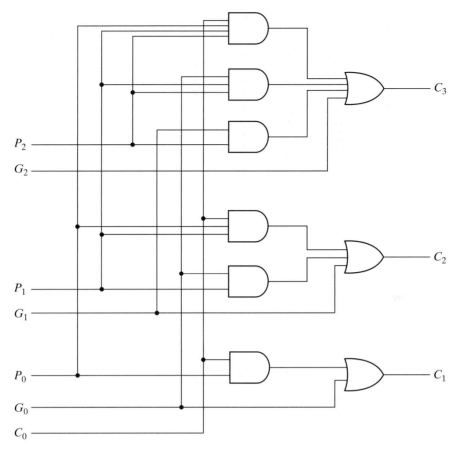

FIGURE 4-11
Logic Diagram of Carry Lookahead Generator

head generator shown in Fig. 4-11. Note that C_3 does not have to wait for C_2 and C_1 to propagate; in fact, C_3 is propagated at the same time as C_1 and C_2.

The construction of a 4-bit adder with a carry lookahead scheme is shown in Fig. 4-12. Each sum output requires two exclusive-OR gates. The output of the first exclusive-OR gate generates the P_i variable, and the AND gate generates the G_i variable. The carries are propagated through the carry lookahead generator (similar to that in Fig. 4-11) and applied as inputs to the second exclusive-OR gate. All output carries are generated after a delay through two levels of gates. Thus, outputs S_1 through S_3 have equal propagation delay times. The two-level circuit for the output carry C_4 is not shown. This circuit can be easily derived by the equation-substitution method.

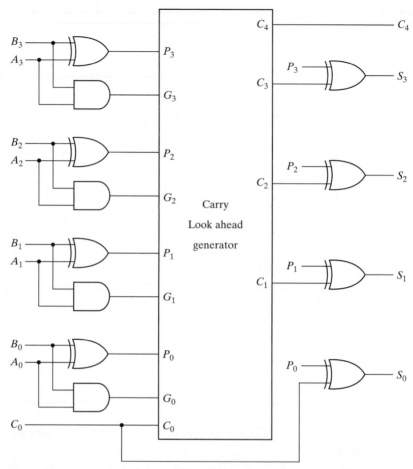

FIGURE 4-12
4-Bit Adder with Carry Lookahead

Each sum output requires two exclusive-OR gates. The output of the first exclusive-OR gate generates the P_i variable, and the AND gate generates the G_i variable. The carries are propagated through the carry lookahead generator (similar to that in Fig. 4-11) and applied as inputs to the second exclusive-OR gate. All output carries are generated after a delay through two levels of gates. Thus, outputs S_1 through S_3 have equal propagation delay times. The two-level circuit for the output carry C_4 is not shown. This circuit can be easily derived by the equation-substitution method.

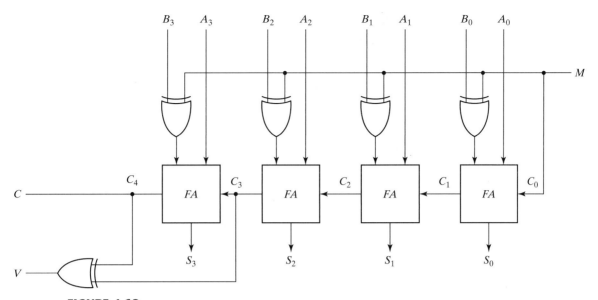

FIGURE 4-13
4-Bit Adder Subtractor

this gives $A - B$ if $A \geq B$ or the 2's complement of $(B - A)$ if $A < B$. For signed numbers, the result is $A - B$, provided that there is no overflow. (See Section 1-6.)

The addition and subtraction operations can be combined into one circuit with one common binary adder. This is done by including an exclusive-OR gate with each full adder. A 4-bit adder-subtractor circuit is shown in Fig. 4-13. The mode input M controls the operation. When $M = 0$, the circuit is an adder, and when $M = 1$, the circuit becomes a subtractor. Each exclusive-OR gate receives input M and one of the inputs of B. When $M = 0$, we have $B \oplus 0 = B$. The full adders receive the value of B, the input carry is 0, and the circuit performs A plus B. When $M = 1$, we have $B \oplus 1 = B'$ and $C_0 = 1$. The B inputs are all complemented and a 1 is added through the input carry. The circuit performs the operation A plus the 2's complement of B. (The exclusive-OR with output V is for detecting an overflow.)

It is worth noting that binary numbers in the signed-complement system are added and subtracted by the same basic addition and subtraction rules as unsigned numbers. Therefore, computers need only one common hardware circuit to handle both types of arithmetic. The user or programmer must interpret the results of such addition or subtraction differently, depending on whether it is assumed that the numbers are signed or unsigned

Overflow

When two numbers of n digits each are added and the sum occupies $n + 1$ digits, we say that an overflow occurred. This is true for binary or decimal numbers whether signed or unsigned. When the addition is performed with paper and pencil, an overflow is not a problem, since there is no limit by the width of the page to write down the sum. Overflow is a problem in digital computers because the number of bits that hold the number is finite and a result that contains $n + 1$ bits cannot be accommodated. For this reason, many computers detect the occurrence of an overflow, and when it occurs, a corresponding flip-flop is set that can then be checked by the user.

The detection of an overflow after the addition of two binary numbers depends on whether the numbers are considered to be signed or unsigned. When two unsigned numbers are added, an overflow is detected from the end carry out of the most significant position. In the case of signed numbers, the leftmost bit always represents the sign and negative numbers are in 2's complement form. When two signed numbers are added, the sign bit is treated as part of the number and the end carry does not indicate an overflow.

An overflow cannot occur after an addition if one number is positive and the other is negative, since adding a positive number to a negative number produces a result which is smaller than the larger of the two original numbers. An overflow may occur if the two numbers added are both positive or both negative. To see how this can happen, consider the following example. Two signed binary numbers, +70 and +80, are stored in two 8-bit registers. The range of numbers that each register can accommodate is from binary +127 to binary −128. Since the sum of the two numbers is +150, it exceeds the capacity of an 8-bit register. This is true if the numbers are both positive or both negative. The two additions in binary are shown next, together with the last two carries;

carries:	0	1			carries:	1	0	
+70	0	1000110			−70	1	0111010
+80	0	1010000			−80	1	0110000
+150	1	0010110			−150	0	1101010

Note that the 8-bit result that should have been positive has a negative sign bit and the 8-bit result that should have been negative has a positive sign bit. If, however, the carry out of the sign bit position is taken as the sign bit of the result, then the 9-bit answer so obtained will be correct. Since the answer cannot be accommodated within 8-bits, we say that an overflow has occurred.

An overflow condition can be detected by observing the carry into the sign bit position and the carry out of the sign bit position. If these two carries are not equal, an overflow has occurred. This is indicated in the examples where the two carries are explicitly shown. If the two carries are applied to an exclusive-OR gate, an overflow is detected when the output of the gate is equal to 1. For this method to work correctly the 2's complement must be computed by taking the 1's complement and adding one. This takes care of the condition when the maximum negative number is complemented.

The binary adder-subtractor circuit with outputs C and V is shown in Fig. 4-13. If the two binary numbers are considered to be unsigned, then the C bit detects a carry after addition or a borrow after subtraction. If the numbers are considered to be signed, then the V bit detects an overflow. If $V = 0$ after an addition or subtraction, it indicates that no overflow occurred and the n-bit result is correct. If $V = 1$, then the result of the operation contains $n + 1$ bits, but only the rightmost n bits of the number fit in the space available, so an overflow has occurred. The $(n + 1)$th bit is the actual sign and has been shifted out of position.

4-5 DECIMAL ADDER

Computers or calculators that perform arithmetic operations directly in the decimal number system represent decimal numbers in binary coded form. An adder for such a computer must employ arithmetic circuits that accept coded decimal numbers and present results in the same code. For binary addition, it is sufficient to consider a pair of significant bits together with a previous carry. A decimal adder requires a minimum of nine inputs and five outputs, since four bits are required to code each decimal digit and the circuit must have an input and output carry. There is a wide variety of possible decimal adder circuits, depending upon the code used to represent the decimal digits. Here we consider a decimal adder for the BCD code. (See Section 1-7.)

BCD Adder

Consider the arithmetic addition of two decimal digits in BCD, together with an input carry from a previous stage. Since each input digit does not exceed 9, the output sum cannot be greater than $9 + 9 + 1 = 19$, the 1 in the sum being an input carry. Suppose we apply two BCD digits to a 4-bit binary adder. The adder will form the sum in *binary* and produce a result that ranges from 0 through 19. These binary numbers are listed in Table 4-5 and are labeled by symbols K, Z_8, Z_4, Z_2, and Z_1. K is the carry, and the subscripts under the letter Z represent the weights 8, 4, 2, and 1 that can be assigned to the four bits in the BCD code. The columns under the binary sum list the binary value that appears in the outputs of the 4-bit binary adder. The output sum

Table 4-5
Derivation of BCD Adder

Binary Sum					BCD Sum					Decimal
K	Z_8	Z_4	Z_2	Z_1	C	S_8	S_4	S_2	S_1	
0	0	0	0	0	0	0	0	0	0	0
0	0	0	0	1	0	0	0	0	1	1
0	0	0	1	0	0	0	0	1	0	2
0	0	0	1	1	0	0	0	1	1	3
0	0	1	0	0	0	0	1	0	0	4
0	0	1	0	1	0	0	1	0	1	5
0	0	1	1	0	0	0	1	1	0	6
0	0	1	1	1	0	0	1	1	1	7
0	1	0	0	0	0	1	0	0	0	8
0	1	0	0	1	0	1	0	0	1	9
0	1	0	1	0	1	0	0	0	0	10
0	1	0	1	1	1	0	0	0	1	11
0	1	1	0	0	1	0	0	1	0	12
0	1	1	0	1	1	0	0	1	1	13
0	1	1	1	0	1	0	1	0	0	14
0	1	1	1	1	1	0	1	0	1	15
1	0	0	0	0	1	0	1	1	0	16
1	0	0	0	1	1	0	1	1	1	17
1	0	0	1	0	1	1	0	0	0	18
1	0	0	1	1	1	1	0	0	1	19

of two decimal digits must be represented in BCD and should appear in the form listed in the columns under BCD sum. The problem is to find a rule by which the binary sum is be converted to the correct BCD digit representation of the number in the BCD sum.

In examining the contents of the table, it is apparent that when the binary sum is equal to or less than 1001, the corresponding BCD number is identical, and therefore no conversion is needed. When the binary sum is greater than 1001, we obtain a non-valid BCD representation. The addition of binary 6 (0110) to the binary sum converts it to the correct BCD representation and also produces an output carry as required.

The logic circuit that detects the necessary correction can be derived from the table entries. It is obvious that a correction is needed when the binary sum has an output carry $K = 1$. The other six combinations from 1010 through 1111 that need a correction have a 1 in position Z_8. To distinguish them from binary 1000 and 1001, which also have a 1 in position Z_8, we specify further that either Z_4 or Z_2 must have a 1. The condition for a correction and an output carry can be expressed by the Boolean function

$$C = K + Z_8 Z_4 + Z_8 Z_2$$

When $C = 1$, it is necessary to add 0110 to the binary sum and provide an output carry for the next stage.

A BCD adder that adds two BCD digits and produces a sum digit in BCD is shown in Fig. 4-14. The two decimal digits, together with the input carry, are first added in the top 4-bit

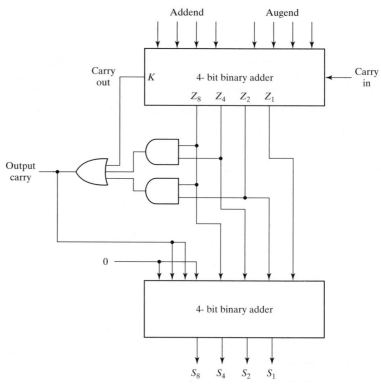

FIGURE 4-14
Block Diagram of a BCD Adder

adder to produce the binary sum. When the output carry is equal to zero, nothing is added to the binary sum. When it is equal to one, binary 0110 is added to the binary sum through the bottom 4-bit adder. The output carry generated from the bottom adder can be ignored, since it supplies information already available at the output carry terminal. A decimal parallel adder that adds n decimal digits needs n BCD adder stages. The output carry from one stage must be connected to the input carry of the next higher-order stage.

4-6 BINARY MULTIPLIER

Multiplication of binary numbers is performed in the same way as in decimal numbers. The multiplicand is multiplied by each bit of the multiplier starting from the least significant bit. Each such multiplication forms a partial product. Successive partial products are shifted one position to the left. The final product is obtained from the sum of the partial products.

To see how a binary multiplier can be implemented with a combinational circuit, consider the multiplication of two 2-bit numbers as shown in Fig. 4-15. The multiplicand bits are B_1 and B_0, the multiplier bits are A_1 and A_0, and the product is $C_3 C_2 C_1 C_0$. The first partial product is formed by multiplying A_0 by $B_1 B_0$. The multiplication of two bits such as A_0 and B_0 produces a 1 if both bits are 1; otherwise, it produces a 0. This is identical to an AND operation. Therefore, the partial product can be implemented with AND gates as shown in the diagram. The second partial product is formed by multiplying A_1 by $B_1 B_0$ and shifted one position to the left. The two partial products are added with two half adder (HA) circuits. Usually there are more bits in the partial products and it is necessary to use full adders to produce the sum of the partial products. Note that the least significant bit of the product does not have to go through an adder since it is formed by the output of the first AND gate.

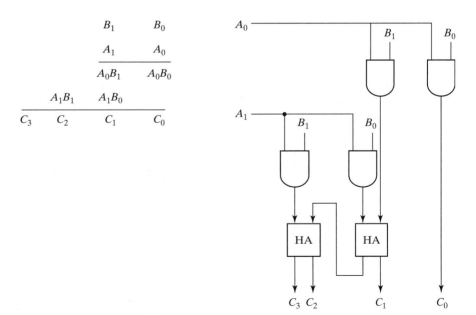

FIGURE 4-15
2-Bit by 2-Bit Binary Multiplier

A combinational circuit binary multiplier with more bits can be constructed in a similar fashion. A bit of the multiplier is ANDed with each bit of the multiplicand in as many levels as there are bits in the multiplier. The binary output in each level of AND gates is added with the partial product of the previous level to form a new partial product. The last level produces the product. For J multiplier bits and K multiplicand bits we need $(J \times K)$ AND gates and $(J - 1)$ K-bit adders to produce a product of $J + K$ bits.

As a second example, consider a multiplier circuit that multiplies a binary number of four bits by a number of three bits. Let the multiplicand be represented by $B_3 B_2 B_1 B_0$ and the multiplier by $A_2 A_1 A_0$. Since $K = 4$ and $J = 3$, we need 12 AND gates and two 4-bit adders to produce a product of seven bits. The logic diagram of the multiplier is shown in Fig. 4-16.

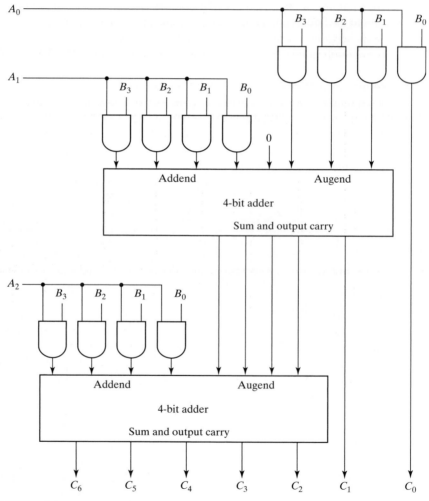

FIGURE 4-16
4-Bit by 3-Bit Binary Multiplier

4-7   MAGNITUDE COMPARATOR

The comparison of two numbers is an operation that determines if one number is greater than, less than, or equal to the other number. A *magnitude comparator* is a combinational circuit that compares two numbers, A and B, and determines their relative magnitudes. The outcome of the comparison is specified by three binary variables that indicate whether $A > B$, $A = B$, or $A < B$.

The circuit for comparing two n-bit numbers has 2^{2n} entries in the truth table and becomes too cumbersome even with $n = 3$. On the other hand, as one may suspect, a comparator circuit possess a certain amount of regularity. Digital functions that possess an inherent well-defined regularity can usually be designed by means of an algorithmic procedure. An algorithm is a procedure that specifies a finite set of steps that, if followed, give the solution to a problem. We illustrate this method here by deriving an algorithm for the design of a 4-bit magnitude comparator.

The algorithm is a direct application of the procedure a person uses to compare the relative magnitudes of two numbers. Consider two numbers, A and B, with four digits each. Write the coefficients of the numbers with descending significance

$$A = A_3 A_2 A_1 A_0$$
$$B = B_3 B_2 B_1 B_0$$

Each subscripted letter represents one of the digits in the number. The two numbers are equal if all pairs of significant digits are equal: $A_3 = B_3$ and $A_2 = B_2$ and $A_1 = B_1$ and $A_0 = B_0$. When the numbers are binary, the digits are either 1 or 0, and the equality relation of each pair of bits can be expressed logically with an exclusive-NOR function as

$$x_i = A_i B_i + A_i' B_i' \qquad \text{for } i = 0, 1, 2, 3$$

where $x_i = 1$ only if the pair of bits in position i are equal (i.e., if both are 1 or both are 0).

The equality of the two numbers, A and B, is displayed in a combinational circuit by an output binary variable that we designate by the symbol $(A = B)$. This binary variable is equal to 1 if the input numbers, A and B, are equal, and it is equal to 0 otherwise. For the equality condition to exist, all x_i variables must be equal to 1. This dictates an AND operation of all variables:

$$(A = B) = x_3 x_2 x_1 x_0$$

The *binary* variable $(A = B)$ is equal to 1 only if all pairs of digits of the two numbers are equal.

To determine if A is greater than or less than B, we inspect the relative magnitudes of pairs of significant digits starting from the most significant position. If the two digits are equal, we compare the next lower significant pair of digits. This comparison continues until a pair of unequal digits is reached. If the corresponding digit of A is 1 and that of B is 0, we conclude that $A > B$. If the corresponding digit of A is 0 and that of B is 1, we have that $A < B$. The sequential comparison can be expressed logically by the two Boolean functions

$$(A > B) = A_3 B_3' + x_3 A_2 B_2' + x_3 x_2 A_1 B_1' + x_3 x_2 x_1 A_0 B_0'$$
$$(A < B) = A_3' B_3 + x_3 A_2' B_2 + x_3 x_2 A_1' B_1 + x_3 x_2 x_1 A_0' B_0$$

The symbols $(A > B)$ and $(A < B)$ are *binary* output variables that are equal to 1 when $A > B$ or $A < B$, respectively.

The gate implementation of the three output variables just derived is simpler than it seems because it involves a certain amount of repetition. The unequal outputs can use the same gates

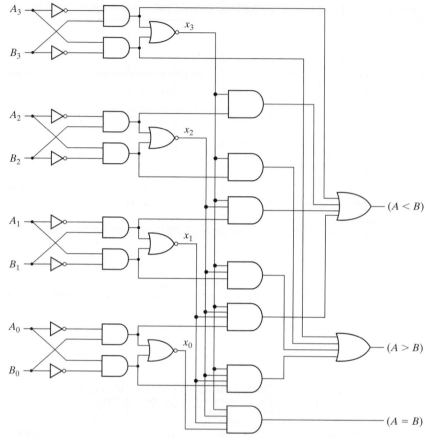

FIGURE 4-17
4-Bit Magnitude Comparator

that are needed to generate the equal output. The logic diagram of the 4-bit magnitude comparator is shown in Fig. 4-17. The four x outputs are generated with exclusive-NOR circuits and applied to an AND gate to give the output binary variable $(A = B)$. The other two outputs use the x variables to generate the Boolean functions listed previously. This is a multilevel implementation and has a regular pattern. The procedure for obtaining magnitude comparator circuits for binary numbers with more than four bits is obvious from this example.

4-8   DECODERS

Discrete quantities of information are represented in digital systems by binary codes. A binary code of n bits is capable of representing up to 2^n distinct elements of coded information. A *decoder* is a combinational circuit that converts binary information from n input lines to a maximum of 2^n unique output lines. If the n-bit coded information has unused combinations, the decoder may have fewer than 2^n outputs.

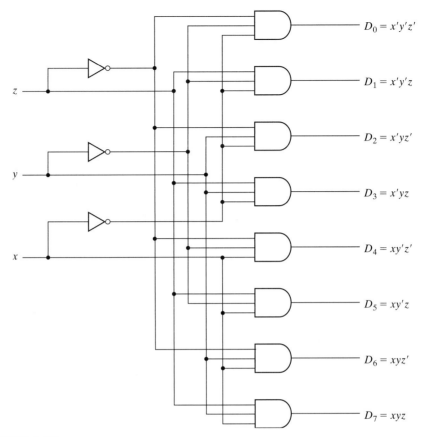

FIGURE 4-18
3-to-8-Line Decoder

The decoders presented here are called *n*-to-*m*-line decoders, where $m \leq 2^n$. Their purpose is to generate the 2^n (or fewer) minterms of *n* input variables. The name *decoder* is also used in conjunction with other code converters such as a BCD-to-seven-segment decoder.

As an example, consider the 3-to-8-line decoder circuit of Fig. 4-18. The three inputs are decoded into eight outputs, each representing one of the minterms of the three input variables. The three inverters provide the complement of the inputs, and each one of the eight AND gates generates one of the minterms. A particular application of this decoder is binary-to-octal conversion. The input variables represent a binary number, and the outputs represent the eight digits in the octal number system. However, a 3-to-8-line decoder can be used for decoding any 3-bit code to provide eight outputs, one for each element of the code.

The operation of the decoder may be clarified by the truth table listed in Table 4-6. For each possible input combination, there are seven outputs that are equal to 0 and only one that is equal to 1. The output whose value is equal to 1 represents the minterm equivalent of the binary number presently available in the input lines.

Table 4-6
Truth Table of a 3-to-8-Line Decoder

Inputs			Outputs							
x	y	z	D_0	D_1	D_2	D_3	D_4	D_5	D_6	D_7
0	0	0	1	0	0	0	0	0	0	0
0	0	1	0	1	0	0	0	0	0	0
0	1	0	0	0	1	0	0	0	0	0
0	1	1	0	0	0	1	0	0	0	0
1	0	0	0	0	0	0	1	0	0	0
1	0	1	0	0	0	0	0	1	0	0
1	1	0	0	0	0	0	0	0	1	0
1	1	1	0	0	0	0	0	0	0	1

Some decoders are constructed with NAND gates. Since a NAND gate produces the AND operation with an inverted output, it becomes more economical to generate the decoder minterms in their complemented form. Furthermore, decoders include one or more *enable* inputs to control the circuit operation. A 2-to-4-line decoder with an enable input constructed with NAND gates is shown in Fig. 4-19. The circuit operates with complemented outputs and a complement enable input. The decoder is enabled when E is equal to 0. As indicated by the truth table, only one output can be equal to 0 at any given time, all other outputs are equal to 1. The output whose value is equal to 0 represents the minterm selected by inputs A and B. The circuit is disabled when E is equal to 1, regardless of the values of the other two

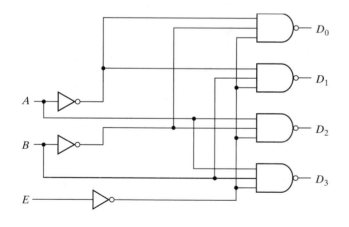

E	A	B	D_0	D_1	D_2	D_3
1	X	X	1	1	1	1
0	0	0	0	1	1	1
0	0	1	1	0	1	1
0	1	0	1	1	0	1
0	1	1	1	1	1	0

(a) Logic diagram

(b) Truth table

FIGURE 4-19
2-to-4-Line Decoder with Enable Input

inputs. When the circuit is disabled, none of the outputs are equal to 0 and none of the minterms are selected. In general, a decoder may operate with complemented or uncomplemented outputs. The enable input may be activated with a 0 or with a 1 signal. Some decoders have two or more enable inputs that must satisfy a given logic condition in order to enable the circuit.

A decoder with enable input can function as a demultiplexer. A *demultiplexer* is a circuit that receives information from a single line and directs it to one of 2^n possible output lines. The selection of a specific output is controlled by the bit combination of n selection lines. The decoder of Fig. 4-19 can function as a 1-to-4-line demultiplexer when E is taken as a data input line and A and B are taken as the selection inputs. The single input variable E has a path to all four outputs, but the input information is directed to only one of the output lines, as specified by the binary combination of the two selection lines A and B. This can be verified from the truth table of the circuit. For example, if the selection lines $AB = 10$, output D_2 will be the same as the input value E, while all other outputs are maintained at 1. Because decoder and demultiplexer operations are obtained from the same circuit, a decoder with an enable input is referred to as a *decoder/demultiplexer*.

Decoders with enable inputs can be connected together to form a larger decoder circuit. Figure 4-20 shows two 3-to-8-line decoders with enable inputs connected to form a 4-to-16-line decoder. When $w = 0$, the top decoder is enabled and the other is disabled. The bottom decoder outputs are all 0's, and the top eight outputs generate minterms 0000 to 0111. When $w = 1$, the enable conditions are reversed; the bottom decoder outputs generate minterms 1000 to 1111, while the outputs of the top decoder are all 0's. This example demonstrates the usefulness of enable inputs in decoders and other combinational logic components. In general, enable inputs are a convenient feature for interconnecting two or more standard components for the purpose of expanding the component into a similar function with more inputs and outputs.

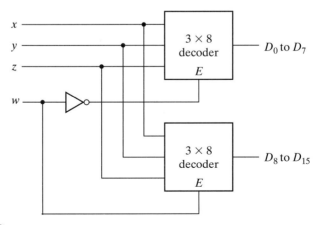

FIGURE 4-20
4 × 16 Decoder Constructed with Two 3 × 8 Decoders

Combinational Logic Implementation

A decoder provides the 2^n minterms of n input variables. Since any Boolean function can be expressed in sum of minterms, one can use a decoder to generate the minterms and an external OR gate to form the logical sum. In this way, any combinational circuit with n inputs and m outputs can be implemented with an n-to-2^n-line decoder and m OR gates.

The procedure for implementing a combinational circuit by means of a decoder and OR gates requires that the Boolean function for the circuit is expressed in sum of minterms. A decoder is then chosen that generates all the minterms of the input variables. The inputs to each OR gate are selected from the decoder outputs according to the list of minterm of each function. This procedure will be illustrated by an example that implements a full adder circuit.

From the truth table of the full adder (see Table 4-4), we obtain the functions for the combinational circuit in sum of minterms:

$$S(x, y, z) = \Sigma(1, 2, 4, 7)$$
$$C(x, y, z) = \Sigma(3, 5, 6, 7)$$

Since there are three inputs and a total of eight minterms, we need a 3-to-8-line decoder. The implementation is shown in Fig. 4-21. The decoder generates the eight minterms for x, y, z. The OR gate for output S forms the logical sum of minterms 1, 2, 4, and 7. The OR gate for output C forms the logical sum of minterms 3, 5, 6, and 7.

A function with a long list of minterms requires an OR gate with a large number of inputs. A function having a list of k minterms can be expressed in its complemented form F' with $2^n - k$ minterms. If the number of minterms in a function is greater than $2^n/2$, then F' can be expressed with fewer minterms. In such a case, it is advantageous to use a NOR gate to sum the minterms of F'. The output of the NOR gate complements this sum and generates the normal output F. If NAND gates are used for the decoder as in Fig. 4-19, then the external gates must be NAND gates instead of OR gates. This is because a two-level NAND gate circuit implements a sum of minterms function and is equivalent to a two-level AND-OR circuit.

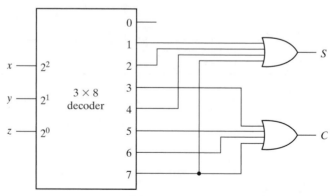

FIGURE 4-21
Implementation of a Full Adder with a Decoder

4-9   ENCODERS

An encoder is a digital circuit that performs the inverse operation of a decoder. An encoder has 2^n (or fewer) input lines and n output lines. The output lines generate the binary code corresponding to the input value. An example of an encoder is the octal-to-binary encoder whose truth table is given in Table 4-7. It has eight inputs (one for each of the octal digits) and three outputs that generate the corresponding binary number. It is assumed that only one input has a value of 1 at any given time.

The encoder can be implemented with OR gates whose inputs are determined directly from the truth table. Output z is equal to 1 when the input octal digit is 1, 3, 5, or 7. Output y is 1 for octal digits 2, 3, 6, or 7 and output x is 1 for digits 4, 5, 6, or 7. These conditions can be expressed by the following output Boolean functions:

$$z = D_1 + D_3 + D_5 + D_7$$
$$y = D_2 + D_3 + D_6 + D_7$$
$$x = D_4 + D_5 + D_6 + D_7$$

The encoder can be implemented with three OR gates.

The encoder defined in Table 4-7 has the limitation that only one input can be active at any given time. If two inputs are active simultaneously, the output produces an undefined combination. For example, if D_3 and D_6 are 1 simultaneously, the output of the encoder will be 111 because all three outputs are equal to 1. This does not represent either binary 3 or binary 6. To resolve this ambiguity, encoder circuits must establish an input priority to ensure that only one input is encoded. If we establish a higher priority for inputs with higher subscript numbers, and if both D_3 and D_6 are 1 at the same time, the output will be 110 because D_6 has higher priority than D_3.

Another ambiguity in the octal-to-binary encoder is that an output with all 0's is generated when all the inputs are 0; this output is the same as when D_0 is equal to 1. The discrepancy can be resolved by providing one more output to indicate that at least one input is equal to 1.

Table 4-7
Truth Table of Octal-to-Binary Encoder

Inputs								Outputs		
D_0	D_1	D_2	D_3	D_4	D_5	D_6	D_7	x	y	z
1	0	0	0	0	0	0	0	0	0	0
0	1	0	0	0	0	0	0	0	0	1
0	0	1	0	0	0	0	0	0	1	0
0	0	0	1	0	0	0	0	0	1	1
0	0	0	0	1	0	0	0	1	0	0
0	0	0	0	0	1	0	0	1	0	1
0	0	0	0	0	0	1	0	1	1	0
0	0	0	0	0	0	0	1	1	1	1

Table 4-8
Truth Table of a Priority Encoder

Inputs				Outputs		
D_0	D_1	D_2	D_3	x	y	V
0	0	0	0	X	X	0
1	0	0	0	0	0	1
X	1	0	0	0	1	1
X	X	1	0	1	0	1
X	X	X	1	1	1	1

Priority Encoder

A priority encoder is an encoder circuit that includes the priority function. The operation of the priority encoder is such that if two or more inputs are equal to 1 at the same time, the input having the highest priority will take precedence. The truth table of a four-input priority encoder is given in Table 4-8. In addition to the two outputs x and y, the circuit has a third output designated by V; this is a *valid* bit indicator that is set to 1 when one or more inputs are equal to 1. If all inputs are 0, there is no valid input and V is equal to 0. The other two outputs are not inspected when V equals 0 and are specified as don't-care conditions. Note that whereas **X**'s in output columns represent don't-care conditions, the **X**'s in the input columns are useful for representing a truth table in condensed form. Instead of listing all 16 minterms of four variables, the truth table uses an **X** to represent either 1 or 0. For example, X100 represents the two minterms 0100 and 1100.

According to Table 4-8, the higher the subscript number, the higher the priority of the input. Input D_3 has the highest priority, so regardless of the values of the other inputs, when this input is 1, the output for xy is 11 (binary 3). D_2 has the next priority level. The output is 10 if $D_2 = 1$ provided that $D_3 = 0$, regardless of the values of the other two lower priority inputs. The output for D_1 is generated only if higher priority inputs are 0, and so on down the priority levels.

The maps for simplifying outputs x and y are shown in Fig. 4-22. The minterms for the two functions are derived from Table 4-8. Although the table has only five rows, when each X in a

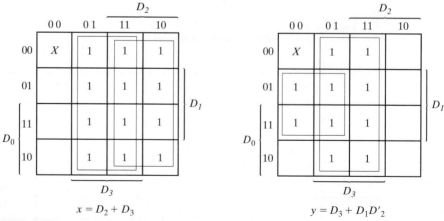

$$x = D_2 + D_3$$

$$y = D_3 + D_1 D'_2$$

FIGURE 4-22
Maps for a Priority Encoder

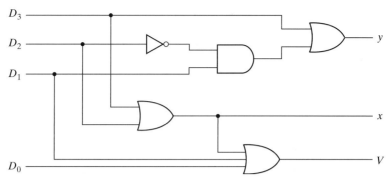

FIGURE 4-23
4-Input Priority Encoder

row is replaced first by 0 and then by 1, we obtain all 16 possible input combinations. For example, the fourth row in the table with XX10 represents the four minterms 0010, 0110, 1010, and 1110. The simplified Boolean expressions for the priority encoder are obtained from the maps. The condition for output V is an OR function of all the input variables. The priority encoder is implemented in Fig. 4-23 according to the following Boolean functions:

$$x = D_2 + D_3$$
$$y = D_3 + D_1 D_2'$$
$$V = D_0 + D_1 + D_2 + D_3$$

4-10   MULTIPLEXERS

A multiplexer is a combinational circuit that selects binary information from one of many input lines and directs it to a single output line. The selection of a particular input line is controlled by a set of selection lines. Normally, there are 2^n input lines and n selection lines whose bit combinations determine which input is selected.

A 2-to-1-line multiplexer connects one of two 1-bit sources to a common destination as shown in Fig. 4-24. The circuit has two data input lines, one output line, and one selection line S. When $S = 0$, the upper AND gate is enabled and I_0 has a path to the output. When $S = 1$, the lower AND gate is enabled and I_1 has a path to the output. The multiplexer acts like an electronic switch that selects one of two sources. The block diagram of a multiplexer is sometimes depicted using a wedge-shaped symbol as shown in Fig 4-24(b). It suggests visually how a selected one of multiple data sources is directed into a single destination. The multiplexer is often labeled as MUX in block diagrams.

A 4-to-1-line multiplexer is shown in Fig. 4-25. Each of the four inputs, I_0 through I_3, is applied to one input of an AND gate. Selection lines S_1 and S_0 are decoded to select a particular AND gate. The outputs of the AND gates are applied to a single OR gate that provides the 1-line output. The function table lists the input that is passed to the output for each combination of the binary selection values. To demonstrate the circuit operation, consider the case when $S_1 S_0 = 10$. The AND gate associated with input I_2 has two of its inputs equal to 1 and the third input connected to I_2. The other three AND gates have at least one input equal to 0, which

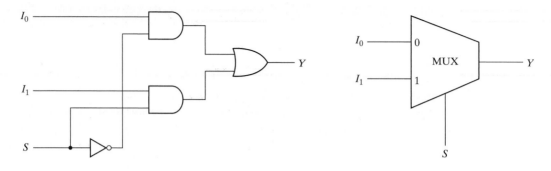

(a) Logic diagram

(b) Block diagram

FIGURE 4-24
2-to-1-Line Multiplexer

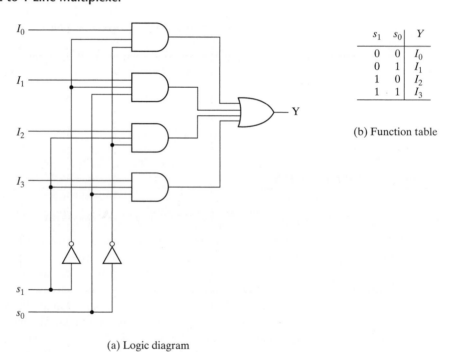

(a) Logic diagram

s_1	s_0	Y
0	0	I_0
0	1	I_1
1	0	I_2
1	1	I_3

(b) Function table

FIGURE 4-25
4-to-1-Line Multiplexer

makes their outputs equal to 0. The OR gate output is now equal to the value of I_2, providing a path from the selected input to the output. A multiplexer is also called a *data selector*, since it selects one of many inputs and steers the binary information to the output line.

The AND gates and inverters in the multiplexer resemble a decoder circuit and, indeed, they decode the selection input lines. In general, a 2^n-to-1-line multiplexer is constructed from an

n-to-2^n decoder by adding to it 2^n input lines, one to each AND gate. The outputs of the AND gates are applied to a single OR gate. The size of a multiplexer is specified by the number 2^n of its data input lines and the single output line. The n selection lines are implied from the 2^n data lines. As in decoders, multiplexers may have an enable input to control the operation of the unit. When the enable input is in the inactive state, the outputs are disabled, and when it is in the active state, the circuit functions as a normal multiplexer.

Multiplexer circuits can be combined with common selection inputs to provide multiple-bit selection logic. As an illustration, a quadruple 2-to-1-line multiplexers are shown in Fig. 4-26. The circuit has four multiplexers, each capable of selecting one of two input lines.

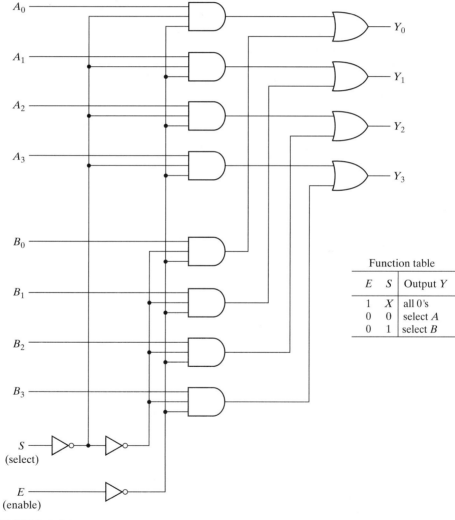

Function table

E	S	Output Y
1	X	all 0's
0	0	select A
0	1	select B

FIGURE 4-26
Quadruple 2-to-1-Line Multiplexer

Output Y_0 can be selected to come from either input A_0 or B_0. Similarly, output Y_1 may have the value of A_1 or B_1, and so on. Input selection line S selects one of the lines in each of the four multiplexers. The enable input E must be active for normal operation. Although the circuit contains four 2-to-1-line multiplexers, we are more likely to view it as a circuit that selects one of two 4-bit sets of data lines. As shown in the function table, the unit is enabled when $E = 0$. Then, if $S = 0$, the four A inputs have a path to the four outputs. On the other hand, if $S = 1$, the four B inputs are applied to the outputs. The outputs have all 0's when $E = 1$, regardless of the value of S.

Boolean Function Implementation

It was shown in Sec. 4-8 that a decoder can be used to implement Boolean functions by employing external OR gates. An examination of the logic diagram of a multiplexer reveals that it is essentially a decoder that includes the OR gate within the unit. The minterms of a function are generated in a multiplexer by the circuit associated with the selection inputs. The individual minterms can be selected by the data inputs. This provides a method of implementing a Boolean function of n variables with a multiplexer that has n selection inputs and 2^n data inputs, one for each minterm.

We will now show a more efficient method for implementing a Boolean function of n variables with a multiplexer that has $n - 1$ selection inputs. The first $n - 1$ variables of the function are connected to the selection inputs of the multiplexer. The remaining single variable of the function is used for the data inputs. If the single variable is denoted by z, each data input of the multiplexer will be z, z', 1, or 0. To demonstrate this procedure, consider the Boolean function of three variables:

$$F(x, y, z) = \Sigma(1, 2, 6, 7)$$

The function can be implemented with a 4-to-1-line multiplexer as shown in Fig. 4-27. The two variables x and y are applied to the selection lines in that order; x is connected to the S_1 input

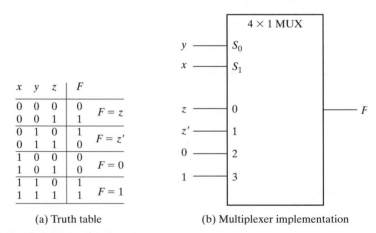

(a) Truth table   (b) Multiplexer implementation

FIGURE 4-27
Implementing a Boolean Function with a Multiplexer

and y to the S_0 input. The values for the data input lines are determined from the truth table of the function. When $xy = 00$, output F is equal to z because $F = 0$ when $z = 0$ and $F = 1$ when $z = 1$. This requires that variable z be applied to data input 0. The operation of the multiplexer is such that when $xy = 00$, data input 0 has a path to the output and that makes F equal to z. In a similar fashion we can determine the required input to data lines 1, 2, and 3 from the value of F when $xy = 01$, 10, and 11, respectively. This particular example shows all four possibilities that can be obtained for the data inputs.

The general procedure for implementing any Boolean function of n variables with a multiplexer with $n - 1$ selection inputs and 2^{n-1} data inputs follows from the previous example. The Boolean function is first listed in a truth table. The first $n - 1$ variables in the table are applied to the selection inputs of the multiplexer. For each combination of the selection variables, we evaluate the output as a function of the last variable. This function can be 0, 1, the variable, or the complement of the variable. These values are then applied to the data inputs in the proper order. As a second example, consider the implementation of the Boolean function

$$F(A, B, C, D) = \Sigma(1, 3, 4, 11, 12, 13, 14, 15).$$

This function is implemented with a multiplexer with three selection inputs as shown in Fig. 4-28. Note that the first variable A must be connected to selection input S_2 so that A, B, and C correspond to selection inputs S_2, S_1, S_0, respectively. The values for the data inputs are determined from the truth table listed in the figure. The corresponding data line number is determined from the binary combination of ABC. For example, when $ABC = 101$ the table shows that $F = D$, so the input variable D is applied to data input 5. The binary constants 0 and 1 correspond to two fixed signal values. When integrated circuits are used, logic 0 corresponds to signal ground and logic 1 is equivalent to the power signal—usually 5 volts.

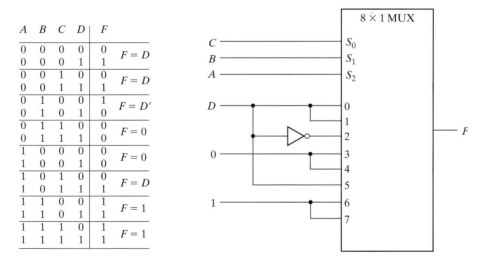

A	B	C	D	F	
0	0	0	0	0	$F = D$
0	0	0	1	1	
0	0	1	0	0	$F = D$
0	0	1	1	1	
0	1	0	0	1	$F = D'$
0	1	0	1	0	
0	1	1	0	0	$F = 0$
0	1	1	1	0	
1	0	0	0	0	$F = 0$
1	0	0	1	0	
1	0	1	0	0	$F = D$
1	0	1	1	1	
1	1	0	0	1	$F = 1$
1	1	0	1	1	
1	1	1	0	1	$F = 1$
1	1	1	1	1	

FIGURE 4-28
Implementing a 4-Input Function with a Multiplexer

Normal input A ——————▷—————— Output $Y = A$ if $C = 1$
High–impedance if $C = 0$

Control input C ——————

FIGURE 4-29
Graphic Symbol for a Three-State Buffer

Three-State Gates

A multiplexer can be constructed with three-state gates. A three-state gate is a digital circuit that exhibits three states. Two of the states are signals equivalent to logic 1 and 0 as in a conventional gate. The third state is a high-impedance state. The *high-impedance* state behaves like an open circuit, which means that the output appears to be disconnected and the circuit has no logic significance. Three-state gates may perform any conventional logic such as AND or NAND. However, the one most commonly used is the buffer gate.

The graphic symbol of a three-state buffer gate is shown in Fig. 4-29. It is distinguished from a normal buffer by an input control line entering the bottom of the gate symbol. The buffer has a normal input, an output, and a control input that determines the state of the output. When the control input is equal to 1, the output is enabled and the gate behaves like a conventional buffer, with the output equal to the normal input. When the control input is 0, the output is disabled and the gate goes to a high-impedance state, regardless of the value in the normal input. The high-impedance state of a three-state gate provides a special feature not available in other gates. Because of this feature, a large number of three-state gate outputs can be connected with wires to form a common line without endangering loading effects.

The construction of multiplexers with three-state buffers is demonstrated in Fig. 4-30. Part (a) of the figure shows the construction of a 2-to-1-line multiplexer with two three-state buffers

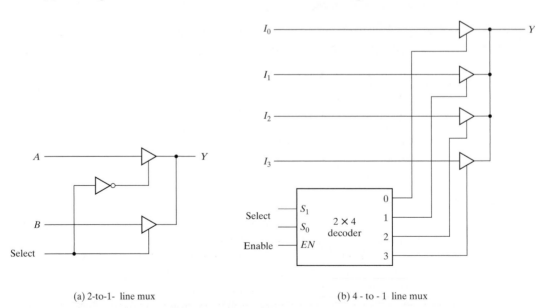

(a) 2-to-1- line mux   (b) 4 - to - 1 line mux

FIGURE 4-30
Multiplexers with Three-State Gates

and an inverter. The two outputs are connected together to form a single output line (It must be realized that this type of connection cannot be done with gates that do not have three-state outputs). When the select input is 0, the upper buffer is enabled by its control input, and the lower buffer is disabled. Output Y is then equal to input A. When the select input is 1, the lower buffer is enabled and Y is equal to B.

The construction of a 4-to-1-line multiplexer is shown in Fig. 4-30(b). The outputs of four three-state buffers are connected together to form a single output line. The control inputs to the buffers determine which one of the four normal inputs I_0 through I_3 will be connected to the output line. No more than one buffer may be in the active state at any given time. The connected buffers must be controlled so that only one three-state buffer has access to the output, while all other buffers are maintained in a high-impedance state. One way to ensure that no more than one control input is active at any given time is to use a decoder as shown in the diagram. When the enable input of the decoder is 0, all of its four outputs are 0, and the bus line is in a high-impedance state because all four buffers are disabled. When the enable input is active, one of the three-state buffers will be active depending on the binary value in the select inputs of the decoder. Careful investigation will reveal that this circuit is another way of constructing a 4-to-1-line multiplexer.

4-11   HDL FOR COMBINATIONAL CIRCUITS

The Verilog hardware description language (HDL) was introduced in Section 3-9. In this section, we present the alternatives available for describing combinational circuits in HDL. Sequential circuits are presented in the next chapter. As mentioned previously, the module is the basic building block of Verilog HDL. A module can be described in any one (or a combination) of the following modeling techniques:

- Gate-level modeling using instantiation of primitive gates and user-defined modules.
- Dataflow modeling using continuous assignment statements with keyword **assign.**
- Behavioral modeling using procedural assignment statements with keyword **always.**

Gate-level modeling describes the circuit by specifying the gates and how they are connected with each other. Dataflow modeling is mostly used for describing combinational circuits. Behavioral modeling is used to describe digital systems at a higher level of abstraction. There is one other modeling style called switch-level modeling. This type of modeling provides the ability to design at the MOS transistor level and is considered in section 10-10.

Gate-Level Modeling

Gate-level modeling was introduced in Section 3-9 with a simple example. In this type of representation, a circuit is specified by its logic gates and their interconnection. It provides a textual description of a schematic diagram. Verilog recognizes 12 basic gates as predefined primitives. Four primitive gates are of the three-state type. The other eight are the same as the ones listed in Section 2-7. They are declared with the lowercase keywords: **and, nand, or, nor, xor, xnor, not, buf.** When the gates are simulated, the system assigns a four-valued logic set to each gate. In

Table 4-9
Truth Table for Predefined Primitive Gates

and	0	1	x	z		or	0	1	x	z
0	0	0	0	0		0	0	1	x	x
1	0	1	x	x		1	1	1	1	1
x	0	x	x	x		x	x	1	x	x
z	0	x	x	x		z	x	1	x	x

xor	0	1	x	z		not	input	output
0	0	1	x	x			0	1
1	1	0	x	x			1	0
x	x	x	x	x			x	x
z	x	x	x	x			z	x

addition to the two logic values of 0 and 1, there are two other values: *unknown* and *high impedance*. An unknown value is denoted by **x** and a high impedance by **z**. An unknown value is assigned during simulation for the case when an input or output is ambiguous, for instance if it has not yet been assigned a value of 0 or 1. A high-impedance condition occurs in the output of three-state gates or if a wire is inadvertently left unconnected. The truth table for the **and, or, xor,** and **not** are shown in Table 4-9. The truth table for the other four gates is the same except that the outputs are complemented. Note that for the **and** gate, the output is 1 only when both inputs are 1, the output is 0 if any input is 0. Otherwise, if one input is **x** or **z**, the output is **x**. The output of the **or** gate is 0 if both inputs are 0, is 1 if any input is 1, and is **x** otherwise.

When a primitive gate is incorporated into a module, we say it is *instantiated* in the module. In general, component instantiations are statements that reference lower-level components in the design, essentially creating unique copies (or *instances*) of those components in the higher-level module. Thus, a module that uses a gate in its description is said to *instantiate* the gate.

We now present two examples of gate-level modeling. Both examples use multiple bit widths called *vectors*. A vector is specified within square brackets and two numbers separated with a colon. The following code specifies two vectors:

output [0:3]D;

wire [7:0]SUM;

The first declares an output vector *D* with four bits 0 through 3. The second declares a wire vector *SUM* with eight bits numbered 7 through 0. The first number listed is the most significant bit of the vector. The individual bits are specified within square brackets, thus *D* [2] specifies bit 2 of *D*. It is also possible to address parts of vectors. For example, *SUM* [2:0] specifies the three least significant bits of vector *SUM*.

HDL Example 4-1 shows the gate-level description of a 2-to-4-line decoder. It has two data inputs *A* and *B* and an enable input *E*. The four outputs are specified with the vector *D*. The **wire** declaration is for internal connections. Three **not** gates produce the complement of the inputs and four **nand** gates provide the outputs for *D*. Remember that the output is always listed first in a gate list, followed by the inputs. This example describes the decoder of Fig. 4-19 and follows the procedures established in Sec. 3-9. Note that the keywords **not** and **nand** are written only once

HDL Example 4-1

```
//Gate-level description of a 2-to-4-line decoder
//Figure 4-19
module decoder_gl (A,B,E,D);
    input A,B,E;
    output [0:3]D;
    wire Anot,Bnot,Enot;
    not
        n1 (Anot,A),
        n2 (Bnot,B),
        n3 (Enot,E);
    nand
        n4 (D[0],Anot,Bnot,Enot),
        n5 (D[1],Anot,B,Enot),
        n6 (D[2],A,Bnot,Enot),
        n7 (D[3],A,B,Enot);
endmodule
```

and do not have to be repeated for each gate, but commas must be inserted at the end of each of the series of gates except for the last statement, which must be terminated with a semicolon.

Two or more modules can be combined to build a hierarchical description of a design. There are two basic types of design methodologies: top-down and bottom-up. In a *top-down* design, the top-level block is defined and then the sub-blocks necessary to build the top-level block are identified. In a *bottom-up* design, the building blocks are first identified and then combined to build the top-level block. Take for example the binary adder of Fig. 4-9. It can be considered as a top-block component built with four full adder blocks, while each full adder is built with two half adder blocks. In a top-down design, the 4-bit adder is defined first, and then the two adders described. In a bottom-up design, the half adder is defined, then the full adder is constructed and then the 4-bit adder is built from the full adders.

A bottom-up hierarchical description of a 4-bit adder is shown in HDL Example 4-2. The half adder is defined by instantiating primitive gates. The next module describes the full adder by instantiating two half adders. The third module describes the 4-bit adder by instantiating four full adders. (Note that identifiers cannot start with a number but can start with an underscore so the module name is: _4bitadder.) The instantiation is done by using the name of the module that is instantiated with a new (or the same) set of port names. For example, the half adder HA1 inside the full adder module is instantiated with ports $S1$, $D1$, x, y. This produces a half adder with outputs $S1$, $D1$, and inputs x, y.

Note that in Verilog, one module definition cannot be placed within another module description. In other words, a module cannot be inserted within the **module** and **endmodule** keywords of another module. The only way one module definition can be incorporated in another module is by instantiating it. Thus, modules are instantiated within other modules to create a hierarchical description of a design. Also, note that names must be specified when defined modules are instantiated (like FA0 for the first full adder in the third module), but using a name is optional when instantiating primitive gates.

HDL Example 4-2

```
//Gate-level hierarchical description of 4-bit adder
// Description of half adder (see Fig 4-5b)
module halfadder (S,C,x,y);
    input x,y;
    output S,C;
//Instantiate primitive gates
    xor (S,x,y);
    and (C,x,y);
endmodule

//Description of full adder (see Fig 4-8)
module fulladder (S,C,x,y,z);
    input x,y,z;
    output S,C;
    wire S1,D1,D2; //Outputs of first XOR and two AND gates
//Instantiate the halfadder
    halfadder HA1 (S1,D1,x,y),
              HA2 (S,D2,S1,z);
    or g1(C,D2,D1);
endmodule

//Description of 4-bit adder (see Fig 4-9)
module _4bit_adder (S,C4,A,B,C0);
    input [3:0] A,B;
    input C0;
    output [3:0] S;
    output C4;
    wire C1,C2,C3;   //Intermediate carries
//Instantiate the fulladder
    fulladder  FA0 (S[0],C1,A[0],B[0],C0),
               FA1 (S[1],C2,A[1],B[1],C1),
               FA2 (S[2],C3,A[2],B[2],C2),
               FA3 (S[3],C4,A[3],B[3],C3);
endmodule
```

Three State Gates

As mentioned in Section 4-10, three-state gates have a control input that can place the gate into a high-impedance state. The high-impedance state is symbolized by **z** in HDL. There are four types of three-state gates as shown in Fig. 4-31. The **bufif1** gate behaves like a normal buffer if control = 1. The output goes to a high-impedance state **z** when control = 0. The **bufif0** gate behaves in a similar fashion except that the high-impedance state occurs when control = 1. The

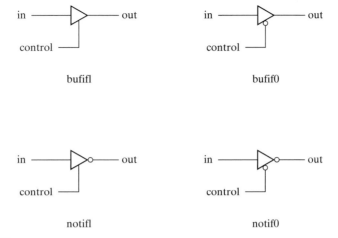

FIGURE 4-31
Three-State Gates

two **not** gates operate in a similar manner except that the output is the complement of the input when the gate is not in a high-impedance state. The gates are instantiated with the statement

gate name (output, input, control);

The gate name can be any one of the four three-state gates. The output can result in 0, 1, or **z**. Two examples of gate instantiation are

```
bufif1    (OUT,A,control);
notif0    (Y,B,enable);
```

In the first example, input A is transferred to OUT when control $= 1$. OUT goes to **z** when control $= 0$. In the second example, output $Y = $ **z** when enable $= 1$ and output $Y = B'$ when enable $= 0$.

The outputs of three-state gates can be connected together to form a common output line. To identify such a connection, HDL uses the keyword **tri** (for tristate) to indicate that the output has multiple drivers. As an example, consider the 2-to-1-line multiplexer with three-state gates shown in Fig. 4-32.

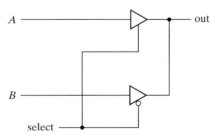

FIGURE 4-32
2-to-1-Line Multiplexer with Three-State Buffers

The HDL description must use a **tri** data type for the output.

```
module muxtri (A,B,select,OUT);
    input A,B,select;
    output OUT;
    tri OUT;
    bufif1 (OUT,A,select);
    bufif0 (OUT,B,select);
endmodule
```

The two three-state buffers have the same output. In order to show that they have a common connection, it is necessary to declare OUT with the keyword **tri.**

Keywords **wire** and **tri** are examples of *net* data type. Nets represent connections between hardware elements. Their value is continuously driven by the output of the device that they represent. The word *net* is not a keyword, but represents a class of data types such as **wire, wor, wand, tri, supply1, and supply0.** The **wire** declaration is used most frequently. The net **wor** models the hardware implementation of the wired-OR configuration. The **wand** models the wired-AND configuration.(See Fig. 3-28). The nets **supply1** and **supply0** represent power supply and ground. They are used in the description of switch-level modeling (see Section 10-10).

Dataflow Modeling

Dataflow modeling uses a number of operators that act on operands to produce desired results. Verilog HDL provides about 30 operator types. Table 4-10 lists some of these operators, their symbols, and the operation that they perform. (A complete list of operators can be found in Table 8-1, Section 8-2.) It is necessary to distinguish between arithmetic and logic operations, so different symbols are used for each. The plus symbol $(+)$ is used for arithmetic addition and logic AND uses the symbol &. There are special symbols for OR, NOT, and XOR. The equality symbol uses two equal signs (without spaces between them) to distinguish it from the equal sign used with the assign statement. The concatenation operator provides a mechanism for appending multiple operands. For example, two operands with two bits each can be concatenated to form an operand with four bits. The conditional operator is explained later in conjunction with HDL Example 4-6.

Table 4-10
Verilog HDL Operators

Symbol	Operation
$+$	binary addition
$-$	binary subtraction
&	bit-wise AND
$\vert$	bit-wise OR
$\wedge$	bit-wise XOR
$\sim$	bit-wise NOT
$==$	equality
$>$	greater than
$<$	less than
{ }	concatenation
? :	conditional

HDL Example 4-3

```
//Dataflow description of a 2-to-4-line decoder
//See Fig. 4-19
module decoder_df (A,B,E,D);
    input A,B,E;
    output [0:3] D;
    assign D[0] = ~(~A & ~B & ~E),
           D[1] = ~(~A &  B & ~E),
           D[2] = ~( A & ~B & ~E),
           D[3] = ~( A &  B & ~E);
endmodule
```

Dataflow modeling uses continuous assignments and the keyword **assign.** A continuous assignment is a statement that assigns a value to a net. The data type *net* is used in Verilog HDL to represent a physical connection between circuit elements. A net defines a gate output declared by an **output** or **wire** statement. The value assigned to the net is specified by an expression that uses operands and operators. As an example, assuming that the variables were declared, a 2-to-1- line multiplexer with data inputs A and B, select input S, and output Y is described with the continuous assignment

$$\textbf{assign } Y = (A \ \& \ S) \ | \ (B \ \& \ {\sim}S);$$

It starts with the keyword assign followed by the target output Y and an equal sign. Following the equal sign is a Boolean expression. In hardware terms, this would be equivalent to connecting the output of the OR ($|$) gate to wire Y.

The next two examples show the dataflow models of the two previous gate-level examples. The dataflow description of a 2-to-4-line decoder is shown in HDL Example 4-3. The circuit is defined with four continuous assignment statements using Boolean expressions, one for each output. The dataflow description of the 4-bit adder is shown in HDL Example 4-4. The addition logic is described by a single statement using the operators of addition and concatenation. The plus symbol ($+$) specifies the binary addition of the four bits of A with the four bits of B and the one bit of Cin. The target output is the concatenation of

HDL Example 4-4

```
//Dataflow description of 4-bit adder
module binary_adder (A,B,Cin,SUM,Cout);
    input [3:0] A,B;
    input Cin;
    output [3:0] SUM;
    output Cout;
    assign {Cout,SUM} = A + B + Cin;
endmodule
```

HDL Example 4-5

```
//Dataflow description of a 4-bit comparator.
module magcomp (A,B,ALSB,AGTB,AEQB);
    input [3:0] A,B;
    output ALTB,AGTB,AEQB;
    assign ALTB=(A < B),
           AGTB = (A > B),
           AEQB = (A == B);
endmodule
```

the output carry *Cout* and the four bits of *SUM*. Concatenation of operands is expressed within braces and a comma separating the operands. Thus, {Cout, SUM} represents the five-bit result of the addition operation.

Dataflow modeling provides the means of describing combinational circuits by their function rather than by their gate structure. To show how dataflow descriptions facilitate digital design, consider the 4-bit magnitude comparator described in HDL Example 4-5. The module specifies two 4-bit inputs *A* and *B* and three outputs. One output (ALTB) is logic 1 if *A* is less than *B*, a second output (AGTB) is logic 1 if *A* is greater than *B*, and a third output (AEQB) if *A* is equal to *B*. (Note that equality is symbolized with two equal signs.) A Verilog HDL synthesis compiler can accept as input this module description and provide an output netlist of a circuit equivalent to Fig. 4-17.

The next example uses the conditional operator (? :). This operator takes three operands:

condition ? true-expression : false-expression ;

The condition is evaluated. If the result is logic 1, the true expression is evaluated. If the result is logic 0, the false expression is evaluated. This is equivalent to an if-else condition. HDL Example 4-6 shows the description of a 2-to-1-line multiplexer using the conditional operator. The continuous assignment

assign OUT = select ? A : B ;

specifies the condition that OUT = *A* if select = 1, else OUT = *B* if select = 0.

HDL Example 4-6

```
//Dataflow description of 2-to-1-line multiplexer
module mux2x1_df (A,B,select,OUT);
    input A,B,select;
    output OUT;
    assign OUT = select ? A : B;
endmodule
```

HDL Example 4-7

```
//Behavioral description of 2-to-1-line multiplexer
module mux2x1_bh(A,B,select,OUT);
    input A,B,select;
    output OUT;
    reg OUT;
    always @ (select or A or B)
          if (select == 1) OUT = A;
          else OUT = B;
endmodule
```

Behavioral Modeling

Behavioral modeling represents digital circuits at a functional and algorithmic level. It is used mostly to describe sequential circuits, but can be used also to describe combinational circuits. Here we present two simple combinational circuit examples to introduce the subject. Behavioral modeling is presented in more detail in Section 5-5 after the study of sequential circuits.

Behavioral descriptions use the keyword **always** followed by a list of procedural assignment statements. The target output of procedural assignment statements must be of the **reg** data type. Contrary to the **wire** data type, where the target output of an assignment may be continuously updated, a **reg** data type retains its value until a new value is assigned.

HDL Example 4-7 shows the behavioral description of a 2-to-1-line multiplexer (compare it with HDL Example 4-6). Since variable OUT is a target output, it must be declared as **reg** data (in addition to the **output** declaration). The procedural assignment statements inside the always block are executed every time there is a change in any of the variables listed after the @ symbol. (Note that there is no (;) at the end of the always statement.) In this case, they are the input variables *A*, *B*, and *select*. Note that the keyword **or** is used between variables instead of the logical OR operator "|". The conditional statement **if-else** provides a decision based upon the value of the *select* input. The **if** statement can be written without the equality symbol:

$$\textbf{if } (select) \text{ OUT = A ;}$$

The statement implies that *select* is checked for logic 1.

HDL Example 4-8 describes the function of a 4-to-1-line multiplexer. The *select* input is defined as a 2-bit vector and output *y* is declared as **reg** data. The **always** statement has a sequential block enclosed between the keywords **case** and **endcase**. The block is executed whenever any of the inputs listed after the @ symbol changes in value. The **case** statement is a multiway conditional branch condition. The case expression (select) is evaluated and compared with the values in the list of statements that follow. The first value that matches the true condition is executed. Since *select* is a 2-bit number, it can be equal to 00, 01, 10, or 11. Binary numbers are specified with the letter **b** preceded by a prime. The size of the number is written first and then its value. Thus, 2'b01 specifies a two-digit binary number whose value is 01. Numbers can be specified also in decimal, octal, or hexadecimal with the letters **'d, 'o,** and **'h,** respectively. If the base of the number is not specified, it defaults to decimal. If the size of the number is not specified, the system assumes that the size of the number is 32 bits.

HDL Example 4-8

```
//Behavioral description of 4-to-1- line multiplexer
//Describes the function table of  Fig. 4-25(b).
module mux4x1_bh (i0,i1,i2,i3,select,y);
    input i0,i1,i2,i3;
    input [1:0] select;
    output y;
    reg y;
    always @ (i0 or i1 or i2 or i3 or select)
              case (select)
                  2'b00: y = i0;
                  2'b01: y = i1;
                  2'b10: y = i2;
                  2'b11: y = i3;
              endcase
endmodule
```

We have shown here simple examples of behavioral descriptions of combinational circuits. Behavioral modeling and procedural assignment statements require knowledge of sequential circuits and are covered in more detail in Section 5-5.

Writing A Simple Test Bench

A test bench is an HDL program used for applying stimulus to an HDL design in order to test it and observe its response during simulation. Test benches can be quite complex and lengthy and may take longer to develop than the design that is tested. However, the ones considered here are relatively simple, since all we want to test is combinational circuits. The examples are presented to demonstrate typical descriptions of HDL stimulus modules.

In addition to the **always** statement, test benches use the **initial** statement to provide stimulus to the circuit under test. The **always** statement executes repeatedly in a loop. The **initial** statement executes only once starting from simulation time=0 and may continue with any operations that are delayed by a given number of time units as specified by the symbol #. For example, consider the initial block

```
initial
    begin
            A = 0; B= 0;
        #10 A = 1;
        #20 A = 0; B=1;
    end
```

The block is enclosed between the keywords **begin** and **end**. At time $= 0$, A and B are set to 0. 10 time units later, A is changed to 1. 20 time units later (at t $= 30$) A is changed to 0 and B to 1. Inputs to a 3-bit truth table can be generated with the initial block:

```
initial
    begin
            D = 3'b000;
            repeat (7)
        #10  D = D + 3'b001;
    end
```

The 3-bit vector D is initialized to 000 at time $= 0$. The keyword **repeat** specifies a looping statement: one is added to D seven times, once every 10 time units. The result is a sequence of binary numbers from 000 to 111.

A stimulus module is an HDL program that has the following form:

module testname.

Declare local **reg** and **wire** identifiers.

Instantiate the design module under test.

Generate stimulus using **initial** and **always** statements.

Display the output response.

endmodule

A test module typically has no inputs or outputs. The signals that are applied as inputs to the design module for simulation are declared in the stimulus module as local **reg** data type. The outputs of the design module that are displayed for testing are declared in the stimulus module as local **wire** data type. The module under test is then instantiated using the local identifiers. Figure 4-33 clarifies this relationship. The stimulus module generates inputs for the design module by declaring identifiers TA and TB as **reg** type, and checks the output of the design unit with the **wire** identifier TC. The local identifiers are then used to instantiate the design module under test.

The response to the stimulus generated by the **initial** and **always** blocks will appear at the output of the simulator as timing diagrams. It is also possible to display numerical outputs

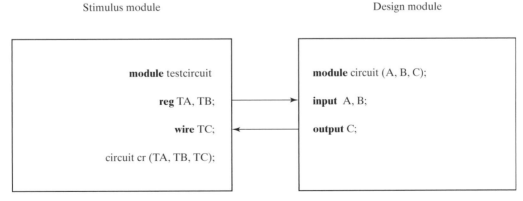

FIGURE 4-33
Stimulus and Design Modules Interaction

using Verilog *system tasks*. These are built in system functions that are recognized by key-words that begin with the symbol $. Some of the system tasks useful for display are

> **$display**—display one-time value of variables or strings with end-of-line return,
>
> **$write**—same as **$display** but without going to next line,
>
> **$monitor**—displays variables whenever a value changes during simulation run,
>
> **$time**—displays simulation time,
>
> **$finish**—terminates the simulation.

The syntax for **$display, $write, and $monitor** is of the form

Task-name (format specification, argument list);

The format specification includes the radix of the numbers that are displayed using the symbol (%) and may have a string enclosed in quotes ("). The base may be binary, decimal, hexa-decimal, or octal, identified with the symbols %b, %d, %h, and %o, respectively. For example, the statement

`$display (%d %b %b, C,A,B);`

specifies the display of *C* in decimal, and of *A* and *B* in binary. Note that there are no commas in the format specification, that the format specification and argument list are separated by a comma, and that the argument list has commas between the variables. An example that speci-fies a string enclosed in quotes may look like the statement

$display ("time = %0d A = %b B = %b", **$time**,A,B);

and will produce the display

`time = 3   A = 10   B = 1`

where $(time =)$, $(A =)$, and $(B =)$ are part of the string to be displayed. The format %0d, %b, and %b specify the base for **$time**, *A*, and *B*, respectively. When displaying time val-ues, it is better to use the format %0d instead of %d. This provides a display of the significant dig-its without the leading spaces that %d will include. (%d will display about 10 leading spaces because time is calculated as a 32-bit number.)

An example of a stimulus module is shown in HDL Example 4-9. The circuit to be tested is the 2 × 1 multiplexer described in Example 4-6. The `testmux` module has no ports. The inputs for the mux are declared with a **reg** keyword and the outputs with a **wire** keyword. The mux is instantiated with the local variables. The **initial** block specifies a sequence of binary values to be applied during the simulation. The output response is checked with the **$monitor** system task. Every time a variable changes value, the simulator displays the inputs, output, and time. The re-sult of the simulation is listed under the simulation log in the example. It shows that *OUT = A* when *S = 1* and *OUT = B* when *S = 0*, verifying the operation of the multiplexer.

Logic simulation is a fast, accurate method of analyzing combinational circuits to verify that they operate properly. There are two types of verification: functional and timing. In *func-tional* verification, we study the circuit logical operation independent of timing considerations. This can be done by deriving the truth table of the combinational circuit. In *timing* verification, we study the circuit operation by including the effect of delays through the gates. This can be done by observing the waveforms at the outputs of the gates when they respond to a given input.

HDL Example 4-9

```
//Stimulus for mux2x1_df.
module testmux;
  reg TA,TB,TS;   //inputs for mux
  wire Y;         //output from mux
  mux2x1_df mx (TA,TB,TS,Y);  // instantiate mux
    initial
      begin
              TS = 1; TA = 0; TB = 1;
          #10 TA = 1; TB = 0;
          #10 TS = 0;
          #10 TA = 0; TB = 1;
        end
    initial
      $monitor("select = %b A = %b B = %b OUT = %b time = %0d",
               TS, TA, TB, Y, $time);
endmodule

//Dataflow description of 2-to-1-line multiplexer
//from Example 4-6
module mux2x1_df (A,B,select,OUT);
    input A,B,select;
    output OUT;
    assign OUT = select ? A : B;
endmodule

Simulation log:

select = 1 A = 0 B = 1 OUT = 0 time = 0
select = 1 A = 1 B = 0 OUT = 1 time = 10
select = 0 A = 1 B = 0 OUT = 0 time = 20
select = 0 A = 0 B = 1 OUT = 1 time = 30
```

An example of a circuit with gate delays was presented in Section 3-9 with HDL Example 3-3. We now show an HDL example that produces the truth table of a combinational circuit.

The analysis of combinational circuits was covered in Section 4-2. A multilevel circuit of a full adder was analyzed and its truth table was derived by inspection. The gate-level description of this circuit is shown in HDL Example 4-10. The circuit has three inputs, two outputs and nine gates. The description of the circuit follows the interconnections between the gates according to the schematic diagram of Fig. 4-2. The stimulus for the circuit is listed in the second module. The inputs for simulating the circuit are specified with a 3-bit **reg** vector D. $D[2]$ is equivalent to input A, $D[1]$ to input B, and $D[0]$ to input C. The outputs of the circuit F_1 and F_2 are declared as **wire.** This procedure follows the steps outlined in Fig. 4-33. The **repeat** loop provides the seven binary numbers after 000 for the truth table. The result of the simulation generates the output truth table displayed with the example. The listed truth table shows that the circuit is a full adder.

HDL Example 4-10

```
//Gate-level description of circuit of Fig. 4-2
module analysis (A,B,C,F1,F2);
    input    A,B,C;
    output   F1,F2;
    wire     T1,T2,T3,F2not,E1,E2,E3;
    or  g1 (T1,A,B,C);
    and g2 (T2,A,B,C);
    and g3 (E1,A,B);
    and g4 (E2,A,C);
    and g5 (E3,B,C);
    or  g6 (F2,E1,E2,E3);
    not g7 (F2not,F2);
    and g8 (T3,T1,F2not);
    or  g9 (F1,T2,T3);
endmodule

//Stimulus to analyze the circuit
module test_circuit;
    reg [2:0]D;
    wire F1,F2;
    analysis fig42(D[2],D[1],D[0],F1,F2);
    initial
      begin
        D = 3'b000;
        repeat(7)
          #10 D = D + 1'b1;
      end
    initial
        $monitor ("ABC = %b F1 = %b F2 =%b ",D, F1, F2);
endmodule


Simulation log:

ABC = 000 F1 = 0 F2 =0
ABC = 001 F1 = 1 F2 =0
ABC = 010 F1 = 1 F2 =0
ABC = 011 F1 = 0 F2 =1
ABC = 100 F1 = 1 F2 =0
ABC = 101 F1 = 0 F2 =1
ABC = 110 F1 = 0 F2 =1
ABC = 111 F1 = 1 F2 =1
```

PROBLEMS

4-1 Consider the combinational circuit shown in Fig. P4-1.
  (a) Derive the Boolean expressions for T_1 through T_4. Evaluate the outputs F_1 and F_2 as a function of the four inputs.
  (b) List the truth table with 16 binary combinations of the four input variables. Then list the binary values for T_1 through T_4 and outputs F_1 and F_2 in the table.
  (c) Plot the output Boolean functions obtained in part (b) on maps and show that the simplified Boolean expressions are equivalent to the ones obtained in part (a).

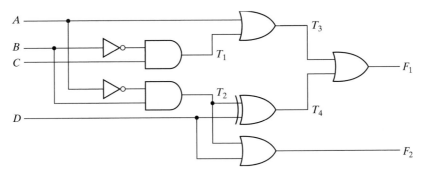

FIGURE P4-1

4-2 Obtain the simplified Boolean expressions for output F and G in terms of the input variables in the circuit of Fig. P4-2.

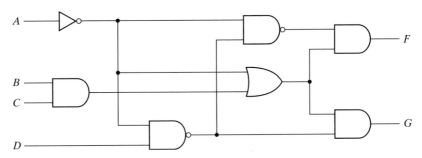

FIGURE P4-2

4-3 For the circuit shown in Fig. 4-26 (Section 4-10),
  (a) Write the Boolean functions for the four outputs in terms of the input variables.
  (b) If the circuit is listed in a truth table, how many rows and columns would there be in the table?

4-4 Design a combinational circuit with three inputs and one output. The output is 1 when the binary value of the inputs is less than 3. The output is 0 otherwise.

4-5 Design a combinational circuit with three inputs, x, y, and z, and three outputs, A, B, and C. When the binary input is 0, 1, 2, or 3, the binary output is one greater than the input. When the binary input is 4, 5, 6, or 7, the binary output is one less than the input.

4-6 A majority circuit is a combinational circuit whose output is equal to 1 if the input variables have more 1's than 0's. The output is 0 otherwise. Design a 3-input majority circuit.

4-7 Design a combinational circuit that converts a 4-bit Gray code (Table 1-6) to a 4-bit binary number. Implement the circuit with exclusive-OR gates.

4-8 Design a code converter that converts a decimal digit from the $8, 4, -2, -1$ code to BCD (see Table 1-5).

4-9 ABCD-to-seven-segment decoder is a combinational circuit that converts a decimal digit in BCD to an appropriate code for the selection of segments in a display indicator used for displaying the decimal digit in a familiar form. The seven outputs of the decoder (a, b, c, d, e, f, g) select the corresponding segments in the display, as shown in Fig. P4-9(a). The numeric display chosen to represent the decimal digit is shown in Fig. P4-9(b). Design the BCD-to-seven-segment decoder using a minimum number of gates. The six invalid combinations should result in a blank display.

(a) Segment designation   (b) Numerical designation for display

FIGURE P4-9

4-10 Design a 4-bit combinational circuit 2's complementer. (The output generates the 2's complement of the input binary number.) Show that the circuit can be constructed using exclusive-OR gates. Can you predict what the output functions are for a 5-bit 2's complementer?

4-11 Design a 4-bit combinational circuit incrementer. (A circuit that adds one to a 4-bit binary number.) The circuit can be designed using four half-adders.

4-12 (a) Design a half-subtractor circuit with inputs x and y and outputs D and B. The circuit subtracts the bits $x - y$ and places the difference in D and the borrow in B.
   (b) Design a full-subtractor circuit with three inputs x, y, z and two outputs D and B. The circuit subtracts $x - y - z$, where z is the input borrow, B is the output borrow, and D is the difference.

4-13 The adder-subtractor circuit of Fig. 4-13 has the following values for mode input M and data inputs A and B. In each case, determine the values of the four SUM outputs, the carry C, and overflow V.

	M	A	B
(a)	0	0111	0110
(b)	0	1000	1001
(c)	1	1100	1000
(d)	1	0101	1010
(e)	1	0000	0001

4-14 Assume that the exclusive-OR gate has a propagation delay of 20 ns and that the AND or OR gates have a propagation delay of 10 ns. What is the total propagation delay time in the 4-bit adder of Fig. 4-12?

4-15 Derive the two-level Boolean expression for the output carry C_4 shown in the look-ahead carry generator of Fig. 4-12.

4-16 Show that the output carry in a full adder circuit can be expressed in the AND-OR-INVERT form

$$C_{i+1} = G_i + P_iC_i = (G_i'P_i' + G_i'C_i')'$$

IC type 74182 is a look-ahead carry generator circuit that generates the carries with AND-OR-INVERT gates (see Section 3-7). The circuit assumes that the input terminals have the complements of the G's, the P's, and of C_1. Derive the Boolean functions for the look-ahead carries C_2, C_3, and C_4 in this IC. (*Hint:* Use the equation-substitution method to derive the carries in terms of C_1'.)

4-17 Define the carry propagate and carry generate as

$$P_i = A_i + B_i$$
$$G_i = A_iB_i$$

respectively. Show that the output carry and output sum of a full adder becomes

$$C_{i+1} = (C_i'G_i' + P_i')'$$
$$S_i = (P_iG_i') \oplus C_i$$

The logic diagram of the first stage of a 4-bit parallel adder as implemented in IC type 74283 is shown in Fig. P4-17. Identify the P_i' and G_i' terminals and show that the circuit implements a

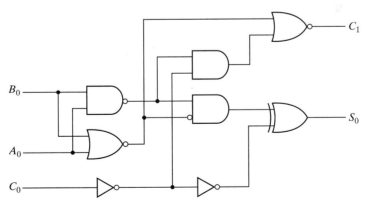

FIGURE P4-17
First Stage of a Parallel Adder

4-18 Design a combinational circuit that generates the 9's complement of a BCD digit.

4-19 Construct a BCD adder-subtractor circuit. Use the BCD adder of Fig. 4-14 and the 9's complementer of problem 4-18. Use block diagrams for the components.

4-20 Design a binary multiplier that multiplies two 4-bit numbers. Use AND gates and binary adders.

4-21 Design a combinational circuit that compares two 4-bit numbers to check if they are equal. The circuit output is equal to 1 if the two numbers are equal and 0 otherwise.

4-22 Design an excess-3-to-binary decoder using the unused combinations of the code as don't-care conditions.

4-23 Draw the logic diagram of a 2-to-4-line decoder using NOR gates only. Include an enable input.

4-24 Design a BCD-to-decimal decoder using the unused combinations of the BCD code as don't-care conditions.

4-25 Construct a 5-to-32-line decoder with four 3-to-8-line decoders with enable and a 2-to-4-line decoder. Use block diagrams for the components.

4-26 Construct a 4-to-16-line decoder with five 2-to-4-line decoders with enable.

4-27 A combinational circuit is specified by the following three Boolean functions:

$$F_1(A, B, C) = \Sigma(2, 4, 7)$$
$$F_2(A, B, C) = \Sigma(0, 3)$$
$$F_3(A, B, C) = \Sigma(0, 2, 3, 4, 7)$$

Implement the circuit with a decoder constructed with NAND gates (similar to Fig. 4-19) and NAND or AND gates connected to the decoder outputs. Use a block diagram for the decoder. Minimize the number of inputs in the external gates.

4-28 A combinational circuit is defined by the following three Boolean functions:

$$F_1 = x'y'z' + xz$$
$$F_2 = xy'z' + x'y$$
$$F_3 = x'y'z + xy$$

Design the circuit with a decoder and external gates.

4-29 Design a 4-input priority encoder with inputs as in Table 4-8, but with input D_0 having the highest priority and input D_3 the lowest priority.

4-30 Specify the truth table of an octal-to-binary priority encoder. Provide an output V to indicate that at least one of the inputs is present. The input with the highest subscript number has the highest priority. What will be the value of the four outputs if inputs D_5 and D_3 are 1 at the same time?

4-31 Construct a 16×1 multiplexer with two 8×1 and one 2×1 multiplexers. Use block diagrams.

4-32 Implement the following Boolean function with a multiplexer:

$$F(A, B, C, D) = \Sigma(0, 1, 3, 4, 8, 9, 15)$$

4-33 Implement a full adder with two 4×1 multiplexers.

4-34 An 8 × 1 multiplexer has inputs A, B, and C connected to the selection inputs S_2, S_1, and S_0, respectively. The data inputs I_0 through I_7, are as follows: $I_1 = I_2 = I_7 = 0$; $I_3 = I_5 = 1$; $I_0 = I_4 = D$; and $I_6 = D'$. Determine the Boolean function that the multiplexer implements.

4-35 Implement the following Boolean function with a 4 × 1 multiplexer and external gates. Connect inputs A and B to the selection lines. The input requirements for the four data lines will be a function of variables C and D. These values are obtained by expressing F as a function of C and D for each of the four cases when $AB = 00, 01, 10,$ and 11. These functions may have to be implemented with external gates.

$$F(A, B, C, D) = \Sigma(1, 3, 4, 11, 12, 13, 14, 15)$$

4-36 Write the HDL gate-level description of the priority encoder circuit shown in Fig. 4-23.

4-37 Write the HDL gate-level hierarchical description of a 4-bit adder-subtractor for unsigned binary numbers. The circuit is similar to Fig. 4-13 but without output V. You can instantiate the 4-bit full adder described in HDL Example 4-2.

4-38 Write the HDL dataflow description of a quadruple 2-to-1-line multiplexers with enable (see Fig. 4-26).

4-39 Write an HDL behavioral description of a 4-bit comparator with a 6-bit output $Y[5:0]$. Bit 5 of Y is for equal, bit 4 for unequal, bit 3 for greater than, bit 2 for less than, bit 1 for greater than or equal, and bit 0 for less than or equal to.

4-40 Write an HDL dataflow description of a 4-bit adder subtractor of unsigned numbers. Use the conditional operator (? :).

4-41 Repeat problem 4-40 using behavioral modeling.

4-42 (a) Write an HDL gate-level description of the BCD-to-excess-3 converter circuit shown in Fig. 4-4.
(b) Write a dataflow description of the BCD-to-excess-3 converter using the Boolean expressions listed in Fig. 4-3.
(c) Write an HDL behavioral description of a BCD-to-excess-3 converter.
(d) Write a test bench to simulate and test the BCD-to-excess-3 converter circuit in order to verify the truth table. Check all three circuits.

4-43 Explain the function of the circuit specified by the following HDL description:

```
module Prob438 (A,B,S,E,Q);
    input  [1:0] A, B;
    input  S, E;
    output [1:0] Q;
    assign Q = E ? (S ? A : B) : 'bz;
endmodule
```

4-44 Write an HDL behavioral description of a 4-bit arithmetic-logic unit (ALU). The circuit performs two arithmetic and two logic operations that are selected by a 2-bit input. The four operations are add, subtract, AND, and OR.

4-45 Write an HDL behavioral description of a 4-input priority encoder. Use a 4-bit vector for the D inputs and an always block with if-else statements. Assume that input $D[3]$ has the highest priority.

REFERENCES

1. Dietmeyer, D. L. 1988. *Logic Design of Digital Systems,* 3rd ed. Boston: Allyn Bacon.

2. Gajski, D. D. 1997. *Principles of Digital Design.* Upper Saddle River, NJ: Prentice Hall.

3. Hayes, J. P. 1993. *Introduction to Digital Logic Design.* Reading, MA: Addison-Wesley.

4. Katz, R. H. 1994. *Conteporary Logic Design.* Upper Saddle River, NJ: Prentice Hall.

5. Mano, M. M. and C. R. Kime. 2000. *Logic and Computer Design Fundamentals,* 2nd ed. Upper Saddle River, NJ: Prentice Hall.

6. Nelson V. P., H. T. Nagle, J. D. Irwin, and B. D. Carroll. 1995. *Digital Logic Circuit Analysis and Design.* Upper Saddle River, NJ: Prentice Hall.

7. Roth, C. H. 1992. *Fundamentals of Logic Design,* 4th ed. St. Paul: West.

8. Wakerly, J. F. 2000. *Digital Design: Principles and Practices,* 3rd ed. Upper Saddle River, NJ: Prentice Hall.

9. Bhasker, J. 1997. *A Verilog HDL Primer.* Allentown, PA: Star Galaxy Press.

10. Bhasker, J. 1998. *Verilog HDL Synthesis.* Allentown, PA: Star Galaxy Press.

11. Ciletti, M. D. 1999. *Modeling, Synthesis, and Rapid Prototyping with Verilog HDL.* Upper Saddle River, NJ: Prentice Hall.

12. Palnitkar, S. 1996. *Verilog HDL: A Guide to Digital Design and Synthesis.* SunSoft Press (A Prentice Hall Title).

13. Thomas, D. E., and P. R. Moorby. 1998. *The Verilog Hardware Description Language* 4th ed. Boston: Kluwer Academic Publishers.

5 Synchronous Sequential Logic

5-1 SEQUENTIAL CIRCUITS

The digital circuits considered thus far have been combinational, where the outputs are entirely dependent on the current inputs. Although every digital system is likely to have combinational circuits, most systems encountered in practice also include storage elements, which require that the system be described in terms of *sequential logic*.

A block diagram of a sequential circuit is shown in Fig. 5-1. It consists of a combinational circuit to which storage elements are connected to form a feedback path. The storage elements are devices capable of storing binary information. The binary information stored in these elements at any given time defines the *state* of the sequential circuit at that time. The sequential circuit receives binary information from external inputs. These inputs, together with the present state of the storage elements, determine the binary value of the outputs. They also determine the condition for changing the state in the storage elements. The block diagram demonstrates that the outputs in a sequential circuit are a function not only of the inputs, but also of the present state of the storage elements. The next state of the storage elements is also

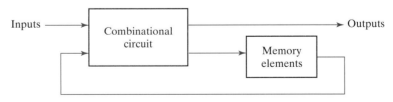

FIGURE 5-1
Block Diagram of Sequential Circuit

167

a function of external inputs and the present state. Thus, a sequential circuit is specified by a time sequence of inputs, outputs, and internal states.

There are two main types of sequential circuits and their classification depends on the timing of their signals. A *synchronous* sequential circuit is a system whose behavior can be defined from the knowledge of its signals at discrete instants of time. The behavior of an *asynchronous* sequential circuit depends upon the input signals at any instant of time and the order in which the inputs change. The storage elements commonly used in asynchronous sequential circuits are time-delay devices. The storage capability of a time-delay device is due to the time it takes for the signal to propagate through the device. In practice, the internal propagation delay of logic gates is of sufficient duration to produce the needed delay so that actual delay units may not be necessary. In gate-type asynchronous systems, the storage elements consist of logic gates whose propagation delay provides the required storage. Thus, an asynchronous sequential circuit may be regarded as a combinational circuit with feedback. Because of the feedback among logic gates, an asynchronous sequential circuit may become unstable at times. The instability problem imposes many difficulties on the designer. Asynchronous sequential circuits are presented in Chapter 9.

A synchronous sequential circuit employs signals that affect the storage elements only at discrete instants of time. Synchronization is achieved by a timing device called a *clock generator* that provides a periodic train of *clock pulses*. The clock pulses are distributed throughout the system in such a way that storage elements are affected only with the arrival of each pulse. In practice, the clock pulses are applied with other signals that specify the required change in the storage elements. Synchronous sequential circuits that use clock pulses in the inputs of storage elements are called *clocked sequential circuits*. Clocked sequential circuits are the type most frequently encountered in practice. They seldom manifest instability problems and their timing is easily broken down into independent discrete steps, each of which can be considered separately.

The storage elements used in clocked sequential circuits are called *flip-flops*. A flip-flop is a binary storage device capable of storing one bit of information. A sequential circuit may use many flip-flops to store as many bits as necessary. The block diagram of a synchronous clocked sequential circuit is shown in Fig. 5-2. The outputs can come either from the combinational cir-

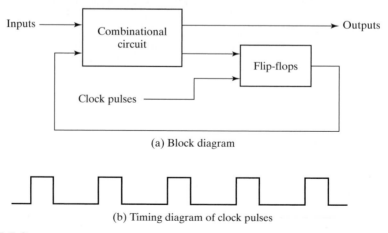

(a) Block diagram

(b) Timing diagram of clock pulses

FIGURE 5-2
Synchronous Clocked Sequential Circuit

cuit or from the flip-flops or both. The flip-flops receive their inputs from the combinational circuit and also from a clock signal with pulses that occur at fixed intervals of time as shown in the timing diagram. The state of the flip-flops can change only during a clock pulse transition. When a clock pulse is not active, the feedback loop is broken because the flip-flop outputs cannot change even if the outputs of the combinational circuit driving their inputs change in value. Thus, the transition from one state to the next occurs only at predetermined time intervals dictated by the clock pulses.

5-2   LATCHES

A flip-flop circuit can maintain a binary state indefinitely (as long as power is delivered to the circuit) until directed by an input signal to switch states. The major differences among various types of flip-flops are in the number of inputs they possess and in the manner in which the inputs affect the binary state. The most basic types of flip-flops operate with signal levels and are referred to as latches. The latches introduced here are the basic circuits from which all flip-flops are constructed. Although latches are useful for storing binary information and for the design of asynchronous sequential circuits (see Sec. 9-3), they are not practical for use in synchronous sequential circuits. The types of flip-flops employed in sequential circuits are presented in the next section.

SR Latch

The SR latch is a circuit with two cross-coupled NOR gates or two cross-coupled NAND gates. It has two inputs labeled S for set and R for reset. The SR latch constructed with two cross-coupled NOR gates is shown in Fig. 5-3. The latch has two useful states. When output $Q = 1$ and $Q' = 0$, it is said to be in the *set state*. When $Q = 0$ and $Q' = 1$, it is in the *reset state*. Output Q and Q' are normally the complement of each other. However, when both inputs are equal to 1 at the same time, an undefined state with both outputs equal to 0 occurs.

Under normal conditions, both inputs of the latch remain at 0 unless the state has to be changed. The application of a momentary 1 to the S input causes the latch to go to the set state. The S input must go back to 0 before any other changes to avoid the occurrence of the undefined state. As shown in the function table of Fig. 5-3(b), two input conditions cause the circuit to

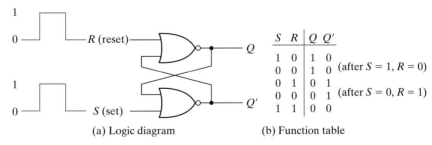

S	R	Q	Q'	
1	0	1	0	
0	0	1	0	(after $S = 1, R = 0$)
0	1	0	1	
0	0	0	1	(after $S = 0, R = 1$)
1	1	0	0	

(a) Logic diagram   (b) Function table

FIGURE 5-3
SR Latch with NOR Gates

be in the set state. The first condition $(S = 1, R = 0)$ is the action that must be taken by input S to bring the circuit to the set state. Removing the active input from S leaves the circuit in the same state. After both inputs return to 0, it is then possible to shift to the reset state by momentary applying a 1 to the R input. The 1 can then be removed from R and the circuit remains in the reset state. Thus, when both inputs S and R are equal to 0, the latch can be in either the set or the reset state, depending on which input was most recently a 1.

If a 1 is applied to both the S and R inputs of the latch, both outputs go to 0. This produces an undefined state because it results in an unpredictable next state when both inputs return to 0. It also violates the requirement that outputs be the complement of each other. In normal operation this condition is avoided by making sure that 1's are not applied to both inputs simultaneously.

The SR latch with two cross-coupled NAND gates is shown in Fig. 5-4. It operates with both inputs normally at 1 unless the state of the latch has to be changed. The application of 0 to the S input causes output Q to go to 1, putting the latch in the set state. When the S input goes back to 1, the circuit remains in the set state. After both inputs go back to 1, we are allowed to change the state of the latch by placing a 0 in the R input. This causes the circuit to go to the reset state and stay there even after both inputs return to 1. The condition that is undefined for the NAND latch is when both inputs are equal to 0 at the same time, an input combination that should be avoided.

Comparing the NAND with the NOR latch note that the input signals for the NAND require the complement of those values used for the NOR latch. Because the NAND latch requires a 0 signal to change its state, it is sometimes referred to as an S'-R' latch. The primes (or bars over the letters) designate the fact that the inputs must be in their complement form to activate the circuit.

The operation of the basic SR latch can be modified by providing an additional control input that determines when the state of the latch can be changed. An SR latch with a control input is shown in Fig. 5-5. It consists of the basic SR latch and two additional NAND gates. The control input C acts as an enable signal for the other two inputs. The output of the NAND gates stay at the logic 1 level as long as the control input remains at 0. This is the quiescent condition for the SR latch. When the control input goes to 1, information from the S or R input is allowed to affect the SR latch. The set state is reached with $S = 1, R = 0$, and $C = 1$. To change to the reset state, the inputs must be $S = 0, R = 1$, and $C = 1$. In either case, when C returns to 0, the circuit remains in its current state. Control input disables the circuit by applying 0 to C, so that the state of the output does not change regardless of the values of S and R. Moreover,

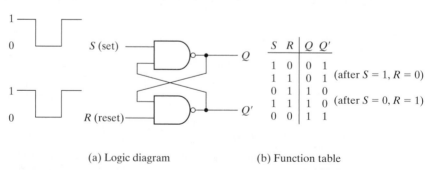

(a) Logic diagram   (b) Function table

FIGURE 5-4
SR Latch with NAND Gates

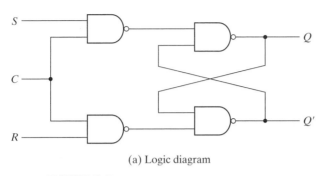

C	S	R	Next state of Q
0	X	X	No change
1	0	0	No change
1	0	1	$Q = 0$; Reset state
1	1	0	$Q = 1$; set state
1	1	1	Indeterminate

(a) Logic diagram

(b) Function table

FIGURE 5-5
SR Latch with Control Input

when $C = 1$ and both the S and R inputs are equal to 0, the state of the circuit does not change. These conditions are listed in the function table accompanying the diagram.

An indeterminate condition occurs when all three inputs are equal to 1. This condition places 0's on both inputs of the basic SR latch, which places it in the undefined state. When the control input goes back to 0, one cannot conclusively determine the next state as it depends on whether the S or R input goes to 0 first. This indeterminate condition makes this circuit difficult to manage and it is seldom used in practice. Nevertheless, it is an important circuit because other latches and flip-flops are constructed from it.

D Latch

One way to eliminate the undesirable condition of the indeterminate state in the SR latch is to ensure that inputs S and R are never equal to 1 at the same time. This is done in the D latch shown in Fig. 5-6. This latch has only two inputs: D (data) and C (control). The D input goes directly to the S input and its complement is applied to the R input. As long as the control input is at 0, the cross-coupled SR latch has both inputs at the 1 level and the circuit cannot change state regardless of the value of D. The D input is sampled when $C = 1$. If $D = 1$, the Q output goes to 1, placing the circuit in the set state. If $D = 0$, output Q goes to 0, placing the circuit in the reset state.

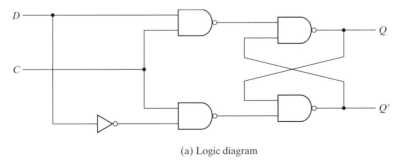

C	D	Next state of Q
0	X	No change
1	0	$Q = 0$; Reset state
1	1	$Q = 1$; Set state

(a) Logic diagram

(b) Function table

FIGURE 5-6
D Latch

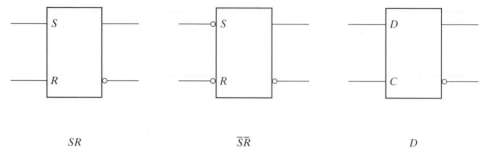

FIGURE 5-7
Graphic Symbols for Latches

The *D* latch receives the designation from its ability to hold data in its internal storage. It is suited for use as a temporary storage for binary information between a unit and its environment. The binary information present at the data input of the *D* latch is transferred to the *Q* output when the control input is enabled. The output follows changes in the data input as long as the control input is enabled. This situation provides a path from input *D* to the output and for this reason, the circuit is often called a *transparent* latch. When the control input is disabled, the binary information that was present at the data input at the time the transition occurred is retained at the *Q* output until the control input is enabled again.

The graphic symbols for the various latches are shown in Fig. 5-7. A latch is designated by a rectangular block with inputs on the left and outputs on the right. One output designates the normal output, and the other (with the bubble designation) designates the complement output. The graphic symbol for the *SR* latch has inputs *S* and *R* indicted inside the block. In the case of a NAND gate latch, bubbles are added to the inputs to indicate that setting and resetting occur with logic 0 signal. The graphic symbol for the *D* latch has inputs *D* and *C* indicated inside the block.

5-3   FLIP-FLOPS

The state of a latch or flip-flop is switched by a change in the control input. This momentary change is called a *trigger* and the transition it causes is said to trigger the flip-flop. The *D* latch with pulses in its control input is essentially a flip-flop that is triggered every time the pulse goes to the logic 1 level. As long as the pulse input remains in this level, any changes in the data input will change the output and the state of the latch.

As seen from the block diagram of Fig. 5-2, a sequential circuit has a feedback path from the outputs of the flip-flops to the input of the combinational circuit. Consequently, the inputs of the flip-flops are derived in part from the outputs of the same and other flip-flops. When latches are used for the storage elements, a serious difficulty arises. The state transitions of the latches start as soon as the clock pulse changes to the logic 1 level. The new state of a latch appears at the output while the pulse is still active. This output is connected to the inputs of the latches through the combinational circuit. If the inputs applied to the latches change while the clock pulse is still in the logic 1 level, the latches will respond to new values and a new output state may occur. The result is an unpredictable situation since the state of latches may keep changing for as long as the clock pulse stays in the active level. Because of this unreliable operation,

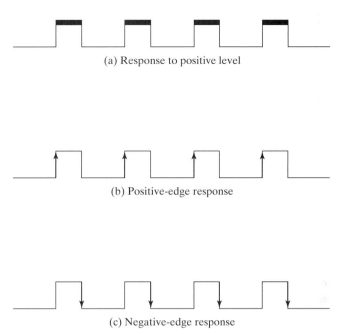

(a) Response to positive level

(b) Positive-edge response

(c) Negative-edge response

FIGURE 5-8
Clock Response in Latch and Flip-Flop

the output of a latch cannot be applied directly or through combinational logic to the input of the same or another latch when all the latches are triggered by a common clock source.

Flip-flop circuits are constructed in such a way as to make them operate properly when they are part of a sequential circuit that employs a common clock. The problem with the latch is that it responds to a change in the *level* of a clock pulse. As shown in Fig. 5-8(a) a positive level response in the control input allows changes, in the output when the D input changes while the clock pulse stays at logic 1. The key to the proper operation of a flip-flop is to trigger it only during a signal *transition*. A clock pulse goes through two transitions from 0 to 1 and the return from 1 to 0. As shown in Fig. 5-8, the positive transition is defined as the positive-edge and the negative transition as the negative-edge. There are two ways that a latch can be modified to form a flip-flop. One way is to employ two latches in a special configuration that isolates the output of the flip-flop from being affected while its input is changing. Another way is to produce a flip-flop that triggers only during a signal transition (from 0 to 1 or from 1 to 0), and is disabled during the rest of the clock pulse duration. We will now proceed to show the implementation of both types of flip-flops.

Edge-Triggered *D* Flip-Flop

The construction of a D flip-flop with two D latches and an inverter is shown in Fig. 5-9. The first latch is called the master and the second the slave. The circuit samples the D input and changes its output Q only at the negative-edge of the controlling clock (designated as CLK). When the clock is 0, the output of the inverter is 1. The slave latch is enabled and its output Q is equal to the master output Y. The master latch is disabled because $CLK = 0$. When the input pulse changes to the logic 1 level, the data from the external D input is transferred to the master. The slave, however,

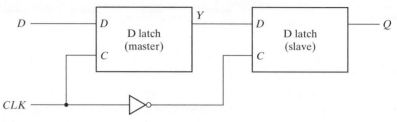

FIGURE 5-9
Master-Slave *D* Flip-Flop

is disabled as long as the clock remains in the 1 level because its *C* input is equal to 0. Any change in the input changes the master output at *Y*, but cannot affect the slave output. When the pulse returns to 0, the master is disabled and is isolated from the *D* input. At the same time, the slave is enabled and the value of *Y* is transferred to the output of the flip flop at *Q*. Thus, the output of the flip-flop can change only during the transition of the clock from 1 to 0.

The behavior of the master-slave flip-flop just described dictates that the output may change only during the negative edge of the clock. It is also possible to design the circuit so that the flip-flop output changes on the positive edge of the clock. This happens in a flip-flop that has an additional inverter between the *CLK* terminal and the junction between the other inverter and input *C* of the master latch. Such flip-flop is triggered with a negative pulse, so that the negative edge of the clock affects the master and the positive edge affects the slave and the output terminal.

Another more efficient construction of an edge-triggered *D* flip-flop uses three *SR* latches as shown in Fig. 5-10. Two latches respond to the external *D* (data) and *CLK* (clock) inputs.

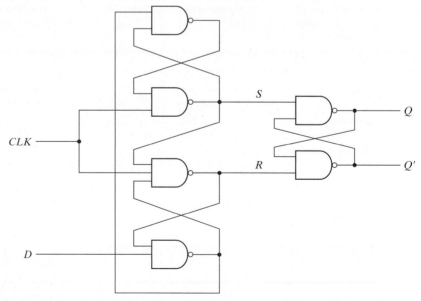

FIGURE 5-10
D-Type Positive-Edge-Triggered Flip-Flop

The third latch provides the outputs for the flip-flop. The S and R inputs of the output latch are maintained at logic 1 level when $CLK = 0$. This causes the output to remain in its present state. Input D may be equal to 0 or 1. If $D = 0$ when CLK becomes 1, R changes to 0. This causes the flip-flop to go to the reset state, making $Q = 0$. If there is a change in the D input while $CLK = 1$, terminal R remains at 0. Thus, the flip-flop is locked out and is unresponsive to further changes in the input. When the clock returns to 0, R goes to 1, placing the output latch in the quiescent condition without changing the output. Similarly, if $D = 1$ when CLK goes from 0 to 1, S changes to 0. This causes the circuit to go to the set state making $Q = 1$. Any change in D while $CLK = 1$ does not affect the output.

In summary, when the input clock in the positive-edge-triggered flip-flop makes a positive transition, the value of D is transferred to Q. A negative transition from 1 to 0 does not affect the output, nor does it when CLK is in the steady logic 1 level or the logic 0 level. Hence, this type of flip-flop responds to the transition from 0 to 1 and nothing else.

The timing of the response of a flip-flop to input data and clock must be taken into consideration when using edge-triggered flip-flops. There is a minimum time, called *setup time,* for which the D input must be maintained at a constant value prior to the occurrence of the clock transition. Similarly, there is a minimum time, called the *hold time*, for which the D input must not change after the application of the positive transition of the clock. The propagation delay time of the flip-flop is defined as the time interval between the trigger edge and the stabilization of the output to a new state. These and other parameters are specified in manufacturer's data books for specific logic families.

The graphic symbol for the edge-triggered D flip-flop is shown in Fig. 5-11. It is similar to the symbol used for the D latch except for the arrowhead-like symbol in front of the letter C designating a *dynamic* input. The *dynamic indicator* denotes the fact that the flip-flop responds to the edge transition of the clock. A bubble outside the block adjacent to the dynamic indicator designates a negative edge for triggering the circuit. The absence of a bubble designates a positive-edge response.

Other Flip-Flops

Very large scale integration circuits contain thousands of gates within one package. Circuits are constructed by interconnecting the various gates to provide a digital system. Each flip-flop is constructed from an interconnection of gates. The most economical and efficient flip-flop constructed in this manner is the edge-triggered D flip-flop because it requires the smallest number

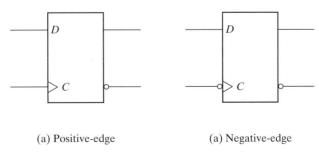

(a) Positive-edge   (a) Negative-edge

FIGURE 5-11
Graphic Symbol for Edge-Triggered *D* Flip-Flop

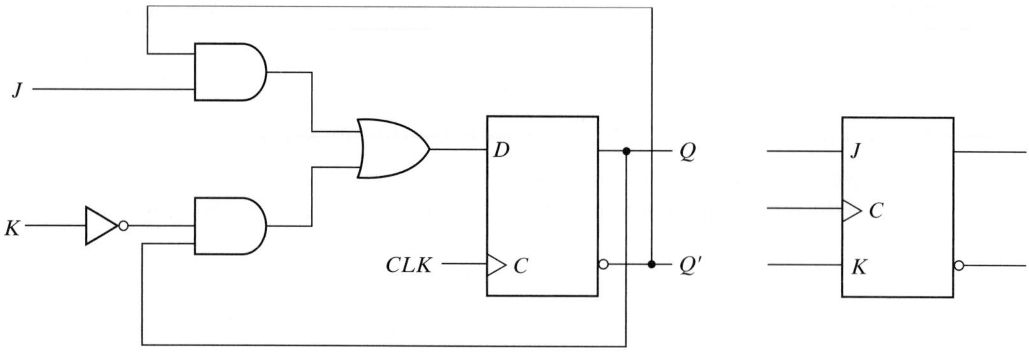

(a) Circuit diagram   (b) Graphic symbol

FIGURE 5-12
JK Flip-Flop

of gates. Other types of flip-flops can be constructed by using the *D* flip-flop and external logic. Two flip-flops widely used in the design of digital systems are the *JK* and *T* flip-flops.

There are three operations that can be performed with a flip-flop: set it to 1, reset it to 0, or complement its output. The *JK* flip-flop performs all three operations. The circuit diagram of a *JK* flip-flop constructed with a *D* flip-flop and gates is shown in Fig. 5-12(a). The *J* input sets the flip-flop to 1, the *K* input resets it to 0, and when both inputs are enabled, the output is complemented. This can be verified by investigating the circuit applied to the *D* input:

$$D = JQ' + K'Q$$

When $J = 1$ and $K = 0$, $D = Q' + Q = 1$, so the next clock edge sets the output to 1. When $J = 0$ and $K = 1$, $D = 0$, so the next clock edge resets the output to 0. When both $J = K = 1$, $D = Q'$, the next clock edge complements the output. When both $J = K = 0$, $D = Q$, the clock edge leaves the output unchanged. The graphic symbol for the *JK* flip-flop is shown in Fig. 5-12(b). It is similar to the graphic symbol of the *D* flip-flop, except that now the inputs are marked *J* and *K*.

The *T* (toggle) flip-flop is a complementing flip-flop and can be obtained from a *JK* flip-flop when inputs *J* and *K* are tied together. This is shown in Fig. 5-13(a). When $T = 0$ $(J = K = 0)$ a clock edge does not change the output. When $T = 1$ $(J = K = 1)$ a clock edge complements the output. The complementing flip-flop is useful for designing binary counters.

The *T* flip-flop can be constructed with a *D* flip-flop and an exclusive-OR gate as shown in Fig. 5-13(b). The expression for the *D* input is

$$D = T \oplus Q = TQ' + T'Q$$

When $T = 0$, then $D = Q$, and there is no change in the output. When $T = 1$, then $D = Q'$ and the output complements. The graphic symbol for this flip-flop has a *T* symbol in the input.

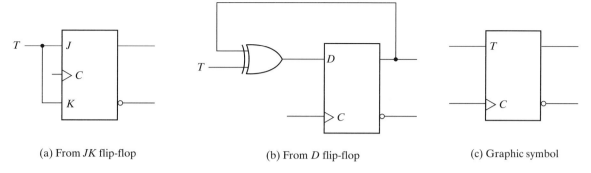

(a) From *JK* flip-flop

(b) From *D* flip-flop

(c) Graphic symbol

FIGURE 5-13
T Flip-Flop

Characteristic Tables

A characteristic table defines the logical properties of a flip-flop by describing its operation in tabular form. The characteristic tables of three types of flip-flops are presented in Table 5-1. They define the next state as a function of the inputs and present state. $Q(t)$ refers to the present state prior to the application of a clock edge. $Q(t + 1)$ is the next state one clock period later. Note that the clock edge input is not included in the characteristic table, but is implied to occur between time t and $t + 1$.

The characteristic table for the *JK* flip-flop shows that the next state is equal to the present state when inputs J and K are both equal to 0. This can be expressed as $Q(t + 1) = Q(t)$, indicating that the clock produces no change of state. When $K = 1$ and $J = 0$, the clock resets

Table 5-1
Flip-Flop Characteristic Tables

JK **Flip-Flop**

J	K	$Q(t + 1)$	
0	0	$Q(t)$	No change
0	1	0	Reset
1	0	1	Set
1	1	$Q'(t)$	Complement

D **Flip-Flop**

D	$Q(t + 1)$	
0	0	Reset
1	1	Set

T **Flip-Flop**

T	$Q(t + 1)$	
0	$Q(t)$	No change
1	$Q'(t)$	Complement

the flip-flop and $Q(t + 1) = 0$. With $J = 1$ and $K = 0$, the flip-flop sets and $Q(t + 1) = 1$. When both J and K are equal to 1, the next state changes to the complement of the present state, which can be expressed as $Q(t + 1) = Q'(t)$.

The next state of a D flip-flop is dependent only on the D input and independent of the present state. This can be expressed as $Q(t + 1) = D$. It means that the next-state value is equal to the value of D. Note that the D flip-flop does not have a "no-change" condition. This condition can be accomplished either by disabling the clock or by leaving the clock and connecting the output back into the D input when the state of the flip-flop must remain the same.

The characteristic table of the T flip-flop has only two conditions. When $T = 0$, the clock edge does not change the state. When $T = 1$, the clock edge complements the state of the flip-flop.

Characteristic Equations

The logical properties of a flip-flop as described in the characteristic table can be expressed also algebraically with a characteristic equation. For the D flip-flop, we have the characteristic equation

$$Q(t + 1) = D$$

It states that the next state of the output will be equal to the value of input D in the present state. The characteristic equation for the JK flip-flop can be derived from the characteristic table or from the circuit of Fig. 5-12. We obtain

$$Q(t + 1) = JQ' + K'Q$$

where Q is the value of the flip-flop output prior to the application of a clock edge. The characteristic equation for the T flip-flop is obtained from the circuit of Fig. 5-13:

$$Q(t + 1) = T \oplus Q = TQ' + T'Q$$

Direct Inputs

Some flip-flops have asynchronous inputs that are used to force the flip-flop to a particular state independent of the clock. The input that sets the flip-flop to 1 is called *preset* or *direct set*. The input that clears the flip-flop to 0 is called *clear* or *direct reset*. When power is turned on in a digital system, the state of the flip-flops is unknown. The direct inputs are useful for bringing all flip-flops in the system to a known starting state prior to the clocked operation.

A positive-edge-triggered D flip-flop with asynchronous reset is shown in Fig. 5-14. The circuit diagram is the same as the one of Fig. 5-10, except for the additional reset input connections to three NAND gates. When the reset input is 0, it forces output Q' to stay at 1, which, in turn, clears output Q to 0, thus resetting the flip-flop. Two other connections from the reset input ensure that the S input of the third SR latch stays at logic 1 while the reset input is at 0 regardless of the values of D and CLK.

The graphic symbol for the D flip-flop with a direct reset has an additional input marked with R. The bubble along the input indicates that the reset is active at the logic 0 level. Flip-flops with a direct set use the symbol S for the asynchronous set input.

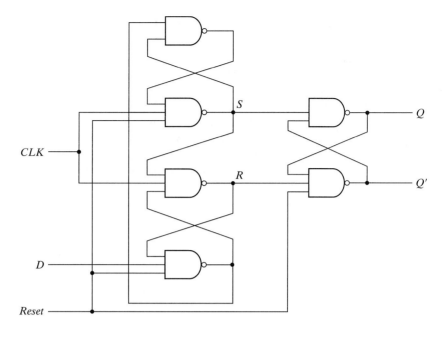

(a) Circuit diagram

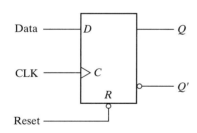

(b) Graphic symbol

R	C	D	Q	Q'
0	X	X	0	1
1	↑	0	0	1
1	↑	1	1	0

(b) Function table

FIGURE 5-14
D Flip-Flop with Asynchronous Reset

The function table specifies the operation of the circuit. When $R = 0$, the output is reset to 0. This state is independent of the values of D or C. Normal clock operation can proceed only after the reset input goes to logic 1. The clock at C is shown with an upward arrow to indicate that the flip-flop triggers on the positive-edge of the clock. The value in D is transferred to Q with every positive-edge clock signal, provided that $R = 1$.

5-4   ANALYSIS OF CLOCKED SEQUENTIAL CIRCUITS

The behavior of a clocked sequential circuit is determined from the inputs, the outputs, and the state of its flip-flops. The outputs and the next state are both a function of the inputs and the present state. The analysis of a sequential circuit consists of obtaining a table or a diagram for the time sequence of inputs, outputs, and internal states. It is also possible to write Boolean expressions that describe the behavior of the sequential circuit. These expressions must include the necessary time sequence, either directly or indirectly.

A logic diagram is recognized as a clocked sequential circuit if it includes flip-flops with clock inputs. The flip-flops may be of any type and the logic diagram may or may not include combinational circuit gates. In this section, we introduce an algebraic representation for specifying the next-state condition in terms of the present state and inputs. A state table and state diagram are then presented to describe the behavior of the sequential circuit. Another algebraic representation is presented for specifying the logic diagram of sequential circuits. Specific examples are used to illustrate the various procedures.

State Equations

The behavior of a clocked sequential circuit can be described algebraically by means of state equations. A *state equation* (also called *transition equation*) specifies the next state as a function of the present state and inputs. Consider the sequential circuit shown in Fig. 5-15. It consists of two D flip-flops A and B, an input x and an output y. Since the D input of a flip-flop determines the value of the next state, it is possible to write a set of state equations for the circuit:

$$A(t + 1) = A(t)x(t) + B(t)x(t)$$
$$B(t + 1) = A'(t)x(t)$$

A state equation is an algebraic expression that specifies the condition for a flip-flop state transition. The left side of the equation with $(t + 1)$ denotes the next state of the flip-flop one clock edge later. The right side of the equation is a Boolean expression that specifies the present state and input conditions that make the next state equal to 1. Since all the variables in the Boolean expressions are a function of the present state, we can omit the designation (t) after each variable for convenience and can express the state equations in the more compact form:

$$A(t + 1) = Ax + Bx$$
$$B(t + 1) = A'x$$

The Boolean expressions for the state equations can be derived directly from the gates that form the combinational circuit part of the sequential circuit, since the D values of the combinational circuit determine the next state. Similarly, the present state value of the output can be expressed algebraically as

$$y(t) = [A(t) + B(t)]x'(t)$$

By removing the symbol (t) for the present state, we obtain the output Boolean equation:

$$y = (A + B)x'$$

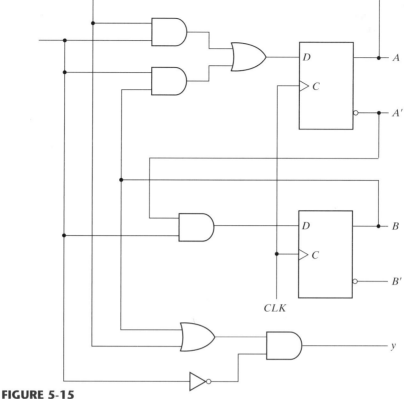

FIGURE 5-15
Example of Sequential Circuit

State Table

The time sequence of inputs, outputs, and flip-flop states can be enumerated in a *state table* (sometimes called *transition table*). The state table for the circuit of Fig. 5-15 is shown in Table 5-2. The table consists of four sections labeled *present state, input, next state*, and *output*. The present state section shows the states of flip-flops A and B at any given time *t*. The input section gives a value of *x* for each possible present state. The next-state section shows the states of the flip-flops one clock cycle later at time $t+1$. The output section gives the value of *y* at time *t* for each present state and input condition.

The derivation of a state table requires listing all possible binary combinations of present state and inputs. In this case, we have eight binary combinations from 000 to 111. The next-state values are then determined from the logic diagram or from the state equations. The next state of flip-flop A must satisfy the state equation

$$A(t+1) = Ax + Bx$$

The next-state section in the state table under column A has three 1's where the present state and input value satisfy the conditions that the present state of *A* and input *x* are both equal to

Table 5-2
State Table for the Circuit of Fig. 5-15

Present State A	B	Input x	Next State A	B	Output y
0	0	0	0	0	0
0	0	1	0	1	0
0	1	0	0	0	1
0	1	1	1	1	0
1	0	0	0	0	1
1	0	1	1	0	0
1	1	0	0	0	1
1	1	1	1	0	0

1 or the present state of B and input x are both equal to 1. Similarly, the next state of flip-flop B is derived from the state equation

$$B(t + 1) = A'x$$

and is equal to 1 when the present state of A is 0 and input x is equal to 1. The output column is derived from the output equation

$$y = Ax' + Bx'$$

The state table of a sequential circuit with D-type flip-flops is obtained by the same procedure outlined in the previous example. In general, a sequential circuit with m flip-flops and n inputs needs 2^{m+n} rows in the state table. The binary numbers from 0 through $2^{m+n} - 1$ are listed under the present-state and input columns. The next-state section has m columns, one for each flip-flop. The binary values for the next state are derived directly from the state equations. The output section has as many columns as there are output variables. Its binary value is derived from the circuit or from the Boolean function in the same manner as in a truth table.

It is sometimes convenient to express the state table in a slightly different form. In the other configuration, the state table has only three sections: present state, next state, and output. The input conditions are enumerated under the next-state and output sections. The state table of Table 5-2 is repeated in Table 5-3 using the second form. For each present state, there are two possible next states and outputs, depending on the value of the input. One form may be preferable over the other, depending on the application.

Table 5-3
Second Form of the State Table

Present State	Next State		Output	
	x = 0	x = 1	x = 0	x = 1
AB	AB	AB	y	y
00	00	01	0	0
01	00	11	1	0
10	00	10	1	0
11	00	10	1	0

State Diagram

The information available in a state table can be represented graphically in the form of a state diagram. In this type of diagram, a state is represented by a circle, and the transitions between states are indicated by directed lines connecting the circles. The state diagram of the sequential circuit of Fig. 5-15 is shown in Fig. 5-16. The state diagram provides the same information as the state table and is obtained directly from Table 5-2 or 5-3. The binary number inside each circle identifies the state of the flip-flops. The directed lines are labeled with two binary numbers separated by a slash. The input value during the present state is labeled first and the number after the slash gives the output during the present state with the given input. (It is important to remember that the bit value listed for the output along the directed line occurs during the present state and the indicated input, and has nothing to do with the transition to the next state.) For example, the directed line from state 00 to 01 is labeled 1/0, meaning that when the sequential circuit is in the present state 00 and the input is 1, the output is 0. After the next clock cycle, the circuit goes to the next state, 01. If the input changes to 0, then the output becomes 1, but if the input remains at 1, the output stays at 0. This information is obtained from the state diagram along the two directed lines emanating from the circle with state 01. A directed line connecting a circle with itself indicates that no change of state occurs.

There is no difference between a state table and a state diagram except in the manner of representation. The state table is easier to derive from a given logic diagram and the state equation. The state diagram follows directly from the state table. The state diagram gives a pictorial view of state transitions and is the form more suitable for human interpretation of the circuit operation. For example, the state diagram of Fig. 5-16 clearly shows that, starting from state 00, the output is 0 as long as the input stays at 1. The first 0 input after a string of 1's gives an output of 1 and transfers the circuit back to the initial state 00.

Flip-Flop Input Equations

The logic diagram of a sequential circuit consists of flip-flops and gates. The interconnections among the gates form a combinational circuit and may be specified algebraically with Boolean expressions. The knowledge of the type of flip-flops and a list of the Boolean expressions of the combinational circuit provide the information needed to draw the logic diagram of the sequential circuit. The part of the combinational circuit that generates external outputs is described algebraically by a set of Boolean functions called *output equations*. The part of the circuit that generates the inputs to flip-flops is described algebraically by a set of Boolean functions called flip-flop

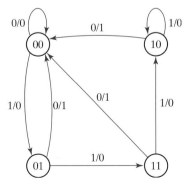

FIGURE 5-16
State Diagram of the Circuit of Fig. 5-15

input equations (sometimes called *excitation equations*). We will adopt the convention of using the flip-flop input symbol to denote the input equation variable and a subscript to designate the name of the flip-flop output. For example, the following input equation specifies an OR gate with inputs x and y connected to the D input of a flip-flop whose output is labeled with the symbol Q:

$$D_Q = x + y$$

The sequential circuit of Fig. 5-15 consists of two D flip-flops A and B, an input x, and an output y. The logic diagram of the circuit can be expressed algebraically with two flip-flop input equations and an output equation:

$$D_A = Ax + Bx$$
$$D_B = A'x$$
$$y = (A + B)x'$$

The three equations provide the necessary information for drawing the logic diagram of the sequential circuit. The symbol D_A specifies a D flip-flop labeled A. D_B specifies a second D flip-flop labeled B. The Boolean expressions associated with these two variables and the expression for output y specify the combinational circuit part of the sequential circuit.

The flip-flop input equations constitute a convenient algebraic form for specifying the logic diagram of a sequential circuit. They imply the type of flip-flop from the letter symbol, and they fully specify the combinational circuit that drives the flip-flops. Note that the expression for the input equation for a D flip-flop is identical to the expression for the corresponding state equation. This is because of the characteristic equation that equates the next state to the value of the D input: $Q(t + 1) = D_Q$.

Analysis with *D* Flip-Flops

We will summarize the procedure for analyzing a clocked sequential circuit with D flip-flops by means of a simple example. The circuit we want to analyze is described by the input equation

$$D_A = A \oplus x \oplus y$$

The D_A symbol implies a D flip-flop with output A. The x and y variables are the inputs to the circuit. No output equations are given, so the output is implied to come from the output of the flip-flop. The logic diagram is obtained from the input equation and is drawn in Fig. 5-17(a).

The state table has one column for the present state for flip-flop A, two columns for the two inputs and one column for the next state of A. The binary numbers under Axy are listed from 000 through 111 as shown in Fig. 5-17(b). The next state values are obtained from the state equation

$$A(t + 1) = A \oplus x \oplus y$$

The expression specifies an odd function and is equal to 1 when only one variable is 1 or when all three variables are 1. This is indicated in the column of the next state of A.

The circuit has one flip-flop and two states. The state diagram consists of two circles—one for each state as shown in Fig. 5-17(c). The present state and the output can be either 0 or 1 as indicated in the number inside the circles. A slash on the directed lines is not needed because there is no output from a combinational circuit. The two inputs can have four possible combinations for each state. Two input combinations during each state transition are separated by a comma to simplify the notation.

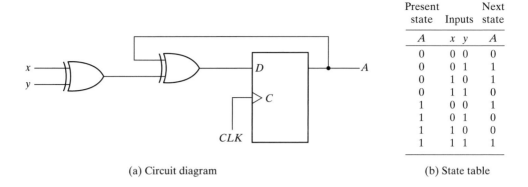

	Present state	Inputs		Next state
	A	x	y	A
	0	0	0	0
	0	0	1	1
	0	1	0	1
	0	1	1	0
	1	0	0	1
	1	0	1	0
	1	1	0	0
	1	1	1	1

(a) Circuit diagram   (b) State table

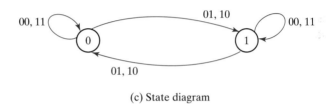

(c) State diagram

FIGURE 5-17
Sequential Circuit with D Flip-Flop

Analysis with JK Flip-Flops

A state table consists of four sections: present state, inputs, next state, and outputs. The first two are obtained by listing all binary combinations. The output section is determined from the output equations. The next-state values are evaluated from the state equations. For a D type flip-flop, the state equation is the same as the input equation. When other than the D type of flip-flop is used, such as JK or T, it is necessary to refer to the corresponding characteristic table or characteristic equation to obtain the next state values. We will illustrate the procedure first by using the characteristic table and again by using the characteristic equation.

The next-state values of a sequential circuit that uses flip-flops such as JK or T type can be derived using the following procedure:

1. Determine the flip-flop input equations in terms of the present state and input variables.

2. List the binary values of each input equation.

3. Use the corresponding flip-flop characteristic table to determine the next state values in the state table.

As an example, consider the sequential circuit with two JK flip-flops A and B and one input x, as shown in Fig. 5-18. The circuit has no outputs and, therefore, the state table does not need an output column. (The outputs of the flip-flops may be considered as the outputs in this case.)

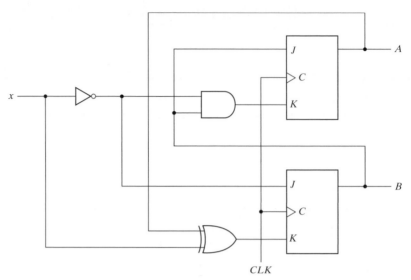

FIGURE 5-18
Sequential Circuit with *JK* Flip-Flop

The circuit can be specified by the flip-flop input equations

$$J_A = B \qquad K_A = Bx'$$
$$J_B = x' \qquad K_B = A'x + Ax' = A \oplus x$$

The state table of the sequential circuit is shown in Table 5-4. The present-state and input columns list the eight binary combinations. The binary values listed under the columns labeled *flip-flop inputs* are not part of the state table, but they are needed for the purpose of evaluating the next state as specified in step 2 of the procedure. These binary values are obtained directly from the four input equations in a manner similar to that for obtaining a truth table from a Boolean expression. The next state of each flip-flop is evaluated from the corresponding *J* and *K* inputs and the characteristic table of the *JK* flip-flop listed in Table 5-1. There are four cases to consider. When $J = 1$ and $K = 0$, the next state is 1. When $J = 0$ and $K = 1$, the next state

Table 5-4
State Table for Sequential Circuit with JK Flip-Flops

Present State		Input	Next State		Flip-Flop Inputs			
A	*B*	*x*	*A*	*B*	J_A	K_A	J_B	K_B
0	0	0	0	1	0	0	1	0
0	0	1	0	0	0	0	0	1
0	1	0	1	1	1	1	1	0
0	1	1	1	0	1	0	0	1
1	0	0	1	1	0	0	1	1
1	0	1	1	0	0	0	0	0
1	1	0	0	0	1	1	1	1
1	1	1	1	1	1	0	0	0

is 0. When $J = K = 0$, there is no change of state and the next-state value is the same as the present state. When $J = K = 1$, the next-state bit is the complement of the present-state bit. Examples of the last two cases occur in the table when the present state AB is 10 and input x is 0. JA and KA are both equal to 0 and the present state of A is 1. Therefore, the next state of A remains the same and is equal to 1. In the same row of the table, JB and KB are both equal to 1. Since the present state of B is 0, the next state of B is complemented and changes to 1.

The next-state values can be obtained also by evaluating the state equations from the characteristic equation. This is done by using the following procedure:

1. Determine the flip-flop input equations in terms of the present state and input variables.
2. Substitute the input equations into the flip-flop characteristic equation to obtain the state equations.
3. Use the corresponding state equations to determine the next state values in the state table.

The input equations for the two JK flip-flops of Fig. 5-18 are listed on the previous page. The characteristic equations for the flip-flops are obtained by substituting A or B for the name of the flip-flop instead of Q:

$$A(t + 1) = JA' + K'A$$
$$B(t + 1) = JB' + K'B$$

Substituting the values of J_A and K_A from the input equations, we obtain the state equation for A:

$$A(t + 1) = BA' + (Bx')'A = A'B + AB' + Ax$$

The state equation provides the bit values for the column under next state of A in the state table. Similarly, the state equation for flip-flop B can be derived from the characteristic equation by substituting the values of J_B and K_B:

$$B(t + 1) = x'B' + (A \oplus x)'B = B'x' + ABx + A'Bx'$$

The state equation provides the bit values for the column under next state of B in the state table. Note that the columns in Table 5-4 under flip-flop inputs are not needed when state equations are used.

The state diagram of the sequential circuit is shown in Fig. 5-19. Note that since the circuit has no outputs, the directed lines out of the circles are marked with one binary number only to designate the value of input x.

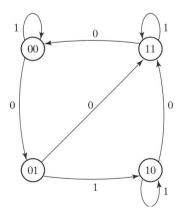

FIGURE 5-19
State Diagram of the Circuit of Fig. 5-18

Analysis With *T* Flip-Flops

The analysis of a sequential circuit with T flip-flops follows the same procedure outlined for JK flip-flops. The next state values in the state table can be obtained either by using the characteristic table listed in Table 5-1 or the characteristic equation

$$Q(t + 1) = T \oplus Q = T'Q + TQ'$$

Consider the sequential circuit shown in Fig. 5-20. It has two flip-flops A and B, one input x, and one output y. It can be described algebraically by two input equations and an output equation:

$$T_A = Bx$$
$$T_B = x$$
$$y = AB$$

The state table for the circuit is listed in Table 5-5. The values for y are obtained from the output equation. The values for the next state can be derived from the state equations by substituting T_A and T_B in the characteristic equations, yielding

$$A(t + 1) = (Bx)'A + (Bx)A' = AB' + Ax' + A'Bx$$
$$B(t + 1) = x \oplus B$$

The next state values for A and B in the state table are obtained from the expressions of the two state equations.

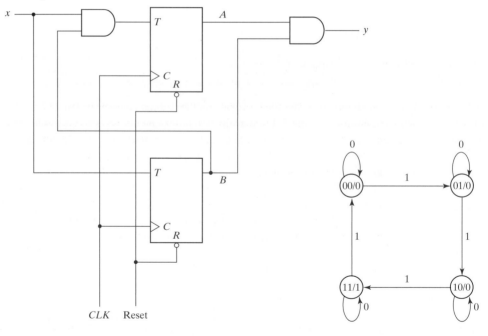

(a) Circuit diagram   (b) State diagram

FIGURE 5-20
Sequential Circuit with *T* Flip-Flops

Table 5-5
State Table for Sequential Circuit with T Flip-Flops

Present State		Input	Next State		Output
A	B	x	A	B	y
0	0	0	0	0	0
0	0	1	0	1	0
0	1	0	0	1	0
0	1	1	1	0	0
1	0	0	1	0	0
1	0	1	1	1	0
1	1	0	1	1	1
1	1	1	0	0	1

The state diagram of the circuit is shown in Fig. 5-20(b). As long as input x is equal to 1, the circuit behaves as a binary counter with a sequence of states 00, 01, 10, 11, and back to 00. When $x = 0$, the circuit remains in the same state. Output y is equal to 1 when the present state is 11. Here the output depends on the present state only and is independent of the input. The two values inside each circle separated by a slash are for the present state and output.

Mealy and Moore Models

The most general model of a sequential circuit has inputs, outputs, and internal states. It is customary to distinguish between two models of sequential circuits: the Mealy model and the Moore model. They differ in the way the output is generated. In the Mealy model, the output is a function of both the present state and input. In the Moore model, the output is a function of the present state only. When dealing with the two models, some books and other technical sources refer to a sequential circuit as a finite state machine abbreviated FSM. The Mealy model of a sequential circuit is referred to as a Mealy FSM or Mealy machine. The Moore model is refereed to as a Moore FSM or Moore machine.

An example of a Mealy model is shown in Fig. 5-15. Output y is a function of both input x and the present state of A and B. The corresponding state diagram in Fig. 5-16 shows both the input and output values separated by a slash along the directed lines between the states.

An example of a Moore model is shown in Fig. 5-18. Here the output is a function of the present state only. The corresponding state diagram in Fig. 5-19 has only inputs marked along the directed lines. The outputs are the flip-flop states marked inside the circles. Another example of a Moore model is the sequential circuit of Fig. 5-20. The output depends only on flip-flop values and that makes it a function of the present state only. The input value in the state diagram is labeled along the directed line, but the output value is indicated inside the circle together with the present state.

In a Moore model, the outputs of the sequential circuit are synchronized with the clock because they depend on only flip-flop outputs that are synchronized with the clock. In a Mealy model, the outputs may change if the inputs change during the clock cycle. Moreover, the outputs may have momentary false values because of the delay encountered from the time that the inputs change and the time that the flip-flop outputs change. In order to synchronize a Mealy type circuit, the inputs of the sequential circuit must be synchronized with the clock and the outputs must be sampled only during the clock edge.

5-5   HDL FOR SEQUENTIAL CIRCUITS

The Verilog hardware description language (HDL) is introduced in Section 3-9. The description of combinational circuits and an introduction to behavioral modeling is presented in Section 4-11. In this section, we continue the discussion of the behavioral modeling and present description examples of flip-flops and sequential circuits.

Behavioral Modeling

There are two kinds of behavioral statements in Verilog HDL: *initial* and *always*. The initial behavior executes once beginning at time = 0. The always behavior executes repeatedly and reexecutes until the simulation terminates. A behavior is declared within a module by using the keywords **initial** or **always**, followed by a statement or a block of statements enclosed by the keywords **begin** and **end**. A module may contain an arbitrary number of initial or always statements. These statements execute concurrently with respect to each other starting at time 0.

An **initial** statement executes only once. It begins its execution at the start of simulation and ends after all the statements have completed execution. As mentioned at the end of Section 4-11, the **initial** statement is useful for generating input signals to simulate a design. In simulating a sequential circuit, it is necessary to generate a clock source for triggering the flip-flops. The following are two possible ways to provide a free-running clock:

```
initial                          initial
   begin                            begin
      clock = 1'b0 ;                   clock = 1'b0;
      repeat (30)                      #300  $finish;
      #10 clock = ~ clock;          end
   end                           always
                                    #10   clock = ~clock;
```

In the first version, the **initial** block is enclosed within the **begin** and **end** keywords. Clock is set to 0 at time = 0. Clock is complemented every 10 time units and is repeated 30 times. This produces 15 clock cycles, each with a cycle time of 20 time units. In the second version, the **initial** block sets clock to 0 at time = 0. After 10 time units, the **always** statement repeatedly complements clock every 10 time units, providing a clock with a cycle time of 20 time units. The simulation terminates in response to the **$finish** system task at time 300.

The **always** statement can be controlled by delays that wait for a certain time or by certain conditions to become true or by events to occur. Here we will explain only the event control condition. This type of statement is of the form

```
always  @ (event control expression)
Procedural assignment statements.
```

The event control expression specifies the condition that must occur to activate the execution of the procedural assignment statements. The variables in the left-hand side of the procedural statements must be of the **reg** data type and must be declared as such. The right-hand side can be any expression that produces a value using Verilog-defined operators.

The event control expression (also called the sensitivity list) specifies the events that must occur to initiate the execution of the procedural statements in the always block. Statements within the block execute sequentially and the execution suspends after the last statement has executed. Then, the always statement waits again for an event to occur. We will consider here two kinds of events: level-sensitive and edge-triggered events. Level-sensitive events occur in combinational circuits and in latches. For example, the statement

always @ (*A* **or** *B* **or** Reset)

will cause the execution of the procedural statements in the always block if a change occurs in *A* or *B* or Reset. In synchronous sequential circuits, changes in flip-flops must occur only in response to a transition of a clock pulse. The transition may be either a positive-edge or a negative-edge trigger. Verilog HDL takes care of these conditions by providing two keywords: **posedge** and **negedge.** For example,

always @(**posedge** clock **or negedge** reset)

will cause the execution of the procedural statements only if the clock goes through a positive transition or if reset goes through a negative transition.

A procedural assignment is an assignment within an **initial** or **always** statement. This is in contrast to a continuous assignment discussed in Sec. 4-11 with dataflow modeling where the statement is continuously evaluated. There are two kinds of procedural assignments: *blocking* and *non-blocking*. The two are distinguished by the symbols that they use. Blocking assignments use the symbol (=) as the assignment operator and non-blocking assignments use the (<=) as the operator. Blocking assignment statements are executed sequentially in the order they are listed in a sequential block. Non-blocking assignments evaluate the expressions on the right-hand side, but do not make the assignment to the left-hand side until all expressions are evaluated. The two types of assignments may be better understood by means of an illustration. Consider these two procedural blocking assignments:

$$B = A$$
$$C = B + 1$$

The first statement transfers *A* into *B*. The second statement increments the new value of *B* and transfers it to *C*. At the completion, *C* contains the value of $A + 1$.

Now consider the two statements as non-blocking assignments:

$$B <= A$$
$$C <= B + 1$$

When the statements are executed, the right-hand side expressions are evaluated and stored in a temporary location. The value of *A* is kept in one storage location and the value of $B + 1$ in another. After all the expressions in the sequential block are evaluated and stored, the assignment to the left-hand-side targets is made. In this case, *C* will contain the original value of *B* plus one. Most of the examples in this and the next chapter can use blocking assignments. Non-blocking assignments are imperative when dealing with register transfer level design as shown in Chapter 8.

Flip-Flops and Latches

HDL Examples 5-1 through 5-4 show descriptions of various flip-flops and a *D* latch. The *D* latch is transparent and responds to a change in data input with a change in output as long as the control input is enabled. The module description of a *D* latch is shown in HDL Example 5-1. It has two inputs, *D* and *control*, and one output *Q*. Since *Q* is evaluated in a procedural statement, it must be declared as **reg** type. Latches respond to input signal levels so the two inputs are listed without edge qualifiers in the event control expression following the @ symbol in the **always** statement. There is only one blocking procedural assignment statement and it specifies the transfer of input *D* to output *Q* if control is true (logic 1). Note that this statement is executed every time there is a change in *D* if control is 1.

HDL Example 5-2 describes two positive-edge *D* flip-flops in two modules. The first responds only to the clock, the second includes an asynchronous reset input. Output *Q* must be declared as a **reg** data type in addition to being listed as an output. This is because it is a target output in a procedural assignment statement. The keyword **posedge** ensures that the transfer of input *D* into *Q* occurs only during the positive-edge transition of CLK. A change in *D* at any other time does not change *Q*.

HDL Example 5-1

```
//Description of D latch (See Fig. 5-6)
module D_latch (Q,D,control);
    output Q;
    input D,control;
    reg Q;
    always @ (control or D)
    if (control) Q = D;       //Same as: if (control == 1)
endmodule
```

HDL Example 5-2

```
//D flip-flop
module D_FF (Q,D,CLK);
    output Q;
    input D,CLK;
    reg Q;
    always @ (posedge CLK)
        Q = D;
endmodule

//D flip-flop with asynchronous reset.
module DFF (Q,D,CLK,RST);
    output Q;
    input D,CLK,RST;
    reg Q;
    always @(posedge CLK or negedge RST)
        if (~RST) Q = 1'b0;      // Same as: if (RST == 0)
        else Q = D;
endmodule
```

The second module includes an asynchronous reset input in addition to the synchronous clock. A special form of **if** statement is used to generate such a flip-flop. The event expression after the @ symbol in the always statement may have any number of edge events, either posedge or negedge. One of the events must be a clock event. The remaining specify conditions under which asynchronous logic is to be executed. Each **if** or **else if** statement in the procedural assignment statements correspond to an asynchronous event. The last **else** statement corresponds to the clock event. There are two edge events in the second module of Example 5-2. The **negedge** RST (reset) event is asynchronous since it matches the **if** ($\sim$RST) statement. As long as RST is 0, Q is cleared to 0. If CLK has a positive transition, its effect is blocked. Only if RST = 1, can the **posedge** clock event synchronously transfer D into Q.

It is usually necessary that flip-flops include a reset (or preset) input signal, otherwise, the initial state of the sequential circuit cannot be determined. A sequential circuit cannot be tested with HDL simulation unless an initial state can be assigned with an input signal.

HDL Example 5-3 describes the construction of a T or JK flip-flop from a D flip-flop and gates. The circuit is described by using the characteristic equations of the flip-flops:

$$Q(t + 1) = Q \oplus T \qquad \text{for a } T \text{ flip-flop}$$
$$Q(t + 1) = JQ' + K'Q \qquad \text{for a } JK \text{ flip-flop}$$

HDL Example 5-3

```
//T flip-flop from D flip-flop and gates
module TFF (Q,T,CLK,RST);
    output Q;
    input T,CLK,RST;
    wire DT;
    assign DT = Q ^ T ;
//Instantiate the D flip-flop
    DFF TF1 (Q,DT,CLK,RST);
endmodule

//JK flip-flop from D flip-flop and gates
module JKFF (Q,J,K,CLK,RST);
    output Q;
    input J,K,CLK,RST;
    wire JK;
    assign JK = (J & ~Q) | (~K & Q);
//Instantiate D flipflop
    DFF JK1 (Q,JK,CLK,RST);
endmodule

//D flip-flop
module DFF (Q,D,CLK,RST);
    output Q;
    input D,CLK,RST;
    reg Q;
    always @ (posedge CLK or negedge RST)
      if (~RST) Q = 1'b0;
      else Q = D;
endmodule
```

HDL Example 5-4

```
// Functional description of JK flip-flop
module  JK_FF (J,K,CLK,Q,Qnot);
    output Q,Qnot;
    input  J,K,CLK;
    reg  Q;
    assign Qnot = ~ Q ;
    always @ (posedge CLK)
            case ({J,K})
                2'b00: Q = Q;
                2'b01: Q = 1'b0;
                2'b10: Q = 1'b1;
                2'b11: Q = ~ Q;
            endcase
endmodule
```

The first module TFF describes a T flip-flop by instantiating DFF (instantiation is explained in Sec. 4-11). The wire declaration DT is assigned the exclusive-OR of Q and T, as required for converting a D flip-flop to a T flip-flop. The instantiation with the value of DT replacing the D in module DFF produces the required T flip-flop. The JK flip-flop is specified in a similar manner by using its characteristic equation to define a replacement for D in the instantiated DFF.

HDL Example 5-4 shows another way to describe a JK flip-flop. Here we choose to describe the flip-flop using the characteristic table rather than the characteristic equation. The **case** multiway branch condition checks the 2-bit number obtained by concatenating the bits of J and K. The **case** value ({J,K}) is evaluated and compared with the values in the list of statements that follow. The first value that matches the true condition is executed. Since the concatenation of J and K produces a two-bit number, it can be equal to 00, 01, 10, or 11. The first bit gives the value of J and the second the value of K. The four possible conditions specify the value of the next state of Q after the application of a positive-edge clock.

State Diagram

The operation of sequential circuits is described in HDL in the same format as a state diagram. A Mealy model state diagram is presented in HDL Example 5-5. The input, output, clock, and reset are declared in the usual manner. The state of the flip-flops is declared with identifiers Prstate and Nxtstate. These variables hold the state value of the sequential circuit. The state binary assignment is done by using a parameter statement. (Verilog allows constants to be defined in a module by the keyword **parameter**). The four states $S0$ through $S3$ are assigned binary 00 through 11. The notation $S2 = 2'b10$ is preferable to the alternative $S2 = 2$. The former uses two bits to store the constant. The second notation results in a binary number with 32 (or 64) bits.

The HDL description uses three **always** blocks that execute concurrently and interact through common variables. The first **always** statement resets the circuit to the initial state $S0 = 00$ and specifies the synchronous clocked operation. The statement Prstate = Nxtstate is executed only in response to a positive-edge transition of the clock. This means that any change

HDL Example 5-5

```
//Mealy state diagram (Fig. 5-16)
module Mealy_mdl (x,y,CLK,RST);
  input x,CLK,RST;
  output y;
  reg y;
  reg [1:0] Prstate, Nxtstate;
  parameter S0 = 2'b00, S1 = 2'b01, S2 = 2'b10, S3 = 2'b11;
   always @ (posedge CLK or negedge RST)
      if (~RST) Prstate = S0;  //Initialize to state S0
      else Prstate = Nxtstate; //Clock operations
   always @ (Prstate or x)     //Determine next state
        case (Prstate)
          S0: if (x) Nxtstate = S1;
                else Nxtstate = S0;
          S1: if (x) Nxtstate = S3;
                else Nxtstate = S0;
          S2: if (~x)Nxtstate = S0;
                else Nxtstate = S2;
          S3: if (x) Nxtstate = S2;
                else Nxtstate = S0;
        endcase
   always @ (Prstate or x)       //Evaluate output
        case (Prstate)
          S0: y = 0;
          S1: if (x) y = 1'b0; else y = 1'b1;
          S2: if (x) y = 1'b0; else y = 1'b1;
          S3: if (x) y = 1'b0; else y = 1'b1;
        endcase
  endmodule
```

that occurs in the `Nxtstate` value in the second **always** block is transferred to `Prstate` as a result of a **posedge** event. The second **always** block determines the next state transition as a function of the present state and input. The multiway branch condition follows the sequence specified in the state diagram of Fig. 5-16. The third **always** block evaluates the output as a function of the present state and input. Although it is listed separately for clarity, it could be combined with the second block. Note that the value of output *y* may change if the value of input *x* changes while the circuit is at any given state.

An example of a Moore model state diagram is described in HDL Example 5-6. This example shows that it is possible to specify the state transitions with only one **always** block. The present state of the circuit is identified by the variable `state`. The state transitions occur with the **posedge** CLK according to the conditions listed in the **case** statements. The output of the circuit is independent of the input and is taken directly from the outputs of the flip-flops. The 2-bit output *AB* is specified with an **assign** statement and is equal to the value of the present state.

HDL Example 5-6

```
//Moore state diagram (Fig. 5-19)
module Moore_mdl (x,AB,CLK,RST);
    input x,CLK,RST;
    output [1:0]AB;
    reg [1:0] state;
    parameter S0 = 2'b00, S1 = 2'b01, S2 = 2'b10, S3 = 2'b11;
        always @ (posedge CLK or negedge RST)
            if (~RST) state = S0;  //Initialize to state S0
            else
            case (state)
              S0: if (~x) state = S1; else state = S0;
              S1: if (x)  state = S2; else state = S3;
              S2: if (~x) state = S3; else state = S2;
              S3: if (~x) state = S0; else state = S3;
            endcase
    assign AB = state;           //Output of flip-flops
endmodule
```

Structural Description

Combinational circuits can be described in HDL by using gate-level or dataflow statements. Sequential circuits use behavioral statements to describe the flip-flop operation. Since a sequential circuit is made up of flip-flops and gates, its structure can be described by a combination of dataflow and behavioral statements. The flip-flops are described with an **always** statement. The combinational part can be described with **assign** statements and Boolean equations. The separate modules can be combined by instantiation.

The structural description of a sequential circuit is shown in HDL Example 5-7. There are two modules in the example. The first describes the circuit of Fig. 5-20(a). The second describes a T flip-flop. Another module provides a stimulus for testing the circuit operation. The sequential circuit is a 2-bit binary counter controlled by input x. Output y is enabled when the count reaches binary 11. Flip-flops A and B are included as outputs in order to check their operation. The flip-flop input equations and the output equation are evaluated with **assign** statements having the corresponding Boolean expressions. The T flip-flop is then instantiated using TA and TB defined by the input equations.

The second module describes the T flip-flop. The RST input resets the flip-flop to 0 with a negative signal. The operation of the flip-flop is specified by its characteristic equation $Q(t + 1) = Q \oplus T$.

The stimulus module provides inputs to the circuit to check the output response. The first **initial** block provides eight clock cycles with period of 10 ns. The second **initial** block specifies an alternate change of input x that occurs at the negative edge transition of the clock. The result of the simulation is shown in Fig. 5-21. Output A and B go through the binary sequence 00, 01, 10, 11, and back to 00. The change in the count occurs during a positive edge of the clock provided $x = 1$. If $x = 0$, the count does not change. Output y is equal to 1 when both A and B are equal to 1. This verifies the operation of the circuit.

HDL Example 5-7

```
//Structural description of sequential circuit
//See Fig. 5-20(a)
module Tcircuit (x,y,A,B,CLK,RST);
   input x,CLK,RST;
   output y,A,B;
   wire TA,TB;
//Flip-flop input equations
   assign TB = x,
          TA = x & B;
//Output equation
   assign y = A & B;
//Instantiate T flip-flops
   T_FF BF (B,TB,CLK,RST);
   T_FF AF (A,TA,CLK,RST);
endmodule

//T flip-flop
module T_FF (Q,T,CLK,RST);
   output Q;
   input T,CLK,RST;
   reg Q;
     always @ (posedge CLK or negedge RST)
       if (~RST) Q = 1'b0;
       else Q = Q ^ T;
endmodule

//Stimulus for testing sequential circuit
module testTcircuit;
  reg x,CLK,RST;   //inputs for circuit
  wire y,A,B;      //output from circuit
  Tcircuit TC (x,y,A,B,CLK,RST);  // instantiate circuit
  initial
    begin
        RST = 0;
        CLK = 0;
     #5 RST = 1;
        repeat (16)
     #5 CLK = ~CLK;
    end
  initial
    begin
        x = 0;
     #15 x = 1;
        repeat (8)
     #10 x = ~ x;
    end
endmodule
```

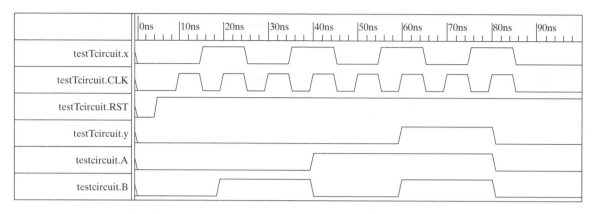

FIGURE 5-21
Simulation Output of HDL Example 5-7

5-6   STATE REDUCTION AND ASSIGNMENT

The analysis of sequential circuits starts from a circuit diagram and culminates in a state table or diagram. The design of a sequential circuit starts from a set of specifications and culminates in a logic diagram. Design procedures are presented starting from Section 5-7. This section discusses certain properties of sequential circuits that may be used to reduce the number of gates and flip-flops during the design.

State Reduction

The reduction of the number of flip-flops in a sequential circuit is referred to as the *state-reduction* problem. State-reduction algorithms are concerned with procedures for reducing the number of states in a state table, while keeping the external input–output requirements unchanged. Since m flip-flops produce 2^m states, a reduction in the number of states may (or may not) result in a reduction in the number of flip-flops. An unpredictable effect in reducing the number of flip-flops is that sometimes the equivalent circuit (with fewer flip-flops) may require more combinational gates.

We will illustrate the state reduction procedure with an example. We start with a sequential circuit whose specification is given in the state diagram of Fig. 5-22. In this example, only the input-output sequences are important; the internal states are used merely to provide the required sequences. For this reason, the states marked inside the circles are denoted by letter symbols instead of their binary values. This is in contrast to a binary counter, where the binary value sequence of the states themselves is taken as the outputs.

There are an infinite number of input sequences that may be applied to the circuit; each results in a unique output sequence. As an example, consider the input sequence 01010110100 starting from the initial state *a*. Each input of 0 or 1 produces an output of 0 or 1 and causes the circuit to go to the next state. From the state diagram, we obtain the output and state sequence for the given input sequence as follows: With the circuit in initial state

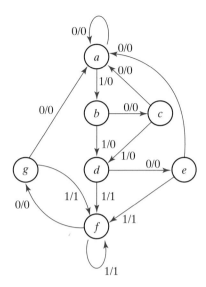

FIGURE 5-22
State Diagram

a, an input of 0 produces an output of 0 and the circuit remains in state *a*. With present state *a* and input of 1, the output is 0 and the next state is *b*. With present state *b* and input of 0, the output is 0 and next state is *c*. Continuing this process, we find the complete sequence to be as follows:

state	*a*	*a*	*b*	*c*	*d*	*e*	*f*	*f*	*g*	*f*	*g*	*a*
input	0	1	0	1	0	1	1	0	1	0	0	
output	0	0	0	0	0	1	1	0	1	0	0	

In each column, we have the present state, input value, and output value. The next state is written on top of the next column. It is important to realize that in this circuit, the states themselves are of secondary importance because we are interested only in output sequences caused by input sequences.

Now let us assume that we have found a sequential circuit whose state diagram has less than seven states and we wish to compare it with the circuit whose state diagram is given by Fig. 5-22. If identical input sequences are applied to the two circuits and identical outputs occur for all input sequences, then the two circuits are said to be equivalent (as far as the input–output is concerned) and one may be replaced by the other. The problem of state reduction is to find ways of reducing the number of states in a sequential circuit without altering the input–output relationships.

We now proceed to reduce the number of states for this example. First, we need the state table; it is more convenient to apply procedures for state reduction using a table rather than a diagram. The state table of the circuit is listed in Table 5-6 and is obtained directly from the state diagram.

Table 5-6
State Table

Present State	Next State		Output	
	$x = 0$	$x = 1$	$x = 0$	$x = 1$
a	a	b	0	0
b	c	d	0	0
c	a	d	0	0
d	e	f	0	1
e	a	f	0	1
f	g	f	0	1
g	a	f	0	1

An algorithm for the state reduction of a completely specified state table is given here without proof: "Two states are said to be equivalent if, for each member of the set of inputs, they give exactly the same output and send the circuit either to the same state or to an equivalent state." When two states are equivalent, one of them can be removed without altering the input–output relationships.

Now apply this algorithm to Table 5-6. Going through the state table, we look for two present states that go to the same next state and have the same output for both input combinations. States g and e are two such states: they both go to states a and f and have outputs of 0 and 1 for $x = 0$ and $x = 1$, respectively. Therefore, states g and e are equivalent and one of these states can be removed. The procedure of removing a state and replacing it by its equivalent is demonstrated in Table 5-7. The row with present state g is removed and state g is replaced by state e each time it occurs in the next-state columns.

Present state f now has next states e and f and outputs 0 and 1 for $x = 0$ and $x = 1$, respectively. The same next states and outputs appear in the row with present state d. Therefore, states f and d are equivalent and state f can be removed and replaced by d. The final reduced table is shown in Table 5-8. The state diagram for the reduced table consists of only five

Table 5-7
Reducing the State Table

Present State	Next State		Output	
	$x = 0$	$x = 1$	$x = 0$	$x = 1$
a	a	b	0	0
b	c	d	0	0
c	a	d	0	0
d	e	f	0	1
e	a	f	0	1
f	e	f	0	1

Table 5-8
Reduced State Table

| | Next State | | Output | |
Present State	x = 0	x = 1	x = 0	x = 1
a	a	b	0	0
b	c	d	0	0
c	a	d	0	0
d	e	d	0	1
e	a	d	0	1

states and is shown in Fig. 5-23. This state diagram satisfies the original input-output specifications and will produce the required output sequence for any given input sequence. The following list derived from the state diagram of Fig. 5-23 is for the input sequence used previously (note that the same output sequence results, although the state sequence is different):

state	a	a	b	c	d	e	d	d	e	d	e	a
input	0	1	0	1	0	1	1	0	1	0	0	
output	0	0	0	0	0	1	1	0	1	0	0	

In fact, this sequence is exactly the same as that obtained for Fig. 5-21, if we replace *g* by *e* and *f* by *d*.

Checking each pair of states for possible equivalency can be done systematically by means of a procedure that employs an implication table. The implication table consists of squares, one for every suspected pair of possible equivalent states. By judicious use of the table, it is possible to determine all pairs of equivalent states in a state table. The use of the implication table for reducing the number of states in a state table is demonstrated in Section 9-5.

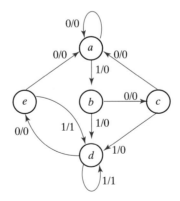

FIGURE 5-23
Reduced State Diagram

The sequential circuit of this example was reduced from seven to five states. In general, reducing the number of states in a state table may result in a circuit with less equipment. However, the fact that a state table has been reduced to fewer states does not guarantee a saving in the number of flip-flops or the number of gates.

State Assignment

In order to design a sequential circuit with physical components, it is necessary to assign coded binary values to the states. For a circuit with m states, the codes must contain n bits where $2^n = \geq m$. For example, with three bits it is possible to assign codes to eight states denoted by binary numbers 000 through 111. If the state table of Table 5-6 is used, we must assign binary values to seven states; the remaining state is unused. If the state table of Table 5-8 is used, only five states need binary assignment, and we are left with three unused states. Unused states are treated as don't-care conditions during the design. Since don't-care conditions usually help in obtaining a simpler circuit, it is more likely that the circuit with five states will require fewer combinational gates than the one with seven states.

The simplest way to code five states is to use the first five integers in binary counting order, as shown in the first assignment of Table 5-9. Another similar assignment is the Gray code shown in assignment 2. Here only one bit in the code group changes when going from one number to the next. This code makes it easier for the Boolean functions to be placed in the map for simplification. Another possible assignment often used in control design is the one-hot assignment. This configuration uses as many bits as there are states in the circuit. At any given time, only one bit is equal to 1 while all others are kept at 0. This type of assignment uses one flip-flop per state.

Table 5-10 is the reduced state table with binary assignment 1 substituted for the letter symbols of the states. A different assignment will result in a state table with different binary values for the states. The binary form of the state table is used to derive the combinational circuit part of the sequential circuit. The complexity of the combinational circuit depends on the binary state assignment chosen.

Sometimes, the name *transition table* is used for a state table with a binary assignment. This distinguishes it from a state table with symbolic names for the states. In this book, we use the same name for both types of state tables.

Table 5-9
Three Possible Binary State Assignments

State	Assignment 1 Binary	Assignment 2 Gray code	Assignment 3 One-hot
a	000	000	00001
b	001	001	00010
c	010	011	00100
d	011	010	01000
e	100	110	10000

Table 5-10
Reduced State Table with Binary Assignment 1

Present State	Next State x = 0	Next State x = 1	Output x = 0	Output x = 1
000	000	001	0	0
001	010	011	0	0
010	000	011	0	0
011	100	011	0	1
100	000	011	0	1

5-7   DESIGN PROCEDURE

The design of a clocked sequential circuit starts from a set of specifications and culminates in a logic diagram or a list of Boolean functions from which the logic diagram can be obtained. In contrast to a combinational circuit, which is fully specified by a truth table, a sequential circuit requires a state table for its specification. The first step in the design of sequential circuits is to obtain a state table or an equivalent representation, such as a state diagram.

A synchronous sequential circuit is made up of flip-flops and combinational gates. The design of the circuit consists of choosing the flip-flops and then finding a combinational gate structure that, together with the flip-flops, produces a circuit that fulfills the stated specifications. The number of flip-flops is determined from the number of states needed in the circuit. The combinational circuit is derived from the state table by evaluating the flip-flop input equations and output equations. In fact, once the type and number of flip-flops are determined, the design process involves a transformation from a sequential circuit problem into a combinational circuit problem. In this way, the techniques of combinational circuit design can be applied.

The procedure for designing synchronous sequential circuits can be summarized by a list of recommended steps.

1. From the word description and specifications of the desired operation, derive a state diagram for the circuit.
2. Reduce the number of states if necessary.
3. Assign binary values to the states.
4. Obtain the binary-coded state table.
5. Choose the type of flip-flops to be used.
6. Derive the simplified flip-flop input equations and output equations.
7. Draw the logic diagram.

The word specification of the circuit behavior usually assumes that the reader is familiar with digital logic terminology. It is necessary that the designer use intuition and experience to arrive at the correct interpretation of the circuit specifications, because word descriptions may be incomplete and inexact. Once such a specification has been set down and the state diagram obtained, it is possible to use known synthesis procedures to complete the design. Although there are formal procedures for state reduction and assignment, they are seldom used by experienced designers.

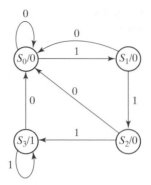

FIGURE 5-24
State Diagram for Sequence Detector

Steps 4 through 7 in the design can be implemented by exact algorithms and therefore can be automated. The part of the design that follows a well-defined procedure is refered to as *synthesis*.

The first step is the most challenging part of the design. We will show here one simple example to demonstrate how a state diagram is obtained from the word specification.

We wish to design a circuit that detects three or more consecutive 1's in a string of bits coming through an input line. The state diagram for the circuit is shown in Fig. 5-24. It is derived by starting with state S_0. If the input is 0, the circuit stays in the same state, but if the input is 1, it goes to state S_1 to indicate that a 1 was detected. If the next input is 1, the change is to state S_2 to indicate the arrival of two consecutive 1's, but if the input is 0, we go back to state S_0. The third consecutive 1 sends the circuit to state S_3. If more 1's are detected, the circuit stays at S_3. Any 0 input sends the circuit back to S_0. In this way, the circuit stays at S_3 as long as there are three or more consecutive 1's received. This is a Moore model sequential circuit since the output is 1 when the circuit is in state S_3 and 0 otherwise.

Synthesis Using *D* Flip-Flops

Once the state diagram has been derived, the rest of the design follows a straightforward synthesis procedure. In fact, we can design the circuit by using an HDL description of the state diagram and the proper HDL synthesis tools to obtain a synthesized net list. (The HDL description of the state diagram will be similar to HDL Example 5-6 in Section 5-5.) To design the circuit by hand, we need to assign binary codes to the states and list the state table. This is done in Table 5-11. The table is derived from the state diagram of Fig. 5-24 with a straight binary assignment. We choose two *D* flip-flops to represent the four states and label their outputs *A* and *B*. There is one input *x* and one output *y*. The characteristic equation of the *D* flip-flop is $Q(t + 1) = D_Q$, which means that the next-state values in the state table specify the *D* input condition for the flip-flop. The flip-flop input equations can be obtained directly from the next-state columns of *A* and *B* and expressed in sum of minterms as

$$A(t + 1) = D_A(A, B, x) = \Sigma(3, 5, 7)$$
$$B(t + 1) = D_B(A, B, x) = \Sigma(1, 5, 7)$$
$$y(A, B, x) = \Sigma(6, 7)$$

Table 5-11
State Table for Sequence Detector

Present State		Input	Next State		Output
A	B	x	A	B	y
0	0	0	0	0	0
0	0	1	0	1	0
0	1	0	0	0	0
0	1	1	1	0	0
1	0	0	0	0	0
1	0	1	1	1	0
1	1	0	0	0	1
1	1	1	1	1	1

where A and B are the present-state values of flip-flops A and B, x is the input, and D_A and D_B are the input equations. The minterms for output y are obtained from the output column in the state table.

The Boolean equations are simplified by means of the maps plotted in Fig. 5-25. The simplified equations are

$$D_A = Ax + Bx$$
$$D_B = Ax + B'x$$
$$y = AB$$

The logic diagram of the sequential circuit is drawn in Fig. 5-26.

Excitation Tables

The design of a sequential circuit with flip-flops other than the D type is complicated by the fact that the input equations for the circuit must be derived indirectly from the state table. When-D type flip-flops are employed, the input equations are obtained directly from the next

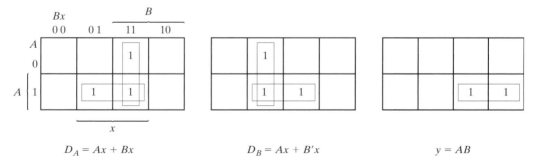

$$D_A = Ax + Bx \qquad\qquad D_B = Ax + B'x \qquad\qquad y = AB$$

FIGURE 5-25
Maps for Sequence Detector

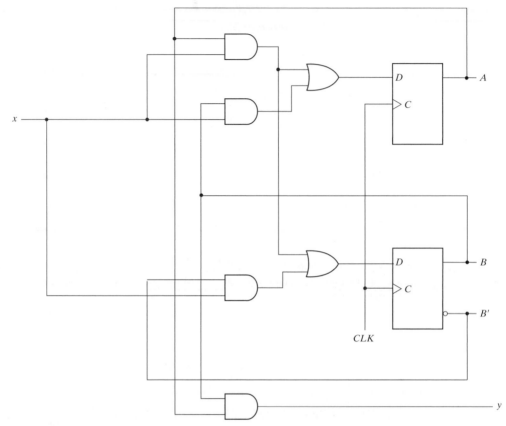

FIGURE 5-26
Logic Diagram of Sequence Detector

state. This is not the case for the JK and T types of flip-flops. In order to determine the input equations for these flip-flops, it is necessary to derive a functional relationship between the state table and the input equations.

The flip-flop characteristic tables presented in Table 5-1 provide the value of the next state when the inputs and present state are known. These tables are useful for the analysis of sequential circuits and for defining the operation of the flip-flops. During the design process we usually know the transition from present state to next state and wish to find the flip-flop input conditions that will cause the required transition. For this reason, we need a table that lists the required inputs for a given change of state. Such a table is called an *excitation table*.

Table 5-12 presents the excitation tables for the two flip-flops. Each table has a column for the present state $Q(t)$, the next state $Q(t + 1)$, and a column for each input to show how the required transition is achieved. There are four possible transitions from present state to next state. The required input conditions for each of the four transitions are derived from the information available in the characteristic table. The symbol X in the tables represents a don't-care condition, which means that it does not matter whether the input is 1 or 0.

The excitation table for the JK flip-flop is shown in part (a). When both present state and next state are 0, the J input must remain at 0 and the K input can be either 0 or 1. Similarly, when

Table 5-12
Flip-Flop Excitation Tables

Q(t)	Q(t + 1)	J	K		Q(t)	Q(t + 1)	T
0	0	0	X		0	0	0
0	1	1	X		0	1	1
1	0	X	1		1	0	1
1	1	X	0		1	1	0

(a) JK (b) T

both present state and next state are 1, the K input must remain at 0, while the J input can be 0 or 1. If the flip-flop is to have a transition from the 0-state to the 1-state, J must be equal to 1, since the J input sets the flip-flop. However, input K may be either 0 or a 1. If $K = 0$, the $J = 1$ condition sets the flip-flop as required; if $K = 1$ and $J = 1$, the flip-flop is complemented and goes from the 0-state to the 1-state as required. Therefore the K input is marked with a don't-care condition for the 0-to-1 transition. For a transition from the 1-state to the 0-state, we must have $K = 1$, since the K input clears the flip-flop. However, the J input may be either 0 or 1, since $J = 0$ has no effect, and $J = 1$ together with $K = 1$ complements the flip-flop with a resultant transition from the 1-state to the 0-state.

The excitation table for the T flip-flop is shown in part (b). From the characteristic table, we find that when input $T = 1$, the state of the flip-flop is complemented; when $T = 0$, the state of the flip-flop remains unchanged. Therefore, when the state of the flip-flop must remain the same, the requirement is that $T = 0$. When the state of the flip-flop has to be complemented, T must equal 1.

Synthesis Using *JK* Flip-Flops

The synthesis procedure for sequential circuits with JK flip-flops is the same as with D flip-flops, except that the input equations must be evaluated from the present-state to next-state transition derived from the excitation table. To illustrate the procedure, we will synthesize the sequential circuit specified by Table 5-13. In addition to having columns for the present state, input, and next state as in a conventional state table, the table also shows the flip-flop input conditions from which the input equations are derived. These flip-flop inputs are derived from the state table in conjunction with the excitation table for the JK flip-flop. For example, in the first row of Table 5-13 we have a transition for flip-flop A from 0 in the present state to 0 in the next state. In Table 5-12 for the JK flip-flop, we find that a transition of states from present state 0 to next state 0 requires that input J be 0 and input K be a don't-care. So 0 and X are entered in the first row under J_A and K_A. Since the first row also shows a transition for flip-flop B from 0 in the present state to 0 in the next state, 0 and X are inserted in the first row under J_B and K_B. The second row of the table shows a transition for flip-flop B from 0 in the present state to 1 in the next state. From the excitation table, we find that a transition from 0 to 1 requires that J be 1 and K be a don't-care, so 1 and X are copied in the second row under J_B and K_B. This process is continued for each row in the table and for each flip-flop, with the input conditions from the excitation table copied into the proper row of the particular flip-flop being considered.

The flip-flop inputs in Table 5-13 specify the truth table for the input equations as a function of present state A and B and input x. The input equations are simplified in the maps of Fig. 5-27. The next-state values are not used during the simplification since the input equations

Table 5-13
State Table and JK Flip-Flop Inputs

Present State		Input	Next State		Flip-Flop Inputs			
A	B	x	A	B	J_A	K_A	J_B	K_B
0	0	0	0	0	0	X	0	X
0	0	1	0	1	0	X	1	X
0	1	0	1	0	1	X	X	1
0	1	1	0	1	0	X	X	0
1	0	0	1	0	X	0	0	X
1	0	1	1	1	X	0	1	X
1	1	0	1	1	X	0	X	0
1	1	1	0	0	X	1	X	1

are a function of the present state and input only. Note the advantage of using JK type flip-flops when designing sequential circuits. The fact that there are so many don't care entries indicates that the combinational circuit for the input equations are likely to be simpler, because don't-care minterms usually help in obtaining simpler expressions. If there are unused states in the state table, there will be additional don't-care conditions in the map.

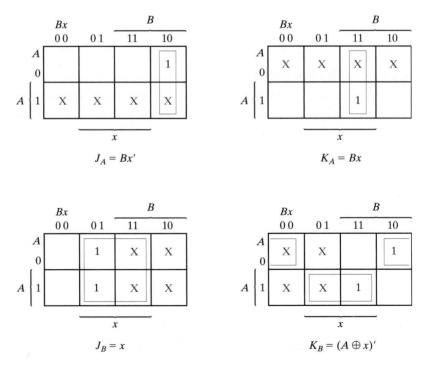

FIGURE 5-27
Maps for J and K Input Equations

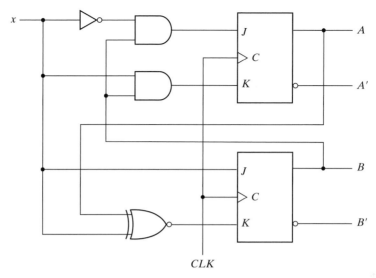

FIGURE 5-28
Logic Diagram for Sequential Circuit with *JK* Flip-Flops

The four input equations for the two JK flip-flops are listed under the maps of Fig. 5-27. The logic diagram of the sequential circuit is drawn in Fig. 5-28.

Synthesis Using *T* Flip-Flops

The synthesis using T flip-flops will be demonstrated by designing a binary counter. An n-bit binary counter consists of n flip-flops that can count in binary from 0 to $2^n - 1$. The state diagram of a 3-bit counter is shown in Fig. 5-29. As seen from the binary states indicated inside the circles, the flip-flop outputs repeat the binary count sequence with a return to 000 after 111. The directed lines between circles are not marked with input and output values as in other state diagrams. Remember that state transitions in clocked sequential circuits occur during a clock edge; the flip-flops remain in their present states if no clock is applied. For this reason, the clock does not appear explicitly as an input variable in a state diagram or state table. From

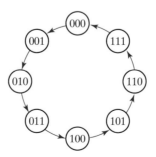

FIGURE 5-29
State Diagram of 3-Bit Binary Counter

Table 5-14
State Table for 3-Bit Counter

Present State			Next State			Flip-Flop Inputs		
A_2	A_1	A_0	A_2	A	A_0	T_{A2}	T_{A1}	T_{A0}
0	0	0	0	0	1	0	0	1
0	0	1	0	1	0	0	1	1
0	1	0	0	1	1	0	0	1
0	1	1	1	0	0	1	1	1
1	0	0	1	0	1	0	0	1
1	0	1	1	1	0	0	1	1
1	1	0	1	1	1	0	1	1
1	1	1	0	0	0	1	1	1

this point of view, the state diagram of a counter does not have to show input and output values along the directed lines. The only input to the circuit is the clock, and the outputs are specified by the present state of the flip-flops. The next state of a counter depends entirely on its present state, and the state transition occurs every time the clock goes through a transition.

Table 5-14 is the state table for the 3-bit binary counter. The three flip-flops are symbolized by A_2, A_1, and A_0. Binary counters are most efficiently constructed with T flip-flops because of their complement property. The flip-flop excitation for the T inputs is derived from the excitation table of the T flip-flop and from inspection of the state transition of the present state to the next state. As an illustration, consider the flip-flop input entries for row 001. The present state here is 001 and the next state is 010, which is the next count in the sequence. Comparing these two counts, we note that A_2 goes from 0 to 0; so T_{A2} is marked with 0 because flip-flop A_2 must not change when a clock occurs. A_1 goes from 0 to 1; so T_{A1} is marked with a 1 because this flip-flop must be complemented in the next clock edge. Similarly, A_0 goes from 1 to 0, indicating that it must be complemented; so T_{A0} is marked with 1. The last row with present state 111 is compared with the first count 000, which is its next state. Going from all 1's to all 0's requires that all three flip-flops be complemented.

The flip-flop input equations are simplified in the maps of Fig. 5-30. Note that T_{A0} has 1's in all eight minterms because the least significant bit of the counter is complemented with

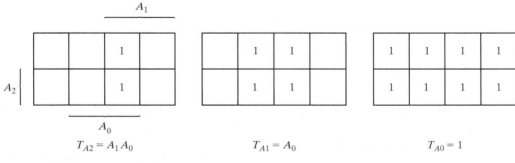

FIGURE 5-30
Maps for 3-Bit Binary Counter

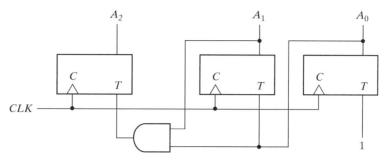

FIGURE 5-31
Logic Diagram of 3-Bit Binary Counter

each count. A Boolean function that includes all minterms defines a constant value of 1. The input equations listed under each map specify the combinational part of the counter. Including these functions with the three flip-flops, we obtain the logic diagram of the counter, as shown in Fig. 5-31.

PROBLEMS

5-1 The D latch of Fig. 5-6 is constructed with four NAND gates and an inverter. Consider the following three other ways for obtaining a D latch. In each case, draw the logic diagram and verify the circuit operation.

(a) Use NOR gates for the SR latch part and AND gates for the other two. An inverter may be needed.

(b) Use NOR gates for all four gates. Inverters may be needed.

(c) Use four NAND gates only (without an inverter). This can be done by connecting the output of the upper gate in Fig. 5-6 (that goes to the SR latch) to the input of the lower gate (instead of the inverter output).

5-2 Construct a JK flip-flop using a D flip-flip, a 2-to-1-line multiplexer and an inverter.

5-3 Show that the characteristic equation for the complement output of a JK flip-flop is

$$Q'(t + 1) = J'Q' + KQ$$

5-4 A PN flip-flop has four operations: clear to 0, no change, complement, and set to 1, when inputs P and N are 00, 01, 10, and 11, respectively.

(a) Tabulate the characteristic table.   (b) Derive the characteristic equation.

(c) Tabulate the excitation table.   (d) Show how the PN flip-flop can be converted to a D flip-flop.

5-5 Explain the differences among a truth table, a state table, a characteristic table, and an excitation table. Also explain the difference among a Boolean equation, a state equation, a characteristic equation, and a flip-flop input equation.

5-6   A sequential circuit with two D flip-flops, A and B; two inputs, x and y; and one output, z, is specified by the following next-state and output equations:

$$A(t + 1) = x'y + xA$$
$$B(t + 1) = x'B + xA$$
$$z = B$$

(a) Draw the logic diagram of the circuit.   (b) List the state table for the sequential circuit.

(c) Draw the corresponding state diagram.

5-7   A sequential circuit has one flip-flop Q, two inputs x and y, and one output S. It consists of a full-adder circuit connected to a D flip-flop, as shown in Fig. P5-7. Derive the state table and state diagram of the sequential circuit.

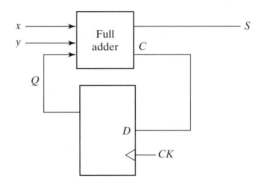

FIGURE P5-7

5-8   Derive the state table and the state diagram of the sequential circuit shown in Fig. P5-8. Explain the function that the circuit performs.

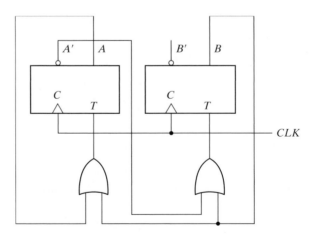

FIGURE P5-8

5-9   A sequential circuit has two JK flip-flops A and B and one input x. The circuit is described by the following flip-flop input equations:

$$J_A = x \qquad K_A = B'$$
$$J_B = x \qquad K_B = A$$

(a) Derive the state equations $A(t + 1)$ and $B(t + 1)$ by substituting the input equations for the J and K variables.

(b) Draw the state diagram of the circuit.

5-10   A sequential circuit has two JK flip-flops A and B, two inputs x and y, and one output z. The flip-flop input equations and circuit output equation are

$$J_A = Bx + B'y' \qquad K_A = B'xy'$$
$$J_B = A'x \qquad K_B = A + xy'$$
$$z = Ax'y' + Bx'y'$$

(a) Draw the logic diagram of the circuit.   (b) Tabulate the state table.

(c) Derive the state equations for A and B.

5-11   Starting from state 00 in the state diagram of Fig. 5-16, determine the state transitions and output sequence that will be generated when an input sequence of 010110111011110 is applied.

5-12   Reduce the number of states in the following state table and tabulate the reduced state table.

Present State	Next State $x = 0$	Next State $x = 1$	Output $x = 0$	Output $x = 1$
a	f	b	0	0
b	d	c	0	0
c	f	e	0	0
d	g	a	1	0
e	d	c	0	0
f	f	b	1	1
g	g	h	0	1
h	g	a	1	0

5-13   Starting from state a, and the input sequence 01110010011, determine the output sequence for

(a) the state table of the previous problem and

(b) the reduced state table from the previous problem. Show that the same output sequence is obtained for both.

5-14 Substitute binary assignment 2 from Table 5-9 to the states in Table 5-8 and obtain the binary state table.

5-15 List a state table for the JK flip-flop using Q as the present and next state and J and K as inputs. Design the sequential circuit specified by the state table and show that it is equivalent to Fig. 5-12(a).

5-16 Design a sequential circuit with two D flip-flops A and B, and one input x. When $x = 0$, the state of the circuit remains the same. When $x = 1$, the circuit goes through the state transitions from 00 to 01 to 11 to 10 back to 00, and repeats.

5-17 Design a one input, one output serial 2's complementer. The circuit accepts a string of bits from the input and generates the 2's complement at the output. The circuit can be reset asynchronously to start and end the operation.

5-18 Design a sequential circuit with two JK flip-flops A and B and two inputs E and x. If $E = 0$, the circuit remains in the same state regardless of the value of x. When $E = 1$ and $x = 1$, the circuit goes through the state transitions from 00 to 01 to 10 to 11 back to 00, and repeats. When $E = 1$ and $x = 0$, the circuit goes through the state transitions from 00 to 11 to 10 to 01 back to 00, and repeats.

5-19 A sequential circuit has three flip-flops A, B, C; one input x; and one output y. The state diagram is shown in Fig. P5-19. The circuit is to be designed by treating the unused states as don't-care conditions. Analyze the circuit obtained from the design to determine the effect of the unused states.

(a) Use D flip-flops in the design.   (b) Use JK flip-flops in the design.

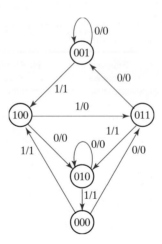

FIGURE P5-19

5-20 Design the sequential circuit specified by the state diagram of Fig. 5-19 using T flip-flops.

5-21 What is the main difference between an initial statement and an always statement in Verilog HDL?

5-22 Draw the waveform generated by the initial statement

```
initial
  begin
  w = 0;   #20 w = 1;   # 50 w = 0;   # 30 w = 1;   #10 w = 0;
  end
```

5-23 Consider the following statements assuming that RegA contains the value of 30 initially.

(a) RegA = 125   (b) RegA <= 125
    RegB = RegA   RegB <= RegA

What are the values of RegA and RegB after execution?

5-24 Write an HDL behavioral description of a D flip-flop with asynchronous preset and clear (This type of flip-flop is shown in Fig. 11-13).

5-25 A special positive-edge-triggered flip-flop has two inputs $D1$ and $D2$ and a control input that chooses between the two. Write an HDL behavioral description of this flip-flop.

5-26 Write an HDL behavioral description of the JK flip-flop using an if-else statement based on the value of the present state. (*Hint:* Consider the characteristic equation when $Q = 0$ or $Q = 1$.)

5-27 Rewrite the description of HDL Example 5-5 by combining the state transitions and output into one **always** block.

5-28 Simulate the sequential circuit shown in Fig. 5-17.

(a) Write the HDL description of the state diagram.

(b) Write the HDL description of the circuit diagram.

(c) Write an HDL stimulus with a sequence of inputs: 00, 01, 11, 10. Verify that the response is the same for both descriptions.

5-29 Write the HDL description of the 2-bit binary counter shown in Fig. 5-20. Use the stimulus module from HDL Example 5-7 and verify that your output response is the same as the waveforms shown in Fig. 5-21.

5-30 Draw the logic diagram for the sequential circuit described by the following HDL module:

```
module Seqcrt (A,B,C,Q,CLK);
   input A,B,C,CLK;
   output Q;
   reg Q,E;
   always @ (posedge CLK)
     begin
     E <= A & B;
     Q <= E | C;
       end
endmodule
```

What changes, if any, must be included in the circuit if the last two statements use blocking instead of non-blocking assignment?

REFERENCES

1. HAYES, J. P. 1993. *Introduction to Digital Logic Design.* Reading, MA: Addison-Wesley.

2. WAKERLY, J. F. 2000. *Digital Design: Principles and Practices,* 3rd ed. Upper Saddle River, NJ: Prentice Hall.

3. KATZ, R. H. 1994. *Contemporary Logic Design.* Upper Saddle River, NJ: Prentice Hall.

4. MANO, M. M. and C. R. KIME. 2000. *Logic and Computer Design Fundamentals,* 2nd ed. Upper Saddle River, NJ: Prentice Hall.

5. NELSON V. P., H. T. NAGLE, J. D. IRWIN, and B. D. CARROLL. 1995. *Digital Logic Circuit Analysis and Design.* Upper Saddle River, NJ: Prentice Hall.

6. DIETMEYER, D. L. 1988. *Logic Design of Digital Systems,* 3rd ed. Boston: Allyn Bacon.

7. GAJSKI, D. D. 1997. *Principles of Digital Design.* Upper Saddle River, NJ: Prentice Hall.

8. ROTH, C. H. 1992. *Fundamentals of Logic Design,* 4th ed. St. Paul: West.

9. BHASKER, J. 1997. *A Verilog HDL Primer.* Allentown, PA: Star Galaxy Press.

10. BHASKER, J. 1998. *VeriLog HDL Synthesis.* Allentown, PA: Star Galaxy Press.

11. CILETTI, M. D. 1999. *Modeling, Synthesis, and Rapid Prototyping with VeriLog HDL.* Upper Saddle River, NJ: Prentice Hall.

12. PALNITKAR, S. 1996. *VeriLog HDL: A Guide to Digital Design and Synthesis.* SunSoft Press (A Prentice Hall Title).

13. THOMAS, D. E., and P. R. MOORBY 1998. *The VeriLog Hardware Description Language* 4th ed. Boston: Kluwer Academic Publishers.

6

Registers and Counters

6-1 REGISTERS

A clocked sequential circuit consists of a group of flip-flops and combinational gates connected to form a feedback path. The flip-flops are essential because in their absence, the circuit reduces to a purely combinational circuit (provided there is no feedback among the gates). A circuit with flip-flops is considered a sequential circuit even in the absence of combinational gates. Circuits that include flip-flops are usually classified by the function they perform rather than by the name of the sequential circuit. Two such circuits are registers and counters.

A register is a group of flip-flops. Each flip–flop is capable of storing one bit of information. An n-bit register consists of a group of n flip-flops capable of storing n bits of binary information. In addition to the flip-flops, a register may have combinational gates that perform certain data processing tasks. In its broadest definition, a register consists of a group of flip-flops and gates that effect their transition. The flip-flops hold the binary information and the gates determine how the information is transferred into the register.

A counter is essentially a register that goes through a predetermined sequence of states. The gates in the counter are connected in such a way as to produce the prescribed sequence of binary states. Although counters are a special type of register, it is common to differentiate them by giving them a different name.

Various types of registers are available commercially. The simplest register is one that consists of only flip-flops without any gates. Fig. 6-1 shows such a register constructed with four D-type flip-flops. The common clock input triggers all flip-flops on the positive edge of each pulse and the binary data available at the four inputs are transferred into the 4-bit register. The four outputs can be sampled at any time to obtain the binary information stored in the register. The clear input goes to the R (reset) input of all four flip-flops. When this input goes to 0, all

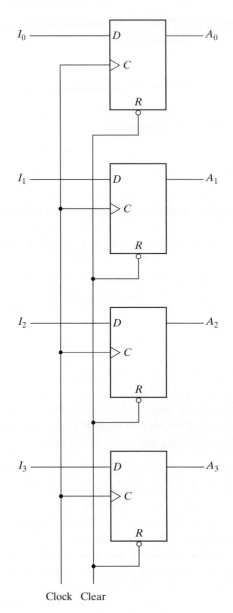

FIGURE 6-1
4-Bit Register

flip-flops are reset asynchronously. The clear input is useful for clearing the register to all 0's prior to its clocked operation. The R inputs must be maintained at logic 1 during normal clocked operation. Note that either *clear* or *reset* can be used to indicate the transfer of the register to an all 0's state.

Register with Parallel Load

Synchronous digital systems have a master clock generator that supplies a continuous train of clock pulses. The clock pulses are applied to all flip-flops and registers in the system. The master clock acts like a pump that supplies a constant beat to all parts of the system. A separate control signal must be used to decide which specific clock pulse will have an effect on a particular register. The transfer of new information into a register is referred to as *loading* the register. If all the bits of the register are loaded simultaneously with a common clock pulse, we say that the loading is done in parallel. A clock edge applied to the C inputs of the register of Fig. 6-1 will load all four inputs in parallel. In this configuration, the clock must be inhibited from the circuit if the content of the register must be left unchanged. The clock can be inhibited from reaching the register by controlling the clock input signal with an enabling gate. However, inserting gates in the clock path means that logic is performed with clock pulses. The insertion of logic gates produces uneven propagation delays between the master clock and the inputs of flip-flops. To fully synchronize the system, we must ensure that all clock pulses arrive at the same time anywhere in the system so that all flip-flops trigger simultaneously. Performing logic with clock pulses inserts variable delays and may cause the system to go out of synchronism. For this reason, it is advisable to control the operation of the register with the D inputs rather than controlling the clock in the C inputs of the flip-flops.

A 4-bit register with a load control input that is directed through gates and into the D inputs of the flip-flops is shown in Fig. 6-2. The load input to the register determines the action to be taken with each clock pulse. When the load input is 1, the data in the four inputs are transferred into the register with the next positive edge of the clock. When the load input is 0, the outputs of the flip-flops are connected to their respective inputs. The feedback connection from output to input is necessary because the D flip-flop does not have a "no change" condition. With each clock edge, the D input determines the next state of the register. To leave the output unchanged, it is necessary to make the D input equal to the present value of the output.

The clock pulses are applied to the C inputs at all times. The load input determines whether the next pulse will accept new information or leave the information in the register intact. The transfer of information from the data inputs or the outputs of the register is done simultaneously with all four bits in response to a clock edge.

6-2   SHIFT REGISTERS

A register capable of shifting its binary information in one or both directions is called a *shift register*. The logical configuration of a shift register consists of a chain of flip-flops in cascade, with the output of one flip-flop connected to the input of the next flip-flop. All flip-flops receive common clock pulses, which activate the shift from one stage to the next.

The simplest possible shift register is one that uses only flip-flops, as shown in Fig. 6-3. The output of a given flip-flop is connected to the D input of the flip-flop at its right. Each clock pulse shifts the contents of the register one bit position to the right. The *serial input* determines what goes into the leftmost flip-flop during the shift. The *serial output* is taken from the output of the rightmost flip-flop. Sometimes it is necessary to control the shift so that it occurs only with certain pulses, but not with others. This can be done by inhibiting the clock from the input

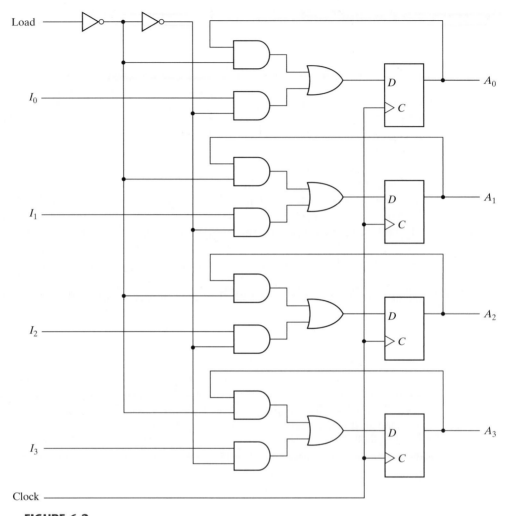

FIGURE 6-2
4-Bit Register with Parallel Load

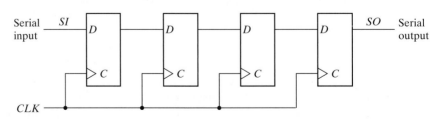

FIGURE 6-3
4-Bit Shift Register

of the register to prevent it from shifting. It will be shown later that the shift operation can be controlled through the D inputs of the flip-flops rather than through the clock input. If however the shift register of Fig. 6-3 is used, the shift can be controlled by connecting the clock through an AND gate with an input that controls the shift.

Serial Transfer

A digital system is said to operate in a serial mode when information is transferred and manipulated one bit at a time. Information is transferred one bit at a time by shifting the bits out of the source register into the destination register. This in contrast to parallel transfer where all the bits of the register are transferred at the same time.

The serial transfer of information from register A to register B is done with shift registers, as shown in the block diagram of Fig. 6-4(a). The serial output (SO) of register A is connected to the serial input (SI) of register B. To prevent the loss of information stored in the source register, the information in register A is made to circulate by connecting the serial output to its serial input. The initial content of register B is shifted out through its serial output and is lost unless it is transferred to a third shift register. The shift control input determines when and how many times the registers are shifted. This is done with an AND gate that allows clock pulses to pass into the CLK terminals only when the shift control is active.

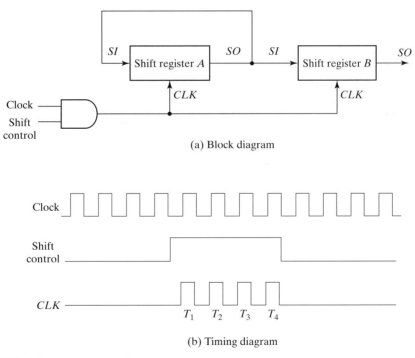

(a) Block diagram

(b) Timing diagram

FIGURE 6-4
Serial Transfer from Register A to register B

Table 6-1
Serial-Transfer Example

Timing Pulse	Shift Register A	Shift Register B
Initial value	1 0 1 1	0 0 1 0
After T_1	1 1 0 1	1 0 0 1
After T_2	1 1 1 0	1 1 0 0
After T_3	0 1 1 1	0 1 1 0
After T_4	1 0 1 1	1 0 1 1

Suppose the shift registers have four bits each. The control unit that supervises the transfer must be designed in such a way that it enables the shift registers, through the shift control signal, for a fixed time of four clock pulses. This is shown in the timing diagram of Fig. 6-4(b). The shift control signal is synchronized with the clock and changes value just after the negative edge of the clock. The next four clock pulses find the shift control signal in the active state, so that the output of the AND gate connected to the *CLK* inputs produces four pulses, T_1, T_2, T_3, and T_4. Each rising edge of the pulse causes a shift in both registers. The fourth pulse changes the shift control to 0 and the shift registers are disabled.

Assume that the binary content of A before the shift is 1011 and that of B is 0010. The serial transfer from A to B occurs in four steps, as shown in Table 6-1. With the first pulse T_1, the rightmost bit of A is shifted into the leftmost bit of B and is also circulated into the leftmost position of A. At the same time, all bits of A and B are shifted one position to the right. The previous serial output from B in the rightmost position is lost and its value changes from 0 to 1. The next three pulses perform identical operations, shifting the bits of A into B, one at a time. After the fourth shift, the shift control goes to 0 and both registers A and B have the value 1011. Thus, the content of A is transferred into B, while the content of A remains unchanged.

The difference between serial and parallel modes of operation should be apparent from this example. In the parallel mode, information is available from all bits of a register and all bits can be transferred simultaneously during one clock pulse. In the serial mode, the registers have a single serial input and a single serial output. The information is transferred one bit at a time while the registers are shifted in the same direction.

Serial Addition

Operations in digital computers are usually done in parallel because this is a faster mode of operation. Serial operations are slower, but have the advantage of requiring less equipment. To demonstrate the serial mode of operation, we present here the design of a serial adder. The parallel counterpart was presented in Section 4-4.

The two binary numbers to be added serially are stored in two shift registers. Bits are added one pair at a time through a single full adder (FA) circuit, as shown in Fig. 6-5. The carry out of the full adder is transferred to a D flip-flop. The output of this flip-flop is then used as the carry input for the next pair of significant bits. The sum bit from the S output of the full adder could be transferred into a third shift register. By shifting the sum into A while the bits of A are shifted out, it is possible to use one register for storing both the augend and the sum bits. The

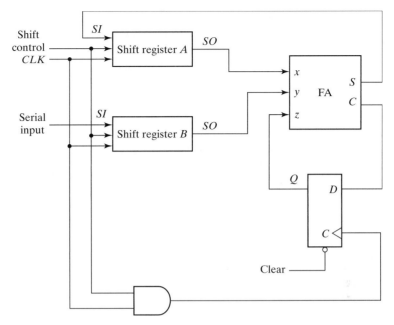

FIGURE 6-5
Serial Adder

serial input of register *B* can be used to transfer a new binary number while the addend bits are shifted out during the addition.

The operation of the serial adder is as follows. Initially register *A* holds the augend, register *B* holds the addend, and the carry flip-flop is cleared to 0. The outputs (*SO*) of *A* and *B* provide a pair of significant bits for the full adder at *x* and *y*. Output *Q* of the flip-flop provides the input carry at *z*. The shift control enables both registers and the carry flip-flop, so at the next clock pulse, both registers are shifted once to the right, the sum bit from *S* enters the leftmost flip-flop of *A*, and the output carry is transferred into flip-flop *Q*. The shift control enables the registers for a number of clock pulses equal to the number of bits in the registers. For each succeeding clock pulse, a new sum bit is transferred to *A*, a new carry is transferred to *Q*, and both registers are shifted once to the right. This process continues until the shift control is disabled. Thus, the addition is accomplished by passing each pair of bits together with the previous carry through a single full adder circuit and transferring the sum, one bit at a time, into register *A*.

Initially, register *A* and the carry flip-flop are cleared to 0 and then the first number is added from *B*. While *B* is shifted through the full adder, a second number is transferred to it through its serial input. The second number is then added to the content of register *A* while a third number is transferred serially into register *B*. This can be repeated to form the addition of two, three, or more numbers and accumulate their sum in register *A*.

Comparing the serial adder with the parallel adder described in Section 4-4, we note several differences. The parallel adder uses registers with parallel load, whereas the serial adder uses shift registers. The number of full adder circuits in the parallel adder is equal to the number of bits in the binary numbers, whereas the serial adder requires only one full adder circuit and a carry flip-flop. Excluding the registers, the parallel adder is a combinational circuit, whereas the serial adder is a sequential circuit. The sequential circuit in the serial adder consists of a full adder and a flip-flop that stores the output carry. This is typical in serial operations because the result of a bit-time operation may depend not only on the present inputs, but also on previous inputs that must be stored in flip-flops.

To show that serial operations can be designed by means of sequential circuit procedure, we will redesign the serial adder using a state table. First, we assume that two shift registers are available to store the binary numbers to be added serially. The serial outputs from the registers are designated by x and y. The sequential circuit to be designed will not include the shift registers, but they will be inserted later to show the complete circuit. The sequential circuit proper has the two inputs, x and y, that provide a pair of significant bits, an output S that generates the sum bit, and flip-flop Q for storing the carry. The state table that specifies the sequential circuit is listed in Table 6-2. The present state of Q is the present value of the carry. The present carry in Q is added together with inputs x and y to produce the sum bit in output S. The next state of Q is equal to the output carry. Note that the state table entries are identical to the entries in a full adder truth table, except that the input carry is now the present state of Q and the output carry is now the next state of Q.

If a D flip-flop is used for Q, the circuit reduces to the one shown in Fig. 6-5. If a JK flip-flop is used for Q, it is necessary to determine the values of inputs J and K by referring to the excitation table (Table 5-12). This is done in the last two columns of Table 6-2. The two flip-flop input equations and the output equation can be simplified by means of maps to obtain

$$J_Q = xy$$
$$K_Q = x'y' = (x + y)'$$
$$S = x \oplus y \oplus Q$$

Table 6-2
State Table for Serial Adder

Present State	Inputs		Next State	Output	Flip-Flop Inputs	
Q	X	y	Q	S	J_Q	K_Q
0	0	0	0	0	0	X
0	0	1	0	1	0	X
0	1	0	0	1	0	X
0	1	1	1	0	1	X
1	0	0	0	1	X	1
1	0	1	1	0	X	0
1	1	0	1	0	X	0
1	1	1	1	1	X	0

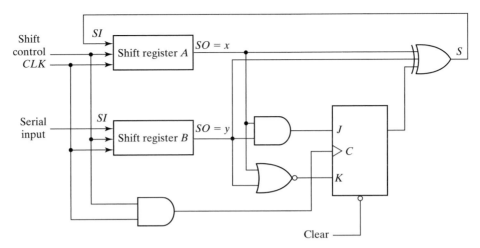

FIGURE 6-6
Second form of Serial Adder

The circuit diagram is shown in Fig. 6-6. The circuit consists of three gates and a *JK* flip-flop. The two shift registers are included in the diagram to show the complete serial adder. Note that output *S* is a function not only of *x* and *y*, but also of the present state of *Q*. The next state of *Q* is a function of the present state of *Q* and the values of *x* and *y* that come out of the serial outputs of the shift registers.

Universal Shift Register

If the flip-flop outputs of a shift register are accessible, then information entered serially by shifting can be taken out in parallel from the outputs of the flip-flops. If a parallel load capability is added to a shift register, then data entered in parallel can be taken out in serial fashion by shifting the data stored in the register.

Some shift registers provide the necessary input and output terminals for parallel transfer. They may also have both shift right and shift left capabilities. The most general shift register has the following capabilities:

1. A *clear* control to clear the register to 0.
2. A *clock* input to synchronize the operations.
3. A *shift-right* control to enable the shift right operation and the *serial input* and *output* lines associated with the shift right.
4. A *shift-left* control to enable the shift left operation and the *serial input* and *output* lines associated with the shift left.
5. A *parallel-load* control to enable a parallel transfer and the *n* input lines associated with the parallel transfer.
6. *n* parallel output lines.
7. A control state that leaves the information in the register unchanged in the presence of the clock.

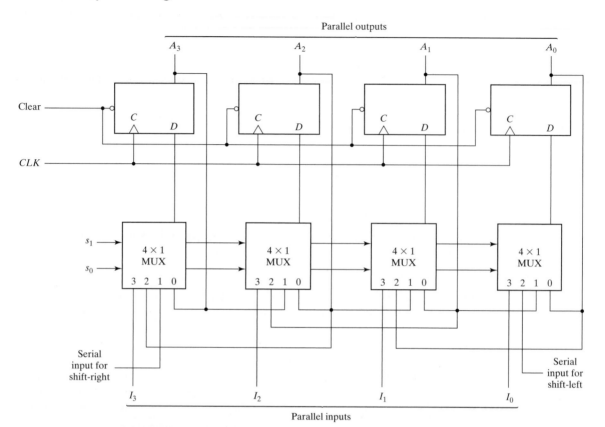

FIGURE 6-7
4-Bit Universal Shift Register

Other shift registers may have only some of the preceding functions, with at least one shift operation.

A register capable of shifting in one direction only is a unidirectional shift register. One that can shift in both directions is a bidirectional shift register. If the register has both shifts and parallel load capabilities, it is referred to as a *universal shift register.*

The diagram of a 4-bit universal shift register that has all the capabilities listed above is shown in Fig. 6-7. It consists of four D flip-flops and four multiplexers. The four multiplexers have two common selection inputs s_1 and s_0. Input 0 in each multiplexer is selected when $s_1 s_0 = 00$, input 1 is selected when $s_1 s_0 = 01$, and similarly for the other two inputs. The selection inputs control the mode of operation of the register according to the function entries in Table 6-3. When $s_1 s_0 = 00$, the present value of the register is applied to the D inputs of the flip-flops. This condition forms a path from the output of each flip-flop into the input of the same flip-flop. The next clock edge transfers into each flip-flop the binary value it held previously, and no change of state occurs. When $s_1 s_0 = 01$, terminal 1 of the multi-

Table 6-3
Function Table for the Register of Fig. 6-7

Mode Control		Register Operation
s_1	s_0	
0	0	No change
0	1	Shift right
1	0	Shift left
1	1	Parallel load

plexer inputs has a path to the D inputs of the flip-flops. This causes a shift-right operation, with the serial input transferred into flip-flop A_4. When $s_1 s_0 = 10$, a shift-left operation results, with the other serial input going into flip-flop A_1. Finally, when $s_1 s_0 = 11$, the binary information on the parallel input lines is transferred into the register simultaneously during the next clock edge.

Shift registers are often used to interface digital systems situated remotely from each other. For example, suppose it is necessary to transmit an n-bit quantity between two points. If the distance is far, it will be expensive to use n lines to transmit the n bits in parallel. It is more economical to use a single line and transmit the information serially, one bit at a time. The transmitter accepts the n-bit data in parallel into a shift register and then transmits the data serially along the common line. The receiver accepts the data serially into a shift register. When all n bits are received, they can be taken from the outputs of the register in parallel. Thus the transmitter performs a parallel-to-serial conversion of data and the receiver does a serial-to-parallel conversion.

6-3   RIPPLE COUNTERS

A register that goes through a prescribed sequence of states upon the application of input pulses is called a counter. The input pulses may be clock pulses or they may originate from some external source and may occur at a fixed interval of time or at random. The sequence of states may follow the binary number sequence or any other sequence of states. A counter that follows the binary number sequence is called a binary counter. An n-bit binary counter consists of n flip-flops and can count in binary from 0 through $2^n - 1$.

Counters are available in two categories: ripple counters and synchronous counters. In a ripple counter, the flip-flop output transition serves as a source for triggering other flip-flops. In other words, the C input of some or all flip-flops are triggered not by the common clock pulses, but rather by the transition that occurs in other flip-flop outputs. In a synchronous counter, the C inputs of all flip-flops receive the common clock. Synchronous counters are presented in the next two sections. Here we present the binary and BCD ripple counters and explain their operation.

Binary Ripple Counter

A binary ripple counter consists of a series connection of complementing flip-flops, with the output of each flip-flop connected to the C input of the next higher-order flip-flop. The flip-flop holding the least significant bit receives the incoming count pulses. A complementing flip-flop can be obtained from a JK flip-flop with the J and K inputs tied together or from a T flip-flop. A third possibility is to use a D flip-flop with the complement output connected to the D input. In this way, the D input is always the complement of the present state and the next clock pulse will cause the flip-flop to complement. The logic diagram of two 4-bit binary ripple counters is shown in Fig. 6-8. The counter is constructed with complementing flip-flops of the T type in part (a) and D type in part (b). The output of each flip-flop is connected to the C input of the next flip-flop in sequence. The flip-flop holding the least significant bit receives the incoming count pulses. The T inputs of all the flip-flops in (a) are connected to a permanent logic-1. This makes each flip-flop complement if the signal in its C input goes through a negative transition. The bubble in front of the dynamic indicator symbol next to C indicates that the flip-flops respond to the negative-edge transition of the input. The negative transition occurs when the output of the previous flip-flop to which C is connected goes from 1 to 0.

To understand the operation of the 4-bit binary ripple counter, refer to the first nine binary numbers listed in Table 6-4. The count starts with binary 0 and increments by one with each count pulse input. After the count of 15, the counter goes back to 0 to repeat the count. The least significant bit A_0 is complemented with each count pulse input. Every time that A_0 goes from 1 to 0, it complements A_1. Every time that A_1 goes from 1 to 0, it complements A_2. Every time that A_2 goes from 1 to 0, it complements A_3, and so on for any other higher order bits of a ripple counter. For example, consider the transition from count 0011 to 0100. A_0 is complemented with the count pulse. Since A_0 goes from 1 to 0, it triggers A_1 and complements it. As a result, A_1 goes from 1 to 0, which in turn complements A_2, changing it from 0 to 1. A_2 does not trigger A_3 because A_2 produces a positive transition and the flip-flop responds only to negative transitions. Thus, the count from 0011 to 0100 is achieved by changing the bits one at a time, so the count goes from 0011 to 0010, then to 0000, and finally to 0100. The flip-flops change one at a time in succession and the signal propagates through the counter in a ripple fashion from one stage to the next.

A binary counter with a reverse count is called a binary count-down counter. In a downward counter, the binary count is decremented by 1 with every input count pulse. The count of a 4-bit count-down counter starts from binary 15 and continues to binary counts 14, 13, 12, ..., 0 and then back to 15. A list of the count sequence of a binary count-down counter shows that the least significant bit is complemented with every count pulse. Any other bit in the sequence is complemented if its previous least significant bit goes from 0 to 1. Therefore, the diagram of a binary count-down counter looks the same as in Fig. 6-8, provided all flip-flops trigger on the positive edge of the clock. (The bubble in the C inputs must be absent.) If negative-edge-triggered flip-flops are used, then the C input of each flip-flop must be connected to the complement output of the previous flip-flop. Then when the true output goes from 0 to 1, the complement will go from 1 to 0 and complement the next flip-flop as required.

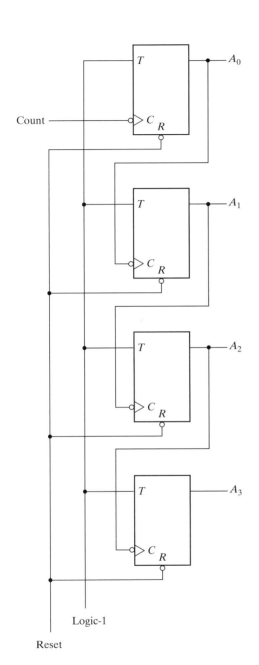

(a) With T flip-flops

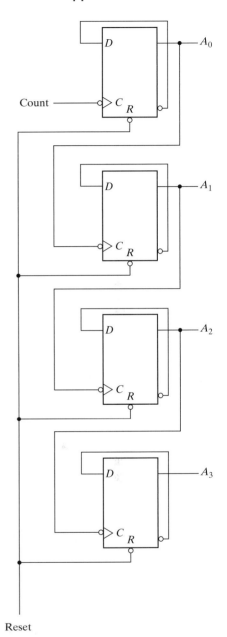

(b) With D flip-flops

FIGURE 6-8
4-Bit Binary Ripple Counter

Table 6-4
Binary Count Sequence

A_3	A_2	A_1	A_0
0	0	0	0
0	0	0	1
0	0	1	0
0	0	1	1
0	1	0	0
0	1	0	1
0	1	1	0
0	1	1	1
1	0	0	0

BCD Ripple Counter

A decimal counter follows a sequence of ten states and returns to 0 after the count of 9. Such a counter must have at least four flip-flops to represent each decimal digit, since a decimal digit is represented by a binary code with at least four bits. The sequence of states in a decimal counter is dictated by the binary code used to represent a decimal digit. If BCD is used, the sequence of states is as shown in the state diagram of Fig. 6-9. This is similar to a binary counter, except that the state after 1001 (code for decimal digit 9) is 0000 (code for decimal digit 0).

The logic diagram of a BCD ripple counter using JK flip-flops is shown in Fig. 6-10. The four outputs are designated by the letter symbol Q with a numeric subscript equal to the binary weight of the corresponding bit in the BCD code. Note that the output of Q_1 is applied to the C inputs of both Q_2 and Q_8 and the output of Q_2 is applied to the C input of Q_4. The J and K inputs are connected either to a permanent 1 signal or to outputs of other flip-flops.

A ripple counter is an asynchronous sequential circuit. Signals that affect the flip-flop transition depend on the way they change from 1 to 0. The operation of the counter can be explained by a list of conditions for flip-flop transitions. These conditions are derived from the logic diagram and from knowledge of how a JK flip-flop operates. Remember that when the C input

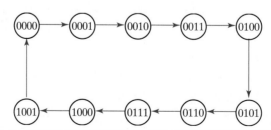

FIGURE 6-9
State Diagram of a Decimal BCD-Counter

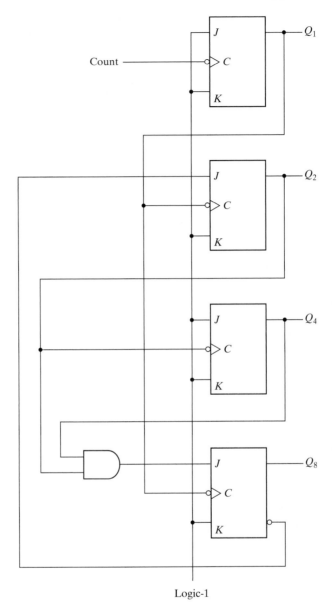

FIGURE 6-10
BCD Ripple Counter

goes from 1 to 0, the flip-flop is set if $J = 1$, is cleared if $K = 1$, is complemented if $J = K = 1$, and is left unchanged if $J = K = 0$.

To verify that these conditions result in the sequence required by a BCD ripple counter, it is necessary to verify that the flip-flop transitions indeed follow a sequence of states as specified by

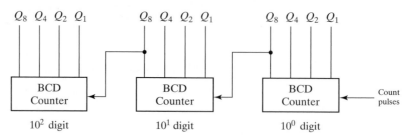

FIGURE 6-11
Block Diagram of a Three-Decade Decimal BCD Counter

the state diagram of Fig. 6-9. Q_1 changes state after each clock pulse. Q_2 complements every time Q_1 goes from 1 to 0 as long as $Q_8 = 0$. When Q_8 becomes 1, Q_2 remains at 0. Q_4 complements every time Q_2 goes from 1 to 0. Q_8 remains at 0 as long as Q_2 or Q_4 is 0. When both Q_2 and Q_4 become 1, Q_8 complements when Q_1 goes from 1 to 0. Q_8 is cleared on the next transition of Q_1.

The BCD counter of Fig. 6-10 is a *decade* counter, since it counts from 0 to 9. To count in decimal from 0 to 99, we need a two-decade counter. To count from 0 to 999, we need a three-decade counter. Multiple decade counters can be constructed by connecting BCD counters in cascade, one for each decade. A three-decade counter is shown in Fig. 6-11. The inputs to the second and third decades come from Q_8 of the previous decade. When Q_8 in one decade goes from 1 to 0, it triggers the count for the next higher-order decade while its own decade goes from 9 to 0.

6-4   SYNCHRONOUS COUNTERS

Synchronous counters are different from ripple counters in that clock pulses are applied to the inputs of all flip-flops. A common clock triggers all flip-flops simultaneously rather than one at a time in succession as in a ripple counter. The decision whether a flip-flop is to be complemented or not is determined from the values of the data inputs such as T or J and K at the time of the clock edge. If $T = 0$ or $J = K = 0$, the flip-flop does not change state. If $T = 1$ or $J = K = 1$, the flip-flop complements.

The design procedure for synchronous counters was presented in Section 5-7 and the design of a 3-bit binary counter was carried out in conjunction with Fig. 5-31. In this section, we present some typical synchronous counters and explain their operation.

Binary Counter

The design of a synchronous binary counter is so simple that there is no need to go through a sequential logic design process. In a synchronous binary counter, the flip-flop in the least significant position is complemented with every pulse. A flip-flop in any other position is complemented when all the bits in the lower significant positions are equal to 1. For example, if the present state of a 4-bit counter is $A_3A_2A_1A_0 = 0011$, the next count is 0100. A_0 is always complemented. A_1 is complemented because the present state of $A_0 = 1$. A_2 is complemented because the present state of $A_1A_0 = 11$. However, A_3 is not complemented because the present state of $A_2A_1A_0 = 011$, which does not give an all-1's condition.

Synchronous binary counters have a regular pattern and can be constructed with complementing flip-flops and gates. The regular pattern can be seen from the 4-bit counter depicted in Fig. 6-12. The C inputs of all flip-flops are connected to a common clock. The counter is enabled with the count enable input. If the enable input is 0, all J and K inputs are equal to 0

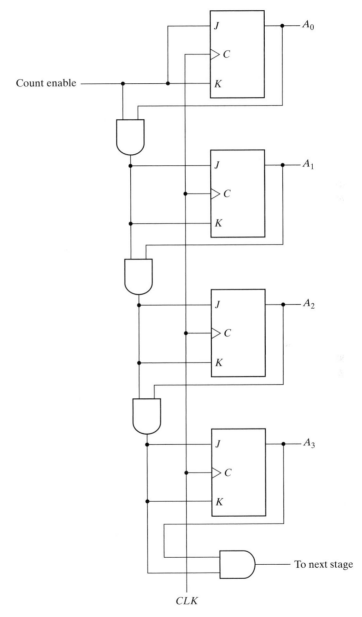

FIGURE 6-12
4-Bit Synchronous Binary Counter

and the clock does not change the state of the counter. The first stage A_0 has its J and K equal to 1 if the counter is enabled. The other J and K inputs are equal to 1 if all previous least significant stages are equal to 1 and the count is enabled. The chain of AND gates generates the required logic for the J and K inputs in each stage. The counter can be extended to any number of stages, with each stage having an additional flip-flop and an AND gate that gives an output of 1 if all previous flip-flop outputs are 1.

Note that the flip-flops trigger on the positive edge of the clock. The polarity of the clock is not essential here as is with the ripple counter. The synchronous counter can be triggered with either the positive or the negative clock edge. The complementing flip-flops in a binary counter can be either of the JK-type or the T-type or the D-type with XOR gates. The equivalency of the three types is indicated in Fig. 5-13.

Up-Down Binary Counter

A synchronous count down binary counter goes through the binary states in reverse order from 1111 down to 0000 and back to 1111 to repeat the count. It is possible to design a count-down counter in the usual manner, but the result is predictable from inspection of the downward binary count. The bit in the least significant position is complemented with each pulse. A bit in any other position is complemented if all lower significant bits are equal to 0. For example, the next state after the present state of 0100 is 0011. The least significant bit is always complemented. The second significant bit is complemented because the first bit is 0. The third significant bit is complemented because the first two bits are equal to 0. But the fourth bit does not change because not all lower significant bits are equal to 0.

A count-down binary counter can be constructed as shown in Fig. 6-12, except that the inputs to the AND gates must come from the complement outputs instead of the normal outputs of the previous flip-flops. The two operations can be combined in one circuit to form a counter capable of counting either up or down. The circuit of an up-down binary counter using T flip-flops is shown in Fig. 6-13. It has an up control input and a down control input. When the up input is 1, the circuit counts up, since the T inputs receive their signals from the values of the previous normal outputs of the flip-flops. When the down input is 1 and the up input is 0, the circuit counts down, since the complemented outputs of the previous flip-flops are applied to the T inputs. When the up and down inputs are both 0, the circuit does not change state and remains in the same count. When the up and down inputs are both 1, the circuit counts up. This ensures that only one operation is performed at any given time.

BCD Counter

A BCD counter counts in binary-coded decimal from 0000 to 1001 and back to 0000. Because of the return to 0 after a count of 9, a BCD counter does not have a regular pattern as in a straight binary count. To derive the circuit of a BCD synchronous counter, it is necessary to go through a sequential circuit design procedure.

The state table of a BCD counter is listed in Table 6-5. The flip-flop input conditions for the T flip-flops are obtained from the present and next state conditions. An output y is also shown in the table. This output is equal to 1 when the present state is 1001. In this way, y can enable

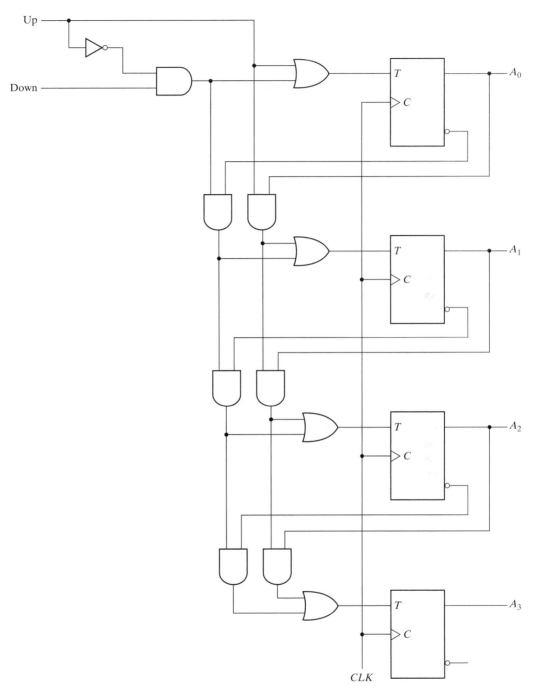

FIGURE 6-13
4-Bit Up-Down Binary Counter

Table 6-5
State Table for BCD Counter

Present State				Next State				Output	Flip-Flop Inputs			
Q_8	Q_4	Q_2	Q_1	Q_8	Q_4	Q_2	Q_1	y	TQ_8	TQ_4	TQ_2	TQ_1
0	0	0	0	0	0	0	1	0	0	0	0	1
0	0	0	1	0	0	1	0	0	0	0	1	1
0	0	1	0	0	0	1	1	0	0	0	0	1
0	0	1	1	0	1	0	0	0	0	1	1	1
0	1	0	0	0	1	0	1	0	0	0	0	1
0	1	0	1	0	1	1	0	0	0	0	1	1
0	1	1	0	0	1	1	1	0	0	0	0	1
0	1	1	1	1	0	0	0	0	1	1	1	1
1	0	0	0	1	0	0	1	0	0	0	0	1
1	0	0	1	0	0	0	0	1	1	0	0	1

the count of the next-higher significant decade while the same pulse switches the present decade from 1001 to 0000.

The flip-flop input equations can be simplified by means of maps. The unused states for minterms 10 to 15 are taken as don't-care terms. The simplified functions are

$$T_{Q1} = 1$$
$$T_{Q2} = Q_8'Q_1$$
$$T_{Q4} = Q_2Q_1$$
$$T_{Q8} = Q_8Q_1 + Q_4Q_2Q_1$$
$$y = Q_8Q_1$$

The circuit can be easily drawn with four T flip-flops, five AND gates, and one OR gate. Synchronous BCD counters can be cascaded to form a counter for decimal numbers of any length. The cascading is done as in Fig. 6-11, except that output y must be connected to the count input of the next-higher significant decade.

Binary Counter with Parallel Load

Counters employed in digital systems quite often require a parallel load capability for transferring an initial binary number into the counter prior to the count operation. Fig. 6-14 shows the logic diagram of a 4-bit register that has a parallel load capability and can operate as a counter. The input load control when equal to 1 disables the count operation and causes a transfer of data from the four data inputs into the four flip-flops. If both control inputs are 0, clock pulses do not change the state of the register.

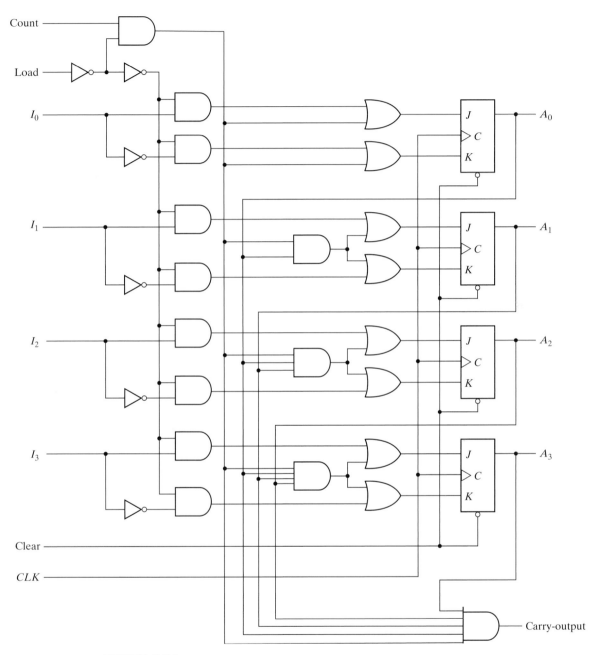

FIGURE 6-14
4-Bit Binary Counter with Parallel Load

Table 6-6
Function Table for the Counter of Fig. 6-14

Clear	CLK	Load	Count	Function
0	X	X	X	Clear to 0
1	↑	1	X	Load inputs
1	↑	0	1	Count next binary state
1	↑	0	0	No change

The carry output becomes a 1 if all the flip-flops are equal to 1 while the count input is enabled. This is the condition for complementing the flip-flop that holds the next significant bit. The carry output is useful for expanding the counter to more than four bits. The speed of the counter is increased when the carry is generated directly from the outputs of all four flip-flops because of the reduced delay for generating the carry. In going from state 1111 to 0000, only one gate delay occurs; whereas, four gate delays occur in the AND gate chain shown in Fig. 6-12. Similarly, each flip-flop is associated with an AND gate that receives all previous flip-flop outputs directly instead of connecting the AND gates in a chain.

The operation of the counter is summarized in Table 6-6. The four control inputs: clear, CLK, load, and count determine the next state. The clear input is asynchronous and, when equal to 0, causes the counter to be cleared regardless of the presence of clock pulses or other inputs. This is indicated in the table by the X entries, which symbolize don't-care conditions for the other inputs. The clear input must be at the 1 state for all other operations. With the load and count inputs both at 0, the outputs do not change, even when clock pulses are applied. A load input of 1 causes a transfer from inputs I_0-I_3 into the register during a positive edge of the clock. The input data are loaded into the register regardless of the value of the count input, because the count input is inhibited when the load input is enabled. The load input must be 0 for the count input to control the operation of the counter.

A counter with parallel load can be used to generate any desired count sequence. Fig. 6-15 shows two ways in which a counter with parallel load is used to generate the BCD count. In each case, the count control is set to 1 to enable the count through the CLK input. Also, remember that the load control inhibits the count and that the clear operation is independent of other control inputs.

The AND gate in Fig. 6-15(a) detects the occurrence of state 1001. The counter is initially cleared to 0 and then the clear and count inputs are set to 1 so the counter is active at all times. As long as the output of the AND gate is 0, each positive-edge clock increments the counter by one. When the output reaches the count of 1001, both A_0 and A_3 become 1, making the output of the AND gate equal to 1. This condition activates the load input; therefore, on the next clock edge the register does not count, but is loaded from its four inputs. Since all four inputs are connected to logic 0, an all 0's value is loaded into the register following the count of 1001. Thus, the circuit goes through the count from 0000 through 1001 and back to 0000 as required in a BCD counter.

In Fig. 6-15(b), the NAND gate detects the count of 1010, but as soon as this count occurs, the register is cleared. The count 1010 has no chance of staying on for any appreciable time because the register goes immediately to 0. A momentary spike occurs in output A_0 as the count

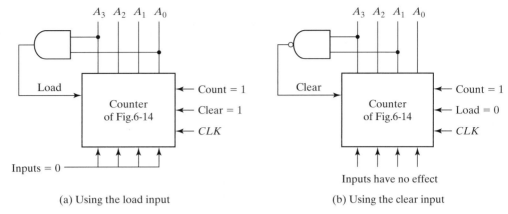

FIGURE 6-15
Two ways to Achieve a BCD Counter Using a Counter with Parallel Load

goes from 1010 to 1011 and immediately to 0000. This momentary spike may be undesirable, and for this reason, this configuration is not recommended. If the counter has a synchronous clear input, it would be possible to clear the counter with the clock after an occurrence of the 1001 count.

6-5   OTHER COUNTERS

Counters can be designed to generate any desired sequence of states. A divide-by-N counter (also known as modulo-N counter) is a counter that goes through a repeated sequence of N states. The sequence may follow the binary count or may be any other arbitrary sequence. Counters are used to generate timing signals to control the sequence of operations in a digital system. Counters can be constructed also by means of shift registers. In this section, we present a few examples of non binary counters.

Counter with Unused States

A circuit with n flip-flops has 2^n binary states. There are occasions when a sequential circuit uses less than this maximum possible number of states. States that are not used in specifying the sequential circuit are not listed in the state table. When simplifying the input equations, the unused states may be treated as don't-care conditions or may be assigned specific next states. Once the circuit is designed and constructed, outside interference may cause the circuit to enter one of the unused states. In that case, it is necessary to ensure that the circuit eventually goes into one of the valid states so it can resume normal operation. Otherwise, if the sequential circuit circulates among unused states, there will be no way to bring it back to its intended sequence of state transitions. If the unused states are treated as don't-care conditions, then once the circuit is designed, it must be investigated to determine the effect

Table 6-7
State Table for Counter

Present State			Next State			Flip-Flop Inputs					
A	B	C	A	B	C	J_A	K_A	J_B	K_B	J_C	K_C
0	0	0	0	0	1	0	X	0	X	1	X
0	0	1	0	1	0	0	X	1	X	X	1
0	1	0	1	0	0	1	X	X	1	0	X
1	0	0	1	0	1	X	0	0	X	1	X
1	0	1	1	1	0	X	0	1	X	X	1
1	1	0	0	0	0	X	1	X	1	0	X

of the unused states. The next state from an unused state can be determined from the analysis of the circuit after it is designed.

As an illustration, consider the counter specified in Table 6-7. The count has a repeated sequence of six states, with flip-flops B and C repeating the binary count 00, 01, 10, and flip-flop A alternating between 0 and 1 every three counts. The count sequence of the counter is not straight binary and two states, 011 and 111, are not included in the count. The choice of JK flip-flops results in the flip-flop input conditions listed in the table. Inputs K_B and K_C have only 1's and X's in their columns, so these inputs are always equal to 1. The other flip-flop input equations can be simplified using minterms 3 and 7 as don't-care conditions. The simplified equations are

$$J_A = B \qquad K_A = B$$
$$J_B = C \qquad K_B = 1$$
$$J_C = B' \qquad K_C = 1$$

The logic diagram of the counter is shown in Fig. 6-16(a). Since there are two unused states, we analyze the circuit to determine their effect. If the circuit happens to be in state 011 because of an error signal, the circuit goes to state 100 after the application of a clock pulse. This is determined from inspection of the logic diagram by noting that when $B = 1$, the next clock edge complements A and clears C to 0, and when $C = 1$, the next clock edge complements B. In a similar manner, we can evaluate the next state from present state 111 to be 000.

The state diagram including the effect of the unused states is shown in Fig. 6-16(b). If the circuit ever goes to one of the unused states because of an outside interference, the next count pulse transfers it to one of the valid states and the circuit continues to count correctly. Thus, the counter is self-correcting. A self correcting counter is one that if it happens to be in one of the unused states, eventually reaches the normal count sequence after one or more clock pulses.

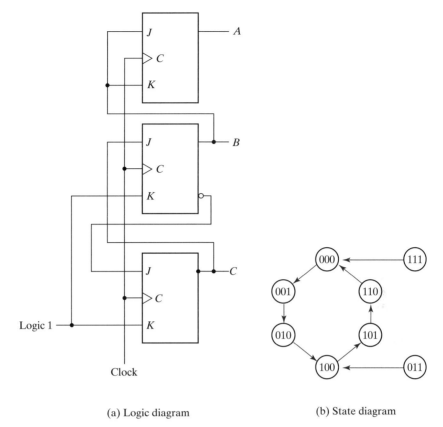

(a) Logic diagram

(b) State diagram

FIGURE 6-16
Counter with Unused States

Ring Counter

Timing signals that control the sequence of operations in a digital system can be generated with a shift register or a counter with a decoder. A *ring counter* is a circular shift register with only one flip-flop being set at any particular time, all others are cleared. The single bit is shifted from one flip-flop to the next to produce the sequence of timing signals. Fig. 6-17(a) shows a 4-bit shift register connected as a ring counter. The initial value of the register is 1000. The single bit is shifted right with every clock pulse and circulates back from T_3 to T_0. Each flip-flop is in the 1 state once every four clock cycles and produces one of the four timing signals shown in Fig. 6-17(c). Each output becomes a 1 after the negative-edge transition of a clock pulse and remains 1 during the next clock cycle.

The timing signals can be generated also by a 2-bit counter that goes through four distinct states. The decoder shown in Fig. 6-17(b) decodes the four states of the counter and generates the required sequence of timing signals.

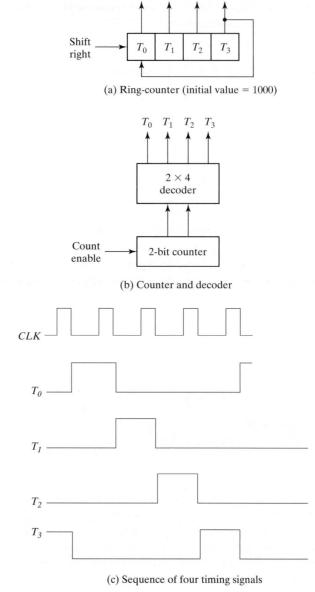

(a) Ring-counter (initial value = 1000)

(b) Counter and decoder

(c) Sequence of four timing signals

FIGURE 6-17
Generation of Timing Signals

To generate 2^n timing signals, we need either a shift register with 2^n flip-flops or an n-bit binary counter together with an n-to-2^n-line decoder. For example, 16 timing signals can be generated with a 16-bit shift register connected as a ring counter or with a 4-bit binary counter and a 4-to-16-line decoder. In the first case, we need 16 flip-flops. In the second, we need four flip-flops and 16 4-input AND gates for the decoder. It is also possible to generate the timing signals with a combination of a shift register and a decoder. In this way, the number of flip-flops is less than a ring counter, and the decoder requires only 2-input gates. This combination is called a *Johnson counter*.

Johnson Counter

A k-bit ring counter circulates a single bit among the flip-flops to provide k distinguishable states. The number of states can be doubled if the shift register is connected as a *switch-tail* ring counter. A switch-tail ring counter is a circular shift register with the complement output of the last flip-flop connected to the input of the first flip-flop. Fig. 6-18(a) shows such a shift register. The circular connection is made from the complement output of the rightmost flip-flop to the input of the leftmost flip-flop. The register shifts its contents once to the right with every clock pulse, and at the same time, the complement value of the E flip-flop is transferred into the A flip-flop. Starting from a cleared state, the switch-tail ring counter goes through a sequence of eight states, as listed in Fig. 6-18(b). In general, a k-bit switch-tail ring counter will go through a sequence of $2k$ states. Starting from all 0's, each shift operation inserts 1's from the left until the register is filled with all 1's. In the following sequences, 0's are inserted from the left until the register is again filled with all 0's.

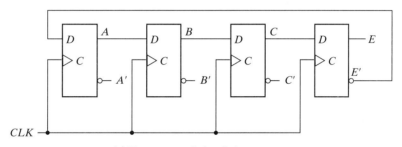

(a) Four-stage switch-tail ring counter

Sequence number	Flip-flop outputs				AND gate required for output
	A	B	C	E	
1	0	0	0	0	$A'E'$
2	1	0	0	0	AB'
3	1	1	0	0	BC'
4	1	1	1	0	CE'
5	1	1	1	1	AE
6	0	1	1	1	$A'B$
7	0	0	1	1	$B'C$
8	0	0	0	1	$C'E$

(b) Count sequence and required decoding

FIGURE 6-18
Construction of a Johnson Counter

A Johnson counter is a k-bit switch-tail ring counter with $2k$ decoding gates to provide outputs for $2k$ timing signals. The decoding gates are not shown in Fig. 6-18, but are specified in the last column of the table. The eight AND gates listed in the table, when connected to the circuit, will complete the construction of the Johnson counter. Since each gate is enabled during one particular state sequence, the outputs of the gates generate eight timing signals in succession.

The decoding of a k-bit switch-tail ring counter to obtain $2k$ timing signals follows a regular pattern. The all-0's state is decoded by taking the complement of the two extreme flip-flop outputs. The all-1's state is decoded by taking the normal outputs of the two extreme flip-flops. All other states are decoded from an adjacent 1, 0 or 0, 1 pattern in the sequence. For example, sequence 7 has an adjacent 0, 1 pattern in flip-flops B and C. The decoded output is then obtained by taking the complement of B and the normal output of C, or $B'C$.

One disadvantage of the circuit in Fig. 6-18(a) is that if it finds itself in an unused state, it will persist in moving from one invalid state to another and never find its way to a valid state. This difficulty can be corrected by modifying the circuit to avoid this undesirable condition. One correcting procedure is to disconnect the output from flip-flop B that goes to the D input of flip-flop C, and instead enable the input of flip-flop C by the function

$$D_C = (A + C)B$$

where D_C is the flip-flop input equation for the D input of flip-flop C.

Johnson counters can be constructed for any number of timing sequences. The number of flip-flops needed is one-half the number of timing signals. The number of decoding gates is equal to the number of timing signals and only 2-input gates are needed.

6-6   HDL FOR REGISTERS AND COUNTERS

Registers and counters can be described in HDL at either the behavioral or the structural level. In the behavioral level, the register is specified by a description of the various operations that it performs similar to a function table. A structural level description shows the circuit in terms of a collection of components such as gates, flip-flops, and multiplexers. The various components are instantiated to form a hierarchical description of the design similar to a representation of a logic diagram. We will use three circuits from this chapter to illustrate the two types of descriptions.

Shift Register

The universal shift register presented in Section 6-2 is a bidirectional shift register with parallel load. The four clocked operations that are performed with the register are specified in Table 6-6. The register also can be cleared asynchronously. The behavioral description of a 4-bit universal shift register is shown in HDL Example 6-1. There are two selection inputs, two serial inputs, a 4-bit parallel input, and a 4-bit parallel output. The **always** block describes the five operations that can be performed with the register. The Clr input clears the register

HDL Example 6-1

```
//Behavioral description of
//Universal shift register
// Fig. 6-7 and Table 6-3
module shftreg (s1,s0,Pin,lfin,rtin,A,CLK,Clr);
    input s1,s0;                        //Select inputs
    input lfin, rtin;                   //Serial inputs
    input CLK,Clr;                      //Clock and Clear
    input [3:0] Pin;                    //Parallel input
    output [3:0] A;                     //Register output
    reg [3:0] A;
    always @ (posedge CLK or negedge Clr)
      if (~Clr) A = 4'b0000;
        else
          case ({s1,s0})
            2'b00: A = A;               //No change
            2'b01: A = {rtin,A[3:1]};   //Shift right
            2'b10: A = {A[2:0],lfin};   //Shift left
            2'b11: A = Pin;             //Parallel load input
          endcase
endmodule
```

asynchronously with a negative signal. Clr must be high for the register to respond to the positive edge of the clock. The four clocked operations of the register are determined from the values of the two select inputs in the case statement (s1 and s0 are concatenated into a 2-bit vector after the **case** keyword). The shifting is specified by the concatenation of the serial input and three flip-flops. For example, the statement

```
A = {rtin, A[3:1]}
```

specifies a concatenation of the serial input for right shift (rtin) with flip-flops $A3$, $A2$, and $A1$ to form a 4-bit number, which is transferred to A [3:0]. This produces a shift right operation. Note that only the function of the circuit has been described irrespective of any particular hardware.

The structure of the register can be described by referring to the logic diagram of Fig. 6-7. The diagram shows that the register is constructed with four multiplexers and four D flip-flops. The structural description of the register is shown in HDL Example 6-2. There are two modules in the example. The first module declares the inputs, outputs, and then instantiates the stages of the register. The four instantiations specify the interconnections between the four stages and provide the detail construction of the register as specified in the logic diagram. The second module has two always blocks. The first always block describes the multiplexer and the second describes the flip-flop. Together they define one stage of the register.

HDL Example 6-2

```
//Structural description of
//Universal shift register(see Fig. 6-7)
module SHFTREG (I,select,lfin,rtin,A,CLK,Clr);
    input [3:0] I;                //Parallel input
    input [1:0] select;          //Mode select
    input lfin,rtin,CLK,Clr;     //Serial inputs,clock,clear
    output [3:0] A;              //Parallel output
  //Instantiate the four stages
    stage ST0 (A[0],A[1],lfin,I[0],A[0],select,CLK,Clr);
    stage ST1 (A[1],A[2],A[0],I[1],A[1],select,CLK,Clr);
    stage ST2 (A[2],A[3],A[1],I[2],A[2],select,CLK,Clr);
    stage ST3 (A[3],rtin,A[2],I[3],A[3],select,CLK,Clr);
endmodule

//One stage of shift register
module stage(i0,i1,i2,i3,Q,select,CLK,Clr);
    input i0,i1,i2,i3,CLK,Clr;
    input [1:0] select;
    output Q;
    reg Q;
    reg D;
//4x1 multiplexer
    always @ (i0 or i1 or i2 or i3 or select)
        case (select)
            2'b00: D = i0;
            2'b01: D = i1;
            2'b10: D = i2;
            2'b11: D = i3;
        endcase
//D flip-flop
    always @ (posedge CLK or negedge Clr)
            if (~Clr) Q = 1'b0;
            else Q = D;
endmodule
```

Synchronous Counter

HDL Example 6-3 describes the synchronous counter with parallel load from Fig. 6-14. Count, Load, CLK, and Clr are inputs that determine the operation of the register according to the function specified in Table 6-6. The counter has four data inputs, four data outputs, and a carry output. The carry output CO is generated by a combinational circuit and is specified with an **assign** statement. $CO = 1$ when the count reaches 15 and the counter is in the count state.

HDL Example 6-3

```
//Binary counter with parallel load
//See Figure 6-14 and Table 6-6
module counter (Count,Load,IN,CLK,Clr,A,CO);
   input Count,Load,CLK,Clr;
   input [3:0] IN;                       //Data input
   output CO;                            //Output carry
   output [3:0] A;                       //Data output
   reg [3:0] A;
   assign CO = Count & ~Load & (A == 4'b1111);
   always @ (posedge CLK or negedge Clr)
     if (~Clr) A = 4'b0000;
     else if (Load)  A = IN;
     else if (Count) A = A + 1'b1;
     else A = A;
endmodule
```

Thus, $CO = 1$ if Count $= 1$, Load $= 0$, and $A = 1111$; otherwise $CO = 0$. The **always** block specifies the operation to be performed in the register depending on the values of Clr, Load, and Count. A negative signal in Clr resets A to 0. Otherwise, if Clr $= 1$, one out of three operations is executed during the positive edge of the clock. The **if**, **else if**, and **else** statements make the decisions as follows:

```
        if Clr = 0                                  Clear A to 0

   else if (Clr = 1 and) Load = 1                   Load inputs to A

   else if (Clr = 1 and Load = 0 and) Count = 1     Increment A

       else (Clr = 1 and Load = 0 and Count = 0)    No change in A
```

The hierarchy implied in the if-else statements complies with the precedence specified in Table 6-6.

Ripple Counter

The structural description of a ripple counter is shown in HDL Example 6-4. The first module instantiates four complementing flip-flops defined in the second module as CF (Q,CLK,Reset). The clock (input C) of the first flip-flop is connected to the external Count input (Count replaces CLK in F0). The clock input of the second flip-flop is connected to the output of the first ($A0$ replaces CLK in $F1$). Similarly, the clock of each of the other flip-flops is connected to the output of the previous flip-flop. In this way, the flip-flops are chained together to create a ripple counter as shown in Fig. 6-8(b).

The second module describes a complementing flip-flop with delay. The circuit of a complementing flip-flop is constructed by connecting the complement output to the D input. A reset

HDL Example 6-4

```verilog
//Ripple counter (See Fig. 6-8(b))
module ripplecounter (A0,A1,A2,A3,Count,Reset);
    output A0,A1,A2,A3;
    input Count,Reset;
//Instantiate complementing flip-flop
    CF F0 (A0,Count,Reset);
    CF F1 (A1,A0,Reset);
    CF F2 (A2,A1,Reset);
    CF F3 (A3,A2,Reset);
endmodule

//Complementing flip-flop with delay
//Input to D flip-flop = Q'
module CF (Q,CLK,Reset);
    output Q;
    input CLK,Reset;
    reg Q;
    always @ (negedge CLK or posedge Reset)
        if (Reset) Q = 1'b0;
        else   Q = #2 (~Q);      // Delay of 2 time units
endmodule

//Stimulus for testing ripple counter
module testcounter;
    reg Count;
    reg Reset;
    wire A0,A1,A2,A3;
//Instantiate ripple counter
    ripplecounter RC (A0,A1,A2,A3,Count,Reset);
always
    #5 Count = ~Count;
initial
 begin
      Count = 1'b0;
      Reset = 1'b1;
    #4 Reset = 1'b0;
    #165 $finish;
 end
endmodule
```

input is included with the flip-flop in order to be able to initialize the counter. HDL simulators cannot provide output values unless they are initialized to some value. The flip-flop is assigned a delay of 2 time units from the time that the clock is applied to the time that the flip-flop complements. This is specified by the statement $Q = $ #2 $(\sim Q)$.

The third module in Example 6-4 provides stimulus for simulating and testing the ripple counter. The **always** statement generates a clock with a cycle of 10 time units. The flip-flops trigger on the negative edge of the clock, which occurs at t = 10, 20, 30, and every 10 time units. The waveforms obtained from this simulation are shown in Fig. 6-19. The Count goes negative every 10 ns. A0 is complemented with each negative edge of Count but is delayed by 2 ns. Each flip-flop is complemented when its previous flip-flop goes from 1 to 0. After *t* = 80 ns, all four flip-flops complement because the counter goes from 0111 to 1000. Each output is delayed by 2 ns and because of that, A3 goes from 0 to 1 at *t* = 88 ns and from 1 to 0 at 168 ns.

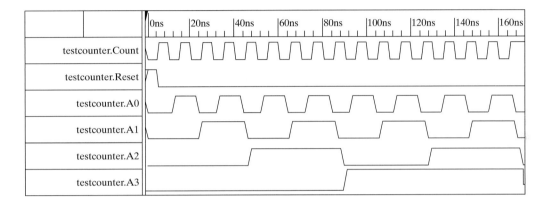

(a) From 0 to 170 ns

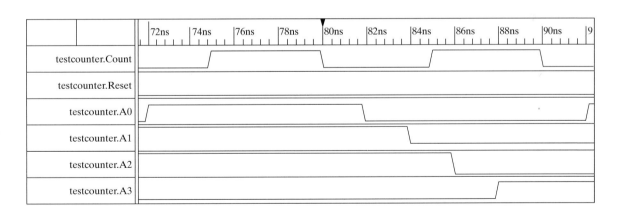

(b) From 70 to 92 ns

FIGURE 6-19
Simulation Output of HDL Example 6-4

PROBLEMS

6-1 Include a 2-input NAND gate with the register of Fig. 6-1 and connect the gate output to the C inputs of all the flip-flops. One input of the NAND gate receives the clock pulses from the clock generator, and the other input of the NAND gate provides a parallel load control. Explain the operation of the modified register.

6-2 Include a synchronous clear input to the register of Fig. 6-2. The modified register will have a parallel load capability and a synchronous clear capability. The register is cleared synchronously when the clock goes through a positive transition and the clear input is equal to 1.

6-3 What is the difference between serial and parallel transfer? Explain how to convert serial data to parallel and parallel data to serial. What type of register is needed?

6-4 The content of a 4-bit register is initially 1101. The register is shifted six times to the right with the serial input being 101101. What is the content of the register after each shift?

6-5 The 4-bit universal shift register shown in Fig. 6-7 is enclosed within one IC package.

(a) Draw a block diagram of the IC showing all inputs and outputs. Include two pins for the power supply.

(b) Draw a block diagram using two ICs to produce an 8-bit universal shift register.

6-6 Design a 4-bit shift register with parallel load using D flip-flops. There are two control inputs: shift and load. When shift $= 1$, the content of the register is shifted by one position. New data is transferred into the register when load $= 1$ and shift $= 0$. If both control inputs are equal to 0, the content of the register does not change.

6-7 Draw the logic diagram of a 4-bit register with four D flip-flops and four 4×1 multiplexers with mode selection inputs s_1 and s_0. The register operates according to the following function table:

s_1	s_0	Register Operation
0	0	No change
0	1	Complement the four outputs
1	0	Clear register to 0 (synchronous with the clock)
1	1	Load parallel data

6-8 The serial adder of Fig. 6-6 uses two 4-bit registers. Register A holds the binary number 0101 and register B holds 0111. The carry flip-flop is initially reset to 0. List the binary values in register A and the carry flip-flop after each shift.

6-9 Two ways for implementing a serial adder $(A + B)$ is shown in Section 6-2. It is necessary to modify the circuits to convert them to serial subtractors $(A - B)$.

(a) Using the circuit of Fig. 6-5, show the changes needed to perform $A +$ 2's complement of B.

(b) Using the circuit of Fig. 6-6, show the changes needed by modifying Table 6-2 from an adder to a subtractor circuit. (See Problem 4-12).

6-10 Design a serial 2's complementer with a shift register and a flip-flop. The binary number is shifted out from one side and it's 2's complement shifted into the other side of the shift register.

6-11 A binary ripple counter uses flip-flops that trigger on the positive-edge of the clock. What will be the count if (a) the normal outputs of the flip-flops are connected to the clock and (b) the complement outputs of the flip-flops are connected to the clock?

6-12 Draw the logic diagram of a 4-bit binary ripple down counter using (a) flip-flops that trigger on the positive-edge of the clock and (b) flip-flops that trigger on the negative-edge of the clock.

6-13 Show that a BCD ripple counter can be constructed using a 4-bit binary ripple counter with asynchronous clear and a NAND gate that detects the occurrence of count 1010.

6-14 How many flip-flop will be complemented in a 10-bit binary ripple counter to reach the next count after the following count: (a) 1001100111; (b) 0011111111; (c) 1111111111.

6-15 A flip-flops has a 5 ns delay from the time the clock edge occurs to the time the output is complemented. What is the maximum delay in a 10-bit binary ripple counter that uses these flip-flops? What is the maximum frequency the counter can operate reliably?

6-16 The BCD ripple counter shown in Fig. 6-10 has four flip-flops and 16 states, of which only 10 are used. Analyze the circuit and determine the next state for each of the other six unused states. What will happen if a noise signal sends the circuit to one of the unused states?

6-17 Design a 4-bit binary synchronous counter with D flip-flops.

6-18 What operation is performed in the up-down counter of Fig. 6-13 when both the up and down inputs are enabled? Modify the circuit so that when both inputs are equal to 1, the counter does not change state, but remains in the same count.

6-19 The flip-flop input equations for a BCD counter using T flip-flops are given in section 6-4. Obtain the input equations for a BCD counter that uses (a) JK flip-flops and (b) D flip-flops. Compare the three designs to determine which one is the most efficient.

6-20 Enclose the binary counter with parallel load of Fig. 6-14 in a block diagram showing all inputs and outputs.

    (a) Show the connections of four such blocks to produce a 16-bit counter with parallel load.

    (b) Construct a binary counter that counts from 0 through binary 64.

6-21 The counter of Fig. 6-14 has two control inputs—Load (L) and Count (C)—and a data input, (I_i).

    (a) Derive the flip-flop input equations for J and K of the first stage in terms of L, C, and I.

    (b) The logic diagram of the first stage of an equivalent integrated circuit (74161) is shown in Fig. P6-21. Verify that this circuit is equivalent to the one in (a).

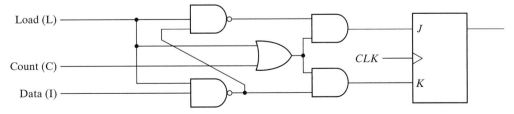

FIGURE P6-21

6-22 Using the circuit of Fig. 6-14, give three alternatives for a mod-12 counter:

    (a) Using an AND gate and the load input.

    (b) Using the output carry.

    (c) Using a NAND gate and the asynchronous clear input.

6-23 Design a timing circuit that provides an output signal that stays on for exactly eight clock cycles. A start signal sends the output to the 1 state, and after eight clock cycles the signal returns to the 0 state.

6-24 Design a counter with T flip-flops that goes through the following binary repeated sequence: 0, 1, 3, 7, 6, 4. Show that when binary states 010 and 101 are considered as don't care conditions, the counter may not operate properly. Find a way to correct the design.

6-25 It is necessary to generate six repeated timing signals T_0 through T_5 similar to the ones shown in Fig. 6-17(c). Design the circuit using:

    (a) Flip-flops only.   (b) A counter and a decoder.

6-26 A digital system has a clock generator that produces pulses at a frequency of 80 MHz. Design a circuit that provides a clock with a cycle time of 50 ns.

6-27 Design a counter with the following repeated binary sequence: 0, 1, 2, 3, 4, 5, 6. Use JK flip-flops.

6-28 Design a counter with the following repeated binary sequence: 0, 1, 2, 4, 6. Use D flip-flops.

6-29 List the eight unused states in the switch-tail ring counter of Fig. 6-18(a).

Determine the next state for each of these states and show that, if the counter finds itself in an invalid state, it does not return to a valid state. Modify the circuit as recommended in the text and show that the counter produces the same sequence of states and that the circuit reaches a valid state from any one of the unused states.

6-30 Show that a Johnson counter with n flip-flops produces a sequence of $2n$ states. List the 10 states produced with five flip-flops and the Boolean terms of each of the 10 AND gate outputs.

6-31 Write the HDL behavioral and structural descriptions of the 4-bit register Fig. 6-1.

6-32 (a) Write the HDL behavioral description of a 4-bit register with parallel load and asynchronous clear.

    (b) Write the HDL structural description of the 4-bit register with parallel load shown in Fig. 6-2. Use a 2×1 multiplexer for the flip-flop inputs. Include an asynchronous clear input.

    (c) Check both descriptions using a test bench.

6-33 The following stimulus program is used to simulate the binary counter with parallel load described in HDL Example 6-3. Going over the program, predict what would be the output of the counter and the carry output from $t = 0$ to $t = 155$ ns.

```
//Stimulus for testing counter
//of Example 6-3
    module testcounter;
        reg Count, Load, CLK, Clr;
        reg [3:0] IN;
        wire C0;
        wire [3:0] A;
        counter cnt (Count, Load, IN, CLK, Clr, A, CO);
        always
            #5 CLK = ~CLK;
          initial
          begin
            Clr = 0;
            CLK = 1;
            Load = 0; Count = 1;
                #5  Clr = 1;
                #50 Load = 1; IN = 4'b1100;
                #10 Load = 0;
                #70 Count = 0;
                #20 $finish;
            end
    endmodule
```

6-34 Write the HDL behavioral description of a 4-bit shift register (Fig. 6-3).

6-35 Write the HDL behavioral and structural descriptions of the 4-bit up-down counter whose logic diagram is shown in Fig. 6-13.

6-36 Write the HDL behavioral description of a 4-bit up-down counter with parallel load using the following control inputs:

(a) The counter has three control inputs for the three operations: Up, Down, and Load. The order of precedence is: Load, Up, and Down.

(b) The counter has two selection inputs to specify four operations: Up, Down, Load, and no-change.

6-37 Write the HDL description of an 8-bit ring-counter similar to the one shown in Fig. 6-17(a).

6-38 Write the HDL description of a 4-bit switch-tail ring counter (Fig. 6-18a).

6-39 Write the HDL behavioral and structural descriptions of the counter of Fig. 6-16.

REFERENCES

1.   MANO, M. M. and C. R. KIME. 2000. *Logic and Computer Design Fundamentals,* 2nd ed. Upper Saddle River, NJ: Prentice Hall.

2.   NELSON V. P., H. T. NAGLE, J. D. IRWIN, and B. D. CARROLL. 1995. *Digital Logic Circuit Analysis and Design.* Upper Saddle River, NJ: Prentice Hall.

3.   HAYES, J. P. 1993. *Introduction to Digital Logic Design.* Reading, MA: Addison-Wesley.

4.   WAKERLY, J. F. 2000. *Digital Design: Principles and Practices,* 3rd ed. Upper Saddle River, NJ: Prentice Hall.

5.   DIETMEYER, D. L. 1988. *Logic Design of Digital Systems,* 3rd ed. Boston: Allyn Bacon.

6.   Gajski, D. D. 1997. *Principles of Digital Design.* Upper Saddle River, NJ: Prentice Hall.

7.   ROTH, C. H. 1992. *Fundamentals of Logic Design,* 4th ed. St. Paul: West.

8.   KATZ, R. H. 1994. *Contemporary Logic Design.* Upper Saddle River, NJ: Prentice Hall.

9.   CILETTI, M. D. 1999. *Modeling, Synthesis, and Rapid Prototyping with Verilog HDL.* Upper Saddle River, NJ: Prentice Hall.

10.   BHASKER, J. 1997. *A Verilog HDL Primer.* Allentown, PA: Star Galaxy Press.

11.   THOMAS, D. E., and P. R. Moorby. 1998. *The VeriLog Hardware Description Language* 4th ed. Boston: Kluwer Academic Publishers.

12.   BHASKER, J. 1998. *Verilog HDL Synthesis.* Allentown, PA: Star Galaxy Press.

13.   PALNITKAR, S. 1996. *Verilog HDL: A Guide to Digital Design and Synthesis.* SunSoft Press (A Prentice Hall Title).

7

Memory and Programmable Logic

7-1 INTRODUCTION

A memory unit is a device to which binary information is transferred for storage and from which information is available when needed for processing. When data processing takes place, information from the memory is transferred to selected registers in the processing unit. Intermediate and final results obtained in the processing unit are transferred back to be stored in memory. Binary information received from an input device is stored in memory and information transferred to an output device is taken from memory. A memory unit is a collection of cells capable of storing a large quantity of binary information.

There are two types of memories that are used in digital systems: *random-access memory* (RAM) and *read-only memory* (ROM). Random-access memory accepts new information for storage to be available later for use. The process of storing new information into memory is referred to as a memory *write* operation. The process of transferring the stored information out of memory is referred to as a memory *read* operation. Random-access memory can perform both the write and read operations. Read-only memory can perform only the read operation. This means that a suitable binary information is already stored inside the memory, which can be retrieved or read at any time. However, the existing information cannot be altered by writing because the read-only memory can only read; it cannot write.

The read-only memory is a *programmable logic device*. The binary information that is stored within a programmable logic device is specified in some fashion and then embedded within the hardware. This process is referred to as *programming* the device. The word "programming" here refers to a hardware procedure that specifies the bits that are inserted into the hardware configuration of the device.

The read-only memory (ROM) is one example of a programmable logic device (PLD). Other such units are the programmable logic array (PLA), the programmable array logic (PAL), and

255

(a) Conventional symbol   (b) Array logic symbol

FIGURE 7-1
Conventional and Array Logic Diagrams for OR Gate

the field-programmable gate array (FPGA). A programmable logic device is an integrated circuit with internal logic gates that are connected through electronic paths that behave similar to fuses. In the original state of the device, all the fuses are intact. Programming the device involves blowing those fuses along the paths that must be removed in order to obtain the particular configuration of the desired logic function. In this chapter, we introduce the configuration of programmable logic devices and indicate procedures for their use in the design of digital systems.

A typical programmable logic device may have hundreds to millions of gates interconnected through hundreds to thousands of internal paths. In order to show the internal logic diagram in a concise form, it is necessary to employ a special gate symbology applicable to array logic. Fig. 7-1 shows the conventional and array symbols for a multiple input OR gate. Instead of having multiple input lines into the gate, we draw a single line along the gate. The input lines are drawn perpendicular to this single line and are connected to the gate through internal fuses. In a similar fashion, we can draw the array logic for an AND gate. This type of graphical representation for the inputs of gates will be used throughout this chapter when drawing array logic diagrams.

7-2   RANDOM-ACCESS MEMORY

A memory unit is a collection of storage cells together with associated circuits needed to transfer information in and out of the device. The time it takes to transfer information to or from any desired random location is always the same, hence, the name *random-access memory* abbreviated RAM.

A memory unit stores binary information in groups of bits called *words*. A word in memory is an entity of bits that move in and out of storage as a unit. A memory word is a group of 1's and 0's and may represent a number, an instruction, one or more alphanumeric characters, or any other binary-coded information. A group of eight bits is called a *byte*. Most computer memories use words that are multiples of eight bits in length. Thus, a 16-bit word contains two bytes, and a 32-bit word is made up of four bytes. The capacity of a memory unit is usually stated as the total number of bytes that it can store.

The communication between a memory and its environment is achieved through data input and output lines, address selection lines, and control lines that specify the direction of transfer. A block diagram of the memory unit is shown in Fig. 7-2. The n data input lines provide the information to be stored in memory and the n data output lines supply the information coming out of memory. The k address lines specify the particular word chosen among the many available. The two control inputs specify the direction of transfer desired: The write input causes binary data to be transferred into the memory, and the read input causes binary data to be transferred out of memory.

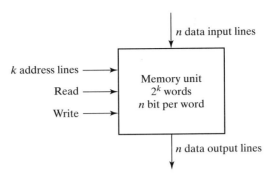

FIGURE 7-2
Block Diagram of a Memory Unit

The memory unit is specified by the number of words it contains and the number of bits in each word. The address lines select one particular word. Each word in memory is assigned an identification number, called an *address*, starting from 0 up to $2^k - 1$, where k is the number of address lines. The selection of a specific word inside memory is done by applying the k-bit address to the address lines. A decoder accepts this address and opens the paths needed to select the word specified. Memories vary greatly in size and may range from 1,024 words, requiring an address of 10 bits, to 2^{32} words, requiring 32 address bits. It is customary to refer to the number of words (or bytes) in a memory with one of the letters K (kilo), M (mega), or G (giga). K is equal to 2^{10}, M is equal to 2^{20}, and G is equal to 2^{30}. Thus, $64K = 2^{16}$, $2M = 2^{21}$, and $4G = 2^{32}$.

Consider, for example, the memory unit with a capacity of 1K words of 16 bits each. Since $1K = 1,024 = 2^{10}$ and 16 bits constitute two bytes, we can say that the memory can accommodate $2,048 = 2K$ bytes. Fig. 7-3 shows the possible content of the first three and the last three

Memory address		Memory content
Binary	decimal	
0000000000	0	1011010101011101
0000000001	1	1010101110001001
0000000010	2	0000110101000110
⋮	⋮	⋮
1111111101	1021	1001110100010100
1111111110	1022	0000110100011110
1111111111	1023	1101111000100101

FIGURE 7-3
Content of a 1024 × 16 Memory

words of this memory. Each word contains 16 bits that can be divided into two bytes. The words are recognized by their decimal address from 0 to 1,023. The equivalent binary address consists of 10 bits. The first address is specified with ten 0's, and the last address is specified with ten 1's. This is because 1,023 in binary is equal to 1111111111. A word in memory is selected by its binary address. When a word is read or written, the memory operates on all 16 bits as a single unit.

The 1K $\times$ 16 memory of Fig. 7-3 has 10 bits in the address and 16 bits in each word. As another example, a 64K $\times$ 10 memory will have 16 bits in the address (since 64K $= 2^{16}$) and each word will consist of 10 bits. The number of address bits needed in a memory is dependent on the total number of words that can be stored in the memory and is independent of the number of bits in each word. The number of bits in the address is determined from the relationship $2^k \geq m$, where m is the total number of words, and k is the number of address bits needed to satisfy the relationship.

Write and Read Operations

The two operations that a random-access memory can perform are the write and read operations. The write signal specifies a transfer-in operation and the read signal specifies a transfer-out operation. On accepting one of these control signals, the internal circuits inside the memory provide the desired operation.

The steps that must be taken for the purpose of transferring a new word to be stored into memory are as follows:

1. Apply the binary address of the desired word to the address lines.

2. Apply the data bits that must be stored in memory to the data input lines.

3. Activate the *write* input.

The memory unit will then take the bits from the input data lines and store them in the word specified by the address lines.

The steps that must be taken for the purpose of transferring a stored word out of memory are as follows:

1. Apply the binary address of the desired word to the address lines.

2. Activate the *read* input.

The memory unit will then take the bits from the word that has been selected by the address and apply them to the output data lines. The content of the selected word does not change after reading.

Commercial memory components available in integrated-circuit chips sometimes provide the two control inputs for reading and writing in a somewhat different configuration. Instead of having separate read and write inputs to control the two operations, most integrated circuits provide two other control inputs: one input selects the unit and the other determines the operation. The memory operations that result from these control inputs are specified in Table 7-1.

The memory enable (sometimes called the chip select) is used to enable the particular memory chip in a multichip implementation of a large memory. When the memory enable is inactive, the memory chip is not selected and no operation is performed. When the memory enable input is active, the read/write input determines the operation to be performed.

Table 7-1
Control Inputs to Memory Chip

Memory Enable	Read/Write	Memory Operation
0	X	None
1	0	Write to selected word
1	1	Read from selected word

Memory Description in HDL

Memory is modeled in Verilog HDL by an array of registers. It is declared with a **reg** keyword using a two-dimensional array. The first number in the array specifies the number of bits in a word and the second gives the number of words in memory. For example, a memory of 1,024 words with 16 bits per word is declared as

$$\textbf{reg}[15:0] \ \texttt{memword}[0:1023];$$

This describes a two-dimensional array of 1,024 registers, each containing 16 bits. The number in memword specifies the total number of words in memory and is equivalent to the address of the memory. For example, memword[512] refers to the 16-bit memory word at address 512.

The operation of a memory unit is illustrated in HDL Example 7-1. The memory has 64 words of four bits each. There are two control inputs: Enable and ReadWrite. The DataIn and DataOut lines have four bits each. The input Address must have six bits (since $2^6 = 64$). The memory is declared as a two-dimensional array of registers with Mem specifying the address

HDL Example 7-1

```
//Read and write operations of memory.
//Memory size is 64 words of 4 bits each.
 module memory (Enable,ReadWrite,Address,DataIn,DataOut);
    input   Enable,ReadWrite;
    input [3:0] DataIn;
    input [5:0] Address;
    output [3:0] DataOut;
    reg [3:0] DataOut;
    reg [3:0] Mem [0:63];            //64 x 4 memory
    always @ (Enable or ReadWrite)
      if (Enable)
      if (ReadWrite)
      DataOut = Mem[Address];   //Read
      else
      Mem[Address] = DataIn;   //Write
      else DataOut = 4'bz;             //High impedance state
endmodule
```

of the 64 words. A memory operation occurs when the Enable input is active. The ReadWrite input determines the type of operation. If ReadWrite is 1, the memory performs a read operation symbolized by the statement

$$\text{DataOut} \leftarrow \text{Mem [Address]};$$

This causes a transfer of four bits from the selected memory word specified by the Address into the DataOut lines. If ReadWrite is 0, the memory performs a write operation symbolized by the statement

$$\text{Mem [Address]} \leftarrow \text{DataIn};$$

This causes a transfer from the 4-bit DataIn lines into the memory word selected by the Address. When Enable is equal to 0, the memory is disabled and the outputs are assumed to be in a high impedance state. This is symbolized by the keyword **z,** indicating that the memory has three-state outputs.

Timing Waveforms

The operation of the memory unit is controlled by an external device such as a central processing unit (CPU). The CPU is usually synchronized by its own clock. The memory, however, does not employ an internal clock. Instead, its read and write operations are specified by control inputs. The *access time* of a memory is the time required to select a word and read it. The *cycle time* of a memory is the time required to complete a write operation. The CPU must provide the memory control signals in such a way as to synchronize its internal clocked operations with the read and write operations of memory. This means that the access time and cycle time of the memory must be within a time equal to a fixed number of CPU clock cycles.

Assume as an example that a CPU operates with a clock frequency of 50 MHz, giving a period for one clock cycle of 20 ns. Suppose now that the CPU communicates with a memory whose access time and cycle time does not exceed 50 ns. That means that the write cycle terminates the storage of the selected word within a 50-ns interval and that the read cycle provides the output data of the selected word within 50 ns or less. (The two numbers are not always the same.) Since the period of the CPU cycle is 20 ns, it will be necessary to devote at least two and a half, and possibly three, clock cycles for each memory request.

The memory timing shown in Fig. 7-4 is for a CPU with 50 MHz clock and a memory with 50 ns maximum cycle time. The write cycle in part (a) shows three 20 ns cycles—$T1$, $T2$, and $T3$. For a write operation, the CPU must provide the address and input data to the memory. This is done at the beginning of $T1$. (The two lines that cross each other in the address and data waveforms designate a possible change in value of the multiple lines.) The memory enable and the read/write signals must be activated after the signals in the address lines are stable to avoid destroying data in other memory words. The memory enable signal switches to the high level and the read/write signal switches to the low level to indicate a write operation. The two control signals must stay active for at least 50 ns. The address and data signals must remain stable for a short time after the control signals are deactivated. At the completion of the third clock cycle, the memory write operation is completed and the CPU can access the memory again with the next $T1$ cycle.

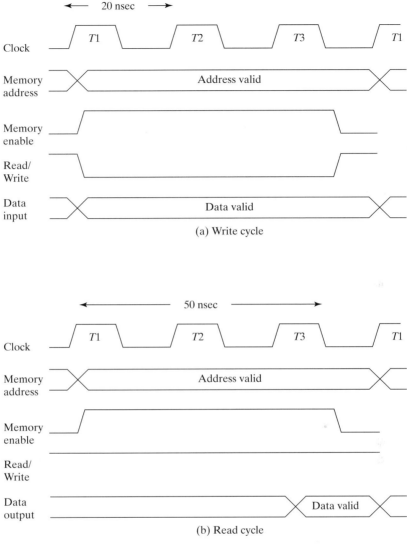

FIGURE 7-4
Memory Cycle Timing Waveforms

The read cycle shown in Fig. 7-4(b) has an address for the memory provided by the CPU. The memory enable and read/write signals must be in their high level for a read operation. The memory places the data of the word selected by the address into the output data lines within a 50 ns interval (or less) from the time that the memory enable is activated. The CPU can transfer the data into one of its internal registers during the negative transition of $T3$. The next $T1$ cycle is available for another memory request.

Types of Memories

The mode of access of a memory system is determined by the type of components used. In a random-access memory, the word locations may be thought of as being separated in space, with each word occupying one particular location. In a sequential-access memory, the information stored in some medium is not immediately accessible, but is available only at certain intervals of time. A magnetic disk or tape unit is of this type. Each memory location passes the read and write heads in turn, but information is read out only when the requested word has been reached. In a random-access memory, the access time is always the same regardless of the particular location of the word. In a sequential-access memory, the time it takes to access a word depends on the position of the word with respect to the reading head position; therefore, the access time is variable.

Integrated circuit RAM units are available in two possible operating modes, *static* and *dynamic*. The static RAM (SRAM) consists essentially of internal latches that store the binary information. The stored information remains valid as long as power is applied to the unit. The dynamic RAM (DRAM) stores the binary information in the form of electric charges on capacitors. The capacitors are provided inside the chip by MOS transistors. The stored charge on the capacitors tends to discharge with time and the capacitors must be periodically recharged by *refreshing* the dynamic memory. Refreshing is done by cycling through the words every few milliseconds to restore the decaying charge. DRAM offers reduced power consumption and larger storage capacity in a single memory chip. SRAM is easier to use and has shorter read and write cycles.

Memory units that lose stored information when power is turned off are said to be *volatile*. Integrated circuit RAMs, both static and dynamic, are of this category since the binary cells need external power to maintain the stored information. In contrast, a nonvolatile memory, such as magnetic disk, retains its stored information after removal of power. This is because the data stored on magnetic components is represented by the direction of magnetization, which is retained after power is turned off. Another nonvolatile memory is the read-only memory (ROM). A nonvolatile property is needed in digital computers to store programs that are needed after the computer is turned off. Programs and data that cannot be altered are stored in ROM. Other large programs are maintained on magnetic disks. When power is turned on, the computer can use the programs from ROM. The other programs residing on a magnetic disk are then transferred into the computer RAM as needed. Before turning the power off, the binary information from the computer RAM is transferred into the disk for the information to be retained.

7-3 MEMORY DECODING

In addition to the storage components in a memory unit, there is a need for decoding circuits to select the memory word specified by the input address. In this section, we present the internal construction of a random-access memory and demonstrate the operation of the decoder. To be able to include the entire memory in one diagram, the memory unit presented here has a small capacity of 16 bits arranged in four words of 4 bits each. An example of a two-dimensional coincident decoding arrangement is presented to show a more efficient decoding scheme that is used in large memories. We then show an example of address multiplexing commonly used in DRAM integrated circuits.

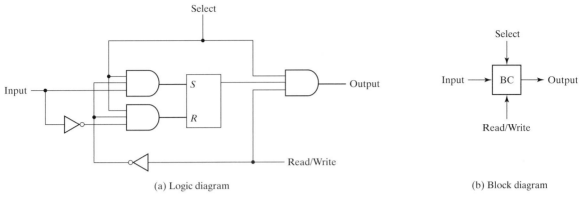

(a) Logic diagram

(b) Block diagram

FIGURE 7-5
Memory Cell

Internal Construction

The internal construction of a random-access memory of m words and n bits per word consists of $m \times n$ binary storage cells and associated decoding circuits for selecting individual words. The binary storage cell is the basic building block of a memory unit. The equivalent logic of a binary cell that stores one bit of information is shown in Fig. 7-5. The storage part of the cell is modeled by an SR latch with associated gates. Actually, the cell is an electronic circuit with four to six transistors. Nevertheless, it is possible and convenient to model it using logic symbols. A binary storage cell must be very small in order to be able to pack as many cells as possible in the small area available in the integrated circuit chip. The binary cell stores one bit in its internal latch. The select input enables the cell for reading or writing and the read/write input determines the cell operation when it is selected. A 1 in the read/write input provides the read operation by forming a path from the latch to the output terminal. A 0 in the read/write input provides the write operation by forming a path from the input terminal to the latch.

The logical construction of a small RAM is shown in Fig. 7-6. It consists of four words of four bits each and has a total of 16 binary cells. The small blocks labeled BC represent the binary cell with its three inputs and one output as specified in Fig. 7-5(b). A memory with four words needs two address lines. The two address inputs go through a 2×4 decoder to select one of the four words. The decoder is enabled with the memory enable input. When the memory enable is 0, all outputs of the decoder are 0 and none of the memory words are selected. With the memory select at 1, one of the four words is selected, dictated by the value in the two address lines. Once a word has been selected, the read/write input determines the operation. During the read operation, the four bits of the selected word go through OR gates to the output terminals. (Note that the OR gates are drawn according to the array logic established in Fig. 7-1.) During the write operation, the data available in the input lines are transferred into the four binary cells of the selected word. The binary cells that are not selected are disabled and their previous binary values remain unchanged. When the memory select input that goes into the decoder is equal to 0, none of the words are selected and the contents of all cells remain unchanged regardless of the value of the read/write input.

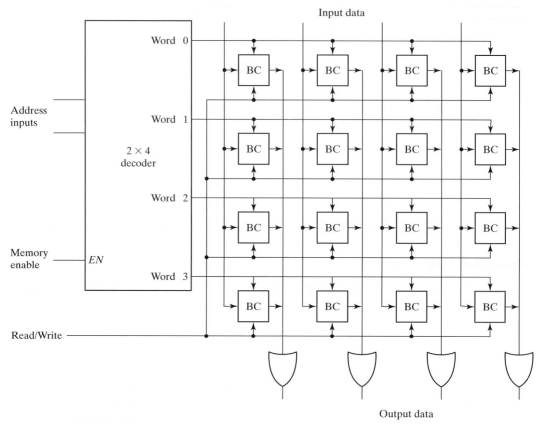

FIGURE 7-6
Diagram of a 4 × 4 RAM

Commercial random-access memories may have a capacity of thousands of words and each word may range from 1 to 64 bits. The logical construction of a large capacity memory would be a direct extension of the configuration shown here. A memory with 2^k words of n bits per word requires k address lines that go into a $k \times 2^k$ decoder. Each one of the decoder outputs selects one word of n bits for reading or writing.

Coincident Decoding

A decoder with k inputs and 2^k outputs requires 2^k AND gates with k inputs per gate. The total number of gates and the number of inputs per gate can be reduced by employing two decoders in a two-dimensional selection scheme. The basic idea in two-dimensional decoding is to arrange the memory cells in an array that is close as possible to square. In this configuration, two $k/2$-input decoders are used instead of one k-input decoder. One decoder performs the row selection and the other the column selection in a two-dimensional matrix configuration.

The two-dimensional selection pattern is demonstrated in Fig. 7-7 for a 1K-word memory. Instead of using a single $10 \times 1,024$ decoder, we use two 5×32 decoders. With the single

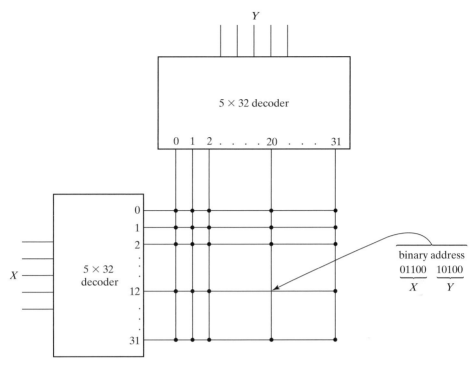

FIGURE 7-7
Two-Dimensional Decoding Structure for a 1K-Word Memory

decoder we would need 1,024 AND gates with 10 inputs in each. In the two-decoder case, we need 64 AND gates with five inputs in each. The five most significant bits of the address go to input X and the five least significant bits go to input Y. Each word within the memory array is selected by the coincidence of one X line and one Y line. Thus, each word in memory is selected by the coincidence between 1 of 32 rows and 1 of 32 columns for a total of 1,024 words. Note that each intersection represents a word that may have any number of bits.

As an example, consider the word whose address is 404. The 10-bit binary equivalent of 404 is 01100 10100. This makes $X = 01100$ (binary 12) and $Y = 10100$ (binary 20). The n-bit word that is selected lies in the X decoder output number 12 and the Y decoder output number 20. All the bits of the word are selected for reading or writing.

Address Multiplexing

The SRAM memory cell modeled in Fig. 7-5 typically contains six transistors. In order to build memories with higher density it is necessary to reduce the number of transistors in a cell. The DRAM cell contains a MOS transistor and a capacitor. The stored charge on the capacitor discharges with time and the memory cells must be periodically recharged by refreshing the memory. Because of their simple cell structure, DRAMs typically have four times the density of SRAM. This allows four times as much memory capacity to be placed on a given size chip. The cost per bit of DRAM storage is three to four times less than SRAM. A further cost savings is realized because of the lower power requirement of DRAM cells. These advantages make DRAM the preferred technology for large memories. DRAM chips are available in capacity of 64K to 256M bits. Most DRAMs have a 1-bit word size, so several chips have to be combined to produce a larger word size.

Because of their large capacity, the address decoding of DRAMs is arranged in two-dimensional array and larger memories often have multiple arrays. To reduce the number of pins in the IC package, designers utilize address multiplexing whereby one set of address input pins accommodates the address components. In a two-dimensional array, the address is applied in two parts at different times, with the row address first and the column address second. Since the same set of pins is used for both parts of the address, the size of the package is decreased significantly.

We will use a 64K-word memory to illustrate the address multiplexing idea. A diagram of the decoding configuration is shown in Fig. 7-8. The memory consists of two-dimensional array of

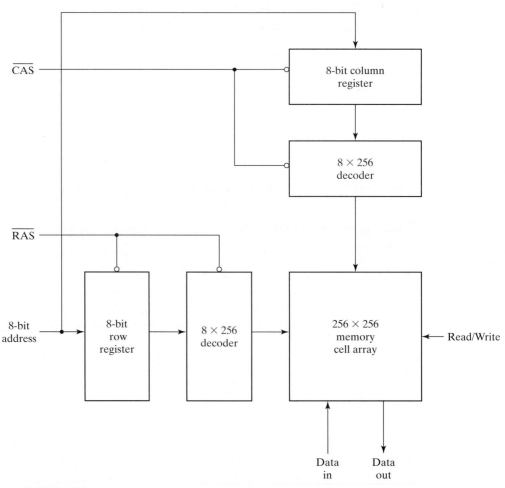

FIGURE 7-8
Address Multiplexing for a 64K DRAM

cells arranged as 256 rows by 256 columns for a total of $2^8 \times 2^8 = 2^{16} = 64K$ words. There is a single data input line, a single data output line, and a Read/Write control. There is an 8-bit address input and two address *strobes*. The address strobes are included for enabling the row and column address into their respective registers. The row address strobe RAS enables the 8-bit row register, and the column address strobe CAS enables the 8-bit column register. The bar on top of the strobe symbol name indicates that the registers are enabled on the zero-level of the signal.

The 16-bit address is applied to the DRAM in two steps using RAS and CAS. Initially both strobes are in the 1 state. The 8-bit row address is applied to the address inputs and RAS is changed to 0. This loads the row address into the row address register. RAS also enables the row decoder so it can decode the row address and select one row of the array. After a time equivalent to the settling time of the row selection, RAS goes back to the 1 level. The 8-bit column address is then applied to the address inputs and CAS is driven to the 0 state. This transfers the column address into the column register and enables the column decoder. At this point, the two parts of the address are in their respective registers, the decoders have decoded them to select the one cell corresponding to the row and column address, and a read or write operation can be performed on that cell. CAS must go back to the 1 level before initiating another memory operation.

7-4 ERROR DETECTION AND CORRECTION

The complexity level of a memory array may cause occasional errors in storing and retrieving the binary information. The reliability of a memory unit may be improved by employing error-detecting and correcting codes. The most common error-detection scheme is the parity bit. (See Section 3-8.) A parity bit is generated and stored along with the data word in memory. The parity of the word is checked after reading it from memory. The data word is accepted if the parity of the bits read out is correct. If the parity checked results in an inversion, an error is detected, but it cannot be corrected.

An error-correcting code generates multiple parity check bits that are stored with the data word in memory. Each check bit is a parity over a group of bits in the data word. When the word is read back from memory, the associated parity bits are also read from memory and compared with a new set of check bits generated from the read data. If the check bits are correct, it signifies that no error has occurred. If the check bits do not compare with the stored parity, they generate a unique pattern, called a *syndrome*, that can be used to identify the bit in error. A single error occurs when a bit changes in value from 1 to 0 or from 0 to 1 during the write and read operation. If the specific bit in error is identified, then the error can be corrected by complementing the erroneous bit.

Hamming Code

One of the most common error-correcting codes used in random-access memories was devised by R. W. Hamming. In the Hamming code, k parity bits are added to an n-bit data word, forming a new word of $n + k$ bits. The bit positions are numbered in sequence from 1 to $n + k$. Those positions numbered as a power of 2 are reserved for the parity bits. The remaining bits are the data bits. The code can be used with words of any length. Before giving the general characteristics of the code, we will illustrate its operation with a data word of eight bits.

Consider, for example, the 8-bit data word 11000100. We include four parity bits with the 8-bit word and arrange the 12 bits as follows:

Bit position:	1	2	3	4	5	6	7	8	9	10	11	12
	P_1	P_2	1	P_4	1	0	0	P_8	0	1	0	0

The 4 parity bits, P_1, P_2, P_4, and P_8, are in positions 1, 2, 4, and 8, respectively. The 8 bits of the data word are in the remaining positions. Each parity bit is calculated as follows:

$$P_1 = \text{XOR of bits } (3, 5, 7, 9, 11) = 1 \oplus 1 \oplus 0 \oplus 0 \oplus 0 = 0$$
$$P_2 = \text{XOR of bits } (3, 6, 7, 10, 11) = 1 \oplus 0 \oplus 0 \oplus 1 \oplus 0 = 0$$
$$P_4 = \text{XOR of bits } (5, 6, 7, 12) = 1 \oplus 0 \oplus 0 \oplus 0 = 1$$
$$P_8 = \text{XOR of bits } (9, 10, 11, 12) = 0 \oplus 1 \oplus 0 \oplus 0 = 1$$

Remember that the exclusive-OR operation performs the odd function. It is equal to 1 for an odd number of 1's in the variables and to 0 for an even number of 1's. Thus, each parity bit is set so that the total number of 1's in the checked positions, including the parity bit, is always even.

The 8-bit data word is stored in memory together with the 4 parity bits as a 12-bit composite word. Substituting the four P bits in their proper positions, we obtain the 12-bit composite word stored in memory

	0	0	1	1	1	0	0	1	0	1	0	0
Bit position:	1	2	3	4	5	6	7	8	9	10	11	12

When the 12 bits are read from memory, they are checked again for possible errors. The parity is checked over the same combination of bits including the parity bit. The 4 check bits are evaluated as follows:

$$C_1 = \text{XOR of bits } (1, 3, 5, 7, 9, 11)$$
$$C_2 = \text{XOR of bits } (2, 3, 6, 7, 10, 11)$$
$$C_4 = \text{XOR of bits } (4, 5, 6, 7, 12)$$
$$C_8 = \text{XOR of bits } (8, 9, 10, 11, 12)$$

A 0 check bit designates an even parity over the checked bits and a 1 designates an odd parity. Since the bits were stored with even parity, the result, $C = C_8 C_4 C_2 C_1 = 0000$, indicates that no error has occurred. However, if $C \neq 0$, then the 4-bit binary number formed by the check bits gives the position of the erroneous bit. For example, consider the following three cases:

Bit position:	1	2	3	4	5	6	7	8	9	10	11	12	
	0	0	1	1	1	0	0	1	0	1	0	0	No error
	1	0	1	1	1	0	0	1	0	1	0	0	Error in bit 1
	0	0	1	1	0	0	0	1	0	1	0	0	Error in bit 5

In the first case, there is no error in the 12-bit word. In the second case, there is an error in bit position number 1 because it changed from 0 to 1. The third case shows an error in bit position 5 with a change from 1 to 0. Evaluating the XOR of the corresponding bits, we determine the four check bits to be as follows:

	C_8	C_4	C_2	C_1
For no error:	0	0	0	0
With error in bit 1:	0	0	0	1
With error in bit 5:	0	1	0	1

Thus, for no error, we have $C = 0000$; with an error in bit 1, we obtain $C = 0001$; and with an error in bit 5, we get $C = 0101$. The binary number of C, when it is not equal to 0000, gives the position of the bit in error. The error can be corrected by complementing the corresponding bit. Note that an error can occur in the data word or in one of the parity bits.

The Hamming code can be used for data words of any length. In general, the Hamming code consists of k check bits and n data bits for a total of $n + k$ bits. The syndrome value C consists of k bits and has a range of 2^k values between 0 and $2^k - 1$. One of these values, usually zero, is used to indicate that no error was detected, leaving $2^k - 1$ values to indicate which of the $n + k$ bits was in error. Each of these $2^k - 1$ values can be used to uniquely describe a bit in error. Therefore, the range of k must be equal to or greater than $n + k$, giving the relationship

$$2^k - 1 \geq n + k$$

Solving for n in terms of k, we obtain

$$2^k - 1 - k \geq n$$

This relationship gives a formula for establishing the number of data bits that can be used in conjunction with k check bits. For example, when $k = 3$, the number of data bits that can be used is $n \leq (2^3 - 1 - 3) = 4$. For $k = 4$, we have $2^4 - 1 - 4 = 11$, giving $n \leq 11$. The data word may be less than 11 bits, but must have at least 5 bits, otherwise, only 3 check bits will be needed. This justifies the use of 4 check bits for the 8 data bits in the previous example. Ranges of n for various values of k are listed in Table 7-2.

The grouping of bits for parity generation and checking can be determined from a list of the binary numbers from 0 through $2^k - 1$. The least significant bit is a 1 in the binary numbers

Table 7-2
Range of Data Bits for k Check Bits

Number of Check Bits, k	Range of Data Bits, n
3	2-4
4	5-11
5	12-26
6	27-57
7	58-120

1, 3, 5, 7, and so on. The second significant bit is a 1 in the binary numbers 2, 3, 6, 7, and so on. Comparing these numbers with the bit positions used in generating and checking parity bits in the Hamming code, we note the relationship between the bit groupings in the code and the position of the 1-bits in the binary count sequence. Note that each group of bits starts with a number that is a power of 2 such as 1, 2, 4, 8, 16, etc. These numbers are also the position numbers for the parity bits.

Single-Error Correction, Double-Error Detection

The Hamming code can detect and correct only a single error. Multiple errors are not detected. By adding another parity bit to the coded word, the Hamming code can be used to correct a single error and detect double errors. If we include this additional parity bit, then the previous 12-bit coded word becomes $001110010100P_{13}$, where P_{13} is evaluated from the exclusive-OR of the other 12 bits. This produces the 13-bit word 0011100101001 (even parity). When the 13-bit word is read from memory, the check bits are evaluated and also the parity P over the entire 13 bits. If $P = 0$, the parity is correct (even parity), but if $P = 1$, then the parity over the 13 bits is incorrect (odd parity). The following four cases can occur:

If $C = 0$ and $P = 0$, no error occurred

If $C \neq 0$ and $P = 1$, a single error occurred that can be corrected

If $C \neq 0$ and $P = 0$, a double error occurred that is detected but that cannot be corrected

If $C = 0$ and $P = 1$ An error occurred in the P_{13} bit

This scheme may detect more than two errors, but is not guaranteed to detect all such errors.

Integrated circuits use a modified Hamming code to generate and check parity bits for a single-error correction, double-error detection. The modified Hamming code uses a more efficient parity configuration that balances the number of bits used to calculate the XOR operation. A typical IC that uses an 8-bit data word and a 5-bit check word is IC type 74637. Other integrated circuits are available for data words of 16 and 32 bits. These circuits can be used in conjunction with a memory unit to correct a single error or detect double errors during the write and read operations.

7-5   READ-ONLY MEMORY

A read-only memory (ROM) is essentially a memory device in which permanent binary information is stored. The binary information must be specified by the designer and is then embedded in the unit to form the required interconnection pattern. Once the pattern is established, it stays within the unit even when power is turned off and on again.

A block diagram of a ROM is shown in Fig. 7-9. It consists of k inputs and n outputs. The inputs provide the address for the memory and the outputs give the data bits of the stored word which is selected by the address. The number of words in a ROM is determined from the fact that k address input lines are needed to specify 2^k words. Note that ROM does not have data

FIGURE 7-9
ROM Block Diagram

inputs because it does not have a write operation. Integrated circuit ROM chips have one or more enable inputs and sometimes come with three-state outputs to facilitate the construction of large arrays of ROM.

Consider for example a 32×8 ROM. The unit consists of 32 words of 8 bits each. There are five input lines that form the binary numbers from 0 through 31 for the address. Fig. 7-10 shows the internal logic construction of the ROM. The five inputs are decoded into 32 distinct outputs by means of a 5×32 decoder. Each output of the decoder represents a memory address. The 32 outputs of the decoder are connected to each of the eight OR gates. The diagram shows the array logic convention used in complex circuits (see Fig. 6-1). Each OR gate must be considered as having 32 inputs. Each output of the decoder is connected to one of the inputs of each OR gate. Since each OR gate has 32 input connections and there are 8 OR gates, the ROM contains $32 \times 8 = 256$ internal connections. In general, a $2^k \times n$ ROM will have an internal $k \times 2^k$ decoder and n OR gates. Each OR gate has 2^k inputs, which are connected to each of the outputs of the decoder.

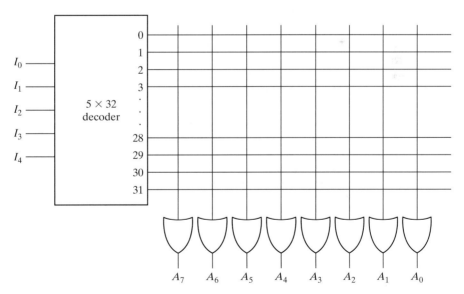

FIGURE 7-10
Internal Logic of a 32 $\times$ 8 ROM

Table 7-3
ROM Truth Table (Partial)

Inputs						Outputs							
I4	I3	I2	I1	I0		A7	A6	A5	A4	A3	A2	A1	A0
0	0	0	0	0		1	0	1	1	0	1	1	0
0	0	0	0	1		0	0	0	1	1	1	0	1
0	0	0	1	0		1	1	0	0	0	1	0	1
0	0	0	1	1		1	0	1	1	0	0	1	0
		$\vdots$						$\vdots$					
1	1	1	0	0		0	0	0	0	1	0	0	1
1	1	1	0	1		1	1	1	0	0	0	1	0
1	1	1	1	0		0	1	0	0	1	0	1	0
1	1	1	1	1		0	0	1	1	0	0	1	1

The 256 intersections in Fig. 7-10 are programmable. A programmable connection between two lines is logically equivalent to a switch that can be altered to either be close (meaning that the two lines are connected) or open (meaning that the two lines are disconnected). The programmable intersection between two lines is sometimes called a crosspoint. Various physical devices are used to implement crosspoint switches. One of the simplest technologies employs a fuse that normally connects the two points, but is opened or "blown" by applying a high-voltage pulse into the fuse.

The internal binary storage of a ROM is specified by a truth table that shows the word content in each address. For example, the content of a 32×8 ROM may be specified with a truth table similar to the one shown in Table 7-3. The truth table shows the five inputs under which are listed all 32 addresses. At each address, there is stored a word of 8 bits, which is listed under the outputs columns. The table shows only the first four and the last four words in the ROM. The complete table must include the list of all 32 words.

The hardware procedure that programs the ROM results in blowing fuse links according to a given truth table. For example, programming the ROM according to the truth table given by Table 7-3 results in the configuration shown in Fig. 7-11. Every 0 listed in the truth table specifies a no connection and every 1 listed specifies a path that is obtained by a connection. For example, the table specifies the 8-bit word 10110010 for permanent storage at address 3. The four 0's in the word are programmed by blowing the fuse links between output 3 of the decoder and the inputs of the OR gates associated with outputs A_6, A_3, A_2, and A_0. The four 1's in the word are marked in the diagram with a $\times$ to denote a connection in place of a dot used for permanent connection in logic diagrams. When the input of the ROM is 00011, all the outputs of the decoder are 0 except for output 3, which is at logic 1. The signal equivalent to logic 1 at decoder output 3 propagates through the connections to the OR gate outputs of A_7, A_5, A_4, and A_1. The other four outputs remain at 0. The result is that the stored word 10110010 is applied to the eight data outputs.

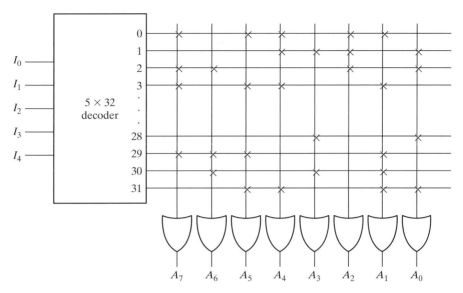

FIGURE 7-11
Programming the ROM According to Table 7-3

Combinational Circuit Implementation

It was shown in Section 4-8 that a decoder generates the 2^k minterms of the k input variables. By inserting OR gates to sum the minterms of Boolean functions, we were able to generate any desired combinational circuit. The ROM is essentially a device that includes both the decoder and the OR gates within a single device. By choosing connections for those minterms that are included in the function, the ROM outputs can be programmed to represent the Boolean functions of the output variables in a combinational circuit.

The internal operation of a ROM can be interpreted in two ways. The first interpretation is that of a memory unit that contains a fixed pattern of stored words. The second interpretation is of a unit that implements a combinational circuit. From this point of view, each output terminal is considered separately as the output of a Boolean function expressed as a sum of minterms. For example, the ROM of Fig. 7-11 may be considered as a combinational circuit with eight outputs, each being a function of the five input variables. Output A_7 can be expressed in sum of minterms as

$$A_7(I_4,I_3,I_2,I_1,I_0) = \Sigma(0, 2, 3, \ldots, 29)$$

(The three dots represent minterms 4 through 27, which are not specified in the figure.) A connection marked with $\times$ in the figure produces a minterm for the sum. All other crosspoint are not connected and are not included in the sum.

In practice, when a combinational circuit is designed by means of a ROM, it is not necessary to design the logic or to show the internal gate connections inside the unit. All that the designer has to do is specify the particular ROM by its IC number and provide the ROM truth table. The truth table gives all the information for programming the ROM. No internal logic diagram is needed to accompany the truth table.

EXAMPLE 7-1

Design a combinational circuit using a ROM. The circuit accepts a 3-bit number and generates an output binary number equal to the square of the input number.

The first step is to derive the truth table of the combinational circuit. In most cases this is all that is needed. In other cases, we can use a partial truth table for the ROM by utilizing certain properties in the output variables. Table 7-4 is the truth table for the combinational circuit. Three inputs and six outputs are needed to accommodate all possible binary numbers. We note that output B_0 is always equal to input A_0; so there is no need to generate B_0 with a ROM since it is equal to an input variable. Moreover, output B_1 is always 0, so this output is a known constant. We actually need to generate only four outputs with the ROM; the other two are readily obtained. The minimum size ROM needed must have three inputs and four outputs. Three inputs specify eight words, so the ROM must be of size 8×4. The ROM implementation is shown in Fig. 7-12. The three inputs specify eight words of four bits each. The truth table in Fig. 7-12(b) specifies the information needed for programming the ROM. The block diagram of Fig. 7-12(a) shows the required connections of the combinational circuit.   ■

Table 7-4
Truth Table for Circuit of Example 7-1

Inputs			Outputs						Decimal
A_2	A_1	A_0	B_5	B_4	B_3	B_2	B_1	B_0	
0	0	0	0	0	0	0	0	0	0
0	0	1	0	0	0	0	0	1	1
0	1	0	0	0	0	1	0	0	4
0	1	1	0	0	1	0	0	1	9
1	0	0	0	1	0	0	0	0	16
1	0	1	0	1	1	0	0	1	25
1	1	0	1	0	0	1	0	0	36
1	1	1	1	1	0	0	0	1	49

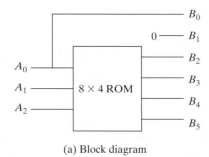

A_2	A_1	A_0	B_5	B_4	B_3	B_2
0	0	0	0	0	0	0
0	0	1	0	0	0	0
0	1	0	0	0	0	1
0	1	1	0	0	1	0
1	0	0	0	1	0	0
1	0	1	0	1	1	0
1	1	0	1	0	0	1
1	1	1	1	1	0	0

(a) Block diagram   (b) ROM truth table

FIGURE 7-12
ROM Implementation of Example 7-1

Types of ROMs

The required paths in a ROM may be programmed in four different ways. The first is called *mask programming* and is done by the semiconductor company during the last fabrication process of the unit. The procedure for fabricating a ROM requires that the customer fill out the truth table he wishes the ROM to satisfy. The truth table may be submitted in a special form provided by the manufacturer or in a specified format on a computer output medium. The manufacturer makes the corresponding mask for the paths to produce the 1's and 0's according to the customer's truth table. This procedure is costly because the vendor charges the customer a special fee for custom masking the particular ROM. For this reason, mask programming is economical only if a large quantity of the same ROM configuration is to be ordered.

For small quantities, it is more economical to use a second type of ROM called programmable read-only memory or PROM. When ordered, PROM units contain all the fuses intact giving all 1's in the bits of the stored words. The fuses in the PROM are blown by application of a high-voltage pulse to the device through a special pin. A blown fuse defines a binary 0 state and an intact fuse gives a binary 1 state. This allows the user to program the PROM in the laboratory to achieve the desired relationship between input addresses and stored words. Special instruments called PROM programmers are available commercially to facilitate this procedure. In any case, all procedures for programming ROMs are hardware procedures even though the word programming is used.

The hardware procedure for programming ROMs or PROMs is irreversible and, once programmed, the fixed pattern is permanent and cannot be altered. Once a bit pattern has been established, the unit must be discarded if the bit pattern is to be changed. A third type of ROM is the erasable PROM or EPROM. The EPROM can be restructured to the initial state even though it has been programmed previously. When the EPROM is placed under a special ultraviolet light for a given period of time, the short wave radiation discharges the internal floating gates that serve as the programmed connections. After erasure, the EPROM returns to its initial state and can be reprogrammed to a new set of values.

The fourth type of ROM is the electrically-erasable PROM (EEPROM or E^2PROM). It is like the EPROM except that the previously programmed connections can be erased with an electrical signal instead of ultraviolet light. The advantage is that the device can be erased without removing it from its socket.

Combinational PLDs

The PROM is a combinational programmable logic device (PLD). A combinational PLD is an integrated circuit with programmable gates divided into an AND array and an OR array to provide an AND-OR sum of product implementation. There are three major types of combinational PLDs and they differ in the placement of the programmable connections in the AND-OR array. Fig. 7-13 shows the configuration of the three PLDs. The programmable read-only memory (PROM) has a fixed AND array constructed as a decoder and programmable OR array. The programmable OR gates implement the Boolean functions in sum of minterms. The programmable array logic (PAL) has a programmable AND array and a fixed OR array. The AND gates are programmed to provide the product terms for the Boolean functions, which are logically summed in each OR gate. The most flexible PLD is the programmable logic array (PLA),

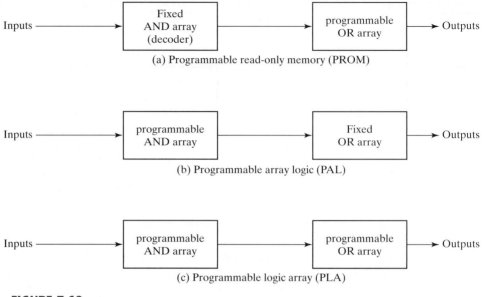

(a) Programmable read-only memory (PROM)

(b) Programmable array logic (PAL)

(c) Programmable logic array (PLA)

FIGURE 7-13
Basic Configuration of Three PLDs

where both the AND and OR arrays can be programmed. The product terms in the AND array may be shared by any OR gate to provide the required sum of products implementation. The names PAL and PLA emerged from different vendors during the development of programmable logic devices. The implementation of combinational circuits with PROM was demonstrated in this section. The design of combinational circuits with PLA and PAL is presented in the next two sections.

7-6   PROGRAMMABLE LOGIC ARRAY

The programmable logic array (PLA) is similar to the PROM in concept except that the PLA does not provide full decoding of the variables and does not generate all the minterms. The decoder is replaced by an array of AND gates that can be programmed to generate any product term of the input variables. The product terms are then connected to OR gates to provide the sum of products for the required Boolean functions.

The internal logic of a PLA with three inputs and two outputs is shown in Fig. 7-14. Such a circuit is too small to be available commercially, but is presented here to demonstrate the typical logic configuration of a PLA. The diagram uses the array logic graphic symbols for complex circuits. Each input goes through a buffer and an inverter shown in the diagram with a composite graphic symbol, which has both the true and complement outputs. Each input and its complement are connected to the inputs of each AND gate as indicated by the intersections between the vertical and horizontal lines. The outputs of the AND gates are connected to the inputs of each OR gate. The output of the OR gate goes to an XOR gate where the other input

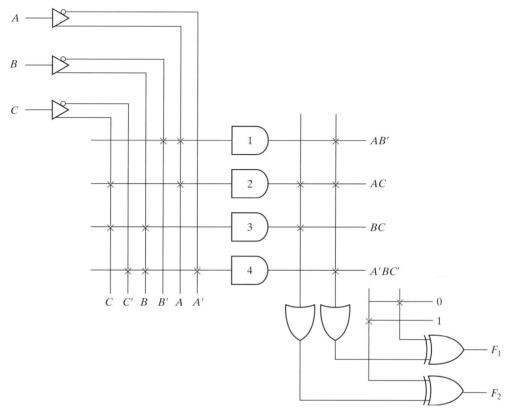

FIGURE 7-14
PLA with 3 Inputs, 4 Product Terms, and 2 Outputs

can be programmed to receive a signal equal to either logic 1 or 0. The output is inverted when the XOR input is connected to 1 (since $x \oplus 1 = x'$). The output does not change when the XOR input is connected to 0 (since $x \oplus 0 = x$). The particular Boolean functions implemented in the PLA of Fig. 7-14 are

$$F_1 = AB' + AC + A'BC'$$
$$F_2 = (AC + BC)'$$

The product terms generated in each AND gate are listed along the output of the gate in the diagram. The product term is determined from the inputs whose crosspoints are connected and marked with a $\times$. The output of an OR gate gives the logic sum of the selected product terms. The output may be complemented or left in its true form depending on the connection for one of the XOR gate inputs.

The fuse map of a PLA can be specified in a tabular form. For example, the programming table that specifies the PLA of Fig. 7-14 is listed in Table 7-5. The PLA programming table consists of three sections. The first section lists the product terms numerically. The second section

Table 7-5
PLA Programming Table

			Inputs			Outputs	
						(T)	(C)
Product Term		A	B	C		F_1	F_2
AB'	1	1	0	–		1	–
AC	2	1	–	1		1	1
BC	3	–	1	1		–	1
A'BC'	4	0	1	0		1	–

specifies the required paths between inputs and AND gates. The third section specifies the paths between the AND and OR gates. For each output variable, we may have a T (for true) or C (for complement) for programming the XOR gate. The product terms listed on the left are not part of the table; they are included for reference only. For each product term, the inputs are marked with 1, 0, or - (dash). If a variable in the product term appears in its true form, the corresponding input variable is marked with a 1. If it appears complemented, the corresponding input variable is marked with a 0. If the variable is absent in the product term, it is marked with a dash.

The paths between the inputs and the AND gates are specified under the column heading *inputs* in the programming table. A 1 in the input column specifies a connection from the input variable to the AND gate. A 0 in the input column specifies a connection from the complement of the variable to the input of the AND gate. A dash specifies a blown fuse in both the input variable and its complement. It is assumed that an open terminal in the input of an AND gate behaves like a 1.

The paths between the AND and OR gates are specified under the column heading *outputs*. The output variables are marked with 1's for those product terms that are included in the function. Each product term that has a 1 in the output column requires a path from the output of the AND gate to the input of the OR gate. Those marked with a dash specify a blown fuse. It is assumed that an open terminal in the input of an OR gate behaves like a 0. Finally, a T (true) output dictates that the other input of the corresponding XOR gate be connected to 0, and a C (complement) specifies a connection to 1.

The size of a PLA is specified by the number of inputs, the number of product terms, and the number of outputs. A typical integrated circuit PLA may have 16 inputs, 48 product terms, and 8 outputs. For n inputs, k product terms, and m outputs the internal logic of the PLA consists of n buffer-inverter gates, k AND gates, m OR gates, and m XOR gates. There are $2n \times k$ connections between the inputs and the AND array, $k \times m$ connections between the AND and OR arrays, and m connections associated with the XOR gates.

When designing a digital system with a PLA, there is no need to show the internal connections of the unit as was done in Fig. 7-14. All that is needed is a PLA programming table from which the PLA can be programmed to supply the required logic. As with a ROM, the PLA may be mask programmable or field programmable. With mask programming, the customer submits a PLA program table to the manufacturer. This table is used by the vendor to produce a custom-made PLA that has the required internal logic specified by the customer. A second type of PLA available is called a field programmable logic array or FPLA. The FPLA can be programmed by the user by means of a commercial hardware programmer unit.

When implementing a combinational circuit with a PLA, careful investigation must be undertaken in order to reduce the number of distinct product terms, since a PLA has a finite number of AND gates. This can be done by simplifying each Boolean function to a minimum number of terms. The number of literals in a term is not important since all the input variables are available anyway. Both the true and complement of each function should be simplified to see which one can be expressed with fewer product terms and which one provides product terms that are common to other functions.

EXAMPLE 7-2

Implement the following two Boolean functions with a PLA:

$$F_1(A, B, C) = \Sigma(0, 1, 2, 4)$$
$$F_2(A, B, C) = \Sigma(0, 5, 6, 7)$$

The two functions are simplified in the maps of Fig. 7-15. Both the true and complement of the functions are simplified in sum of products. The combination that gives a minimum number of product terms is

$$F_1 = (AB + AC + BC)'$$

and

$$F_2 = AB + AC + A'B'C'$$

This gives four distinct product terms: AB, AC, BC, and $A'B'C'$. The PLA programming table for this combination is shown in the figure. Note that output F_1 is the true output even though a C is marked over it in the table. This is because F_1 is generated with an AND-OR circuit and is available at the output of the OR gate. The XOR gate complements the function to produce the true F_1 output.

◼

The combinational circuit used in Example 7-2 is too simple for implementing with a PLA. It was presented merely for illustration purposes. A typical PLA has a large number of inputs and product terms. The simplification of Boolean functions with so many variables should be carried out by means of computer-assisted simplification procedures. The computer-aided design program simplifies each function and its complement to a minimum number of terms. The program then selects a minimum number of product terms that cover all functions in their true or complement form. The PLA programming table is then generated, and the required fuse map is obtained. The fuse map is applied to an FPLA programmer that goes through the hardware procedure of blowing the internal fuses in the integrated circuit.

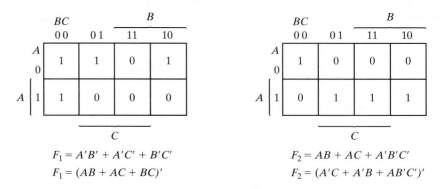

$$F_1 = A'B' + A'C' + B'C'$$
$$F_1 = (AB + AC + BC)'$$

$$F_2 = AB + AC + A'B'C'$$
$$F_2 = (A'C + A'B + AB'C')'$$

PLA programming table

Product term	Inputs A B C	Outputs (C) F_1	(T) F_2
AB	1 1 1 –	1	1
AC	2 1 – 1	1	1
BC	3 – 1 1	1	–
A'B'C'	4 0 0 0	–	1

FIGURE 7-15
Solution to Example 7-2

7-7   PROGRAMMABLE ARRAY LOGIC

The programmable array logic (PAL) is a programmable logic device with a fixed OR array and a programmable AND array. Because only the AND gates are programmable, the PAL is easier to program, but is not as flexible as the PLA. Fig. 7-16 shows the logic configuration of a typical PAL. It has four inputs and four outputs. Each input has a buffer-inverter gate and each output is generated by a fixed OR gate. There are four sections in the unit, each being composed of a three-wide AND-OR array. This is the term used to indicate that there are three programmable AND gates in each section and one fixed OR gate. Each AND gate has 10 programmable input connections. This is shown in the diagram by 10 vertical lines intersecting each horizontal line. The horizontal line symbolizes the multiple-input configuration of the AND gate. One of the outputs is connected to a buffer-inverter gate and then fed back into two inputs of the AND gates.

Commercial PAL devices contain more gates than the one shown in Fig. 7-16. A typical PAL integrated circuit may have eight inputs, eight outputs, and eight sections, each consisting of an eight-wide AND-OR array. The output terminals are sometimes driven by three-state buffers or inverters.

When designing with a PAL, the Boolean functions must be simplified to fit into each section. Unlike the PLA, a product term cannot be shared among two or more OR gates.

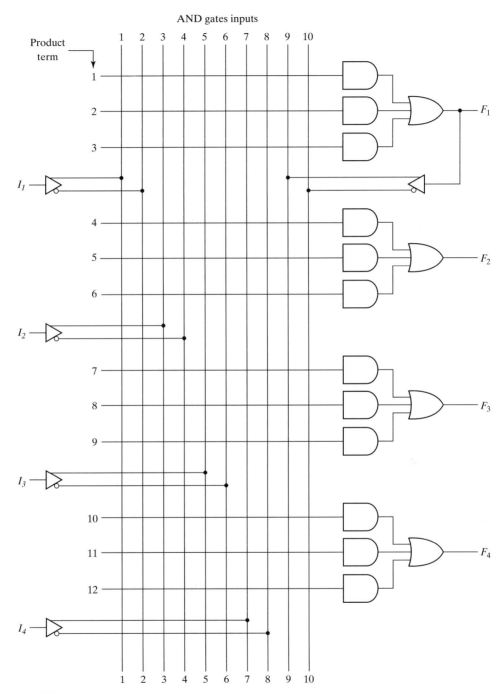

FIGURE 7-16
PAL with Four Inputs, Four Outputs, and Three-Wide AND-OR Structure

Therefore, each function can be simplified by itself without regard to common product terms. The number of product terms in each section is fixed, and if the number of terms in the function is too large, it may be necessary to use two sections to implement one Boolean function.

As an example of using a PAL in the design of a combinational circuit, consider the following Boolean functions, given in sum of minterms:

$$w(A, B, C, D) = \Sigma(2, 12, 13)$$
$$x(A, B, C, D) = \Sigma(7, 8, 9, 10, 11, 12, 13, 14, 15)$$
$$y(A, B, C, D) = \Sigma(0, 2, 3, 4, 5, 6, 7, 8, 10, 11, 15)$$
$$z(A, B, C, D) = \Sigma(1, 2, 8, 12, 13)$$

Simplifying the four functions to a minimum number of terms results in the following Boolean functions:

$$w = ABC' + A'B'CD'$$
$$x = A + BCD$$
$$y = A'B + CD + B'D'$$
$$z = ABC' + A'B'CD' + AC'D' + A'B'C'D$$
$$= w + AC'D' + A'B'C'D$$

Note that the function for z has four product terms. The logical sum of two of these terms is equal to w. By using w, it is possible to reduce the number of terms for z from four to three.

The PAL programming table is similar to the one used for the PLA except that only the inputs of the AND gates need to be programmed. Table 7-6 lists the PAL programming table for the four Boolean functions. The table is divided into four sections with three product terms

Table 7-6
PAL Programming Table

Product Term	AND Inputs					Outputs
	A	B	C	D	W	
1	1	1	0	–	–	$w = ABC'$
2	0	0	1	0	–	$+ A'B'CD'$
3	–	–	–	–	–	
4	1	–	–	–	–	$x = A$
5	–	1	1	1	–	$+ BCD$
6	–	–	–	–	–	
7	0	1	–	–	–	$y = A'B$
8	–	–	1	1	–	$+ CD$
9	–	0	–	0	–	$+ B'D'$
10	–	–	–	–	1	$z = w$
11	1	–	0	0	–	$+ AC'D'$
12	0	0	0	1	–	$+ A'B'C'D$

in each to conform with the PAL of Fig. 7-16. The first two sections need only two product terms to implement the Boolean function. The last section for output z needs four product terms. Using the output from w, we can reduce the function to three terms.

The fuse map for the PAL as specified in the programming table is shown in Fig. 7-17. For each 1 or 0 in the table, we mark the corresponding intersection in the diagram with the symbol for an intact fuse. For each dash, we mark the diagram with blown fuses in both the true and complement inputs. If the AND gate is not used, we leave all its input fuses intact. Since the corresponding input receives both the true and complement of each input variable, we have $AA' = 0$ and the output of the AND gate is always 0.

As with all PLDs, the design with PALs is facilitated by using computer-aided design techniques. The blowing of internal fuses is a hardware procedure done with the help of special electronic instruments.

7-8   SEQUENTIAL PROGRAMMABLE DEVICES

Digital systems are designed using flip-flops and gates. Since the combinational PLD consists of only gates, it is necessary to include external flip-flops when they are used in the design. Sequential programmable devices include both gates and flip-flops. In this way, the device can be programmed to perform a variety of sequential-circuit functions. There are several types of sequential programmable devices available commercially and each device has vendor-specific variant within each type. The internal logic of these devices is too complex to be shown here. Therefore, we will describe three major types without going into their detailed construction:

1. Sequential (or simple) programmable logic device (SPLD)
2. Complex programmable logic device (CPLD)
3. Field programmable gate array (FPGA)

The sequential PLD is sometimes referred to as a simple PLD to differentiate it from the complex PLD. SPLD includes flip-flops within the integrated circuit chip in addition to the AND-OR array. The result is a sequential circuit as shown in Fig. 7-18. A PAL or PLA is modified by including a number of flip-flops connected to form a register. The circuit outputs can be taken from the OR gates or from the outputs of the flip-flops. Additional programmable connections are available to include the flip-flop outputs in the product terms formed with the AND array. The flip-flops may be of the D or the JK type.

The first programmable device developed to support sequential circuit implementation is the field-programmable logic sequencer (FPLS). A typical FPLS is organized around a PLA with several outputs driving flip-flops. The flip-flops are flexible in that they can be programmed to operate as either JK or D type. The FPLS did not succeed commercially because it has too many programmable connections. The configuration mostly used for SPLD is the combinational PAL together with D flip-flops. A PAL that includes flip-flops is referred to as a registered PAL to signify that the device contains flip-flops in addition to the AND-OR array. Each section of an SPLD is called a *macrocell*. A macrocell is a circuit that contains a sum-of-products combinational logic function and an optional flip-flop. We will assume an AND-OR sum of products but in practice, it can be any one of the two-level implementation presented in Sec. 3-7.

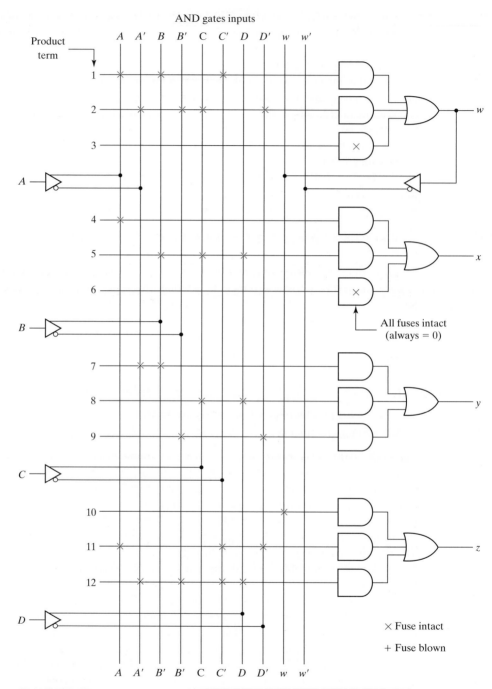

FIGURE 7-17
Fuse Map for PAL as Specified in Table 7-6

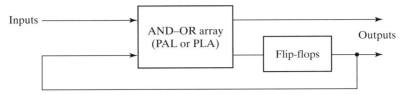

FIGURE 7-18
Sequential Programmable Logic Device

Fig. 7-19 shows the logic of a basic macrocell. The AND-OR array is the same as in the combinational PAL shown in Fig. 7-16. The output is driven by an edge-triggered D flip-flop. The flip-flop is connected to a common clock input and changes state on a clock edge. The output of the flip-flop is connected to a three-state buffer (or inverter) controlled by an output-enable signal marked in the diagram as OE. The output of the flip-flop is fed back into one of the inputs of the programmable AND gates to provide the present-state condition for the sequential circuit. A typical SPLD has from 8 to 10 macrocells within one IC package. All the flip-flops are connected to the common CLK input and all three-state buffers are controlled by the EO input.

In addition to programming the AND array, a macrocell may have other programming features. Typical programming options include the ability to either use or bypass the flip-flop, selection of clock edge polarity, selection of preset and clear for the register, and selection of

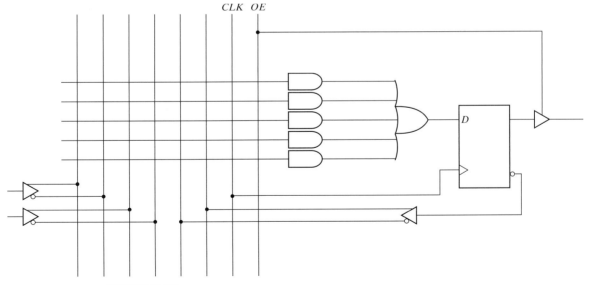

FIGURE 7-19
Basic Macrocell Logic

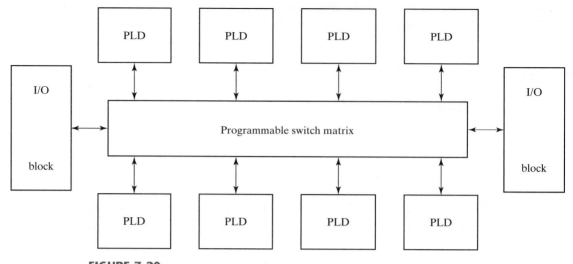

FIGURE 7-20
General CPLD Configuration

the true or complement of an output. An XOR gate is used to program a true/complement condition. Multiplexers are used to select between two or four distinct paths by programming the selection inputs.

The design of a digital system using PLD often requires the connection of several devices to produce the complete specification. For this type of application, it is more economical to use a complex programmable logic device (CPLD). A CPLD is a collection of individual PLDs on a single integrated circuit. A programmable interconnection structure allows the PLDs to be connected to each other in the same way that can be done with individual PLDs.

Fig. 7-20 shows a general configuration of a CPLD. It consists of multiple PLDs interconnected through a programmable switch matrix. The input/output (I/O) blocks provide the connections to the IC pins. Each I/O pin is driven by a three-state buffer and can be programmed to act as input or output. The switch matrix receives inputs from the I/O block and directs it to the individual macrocells. Similarly, selected outputs from macrocells are sent to the outputs as needed. Each PLD typically contains from 8 to 16 macrocells. The macrocells within each PLD are usually fully connected. If a macrocell has unused product terms they can be used by other nearby macrocells. In some cases the macrocell flip-flop is programmed to act as a D, JK, or T flip-flop.

Different manufacturers have taken different approaches to the general architecture of CPLDs. Areas in which they differ include the individual PLDs (sometimes called *function blocks*), the type of macrocells, The I/O blocks, and the programmable interconnection structure. The best way to investigate a vendor-specific device is to look at the manufacturer's literature.

The basic component used in VLSI design is the *gate array*. A gate array consists of a pattern of gates fabricated in an area of silicon that is repeated thousands of times until the entire chip is covered with the gates. Arrays of one thousand to hundred thousand gates are fabricated within a single IC chip depending on the technology used. The design with gate arrays requires that the customer provide the manufacturer the desired interconnection pattern. The first few levels of fabrication process are common and independent of the final logic function. Additional fabrication steps are required to interconnect the gates according to the specifications given by the designer.

A field programmable gate array (FPGA) is a VLSI circuit that can be programmed in the user's location. A typical FPGA consists of an array of hundreds or thousands of logic blocks, surrounded by programmable input and output blocks and connected together via programmable interconnections. There is a wide variety of internal configurations within this group of devices. The performance of each device type depends on the circuit contained in their logic blocks and the efficiency of their programmed interconnections.

A typical FPGA logic block consists of look-up tables, multiplexers, gates, and flip-flops. The look-up table is a truth table stored in a SRAM and provides the combinational circuit functions for the logic block. These functions are realized from the truth table stored in the SRAM, similar to the manner that combinational circuit functions are implemented with ROM, as described in Sec. 7-5. For example, a 16×2 SRAM can store the truth table of a combinational circuit that has four inputs and two outputs. The combinational logic section along with a number of programmable multiplexers are used to configure the input equations for the flip-flop and the output of the logic block.

The advantage of using RAM instead of ROM to store the truth table is that the table can be programmed by writing into memory. The disadvantage is that the memory is volatile and presents the need for the look-up table content to be reloaded in the event that power is disrupted. The program can be downloaded either from a host computer or from an on-board PROM. The program remains in SRAM until the FPGA is reprogrammed or the power is turned off. The device must be reprogrammed every time power is turned on. The ability to reprogram the FPGA can serve a variety of applications by using different logic implementations in the program.

The design with PLD, CPLD, or FPGA requires extensive computer-aided design (CAD) tools to facilitate the synthesis procedure. A variety of tools are available such as schematic entry package and hardware description languages (HDL) such as ABEL, VHDL, and Verilog. Synthesis tools are available that allocate, configure, and connect logic blocks to match a high-level design description written in HDL.

PROBLEMS

7-1   The following memory units are specified by the number of words times the number of bits per word. How many address lines and input-output data lines are needed in each case? (a) $4K \times 16$, (b) $2G \times 8$, (c) $16M \times 32$, (d) $256K \times 64$.

7-2   Give the number of bytes stored in the memories listed in Problem 7-1.

7-3   Word number 723 in the memory shown in Fig. 7-3 contains the binary equivalent of 3,451. List the 10-bit address and the 16-bit memory content of the word.

7-4   Show the memory cycle timing waveforms for the write and read operations. Assume a CPU clock of 25 MHz and a memory cycle time of 60 ns.

7-5 Write a test bench for the memory described in HDL Example 7-1. The test program stores binary 7 in address 0 and binary 14 at address 60. Then the two addresses are read to verify their stored content.

7-6 Enclose the 4 × 4 RAM of Fig. 7-6 in a block diagram showing all inputs and outputs. Assuming three-state outputs, construct an 8 × 8 memory using four 4 × 4 RAM units.

7-7 A 16K × 4 memory uses coincident decoding by splitting the internal decoder into X-selection and Y-selection.

    (a) What is the size of each decoder and how many AND gates are required for decoding the address?

    (b) Determine the X and Y selection lines that are enabled when the input address is the binary equivalent of 6,000.

7-8 (a) How many 32K × 8 RAM chips are needed to provide a memory capacity of 256K bytes?

    (b) How many lines of the address must be used to access 256K bytes? How many of these lines are connected to the address inputs of all chips?

    (c) How many lines must be decoded for the chip select inputs? Specify the size of the decoder.

7-9 A DRAM chip uses two-dimensional address multiplexing. It has 13 common address pins with the row address having 1 bit more than the column address. What is the capacity of the memory?

7-10 Given the 8-bit data word 01011011, generate the 13-bit composite word for the Hamming code that corrects single errors and detects double errors.

7-11 Obtain the 15-bit Hamming code word for the 11-bit data word 11001001010.

7-12 A 12-bit Hamming code word containing 8 bits of data and 4 parity bits is read from memory. What was the original 8-bit data word that was written into memory if the 12-bit word read out is as follows:

    (a) 000011101010   (b) 101110000110

    (c) 101111110100

7-13 How many parity check bits must be included with the data word to achieve single error-correction and double-error detection when the data word contains (a) 16 bits, (b) 32 bits, (c) 48 bits.

7-14 It is necessary to formulate the Hamming code for four data bits, D_3, D_5, D_6, and D_7, together with three parity bits, P_1, P_2, and P_4.

    (a) Evaluate the 7-bit composite code word for the data word 0010.

    (b) Evaluate three check bits, C_4, C_2, and C_1, assuming no error.

    (c) Assume an error in bit D_5 during writing into memory. Show how the error in the bit is detected and corrected.

    (d) Add parity bit P_8 to include a double-error detection in the code. Assume that errors occurred in bits P_2 and D_5. Show how the double error is detected.

7-15 Given a 32 × 8 ROM chip with an enable input, show the external connections necessary to construct a 128 × 8 ROM with four chips and a decoder.

7-16 A ROM chip of 4,096 × 8 bits has two chip select inputs and operates from a 5-volt power supply. How many pins are needed for the integrated circuit package? Draw a block diagram and label all input and output terminals in the ROM.

7-17 The 32 × 6 ROM together with the 2^0 line as shown in Fig. P7-17 converts a 6-bit binary number to its corresponding 2-digit BCD number. For example, binary 100001 converts to BCD 011 0011 (decimal 33). Specify the truth table for the ROM.

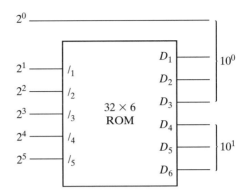

FIGURE P7-17

7-18 Specify the size of a ROM (number of words and number of bits per word) that will accommodate the truth table for the following combinational circuit components:

(a) a binary multiplier that multiplies two 4-bit,

(b) a 4-bit adder-subtractor,

(c) a quadruple 2-to-1-line multiplexers with common select and enable inputs, and

(d) a BCD-to-seven-segment decoder with an enable input.

7-19 Tabulate the truth table for an 8 × 4 ROM that implements the Boolean functions

$$A(x, y, z) = \Sigma(1, 2, 4, 6)$$
$$B(x, y, z) = \Sigma(0, 1, 6, 7)$$
$$C(x, y, z) = \Sigma(2, 6)$$
$$D(x, y, z) = \Sigma(1, 2, 3, 5, 7)$$

Considering now the ROM as a memory, specify the memory contents at addresses 1 and 4.

7-20 Tabulate the PLA programming table for the four Boolean functions listed in Problem 7-19. Minimize the number of product terms.

7-21 Derive the PLA programming table for the combinational circuit that squares a 3-bit number. Minimize the number of product terms. (See Fig. 7-12 for the equivalent ROM implementation.)

7-22 List the PLA programming table for the BCD-to-excess-3-code converter whose Boolean functions are simplified in Fig. 4-3.

7-23 Repeat Problem 7-22 using a PAL.

7-24 The following is a truth table of a 3-input, 4-output combinational circuit. Tabulate the PAL programming table for the circuit and mark the fuse map in a PAL diagram similar to the one shown in Fig. 7-17.

Inputs			Outputs			
x	y	z	A	B	C	D
0	0	0	0	1	0	0
0	0	1	1	1	1	1
0	1	0	1	0	1	1
0	1	1	0	1	0	1
1	0	0	1	0	1	0
1	0	1	0	0	0	1
1	1	0	1	1	1	0
1	1	1	0	1	1	1

7-25 Using the registered macrocell of Fig. 7-19, show the fuse map for a sequential circuit with two inputs x, y and one flip-flop A described by the input equation

$$D_A = x \oplus y \oplus A$$

7-26 Modify the PAL diagram of Fig. 7-16 by including three clocked D-type flip-flops between the OR gates and outputs as in Fig. 7-19. The diagram should conform with the block diagram of a sequential circuit. This will require three additional buffer-inverter gates and six vertical lines for the flip-flop outputs to be connected to the AND array through programmable connections. Using the modified registered PAL diagram, show the fuse map that will implement a 3-bit binary counter with an output carry.

REFERENCES

1. TOCCI, R. J. and N. S. WIDMER. 2001. *Digital Systems Principles and Applications*, 8th ed. Upper Saddle River, NJ: Prentice Hall.

2. KITSON, B. 1984. *Programmable Array Logic Handbook*. Sunnyvale, CA: Advanced Micro Devices.

3. WAKERLY, J. F. 2000. *Digital Design: Principles and Practices,* 3rd ed. Upper Saddle River, NJ: Prentice Hall.

4. NELSON, V. P., H. T. NAGLE, J. D. IRWIN, and B. D. CARROLL. 1995. *Digital Logic Circuit Analysis and Design.* Upper Saddle River, NJ: Prentice Hall.

5. HAMMING, R. W. 1950. Error Detecting and Error Correcting Codes. *Bell Syst. Tech. J.* 29: 147-160.

6. LIN, S., and D. J. COSTELLO, J R. 1983. *Error Control Coding.* Englewood Cliffs, NJ: Prentice-Hall.

7. 1988. *Programmable Logic Data Book.* Dallas: Texas Instruments.

8. TRIMBERGER, S. M. 1994. *Field Programmable Gate Array Technology.* Boston: Kluwer Academic Pub.

9. 1994. *The Programmable Logic Data Book,* 2nd ed. San Jose, CA: Xilinx, Inc.

10. 1986. *Memory Components Handbook.* Santa Clara, CA: Intel.

8 Register Transfer Level

8-1 REGISTER TRANSFER LEVEL (RTL) NOTATION

A digital system is a sequential logic system constructed with flip-flops and gates. Sequential circuits can be specified by means of state tables as shown in Chapter 5. To specify a large digital system with a state table is very difficult, if not impossible, because the number of states would be prohibitively large. To overcome this difficulty, digital systems are designed using a modular approach. The system is partitioned into modular subsystems, each of which performs some functional task. The modules are constructed from such digital devices as registers, decoders, multiplexers, arithmetic elements, and control logic. The various modules are interconnected with common data and control paths to form a digital system.

Digital modules are best defined by a set of registers and the operations that are performed on the binary information stored in them. Examples of register operations are shift, count, clear, and load. The registers are assumed to be the basic components of the digital system. The information flow and processing perform on the data stored in the registers is referred to as register transfer operations. A digital system is represented at the *register transfer level* (RTL) when it is specified by the following three components:

1. The set of registers in the system.
2. The operations that are performed on the data stored in the registers.
3. The control that supervises the sequence of operations in the system.

A register is a group of flip-flops that stores binary information and has the capability of performing one or more elementary operations. A register can load new information or shift the information to the right or the left. A counter is considered a register that increments a number by one. A flip-flop standing alone is considered as a 1-bit register that can be set, cleared,

291

or complemented. In fact, the flip-flops and associated gates of any sequential circuit can be called registers by this definition.

The operations executed on the information stored in registers are elementary operations that are performed in parallel on a string of bits during one clock cycle. The result of the operation may replace the previous binary information in a register. Alternatively, the result may be transferred to another register, leaving the previous data unchanged. The digital circuits introduced in Chapters 6 are registers that implement elementary operations. A counter with parallel load is able to perform the increment by one and load operations. A bidirectional shift register is able to perform the shift right and shift left operations.

The control that initiates the sequence of operations consists of timing signals that sequence the operations in a prescribed manner. Certain conditions that depend on results of previous operations may determine the sequence of future operations. The outputs of the control logic are binary variables that initiate the various operations in the register.

Information transfer from one register to another is designated in symbolic form by means of a replacement operator. The statement

$$R2 \leftarrow R1$$

denotes a transfer of the contents of register $R1$ into register $R2$. It specifies a replacement of the contents of $R2$ by the contents of $R1$. By definition, the contents of the source register $R1$ do not change after the transfer. The arrow symbolizes the transfer and the direction of transfer.

A statement that specifies a register transfer implies that circuit connections are available from the outputs of the source register to the inputs of the destination register and that the destination register has a parallel load capability. Normally, we do not want the transfer to occur with every clock cycle, but only under a predetermined condition. A conditional statement is symbolized with an if-then statement such as

$$\text{If } (T1 = 1) \text{ then } (R2 \leftarrow R1)$$

where $T1$ is a control signal generated in the control section. Note that the clock is not included as a variable in the register transfer statements. It is assumed that all transfers occur during a clock-edge transition. Although a control condition such as $T1$ may become true before the clock transition, the actual transfer does not occur until the clock transition is completed.

A comma may be used to separate two or more operations that are executed at the same time. Consider the statement

$$\text{If } (T3 = 1) \text{ then } (R2 \leftarrow R1, R1 \leftarrow R2)$$

This statement denotes an operation that exchanges the contents of two registers during the same clock edge, provided that $T3 = 1$. This simultaneous operation is possible with registers that have edge-triggered flip-flops. Other examples of register transfers are as follows:

$R1 \leftarrow R1 + R2$	Add content of $R2$ to $R1$
$R3 \leftarrow R3 + 1$	Increment $R3$ by 1 (count up)
$R4 \leftarrow \text{shr } R4$	Shift right $R4$
$R5 \leftarrow 0$	Clear $R5$ to 0

The addition is done with a binary parallel adder, the incrementing with a counter, and the shift with a shift register. The type of operations most often encountered in digital systems can be classified into four categories:

1. Transfer operations that transfer data from one register to another.
2. Arithmetic operations that perform arithmetic on data in registers.
3. Logic operations that perform bit manipulation of non-numeric data in registers.
4. Shift operations that shift data in registers.

The transfer operation does not change the information content of the data being moved from the source register to the destination register. The other three types change the information content during the transfer. The register transfer notation and the symbols used to represent the various register transfer operations are not standardized. Here we employ two types of notation. The notation introduced in this section will be used informally to specify and explain digital systems at the register transfer level. The next section introduces the RTL symbols used in Verilog HDL.

8-2   REGISTER TRANSFER LEVEL IN HDL

Digital systems can be described at the register transfer level by means of a hardware description language. In Verilog HDL, RTL descriptions use a combination of behavioral and dataflow constructs. Register transfers are specified by means of procedural assignment statements. Combinational circuit functions are specified by means of continuous assignment or procedural assignment statements. The symbol used to designate a transfer is either an equal sign or an arrow. Synchronization with the clock is achieved by using an always statement with an event control of posedge or negedge. The following examples show the possible ways that are available to specify a transfer in Verilog HDL:

```
assign  S = A + B;          Continuous assignment

always @ (A or B)           Procedural assignment (without a clock)
   S = A + B;

always @ (posedge clock)    Blocking procedural assignment
  begin
   RA = RA + RB;
   RD = RA;
  end

always @ (negedge clock)    Non-blocking procedural assignment
  begin
   RA <= RA + RB;
   RD <= RA;
  end
```

Continuous assignments are used to specify combinational circuits. The preceding assign statement describes a binary adder with inputs A and B and output S. The target operand in an assign statement (S in this case) cannot be a register. Outputs of combinational circuits can be transferred to a register by means of a clocked procedural assignment. The non-clocked procedural assignment in the second example shows an alternate way of specifying a combinational circuit.

There are two kinds of procedural assignments: *blocking* and *non-blocking*. The two are distinguished by the symbols that they use. Blocking assignments use the symbol (=) as the transfer operator and non-blocking assignments use the (<=) as the operator. Blocking assignment statements are executed sequentially in the order they are listed in a sequential block. Non-blocking assignments evaluate the expressions on the right-hand side, but do not make the assignment to the left-hand side until all expressions are evaluated. Consider the two examples shown above. In the blocking procedural assignment, the first statement transfers the sum to *RA* and the second statement transfers the new value of *RA* into *RD*. At the completion, both *RA* and *RD* have the same value. In the non-blocking procedural assignment, the two operations are performed concurrently so that *RD* receives the original value of *RA*.

To ensure synchronous operations in RTL design, it is necessary that non-blocking procedural assignments be used for variables that follow an always-clocked statement. This is to prevent any possibility of functional mismatch between the design model and the HDL description. The non-blocking assignment that appears in an always-clocked statement accurately models the behavior of a synchronous sequential circuit.

HDL Operators

The Verilog HDL operators and their symbols used in RTL design are listed in Table 8-1. The arithmetic, logic, and shift operators are required for describing register transfer operations. The logical and relational operators are useful for specifying control conditions. The arithmetic operations are done with binary numbers. Negative numbers are represented in 2's complement. The modulus operator produces the remainder from the division of two numbers. For example, 14 % 3 evaluates to 2.

There are two types of logic operators: bit-wise and reduction. Bit-wise operators perform a bit-by-bit logic operation on two operands. They take each bit in one operand and perform the operation with the corresponding bit in the other operand. The reduction operators perform the logic operation on a single operand. They perform the operation bit by bit from right to left and yield a 1-bit result. For example, the reduction NOR ($\sim|$) results in 0 with operand 00101 and in 1 with operand 00000. Negation is not used as a reduction operator. Truth tables for the bit-wise operators are listed in Table 4-9 in Section 4-11.

The logical and relational operators can take variables or expressions as operands. They are basically used for determining true or false conditions. They evaluate to 1 if the condition is true, and to 0 if the condition is false. If the condition is ambiguous, they evaluate to x. When the operand is a number, it evaluates to 0 if the number is equal to zero and to 1 if the number is not equal to zero. For example, if $A = 1010$ and $B = 0000$, then A is taken as 1 (the number is not equal to 0) and B is taken as 0. Results of other operations with these values are:

```
A && B = 0
A || B = 1
!A = 0
!B = 1
(A > B) = 1
(A == B) = 0
```

Table 8-1
Verilog HDL Operators

Operator Type	Symbol	Operation Performed
Arithmetic	+	addition
	−	subtraction
	*	multiplication
	/	division
	%	modulus
Logic	~	negation (complement)
(bit-wise	&	AND
or	|	OR
reduction)	^	Exclusive-OR (XOR)
Logical	!	negation
	&&	AND
	| |	OR
Shift	>>	shift right
	<<	shift left
	{ , }	concatenation
Relational	>	greater than
	<	less than
	==	equality
	! =	inequality
	>=	greater than or equal
	<=	less than or equal

The shift operators shift a vector operand to the right or the left by a specified number of bits. The vacant bit positions are filled with zeros. For example, if $R = 11010$, the statement

```
R = R >> 1;
```

shifts R to the right one position. The new value of R is 01101. The concatenation operator provides a mechanism for appending multiple operands. It can be used to specify a shift including the bits transferred into the vacant positions. This was shown in HDL Example 6-1 for the shift register.

Loop Statements

Verilog HDL has four types of loops that allow procedural statements to be executed repeatedly: *repeat, forever, while,* and *for.* All looping statements must appear inside an **initial** or **always** block.

The **repeat** loop executes the associated statements a specified number of times. The following is an example that was used previously:

```
initial
   begin
        clock = 1'b0;
        repeat (16)
        #5 clock = ~ clock;
   end
```

This produces eight clock cycles with a cycle time of 10 time units.

The **forever** loop causes a continuous repetitive execution of the procedural statement. For example, the following loop produces a continuous clock:

```
initial
   begin
      clock = 1'b0;
      forever
      # clock = ~ clock;
   end
```

The **while** loop executes a statement or block of statements repeatedly while an expression is true. If the expression is false to begin with, the statement is never executed. The following example illustrates the use of the **while** loop:

```
integer count;
initial
   begin
      count = 0;
      while (count < 64)
   #5 count = count + 1;
   end
```

The value of count is incremented from 0 to 63. The loop exits at the count of 64.

In dealing with looping statements, it is sometimes convenient to use integer data type for manipulating quantities. Integers are declared with the keyword **integer** as done in the previous example. Although it is possible to use the **reg** keyword for variables, it is more convenient to declare an integer variable for counting purposes. Variables declared as data type **reg** are stored as unsigned numbers. Those declared as data type **integer** are store as signed numbers in 2's complement format. The default width of an integer is a minimum of 32 bits.

The **for** loop contains three parts separated by two semicolons:

- An initial condition.

- An expression to check for the terminating condition.

- An assignment to change the control variable.

HDL Example 8-1

```
//description of 2x4 decoder
//using for loop statement
module decoder (IN, Y);
    input   [1:0] IN;     //Two binary inputs
    output [3:0] Y;       //Four binary outputs
    reg [3:0] Y;
    integer I;                //control variable for loop
    always @ (IN)
      for (I = 0; I <= 3; I = I + 1)
        if (IN == I) Y[I] = 1;
        else Y[I] = 0;
endmodule
```

The following is an example of a **for** loop:

```
for (i = 0; i < 8; i = i + 1)
procedural statements
```

The loop statement repeats the execution of the procedural statements eight times. The control variable is i, the initial condition is $i = 0$, the loop is repeated as long as i is less than 8. Every time the loop is executed, i is incremented by 1.

The description of a 2-to-4-line decoder using a **for** loop is shown in HDL Example 8-1. Since output Y is evaluated in a procedural statement, it must be declared as **reg** type. The control variable for the loop is the **integer** I. When the loop is expanded, we get the following four conditions (IN and Y are in binary, the index for Y is in decimal):

$$\text{if } IN = 00 \text{ then } Y(0) = 1 \quad \text{else } Y(0) = 0$$
$$\text{if } IN = 01 \text{ then } Y(1) = 1 \quad \text{else } Y(1) = 0$$
$$\text{if } IN = 10 \text{ then } Y(2) = 1 \quad \text{else } Y(2) = 0$$
$$\text{if } IN = 11 \text{ then } Y(3) = 1 \quad \text{else } Y(3) = 0$$

Logic Synthesis

Logic synthesis is the automatic process of transforming a high-level language description such as HDL into an optimized netlist of gates that perform the operations specified by the source code. There are various target technologies that implement the synthesized design. Effective use of an HDL description requires that designers adopt a vendor-specific style suitable for the particular synthesis tools. The type of ICs that implement the design may be an application-specific integrated circuit (ASIC), a programmable logic device (PLD), or a field-programmable gate array (FPGA).

Logic synthesis tools are programs that interpret the source code of the hardware description language and translates it into a gate structure. Designs written in HDL for the purpose of logic synthesis tend to be at the register transfer level. This is because HDL constructs used in RTL description can be converted into a gate-level description in a straightforward manner.

The following examples show how a logic synthesizer can interpret a HDL construct and convert it into a gate structure.

The **assign** statement is used to describe combinational circuits. An assign statement with Boolean equations is interpreted into the corresponding gate circuit. A statement with a plus (+) is interpreted as a binary adder with full adder circuits. A statement with a minus (−) is converted into a subtractor consisting of full adders and exclusive-OR gates (Fig. 4-13). A statement with the conditional operator such as

```
assign Y = S ? I1 : I0;
```

translates into a 2-to-1-line multiplexer with control input S and data inputs I1 and I0. A statement with multiple conditional operators specifies a larger multiplexer.

The **always** statement may imply a combinational or sequential circuit. For sequential circuits, the event control must be posedge or negedge of a clock, otherwise the procedural statement specify a combinational circuit. For example,

```
always @ (I1 or I0 or S)
      if (S) Y = I1;
      else   Y = I0;
```

translates into a 2-to-1-line multiplexer. The **case** statement may be used to imply large multiplexers.

The **always @ posedge** or **negedge** clock specifies clocked sequential circuits. The corresponding circuits consists of D flip-flops and the gates that implement the register transfer operations. Examples of such circuits are registers and counters. A sequential circuit description with a **case** statement translates into a control circuit with D flip-flops and gates. Thus, each statement in an RTL description is interpreted by the synthesizer and assigned to a corresponding gate and flip-flop circuit.

A simplified flow chart of the design process is shown in Fig. 8-1. The RTL description of the HDL design is simulated and checked for proper operation. The test bench provides the stimulus signals to the simulator. If the result of the simulation is not satisfactory, the HDL description is corrected and checked again. When the result of the simulation shows a valid design, the RTL description is applied to the logic synthesizer. The synthesis tools generate a netlist equivalent to a gate-level description of the design. The gate-level circuit is simulated with the same set of stimuli used to check the RTL design. If any corrections are needed, the process is repeated until a satisfactory simulation is achieved. The results of the two simulations are compared to see if they match. If they don't match, the designer goes back and changes the RTL description to correct any faults in the design. Then the description is again read into the logic synthesizer to generate a new gate-level description. Once the designer is satisfied with the results of all simulation tests, the circuit can be fabricated with an integrated circuit.

Logic synthesis provides several advantages to the designer. It takes less time to write an HDL description and synthesize a gate-level realization than it does to develop the circuit by manual entry from schematic diagrams. The ease of changing the description facilitates the exploration of design alternatives. It is easier to check the validity of the design by simulation rather than produce a hardware prototype for evaluation. The database for fabricating the integrated circuit can be generated automatically by the synthesis tools.

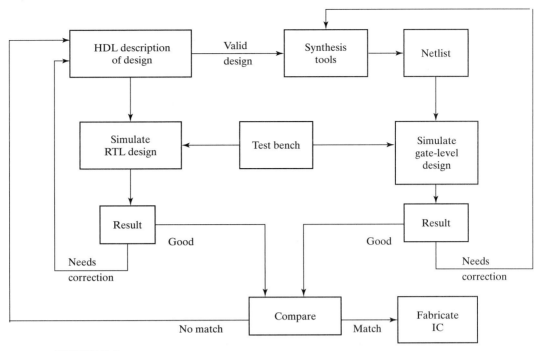

FIGURE 8-1
Process of HDL Simulation and Synthesis

8-3   ALGORITHMIC STATE MACHINES (ASM)

The binary information stored in a digital system can be classified as either data or control information. Data are discrete elements of information that are manipulated to perform arithmetic, logic, shift, and other similar data processing tasks. These operations are implemented with digital components such as adders, decoders, multiplexers, counters, and shift registers. Control information provides command signals that supervise the various operations in the data section in order to accomplish the desired data processing tasks. The logic design of a digital system can be divided into two distinct parts. One part is concerned with the design of the digital circuits that perform the data processing operations. The other part is concerned with the design of the control circuits that determines the sequence in which the various actions are performed.

The relationship between the control logic and the data processessing in a digital system is shown in Fig. 8-2. The data processessing path, commonly referred to as the *datapath*, manipulates data in registers according to the system's requirements. The control logic initiates a sequence of commands to the datapath. The control logic uses status conditions from the datapath to serve as decision variables for determining the sequence of control signals.

The control logic that generates the signals for sequencing the operations in the datapath is a sequential circuit whose internal states dictate the control commands for the system. At any

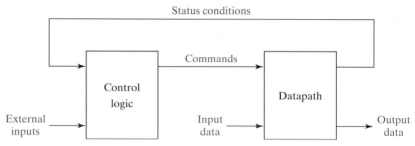

FIGURE 8-2
Control and Datapath Interaction

given time, the state of the sequential control initiates a prescribed set of commands. Depending on status conditions and other external inputs, the sequential control goes to the next state to initiate other operations. The digital circuits that act as the control logic provide a time sequence of signals for initiating the operations in the datapath and also determine the next state of the control subsystem itself.

The control sequence and datapath tasks of a digital system are specified by means of a hardware algorithm. An algorithm consists of a finite number of procedural steps that specify how to obtain a solution to a problem. A hardware algorithm is a procedure for implementing the problem with a given piece of equipment. The most challenging and creative part of digital design is the formulation of hardware algorithms for achieving required objectives.

A flowchart is a convenient way to specify the sequence of procedural steps and decision paths for an algorithm. A flowchart for a hardware algorithm translates the word statement to an information diagram that enumerates the sequence of operations together with the conditions necessary for their execution. A special flowchart that has been developed specifically to define digital hardware algorithms is called an *algorithmic state machine* (ASM) chart. A *state machine* is another term for a sequential circuit, which is the basic structure of a digital system.

The ASM chart resembles a conventional flowchart, but is interpreted somewhat differently. A conventional flowchart describes the sequence of procedural steps and decision paths for an algorithm in a sequential manner without taking into consideration their time relationship. The ASM chart describes the sequence of events as well as the timing relationship between the states of a sequential controller and the events that occur while going from one state to the next. It is specifically adapted to specify accurately the control sequence and datapath operations in a digital system, taking into consideration the constraints of digital hardware.

ASM Chart

The ASM chart is a special type of flowchart suitable for describing the sequential operations of a digital system. The chart is composed of three basic elements: the state box, the decision box, and the conditional box. A state in the control sequence is indicated by a state box, as shown in Fig. 8-3. The shape of the state box is a rectangle within which are written register operations or output signal names that the control generates while being in this state. The state

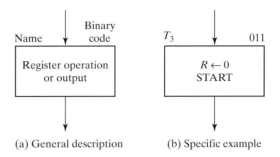

(a) General description   (b) Specific example

FIGURE 8-3
State Box

is given a symbolic name, which is placed at the upper left corner of the box. The binary code assigned to the state is placed at the upper right corner. Fig. 8-3(b) shows a specific example of a state box. The state has the symbolic name T_3, and the binary code assigned to it is 011. Inside the box is written the register operation $R \leftarrow 0$, which indicates that register R is to be cleared to 0 when the system is in state T_3. The START name inside the box may indicate, for example, an output signal that starts a certain operation.

The decision box describes the effect of an input on the control subsystem. It has a diamond-shaped box with two or more exit paths, as shown in Fig. 8-4. The input condition to be tested is written inside the box. One exit path is taken if the condition is true and another when the condition is false. When an input condition is assigned a binary value, the two paths are indicated by 1 and 0.

The state and decision boxes are familiar from use in conventional flowcharts. The third element, the conditional box, is unique to the ASM chart. The oval shape of the conditional box is shown in Fig. 8-5. The rounded corners differentiate it from the state box. The input path to the conditional box must come from one of the exit paths of a decision box. The register operations or outputs listed inside the conditional box are generated during a given state, provided that the input condition is satisfied. Fig. 8-5(b) shows an example with a conditional box. The control generates a START output signal when in state T_1. While in state T_1, the control checks the status of input E. If $E = 1$, then R is cleared to 0; otherwise, R remains unchanged. In either case, the next state is T_2.

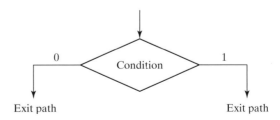

Exit path   Exit path

FIGURE 8-4
Decision Box

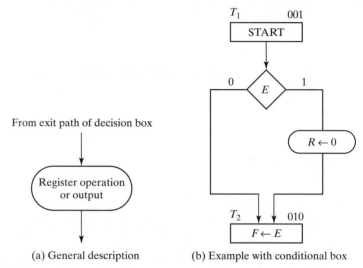

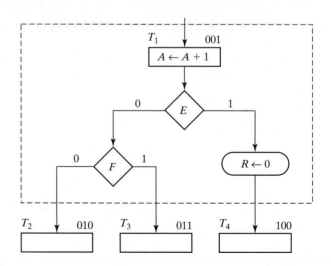

FIGURE 8-5
Conditional Box

ASM Block

An ASM block is a structure consisting of one state box and all the decision and conditional boxes connected to its exit path. An ASM block has one entrance and any number of exit paths represented by the structure of the decision boxes. An ASM chart consists of one or more interconnected blocks. An example of an ASM block is shown in Fig. 8-6. Associated with state

FIGURE 8-6
ASM Block

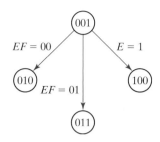

FIGURE 8-7
State Diagram Equivalent to the ASM Chart of Fig. 8-6

T_1 are two decision boxes and one conditional box. The diagram distinguishes the block with dashed lines around the entire structure, but this is not usually done, since the ASM chart uniquely defines each block from its structure. A state box without any decision or conditional boxes constitutes a simple block.

Each block in the ASM chart describes the state of the system during one clock-pulse interval. The operations within the state and conditional boxes in Fig. 8-6 are executed with a common clock pulse while the system is in state T_1. The same clock pulse also transfers the system controller to one of the next states—T_2, T_3, or T_4—as dictated by the binary values of E and F.

The ASM chart is very similar to a state diagram. Each state block is equivalent to a state in a sequential circuit. The decision box is equivalent to the binary information written along the directed lines that connect two states in a state diagram. As a consequence, it is sometimes convenient to convert the chart into a state diagram and then use sequential circuit procedures to design the control logic. As an illustration, the ASM chart of Fig. 8-6 is drawn as a state diagram in Fig. 8-7. The three states are symbolized by circles, with their binary values written inside the circles. The directed lines indicate the conditions that determine the next state. The unconditional and conditional operations that must be performed are not indicated in the state diagram.

Timing Considerations

The timing for all registers and flip-flops in a digital system is controlled by a master-clock generator. The clock pulses are applied not only to the registers of the datapath, but also to all the flip-flops in the control logic. Inputs are also synchronized with the clock because they are normally generated as outputs of another circuit that uses the same clock signals. If the input signal changes at an arbitrary time independent of the clock, we call it an asynchronous input. Asynchronous inputs may cause a variety of problems, as discussed in Chapter 9. To simplify the design, we will assume that all inputs are synchronized with the clock and change state in response to an edge transition.

The major difference between a conventional flow chart and an ASM chart is in interpreting the time relationship among the various operations. For example, if Fig. 8-6 were a conventional flowchart, then the listed operations would be considered to follow one after another in time sequence: Register A is first incremented and only then is E evaluated. If $E = 1$, then register R is cleared and control goes to state T_4. Otherwise, if $E = 0$, the next step is to evaluate F and go to state T_2 or T_3. In contrast, an ASM chart considers the entire block as one unit.

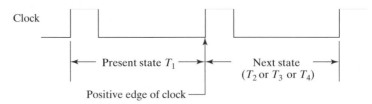

FIGURE 8-8
Transition Between States

All the operations that are specified within the block must occur in synchronism during the edge transition of the same clock pulse while the system changes from T_1 to the next state. This is presented pictorially in Fig. 8-8. We assume positive-edge triggering of all flip-flops. The first positive transition of the clock transfers the control circuit into state T_1. While in state T_1, the control circuits check inputs E and F and generate appropriate signals accordingly. The following operations occur simultaneously during the next positive edge of the clock:

1. Register A is incremented.
2. If $E = 1$, register R is cleared.
3. Control transfers to the next state as specified in Fig. 8-7.

Note that the two operations in the datapath and the change of state in the control logic occur at the same time.

8-4 DESIGN EXAMPLE

We will now demonstrate the components of the ASM chart and the register transfer representation by going over a specific design example. We start from the initial specifications and proceed with the development of an appropriate ASM chart from which the digital hardware is then designed.

We wish to design a digital system with two flip-flops, E and F, and one 4-bit binary counter A. The individual flip-flops in A are denoted by A_4, A_3, A_2, A_1, with A_4 holding the most significant bit of the count. A start signal S initiates the system operation by clearing the counter A and flip-flop F. The counter is then incremented by one starting from the next clock pulse and continues to increment until the operations stop. Counter bits A_3 and A_4 determine the sequence of operations:

If $A_3 = 0$, E is cleared to 0 and the count continues.

If $A_3 = 1$, E is set to 1; then if $A_4 = 0$, the count continues, but if $A_4 = 1$, F is set to 1 on the next clock pulse and the system stops counting.

Then if $S = 0$, the system remains in the initial state, but if $S = 1$, the operation cycle repeats.

ASM Chart

The ASM chart is shown in Fig. 8-9. When no operations are performed, the system is in the initial state T_0, waiting for the start signal S. When input S is equal to 1, counter A and flip-flop F are cleared to 0 and the controller goes to state T_1. Note the conditional box that follows the decision box for S. This means that the counter and flip-flop will be cleared during T_0 if $S = 1$, and at the same time, control transfers to state T_1.

The block associated with state T_1 has two decision boxes and two conditional boxes. The counter is incremented with every clock pulse. At the same time, one of three possible operations occur during the same clock edge:

Either E is cleared and control stays in state T_1 $(A_3 = 0)$; or

E is set and control stays in state T_1 $(A_3A_4 = 10)$; or

E is set and control goes to state T_2 $(A_3A_4 = 11)$.

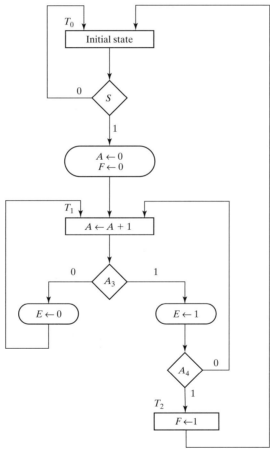

FIGURE 8-9
ASM Chart for Design Example

When the control is in state T_2, flip-flop F is set to 1 and the circuit goes back to the initial state, T_0.

The ASM chart consists of three states and three blocks. The block associated with T_0 consists of the state box, one decision box, and one conditional box. The block associated with T_2 consists of only the state box. The control logic has one external input, S, and two status inputs, A_3 and A_4.

We have shown here the way that a word description of a design is translated into an ASM chart. It must be realized that the design example formulated in the ASM chart does not have a practical application and, depending on the interpretation, may be simplified and formulated differently. However, once the ASM chart is established, the procedure for designing the circuit is straightforward.

Timing Sequence

Every block in an ASM chart specifies the operations that are to be performed during one common clock pulse. The operations specified within the state and conditional boxes in the block are performed in the datapath subsection. The change from one state to the next is performed in the control logic. In order to appreciate the timing relationship involved, we will list the step-by-step sequence of operations after each clock edge from the time the start signal occurs until the system goes back to the initial state.

Table 8-2 shows the binary values of the counter and the two flip-flops after every clock pulse. The table also shows separately the status of A_3 and A_4 as well as the present state of the controller. We start with state T_1 right after the input signal S has caused the counter and flip-flop F to be cleared. The value of E is assumed to be 1, because E is equal to 1 at T_0 (as shown at the end of the table) and because E does not change during the transition from T_0 to T_1. The system stays in state T_1 during the next 13 clock pulses. Each pulse increments the counter and either clears or sets E. Note the relationship between the time at which A_3 becomes a 1 and the time at which E is set to 1. When $A = 0011$, the next clock pulse increments the counter to 0100, but that same clock edge sees the value of A_3 as 0, so E is cleared. The next pulse changes the counter from 0100 to 0101, and now A_3 is initially equal to 1, so E is set to 1. Similarly, E is cleared to 0 not when the count goes from 0111 to 1000, but when it goes from 1000 to 1001, which is when A_3 is 0 in the present value of the counter.

When the count reaches 1100, both A_3 and A_4 are equal to 1. The next clock edge increments A by 1, sets E to 1, and transfers control to state T_2. Control stays in T_2 for only one clock period. The clock edge associated with T_2 sets flip-flop F to 1 and transfers control to state T_0. The system stays in the initial state T_0 as long as S is equal to 0.

From observation of Table 8-2, it may seem that the operations performed on E are delayed by one clock pulse. This is the difference between an ASM chart and a conventional flow chart. If Fig. 8-9 were a conventional flowchart, we would assume that A is first incremented and the incremented value would have been used to check the status of A_3. The operations that are performed in the digital hardware as specified by a block in the ASM chart occur during the same clock cycle and not in a sequence of operations following each other in time, as is usually interpreted in a conventional flowchart. Thus, the value of A_3 to be considered in the decision box is taken from the value of the counter in the present state and before it is incremented. This is because the decision box for E belongs with the same block as state T_1. The digital circuits in

Table 8-2
Sequence of Operations for Design Example

	Counter			Flip-Flops			
A_4	A_3	A_2	A_1	E	F	Conditions	State
0	0	0	0	1	0	$A_3 = 0, A_4 = 0$	T_1
0	0	0	1	0	0		
0	0	1	0	0	0		
0	0	1	1	0	0		
0	1	0	0	0	0	$A_3 = 1, A_4 = 0$	
0	1	0	1	1	0		
0	1	1	0	1	0		
0	1	1	1	1	0		
1	0	0	0	1	0	$A_3 = 0, A_4 = 1$	
1	0	0	1	0	0		
1	0	1	0	0	0		
1	0	1	1	0	0		
1	1	0	0	0	0	$A_3 = 1, A_4 = 1$	
1	1	0	1	1	0		T_2
1	1	0	1	1	1		T_0

the control generate the signals for all the operations specified in the present block prior to the arrival of the next clock pulse. The next clock edge executes all the operations in the registers and flip-flops, including the flip-flops in the controller that determine the next state.

Datapath Design

The ASM chart gives all the information necessary to design the digital system. The requirements for the design of the datapath are specified inside the state and conditional boxes. The control logic is determined from the decision boxes and the required state transitions. A diagram showing the hardware for the design example is shown in Fig. 8-10. The control subsystem is shown with only its inputs and outputs. The detailed design of the control is considered subsequently. The datapath consists of a four bit binary counter, two flip-flops, and a number of gates. The counter is similar to the one shown in Fig. 6-12 except that additional gates are required for the synchronous clear operation. The counter is incremented with every clock cycle when control is in state T_1. It is cleared only when control is at state T_0 and S is equal to 1. This conditional operation requires an AND gate to guarantee that both conditions are present. The other two conditional operations use two other AND gates for setting or clearing flip-flop E. Flip-flop F is set unconditionally during state T_2. Note that all flip-flops and registers including the flip-flops in the control use a common clock.

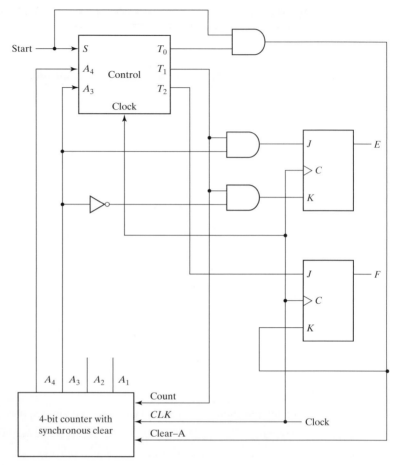

FIGURE 8-10
Datapath for Design Example

Register Transfer Representation

A digital system is represented in the register transfer level by specifying the registers in the system, the operations performed, and the control sequence. The register operations and control information can be specified with an ASM chart. It is sometimes convenient to separate the control logic and the register operations for the datapath. The control information and register transfer operations can be represented separately as shown in Fig. 8-11. The state diagram specifies the control sequence and the register operations are symbolized with the notation introduced in Section 8-1. This representation is an alternative to the representation of the system described in the ASM chart of Fig. 8-9. The information for the state diagram is taken directly from the ASM chart. The state names are specified in each state box. The conditions that cause a change of state are specified inside the diamond-shaped decision boxes. The directed lines between states and the condition associated with each follow the same path as in the ASM chart. The register transfer operations for each of the three states are listed following the name of the state and a colon(:). They are taken from the corresponding rectangular-shaped state boxes and the oval-shaped conditional boxes in the ASM chart.

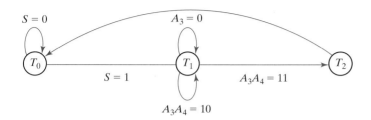

T_0: if $(S = 1)$ then $A \leftarrow 0, F \leftarrow 0$

T_1: $A \leftarrow A + 1$

    if $(A_3 = 1)$ then $E \leftarrow 1$

    if $(A_3 = 0)$ then $E \leftarrow 0$

T_2: $F \leftarrow 1$

(a) State diagram for control   (b) Register transfer operations

FIGURE 8-11
Register Transfer Level Description of Design Example

State Table

The state diagram can be converted into a state table from which the sequential circuit of the controller can be designed. First, we must assign binary values to each state in the ASM chart. For n flip-flops in the control sequential circuit, the ASM chart can accommodate up to 2^n states. A chart with three or four states requires a sequential circuit with two flip-flops. With five to eight states, there is a need for three flip-flops. Each combination of flip-flop values represents a binary number for one of the states.

A state table for a controller is a list of present states and inputs and their corresponding next states and outputs. In most cases, there are many don't-care input conditions that must be included, so it is advisable to arrange the state table to take this into consideration. We assign the following binary values to the three states: $T_0 = 00, T_1 = 01, T_2 = 11$. Binary state 10 is not used and will be treated a don't-care condition. The state table corresponding to the state diagram is shown in Table 8-3. Two flip-flops are needed, and they are labeled G_1 and G_0. There are three inputs and three outputs. The inputs are taken from the conditions in the decision boxes. The outputs are equivalent to the present state of the control. Note that there is a row in the table for each

Table 8-3
State Table for Control of Fig. 8-10

Present-State Symbol	Present State		Inputs			Next State		Outputs		
	G_1	G_0	S	A_3	A_4	G_1	G_0	T_0	T_1	T_2
T_0	0	0	0	X	X	0	0	1	0	0
T_0	0	0	1	X	X	0	1	1	0	0
T_1	0	1	X	0	X	0	1	0	1	0
T_1	0	1	X	1	0	0	1	0	1	0
T_1	0	1	X	1	1	1	1	0	1	0
T_2	1	1	X	X	X	0	0	0	0	1

possible transition between states. Initial state 00 goes to state 01 or stays in 00, depending on the value of input S. The other two inputs are marked with don't-care X's, as they do not determine the next state in this case. While the system is in binary state 00, the control provides an output labeled T_0 to initiate the required register operations. The transition from binary state 01 depends on inputs A_3 and A_4. The system goes to binary state 11 only if $A_3A_4 = 11$; otherwise, it remains in binary state 01. Finally, binary state 11 goes to 00 independently of the input variables.

Control Logic

The procedure for designing a sequential circuit starting from a state table is presented in Chapter 5. If this procedure is applied to Table 8-3, we need to use five-variable maps to simplify the input equations. This is because there are five variables listed under the present-state and input columns in the table. Instead of using maps to simplify the input equations, we can obtain them directly from the state table by inspection. To design the sequential circuit with D flip-flops, it is necessary to go over the next state columns in the state table and derive all the conditions that must set each flip-flop to 1. From Table 8-3, we note that the next state column of G_1 has a single 1 in the fifth row. The D input of flip-flop G_1 must be equal to 1 during present state T_1 when both inputs A_3 and A_4 are equal to 1. This is expressed with the D flip-flop input equation.

$$D_{G1} = T_1A_3A_4$$

Similarly, the next state column of G_0 has four 1's, and the condition for setting this flip-flop is

$$D_{G0} = T_0S + T_1$$

To derive the three output functions, we can utilize the fact that binary state 10 is not used and obtain the following simplified set of output equations:

$$T_0 = G_0'$$
$$T_1 = G_1'G_0$$
$$T_2 = G_1$$

The logic diagram of the control is drawn in Fig. 8-12. This circuit shows the internal construction of the control block in Fig. 8-10 together with the AND gate that generates the Clear-A signal.

8-5   HDL DESCRIPTION OF DESIGN EXAMPLE

In previous chapters, we have shown examples of HDL descriptions of combinational circuits, sequential circuits, and various standard components such as multiplexers, counters, and registers. We are now in a position to incorporate these components into the description of a specific design. As mentioned previously, a design can be described either at the structural or behavioral level. Behavioral descriptions may be classified as being either at the register transfer level or at an abstract algorithmic level. Consequently, we now consider three levels of design: structural description, RTL description, and algorithmic-based behavioral description.

The *structural* description is the lowest and most detailed level. The digital system is specified in terms of the physical components and their interconnection. The various components may include gates, flip-flops, and standard circuits such as multiplexers and counters. The design is

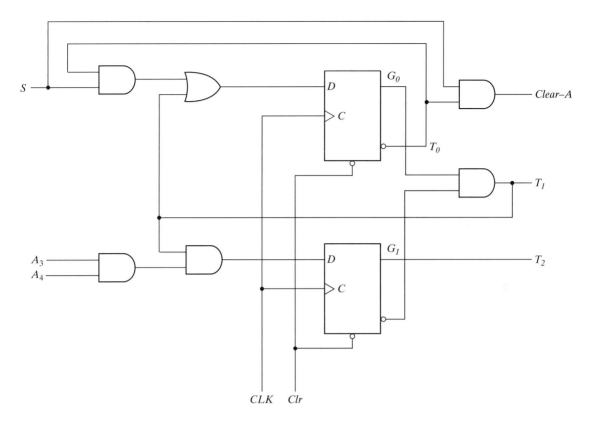

FIGURE 8-12
Logic Diagram of Control

hierarchically decomposed into functional units, and each unit is described by an HDL module. A top-level module combines the entire system by instantiating all the lower-level modules.

The *RTL* description specifies the digital system in terms of the registers, the operations performed, and the control that sequences the operations. This type of description consists of procedural statements that determine the relationship between the various operations of the design without reference to specific structure. The RTL description implies a certain hardware configuration among the registers. This allows the designer to create a design that can be synthesized into standard digital components.

The *algorithmic-based behavioral* description is the most abstract level. It describes the function of the design in a procedural algorithmic form similar to a programming language. It does not provide any detail on how the design is to be implemented with hardware. It is most appropriate for simulation of complex systems to verify design ideas. Descriptions at this level can be accessible to non-technical users that understand programming languages. Some of the constructs at this level might not be synthesizable.

We will now demonstrate the RTL and structural descriptions by using the design example of the previous section. An algorithmic-based description is illustrated in Section 8-8.

RTL Description

The HDL description of an RTL design can be divided into three sections. The first section defines the inputs, outputs, and registers in the design. The second section specifies the control sequence. The third section provides the register transfer operations and outputs. The RTL description of the design example is shown in HDL Example 8-2. It follows the ASM chart of Fig. 8-9 and the register transfer specifications of Fig. 8-11. The inputs are S (start), CLK (clock), and Clr (clear). The clear input is needed for initializing the state of the control to $T0$. The outputs are flip-flops E and F, and register A. The control register is specified with a 2-bit vector that holds the binary value of the present and next state conditions. The three control states are given symbolic names and are encoded into binary values.

The next section of the RTL description specifies the control sequence with two always statements. The first always block provides two operations: the Clr input initializes the present state to $T0$, and the posedge CLK synchronizes the state transition with the clock. The second always block consists of a case condition that specifies the transition from present state to next state. For example, if the present state is $T0$ and $S = 1$, the next state is set to $T1$. If $S = 0$, state $T0$ does not change. The change from $T0$ to $T1$ (if $S = 1$) is executed only when the event posedge CLK occurs as dictated by the first always statement.

The third section of the RTL description specifies the register transfer operations in each of the three control states. This follows the register transfer operations listed in Figure 8-11(b). Note that non-blocking assignments are used (with symbol <=) for the register transfer operations. This is crucial especially during control state $T1$. While in this state, A is incremented by one and the value of $A[3]$ is checked to determine the status of E. To accomplish a valid synchronous design, it is necessary to ensure that $A[3]$ is checked before A is incremented. If blocking assignment were used, one would have to place the two statements that check E first and the increment A statement last. However, by using non-blocking assignments, we accomplish the required synchronization without being concerned about the order in which the statements are listed.

Testing the Design Description

The sequence of operations for the design example was investigated in the previous section. Table 8-2 shows the values of E and F while register A is incremented. It would be instructive to devise a test that checks the circuit to verify the validity of the HDL description. The test bench in HDL Example 8-3 provides such a module. (The procedure for writing test benches is explained in Section 4-11.) The test module generates signals for S, CLK, Clr, and checks the results obtained from registers A, E, and F. Initially, the Clr signal is set to 0 to initialize the control and S and CLK are set to 0. At time $t = 5$, the Clr signal is disabled by setting it to 1, the S input is enabled by setting it to 1, and the clock is then repeated for 16 cycles. The **$monitor** statement displays the values of A, E, and F every 10 ns. The output of the simulation is listed in the example under the simulation log. Initially, at time $t = 0$, the values of the registers are unknown so they are marked with the symbol **x**. The first positive clock transition at time $= 10$, clears A and F but does not affect E, so E is unknown at this time. The rest of the table is identical to Table 8-2. Note that since S is still equal to 1 at time $= 160$, the last entry in the table shows that A and F are cleared to 0 and E does not change and remains at 1. This occurs during the second transition from $T0$ to $T1$.

HDL Example 8-2

```
//RTL description of design example (Fig.8-11)
module Example_RTL (S,CLK,Clr,E,F,A);
//Specify inputs and outputs
//See block diagram Fig. 8-10
   input S,CLK,Clr;
   output E,F;
   output [4:1] A;
//Specify system registers
   reg [4:1] A;                 //A register
   reg E, F;                    //E and F flip-flops
   reg [1:0] pstate, nstate;    //control register
//Encode the states
   parameter T0 = 2'b00, T1 = 2'b01, T2 = 2'b11;
//State transition for control logic
//See state diagram Fig. 8-11(a)
   always @(posedge CLK or negedge Clr)
      if (~Clr) pstate = T0;    //Initial state
      else pstate <= nstate;    //Clocked operations
   always @ (S or A or pstate)
      case (pstate)
        T0: if(S) nstate = T1; else nstate = T0;
        T1: if(A[3] & A[4]) nstate = T2; else nstate = T1;
        T2: nstate = T0;
      endcase
//Register transfer operations
//See list of operations Fig.8-11(b)
   always @(posedge CLK)
      case (pstate)
        T0: if(S)
               begin
                  A <= 4'b0000;
                  F <= 1'b0;
               end
        T1:
               begin
                  A <= A + 1'b1;
                  if (A[3]) E <= 1'b1;
                  else  E <= 1'b0;
               end
        T2:  F <= 1'b1;
      endcase
endmodule
```

HDL Example 8-3

```
//Test bench for design example
module test_design_example;
  reg S, CLK, Clr;
  wire [4:1] A;
  wire E, F;
//Instantiate design example
    Example_RTL dsexp (S,CLK,Clr,E,F,A);
      initial
        begin
              Clr = 0;
              S = 0;
              CLK = 0;
          #5 Clr = 1; S = 1;
              repeat (32)
              begin
                #5 CLK = ~ CLK;
              end
        end
      initial
        $monitor("A = %b E = %b F = %b time = %0d", A,E,F,$time);
endmodule
```

```
Simulation log:

A = xxxx E = x F = x time = 0
A = 0000 E = x F = 0 time = 10
A = 0001 E = 0 F = 0 time = 20
A = 0010 E = 0 F = 0 time = 30
A = 0011 E = 0 F = 0 time = 40
A = 0100 E = 0 F = 0 time = 50
A = 0101 E = 1 F = 0 time = 60
A = 0110 E = 1 F = 0 time = 70
A = 0111 E = 1 F = 0 time = 80
A = 1000 E = 1 F = 0 time = 90
A = 1001 E = 0 F = 0 time = 100
A = 1010 E = 0 F = 0 time = 110
A = 1011 E = 0 F = 0 time = 120
A = 1100 E = 0 F = 0 time = 130
A = 1101 E = 1 F = 0 time = 140
A = 1101 E = 1 F = 1 time = 150
A = 0000 E = 1 F = 0 time = 160
```

Structural Description

The RTL description of a design consists of procedural statements that determine the functional behavior of the digital circuit. This type of presentation can be compiled by HDL synthesis tools from which it is possible to obtain the equivalent gate-level circuit of the design. It is also possible to describe the design by its structure rather than its function. A structural description of a design consists of instantiation of components that define the interconnection structure of the circuit. In this regard, a structural description is equivalent to a schematic diagram or a block diagram of the circuit.

The block diagram of Fig. 8-10 gives the information needed for the structural description. For convenience, the circuit is decomposed into three parts:

1. The control block.
2. The E and F flip-flops and associated gates.
3. The counter with synchronous clear.

A hierarchical description of the design can be accomplished by a nested instantiation of the three parts.

HDL Example 8-4 shows the structural description of the design example. It consists of six modules that can be separated into four parts:

1. The first module instantiates the three components.
2. The next two modules describe the control and its D flip-flop.
3. The next two modules describe E and F and their JK flip-flop.
4. The last module describes the counter.

The first module declares the inputs and outputs of the circuit. The port list is identical to the list used in the RTL description. The outputs are not declared as **reg** type here because they are declared as **reg** in the lower-level modules. The top-level module encapsulates the entire design by instantiating the three lower-level components. Some of the ports in the instantiated modules are the circuit inputs or outputs. Other ports are inputs generated from other modules or outputs needed for other modules. For example, the control module ctl has inputs $A[3]$ and $A[4]$ that come from the $A[4:1]$ output of the counter ctr module. Outputs $T1$ and $T2$ in the ctl module are used as inputs in the EF module.

The control module describes the circuit of Fig. 8-12. The outputs of the two flip-flops $G1$ and $G0$ and their inputs $DG1$ and $DG0$ are declared as **wire** data type. $G1$ and $G0$ cannot be declared as **reg** data type because they are outputs of the instantiated D flip-flop. $DG1$ and $DG0$ cannot be declared as **reg** type because they are used in continuous assignment statements. The five **assign** statements specify the combinational part of the circuit. There are two flip-flop input equations and three output equations. The outputs of the flip-flops $G1$ and $G0$, and the input equations $DG1$ and $DG0$ replace output Q and input D in the instantiated flip-flops. The D flip-flop is then described in the next module. The EF module follows the same pattern for the two JK flip-flops. The flip-flop input equations are first derived, and the JK flip-flop is instantiated with these values as inputs. The last module describes the counter with synchronous clear.

HDL Example 8-4

```
//Structural description of design example
//See block diagram Fig. 8-10
module Example_Structure (S,CLK,Clr,E,F,A);
    input S,CLK,Clr;
    output E,F;
    output [4:1] A;
//Instantiate control circuit
    control ctl (S,A[3],A[4],CLK,Clr,T2,T1,Clear);
//Instantiate E and F flip-flips
    E_F EF (T1,T2,Clear,CLK,A[3],E,F);
//Instantiate counter
    counter ctr (T1,Clear,CLK,A);
endmodule

//Control circuit (Fig. 8-12)
module control (Start,A3,A4,CLK,Clr,T2,T1,Clear);
    input Start,A3,A4,CLK,Clr;
    output T2,T1,Clear;
    wire G1,G0,DG1,DG0;
//Combinational circuit
    assign  DG1 = A3 & A4 & T1,
            DG0 = (Start & ~G0) | T1,
            T2  = G1,
            T1  = G0 & ~G1,
            Clear = Start & ~G0;
//Instantiate D flip-flop
    DFF G1F (G1,DG1,CLK,Clr),
        G0F (G0,DG0,CLK,Clr);
endmodule

//D flip-flop
module DFF (Q,D,CLK,Clr);
    input D,CLK,Clr;
    output Q;
    reg Q;
    always @ (posedge CLK or negedge Clr)
      if (~Clr) Q = 1'b0;
      else Q = D;
endmodule

//E and F flip-flops
module E_F (T1,T2,Clear,CLK,A3,E,F);
    input T1,T2,Clear,CLK,A3;
    output E,F;
    wire E,F,JE,KE,JF,KF;
```

(continued)

```
//Combinational circuit
    assign JE = T1 & A3,
           KE = T1 & ~A3,
           JF = T2,
           KF = Clear;
//Instantiate JK flip-flop
    JKFF EF (E,JE,KE,CLK),
         FF (F,JF,KF,CLK);
endmodule

//JK flip-flop
module JKFF (Q,J,K,CLK);
    input J,K,CLK;
    output Q;
    reg Q;
    always @ (posedge CLK)
      case ({J,K})
        2'b00: Q = Q;
        2'b01: Q = 1'b0;
        2'b10: Q = 1'b1;
        2'b11: Q = ~Q;
      endcase
endmodule

//counter with synchronous clear
module counter (Count,Clear,CLK,A);
    input Count,Clear,CLK;
    output [4:1] A;
    reg [4:1] A;
    always @ (posedge CLK)
      if (Clear) A<= 4'b0000;
      else if (Count) A <= A + 1'b1;
      else A <= A;
endmodule
```

The structural description was tested using the test bench of Example 8-3. The only change necessary is the replacement of the instantiation of the example from Example_RTL to Example_Structure. The result of the simulation for the structural description is the same as the output simulation obtained from the RTL description.

8-6   BINARY MULTIPLIER

This section introduces a second design example. It presents a hardware algorithm for binary multiplication, proposes the register configuration for its implementation, and then proceeds to show the design of the datapath and control by use of an ASM chart.

The system we will examine multiplies two unsigned binary numbers. In Section 4-6, a hardware algorithm to execute the multiplication was developed that resulted in a combinational circuit multiplier with many adders and AND gates. In contrast, in this section, the hardware algorithm is to result in a sequential multiplier that uses only one adder and a shift register.

The multiplication of two binary numbers is done with paper and pencil by successive additions and shifting. This process is best illustrated with a numerical example. Let us multiply the two binary numbers 10111 and 10011:

23	10111	multiplicand
19	10011	multiplier
	10111	
	10111	
	00000	
	00000	
	10111	
437	110110101	product

The process consists of looking at successive bits of the multiplier, least significant bit first. If the multiplier bit is 1, the multiplicand is copied down; otherwise, 0's are copied down. The numbers copied in successive lines are shifted one position to the left from the previous number. Finally, the numbers are added and their sum forms the product. The product obtained from the multiplication of two binary numbers of n bits each can have up to $2n$ bits.

When the multiplication procedure is implemented with digital hardware, it is convenient to change the process slightly. First, instead of providing digital circuits to store and add simultaneously as many binary numbers as there are 1's in the multiplier, it is less expensive to provide circuits for the summation of only two binary numbers and successively accumulate the partial products in a register. Second, instead of shifting the multiplicand to the left, the partial product being formed is shifted to the right. This leaves the partial product and the multiplicand in the required relative positions. Third, when the corresponding bit of the multiplier is 0, there is no need to add all 0's to the partial product, since this will not alter its resulting value.

Register Configuration

The block diagram for the binary multiplier is shown in Fig. 8-13. The multiplicand is stored in register B, the multiplier is stored in register Q, and the partial product is formed in register A and stored in A and Q. A parallel adder adds the contents of register B to register A. The C flip-flop stores the carry after the addition. The P counter is initially set to hold a binary number equal to the number of bits in the multiplier. This counter is decremented after the formation of each partial product. When the content of the counter reaches zero, the product is formed in the double register A and Q and the process stops. The control logic stays in an initial state until the start signal S becomes 1. The system then performs the multiplication. The sum of A and B forms the n most significant bits of the partial product, which is transferred to A. The output carry from the addition, whether 0 or 1, is transferred to C. Both the partial product in A and the multiplier in Q are shifted to the right. The least significant bit of A is shifted into the

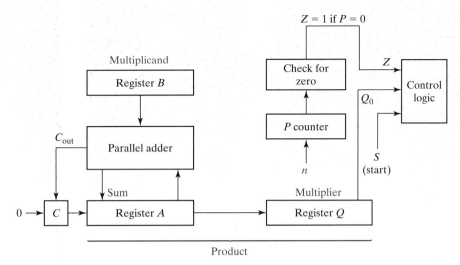

FIGURE 8-13
Block Diagram of Binary Multiplier

most significant position of Q; the carry from C is shifted into the most significant position of A; and 0 is shifted into C. After the shift right operation, one bit of the partial product is transferred into Q while the multiplier bits in Q are shifted one position to the right. In this manner, the least significant bit of register Q, designated by Q_0, holds the bit of the multiplier that must be inspected next. The control logic determines whether to add or not, based on this input bit. The control logic also receives signal Z from a circuit that checks counter P for zero. Q_0 and Z are status inputs for the control unit. The start input S is an external control input. The outputs of the control logic activate the required operations in the registers.

ASM Chart

The ASM chart for the binary multiplier is shown in Fig. 8-14. Initially, the multiplicand is in B and the multiplier in Q. As long as the circuit is in the initial state and $S = 0$, no action occurs and the system remains in an initial state T_0. The multiplication process starts when $S = 1$ and control goes to state T_1. Register A and carry flip-flop C are cleared to 0 and the sequence counter P is set to a binary number n, equal to the number of bits in the multiplier. The system then goes to state T_2. The multiplier bit in Q_0 is checked, and if it is equal to 1, the multiplicand in B is added to the partial product in A. The carry from the addition is transferred to C. The partial product in A and C is left unchanged if $Q_0 = 0$. The P counter is decremented by 1 regardless of the value of Q_0. In both cases, the next state is T_3. Registers C, A, and Q are combined into one composite register CAQ, and its contents are shifted once to the right to obtain a new partial product. This shift operation is symbolized in the flowchart in compact form with the statement

$$\text{Shift right } CAQ, C \leftarrow 0$$

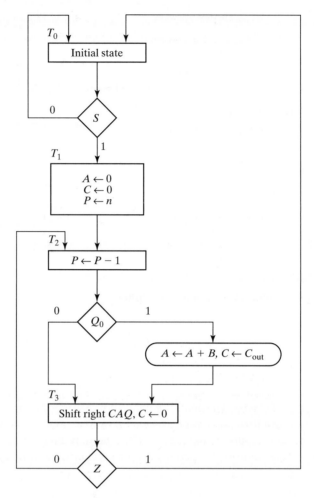

FIGURE 8-14
ASM Chart for Binary Multiplier

Using the individual register symbols, the shift operation can be described by the following register operations:

$$A \leftarrow shr\ A, A_{n-1} \leftarrow C$$
$$Q \leftarrow shr\ Q, Q_{n-1} \leftarrow A_0$$
$$C \leftarrow 0$$

Both registers A and Q are shifted right. The leftmost bit of A, designated by A_{n-1}, receives the carry from C. The leftmost bit of Q, or Q_{n-1}, receives the bit from the rightmost position of A in A_0; and C is reset to 0. In essence, this is a long shift of the composite register CAQ with 0 inserted into the serial input which is at C.

Table 8-4

Numerical Example For Binary Multiplier

Multiplicand B = 10111

	C	A	Q	P
Multiplier in Q	0	00000	10011	101
$Q_0 = 1$; add B		10111		
First partial product	0	10111		100
Shift right CAQ	0	01011	11001	
$Q_0 = 1$; add B		10111		
Second partial product	1	00010		011
Shift right CAQ	0	10001	01100	
$Q_0 = 0$; shift right CAQ	0	01000	10110	010
$Q_0 = 0$; shift right CAQ	0	00100	01011	001
$Q_0 = 1$; add B		10111		
Fifth partial product	0	11011		
Shift right CAQ	0	01101	10101	000
Final product in $AQ = 0110110101$				

The value in the P counter is checked after the formation of each partial product. If the content of P is not zero, status bit Z is equal to 0 and the process is repeated to form a new partial product. The process stops when the P counter reaches 0 and the control input Z is equal to 1. Note that the partial product formed in A is shifted into Q one bit at a time and eventually replaces the multiplier. The final product is available in A and Q, with A holding the most significant bits and Q the least significant bits of the product.

The previous numerical example is repeated in Table 8-4 to clarify the multiplication process. The procedure follows the steps outlined in the ASM chart.

The type of registers needed for the data processor subsystem can be derived from the register operations listed in the ASM chart. Register A is a shift register with parallel load to accept the sum from the adder and must have a synchronous clear capability to reset the register to 0. Register Q is a shift register. The counter P is a binary down counter with a facility to parallel load a binary constant. The C flip-flop must be designed to accept the input carry and have a synchronous clear. Registers B and Q need a parallel load capability in order to receive the multiplicand and multiplier prior to the start of the multiplication process.

8-7   CONTROL LOGIC

The design of a digital system can be divided into two parts: the design of the register transfers in the datapath and the design of the control logic. The control logic design is a sequential circuit design problem. As such, it may be convenient to formulate the state diagram of the sequential control. An ASM chart is similar to a state diagram. The rectangular blocks that designate state boxes are the states of the sequential circuit. The diamond shaped blocks that designate decision boxes determine the conditions for the next state transition in the state

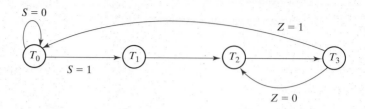

(a) State diagram

T_0: Initial state

T_1: $A \leftarrow 0, C \leftarrow 0, P \leftarrow n$

T_2: $P \leftarrow P - 1$

if $(Q_0) = 1$ then $(A \leftarrow A + B, C \leftarrow C_{out})$

T_3: shift right$CAQ, C \leftarrow 0$

(b) Register transfer operations

FIGURE 8-15
Control Specifications for Binary Multiplier

diagram. As an example, the control state diagram for the binary multiplier developed in the previous section is shown in Fig. 8-15. The information for the diagram is taken directly from the ASM chart of Fig. 8-14. The four states T_0 through T_3 are taken from the rectangular state boxes. The inputs S and Z are taken from the diamond-shaped decision boxes. The register transfer operations for each of the four states are listed below the state diagram. They are taken from the corresponding state and conditional boxes in the ASM chart.

There are two distinct aspects with which we have to deal when implementing the control logic: establish the required sequence of states and provide signals to control the register operations. The sequence of states is specified in the state diagram. The signals for controlling the operations in the registers are specified in the register transfer statements. For the multiplier, these signals are T_1 (for clearing A and C and loading a number into P), T_2 (for decrementing P), T_3 (for shifting register CAQ), and Q_0 to determine whether B is added to A or not. The block diagram of the control is shown in Fig. 8-16. The inputs for the sequential control are S and Z, and the outputs are T_0, T_1, T_2, T_3, as specified in the state diagram. The AND gate that generates signal $L = T_2 Q_0$ is required for loading the sum into register A if $Q_0 = 1$ while in state T_2.

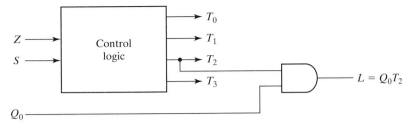

FIGURE 8-16
Control Block Diagram

An important step in the design is the assignment of coded binary values to the states. The simplest assignment is the straight binary numbers as shown in Table 8-5. Another similar assignment is the Gray code where only one bit changes when going from one number to the next. A state assignment often used in control design is the *one-hot* assignment. This assignment uses as many bits as there are states in the circuit. At any given time, only one bit is equal to 1 (the one hot) while all others are kept at 0 (all cold). This type of assignment uses a flip-flop for each state.

Table 8-5
State Assignment for Control

State	Binary	Gray Code	One-Hot
T_0	00	00	0001
T_1	01	01	0010
T_2	10	11	0100
T_3	11	10	1000

Since the control is a sequential circuit, it can be designed by the sequential logic procedure as outlined in Chapter 5. However, in most cases this method is difficult to carry out because of the large number of states and inputs that a typical control circuit may have. As a consequence, it is necessary to use specialized methods for control logic design that may be considered as variations of the classical sequential logic method. We will now present two such design procedures. One uses a sequence register and decoder and the other uses one flip-flop per state.

Sequence Register and Decoder

The sequence register and decoder method, as the name implies, uses a register for the control states and a decoder to provide an output corresponding to each of the states. A register with n flip-flops can have up to 2^n states and an n-to-2^n-line decoder has up to 2^n outputs. An n-bit sequence register is essentially a circuit with n flip-flops together with the associated gates that effect their state transition.

The control state diagram for the binary multiplier has four states and two inputs. To implement it with a sequence register and decoder, we need two flip-flops for the register and a

Table 8-6
State Table for Control Circuit

Present State		Input		Next State		Outputs			
G_1	G_0	S	Z	G_1	G_0	T_0	T_1	T_2	T_3
0	0	0	X	0	0	1	0	0	0
0	0	1	X	0	1	1	0	0	0
0	1	X	X	1	0	0	1	0	0
1	0	X	X	1	1	0	0	1	0
1	1	X	0	1	0	0	0	0	1
1	1	X	1	0	0	0	0	0	1

2-to-4- line decoder. Although this is a simple example, the procedure to be outlined applies to more complex situations as well.

The state table for the sequential control is shown in Table 8-6. It is derived directly from the state diagram of Fig. 8-15(a). We designate the two flip-flops as G_1 and G_0 and assign the binary state 00, 01, 10, and 11, to T_0, T_1, T_2, and T_3, respectively. Note that the input columns have don't-care entries whenever the input variable is not used to determine the next state. The outputs of the control circuit are designated by the state names. The particular output variable that is equal to 1 at any given time is determined from the equivalent binary value of the present state. Thus, when the present state is $G_1 G_0 = 00$, output T_0 must be equal to 1, while the other outputs remain at 0. Since the outputs are a function of only the present state, they can be generated with a decoder circuit having the two inputs G_1 and G_0 and the four outputs T_0 through T_3.

The sequential circuit can be designed from the state table by means of the classical procedure presented in Chapter 5. This example has a small number of states and inputs so we could use maps to simplify the Boolean functions. In most control logic applications, the number of states and inputs is much larger. The application of the classical method requires an excessive amount of work to obtain the simplified input equations for the flip-flops. The design can be simplified if we take into consideration the fact that the decoder outputs are available for use in the design. Instead of using flip-flop outputs as the present state conditions, we might as well use the outputs of the decoder to supply the present state conditions for the sequential circuit. Moreover, instead of using maps to simplify the flip-flop equations, we can obtain them directly from inspection of the state table. For example, from the next state conditions in the state table, we find that the next state of G_1 is equal to 1 when the present state is T_1, when the present state is T_2, or when the present state is T_3, provided that $Z = 0$. These conditions can be specified by the equation:

$$D_{G1} = T_1 + T_2 + T_3 Z'$$

where D_{G1} is the D input of flip-flop G_1. Similarly, the D input of G_0 is

$$D_{G0} = T_0 S + T_2$$

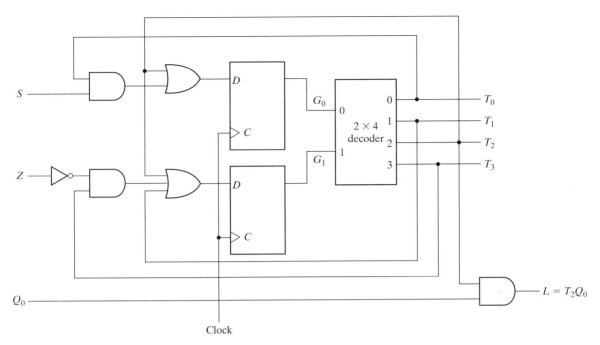

FIGURE 8-17
Logic Diagram of Control for Binary Multiplier Using a Sequence Register
and Decoder

When deriving input equations by inspection from the state table, we cannot be sure that the Boolean functions have been simplified in the best possible way. For this reason, it is advisable to analyze the circuit to ensure that the derived equations do indeed produce the required state transitions.

The logic diagram of the control circuit is drawn in Fig. 8-17. It consists of a register with two flip-flops G_1 and G_0 and a 2×4 decoder. The outputs of the decoder are used to generate the inputs to the next state logic as well as the control outputs. The outputs of the controller should be connected to the datapath to activate the required register operations.

One Flip-Flop per State

Another possible method of control logic design is the use of the one-hot assignment that results in a sequential circuit with one flip-flop per state. Only one of the flip-flops contains a 1 at any time; all others are reset to 0. The single 1 propagates from one flip-flop to another under the control of decision logic. In such a configuration, each flip-flop represents a state that is present only when the control bit is transferred to it.

This method uses the maximum number of flip-flops for the sequential circuit. For example, a sequential circuit with 12 states requires a minimum of four flip-flops. With the one flip-flop per state method, the circuit requires 12 flip-flops, one for each state. At first glance, it may seem that this method would increase system cost since more flip-flops are used. But the method offers some advantages that may not be apparent. One advantage is the simplicity with which the logic can be designed from inspection of the ASM chart or the state diagram. No state or excitation tables are needed if D type flip-flops are employed. It offers a savings in design effort, an increase in operational simplicity, and a possible decrease in the total number of gates since a decoder is not needed.

The design procedure will be demonstrated by obtaining the control circuit specified by the state diagram of Fig. 8-15(a). Since there are four states in the state diagram, we choose four D flip-flops and label their outputs T_0, T_1, T_2, and T_3. The input equations for setting each flip-flop to 1 is determined from the present state and the input conditions along the corresponding directed lines going into the state. For example, flip-flop T_0 is set to 1 with the next clock edge if the circuit is in present state T_3 and input Z is equal to 1 or if the circuit is in present state T_0 and S is equal to 0. These conditions are specified by the input equation:

$$D_{T0} = T_0 S' + T_3 Z$$

where D_{T0} denotes the D input of flip-flop T_0. In fact, the condition for setting a flip-flop to 1 is obtained directly from the state diagram from the condition specified in the directed lines going into the corresponding flip-flop state ANDed with the previous flip-flop state. If there are more than one directed lines going into a state, all conditions must be ORed. Using this procedure for the other three flip-flops, we obtain the input equations:

$$D_{T1} = T_0 S$$
$$D_{T2} = T_1 + T_3 Z'$$
$$D_{T3} = T_2$$

The logic diagram of the controller is shown in Fig. 8-18. It consists of four D flip-flops T_0 through T_3 and the associated gates specified by the input equations. Initially, flip-flop T_0 must be set to 1 and all other flip-flops must be reset to 0 so that the flip-flop representing the initial state is enabled. This can be done by using an asynchronous preset on flip-flop T_0 and an asynchronous clear for the other flip-flops. Once started, the one flip-flop per state controller will propagate from one state to the other in the proper manner. Only one flip-flop will be set to 1 with each clock edge; all others are reset to 0 because their D inputs are equal to 0.

8-8   HDL DESCRIPTION OF BINARY MULTIPLIER

A second example of an HDL description of an RTL design is shown in Example 8-5. The example is for the binary multiplier designed in Section 8-6. The description can be divided into five parts with each part preceded by an explanatory comment. The first part lists all inputs and outputs as specified in the block diagram of Fig. 8-13. The data inputs to B and Q and the data outputs from A and Q are 5-bit vectors. Five bits are chosen for this example in order to be able to compare the result of the multiplication with the numerical example listed in Table 8-4. The second part declares all registers including the control register and the encoding of the four states. The third part specifies a combinational circuit with an **assign** statement. There are two combinational circuits in the multiplier. One circuit is for checking the output of the counter

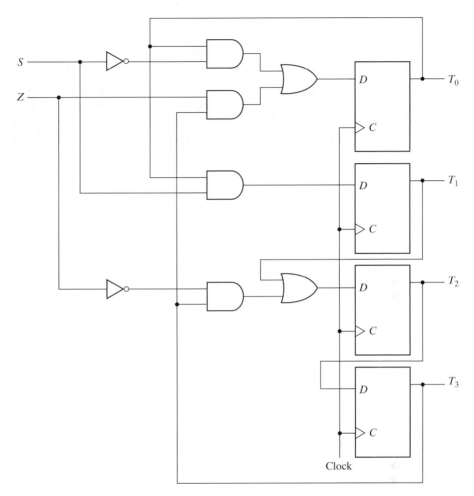

FIGURE 8-18
One Flip-Flop Per State Controller

to detect a zero output; the other is a parallel adder. The adder can be specified later as part of the register transfer operation that adds the multiplicand to the partial product. The zero detection is implemented with a 5-input NOR gate. This is specified in the assign statement with a NOR reduction operator.

The fourth part describes the state transition for the control and follows the state diagram of Fig. 8-15(a). The last part is a description of the register transfer operations for the datapath. This follows the operations listed in the ASM chart of Fig. 8-15(b). The data inputs are not listed in the ASM chart, but they must be provided here for checking the circuit operation. The multiplicand is transferred to B register during the initial state $T0$. The multiplier is transferred during state $T1$. At $T2$, the multiplicand is added to the partial product if $Q[0] = 1$. At $T3$, the partial product is shifted to the right.

HDL Example 8-5

```
//RTL description of binary multiplier
//Block diagram Fig. 8-13 and ASM chart Fig. 8-14
//n = 5 to compare with Table 8-4
module mltp(S,CLK,Clr,Binput,Qinput,C,A,Q,P);
   input S,CLK,Clr;
   input [4:0] Binput,Qinput;              //Data inputs
   output C;
   output [4:0] A,Q;
   output [2:0] P;
//System registers
   reg C;
   reg [4:0] A,Q,B;
   reg [2:0] P;
   reg [1:0] pstate, nstate;               //control register
   parameter T0=2'b00, T1=2'b01, T2=2'b10, T3=2'b11;
//Combinational circuit
   wire Z;
   assign Z = ~|P;                         //Check for zero
//State transition for control
//See state diagram Fig. 8-15(a)
   always @(negedge CLK or negedge Clr)
     if (~Clr) pstate = T0;
     else pstate <= nstate;
   always @(S or Z or pstate)
     case (pstate)
       T0: if (S) nstate = T1; else nstate = T0;
       T1: nstate = T2;
       T2: nstate = T3;
       T3: if (Z) nstate = T0;
           else    nstate = T2;
     endcase
//Register transfer operations
//See register operation Fig. 8-15(b)
   always @(negedge CLK)
     case (pstate)
       T0: B <= Binput;                    //Input multiplicand
       T1: begin
             A <= 5'b00000;
             C <= 1'b0;
             P <= 3'b101;                  //Initialize counter to n=5
             Q <= Qinput;                  //Input multiplier
           end
       T2: begin
             P <= P - 3'b001;              //Decrement counter
             if (Q[0])
             {C,A} <= A + B;               //Add multiplicand
           end
       T3: begin
             C <= 1'b0;                    //Clear C
             A <= {C,A[4:1]};              //Shift right A
             Q <= {A[0],Q[4:1]};           //Shift right Q
           end
     endcase
endmodule
```

Testing the Multiplier

HDL Example 8-6 shows a test bench for testing the multiplier. The inputs are the multiplicand and the multiplier in B and Q. The output is the product in A and Q. We also check the values of carry C and counter P. The 5-bit binary inputs are the same as the ones used in Table 8-4. The second initial statement provides 13 clock cycles of 10 time units each. Inspection of the state transitions shows that states $T2$ and $T3$ cycle in a loop five times (once for each partial product). This requires 10 clock cycles. Three more clock cycles are needed for $T0$, $T1$, and the return to $T0$ when $Z = 1$.

The result of the computation is displayed using the system task **$strobe**. This task is similar to the **$display** and **$monitor** tasks explained in Sec. 4-11. The **$strobe** system task provides a synchronization mechanism to ensure that data are displayed only after all assignments in a given time step are executed. This is very useful in synchronous sequential circuits where the time step begins at a clock edge. Using **$strobe** after the **always** @ **negedge** CLK statement ensures that the display shows signal values as they are after a negative transition of the clock.

The module test_mltp in HDL Example 8-6 instantiates the module mltp of Example 8-5. Both modules must be included when simulating the multiplier with a Verilog HDL simulator. The result of this simulation displays a simulation log with numbers identical to the ones in Table 8-4.

Behavioral Description of Multiplier

The binary multiplier can be described in the behavioral level as shown in HDL Example 8-7. The two inputs are declared as 8-bit vectors and the output as a 16-bit vector. No specific hardware is implied as in the RTL or structural descriptions. The operation is specified using just one multiplication statement. In this case, the description may be synthesized to a combinational circuit multiplier (see Section 4-6) if the synthesis software was so designed. In general, the algorithmic-based behavioral descriptions are not always synthesizable.

8-9 DESIGN WITH MULTIPLEXERS

The sequence register and decoder control consists of three components: the flip-flops that hold the binary state value, the decoder that generates the control outputs, and the gates that determine the next state and output signals. In Sec. 4-10 it was shown that a combinational circuit can be implemented with multiplexers instead of individual gates. Replacing the gates with multiplexers results in a regular pattern of three levels of components. The first level consists of multiplexers that determine the next state of the register. The second level contains a register that holds the present binary state. The third level has a decoder that provides a separate output for each control state. These three components are predefined standard cells in many integrated circuits.

Consider, for example, the ASM chart of Fig. 8-19. It consists of four states and four control inputs. The state boxes are left empty in this case because we are interested only in the control sequence, which is independent of the register operations. The binary assignment for each state is indicated at the upper right corner of the state boxes. The decision boxes specify the state transitions as a function of the four control inputs—w, x, y, and z. The three-level control

HDL Example 8-6

```
//Testing binary multiplier
module test_mltp;
//Inputs for multiplier
    reg S,CLK,Clr;
    reg [4:0] Binput,Qinput;
//Data for display
    wire C;
    wire [4:0] A,Q;
    wire [2:0] P;
//Instantiate multiplier
    mltp mp(S,CLK,Clr,Binput,Qinput,C,A,Q,P);
    initial
      begin
            S=0; CLK=0; Clr=0;
        #5  S=1; Clr=1;
            Binput = 5'b10111;
            Qinput = 5'b10011;
        #15 S = 0;
      end
    initial
      begin
            repeat (26)
        #5 CLK = ~CLK;
      end
//Display computations and compare with Table 8-4
    always @(negedge CLK)
        $strobe ("C=%b  A=%b  Q=%b  P=%b  time=%0d",C,A,Q,P,$time);
endmodule


Simulation log:

C=x  A=xxxxx  Q=xxxxx  P=xxx  time=10
C=0  A=00000  Q=10011  P=101  time=20
C=0  A=10111  Q=10011  P=100  time=30
C=0  A=01011  Q=11001  P=100  time=40
C=1  A=00010  Q=11001  P=011  time=50
C=0  A=10001  Q=01100  P=011  time=60
C=0  A=10001  Q=01100  P=010  time=70
C=0  A=01000  Q=10110  P=010  time=80
C=0  A=01000  Q=10110  P=001  time=90
C=0  A=00100  Q=01011  P=001  time=100
C=0  A=11011  Q=01011  P=000  time=110
C=0  A=01101  Q=10101  P=000  time=120
C=0  A=01101  Q=10101  P=000  time=130
```

HDL Example 8-7

```
//Behavioral description of multiplier (n = 8)
module Mult (A,B,Q);
    input [7:0] B,Q;
    output [15:0] A;
    reg [15:0] A;
    always @ (B or Q)
       A = B * Q;
endmodule
```

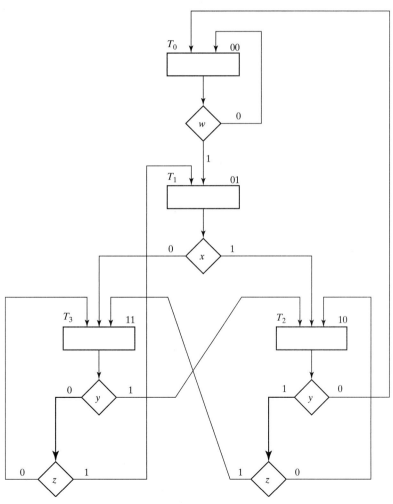

FIGURE 8-19
Example of ASM Chart with Four Control Inputs

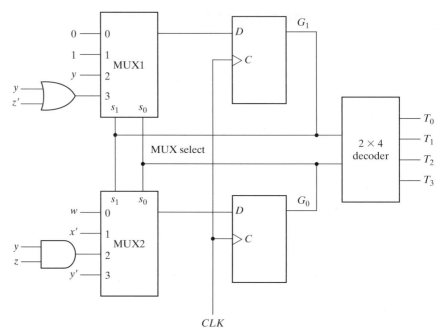

FIGURE 8-20
Control Implementation with Multiplexers

implementation is shown in Fig. 8-20. It consists of two multiplexers, MUX1 and MUX2; a register with two flip-flops, G_1 and G_0; and a decoder with four outputs. The outputs of the register are applied to the decoder inputs and also to the select inputs of the multiplexers. In this way, the present state of the register is used to select one of the inputs from each multiplexer. The outputs of the multiplexers are then applied to the D inputs of G_1 and G_0. The purpose of each multiplexer is to produce an input to its corresponding flip-flop equal to the binary value of the next state. The inputs of the multiplexers are determined from the decision boxes and state transitions given in the ASM chart. For example, state 00 stays at 00 or goes to 01, depending on the value of input w. Since the next state of G_1 is 0 in either case, we place a signal equivalent to logic-0 in MUX1 input 0. The next state of G_0 is 0 if $w = 0$ and 1 if $w = 1$. Since the next state of G_0 is equal to w, we apply control input w to MUX2 input 0. What this means is that when the select inputs of the multiplexers are equal to present state 00, the outputs of the multiplexers provide the binary value that is transferred to the register during the next clock pulse.

   To facilitate the evaluation of the multiplexer inputs, we prepare a table showing the input conditions for each possible transition in the ASM chart. Table 8-7 gives this information for the ASM chart of Fig. 8-19. There are two transitions from present state 00 or 01 and three transitions from present state 10 or 11. These are separated by horizontal lines across the table. The input conditions listed in the table are obtained from the decision boxes in the ASM chart. For example, from Fig. 8-19, we note that present state 01 will go to next state 10 if $x = 1$ or to next state 11 if $x = 0$. In the table, we mark these input conditions as x and x', respectively. The two columns under "multiplexer inputs" in the table specify the input values that must be applied to MUX1 and MUX2. The multiplexer input for each present state is determined from the input conditions when the next state of the flip-flop is equal to 1. Thus, after present state 01, the next state of G_1 is always equal to 1 and the

Table 8-7
Multiplexer Input Conditions

Present State		Next State		Input Conditions	Inputs	
G_1	G_0	G_1	G_0		MUX1	MUX2
0	0	0	0	w'		
0	0	0	1	w	0	w
0	1	1	0	x		
0	1	1	1	x'	1	x'
1	0	0	0	y'		
1	0	1	0	yz'	$yz' + yz = y$	yz
1	0	1	1	yz		
1	1	0	1	$y'z$		
1	1	1	0	y		
1	1	1	1	$y'z'$	$y + y'z' = y + z'$	$y'z + y'z' = y'$

next state of G_0 is equal to the complement value of x. Therefore, the input of MUX1 is made equal to 1 and that of MUX2 to x' when the present state of the register is 01. As another example, after present state 10, the next state of G_1 must be equal to 1 if the input conditions are yz' or yz. When these two Boolean terms are ORed together and then simplified, we obtain the single binary variable y, as indicated in the table. The next state of G_0 is equal to 1 if the input conditions are $yz = 11$. If the next state of G_1 remains at 0 after a given present state, we place a 0 in the multiplexer input as shown in present state 00 for MUX1. If the next state of G_1 is always 1, we place a 1 in the multiplexer input as shown in present state 01 for MUX1. The other entries for MUX1 and MUX2 are derived in a similar manner. The multiplexer inputs from the table are then used in the control implementation of Fig. 8-20. Note that if the next state of a flip-flop is a function of two or more control variables, the multiplexer may require one or more gates in its input. Otherwise, the multiplexer input is equal to the control variable, or the complement of the control variable, or 0, or 1.

Design Example–Count the Number of Ones in a Register

We will demonstrate the multiplexer control implementation by means of a design example. The example will also demonstrate the formulation of the ASM chart and the implementation of the datapath subsystem.

The digital system to be designed consists of two registers, $R1$ and $R2$, and a flip-flop, E. The system counts the number of 1's in the number loaded into register $R1$ and sets register $R2$ to that number. For example, if the binary number loaded into $R1$ is 10111001, the circuit counts the five 1's in $R1$ and sets register $R2$ to the binary count 101. This is done by shifting each bit from register $R1$ one at a time into flip-flop E. The value in E is checked by the control, and each time it is equal to 1, register $R2$ is incremented by 1.

The control uses one external input S to start the operation and two status inputs E and Z from the datapath. E is the output of the flip-flop. Z is the output of a circuit that checks the contents of register $R1$ for all 0's. The circuit produces an output $Z = 1$ when $R1$ is equal to 0.

The ASM chart for the circuit is shown in Fig. 8-21. The binary number is loaded into $R1$, and register $R2$ is set to an all-1's value. Note that a number with all 1's in a register when incremented

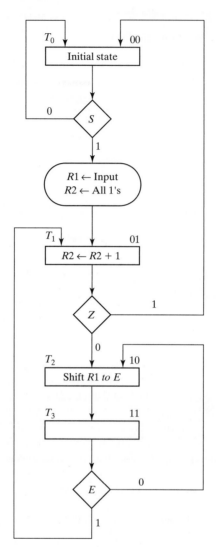

FIGURE 8-21
ASM Chart for Count-of-Ones Circuit

produces a number with all 0's. In state T_1, register $R2$ is incremented and the content of $R1$ is examined. If the content is zero, then $Z = 1$, and it signifies that there are no 1's stored in the register; so the operation terminates with $R2$ equal to 0. If the content of $R1$ is not zero, then $Z = 0$, and it indicates that there are some 1's stored in the register. The number in $R1$ is shifted and its leftmost bit transferred into E. This is done as many times as necessary until a 1 is transferred into E. For every 1 detected in E, register $R2$ is incremented and register $R1$ is checked again for more 1's. The major loop is repeated until all the 1's in $R1$ are counted. Note that the state box of T_3 has no register operations, but the block associated with it contains the decision box for E. Also note that the serial input to shift register $R1$ must be equal to 0 because we don't want to shift external 1's into $R1$.

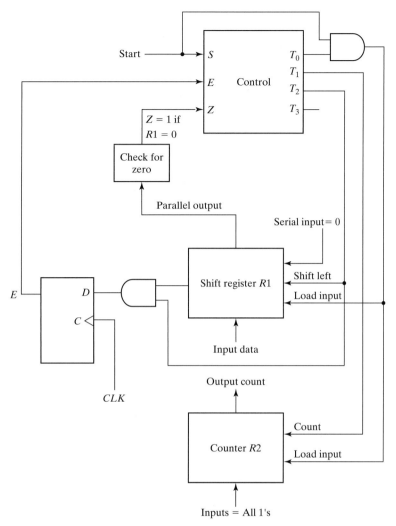

FIGURE 8-22
Block Diagram for Count-of-Ones

The block diagram of the circuit is shown in Fig. 8-22. The control has three inputs and four outputs. Only three outputs are used by the datapath. Register $R1$ is a shift register. Register $R2$ is a counter with parallel load. In order not to complicate the diagram, the clock is not shown, but it must be applied to the two registers, the E flip-flop, and the flip-flops in the control.

The multiplexer input conditions for the control are determined from Table 8-8. The input conditions are obtained from the ASM chart for each possible binary state transition. The four states are assigned binary values 00 through 11. The transition from present state 00 depends on S. The transition from present state 01 depends on Z, and the transition from present state 11 on E. Present state 10 goes to next state 11 unconditionally. The values under MUX1 and MUX2 in the table are determined from the input Boolean conditions for the next state of G_1 and G_0, respectively.

Table 8-8
Multiplexer Input Conditions for Design Example

Present State		Next State		Input Conditions	Multiplexer Inputs	
G_1	G_0	G_1	G_0		MUX1	MUX2
0	0	0	0	S'		
0	0	0	1	S	0	S
0	1	0	0	Z		
0	1	1	0	Z'	Z'	0
1	0	1	1	None	1	1
1	1	1	0	E'		
1	1	0	1	E	E'	E

The control implementation of the design example is shown in Fig. 8-23. This is a three-level implementation with the multiplexers in the first level. The inputs to the multiplexers are obtained from Table 8-8.

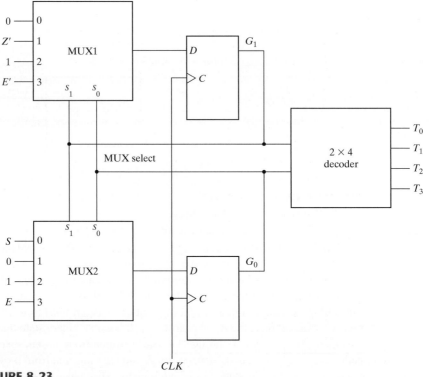

FIGURE 8-23
Control Implementation for Count-of-Ones Circuit

PROBLEMS

8-1 Explain in words the operations specified by the following register transfer notation:

(a) $R2 \leftarrow R2 + 1$, $R1 \leftarrow R2$

(b) $R3 \leftarrow R3 - 1$

(c) If $(T_1 = 1)$ then $(R0 \leftarrow R1)$ else if $(T_2 = 1)$ then $(R0 \leftarrow R2)$

8-2 Draw the portion of an ASM chart starting from an initial state. There are two control signals x and y. If $xy = 10$, register R is incremented by one and control goes to a second state. If $xy = 01$, register R is cleared to zero and control goes from the initial state to a third state. Otherwise, control stays in the initial state.

8-3 Draw the ASM charts for the following state transitions:

(a) If $x = 0$, control goes from state T_1 to state T_2; if $x = 1$, generate a conditional operation and go from T_1 to T_2.

(b) If $x = 1$, control goes from T_1 to T_2 and then to T_3; if $x = 0$, control goes from T_1 to T_3.

(c) Start from state T_1; then: if $xy = 00$, go to T_2; if $xy = 01$, go to T_3; if $xy = 10$, go to T_1; otherwise, go to T_3.

8-4 Show the eight exit paths in an ASM block emanating from the decision boxes that check the eight possible binary values of three control variables x, y, and z.

8-5 Explain how the ASM chart differs from a conventional flow chart. Using Fig. 8-5 as an illustration, show the difference in interpretation.

8-6 Construct an ASM chart for a digital system that counts the number of people in a room. People enter the room from one door with a photocell that changes a signal x from 1 to 0 when the light is interrupted. They leave the room from a second door with a similar photocell that changes a signal y from 1 to 0 when the light is interrupted. The circuit consists of an up–down counter with a display that shows how many people are in the room.

8-7 Draw an ASM chart for a circuit with two 8-bit registers RA and RB that receive two unsigned binary numbers and performs the subtraction operation:

$$RA \leftarrow RA - RB$$

Use the method for subtraction described in Section 1-5 and set a borrow flip-flop to 1 if the answer is negative.

8-8 Design a digital circuit with three 16-bit registers AR, BR, and CR to perform the following operations:

(a) Transfer two 16-bit signed numbers (in 2's complement representation) to AR and BR.

(b) If the number in AR is negative, divide the number in AR by two and transfer the result to register CR.

(c) If the number in AR is positive but nonzero, multiply the number in BR by two and transfer the result to register CR.

(d) If the number in AR is zero, clear register CR to 0.

8-9 Design the control whose state diagram is given by Fig. 8-11(a) using one flip-flop per state (one-hot assignment).

8-10 The state diagram of a control unit is shown in Fig. P8-10. It has four states and two inputs x and y. Draw the equivalent ASM chart, leaving the state boxes empty.

8-11 Design the control whose state diagram is shown in Fig. P8-10 using D flip-flops.

8-12 Assume that $R1$ in Fig. 8-22 is the 4-bit shift register shown in Fig. 6-7. Show how the shift and load inputs are to be connected to the s_1 and s_0 inputs of the shift register.

8-13 Design the 4-bit counter with synchronous clear specified in Fig. 8-10.

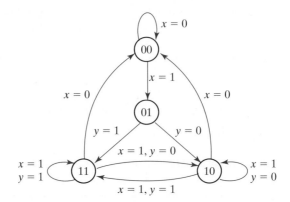

FIGURE P8-10
Control State Diagram for Problems 8-10 and 8-11

8-14 Design a digital circuit that multiplies two binary numbers by the repeated addition method. For example, to multiply 5×4, the digital system evaluates the product by adding the multiplicand four times: $5 + 5 + 5 + 5 = 20$. Let the multiplicand be in register BR, the multiplier in register AR, and the product in register PR. An adder circuit adds the contents of BR to PR. A zero-detection circuit Z checks when AR becomes 0 after each time that it is decremented.

8-15 Prove that the multiplication of two n-bit numbers gives a product of length less than or equal to $2n$ bits.

8-16 In Fig. 8-13, the Q register holds the multiplier and the B register holds the multiplicand. Assume that each number consists of 16 bits.

(a) How many bits can be expected in the product, and where is it available?

(b) How many bits are in the P counter, and what is the binary number loaded into it initially?

(c) Design the circuit that checks for zero in the P counter.

8-17 List the contents of registers C, A, Q, and P similar to Table 8-4 during the process of multiplying the two numbers 11111 (multiplicand) and 10101 (multiplier).

8-18 Determine the time it takes to process the multiplication operation in the binary multiplier described in Section 8-6. Assume that the Q register has n bits and the clock cycle is t nanoseconds.

8-19 Design the control circuit of the binary multiplier specified by the state diagram of Fig. 8-15 using multiplexers, decoder and a register.

8-20 Consider the ASM chart of Fig. P8-20. The register operations are not specified, because we are interested only in designing the control logic.

   (a) Draw the equivalent state diagram.

   (b) Design the control with one flip-flop per state.

   (c) List the state table for the control.

   (d) Design the control with three D flip-flops, a decoder, and gates.

   (e) Derive a table showing the multiplexer input conditions for the control.

   (f) Design the control with three multiplexers, a register with three flip-flops, and a 3×8 decoder.

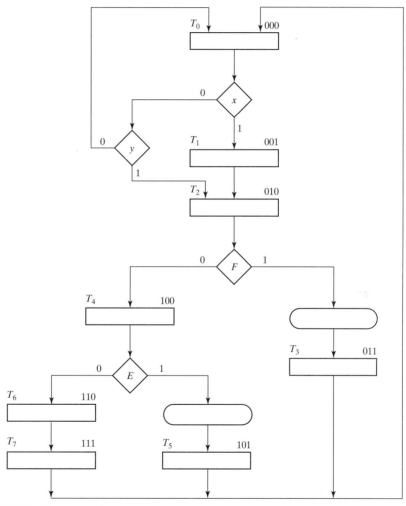

FIGURE P8-20
ASM Chart for Problems 8-20

8-21 What is the value of E in each HDL block assuming that $RA = 1$?

    (a)
```
RA = RA - 1;
if (RA == 0) E = 1;
else E = 0;
```
    (b)
```
RA <= RA - 1;
if (RA == 0) E <= 1;
else E <= 0;
```

8-22 Using the Verilog HDL operators listed in Table 8-1, evaluate the result of the following operations. Assume that $A = 4\text{'b}0110$, $B = 4\text{'b}0010$, and $C = 4\text{'b}0000$.

```
A * B; A + B; A - B; ~C; A & B; A | B; A ^ B; & A; ~|C; A || B;
A && C; |A; A < B; A > B; A != B;
```

8-23 Consider the following always block:

```
always @ (posedge CLK)
if (T1) R1 <= R1 + R2;
else if (T2) R1 <= R1 + 1;
else R1 <= R1;
```

Using a 4-bit counter with parallel load for $R1$ (as in Fig. 6-14) and a 4-bit adder, draw a block diagram showing the connections of components and control signals for a possible synthesis of the block.

8-24 The multilevel case statement is often translated by a logic synthesizer into hardware multiplexers. How would you translate the following **case** block into hardware? Assume registers of 8-bits each.

```
case (state)
T0:   R4 = R0;
T1:   R4 = R1;
T2:   R4 = R2;
T3:   R4 = R3;
endcase
```

8-25 The design of a circuit that counts the number of ones in a register is carried out in Section 8-9. The ASM chart for this circuit is shown in Fig. 8-21 and the block diagram in Fig. 8-22.

    (a) Write the HDL register transfer level description of the circuit.

    (b) Design the control logic using one flip-flop per state (one-hot assignment). List the input equations for the four flip-flops.

    (c) Write the HDL structural description of the circuit using the control designed in part (b) and the block diagram of Fig. 8-22.

    (d) Write a test bench to test the circuit. Simulate the circuit to verify the operation described in both the RTL and the structural programs.

8-26 Write the HDL structural description of the multiplier designed in Section 8-6. Use the block diagram of Fig. 8-13 and the control circuit of Fig. 8-17. Simulate the design and check the operation by using the test bench of HDL Example 8-6.

8-27 The addition of two signed binary numbers in the signed-magnitude representation follows the rules of ordinary arithmetic. If the two numbers have the same sign (both positive or both negative), the two magnitudes are added and the sum has the common sign. If the two numbers have opposite signs, the smaller magnitude is subtracted from the larger and the result has the sign of the larger magnitude. Write an HDL behavioral description for adding two 8-bit signed numbers in signed-magnitude representation. The left-most bit of the number holds the sign and the other 7 bits hold the magnitude.

8-28 Write the HDL description of the circuit designed in Problem 8-14.

REFERENCES

1. PALNITKAR, S. 1996. *Verilog HDL: A Guide to Digital Design and Synthesis.* SunSoft Press (A Prentice Hall Title).

2. BHASKER, J. 1997. *A Verilog HDL Primer.* Allentown, PA: Star Galaxy Press.

3. BHASKER, J. 1998. *Verilog HDL Synthesis.* Allentown, PA: Star Galaxy Press.

4. THOMAS, D. E., and P. R. MOORBY. 1998. *The Verilog Hardware Description Language* 4th ed. Boston: Kluwer Academic Publishers.

5. CILETTI, M. D. 1999. *Modeling, Synthesis, and Rapid Prototyping with Verilog HDL.* Upper Saddle River, NJ: Prentice Hall.

6. ARNOLD, M. G. 1999. *Verilog Digital Computer Design.* Upper Saddle River, NJ: Prentice Hall.

7. SMITH, D. J. 1996. *HDL Chip Design.* Madison, AL: Doone Publications.

8. 1995. *IEEE Standard Hardware Description Language Based on the Verilog Hardware Description Language* (IEEB Std 1364-1995). New York: The Institute of Electrical and Electronics Engineers.

9. MANO, M. M. 1993. *Computer System Architecture,* 3rd ed. Upper Saddle River, NJ: Prentice Hall.

10. MANO, M. M. and C. R. KIME. 2000. *Logic and Computer Design Fundamentals,* 2nd ed. Upper Saddle River, NJ: Prentice Hall.

11. HAYES, J. P. 1993. *Introduction to Digital Logic Design.* Reading, MA: Addison-Wesley.

12. CLARE, C. R. 1971. *Designing Logic Systems Using State Machines.* New York: McGraw-Hill.

13. WINKLER, D. and F. PROSSER. 1987. *The Art of Digital Design,* 2nd Ed. Englewood Cliffs, NJ: Prentice-Hall.

9 Asynchronous Sequential Logic

9-1 INTRODUCTION

A sequential circuit is specified by a time sequence of inputs, outputs, and internal states. In synchronous sequential circuits, the change of internal state occurs in response to the synchronized clock pulses. Asynchronous sequential circuits do not use clock pulses. The change of internal state occurs when there is a change in the input variables. The memory elements in synchronous sequential circuits are clocked flip-flops. The memory elements in asynchronous sequential circuits are either unclocked flip-flops or time-delay elements. The memory capability of a time-delay device is due to the finite time it takes for the signal to propagate through digital gates. An asynchronous sequential circuit quite often resembles a combinational circuit with feedback.

The design of asynchronous sequential circuits is more difficult than that of synchronous circuits because of the timing problems involved in the feedback path. In a properly designed synchronous system, timing problems are eliminated by triggering all flip–flops with the pulse edge. The change from one state to the next occurs during the short time of the pulse transition. Since the asynchronous circuit does not use a clock, the state of the system is allowed to change immediately after the input changes. Care must be taken to ensure that each new state keeps the circuit in a stable condition even though a feedback path exists.

Asynchronous sequential circuits are useful in a variety of applications. They are used when speed of operation is important, especially in those cases where the digital system must respond quickly without having to wait for a clock pulse. They are more economical to use in small independent systems that require only a few components, as it may not be practical to go to the expense of providing a circuit for generating clock pulses. Asynchronous circuits are useful in applications where the input signals to the system may change at any time, independently of an internal clock. The communication between two units, with each unit having its own

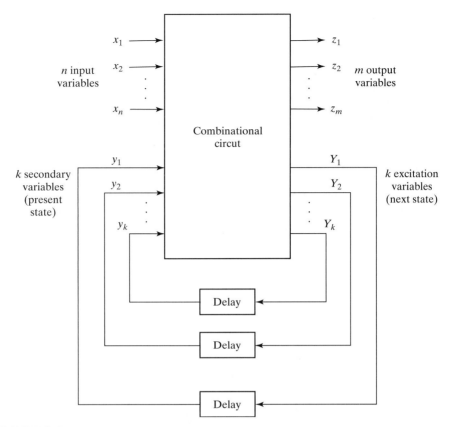

FIGURE 9-1
Block Diagram of an Asynchronous Sequential Circuit

independent clock, must be done with asynchronous circuits. Digital designers often produce a mixed system where some part of the synchronous system has the characteristics of an asynchronous circuit. Knowledge of asynchronous sequential logic behavior is helpful in verifying that the total digital system is operating in the proper manner.

Fig. 9-1 shows the block diagram of an asynchronous sequential circuit. It consists of a combinational circuit and delay elements connected to form feedback loops. There are n input variables, m output variables, and k internal states. The delay elements can be visualized as providing short-term memory for the sequential circuit. In a gate-type circuit, the propagation delay that exists in the combinational circuit path from input to output provides sufficient delay along the feedback loop so that no specific delay elements are actually inserted in the feedback path. The present-state and nextstate variables in asynchronous sequential circuits are customarily called secondary variables and excitation variables, respectively. The excitation variables should not be confused with the excitable table used in the design of clocked sequential circuits.

When an input variable changes in value, the y secondary variables do not change instantaneously. It takes a certain amount of time for the signal to propagate from the input terminals through the combinational circuit to the Y excitation variables where new values are generated for the next state. These values propagate through the delay elements and become the new present state for the secondary variables. Note the distinction betwen the y's and the Y's. In the steady-state condition, they are the same, but during transition they are not. For a given value of input variables, the system is stable if the circuit reaches a steady-state condition with $y_i = Y_i$ for $i = 1, 2, \ldots, k$. Otherwise, the circuit is in a continuous transition and is said to be unstable. It is important to realize that a transition from one stable state to another occurs only in response to a change in an input variable. This is in contrast to synchronous systems, where the state transitions occur in response to the application of a clock pulse.

To ensure proper operation, asynchronous sequential circuits must be allowed to attain a stable state before the input is changed to a new value. Because of delays in the wires and the gate circuits, it is impossible to have two or more input variables change at exactly the same instant of time without an uncertainty as to which one changes first. Therefore, simultaneous changes of two or more variables are usually prohibited. This restriction means that only one input variable can change at any one time and the time between two input changes must be longer than the time it takes the circuit to reach a stable state. This type of operation is defined as *fundamental mode*. Fundamental-mode operation assumes that the input signals change one at a time and only when the circuit is in a stable condition.

9-2   ANALYSIS PROCEDURE

The analysis of asynchronous sequential circuits consists of obtaining a table or a diagram that describes the sequence of internal states and outputs as a function of changes in the input variables. A logic diagram manifests an asynchronous-sequential-circuit behavior if it has one or more feedback loops or if it includes unclocked flip-flops. In this section, we will investigate the behavior of asynchronous sequential circuits that have feedback paths without employing flip-flops. Unclocked flip-flops are called latches, and their use in asynchronous sequential circuits will be explained in the next section.

The analysis procedure will be presented by means of three specific examples. The first example introduces the transition table. The second example defines the flow table. The third example investigates the stability of asynchronous sequential circuits.

Transition Table

An example of an asynchronous sequential circuit with only gates is shown in Fig. 9-2. The diagram clearly shows two feedback loops from the OR gate outputs back to the AND-gate inputs. The circuit consists of one input variable x and two internal states. The internal states have two excitation variables, Y_1 and Y_2, and two secondary variables, y_1 and y_2. The delay associated with each feedback loop is obtained from the propagation delay between each y input and its corresponding Y output. Each logic gate in the path introduces a propagation delay of about 2 to 10 ns. The wires that conduct electrical signals introduce an approximately one-nanosecond delay for each foot of wire. Thus, no additional external delay elements are necessary when the combinational circuit and the wires in the feedback path provide sufficient delay.

The analysis of the circuit starts by considering the excitation variables as outputs and the secondary variables as inputs. We then derive the Boolean expressions for the excitation

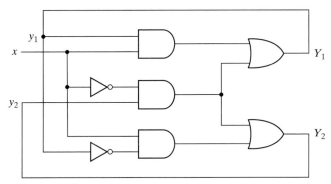

FIGURE 9-2
Example of an Asynchronous Sequential Circuit

variables as a function of the input and secondary variables. These can be readily obtained from the logic diagram.

$$Y_1 = xy_1 + x'y_2$$
$$Y_2 = xy_1' + x'y_2$$

The next step is to plot the Y_1 and Y_2 functions in a map, as shown in Fig. 9-3(a) and (b). The encoded binary values of the y variables are used for labeling the rows, and the input x variable is used to designate the columns. This configuration results in a slightly different three-variable map from the one used in previous chapters. However, it is still a valid map, and this type of configuration is more convenient when dealing with asynchronous sequential circuits. Note that the variables belonging to the appropriate squares are not marked along the sides of the map as done in previous chapters.

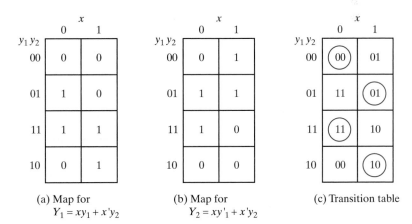

(a) Map for
$Y_1 = xy_1 + x'y_2$

(b) Map for
$Y_2 = xy'_1 + x'y_2$

(c) Transition table

FIGURE 9-3
Maps and Transition Table for the Circuit of Fig. 9-2

The transition table shown in Fig. 9-3(c) is obtained from the maps by combining the binary values in corresponding squares. The transition table shows the value of $Y = Y_1 Y_2$ inside each square. The first bit of Y is obtained from the value of Y_1, and the second bit is obtained from the value of Y_2 in the same square position. For a state to be stable, the value of Y must be the same as that of $y = y_1 y_2$. Those entries in the transition table where $Y = y$ are circled to indicate a stable condition. An uncircled entry represents an unstable state.

Now consider the effect of a change in the input variable. The square for $x = 0$ and $y = 00$ in the transition table shows that $Y = 00$. Since Y represents the next value of y, this is a stable condition. If x changes from 0 to 1 while $y = 00$, the circuit changes the value of Y to 01. This represents a temporary unstable condition because Y is not equal to the present value of y. What happens next is that as soon as the signal propagates to make $Y = 01$, the feedback path in the circuit causes a change in y to 01. This is manifested in the transition table by a transition from the first row ($y = 00$) to the second row, where $y = 01$. Now that $y = Y$, the circuit reaches a stable condition with an input of $x = 1$. In general, if a change in the input takes the circuit to an unstable state, the value of y will change (while x remains the same) until it reaches a stable (circled) state. Using this type of analysis for the remaining squares of the transition table, we find that the circuit repeats the sequence of states 00, 01, 11, 10 when the input repeatedly alternates between 0 and 1.

Note the difference between a synchronous and an asynchronous sequential circuit. In a synchronous system, the present state is totally specified by the flip-flop values and does not change if the input changes while the clock pulse is inactive. In an asynchronous circuit, the internal state can change immediately after a change in the input. Because of this, it is sometimes convenient to combine the internal state with the input value together and call it the *total state* of the circuit. The circuit whose transition table is shown in Fig. 9-3(c) has four stable total states—$y_1 y_2 x = 000, 011, 110$, and 101—and four unstable total states—001, 010, 111, and 100.

The transition table of asynchronous sequential circuits is similar to the state table used for synchronous circuits. If we regard the secondary variables as the present state and the excitation variables as the next state, we obtain the state table, as shown in Table 9-1. This table provides the same information as the transition table. There is one restriction that applies to the asynchronous case, but not the synchronous case. In the asynchronous transition table, there usually is at least one next state entry that is the same as the present-state value in each row. Otherwise, all the total states in that row will be unstable.

Table 9-1
State Table for the Circuit of Fig.9-2

Present State		Next State			
		x = 0		x = 1	
0	0	0	0	0	1
0	1	1	1	0	1
1	0	0	0	1	0
1	1	1	1	1	0

The procedure for obtaining a transition table from the circuit diagram of an asynchronous sequential circuit is as follows:

1. Determine all feedback loops in the circuit.
2. Designate the output of each feedback loop with variable Y_i and its corresponding input with y_i for $i = 1, 2, \ldots, k$, where k is the number of feedback loops in the circuit.
3. Derive the Boolean functions of all Y's as a function of the external inputs and the y's.
4. Plot each Y function in a map, using the y variables for the rows and the external inputs for the columns.
5. Combine all the maps into one table showing the value of $Y = Y_1 Y_2 \cdots Y_k$ inside each square.
6. Circle those values of Y in each square that are equal to the value of $y = y_1 y_2 \cdots y_k$ in the same row.

Once the transition table is available, the behavior of the circuit can be analyzed by observing the state transition as a function of changes in the input variables.

Flow Table

During the design of asynchronous sequential circuits, it is more convenient to name the states by letter symbols without making specific reference to their binary values. Such a table is called a *flow table*. A flow table is similar to a transition table except that the internal states are symbolized with letters rather than binary numbers. The flow table also includes the output values of the circuit for each stable state.

Examples of flow tables are shown in Fig. 9-4. The one in Fig. 9-4(a) has four states designated by the letters a, b, c, and d. It reduces to the transition table of Fig. 9-3(c) if we assign

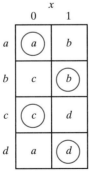

(a) Four states with
one input

	$x_1 x_2$			
	00	01	11	10
a	$\textcircled{a}, 0$	$\textcircled{a}, 0$	$\textcircled{a}, 0$	$b , 0$
b	$a , 0$	$a , 0$	$\textcircled{b}, 1$	$\textcircled{b}, 0$

(b) Two states with two
inputs and one output

FIGURE 9-4
Examples of Flow Tables

the following binary values to the states: $a = 00$, $b = 01$, $c = 11$, and $d = 10$. The table of Fig. 9-4(a) is called a *primitive* flow table because it has only one stable state in each row. Figure 9-4(b) shows a flow table with more than one stable state in the same row. It has two states, a and b; two inputs, x_1 and x_2; and one output, z. The binary value of the output variable is indicated inside the square next to the state symbol and is separated by a comma. From the flow table, we observe the following behavior of the circuit. If $x_1 = 0$, the circuit is in state a. If x_1 goes to 1 while x_2 is 0, the circuit goes to state b. With inputs $x_1 x_2 = 11$, the circuit may be either in state a or state b. If in state a, the output is 0, and if in state b, the output is 1. State b is maintained if the inputs change from 10 to 11. The circuit stays in state a if the inputs change from 01 to 11. Remember that in fundamental mode, two input variables cannot change simultaneously, and therefore we do not allow a change of inputs from 00 to 11.

In order to obtain the circuit described by a flow table, it is necessary to assign to each state a distinct binary value. This assignment converts the flow table into a transition table from which we can derive the logic diagram. This is illustrated in Fig. 9-5 for the flow table of Fig. 9-4(b). We assign binary 0 to state a and binary 1 to state b. The result is the transition table of Fig. 9-5(a). The output map shown in Fig. 9-5(b) is obtained directly from the output values in the flow table. The excitation function Y and the output function z are simplified by means of the two maps. The logic diagram of the circuit is shown in Fig. 9-5(c).

This example demonstrates the procedure for obtaining the logic diagram from a given flow table. This procedure is not always as simple as in this example. There are several difficulties

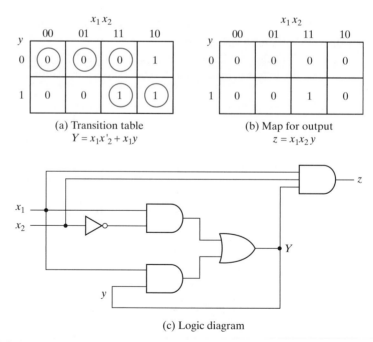

(a) Transition table
$$Y = x_1 x'_2 + x_1 y$$

(b) Map for output
$$z = x_1 x_2 y$$

(c) Logic diagram

FIGURE 9-5
Derivation of a Circuit Specified by the Flow Table of Fig. 9-4(b)

associated with the binary state assignment and with the output assigned to the unstable states. These problems are discussed in detail in the following sections.

Race Conditions

A *race* condition is said to exist in an asynchronous sequential circuit when two or more binary state variables change value in response to a change in an input variable. When unequal delays are encountered, a race condition may cause the state variables to change in an unpredictable manner. For example, if the state variables must change from 00 to 11, the difference in delays may cause the first variable to change faster than the second, with the result that the state variables change in sequence from 00 to 10 and then to 11. If the second variable changes faster than the first, the state variables will change from 00 to 0 1 and then to 11. Thus, the order by which the state variables change may not be known in advance. If the final stable state that the circuit reaches does not depend on the order in which the state variables change, the race is called a *noncritical* race. If it is possible to end up in two or more different stable states, depending on the order in which the state variables change, then it is a critical race. For proper operation, *critical* races must be avoided.

The two examples in Fig. 9-6 illustrate noncritical races. We start with the total stable state $y_1 y_2 x = 000$ and then change the input from 0 to 1. The state variables must change from 00 to 11, which defines a race condition. The listed transitions under each table show three possible ways that the state variables may change. They can either change simultaneously from 00 to 11, or they may change in sequence from 00 to 01 and then to 11, or they may change in sequence from 00 to 10 and then to 11. In all cases, the final stable state is the same, which results in a noncritical race condition. In (a), the final total state is $y_1 y_2 x = 111$, and in (b), it is 011.

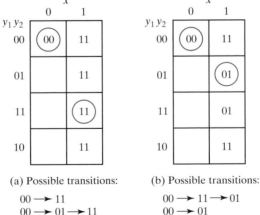

(a) Possible transitions:

00 ⟶ 11
00 ⟶ 01 ⟶ 11
00 ⟶ 10 ⟶ 11

(b) Possible transitions:

00 ⟶ 11 ⟶ 01
00 ⟶ 01
00 ⟶ 10 ⟶ 11 ⟶ 01

FIGURE 9-6
Examples of Noncritical Races

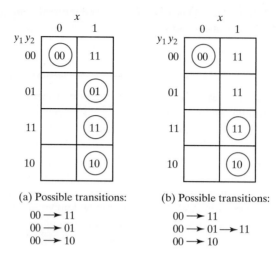

FIGURE 9-7
Examples of Critical Races

The transition tables of Fig. 9-7 illustrate critical races. Here again we start with the total stable state $y_1 y_2 x = 000$ and then change the input from 0 to 1. The state variables must change from 00 to 11. If they change simultaneously, the final total stable state is 111. In the transition table of part (a), if Y_2 changes to 1 before Y_1 because of unequal propagation delay, then the circuit goes to the total stable state 011 and remains there. On the other hand, if Y_1 changes first, the internal state becomes 10 and the circuit will remain in the stable total state 101. Hence, the race is critical because the circuit goes to different stable states depending on the order in which the state variables change. The transition table of Fig. 9-7(b) illustrates another critical race, where two possible transitions result in one final total state, but the third possible transition goes to a different total state.

Races may be avoided by making a proper binary assignment to the state variables. The state variables must be assigned binary numbers in such a way that only one state variable can change at any one time when a state transition occurs in the flow table. The subject of race-free state assignment is discussed in Section 9-6.

Races can be avoided by directing the circuit through intermediate unstable states with a unique state-variable change. When a circuit goes through a unique sequence of unstable states, it is said to have a *cycle*. Fig. 9-8 illustrates the occurrence of cycles. Again we start with $y_1 y_2 = 00$ and then change the input from 0 to 1. The transition table of part (a) gives a *unique* sequence that terminates in a total stable state 101. The table in (b) shows that even though the state variables change from 00 to 11, the cycle provides a unique transition from 00 to 0 1 and then to 11. Care must be taken when using a cycle that it terminates with a stable state. If a cycle does not terminate with a stable state, the circuit will keep going from one unstable state to another, making the entire circuit unstable. This is demonstrated in Fig. 9-8(c) and also in the following example.

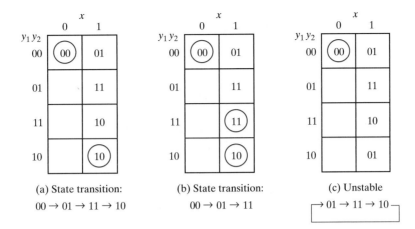

(a) State transition:
$00 \rightarrow 01 \rightarrow 11 \rightarrow 10$

(b) State transition:
$00 \rightarrow 01 \rightarrow 11$

(c) Unstable
$\rightarrow 01 \rightarrow 11 \rightarrow 10 \rightarrow$

FIGURE 9-8
Examples of Cycles

Stability Considerations

Because of the feedback connection that exists in asynchronous sequential circuits, care must be taken to ensure that the circuit does not become unstable. An unstable condition will cause the circuit to oscillate between unstable states. The transition-table method of analysis can be useful in detecting the occurrence of instability.

Consider, for example, the circuit of Fig. 9-9(a). The excitation function is

$$Y = (x_1 y)' x_2 = (x_1' + y') x_2 = x_1' x_2 + x_2 y'$$

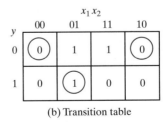

(a) Logic diagram

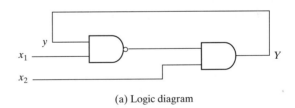

(b) Transition table

FIGURE 9-9
Example of an Unstable Circuit

The transition table for the circuit is shown in Fig. 9-9(b). Those values of Y that are equal to y are circled and represent stable states. The uncircled entries indicate unstable conditions. Note that column 11 has no stable states. This means that with input $x_1 x_2$ fixed at 11, the values of Y and y are never the same. If $y = 0$, then $Y = 1$, which causes a transition to the second row of the table with $y = 1$ and $Y = 0$. This causes a transition back to the first row, with the result that the state variable alternates between 0 and 1 indefinitely as long as the input is 11.

The instability condition can be detected directly from the logic diagram. Let $x_1 = 1$, $x_2 = 1$, and $y = 1$. The output of the NAND gate is equal to 0, and the output of the AND gate is equal to 0, making Y equal to 0, with the result that $Y \neq y$. Now if $y = 0$, the output of the NAND gate is 1, the output of the AND gate is 1, making Y equal to 1, with the result that $Y \neq y$. If it is assumed that each gate has a propagation delay of 5 ns (including the wires), we will find that Y will be 0 for 10 ns and 1 for the next 10 ns. This will result in a square-wave waveform with a period of 20 ns. The frequency of oscillation is the reciprocal of the period and is equal to 50 MHz. Unless one is designing a square-wave generator, the instability that may occur in asynchronous sequential circuits is undesirable and must be avoided.

9-3   CIRCUITS WITH LATCHES

Historically, asynchronous circuits were known and used before synchronous circuits were developed. The first practical digital circuits were constructed with relays, which are more adaptable to asynchronous type operations. For this reason, the traditional method of asynchronous circuit configuration has been with components that are connected to form one or more feedback loops. When digital circuits are constructed with electronic components, it is convenient to employ the SR latch (introduced in Section 5-2) as a memory element. The use of SR latches in asynchronous sequential circuits produces an orderly pattern in the logic diagrams with the memory elements clearly visible. In this section, the operation of the SR latch is analyzed using the technique introduced in the previous section. We will then show a procedure for implementing asynchronous sequential circuits using SR latches.

SR Latch

The SR latch is a digital circuit with two inputs S and R and two cross-coupled NOR gates or two cross-coupled NAND gates. The cross-coupled NOR gate circuit is shown in Fig. 9-10. This circuit and its truth table are taken from Fig. 5-3. In order to analyze the circuit by the transition table method, it is first redrawn in Fig. 9-10(c) to see the feedback path from the output of gate 1 to the input of gate 2. The output Q is equivalent to the excitation variable Y and the secondary variable y. The Boolean function for the output is

$$Y = \left[(S + y)' + R \right]' = (S + y)R' = SR' + R'y$$

Plotting Y as in Fig. 9-10(d), we obtain the transition table for the circuit.

We can now investigate the behavior of the SR latch from the transition table. With $SR = 10$, the output $Q = Y = 1$ and the latch is said to be set. Changing S to 0 leaves the circuit in the set state. With $SR = 01$, the output $Q = Y = 0$ and the latch is said to be reset. A change of

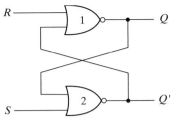

(a) Crossed-coupled circuit

S	R	Q	Q'	
1	0	1	0	
0	0	1	0	(After $SR = 10$)
0	1	0	1	
0	0	0	1	(After $SR = 01$)
1	1	0	0	

(b) Truth table

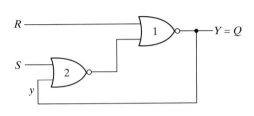

(c) Circuit showing feedback

SR

	00	01	11	10
y				
0	0	0	0	1
1	1	0	0	1

$Y = SR' + R'y$
$Y = S + R'y$ when $SR = 0$

(d) Transition table

FIGURE 9-10
SR Latch with NOR Gates

R back to 0 leaves the circuit in the reset state. These conditions are also listed in the truth table. The circuit exhibits some difficulty when both S and R are equal to 1. From the truth table, we see that both Q and Q' are equal to 0, a condition that violates the requirement that these two outputs be the complement of each other. Moreover, from the transition table, we note that going from $SR = 11$ to $SR = 00$ produces an unpredictable result. If S goes to 0 first, the output remains at 0, but if R goes to 0 first, the output goes to 1. In normal operation, we must make sure that 1's are not applied to both the S and R inputs simultaneously. This condition can be expressed by the Boolean function $SR = 0$, which states that the ANDing of S and R must always result in a 0.

Coming back to the excitation function, we note that when we OR the Boolean expression SR' with SR, the result is the single variable S.

$$SR' + SR = S(R' + R) = S$$

From this, we deduce that $SR' = S$ when $SR = 0$. Therefore, the excitation function derived previously,

$$Y = SR' + R'y$$

can be expressed as

$$Y = S + R'y \qquad \text{when } SR = 0$$

To analyze a circuit with an SR latch, we must first check that the Boolean condition $SR = 0$ holds at all times. We then use the reduced excitation function to analyze the circuit. However, if it is found that both S and R can be equal to 1 at the same time, then it is necessary to use the original excitation function.

The analysis of the SR latch with NAND gates is carried out in Fig. 9-11. The NAND latch operates with both inputs normally at 1 unless the state of the latch has to be changed. The application of 0 to R causes the output Q to go to 0, thus putting the latch in the reset state. After the R input returns to 1, a change of S to 0 causes a change to the set state. The condition to be avoided here is that both S and R not be 0 simultaneously. This condition is satisfied when $S'R' = 0$. The excitation function for the circuit is

$$Y = [S(Ry)']' = S' + Ry$$

Comparing it with the excitation function of the NOR latch, we note that S has been replaced with S' and R' with R. Hence, the input variables for the NAND latch require the complemented values of those used in the NOR latch. For this reason, the NAND latch is sometimes referred to as an $S'R'$ latch (or $\overline{S}$–$\overline{R}$ latch).

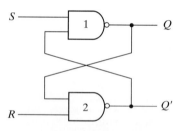

(a) Crossed-coupled circuit

S	R	Q	Q'	
1	0	0	1	
1	1	0	1	(After SR = 10)
0	1	1	0	
1	1	1	0	(After SR = 01)
0	0	1	1	

(b) Truth table

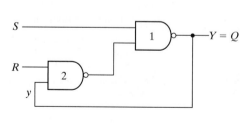

(c) Circuit showing feedback

SR

y	00	01	11	10
0	1	1	0	0
1	1	1	1	0

$Y = S' + Ry$ when $S'R' = 0$

(d) Transition table

FIGURE 9-11
SR Latch with NAND Gates

Analysis Example

Asynchronous sequential circuits can be constructed with the use of SR latches with or without external feedback paths. Of course, there is always a feedback loop within the latch itself. The analysis of a circuit with latches will be demonstrated by means of a specific example. From this example, it will be possible to generalize the procedural steps necessary to analyze other, similar circuits.

The circuit shown in Fig. 9-12 has two SR latches with outputs Y_1 and Y_2. There are two inputs, x_1 and x_2, and two external feedback loops giving rise to the secondary variables, y_1 and y_2. Note that this circuit resembles a conventional sequential circuit with latches behaving like flip-flops without clock pulses. The analysis of the circuit requires that we first obtain the Boolean functions for the S and R inputs in each latch.

$$S_1 = x_1 y_2 \qquad S_2 = x_1 x_2$$
$$R_1 = x_1' x_2' \qquad R_2 = x_2' y_1$$

We then check whether the condition $SR = 0$ is satisfied to ensure proper operation of the circuit:

$$S_1 R_1 = x_1 y_2 x_1' x_2' = 0$$
$$S_2 R_2 = x_1 x_2 x_2' y_1 = 0$$

The result is 0 because $x_1 x_1' = x_2 x_2' = 0$.

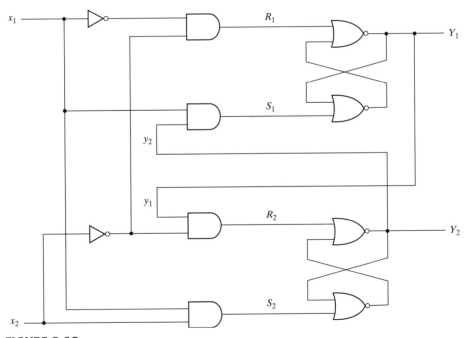

FIGURE 9-12
Example of a Circuit with SR Latches

The next step is to derive the transition table of the circuit. Remember that the transition table specifies the value of Y as a function of y and x. The excitation functions are derived from the relation $Y = S + R'y$.

$$Y_1 = S_1 + R_1'y_1 = x_1y_2 + (x_1 + x_2)y_1 = x_1y_2 + x_1y_1 + x_2y_1$$
$$Y_2 = S_2 + R_2'y_2 = x_1x_2 + (x_2 + y_1')y_2 = x_1x_2 + x_2y_2 + y_1'y_2$$

We now develop a composite map for $Y = Y_1Y_2$. The y variables are assigned to the rows in the map, and the x variables are assigned to the columns, as shown in Fig. 9-13. The Boolean functions of Y_1 and Y_2 as expressed above are used to plot the composite map for Y. The entries of Y in each row that have the same value as that given to Y are circled and represent stable states. From investigation of the transition table, we deduce that the circuit is stable. There is a critical race condition when the circuit is initially in total state $y_1y_2x_1x_2 = 1101$ and x_2 changes from 1 to 0. If Y_1 changes to 0 before Y_2, the circuit goes to total state 0100 instead of 0000. However, with approximately equal delays in the gates and latches, this undesirable situation is not likely to occur.

The procedure for analyzing an asynchronous sequential circuit with SR latches can be summarized as follows:

1. Label each latch output with Y_i and its external feedback path (if any) with y_i for $i = 1, 2, \ldots, k$.

2. Derive the Boolean functions for the S_i and R_i inputs in each latch.

3. Check whether $SR = 0$ for each NOR latch or whether $S'R' = 0$ for each NAND latch. If this condition is not satisfied, there is a possibility that the circuit may not operate properly.

4. Evaluate $Y = S + R'y$ for each NOR latch or $Y = S' + Ry$ for each NAND latch.

5. Construct a map with the y's representing the rows and the x inputs representing the columns.

6. Plot the value of $Y = Y_1Y_2\cdots Y_k$ in the map.

7. Circle all stable states where $Y = y$. The resulting map is then the transition table.

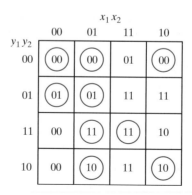

FIGURE 9-13
Transition Table for the Circuit of Fig. 9-12

Latch Excitation Table

The transition table of the SR latch is useful for analysis and for defining the operation of the latch. It specifies the excitation variable Y when the secondary variable y and the inputs S and R are known. During the implementation process, the transition table of the circuit is available and we wish to find the values of S and R. For this reason, we need a table that lists the required inputs S and R for each of the possible transitions from y to Y. Such a list is called an *excitation table*.

The excitation table of the SR latch is shown in Fig. 9-14(b). The first two columns list the four possible transitions from y to Y. The next two columns specify the required input values that will result in the specified transition. For example, in order to provide a transition from $y = 0$ to $Y = 1$, it is necessary to ensure that input $S = 1$ and input $R = 0$. This is shown in the second row of the transition table.

The required input conditions for each of the four transitions in the excitation table can be derived directly from the latch transition table of Fig. 9-10(d) after removing the unstable condition $SR = 11$. For example, in order to change from $y = 0$ to $Y = 0$, the transition table shows that SR can be either 00 or 01. This means that S must be 1 and R may be either 0 or 1. Therefore, the first row in the excitation table shows $S = 0$ and $R = X$, where X is a don't-care condition signifying either a 0 or a 1.

Implementation Example

The implementation of a sequential circuit with SR latches is a procedure for obtaining the logic diagram from a given transition table. The procedure requires that we determine the Boolean functions for the S and R inputs of each latch. The logic diagram is then obtained by drawing the SR latches and the logic gates that implement the S and R functions. To demonstrate the procedure, we will repeat the implementation example of Fig. 9-5. The output circuit remains the same and will not be repeated again.

The transition table from Fig. 9-5(a) is duplicated in Fig. 9-14(a). From the information given in the transition table and from the latch excitation table conditions in Fig. 9-14(b), we can obtain the maps for the S and R inputs of the latch, as shown in Fig. 9-14(c) and (d). For example, the square in the second row and third column $(yx_1x_2 = 111)$ in Fig. 9-14(a) requires a transition from $y = 1$ to $Y = 1$. The excitation table specifies $S = X, R = 0$ for this change. Therefore, the corresponding square in the S map is marked with an X and the one in the R map with a 0. All other squares are filled with values in a similar manner. The maps are then used to derive the simplified Boolean functions

$$S = x_1 x_2' \qquad \text{and} \qquad R = x_1'$$

The logic diagram consists of an SR latch and the gates required to implement the S and R Boolean functions. The circuit is as shown in Fig. 9-14(e) when a NOR latch is used. With a NAND latch, we must use the complemented values for S and R.

$$S = (x_1 x_2')' \qquad \text{and} \qquad R = x_1$$

This circuit is shown in Fig. 9-14(f).

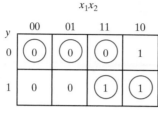

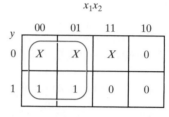

(a) Transition table
$Y = x_1 x'_2 + x_1 y$

(b) Latch excitation table

y	Y	S	R
0	0	0	X
0	1	1	0
1	0	0	1
1	1	X	1

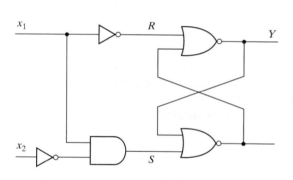

(c) Map for $S = x_1 x'_2$

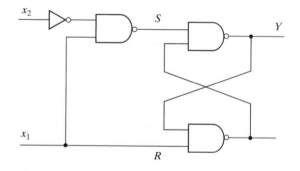

(d) Map for $R = x'_1$

(e) Circuit with NOR latch

(f) Circuit with NAND latch

FIGURE 9-14
Derivation of a Latch Circuit from a Transition Table

The general procedure for implementing a circuit with SR latches from a given transition table can now be summarized as follows:

1. Given a transition table that specifies the excitation function $Y = Y_1 Y_2 \cdots Y_k$, derive a pair of maps for S_i and R_i for each $i = 1, 2, \ldots, k$. This is done by using the conditions specified in the latch excitation table of Fig. 9-14(b).

2. Derive the simplified Boolean functions for each S_i and R_i. Care must be taken not to make S_i and R_i equal to 1 in the same minterm square.

3. Draw the logic diagram using k latches together with the gates required to generate the S and R Boolean functions. For NOR latches, use the S and R Boolean functions obtained in step 2. For NAND latches, use the complemented values of those obtained in step 2.

Another useful example of latch implementation can be found in Section 9-7 in conjunction with Fig. 9-38.

Debounce Circuit

Input binary information in a digital system can be generated manually by means of mechanical switches. One position of the switch provides a voltage equivalent to logic 1, and the other position provides a second voltage equivalent to logic 0. Mechanical switches are also used to start, stop, or reset the digital system. When testing digital circuits in the laboratory, the input signals will normally come from switches. A common characteristic of a mechanical switch is that when the arm is thrown from one position to the other, the switch contact vibrates or bounces several times before coming to a final rest. In a typical switch, the contact bounce may take several milliseconds to die out. This may cause the signal to oscillate between 1 and 0 because the switch contact is vibrating.

A debounce circuit is one that removes the series of pulses that result from a contact bounce and produces a single smooth transition of the binary signal from 0 to 1 or from 1 to 0. One such circuit consists of a single-pole double-throw switch connected to an SR latch, as shown in Fig. 9-15. The center contact is connected to ground that provides a signal equivalent to logic-0. When one of the two contacts, A or B, is not connected to ground through the switch, it behaves like a logic-1 signal. A resistor is sometimes connected from each contact to a fixed voltage to provide a firm logic-1 signal. When the switch is thrown from position A to position B and back, the outputs of the latch produce a single pulse as shown, negative for Q and positive for Q'. The switch is usually a pushbutton whose contact rests in position A. When the pushbutton is depressed, it goes to position B and when released, it returns to position A.

The operation of the debounce circuit is as follows. When the switch rests in position A, we have the condition $S = 0$, $R = 1$ and $Q = 1$, $Q' = 0$ (see Fig. 9-11(b)). When the switch is moved to position B, the ground connection causes R to go to 0 while S becomes a 1 because

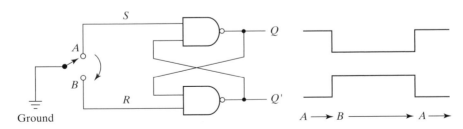

FIGURE 9-15
Debounce Circuit

contact A is open. This condition causes output Q to go to 0 and Q' to go to 1. After the switch makes an initial contact with B, it bounces several times, but for proper operation, we must assume that it does not bounce back far enough to reach point A. The output of the latch will be unaffected by the contact bounce because Q' remains 1 (and Q remains 0) whether R is equal to 0 (contact with ground) or equal to 1 (no contact with ground). When the switch returns to position A, S becomes 0 and Q returns to 1. The output again will exhibit a smooth transition even if there is a contact bounce in position A.

9-4   DESIGN PROCEDURE

The design of an asynchronous sequential circuit starts from the statement of the problem and culminates in a logic diagram. There are a number of design steps that must be carried out in order to minimize the circuit complexity and to produce a stable circuit without critical races. Briefly, the design steps are as follows. A primitive flow table is obtained from the design specifications. The flow table is reduced to a minimum number of states. The states are then given a binary assignment from which we obtain the transition table. From the transition table, we derive the logic diagram as a combinational circuit with feedback or as a circuit with SR latches.

The design process will be demonstrated by going through a specific example. Once this example is mastered, it will be easier to understand the design steps that are enumerated at the end of this section. Some of the steps require the application of formal procedures, and these are discussed in greater detail in the following sections.

Design Example

It is necessary to design a gated latch circuit with two inputs, G (gate) and D (data), and one output, Q. Binary information present at the D input is transferred to the Q output when G is equal to 1. The Q output will follow the D input as long as $G = 1$. When G goes to 0, the information that was present at the D input at the time the transition occurred is retained at the Q output. The gated latch is a memory element that accepts the value of D when $G = 1$ and retains this value after G goes to 0. Once $G = 0$, a change in D does not change the value of the output Q.

Primitive Flow Table

As defined previously, a primitive flow table is a flow table with only one stable total state in each row. Remember that a total state consists of the internal state combined with the input. The derivation of the primitive flow table can be facilitated if we first form a table with all possible total states in the system. This is shown in Table 9-2 for the gated latch. Each row in the table specifies a total state, which consists of a letter designation for the internal state and a possible input combination for D and G. The output Q is also shown for each total state. We start with the two total states that have $G = 1$. From the design specifications, we know that $Q = 0$ if $DG = 01$ and $Q = 1$ if $DG = 11$ because D must be equal to Q when $G = 1$. We assign these conditions to states a and b. When G goes to 0, the output depends on the last value of

Table 9-2
Gated-Latch Total States

	Inputs		Output	
State	*D*	*G*	*Q*	**Comments**
a	0	1	0	$D = Q$ because $G = 1$
b	1	1	1	$D = Q$ because $G = 1$
c	0	0	0	After state *a* or *d*
d	1	0	0	After state *c*
e	1	0	1	After state *b* or *f*
f	0	0	1	After state *e*

D. Thus, if the transition of *DG* is from 01 to 00 to 10, then *Q* must remain 0 because *D* is 0 at the time of the transition from 1 to 0 in *G*. If the transition of *DG* is from 11 to 10 to 00, then *Q* must remain 1. This information results in six different total states, as shown in the table. Note that simultaneous transitions of two input variables, such as from 01 to 10 or from 11 to 00, are not allowed in fundamental-mode operation.

The primitive flow table for the gated latch is shown in Fig. 9-16. It has one row for each state and one column for each input combination. First, we fill in one square in each row belonging to the stable state in that row. These entries are determined from Table 9-2. For example, state *a* is stable and the output is 0 when the input is 01. This information is entered in the flow table in the first row and second column. Similarly, the other five stable states together with their output are entered in the corresponding input columns.

DG	00	01	11	10
a	*c*, –	(*a*), 0	*b*, –	–, –
b	–, –	*a*, –	(*b*), 1	*e*, –
c	(*c*), 0	*a*, –	–, –	*d*, –
d	*c*, –	–, –	*b*, –	(*d*), 0
e	*f*, –	–, –	*b*, –	(*e*), 1
f	(*f*), 1	*a*, –	–, –	*e*, –

FIGURE 9-16
Primitive Flow Table

Next we note that since both inputs are not allowed to change simultaneously, we can enter dash marks in each row that differs in two or more variables from the input variables associated with the stable state. For example, the first row in the flow table shows a stable state with an input of 01. Since only one input can change at any given time, it can change to 00 or 11, but not to 10. Therefore, we enter two dashes in the 10 column of row a. This will eventually result in a don't care condition for the next state and output in this square. Following this procedure, we fill in a second square in each row of the primitive flow table.

Next it is necessary to find values for two more squares in each row. The comments listed in Table 9-2 may help in deriving the necessary information. For example, state c is associated with input 00 and is reached after an input change from state a or d. Therefore, an unstable state c is shown in column 00 and rows a and d in the flow table. The output is marked with a dash to indicate a don't-care condition. The interpretation of this is that if the circuit is in stable state a and the input changes from 01 to 00, the circuit first goes to an unstable next state c, which changes the present state value from a to c, causing a transition to the third row and first column of the flow table. The unstable state values for the other squares are determined in a similar manner. All outputs associated with unstable states are marked with a dash to indicate don't-care conditions. The assignment of actual values to the outputs is discussed further after the design example is completed.

Reduction of the Primitive Flow Table

The primitive flow table has only one stable state in each row. The table can be reduced to a smaller number of rows if two or more stable states are placed in the same row of the flow table. The grouping of stable states from separate rows into one common row is called *merging*. Merging a number of stable states in the same row means that the binary state variable that is ultimately assigned to the merged row will not change when the input variable changes. This is because in a primitive flow table, the state variable changes every time the input changes, but in a reduced flow table, a change of input will not cause a change in the state variable if the next stable state is in the same row.

A formal procedure for reducing a flow table is given in the next section. In order to complete the design example without going through the formal procedure, we will apply the merging process by using a simplified version of the merging rules. Two or more rows in the primitive flow table can be merged into one row if there are non-conflicting states and outputs in each of the columns. Whenever one state symbol and don't-care entries are encountered in the same column, the state is listed in the merged row. Moreover, if the state is circled in one of the rows, it is also circled in the merged row. The output value is included with each stable state in the merged row.

We now apply these rules to the primitive flow table of Fig. 9-16. To see how this is done, the primitive flow table is separated into two parts of three rows each, as shown in Fig. 9-17(a). Each part shows three stable states that can be merged because there are no conflicting entries in each of the four columns. The first column shows state c in all the rows and 0 or a dash for the output. Since a dash represents a don't-care condition, it can be associated with any state or output. The two dashes in the first column can be taken as 0 output to make all three rows identical to a stable state c with a 0 output. The second column shows that the dashes can be

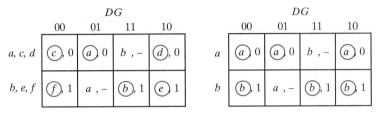

(a) States that are candidates for merging

(b) Reduced table (two alternatives)

FIGURE 9-17
Reduction of the Primitive Flow Table

assigned to correspond to a stable state a with a 0 output. Note that if the state is circled in one of the rows, it is also circled in the merged row. Similarly, the third column can be merged into an unstable state b with a don't-care output and the fourth column can be merged into stable state d and a 0 output. Thus, the three rows, a, c, and d, can be merged into one row with three stable states and one unstable state, as shown in the first row of Fig. 9-17(b). The second row of the reduced table results from the merging of rows b, e, and f of the primitive flow table. There are two ways that the reduced table can be drawn. The letter symbols for the states can be retained to show the relationship between the reduced and primitive flow tables. The other alternative is to define a common letter symbol for all the stable states of the merged rows. Thus, states c and d are replaced by state a, and states e and f are replaced by state b. Both alternatives are shown in Fig. 9-17(b).

Transition Table and Logic Diagram

In order to obtain the circuit described by the reduced flow table, it is necessary to assign to each state a distinct binary value. This assignment converts the flow table into a transition table. In the general case, a binary state assignment must be made to ensure that the circuit will be free of critical races. The state-assignment problem in asynchronous sequential circuits and ways to solve it are discussed in Section 9-6. Fortunately, there can be no critical races in a two-row flow table, and therefore, we can finish the design of the gated latch prior to studying Section 9-6. Assigning 0 to state a and 1 to state b in the reduced flow table of Fig. 9-17(b), we

DG

y	00	01	11	10
0	0	0	1	0
1	1	0	1	1

(a) $Y = DG + G'y$

DG

y	00	01	11	10
0	0	0	1	0
1	1	0	1	1

(b) $Q = Y$

FIGURE 9-18
Transition Table and Output Map for Gated Latch

obtain the transition table of Fig. 9-18(a). The transition table is, in effect, a map for the excitation variable Y. The simplified Boolean function for Y is then obtained from the map.

$$Y = DG + G'y$$

There are two don't-care outputs in the final reduced flow table. If we assign values to the output, as shown in Fig. 9-18(b), it is possible to make output Q equal to the excitation function Y. If we assign the other possible values to the don't-care outputs, we can make output Q equal to y. In either case, the logic diagram of the gated latch is as shown in Fig. 9-19.

The diagram can be implemented also by means of an SR latch. Using the procedure outlines in Section 9-3, we first obtain the Boolean functions for S and R, as shown in Fig. 9-20(a). The logic diagram with NAND gates is shown in Fig. 9-20(b). Note that the gated latch is a level-sensitive D-latch introduced in Section 5-2 and Fig. 5-6.

Assigning Outputs to Unstable States

The stable states in a flow table have specific output values associated with them. The unstable states have unspecified output entries designated by a dash. The output values for the unstable states must be chosen so that no momentary false outputs occur when the circuit switches between stable states. This means that if an output variable is not supposed to change as the result of a transition, then an unstable state that is a transient state between two stable states must

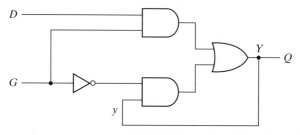

FIGURE 9-19
Gated-Latch Logic Diagram

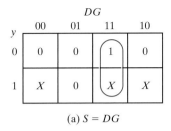

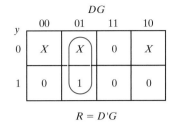

(a) $S = DG$ $R = D'G$

(a) Maps for S and R

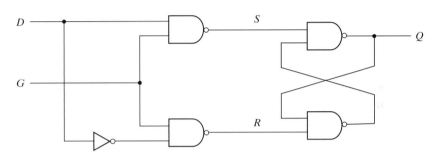

(b) Logic diagram

FIGURE 9-20
Circuit with SR Latch

have the same output value as the stable states. Consider, for example, the flow table of Fig. 9-21(a). A transition from stable state a to stable state b goes through the unstable state b. If the output assigned to the unstable b is a 1, then a momentary short pulse will appear on the output as the circuit shifts from an output of 0 in state a to an output of 1 for the unstable b and

a	a , 0	b , –
b	c , –	b 0
c	c , 1	d , –
d	a , –	d 1

0	0
X	0
1	1
X	1

(a) Flow table   (b) Output assignment

FIGURE 9-21
Assigning Output Values to Unstable States

back to 0 when the circuit reaches stable state b. Thus the output corresponding to unstable state b must be specified as 0 to avoid a momentary false output.

If an output variable is to change value as a result of a state change, then this variable is assigned a don't-care condition. For example, the transition from stable state b to stable state c in Fig. 9-21(a) changes the output from 0 to 1. If a 0 is entered as the output value for unstable c, then the change in the output variable will not take place until the end of the transition. If a 1 is entered, the change will take place at the start of the transition. Since it makes no difference when the output change occurs, we place a don't-care entry for the output associated with unstable state c. Fig. 9-21(b) shows the output assignment for the flow table. It demonstrates the four possible combinations in output change that can occur. The procedure for making the assignment to outputs associated with unstable states can be summarized as follows:

1. Assign a 0 to an output variable associated with an unstable state that is a transient state between two stable states that have a 0 in the corresponding output variable.

2. Assign a 1 to an output variable associated with an unstable state that is a transient state between two stable states that have a 1 in the corresponding output variable.

3. Assign a don't-care condition to an output variable associated with an unstable state that is a transient state between two stable states that have different values (0 and 1 or 1 and 0) in the corresponding output variable.

Summary of Design Procedure

The design of asynchronous sequential circuits can be carried out by using the procedure illustrated in the previous example. Some of the design steps need further elaboration and are explained in the following sections. The procedural steps are as follows:

1. Obtain a primitive flow table from the given design specifications. This is the most difficult part of the design because it is necessary to use intuition and experience to arrive at the correct interpretation of the problem specifications.

2. Reduce the flow table by merging rows in the primitive flow table. A formal procedure for merging rows in the flow table is given in Section 9-5.

3. Assign binary state variables to each row of the reduced flow table to obtain the transition table. The procedure of state assignment that eliminates any possible critical races is given in Section 9-6.

4. Assign output values to the dashes associated with the unstable states to obtain the output maps. This procedure was explained previously.

5. Simplify the Boolean functions of the excitation and output variables and draw the logic diagram, as shown in Section 9-2. The logic diagram can be drawn using SR latches, as shown in Section 9-3 and also at the end of Section 9-7.

9-5   REDUCTION OF STATE AND FLOW TABLES

The procedure for reducing the number of internal states in an asynchronous sequential circuit resembles the procedure that is used for synchronous circuits. An algorithm for state reduction of a completely specified state table is given in Section 5-6. We will review this algorithm and apply it to a state-reduction method that uses an implication table. The algorithm and the implication table will then be modified to cover the state reduction of incompletely specified state tables. This modified algorithm will be used to explain the procedure for reducing the flow table of asynchronous sequential circuits.

Implication Table

The state-reduction procedure for completely specified state tables is based on the algorithm that two states in a state table can be combined into one if they can be shown to be equivalent. Two states are equivalent if for each possible input, they give exactly the same output and go to the same next states or to equivalent next states. Table 6-6 shows an example of equivalent states that have the same next states and outputs for each combination of inputs. There are occasions when a pair of states do not have the same next states, but, nonetheless, go to equivalent next states. Consider, for example, the state table shown in Table 9-3. The present states a and b have the same output for the same input. Their next states are c and d for $x = 0$ and b and a for $x = 1$. If we can show that the pair of states (c, d) are equivalent, then the pair of states (a, b) will also be equivalent because they will have the same or equivalent next states. When this relationship exists, we say that (a, b) *imply* (c, d). Similarly, from the last two rows of Table 9-3, we find that the pair of states (c, d) imply the pair of states (a, b). The characteristic of equivalent states is that if (a, b) imply (c, d) and (c, d) imply (a, b), then both pairs of states are equivalent; that is, a and b are equivalent as well as c and d. As a consequence, the four rows of Table 9-3 can be reduced to two rows by combining a and b into one state and c and d into a second state.

The checking of each pair of states for possible equivalence in a table with a large number of states can be done systematically by means of an implication table. The implication table is a chart that consists of squares, one for every possible pair of states, that provide spaces for listing any possible implied states. By judicious use of the table, it is possible to determine all

Table 9-3
State Table to Demonstrate Equivalent States

Present State	Next State		Output	
	x = 0	x = 1	x = 0	x = 1
a	c	b	0	1
b	d	a	0	1
c	a	d	1	0
d	b	d	1	0

Table 9-4
State Table to Be Reduced

Present State	Next State x = 0	Next State x = 1	Output x = 0	Output x = 1
a	d	6	0	0
b	e	a	0	0
c	g	f	0	1
d	a	d	1	0
e	a	d	1	0
f	c	b	0	0
g	a	e	1	0

pairs of equivalent states. The state table of Table 9-4 will be used to illustrate this procedure. The implication table is shown in Fig. 9-22. On the left side along the vertical are listed all the states defined in the state table except the first, and across the bottom horizontally are listed all the states except the last. The result is a display of all possible combinations of two states with a square placed in the intersection of a row and a column where the two states can be tested for equivalence.

Two states that are not equivalent are marked with a cross (×) in the corresponding square, whereas their equivalence is recorded with a check mark (√). Some of the squares have entries of implied states that must be further investigated to determine whether they are equivalent or not. The step-by-step procedure of filling in the squares is as follows. First, we place a cross in any square corresponding to a pair of states whose outputs are not equal for every input. In

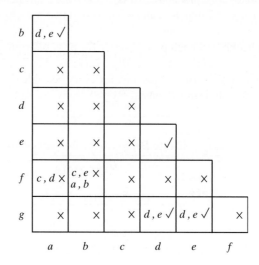

FIGURE 9-22
Implication Table

this case, state c has a different output than any other state, so a cross is placed in the two squares of row c and the four squares of column c. There are nine other squares in this category in the implication table.

Next, we enter in the remaining squares the pairs of states that are implied by the pair of states representing the squares. We do that starting from the top square in the left column and going down and then proceeding with the next column to the right. From the state table, we see that pair (a, b) imply (d, e), so (d, e) is recorded in the square defined by column a and row b. We proceed in this manner until the entire table is completed. Note that states (d, e) are equivalent because they go to the same next state and have the same output. Therefore, a check mark is recorded in the square defined by column d and row e, indicating that the two states are equivalent and independent of any implied pair.

The next step is to make successive passes through the table to determine whether any additional squares should be marked with a cross. A square in the table is crossed out if it contains at least one implied pair that is not equivalent. For example, the square defined by a and f is marked with a cross next to c, d because the pair (c, d) defines a square that contains a cross. This procedure is repeated until no additional squares can be crossed out. Finally, all the squares that have no crosses are recorded with check marks. These squares define pairs of equivalent states. In this example, the equivalent states are

$$(a, b)   (d, e)   (d, g)   (e, g)$$

We now combine pairs of states into larger groups of equivalent states. The last three pairs can be combined into a set of three equivalent states (d, e, g) because each one of the states in the group is equivalent to the other two. The final partition of the states consists of the equivalent states found from the implication table, together with all the remaining states in the state table that are not equivalent to any other state.

$$(a, b)   (c)   (d, e, g)   (f)$$

This means that Table 9-4 can be reduced from seven states to four states, one for each member of the above partition. The reduced table is obtained by replacing state b by a and states e and g by d. The reduced state table is shown in Table 9-5.

Table 9-5
Reduced State Table

Present State	Next State		Output	
	x = 0	x = 1	x = 0	x = 1
a	d	a	0	0
c	d	f	0	1
d	a	d	1	0
f	c	a	0	0

Merging of the Flow Table

There are occasions when the state table for a sequential circuit is incompletely specified. This happens when certain combinations of inputs or input sequences may never occur because of external or internal constraints. In such a case, the next states and outputs that should have occurred if all inputs were possible are never attained and are regarded as don't-care conditions. Although synchronous sequential circuits may sometimes be represented by incompletely specified state tables, our interest here is with asynchronous sequential circuits where the primitive flow table is always incompletely specified.

Incompletely specified states can be combined to reduce the number of states in the flow table. Such states cannot be called equivalent, because the formal definition of equivalence requires that all outputs and next states be specified for all inputs. Instead, two incompletely specified states that can be combined are said to be *compatible*. Two states are compatible if for each possible input they have the same output whenever specified and their next states are compatible whenever they are specified. All don't-care conditions marked with dashes have no effect when searching for compatible states as they represent unspecified conditions.

The process that must be applied in order to find a suitable group of compatibles for the purpose of merging a flow table can be divided into three procedural steps:

1. Determine all compatible pairs by using the implication table.

2. Find the maximal compatibles using a merger diagram.

3. Find a minimal collection of compatibles that covers all the states and is closed.

The minimal collection of compatibles is then used to merge the rows of the flow table. We will now proceed to show and explain the three procedural steps using the primitive flow table from the design example in the previous section.

Compatible Pairs

The procedure for finding compatible pairs is illustrated in Fig. 9-23. The primitive flow table in (a) is the same as Fig. 9-16. The entries in each square represent the next state and output. The dashes represent the unspecified states or outputs. The implication table is used to find compatible states just as it is used to find equivalent states in the completely specified case. The only difference is that when comparing rows, we are at liberty to adjust the dashes to fit any desired condition.

Two states are compatible if in every column of the corresponding rows in the flow table, there are identical or compatible states and if there is no conflict in the output values. For example, rows a and b in the flow table are found to be compatible, but rows a and f will be compatible only if c and f are compatible. However, rows c and f are not compatible because they have different outputs in the first column. This information is recorded in the implication table. A check mark designates a square whose pair of states are compatible. Those states that are not compatible are marked with a cross. The remaining squares are recorded with the implied pairs that need further investigation.

	00	01	11	10
a	c , –	ⓐ, 0	b , –	– , –
b	– , –	a , –	ⓑ, 1	e , –
c	ⓒ, 0	a , –	– , –	d , –
d	c , –	– , –	b , –	ⓓ, 0
e	f , –	– , –	b , –	ⓔ, 1
f	ⓕ, 1	a , –	– , –	e , –

(a) Primitive flow table

	a	b	c	d	e
b	✓				
c	✓	d , e ×			
d	✓	d , e ×	✓		
e	c , f ×	✓	d , e × c , f ×	×	
f	c , f ×	✓	×	d , e × c , f ×	✓

(b) Implication table

FIGURE 9-23
Flow and Implication Tables

Once the initial implication table has been filled, it is scanned again to cross out the squares whose implied states are not compatible. The remaining squares that contain check marks define the compatible pairs. In the example of Fig. 9-23, the compatible pairs are

$$(a, b) \quad (a, c) \quad (a, d) \quad (b, e) \quad (b, f) \quad (c, d) \quad (e, f)$$

Maximal Compatibles

Having found all the compatible pairs, the next step is to find larger sets of states that are compatible. The *maximal compatible* is a group of compatibles that contains all the possible combinations of compatible states. The maximal compatible can be obtained from a merger diagram, as shown in Fig. 9-24. The merger diagram is a graph in which each state is represented by a dot placed along the circumference of a circle. Lines are drawn between any two corresponding dots that form a compatible pair. All possible compatibles can be obtained from the merger diagram by observing the geometrical patterns in which states are connected to each other. An isolated dot represents a state that is not compatible to any other state. A line represents a compatible pair. A triangle constitutes a compatible with three states. An *n*-state compatible is represented in the merger diagram by an *n*-sided polygon with all its diagonals connected.

The merger diagram of Fig. 9-24(a) is obtained from the list of compatible pairs derived from the implication table of Fig. 9-23. There are seven straight lines connecting the dots, one for each compatible pair. The lines form a geometrical pattern consisting of two triangles connecting (a, c, d) and (b, e, f) and a line (a, b). The maximal compatibles are

$$(a, b) \quad (a, c, d) \quad (b, e, f)$$

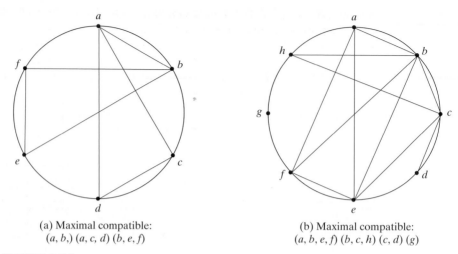

(a) Maximal compatible:
    $(a, b,) (a, c, d) (b, e, f)$

(b) Maximal compatible:
    $(a, b, e, f) (b, c, h) (c, d) (g)$

FIGURE 9-24
Merger Diagrams

Fig. 9-24(b) shows the merger diagram of an 8-state flow table. The geometrical patterns are a rectangle with its two diagonals connected to form the 4-state compatible (a, b, e, f), a triangle (b, c, h), a line (c, d), and a single state g that is not compatible to any other state. The maximal compatibles are

$$(a, b, e, f)   (b, c, h)   (c, d)   (g)$$

The maximal compatible set can be used to merge the flow table by assigning one row in the reduced table to each member of the set. However, quite often the maximal compatibles do not necessarily constitute the set of compatibles that is minimal. In many cases, it is possible to find a smaller collection of compatibles that will satisfy the condition for row merging.

Closed Covering Condition

The condition that must be satisfied for row merging is that the set of chosen compatibles must *cover* all the states and must be *closed*. The set will cover all the states if it includes all the states of the original state table. The closure condition is satisfied if there are no implied states or if the implied states are included within the set. A closed set of compatibles that covers all the states is called a *closed covering*. The closed-covering condition will be explained by means of two examples.

Consider the maximal compatibles from Fig. 9-24(a). If we remove (a, b), we are left with a set of two compatibles:

$$(a, c, d)   (b, e, f)$$

All six states from the flow table in Fig. 9-23 are included in this set. This satisfies the covering condition. There are no implied states for (a, c); (a, d); (c, d); (b, e); (b, f); and (e, f), as seen from the implication table of Fig. 9-23(b), so the closure condition is also satisfied.

Therefore, the primitive flow table can be merged into two rows, one for each of the compatibles. The detailed construction of the reduced table for this particular example was done in the previous section and is shown in Fig. 9-17(b).

The second example is from a primitive flow table (not shown) whose implication table is given in Fig. 9-25(a). The compatible pairs derived from the implication table are

$$(a, b) \ (a, d) \ (b, c) \ (c, d) \ (c, e) \ (d, e)$$

From the merger diagram of Fig. 9-25(b), we determine the maximal compatibles:

$$(a, b) \quad (a, d) \quad (b, c) \quad (c, d, e)$$

If we choose the two compatibles

$$(a, b) \quad (c, d, e)$$

then the set will cover all five states of the original table. The closure condition can be checked by means of a closure table, as shown in Fig. 9-25(c). The implied pairs listed for each compatible are taken directly from the implication table. The implied states for (a, b) are (b, c). But (b, c) is not included in the chosen set of $(a, b) \ (c, d, e)$, so this set of compatibles is not closed. A set of compatibles that will satisfy the closed covering condition is

$$(a, d) \quad (b, c) \quad (c, d, e)$$

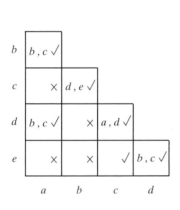

(a) Implication table

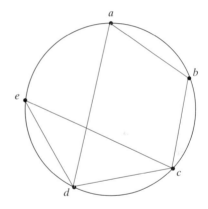

(b) Merger diagram

Compatibles	(a, b)	(a, d)	(b, c)	(c, d, e)
Implied states	(b, c)	(b, c)	(d, e)	(a, d,) (b, c,)

(c) Closure table

FIGURE 9-25
Choosing a Set of Compatibles

The set is covered because it contains all five states. Note that the same state can be repeated more than once. The closure condition is satisfied because the implied states are (b, c) (d, e) and (a, d), which are included in the set. The original flow table (not shown here) can be reduced from five rows to three rows by merging rows a and d, b and c, and c, d, and e. Note that an alternative satisfactory choice of closed-covered compatibles would be (a, b) (b, c) (d, e). In general, there may be more than one possible way of merging rows when reducing a primitive flow table.

9-6   RACE-FREE STATE ASSIGNMENT

Once a reduced flow table has been derived for an asynchronous sequential circuit, the next step in the design is to assign binary variables to each stable state. This assignment results in the transformation of the flow table into its equivalent transition table. The primary objective in choosing a proper binary state assignment is the prevention of critical races. The problem of critical races was demonstrated in Section 9-2 in conjunction with Fig. 9-7.

Critical races can be avoided by making a binary state assignment in such a way that only one variable changes at any given time when a state transition occurs in the flow table. To accomplish this, it is necessary that states between which transitions occur be given adjacent assignments. Two binary values are said to be adjacent if they differ in only one variable. For example, 010 and 011 are adjacent because they only differ in the third bit.

In order to ensure that a transition table has no critical races, it is necessary to test each possible transition between two stable states and verify that the binary state variables change one at a time. This is a tedious process, especially when there are many rows and columns in the table. To simplify matters, we will explain the procedure of binary state assignment by going through examples with only three and four rows in the flow table. These examples will demonstrate the general procedure that must be followed to ensure a race-free state assignment. The procedure can then be applied to flow tables with any number of rows and columns.

Three-Row Flow-Table Example

The assignment of a single binary variable to a flow table with two rows does not impose critical race problems. A flow table with three rows requires an assignment of two binary variables. The assignment of binary values to the stable states may cause critical races if not done properly. Consider, for example, the reduced flow table of Fig. 9-26(a). The outputs have been omitted from the table for simplicity. Inspection of row a reveals that there is a transition from state a to state b in column 01 and from state a to state c in column 11. This information is transferred into a *transition diagram,* as shown in Fig. 9-26(b). The directed lines from a to b and from a to c represent the two transitions just mentioned. Similarly, the transitions from the other two rows are represented by directed lines in the transition diagram. The transition diagram is a pictorial representation of all required transitions between rows.

To avoid critical races, we must find a binary state assignment such that only one binary variable changes during each state transition. An attempt to find such assignment is shown in the transition diagram. State a is assigned binary 00, and state c is assigned binary 11. This assignment will cause a critical race during the transition from a to c because there are two changes in the binary state variables. Note that the transition from c to a also causes a race condition, but it is noncritical.

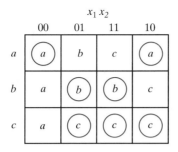

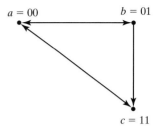

(a) Flow table   (b) Transition diagram

FIGURE 9-26
Three-Row Flow-Table Example

A race-free assignment can be obtained if we add an extra row to the flow table. The use of a fourth row does not increase the number of binary state variables, but it allows the formation of cycles between two stable states. Consider the modified flow table in Fig. 9-27. The first three rows represent the same conditions as the original three-row table. The fourth row, labeled d, is assigned the binary value 10, which is adjacent to both a and c. The transition from a to c must now go through d, with the result that the binary variables change from $a = 00$ to $d = 10$ to $c = 11$, thus avoiding a critical race. This is accomplished by changing row a, column 11 to d and row d, column 11 to c. Similarly, the transition from c to a is shown to go through unstable state d even though column 00 constitutes a noncritical race.

The transition table corresponding to the flow table with the indicated binary state assignment is shown in Fig. 9-28. The two dashes in row d represent unspecified states that can be considered don't-care conditions. However, care must be taken not to assign 10 to these squares in order to avoid the possibility of an unwanted stable state being established in the fourth row.

This example demonstrates the use of an extra row in the flow table for the purpose of achieving

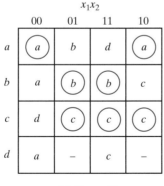

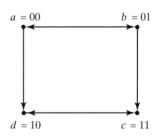

(a) Flow table   (b) Transition diagram

FIGURE 9-27
Flow Table with an Extra Row

$$x_1x_2$$

	00	01	11	10
a = 00	(00)	01	10	(00)
b = 01	00	(01)	(01)	11
c = 11	10	(11)	(11)	(11)
d = 10	00	–	11	–

FIGURE 9-28
Transition Table

a race-free assignment. The extra row is not assigned to any specific stable state, but instead is used to convert a critical race into a cycle that goes through adjacent transitions between two stable states. Sometimes, just one extra row may not be sufficient to prevent critical races, and it may be necessary to add two or more extra rows in the flow table. This is demonstrated in the next example.

Four-Row Flow-Table Example

A flow table with four rows requires a minimum of two state variables. Although race-free assignment is sometimes possible with only two binary state variables, in many cases, the requirement of extra rows to avoid critical races will dictate the use of three binary state variables. Consider, for example, the flow table and its corresponding transition diagram, shown in Fig. 9-29. If there were no transitions in the diagonal direction (from b to d or from c to a), it would be possible to find an adjacent assignment for the remaining four transitions. With one or two diagonal transitions, there is no way of assigning two binary variables that satisfy the adjacency requirement. Therefore, at least three binary state variables are needed.

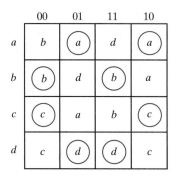

(a) Flow table

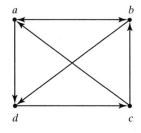

(b) Transition diagram

FIGURE 9-29
Four-Row Flow-Table Example

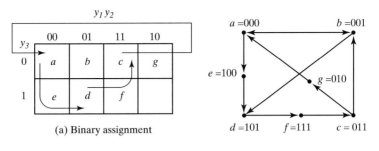

(a) Binary assignment

(b) Transition diagram

FIGURE 9-30
Choosing Extra Rows for the Flow Table

Fig. 9-30 shows a state assignment map that is suitable for any four-row flow table. States a, b, c, and d are the original states, and e, f, and g are extra states. States placed in adjacent squares in the map will have adjacent assignments. State b is assigned binary 001 and is adjacent to the other three original states. The transition from a to d must be directed through the extra state e to produce a cycle so that only one binary variable changes at a time. Similarly, the transition from c to a is directed through g and the transition from d to c goes through f. By using the assignment given by the map, the four-row table can be expanded to a seven-row table that is free of critical races, as shown in Fig. 9-31. Note that although the flow table has seven rows, there are only four stable states. The uncircled states in the three extra rows are there merely to provide a race-free transition between the stable states.

	00	01	11	10
000 = a	b	(a)	e	(a)
001 = b	(b)	d	(b)	a
011 = c	(c)	g	b	(c)
010 = g	–	a	–	–
110 –	–	–	–	–
111 = f	c	–	–	c
101 = d	f	(d)	(d)	f
100 = e	–	–	d	–

FIGURE 9-31
State Assignment to Modified Flow Table

This example demonstrates a possible way of selecting extra rows in a flow table in order to achieve a race-free assignment. A state-assignment map similar to the one used in Fig. 9-30(a) can be helpful in most cases. Sometimes it is possible to take advantage of unspecified entries in the flow table. Instead of adding rows to the table, it may be possible to eliminate critical races by directing some of the state transitions through the don't-care entries. The actual assignment is done by trial and error until a satisfactory assignment is found that resolves all critical races.

Multiple-Row Method

The method for making race-free state assignments by adding extra rows in the flow table, as demonstrated in the previous two examples, is sometimes referred to as the *shared-row* method. There is a second method that is not as efficient, but is easier to apply, called the *multiple-row* method. In the multiple-row assignment, each state in the original flow table is replaced by two or more combinations of state variables. The state-assignment map of Fig. 9-32(a) shows a

y_1 \ y_2y_3	00	01	11	10
0	a_1	b_1	c_1	d_1
1	c_2	d_2	a_2	b_2

(a) Binary assignment

	00	01	11	10
$000 = a_1$	b_1	(a_1)	d_1	(a_1)
$111 = a_2$	b_2	(a_2)	d_2	(a_2)
$001 = b_1$	(b_1)	d_2	(b_1)	a_1
$110 = b_2$	(b_2)	d_1	(b_2)	a_2
$011 = c_1$	(c_1)	a_2	b_1	(c_1)
$100 = c_2$	(c_2)	a_1	b_2	(c_2)
$010 = d_1$	c_1	(d_1)	(d_1)	c_1
$101 = d_2$	c_2	(d_2)	(d_2)	c_2

(b) Flow table

FIGURE 9-32
Multiple-Row Assignment

multiple-row assignment that can be used with any four-row flow table. There are two binary state variables for each stable state, each being the logical complement of each other. For example, the original state a is replaced with two equivalent states $a_1 = 000$ and $a_2 = 111$. The output values, not shown here, must be the same in a_1 and a_2. Note that a_1 is adjacent to b_1, c_2, and d_1 and a_2 is adjacent to c_1, b_2, and d_2, and, similarly, each state is adjacent to three states of different letter designation. The behavior of the circuit is the same whether the internal state is a_1 or a_2, and so on for the other states.

Fig. 9-32(b) shows the multiple-row assignment for the original flow table of Fig. 9-29(a). The expanded table is formed by replacing each row of the original table with two rows. For example, row b is replaced by rows b_1 and b_2 and stable state b is entered in columns 00 and 11 in both rows b_1 and b_2. After all the stable states have been entered, the unstable states are filled in by reference to the assignment specified in the map of part (a). When choosing the next state for a given present state, a state that is adjacent to the present state is selected from the map. In the original table, the next states of b are a and d for inputs 10 and 01, respectively. In the expanded table, the next states for b_1 are a_1 and d_2 because these are the states adjacent to b_1. Similarly, the next states for b_2 are a_2 and d_1 because they are adjacent to b_2.

In the multiple-row assignment, the change from one stable state to another will always cause a change of only one binary state variable. Each stable state has two binary assignments with exactly the same output. At any given time, only one of the assignments is in use. For example, if we start with state a_1 and input 01 and then change the input to 11, 01, 00, and back to 01, the sequence of internal states will be a_1, d_1, c_1, and a_2. Although the circuit starts in state a_1 and terminates in state a_2, as far as the input–output relationship is concerned, the two states, a_1 and a_2, are equivalent to state a of the original flow table.

9-7 HAZARDS

When designing asynchronous sequential circuits, care must be taken to conform with certain restrictions and precautions to ensure proper operation. The circuit must be operated in fundamental mode with only one input changing at any time and must be free of critical races. In addition, there is one more phenomenon, called *hazard,* that may cause the circuit to malfunction. Hazards are unwanted switching transients that may appear at the output of a circuit because different paths exhibit different propagation delays. Hazards occur in combinational circuits, where they may cause a temporary false-output value. When this condition occurs in asynchronous sequential circuits, it may result in a transition to a wrong stable state. It is therefore necessary to check for possible hazards and determine whether they cause improper operations. Steps must then be taken to eliminate their effect.

Hazards in Combinational Circuits

A hazard is a condition where a single variable change produces a momentary output change when no ouput change should occur. The circuit of Fig. 9-33(a) demonstrates the occurrence of a hazard. Assume that all three inputs are initially equal to 1. This causes the output of gate 1 to be 1, that of gate 2 to be 0, and the output of the circuit to be equal to 1. Now consider a change of x_2 from 1 to 0. The output of gate 1 changes to 0 and that of gate 2 changes to 1, leaving the output at 1. However, the output may momentarily go to 0 if the propagation delay

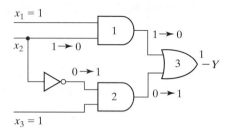

(a) AND-OR circuit

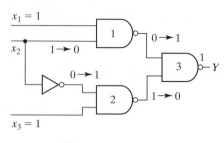

(b) NAND circuit

FIGURE 9-33
Circuits with Hazards

through the inverter is taken into consideration. The delay in the inverter may cause the output of gate 1 to change to 0 before the output of gate 2 changes to 1. In that case, both inputs of gate 3 are momentarily equal to 0, causing the output to go to 0 for the short interval of time that the input signal from x_2 is delayed while it is propagating through the inverter circuit.

The circuit of Fig. 9-33(b) is a NAND implementation of the same Boolean function. It has a hazard for the same reason. Because gates 1 and 2 are NAND gates, their outputs are the complement of the outputs of the corresponding AND gates. When x_2 changes from 1 to 0, both inputs of gate 3 may be equal to 1, causing the output to produce a momentary change to 0 when it should have stayed at 1.

The two circuits shown in Fig. 9-33 implement the Boolean function in sum of products:

$$Y = x_1 x_2 + x_2' x_3$$

This type of implementation may cause the output to go to 0 when it should remain a 1. If the circuit is implemented in product of sums (see Section 3-5), namely,

$$Y = (x_1 + x_2')(x_2 + x_3)$$

then the output may momentarily go to 1 when it should remain 0. The first case is referred to as *static 1-hazard* and the second case as *static 0-hazard.* A third type of hazard, known as *dynamic hazard,* causes the output to change three or more times when it should change from 1 to 0 or from 0 to 1. Fig. 9-34 demonstrates the three types of hazards. When a circuit is

(a) Static 1-hazard

(b) Static 0-hazard

(c) Dynamic hazard

FIGURE 9-34
Types of Hazards

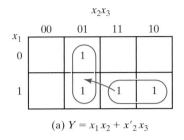
(a) $Y = x_1 x_2 + x'_2 x_3$

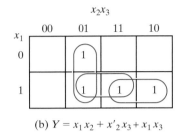
(b) $Y = x_1 x_2 + x'_2 x_3 + x_1 x_3$

FIGURE 9-35
Maps Demonstrating a Hazard and its Removal

implemented in sum of products with AND–OR gates or with NAND gates, the removal of static 1-hazard guarantees that no static 0-hazards or dynamic hazards will occur.

The occurrence of the hazard can be detected by inspecting the map of the particular circuit. To illustrate, consider the map in Fig. 9-35(a), which is a plot of the function implemented in Fig. 9-33. The change in x_2 from 1 to 0 moves the circuit from minterm 111 to minterm 101. The hazard exists because the change of input results in a different product term covering the two minterms. Minterm 111 is covered by the product term implemented in gate 1, and minterm 101 is covered by the product term implemented in gate 2 of Fig. 9-33. Whenever the circuit must move from one product term to another, there is a possibility of a momentary interval when neither term is equal to 1, giving rise to an undesirable 0 output.

The remedy for eliminating a hazard is to enclose the two minterms in question with another product term that overlaps both groupings. This is shown in the map of Fig. 9-35(b), where the two minterms that cause the hazard are combined into one product term. The hazard-free circuit obtained by this configuration is shown in Fig. 9-36. The extra gate in the circuit generates the product term $x_1 x_3$. In general, hazards in combinational circuits can be removed by covering any two minterms that may produce a hazard with a product term common to both. The removal of hazards requires the addition of redundant gates to the circuit.

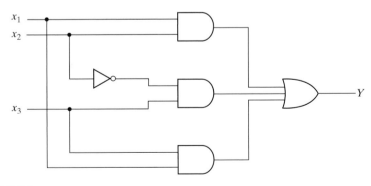

FIGURE 9-36
Hazard-Free Circuit

Hazards in Sequential Circuits

In normal combinational-circuit design associated with synchronous sequential circuits, hazards are not of concern, since momentary erroneous signals are not generally troublesome. However, if a momentary incorrect signal is fed back in an asynchronous sequential circuit, it may cause the circuit to go to the wrong stable state. This is illustrated in the example of Fig. 9-37. If the circuit is in total stable state $yx_1x_2 = 111$ and input x_2 changes from 1 to 0, the next total stable state should be 110. However, because of the hazard, output Y may go to 0 momentarily. If this false signal feeds back into gate 2 before the output of the inverter goes to 1, the output of gate 2 will remain at 0 and the circuit will switch to the incorrect total stable state 010. This malfunction can be eliminated by adding an extra gate, as done in Fig. 9-36.

Implementation with *SR* Latches

Another way to avoid static hazards in asynchronous sequential circuits is to implement the circuit with *SR* latches. A momentary 0 signal applied to the *S* or *R* inputs of a NOR latch will have no effect on the state of the circuit. Similarly, a momentary 1 signal applied to the *S* and *R* inputs of a NAND latch will have no effect on the state of the latch. In Fig. 9-33(b), we observed that a two-level sum of product expression implemented with NAND gates may have a static 1-hazard if both inputs of gate 3 go to 1, changing the output from 1 to 0 momentarily. But if gate 3 is part of a latch, the momentary 1 signal will have no effect on the output because a third input to the gate will come from the complemented side of the latch that will be equal

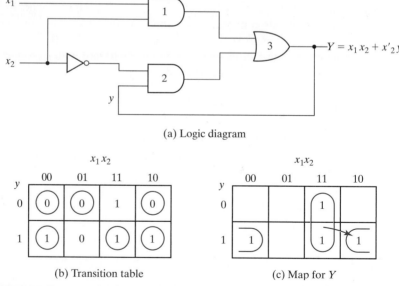

(a) Logic diagram

(b) Transition table   (c) Map for Y

FIGURE 9-37
Hazard in an Asynchronous Sequential Circuit

to 0 and thus maintain the output at 1. To clarify what was just said, consider a NAND *SR* latch with the following Boolean functions for *S* and *R*:

$$S = AB + CD$$
$$R = A'C$$

Since this is a NAND latch, we must apply the complemented values to the inputs:

$$S = (AB + CD)' = (AB)'(CD)'$$
$$R = (A'C)'$$

This implementation is shown in Fig. 9-38(a). *S* is generated with two NAND gates and one AND gate. The Boolean function for output *Q* is

$$Q = (Q'S)' = \left[Q'(AB)'(CD)' \right]'$$

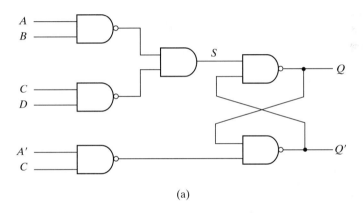

(a)

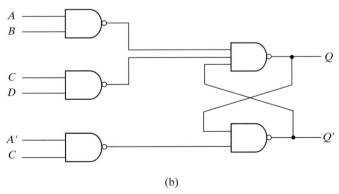

(b)

FIGURE 9-38
Latch Implementation

This function is generated in Fig. 9-38(b) with two levels of NAND gates. If output Q is equal to 1, then Q' is equal to 0. If two of the three inputs go momentarily to 1, the NAND gate associated with output Q will remain at 1 because Q' is maintained at 0.

Figure 9-38(b) shows a typical circuit that can be used to construct asynchronous sequential circuits. The two NAND gates forming the latch normally have two inputs. However, if the S or R functions contain two or more product terms when expressed in sum of products, then the corresponding NAND gate of the SR latch will have three or more inputs. Thus, the two terms in the original sum of products expression for S are AB and CD and each is implemented with a NAND gate whose output is applied to the input of the NAND latch. In this way, each state variable requires a two-level circuit of NAND gates. The first level consists of NAND gates that implement each product term in the original Boolean expression of S and R. The second level forms the cross-coupled connection of the SR latch with inputs that come from the outputs of each NAND gate in the first level.

Essential Hazards

Thus far we have considered what are known as static and dynamic hazards. There is another type of hazard that may occur in asynchronous sequential circuits, called *essential hazard*. An essential hazard is caused by unequal delays along two or more paths that originate from the same input. An excessive delay through an inverter circuit in comparison to the delay associated with the feedback path may cause such a hazard. Essential hazards cannot be corrected by adding redundant gates as in static hazards. The problem that they impose can be corrected by adjusting the amount of delay in the affected path. To avoid essential hazards, each feedback loop must be handled with individual care to ensure that the delay in the feedback path is long enough compared to delays of other signals that originate from the input terminals. This problem tends to be specialized, as it depends on the particular circuit used and the amount of delays that are encountered in its various paths.

9-8   DESIGN EXAMPLE

We are now in a position to examine a complete design example of an asynchronous sequential circuit. This example may serve as a reference for the design of other similar circuits. We will demonstrate the method of design by following the recommended procedural steps that were listed at the end of Section 9-4 and are repeated here:

1. State the design specifications.
2. Derive a primitive flow table.
3. Reduce the flow table by merging the rows.
4. Make a race-free binary state assignment.
5. Obtain the transition table and output map.
6. Obtain the logic diagram using SR latches.

Design Specifications

It is necessary to design a negative-edge-triggered T flip-flop. The circuit has two inputs, T (toggle) and C (clock), and one output, Q. The output state is complemented if $T = 1$ and the clock C changes from 1 to 0 (negative-edge triggering). Otherwise, under any other input condition, the output Q remains unchanged. Although this circuit can be used as a flip-flop in clocked sequential circuits, the internal design of the flip-flop (as is the case with all other flip-flops) is an asynchronous problem.

Primitive Flow Table

The derivation of the primitive flow table can be facilitated if we first derive a table that lists all the possible total states in the circuit. This is shown in Table 9-6. We start with the input condition $TC = 11$ and assign to it state a. The circuit goes to state b and the output Q complements from 0 to 1 when C changes from 1 to 0 while T remains a 1. Another change in the output occurs when the circuit goes from state c to state d. In this case, $T = 1$, C changes from 1 to 0, and the output Q complements from 1 to 0. The other four states in the table do not change the output, because T is equal to 0. If Q is initially 0, it stays at 0, and if initially at 1, it stays at 1 even though the clock input changes. This information results in six total states. Note that simultaneous transitions of two input variables, such as from 01 to 10, are not included, as they violate the condition for fundamental-mode operation.

The primitive flow table is shown in Fig. 9-39. The information for the flow table can be obtained directly from the conditions listed in Table 9-6. We first fill in one square in each row belonging to the stable state in that row as listed in the table. Then we enter dashes in those squares whose input differs by two variables from the input corresponding to the stable state. The unstable conditions are then determined by utilizing the information listed under the comments in Table 9-6.

Table 9-6
Specification of Total States

	Inputs		Output	
State	**T**	**C**	**Q**	**Comments**
a	1	1	0	Initial output is 0
b	1	0	1	After state a
c	1	1	1	Initial output is 1
d	1	0	0	After state c
e	0	0	0	After state d or f
f	0	1	0	After state e or a
g	0	0	1	After states b or h
h	0	1	1	After states g or c

$$TC$$

	00	01	11	10
a	– , –	f , –	ⓐ, 0	b , –
b	g , –	– , –	c , –	ⓑ, 1
c	– , –	h , –	ⓒ, 1	d , –
d	e , –	– , –	a , –	ⓓ, 0
e	ⓔ, 0	f , –	– , –	d , –
f	e , –	ⓕ, 0	a , –	– , –
g	ⓖ, 1	h , –	– , –	b , –
h	g , –	ⓗ, 1	c , –	– , –

FIGURE 9-39
Primitive Flow Table

Merging of the Flow Table

The rows in the primitive flow table are merged by first obtaining all compatible pairs of states. This is done by means of the implication table shown in Fig. 9-40. The squares that contain check marks define the compatible pairs:

$$(a, f) \quad (b, g) \quad (b, h) \quad (c, h) \quad (d, e) \quad (d, f) \quad (e, f) \quad (g, h)$$

The maximal compatibles are obtained from the merger diagram shown in Fig. 9-41. The geometrical patterns that are recognized in the diagram consist of two triangles and two straight lines. The maximal compatible set is

$$(a, f) \quad (b, g, h) \quad (c, h) \quad (d, e, f)$$

In this particular example, the minimal collection of compatibles is also the maximal compatible set. Note that the closed condition is satisfied because the set includes all the original eight states listed in the primitive flow table, although states h and f are repeated. The covering condition is also satisfied because all the compatible pairs have no implied states, as can be seen from the implication table.

The reduced flow table is shown in Fig. 9-42. The one shown in part (a) of the figure retains the original state symbols but merges the corresponding rows. For example, states a and f are compatible and are merged into one row that retains the original letter symbols of the states. Similarly, the other three compatible sets of states are used to merge the flow table into four

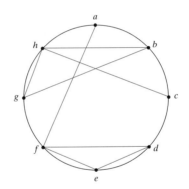

b	a,c ×						
c	×	b,d ×					
d	b,d ×	×	a,c ×				
e	b,d ×	e,g × / b,d ×	f,h ×	✓			
f	✓	e,g × / a,c ×	f,h × / a,c ×	✓	✓		
g	f,h ×	✓	b,d ×	e,g × / b,d ×	×	e,g × / f,h ×	
h	f,h × / a,c ×	✓	✓	d,e × / c,f ×	e,g × / f,h ×	×	✓
	a	b	c	d	e	f	g

FIGURE 9-40
Implication Table

FIGURE 9-41
Merger Diagram

_TC_

	00	01	11	10
a, f	e,–	(f), 0	(a), 0	b,–
b, g, h	(g), 1	(h), 1	c,–	(b), 1
c, h	g, 1	(h), 1	(c), 1	d,–
d, e, f	(e), 0	(f), 0	a,–	(d), 0

(a)

_TC_

	00	01	11	10
a	d,–	(a), 0	(a), 0	(b),–
b	(b), 1	(b), 1	c,–	(b), 1
c	b,–	(c), 1	(c), 1	d,–
d	(d), 0	(d), 0	a,–	(d), 0

(b)

FIGURE 9-42
Reduced Flow Table

rows, retaining the eight original letter symbols. The other alternative for drawing the merged flow table is shown in part (b) of the figure. Here we assign a common letter symbol to all the stable states in each merged row. Thus, the symbol f is replaced by a, and g and h are replaced by b, and similarly for the other two rows. The second alternative shows clearly a four-state flow table with only four letter symbols for the states.

State Assignment and Transition Table

The next step in the design is to find a race-free binary assignment for the four stable states in the reduced flow table. In order to find a suitable adjacent assignment, we draw the transition diagram, as shown in Fig. 9-43. For this example, it is possible to obtain a suitable adjacent assignment without the need of extra states. This is because there are no diagonal lines in the transition diagram.

Substituting the binary assignment indicated in the transition diagram into the reduced flow table, we obtain the transition table shown in Fig. 9-44. The output map is obtained from the reduced flow table. The dashes in the output section are assigned values according to the rules established in Section 9-4.

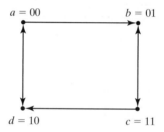

FIGURE 9-43
Transition Diagram

(a) Transition table

$y_1 y_2$	TC 00	01	11	10
$a = 00$	10	(00)	(00)	01
$b = 01$	(01)	(01)	11	(01)
$c = 11$	01	(11)	(11)	10
$d = 10$	(10)	(10)	00	(10)

(b) Output map $Q = y_2$

$y_1 y_2$	TC 00	01	11	10
00	0	0	0	X
01	1	1	1	1
11	1	1	1	X
10	0	0	0	0

FIGURE 9-44
Transition Table and Output Map

Logic Diagram

The circuit to be designed has two state variables, Y_1 and Y_2, and one output, Q. The output map in Fig. 9-44 shows that Q is equal to the state variable y_2. The implementation of the circuit requires two SR latches, one for each state variable. The maps for inputs S and R of the two latches are shown in Fig. 9-45. The maps are obtained from the information given in the transition table by using the conditions specified in the latch excitation table shown in Fig. 9-14(b). The simplified Boolean functions are listed under each map.

The logic diagram of the circuit is shown in Fig. 9-46. Here we use two NAND latches with two or three inputs in each gate. This implementation is according to the pattern established in Section 9-7 in conjunction with Fig. 9-38(b). The S and R input functions require six NAND gates for their implementation.

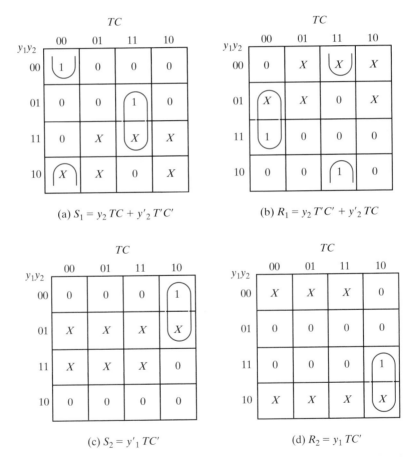

(a) $S_1 = y_2\, TC + y'_2\, T'C'$

(b) $R_1 = y_2\, T'C' + y'_2\, TC$

(c) $S_2 = y'_1\, TC'$

(d) $R_2 = y_1\, TC'$

FIGURE 9-45
Maps for Latch Inputs

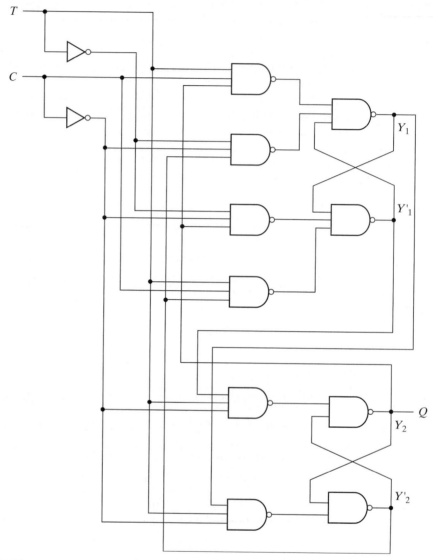

FIGURE 9-46
Logic Diagram of Negative-Edge-Triggered T Flip-Flop

This example demonstrates the complexity involved in designing asynchronous sequential circuits. It was necessary to go through ten diagrams in order to obtain the final circuit diagram. Although most digital circuits are synchronous, there are occasions when one has to deal with asynchronous behavior. The basic properties presented in this chapter are essential to understand fully the internal behavior of digital circuits.

PROBLEMS

9-1 (a) Explain the difference between asynchronous and synchronous sequential circuits.

(b) Define fundamental-mode operation.

(c) Explain the difference between stable and unstable states.

(d) What is the difference between an internal state and a total state?

9-2 Derive the transition table for the asynchronous sequential circuit shown in Fig. P9-2. Determine the sequence of internal states $Y_1 Y_2$ for the following sequence of inputs $x_1 x_2$: 00, 10, 11, 01, 11, 10, 00.

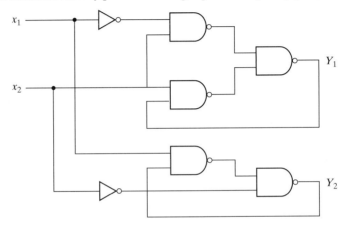

FIGURE P9-2

9.3 An asynchronous sequential circuit is described by the excitation and output functions

$$Y = x_1 x_2' + (x_1 + x_2')y$$

$$z = y$$

(a) Draw the logic diagram of the circuit.   (b) Derive the transition table and output map.

(c) Obtain a two-state flow table.   (d) Describe in words the behavior of the circuit.

9-4 An asynchronous sequential circuit has two internal states and one output. The excitation and output functions describing the circuit are

$$Y_1 = x_1 x_2 + x_1 y_2' + x_2' y_1$$

$$Y_2 = x_2 + x_1 y_1' y_2 + x_1' y_1$$

$$z = x_2 + y_1$$

(a) Draw the logic diagram of the circuit.   (b) Derive the transition table and output map.

(c) Obtain a flow table for the circuit.

9-5 Convert the flow table of Fig. P9-5 into a transition table by assigning the following binary values to the states: $a = 00$, $b = 11$, and $c = 01$.

(a) Assign values to the extra fourth state to avoid critical races.

(b) Assign outputs to the don't-care states to avoid momentary false outputs.

(c) Derive the logic diagram of the circuit.

x_1x_2

	00	01	11	10
a	$\boxed{a}$, 0	b , –	c , –	$\boxed{a}$, 1
b	a , –	$\boxed{b}$, 0	$\boxed{b}$, 0	c , –
c	a , –	b , –	$\boxed{c}$, 1	$\boxed{c}$, 0

FIGURE P9-5

9-6   Investigate the transition table of Fig. P9-6 and determine all race conditions and whether they are critical or noncritical. Also determine whether there are any cycles.

x_1x_2

y_1y_2	00	01	11	10
00	10	(00)	11	10
01	(01)	00	10	10
11	01	00	(11)	(11)
10	11	00	(10)	(10)

FIGURE P9-6

9-7   Analyze the SR latch with control shown in Fig. 5-5. Obtain the transition table and show that the circuit is unstable when all three inputs are equal to 1.

9-8   Modify the diagram of Fig. 5-5(a) to convert it into a JK type latch by inserting two feedback connections from the outputs to the inputs. Show that the circuit is unstable when $J = K = 1$ while the control input C remains in the 1 state.

9-9   For the asynchronous sequential circuit shown in Fig. P9-9,

(a) Derive the Boolean functions for the outputs of the two SR latches Y_1 and Y_2. Note that the S input of the second latch is $x_1'y_1'$.

(b) Derive the transition table and output map of the circuit.

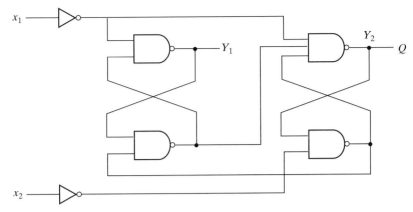

FIGURE P9-9

9-10 Implement the circuit defined in Problem 9-3 with a NOR SR latch. Repeat with a NAND SR latch.

9-11 Implement the circuit defined in Problem 9-4 with NAND SR latches.

9-12 Obtain a primitive flow table for a circuit with two inputs, x_1 and x_2, and two outputs, z_1 and z_2, that satisfy the following four conditions:

(a) When $x_1 x_2 = 00$, the output is $z_1 z_2 = 00$.

(b) When $x_1 = 1$ and x_2 changes from 0 to 1, the output is $z_1 z_2 = 01$.

(c) When $x_2 = 1$ and x_1 changes from 0 to 1, the output is $z_1 z_2 = 10$.

(d) Otherwise, the output does not change.

9-13 A traffic light is installed at a junction of a railroad and a road. The traffic light is controlled by two switches in the rails placed one mile apart on either side of the junction. A switch is turned on when the train is over it and is turned off otherwise. The traffic light changes from green (logic-0) to red (logic-1) when the beginning of the train is one mile from the junction. The light changes back to green when the end of the train is one mile away from the junction. Assume that the length of the train is less than two miles.

(a) Obtain a primitive flow table for the circuit.

(b) Show that the flow table can be reduced to four rows.

9-14 It is necessary to design an asynchronous sequential circuit with two inputs, x_1 and x_2, and one output, z. Initially, both inputs and output are equal to 0. When x_1 or x_2 becomes 1, z becomes 1. When the second input also becomes 1, the output changes to 0. The output stays at 0 until the circuit goes back to the initial state.

(a) Obtain a primitive flow table for the circuit and show that it can be reduced to the flow table shown in Fig. P9-14.

(b) Complete the design of the circuit.

	00	01	11	10
a	(a), 0	(a), 1	b , –	(a), 1
b	a , –	(b), 0	(b), 0	(b), 0

FIGURE P9-14

9-15 Assign output values to the don't-care states in the flow tables of Fig. P9-15 in such a way as to avoid transient output pulses.

	00	01	11	10
a	(a), 0	b , –	– , –	d , –
b	a , –	(b), 1	(b), 1	c , –
c	b , –	– , –	b , –	(c), 0
d	c , –	(d), 1	c , –	(d), 1

(a)

	00	01	11	10
a	(a), 0	b , –	b , –	(a), 0
b	a , –	(b), 0	(b), 1	c , –
c	b , –	d , –	(c), 1	(c), 1
d	(d), 0	(d), 1	c , –	a , –

(b)

FIGURE P9-15

9-16 Using the implication-table method, show that the state table listed in Table 5-7 cannot be reduced any further.

9-17 Reduce the number of states in the state table listed in Problem 5-12. Use an implication table.

9-18 Merge each of the primitive flow tables shown in Fig. P9-18. Proceed as follows:
   (a) Find all compatible pairs by means of an implication table.
   (b) Find the maximal compatibles by means of a merger diagram.
   (c) Find a minimal set of compatibles that covers all the states and is closed.

	00	01	11	10
a	ⓐ,1	f ,–	– ,–	e ,–
b	c ,–	– ,–	j ,–	ⓑ,0
c	ⓒ,0	d ,–	– ,–	b ,–
d	c ,–	ⓓ,0	g ,–	– ,–
e	a ,–	– ,–	g ,–	ⓔ,1
f	a ,–	ⓕ,1	g ,–	– ,–
g	– ,–	d ,–	ⓖ,0	k ,–
h	ⓗ,0	d ,–	– ,–	k ,–
j	– ,–	f ,–	ⓙ,1	b ,–
k	a ,–	– ,–	j ,1	ⓚ,0

	00	01	11	10
a	ⓐ,0	b ,–	– ,–	e ,–
b	a ,–	ⓑ,0	c ,–	– ,–
c	– ,–	d ,–	ⓒ,0	h ,–
d	a ,–	ⓓ,1	– ,–	– ,–
e	a ,–	– ,–	f ,–	ⓔ,0
f	– ,–	g ,–	ⓕ,0	h ,–
g	a ,–	ⓖ,0	– ,–	– ,–
h	a ,–	– ,–	– ,–	ⓗ,0

(a)

(b)

FIGURE P9-18

9-19 (a) Obtain a binary state assignment for the reduced flow table shown in Fig. P9-19. Avoid critical race conditions.

(b) Obtain the logic diagram of the circuit using NAND latches and gates.

x_1x_2

	00	01	11	10
a	ⓐ,0	ⓐ,1	b ,–	d ,–
b	a ,–	ⓑ,0	ⓑ,0	c ,–
c	a ,–	– ,–	d ,–	ⓒ,0
d	a ,–	a ,–	ⓓ,1	ⓓ,1

FIGURE P9-19

9-20 Find a critical race-free state assignment for the reduced flow table shown in Fig. P9-20.

	00	01	11	10
a	(a)	d	(a)	c
b	a	(b)	(b)	d
c	d	(c)	b	(c)
d	(d)	(d)	e	(d)
e	f	c	(e)	c
f	(f)	b	a	(f)

FIGURE P9-20

9-21 Consider the reduced flow table shown in Fig. P9-21.

  (a) Obtain the transition diagram and show that three state variables are needed for a race-free binary state assignment.

  (b) Obtain the expanded flow table using the multiple-row-method assignment as specified in Fig. 9-32(a).

	00	01	11	10
a	(a)	c	(a)	d
b	a	(b)	c	(b)
c	(c)	(c)	(c)	d
d	(d)	b	a	(d)

FIGURE P9-21

9-22 Find a circuit that has no static hazards and implements the Boolean function

$$F(A, B, C, D) = \Sigma(0, 2, 6, 7, 8, 10, 12)$$

9-23 Draw the logic diagram of the product of sums expression:

$$Y = (x_1 + x_2')(x_2 + x_3)$$

Show that there is a static 0-hazard when x_1 and x_3 are equal to 0 and x_2 goes from 0 to 1. Find a way to remove the hazard by adding one more OR gate.

9-24 The Boolean functions for the inputs of an *SR* latch are

$$S = x_1'x_2'x_3 + x_1x_2x_3$$
$$R = x_1x_2' + x_2x_3'$$

Obtain the circuit diagram using a minimum number of NAND gates.

9-25 Complete the design of the circuit specified in Problem 9-13.

REFERENCES

1. HILL, F. J., and G. R. PETERSON. 1981. *Introduction to Switching Theory and Logical Design,* 3rd Ed. New York: John Wiley.

2. KOHAVI, Z. 1978. *Switching and Automata Theory,* 2nd Ed. New York: McGraw-Hill.

3. McCLUSKEY, E. J. 1986. *Logic Design Principles.* Englewood Cliffs, NJ: Prentice-Hall.

4. UNGER, S. H. 1969. *Asynchronous Sequential Switching Circuits.* New York: John Wiley.

5. BREEDING, K. J. 1989. *Digital Design Fundamentals.* Englewood Cliffs, NJ: Prentice-Hall.

6. FRIEDMAN, A. D. 1986. *Fundamentals of Logic Design and Switching Theory.* Rockville, MD: Computer Science Press.

7. NELSON, V. P., H. T. NAGLE, J. D. IRWIN, and B. D. CARROLL. 1995. *Digital Logic Circuits Analysis and Design,* Prentice Hall.

10 Digital Integrated Circuits

10-1 INTRODUCTION

The integrated circuit (IC) and the digital logic families were introduced in Section 2-8. This chapter presents the electronic circuits in each IC digital logic family and analyzes their electrical operation. A basic knowledge of electrical circuits is assumed.

The IC digital logic families to be considered here are

RTL	Resistor-transistor logic
DTL	Diode-transistor logic
TTL	Transistor-transistor logic
ECL	Emitter-coupled logic
MOS	Metal-oxide semiconductor
CMOS	Complementary metal-oxide semiconductor

The first two, RTL and DTL, have only historical significance since they are no longer used in the design of digital systems. RTL was the first commercial family to have been used extensively. It is included here because it represents a useful starting point for explaining the basic operation of digital gates. DTL circuits have been replaced by TTL. In fact, TTL is a modification of the DTL gate. The operation of the TTL gate will be easier to understand after the DTL gate is analyzed. TTL, ECL, and CMOS have a large number of SSI circuits, as well as MSI, LSI, and VLSI components.

The basic circuit in each IC digital logic family is either a NAND or NOR gate. This basic circuit is the primary building block from which all other more complex digital components are obtained. Each IC logic family has available a data book that lists all the integrated circuits in that family. The differences in the logic functions available from each logic family are not so

Inputs		Output
x	y	z
L	L	H
L	H	H
H	L	H
H	H	L

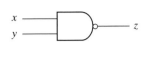

FIGURE 10-1
Positive Logic NAND Gate

much in the functions that they achieve as in the specific electrical characteristics of the basic gate from which the circuit is constructed.

NAND and NOR gates are usually defined by the Boolean functions that they implement in terms of binary variables. When analyzing them as electronic circuits, it is necessary to investigate their input–output relationships in terms of two voltage levels: a *high* level designated by H and a *low* level designated by L. As mentioned in Section 2-8, the assignment of binary 1 to H results in a positive logic system and the assignment of binary 1 to L results in a negative logic system. The truth table in terms of H and L of a positive logic NAND gate is shown in Fig. 10-1. We notice that the output of the gate is high as long as one or more inputs are low. The output is low only when both inputs are high. The behavior of a positive logic NAND gate in terms of high and low signals can be stated as follows:

If *any* input of a NAND gate is low, the output its high.

If *all* inputs of a NAND gate are high, the output is low.

The corresponding truth table for a positive logic NOR gate is shown in Fig. 10-2. The output of the NOR gate is low when one or more inputs are high. The output is high when both inputs are low. The behavior of a positive logic NOR gate in terms, of high and low signals can be stated as follows:

If *any* input of a NOR gate is high, the output is low.

If *all* inputs of a NOR gate are low, the output is high.

These statements for NAND and NOR gates must be remembered because they will be used during the analysis of the electronic gates in this chapter.

Inputs		Output
x	y	z
L	L	H
L	H	L
H	L	L
H	H	L

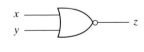

FIGURE 10-2
Positive Logic NOR Gate

A bipolar junction transistor (BJT) can be either an *npn* or a *pnp* junction transistor. In contrast, the field-effect transistor (FET) is said to be unipolar. The operation of a bipolar transistor depends on the flow of two types of carriers: electrons and holes. A unipolar transistor depends on the flow of only one type of majority carrier, which may be electrons (*n*-channel) or holes (*p*-channel). The first four digital logic families listed—RTL, DTL, TTL, and ECL—use bipolar transistors. The last two families—MOS and CMOS—employ a type of unipolar transistor called a metal-oxide-semiconductor field-effect transistor, abbreviated MOSFET or MOS for short.

In this chapter, we first introduce the most common characteristics by which the digital logic families are compared. We then describe the properties of the bipolar transistor and analyze the basic gates in the bipolar logic families. We then explain the operation of the MOS transistor and introduce the basic gates of its two logic families.

10-2   SPECIAL CHARACTERISTICS

The characteristics of IC digital logic families are usually compared by analyzing the circuit of the basic gate in each family. The most important parameters that are evaluated and compared are fan-out, power dissipation, propagation delay, and noise margin. We first explain the properties of these parameters and then use them to compare the IC logic families.

Fan-Out

The fan-out of a gate specifies the number of standard loads that can be connected to the output of the gate without degrading its normal operation. A standard load is usually defined as the amount of current needed by an input of another gate in the same logic family. Sometimes the term *loading* is used instead of fan-out. This term is derived because the output of a gate can supply a limited amount of current, above which it ceases to operate properly and is said to be overloaded. The output of a gate is usually connected to the inputs of other gates. Each input consumes a certain amount of current from the gate output, so that each additional connection adds to the load of the gate. Loading rules are sometimes specified for a family of digital circuits. These rules give the maximum amount of loading allowed for each output of each circuit in the family. Exceeding the specified maximum load may cause a malfunction because the circuit cannot supply the power demanded from it. The fan-out is the maximum number of inputs that can be connected to the output of a gate, and is expressed by a number.

The fan-out is calculated from the amount of current available in the output of a gate and the amount of current needed in each input of a gate. Consider the connections shown in Fig. 10-3. The output of one gate is connected to one or more inputs of other gates. The output of the gate is in the high voltage level in Fig. 10-3(a). It provides a current source I_{OH} to all the gate inputs connected to it. Each gate input requires a current I_{IH} for proper operation. Similarly, the output of the gate is in the low voltage level in Fig. 10-3(b). It provides a current sink I_{OL} for all the gate inputs connected to it. Each gate input supplies a current I_{IL}. The fan-out

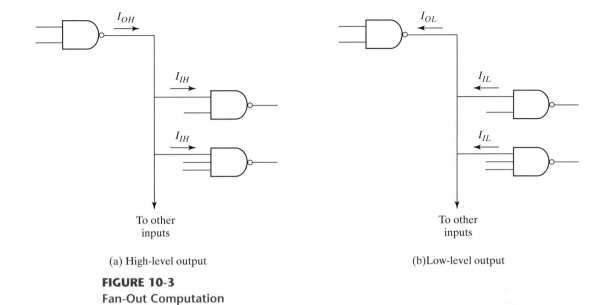

(a) High-level output   (b)Low-level output

FIGURE 10-3
Fan-Out Computation

of the gate is calculated from the ratio I_{OH}/I_{IH} or I_{OL}/I_{IL}, whichever is smaller. For example, the standard TTL gates have the following values for the currents:

$$I_{OH} = 400 \; \mu A$$
$$I_{IH} = 40 \; \mu A$$
$$I_{OL} = 16 \; mA$$
$$I_{IL} = 1.6 \; mA$$

The two ratios give the same number in this case:

$$\frac{400 \; \mu A}{40 \; \mu A} = \frac{16 \; mA}{1.6 \; mA} = 10$$

Therefore, the fan-out of standard TTL is 10. This means that the output of a TTL gate can be connected to no more than ten inputs of other gates in the same logic family. Otherwise, the gate may not be able to drive or sink the amount of current needled from the inputs that are connected to it.

Power Dissipation

Every electronic circuit requires a certain amount of power to operate. The power dissipation is a parameter expressed in milliwatts (mW) and represents the amount of power needed by the gate. The number that represents this parameter does not include the power delivered from another gate; rather, it represents the power delivered to the gate from the power supply. An IC with four gates will require, from its power supply, four times the power dissipated in each gate.

The amount of power that is dissipated in a gate is calculated from the supply voltage V_{CC} and the current I_{CC} that is drawn by the circuit. The power is the product $V_{CC} \times I_{CC}$. The current drain from the power supply depends on the logic state of the gate. The current drawn from the power supply when the output of the gate is in the high-voltage level is termed I_{CCH}. When the output is in the low-voltage level, the current is I_{CCL}. The average current is

$$I_{CC}(\text{avg}) = \frac{I_{CCH} + I_{CCL}}{2}$$

and is used to calculate the average power dissipation:

$$P_D(\text{avg}) = I_{CC}(\text{avg}) \times V_{CC}$$

For example, a standard TTL NAND gate uses a supply voltage V_{CC} of 5 V and has current drains $I_{CCH} = 1$ mA and $I_{CCL} = 3$ mA. The average current is $(3 + 1)/2 = 2$ mA. The average power dissipation is $5 \times 2 = 10$ mW. An IC that has four NAND gates dissipates a total of $10 \times 4 = 40$ mW. In a typical digital system there will be many ICs, and the power required by each IC must be considered. The total power dissipation in the system is the sum total of the power dissipated in all ICs.

Propagation Delay

The propagation delay of a gate is the average transition-delay time for the signal to propagate from input to output when the binary signal changes in value. The signals through a gate take a certain amount of time to propagate from the inputs to the output. This interval of time is defined as the propagation delay of the gate. Propagation delay is measured in nanoseconds (ns). 1 ns is equal to 10^{-9} of a second.

The signals that travel from the inputs of a digital circuit to its outputs pass through a series of gates. The sum of the propagation delays through the gates is the total delay of the circuit. When speed of operation is important, each gate must have a short propagation delay and the digital circuit must have a minimum number of gates between inputs and outputs.

The average propagation delay time of a gate is calculated from the input and output waveforms, as shown in Fig. 10-4. The signal-delay time between the input and output when the output changes from the high to the low level is referred to as t_{PHL}. Similarly, when the output goes from the low to the high level, the delay is t_{PLH}. It is customary to measure the time between the 50 percent point on the input and output transitions. In general, the two delays are not the same, and both will vary with loading conditions. The average propagation-delay time is calculated as the average of the two delays.

As an example, the delays for a standard TTL gate are $t_{PHL} = 7$ ns and $t_{PLH} = 11$ ns. These quantities are given in the TTL data book and are measured with a load resistance of 400 ohms and a load capacitance of 15 pF. The average propagation delay of the TTL gate is $(11 + 7)/2 = 9$ ns.

Under certain conditions, it is more important to know the maximum delay time of a gate rather than the average value. The TTL data book lists the following maximum propagation delays for a standard NAND gate: $t_{PHL} = 15$ ns and $t_{PLH} = 22$ ns. When speed of operation is critical, it is necessary to take into account the maximum delay to ensure proper operation.

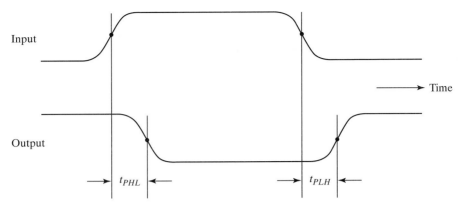

FIGURE 10-4
Measurement of Propagation Delay

The input signals in most digital circuits are applied simultaneously to more than one gate. All the gates that are connected to external inputs constitute the first logic level of the circuit. Gates that receive at least one input from an output of a first level gate are considered to be in the second logic level, and similarly for the third and higher logic levels. The total propagation delay of the circuit is equal to the propagation delay of a gate times the number of logic levels in the circuit. Thus, a reduction in the number of logic levels results in a reduction of signal delay and faster circuits. The reduction of the propagation delay in circuits may be more important than the reduction of the total number of gates if speed of operation is a major factor.

Noise Margin

Spurious electrical signals from industrial and other similar sources can induce undesirable voltages on the connecting wires between logic circuits. These unwanted signals are referred to as *noise*. There are two types of noise to be considered. DC noise is caused by a drift in the voltage levels of a signal. AC noise is a random pulse that may be created by other switching signals. Thus, noise is a term used to denote an undesirable signal that is superimposed upon the normal operating signal. *Noise margin* is the maximum noise voltage added to an input signal of a digital circuit that does not cause an undesirable change in the circuit output. The ability of circuits to operate reliably in a noise environment is important in many applications. Noise margin is expressed in volts and represents the maximum noise signal that can be tolerated by the gate.

The noise margin is calculated from knowledge of the voltage signal available in the output of the gate and the voltage signal required in the input of the gate. Fig. 10-5 illustrates the signals for computing noise margin. Part (a) shows the range of output voltages that can occur in a typical gate. Any voltage in the gate output between V_{CC} and V_{OH} is considered as the high-level state and any voltage between 0 and V_{OL} in the gate output is considered as the low-level state. Voltages between V_{OL} and V_{OH} are indeterminate and do not appear under normal operating conditions except during transition between the two levels. The corresponding two voltage ranges that are recognized by the input of the gate are indicated in Fig. 10-5(b). In order to compensate for any noise signal, the circuit must be designed so that V_{IL} is greater than V_{OL} and V_{IH} is less than V_{OH}. The noise margin is the difference $V_{OH} - V_{IH}$ or $V_{IL} - V_{OL}$, whichever is smaller.

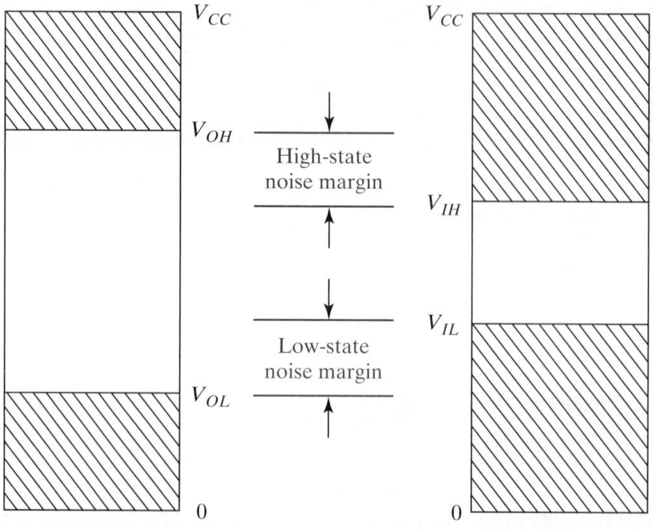

(a) Output voltage range

(b) Input voltage range

FIGURE 10-5
Signals for Evaluating Noise Margin

As illustrated in Fig. 10-5, V_{OL} is the maximum voltage that the output can be when in the low-level state. The circuit can tolerate any noise signal that is less than the noise margin $(V_{IL} - V_{OL})$ because the input will recognize the signal as being in the low-level state. Any signal greater than V_{OL} plus the noise-margin figure will send the input voltage into the indeterminate range, which may cause an error in the output of the gate. In a similar fashion, a negative-voltage noise greater than $V_{OH} - V_{IH}$ will send the input voltage into the indeterminate range.

The parameters for the noise margin in a standard TTL NAND gate are $V_{OH} = 2.4$ V, $V_{OL} = 0.4$ V, $V_{IH} = 2$ V, and $V_{IL} = 0.8$ V. The high-state noise margin is $2.4 - 2 = 0.4$ V, and the low-state noise margin is $0.8 - 0.4 = 0.4$ V. In this case, both values are the same.

10-3 BIPOLAR-TRANSISTOR CHARACTERISTICS

This section is devoted to a review of the bipolar transistor as applied to digital circuits. This information will be used for the analysis of the basic circuit in the four bipolar logic families. Bipolar transistors may be of the *npn* or *pnp* type. Moreover, they are constructed either with germanium or silicon semiconductor material. IC transistors, however, are made with silicon and are usually of the *npn* type.

The basic data needed for the analysis of digital circuits may be obtained from inspection of the typical characteristic curves of a common-emitter *npn* silicon transistor, shown in Fig. 10-6. The circuit in (a) is a simple inverter with two resistors and a transistor. The current marked I_C flows through resistor R_C and the collector of the transistor. Current I_B flows through

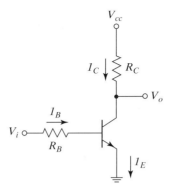

(a) Inverter circuit

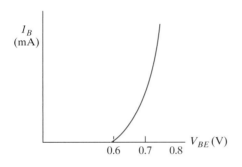

(b) Transistor-base characteristic

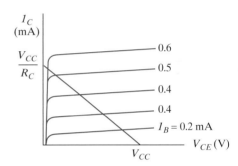

(c) Transistor-collector characteristic

FIGURE 10-6
Silicon *npn* Transistor Characteristics

resistor R_B and the base of the transistor. The emitter is connected to ground and its current $I_E = I_C + I_B$. The supply voltage is between V_{CC} and ground. The input is between V_i and ground, and the output is between V_o and ground.

We have assumed a positive direction for the currents as indicated. These are the directions in which the currents normally flow in an *npn* transistor. Collector and base currents, I_C and I_B, respectively, are positive when they flow into the transistor. Emitter current I_E is positive when it flows out of the transistor, as indicated by the arrow in the emitter terminal. The symbol V_{CE} stands for the voltage drop from collector to emitter and is always positive. Correspondingly, V_{BE} is the voltage drop across the base-to-emitter junction. This junction is forward biased when V_{BE} is positive. It is reverse biased when V_{BE} is negative.

The base-emitter graphical characteristic is shown in Fig. 10-6(b). This is a plot of V_{BE} versus I_B. If the base-emitter voltage is less than 0.6 V, the transistor is said to be *cut off* and no base current flows. When the base-emitter junction is forward biased with a voltage greater than 0.6 V, the transistor conducts and I_B starts rising very fast whereas V_{BE} changes very little. The voltage V_{BE} across a conducting transistor seldom exceeds 0.8 V.

The graphical collector-emitter characteristics, together with the load line, are shown in Fig. 10-6(c). When V_{BE} is less than 0.6 V, the transistor is cut off with $I_B = 0$ and a negligible current flows in the collector. The collector-to-emitter circuit then behaves like an open circuit. In the *active* region, collector voltage V_{CE} may be anywhere from about 0.8 V up to V_{CC}. Collector current I_C in this region can be calculated to be approximately equal to $I_B h_{FE}$, where h_{FE} is a transistor parameter called the *dc current gain*. The maximum collector current depends not on I_B, but rather on the external circuit connected to the collector. This is because V_{CE} is always positive and its lowest possible value is 0 V. For example, in the inverter shown, the maximum I_C is obtained by making $V_{CE} = 0$ to obtain $I_C = V_{CC}/R_C$.

It was stated that $I_C = h_{FE}I_B$ in the active region. The parameter h_{FE} varies widely over the operating range of the transistor, but still it is useful to employ an average value for the purpose of analysis. In a typical operating range, h_{FE} is about 50, but under certain conditions, it could be as low as 20. It must be realized that the base current I_B may be increased to any desirable value, but the collector current I_C is limited by external circuit parameters. As a consequence, a situation can be reached where $h_{FE}I_B$ is greater than I_C. If this condition exists, then the transistor is said to be in the *saturation* region. Thus, the condition for saturation is determined from the relationship

$$I_B \geq \frac{I_{CS}}{h_{FE}}$$

where I_{CS} is the maximum collector current flowing during saturation. V_{CE} is not exactly zero in the saturation region, but is normally about 0.2 V.

The basic data needed for analyzing bipolar transistor digital circuits are listed in Table 10-1. In the cutoff region, V_{BE} is less than 0.6 V, V_{CE} is considered as an open circuit, and both currents are negligible. In the active region, V_{BE} is about 0.7 V, V_{CE} may vary over a wide range, and I_C can be calculated as a function of I_B. In the saturation region, V_{BE} hardly changes, but V_{CE} drops to 0.2 V. The base current must be large enough to satisfy the inequality listed. To simplify the analysis, we will assume that $V_{BE} = 0.7$ V if the transistor is conducting, whether in the active or saturation region.

The analysis of digital circuits may be undertaken using the following prescribed procedure: For each transistor in the circuit, determine if its V_{BE} is less than 0.6 V. If so, then the transistor is cut off and the collector-to-emitter circuit is considered an open circuit. If V_{BE} is greater than 0.6 V, the transistor may be in the active or saturation region. Calculate the base current, assuming that $V_{BE} = 0.7$ V. Then calculate the maximum possible value of collector current I_{CS}, assuming $V_{CE} = 0.2$ V. These calculations will be in terms of voltages applied and resistor

Table 10-1
Typical npn Silicon Transistor Parameters

Region	V_{BE} (V)	V_{CE} (V)	Current Relationship
Cutoff	< 0.6	Open circuit	$I_B = I_C = 0$
Active	0.6–0.7	> 0.8	$I_C = h_{FE}I_B$
Saturation	0.7–0.8	0.2	$I_B \geq I_{CS}/h_{FE}$

values. Then, if the base current is large enough that $I_B \geq I_{CS}/h_{FE}$, we deduce that the transistor is in the saturation region with $V_{CE} = 0.2$ V. However, if the base current is smaller and the above relationship is not satisfied, the transistor is in the active region and we recalculate collector current I_C using the equation $I_C = h_{FE}I_B$.

To demonstrate with an example, consider the inverter circuit of Fig. 10-6(a) with the following parameters:

$$R_C = 1 \ k\Omega \qquad\qquad V_{CC} = 5 \ V \ \text{(voltage supply)}$$
$$R_B = 22 \ k\Omega \qquad\qquad H = 5 \ V \ \text{(high-level voltage)}$$
$$h_{FE} = 50 \qquad\qquad L = 0.2 \ V \ \text{(low-level voltage)}$$

With input voltage $V_i = L = 0.2$ V, we have that $V_{BE} < 0.6$ V and the transistor is cut off. The collector-emitter circuit behaves like an open circuit, so output voltage $V_o = 5$ V $= H$.

With input voltage $V_i = H = 5$ V, we deduce that $V_{BE} > 0.6$ V. Assuming that $V_{BE} = 0.7$, we calculate the base current:

$$I_B = \frac{V_i - V_{BE}}{R_B} = \frac{5 - 0.7}{22 \ k\Omega} = 0.195 \ \text{mA}$$

The maximum collector current, assuming $V_{CE} = 0.2$ V, is

$$I_{CS} = \frac{V_{CC} - V_{CE}}{R_C} = \frac{5 - 0.2}{1 \ k\Omega} = 4.8 \ \text{mA}$$

We then check for saturation, using the condition

$$0.195 = I_B \geq \frac{I_{CS}}{h_{FE}} = \frac{4.8}{50} = 0.096 \ \text{mA}$$

whereupon we find that the inequality is satisfied, since $0.195 > 0.096$. We conclude that the transistor is saturated and output voltage $V_o = V_{CE} = 0.2$ V $= L$. Thus, the circuit behaves as an inverter.

The procedure just described will be used extensively during the analysis of the circuits in the following sections. This will be done by means of a qualitative analysis, i.e., without writing down the specific numerical equations. The quantitative analysis and specific calculations will be left as exercises in the Problems section at the end of the chapter.

There are occasions where not only transistors but also diodes are used in digital circuits. An IC diode is usually constructed from a transistor with its collector connected to the base, as shown in Fig. 10-7(a). The graphic symbol employed for a diode is shown in Fig. 10-7(b). The diode behaves essentially like the base-emitter junction of a transistor. Its graphical characteristic, shown in Fig. 10-7(c), is similar to the base-emitter characteristic of a transistor. We can then conclude that a diode is off and non-conducting when its forward voltage, V_D, is less than 0.6 V. When the diode conducts, current I_D flows in the direction shown in Fig. 10-7(b), and V_D stays at about 0.7 V. One must always provide an external resistor to limit the current in a conducting diode, since its voltage remains fairly constant at a fraction of a volt.

1 o——

2 o——

(a) Transistor adapted for
use as a diode

I_D

1 o——▷|——o 2
  + V_D −

(b) Diode graphic symbol

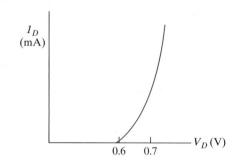

I_D
(mA)

0.6   0.7   —V_D (V)

(c) Diode characteristic

FIGURE 10-7
Silicon Diode Symbol and Characteristic

10-4   RTL AND DTL CIRCUITS

RTL Basic Gate

The basic circuit of the RTL digital logic family is the NOR gate shown in Fig. 10-8. Each input is associated with one resistor and one transistor. The collectors of the transistors are tied together at the output. The voltage levels for the circuit are 0.2 V for the low level and from 1 to 3.6 V for the high level.

The analysis of the RTL gate is very simple and follows the procedure outlined in the previous section. If any input of the RTL gate is high, the corresponding transistor is driven into saturation.

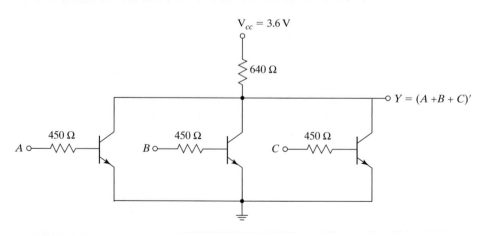

$V_{cc} = 3.6$ V

640 Ω

o $Y = (A + B + C)'$

450 Ω   450 Ω   450 Ω

A o—WW— B o—WW— C o—WW—

FIGURE 10-8
RTL Basic NOR Gate

This causes the output to be low, regardless of the states of the other transistors. If all inputs are low at 0.2 V, all transistors are cut off because $V_{BE} < 0.6$ V. This causes the output of the circuit to be high, approaching the value of supply voltage V_{CC}. This confirms the conditions stated in Fig. 10-2 for the NOR gate. Note that the noise margin for low signal input is $0.6 - 0.2 = 0.4$ V.

The fan-out of the RTL gate is limited by the value of the output voltage when high. As the output is loaded with inputs of other gates, more current is consumed by the load. This current must flow through the 640-Ω resistor. A simple calculation (see Problem 10-2) will show that if h_{FE} drops to 20, the output voltage drops to about 1 V when the fan-out is 5. Any voltage below 1 V in the output may not drive the next transistor into saturation as required. The power dissipation of the RTL gate is about 12 mW and the propagation delay averages 25 ns.

DTL Basic Gates

The basic circuit in the DTL digital logic family is the NAND gate shown in Fig. 10-9. Each input is associated with one diode. The diodes and the 5-kΩ resistor form an AND gate. The transistor serves as a current amplifier while inverting the digital signal. The two voltage levels are 0.2 V for the low level and between 4 and 5 V for the high level.

The analysis of the DTL gate should conform to the conditions listed in Fig. 10-1 for the NAND gate. If any input of the gate is low at 0.2 V, the corresponding input diode conducts current through V_{CC} and the 5-kΩ resistor into the input node. The voltage at point P is equal to the input voltage of 0.2 V plus a diode drop of 0.7 V, for a total of 0.9 V. In order for the transistor to start conducting, the voltage at point P must overcome a potential of one V_{BE} drop in $Q1$ plus two diode drops across $D1$ and $D2$, or $3 \times 0.6 = 1.8$ V. Since the voltage at P is maintained at 0.9 V by the input conducting diode, the transistor is cut off and the output voltage is high at 5 V.

If all inputs of the gate are high, the transistor is driven into the saturation region. The voltage at P now is equal to V_{BE} plus the two diode drops across $D1$ and $D2$, or $0.7 \times 3 = 2.1$ V. Since all inputs are high at 5 V and $V_P = 2.1$ V, the input diodes are reverse biased and off. The base current is equal to the difference of currents flowing in the two 5-kΩ resistors and is

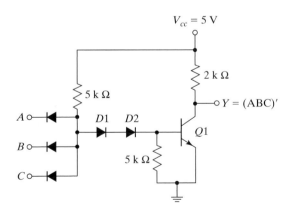

FIGURE 10-9
DTL Basic NAND Gate

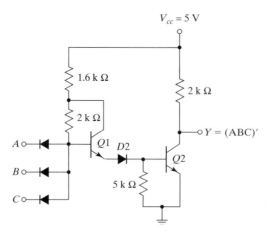

FIGURE 10-10
Modified DTL Gate

sufficient to drive the transistor into saturation. (See Problem 10-3.) With the transistor saturated, the output drops to V_{CE} of 0.2 V, which is the low level for the gate.

The power dissipation of a DTL gate is about 12 mW and the propagation delay averages 30 ns. The noise margin is about 1 V and a fan-out as high as 8 is possible. The fan-out of the DTL gate is limited by the maximum current that can flow in the collector of the saturated transistor. (See Problem 10-4.)

The fan-out of a DTL gate may be increased by replacing one of the diodes in the base circuit with a transistor, as shown in Fig. 10-10. Transistor $Q1$ is maintained in the active region when output transistor $Q2$ is saturated. As a consequence, the modified circuit can supply a larger amount of base current to the output transistor. The output transistor can now draw a larger amount of collector current before it goes out of saturation. Part of the collector current comes from the conducting diodes in the loading gates when $Q2$ is saturated. Thus, an increase in allowable collector saturated current allows more loads to be connected to the output, which increases the fan-out capability of the gate.

10-5   TRANSISTOR-TRANSISTOR LOGIC (TTL)

The original basic TTL gate was a slight improvement over the DTL gate. As the TTL technology progressed, additional improvements were added to the point where this logic family is widely used in the design of digital systems. There are several subfamilies or series of the TTL technology. The names and characteristics of eight TTL series appear in Table 10-2. Commercial TTL ICs have a number designation that starts with 74 and follows with a suffix that identifies the series type. Examples are 7404, 74S86, and 74ALS161. Fan-out, power dissipation, and propagation delay were defined in Section 10-2. The speed-power product is an important parameter for comparing the various TTL series. This is the product of the propagation delay and power dissipation and is measured in picojoules (pJ). A low value for this parameter is desirable, because it indicates that a given propagation delay can be achieved without excessive power dissipation, and vice versa.

Table 10-2
TTL Series and Their Characteristics

TTL Series Name	Prefix	Fan-out	Power Dissipation (mW)	Propagation Delay (ns)	Speed-Power Product (pJ)
Standard	74	10	10	9	90
Low-power	74L	20	1	33	33
High-speed	74H	10	22	6	132
Schottky	74S	10	19	3	57
Low-power Schottky	74LS	20	2	9.5	19
Advanced Schottky	74AS	40	10	1.5	15
Advanced low-power Schottky	74ALS	20	1	4	4
Fast	74F	20	4	3	12

The standard TTL gate was the first version in the TTL family. This basic gate was then de-signed with different resistor values to produce gates with lower power dissipation or with higher speed. The propagation delay of a transistor circuit that goes into saturation depends mostly on two factors: storage time and *RC* time constants. Reducing the storage time de-creases the propagation delay. Reducing resistor values in the circuit reduces the *RC* time constants and decreases the propagation delay. Of course, the trade-off is higher power dissipation because lower resistances draw more current from the power supply. The speed of the gate is inversely proportional to the propagation delay.

In the low-power TTL gate, the resistor values are higher than in the standard gate to re-duce the power dissipation, but the propagation delay is increased. In the high-speed TTL gate, resistor values are lowered to reduce the propagation delay, but the power dissipation is increased. The Schottky TTL gate was the next improvement in the technology. The effect of the Schottky transistor is to remove the storage time delay by preventing the transistor from going into saturation. This series increases the speed of operation without an excessive increase in power dissipation. The low-power Schottky TTL sacrifices some speed for reduced power dissipation. It is equal to the standard TTL in propagation delay, but has only one-fifth the power dissipation. Recent innovations have led to the development of the advanced Schottky series. It provides an improvement in propagation delay over the Schottky series and also lowers the power dissipation. The advanced low-power Schottky has the lowest speed-power product and is the most efficient series. The Fast TTL family is the best choice for high-speed designs.

All TTL series are available in SSI and in more complex forms such as MSI and LSI com-ponents. The differences in the TTL series are not in the digital logic that they perform, but rather in the internal construction of the basic NAND gate. In any case, TTL gates in all the available series come in three different types of output configuration:

1. Open-collector output
2. Totem-pole output
3. Three-state (or tristate) output

These three types of outputs will be considered in conjunction with the circuit description of the basic TTL gate.

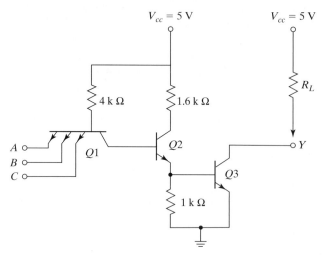

FIGURE 10-11
Open-Collector TTL Gate

Open-Collector Output Gate

The basic TTL gate shown in Fig. 10-11 is a modified circuit of the DTL gate. The multiple emitters in transistor $Q1$ are connected to the inputs. These emitters behave most of the time like the input diodes in the DTL gate since they form a *pn* junction with their common base. The base-collector junction of $Q1$ acts as another *pn* junction diode corresponding to $D1$ in the DTL gate (see Fig. 10-5). Transistor $Q2$ replaces the second diode, $D2$, in the DTL gate. The output of the TTL gate is taken from the open collector of $Q3$. A resistor connected to V_{CC} must be inserted externally to the IC package for the output to "pull up" to the high voltage level when $Q3$ is off; otherwise, the output acts as an open circuit. The reason for not providing the resistor internally will be discussed later.

The two voltage levels of the TTL gate are 0.2 V for the low level and from 2.4 to 5 V for the high level. The basic circuit is a NAND gate. If any input is low, the corresponding base-emitter junction in $Q1$ is forward biased. The voltage at the base of $Q1$ is equal to the input voltage of 0.2 V plus a V_{BE} drop of 0.7 or 0.9 V. In order for $Q3$ to start conducting, the path from $Q1$ to $Q3$ must overcome a potential of one diode drop in the base-collector *pn* junction of $Q1$ and two V_{BE} drops in $Q2$ and $Q3$, or $3 \times 0.6 = 1.8$ V. Since the base of $Q1$ is maintained at 0.9 V by the input signal, the output transistor cannot conduct and is cut off. The output level will be high if an external resistor is connected between the output and V_{CC} (or an open circuit if a resistor is not used).

If all inputs are high, both $Q2$ and $Q3$ conduct and saturate. The base voltage of $Q1$ is equal to the voltage across its base-collector *pn* junction plus two V_{BE} drops in $Q2$ and $Q3$, or about $0.7 \times 3 = 2.1$ V. Since all inputs are high and greater than 2.4 V, the base-emitter junctions of $Q1$ are all reverse biased. When output transistor $Q3$ saturates (provided it has a current path), the output voltage goes low to 0.2 V. This confirms the conditions of a NAND operation.

In this analysis, we said that the base-collector junction of $Q1$ acts like a *pn* diode junction. This is true in the steady-state condition. However, during the turn-off transition, $Q1$ does exhibit transistor action, resulting in a reduction in propagation delay. When all inputs are high and then one of the inputs is brought to a low level, both $Q2$ and $Q3$ start turning off. At this time, the collector junction of $Q1$ is reverse biased and the emitter is forward biased; so transistor $Q1$ goes momentarily into the active region. The collector current of $Q1$ comes from the base of $Q2$ and quickly removes the excess charge stored in $Q2$ during its previous saturation state. This causes a reduction in the storage time of the circuit as compared to the DTL type of input. The result is a reduction of the turn-off time of the gate.

The open-collector TTL gate will operate without the external resistor when connected to inputs of other TTL gates, although this is not recommended because of the low noise immunity encountered. Without an external resistor, the output of the gate will be an open circuit when $Q3$ is off. An open circuit to an input of a TTL gate behaves as if it has a high-level input (but a small amount of noise can change this to a low level). When $Q3$ conducts, its collector will have a current path supplied by the input of the loading gate through V_{CC}, the 4-kΩ resistor, and the forward-biased base–emitter junction.

Open-collector gates are used in three major applications: driving a lamp or relay, performing wired logic, and construction of a common-bus system. An open-collector output can drive a lamp placed in its output through a limiting resistor. When the output is low, the saturated transistor $Q3$ forms a path for the current that turns the lamp on. When the output transistor is off, the lamp turns off because there is no path for the current.

If the outputs of several open-collector TTL gates are tied together with a single external resistor, a wired-AND logic is performed. Remember that a positive-logic AND function gives a high level only if all variables are high; otherwise, the function is low. With outputs of open-collector gates connected together, the common output is high only when all output transistors are off (or high). If an output transistor conducts, it forces the output to the low state.

The wired logic performed with open-collector TTL gates is depicted in Fig. 10-12. The physical wiring in (a) shows how the outputs must be connected to a common resistor. The graphic

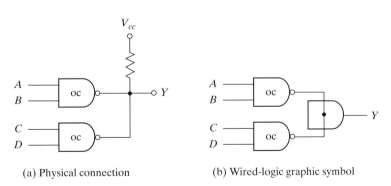

(a) Physical connection   (b) Wired-logic graphic symbol

FIGURE 10-12
Wired-AND of two Open-Collector (oc) Gates, $Y = (AB + CD)'$

symbol for such a connection is demonstrated in (b). The AND function formed by connecting together the two outputs is called a wired-AND function. The AND gate is drawn with the lines going through the center of the gate to distinguish it from a conventional gate. The wired-AND gate is not a physical gate, but only a symbol to designate the function obtained from the indicated connection. The Boolean function obtained from the circuit of Fig. 10-12 is the AND operation between the outputs of the two NAND gates:

$$Y = (AB)' \cdot (CD)' = (AB + CD)'$$

The second expression is preferred since it shows an operation commonly referred to as an AND-OR-INVERT function (see Section 3-7).

Open-collector gates can be tied together to form a common bus. At any time, all gate outputs tied to the bus, except one, must be maintained in their high state. The selected gate may be either in the high or low state, depending on whether we want to transmit a 1 or 0 on the bus. Control circuits must be used to select the particular gate that drives the bus at any given time.

Fig. 10-13 demonstrates the connection of four sources tied to a common bus line. Each of the four inputs drives an open-collector inverter, and the outputs of the inverters are tied together to form a single bus line. The figure shows that three of the inputs are 0, which produces a 1 or high level on the bus. The fourth input, I_4, can now transmit information through the common-bus line into inverter 5. Remember that an AND operation is performed in the wired logic. If $I_4 = 1$, the output of gate 4 is 0 and the wired-AND operation produces a 0. If $I_4 = 0$, the output of gate 4 is 1 and the wired-AND operation produces a 1. Thus, if all other outputs are maintained at 1, the selected gate can transmit its value through the bus. The value transmitted is the complement of I_4, but inverter 5 in the receiving end can easily invert this signal again to make $Y = I_4$.

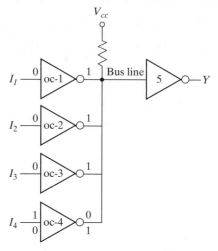

FIGURE 10-13
Open-Collector Gates Forming a Common Bus Line

Totem-Pole Output

The output impedance of a gate is normally a resistive plus a capacitive load. The capacitive load consists of the capacitance of the output transistor, the capacitance of the fan-out gates, and any stray wiring capacitance. When the output changes from the low to the high state, the output transistor of the gate goes from saturation to cutoff and the total load capacitance C charges exponentially from the low to the high voltage level with a time constant equal to RC. For the open-collector gate, R is the external resistor marked R_L. For a typical operating value of $C = 15$ pF and $R_L = 4$ kΩ, the propagation delay of a TTL open-collector gate during the turn-off time is 35 ns. With an *active pull-up* circuit replacing the passive pull-up resistor R_L, the propagation delay is reduced to 10 ns. This configuration, shown in Fig. 10-14, is called a *totem-pole* output because transistor $Q4$ "sits" upon $Q3$.

The TTL gate with the totem-pole output is the same as the open-collector gate, except for the output transistor $Q4$ and the diode $D1$. When the output Y is in the low state, $Q2$ and $Q3$ are driven into saturation as in the open-collector gate. The voltage in the collector of $Q2$ is $V_{BE}(Q3) + V_{CE}(Q2)$ or $0.7 + 0.2 = 0.9$ V. The output $Y = V_{CE}(Q3) = 0.2$ V. Transistor $Q4$ is cutoff because its base must be one V_{BE} drop plus one diode drop, or $2 \times 0.6 = 1.2$ V, to start conducting. Since the collector of $Q2$ is connected to the base of $Q4$, the latter's voltage is only 0.9 V instead of the required 1.2 V, and so $Q4$ is cut off. The reason for placing the diode in the circuit is to provide a diode drop in the output path and thus ensure that $Q4$ is cut off when $Q3$ is saturated.

When the output changes to the high state because one of the inputs drops to the low state, transistors $Q2$ and $Q3$ go into cutoff. However, the output remains momentarily low because

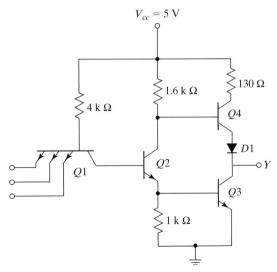

FIGURE 10-14
TTL Gate with Totem-Pole Output

the voltages across the load capacitance cannot change instantaneously. As soon as $Q2$ turns off, $Q4$ conducts because its base is connected to V_{CC} through the 1.6-kΩ resistor. The current needed to charge the load capacitance causes $Q4$ to momentarily saturate, and the output voltage rises with a time constant RC. But R in this case is equal to 130 Ω, plus the saturation resistance of $Q4$, plus the resistance of the diode, for a total of approximately 150 Ω. This value of R is much smaller than the passive pull-up resistance used in the open-collector circuit. As a consequence, the transition from the low to high level is much faster.

As the capacitive load charges, the output voltage rises and the current in $Q4$ decreases, bringing the transistor into the active region. Thus, in contrast to the other transistors, $Q4$ is in the *active* region when in a steady-state condition. The final value of the output voltage is then 5 V, minus a V_{BE} drop in $Q4$, minus a diode drop in $D1$ to about 3.6 V. Transistor $Q3$ goes into cutoff very fast, but during the initial transition time, both $Q3$ and $Q4$ are on and a peak current is drawn from the power supply. This current spike generates noise in the power-supply distribution system. When the change of state is frequent, the transient-current spikes increase the power-supply current requirement and the average power dissipation of the circuit increases.

The wired-logic connection is not allowed with totem-pole output circuits. When two totem-poles are wired together with the output of one gate high and the output of the second gate low, the excessive amount of current drawn can produce enough heat to damage the transistors in the circuit (see Problem 10-7). Some TTL gates are constructed to withstand the amount of current that flows under this condition. In any case, the collector current in the low gate may be high enough to move the transistor into the active region and produce an output voltage in the wired connection greater than 0.8 V, which is not a valid binary signal for TTL gates.

Schottky TTL Gate

As mentioned before, a reduction in storage time results in a reduction of propagation delay. This is because the time needed for a transistor to come out of saturation delays the switching of the transistor from the on condition to the off condition. Saturation can be eliminated by placing a Schottky diode between the base and collector of each saturated transistor in the circuit. The Schottky diode is formed by the junction of a metal and semiconductor, in contrast to a conventional diode, which is formed by the junction of *p*-type and *n*-type semiconductor material. The voltage across a conducting Schottky diode is only 0.4 V, as compared to 0.7 V in a conventional diode. The presence of a Schottky diode between the base and collector prevents the transistor from going into saturation. The resulting transistor is called a *Schottky transistor.* The use of Schottky transistors in a TTL decreases the propagation delay without a sacrifice of power dissipation.

The Schottky TTL gate is shown in Fig. 10-15. Note the special symbol used for the Schottky transistors and diodes. The diagram shows all transistors to be of the Schottky type except $Q4$. An exception is made of $Q4$ since it does not saturate, but stays in the active region. Note also that resistor values have been reduced to further decrease the propagation delay.

In addition to using Schottky transistors and lower resistor values, the circuit of Fig. 10-15 includes other modifications not available in the standard gate of Fig. 10-14. Two new transistors,

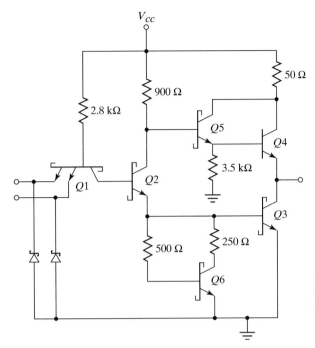

FIGURE 10-15
Schottky TTL Gate

$Q5$ and $Q6$ have been added, and Schottky diodes are inserted between each input terminal and ground. There is no diode in the totem-pole circuit. However, the new combination of $Q5$ and $Q4$ still gives the two V_{BE} drops necessary to prevent $Q4$ from conducting when the output is low. This combination comprises a double emitter-follower called a *Darlington pair.* The Darlington pair provides a very high current gain and extremely low resistance. This is exactly what is needed during the low-to-high swing of the output, resulting in a decrease of propagation delay.

The diodes in each input shown in the circuit help clamp any ringing that may occur in the input lines. Under transient switching conditions, signal lines appear inductive; this, along with stray capacitance, causes signals to oscillate or "ring." When the output of a gate switches from the high to the low state, the ringing waveform at the input may have excursions below ground as great as 2-3 V, depending on line length. The diodes connected to ground help clamp this ringing since they conduct as soon as the negative voltage exceeds 0.4 V. When the negative excursion is limited, the positive swing is also reduced. The clamp diodes have been so successful in limiting line effects, that all versions of TTL gates use them.

The emitter resistor of $Q2$ in Fig. 10-14 has been replaced in Fig. 10-15 by a circuit consisting of transistor $Q6$ and two resistors. The effect of this circuit is to reduce the turn-off current spikes discussed previously. The analysis of this circuit, which helps to reduce the propagation time of the gate, is too involved to present in this brief discussion.

Three-State Gate

As mentioned earlier, the outputs of two TTL gates with totem-pole structures cannot be connected together as in open-collector outputs. There is, however, a special type of totem-pole gate that allows the wired connection of outputs for the purpose of forming a common-bus system. When a totem-pole output TTL gate has this property, it is called a *three-state* (or tristate) gate.

A three-state gate exhibits three output states: (1) a low-level state when the lower transistor in the totem-pole is on and the upper transistor is off, (2) a high-level state when the upper transistor in the totem-pole is on and the lower transistor is off, and (3) a third state when both transistors in the totem-pole are off. The third state provides an open circuit or high-impedance state that allows a direct wire connection of many outputs to a common line. Three-state gates eliminate the need for open-collector gates in bus configurations.

Fig. 10-16(a) shows the graphic symbol of a three-state buffer gate. When the control input C is high, the gate is enabled and behaves like a normal buffer with the output equal to the input binary value. When the control input is low, the output is an open circuit, which gives a high impedance (the third state) regardless of the value of input A. Some three-state gates produce a high-impedance state when the control input is high. This is shown symbolically in Fig. 10-16(b). Here we have two small circles, one for the inverter output and the other to indicate that the gate is enabled when C is low.

The circuit diagram of the three-state inverter is shown in Fig. 10-16(c). Transistors $Q6$, $Q7$, and $Q8$ associated with the control input form a circuit similar to the open-collector gate. Transistors $Q1$-$Q5$, associated with the data input, form a totem-pole TTL circuit. The two circuits are connected together through diode $D1$. As in an open-collector circuit, transistor $Q8$ turns off when the control input at C is in the low-level state. This prevents diode $D1$ from conducting. In addition, the emitter in $Q1$ connected to $Q8$ has no conduction path. Under this condition, transistor $Q8$ has no effect on the operation of the gate and the output in Y depends only on the data input at A.

When the control input is high, transistor $Q8$ turns on, and the current flowing from V_{CC} through diode $D1$ causes transistor $Q8$ to saturate. The voltage at the base of $Q5$ is now equal to the voltage across the saturated transistor, $Q8$, plus one diode drop, or 0.9 V. This voltage turns off $Q5$ and $Q4$ since it is less than two V_{BE} drops. At the same time, the low input to one of the emitters of $Q1$ forces transistor $Q3$ (and $Q2$) to turn off. Thus, both $Q3$ and $Q4$ in the totem-pole are turned off and the output of the circuit behaves like an open circuit with a very high output impedance.

A three-state bus is created by wiring several three-state outputs together. At any given time, only one control input is enabled while all other outputs are in the high-impedance state. The single gate not in a high-impedance state can transmit binary information through the common bus. Extreme care must be taken that all except one of the outputs are in the third state; otherwise, we have the undesirable condition of having two active totem-pole outputs connected together.

An important feature of most three-state gates is that the output enable delay is longer than the output disable delay. If a control circuit enables one gate and disables another at the same time, the disabled gate enters the high-impedance state before the other gate is enabled. This eliminates the situation of both gates being active at the same time.

There is a very small leakage current associated with the high-impedance condition in a three-state gate. Nevertheless, this current is so small that as many as 100 three-state outputs can be connected together to form a common-bus line.

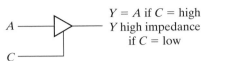

$Y = A$ if C = high
Y high impedance
if C = low

(a) Three-state buffer gate

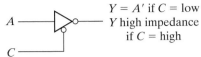

$Y = A'$ if C = low
Y high impedance
if C = high

(b) Three-state inverter gate

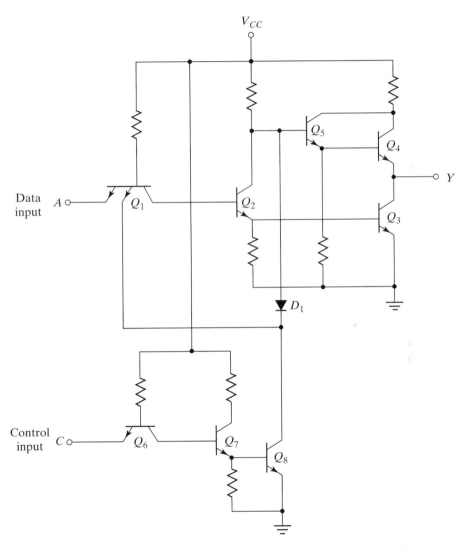

(c) Circuit diagram for the three-state inverter of (b)

FIGURE 10-16
Three-State TTL Gate

10-6   EMITTER-COUPLED LOGIC (ECL)

Emitter-coupled logic (ECL) is a nonsaturated digital logic family. Since transistors do not saturate, it is possible to achieve propagation delays as low as 1–2 ns. This logic family has the lowest propagation delay of any family and is used mostly in systems requiring very high-speed operation. Its noise immunity and power dissipation, however, are the worst of all the logic families available.

A typical basic circuit of the ECL family is shown in Fig. 10-17. The outputs provide both the OR and NOR functions. Each input is connected to the base of a transistor. The two voltage levels are about −0.8 V for the high state and about −1.8 V for the low state. The circuit consists of a differential amplifier, a temperature- and voltage-compensated bias network, and an emitter-follower output. The emitter outputs require a pull-down resistor for current to flow. This is obtained from the input resistor R_P of another similar gate or from an external resistor connected to a negative voltage supply.

The internal temperature- and voltage-compensated bias circuit supplies a reference voltage to the differential amplifier. Bias voltage V_{BB} is set at −1.3 V, which is the midpoint of the signal logic swing. The diodes in the voltage divider, together with $Q6$, provide a circuit that maintains a constant V_{BB} value despite changes in temperature or supply voltage. Any one of the power supply inputs could be used as ground. However, the use of the V_{CC} node as ground and V_{EE} at −5.2 V results in best noise immunity.

If any input in the ECL gate is high, the corresponding transistor is turned on and $Q5$ is turned off. An input of −0.8 V causes the transistor to conduct and places −1.6 V on the emitters of all transistors (V_{BE} drop in ECL transistors is 0.8 V). Since $V_{BB} = -1.3$ V, the base voltage of $Q5$ is only

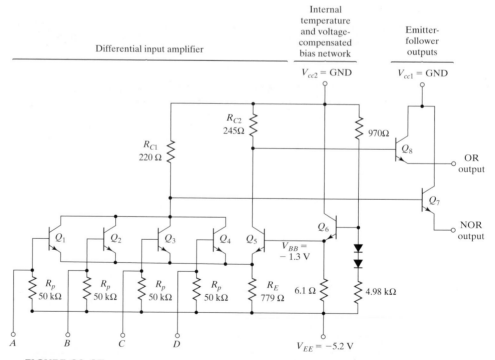

FIGURE 10-17
ECL Basic Gate

0.3 V more positive than its emitter. $Q5$ is cut off because its V_{BE} voltage needs at least 0.6 V to start conducting. The current in resistor R_{C2} flows into the base of $Q8$ (provided there is a load resistor). This current is so small that only a negligible voltage drop occurs across R_{C2}. The OR output of the gate is one V_{BE} drop below ground, or −0.8 V, which is the high state. The current flowing through R_{C1} and the conducting transistor causes a drop of about 1 V below ground (see Problem 10-9). The NOR output is one V_{BE} drop below this level, or at −1.8 V, which is the low state.

If all inputs are at the low level, all input transistors turn off and $Q5$ conducts. The voltage in the common-emitter node is one V_{BE} drop below V_{BB}, or −2.1 V. Since the base of each input is at a low level of −1.8 V, each base-emitter junction has only 0.3 V and all input transistors are cut off. R_{C2} draws current through $Q5$ that results in a voltage drop of about 1 V, making the OR output one V_{BE} drop below this, at −1.8 V or the low level. The current in R_{C1} is negligible and the NOR output is one V_{BE} drop below ground, at −0.8 V or the high level. This verifies the OR and NOR operations of the circuit.

The propagation delay of the ECL gate is 2 ns, and the power dissipation is 25 mW. This gives a speed-power product of 50, which is about the same as for the Schottky TTL. The noise margin is about 0.3 V and not as good as in the TTL gate. High fan-out is possible in the ECL gate because of the high input impedance of the differential amplifier and the low output impedance of the emitter-follower. Because of the extreme high speed of the signals, external wires act like transmission lines. Except for very short wires of a few centimeters, ECL outputs must use coaxial cables with a resistor termination to reduce line reflections.

The graphic symbol for the ECL gate is shown in Fig. 10-18(a). Two outputs are available: one for the NOR function and the other for the OR function. The outputs of two or more ECL gates can be connected together to form wired logic. As shown in Fig. 10-18(b), an *external* wired connection of two NOR outputs produces a wired-OR function. An *internal* wired connection of two OR outputs is employed in some ECL ICs to produce a wired-AND (sometimes called dot-AND) logic. This property may be utilized when ECL gates are used to form the OR-AND-INVERT and the OR-AND functions.

10-7   METAL-OXIDE SEMICONDUCTOR (MOS)

The field-effect transistor (FET) is a unipolar transistor, since its operation depends on the flow of only one type of carrier. There are two types of field-effect transistors: the junction field-effect transistor (JFET) and the metal-oxide semi-conductor (MOS). The former is used in linear circuits and the latter in digital circuits. MOS transistors can be fabricated in less area than bipolar transistors.

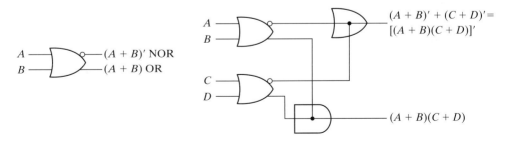

(a) Single gate   (b) Wired combination of two gates

FIGURE 10-18
Graphic Symbols of ECL Gates

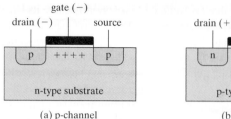
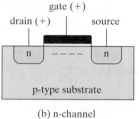

(a) p-channel   (b) n-channel

FIGURE 10-19
Basic Structure of MOS Transistor

The basic structure of the MOS transistor is shown in Fig. 10-19. The *p*-channel MOS consists of a lightly doped substrate of *n*-type silicon material. Two regions are heavily doped by diffusion with *p*-type impurities to form the *source* and *drain*. The region between the two *p*-type sections serves as the *channel*. The *gate* is a metal plate separated from the channel by an insulated dielectric of silicon dioxide. A negative voltage (with respect to the substrate) at the gate terminal causes an induced electric field in the channel that attracts *p*-type carriers from the substrate. As the magnitude of the negative voltage on the gate increases, the region below the gate accumulates more positive carriers, the conductivity increases, and current can flow from source to drain, provided a voltage difference is maintained between these two terminals.

There are four basic types of MOS structures. The channel can be a *p*- or *n*-type, depending on whether the majority carriers are holes or electrons. The mode of operation can be enhancement or depletion, depending on the state of the channel region at zero gate voltage. If the channel is initially doped lightly with *p*-type impurity (diffused channel), a conducting channel exists at zero gate voltage and the device is said to operate in the *depletion* mode. In this mode, current flows unless the channel is depleted by an applied gate field. If the region beneath the gate is left initially uncharged, a channel must be induced by the gate field before current can flow. Thus, the channel current is enhanced by the gate voltage and such a device is said to operate in the *enhancement* mode.

The source is the terminal through which the majority carriers enter the bar. The drain is the terminal through which the majority carriers leave the bar. In a *p*-channel MOS, the source terminal is connected to the substrate and a negative voltage is applied to the drain terminal. When the gate voltage is above a threshold voltage V_T (about -2 V), no current flows in the channel and the drain-to-source path is like an open circuit. When the gate voltage is sufficiently negative below V_T, a channel is formed and *p*-type carriers flow from source to drain. *p*-type carriers are positive and correspond to a positive current flow from source to drain.

In the *n*-channel MOS, the source terminal is connected to the substrate and a positive voltage is applied to the drain terminal. When the gate voltage is below the threshold voltage V_T (about 2 V), no current flows in the channel. When the gate voltage is sufficiently positive above V_T to form the channel, *n*-type carriers flow from source to drain. *n*-type carriers are negative, which corresponds to a positive current flow from drain to source. The threshold voltage may vary from 1 to 4 V, depending on the particular process used.

The graphic symbols for the MOS transistors are shown in Fig. 10-20. The symbol for the enhancement type is the one with the broken line connection between source and drain. In this symbol, the substrate can be identified and is shown connected to the source. An alternative symbol omits the substrate and instead, an arrow is placed in the source terminal to show the direction of *positive* current flow (from source to drain in the *p*-channel and from drain to source in the *n*-channel).

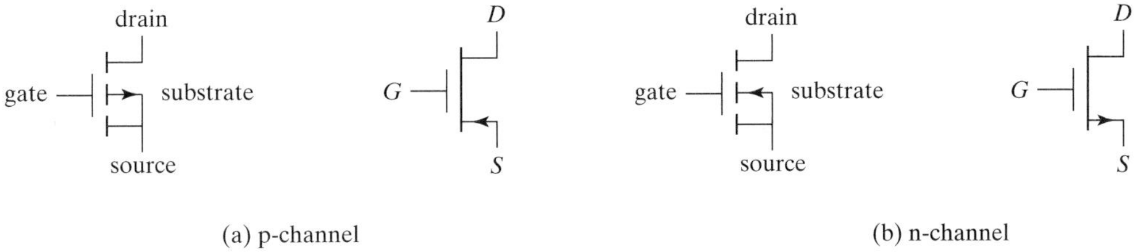

(a) p-channel   (b) n-channel

FIGURE 10-20
Symbols for MOS Transistors

Because of the symmetrical construction of source and drain, the MOS transistor can be operated as a bilateral device. Although normally operated so that carriers flow from source to drain, there are circumstances when it is convenient to allow carrier flow from drain to source (see Problem 10-12).

One advantage of the MOS device is that it can be used not only as a transistor, but as a resistor as well. A resistor is obtained from the MOS by permanently biasing the gate terminal for conduction. The ratio of the source-drain voltage to the channel current then determines the value of the resistance. Different resistor values may be constructed during manufacturing by fixing the channel length and width of the MOS device.

Three logic circuits using MOS devices are shown in Fig. 10-21. For an n-channel MOS, supply voltage V_{DD} is positive (about 5 V) to allow positive current flow from drain to source. The two voltage levels are a function of the threshold voltage V_T. The low level is anywhere from zero to V_T, and the high level ranges from V_T to V_{DD}. The n-channel gates usually employ positive logic. The p-channel MOS circuits use a negative voltage for V_{DD} to allow positive current flow from source to drain. The two voltage levels are both negative above and below the negative threshold voltage V_T. p-channel gates usually employ negative logic.

The inverter circuit shown in Fig. 10-21(a) uses two MOS devices. $Q1$ acts as the load resistor and $Q2$ as the active device. The load resistor MOS has its gate connected to V_{DD}, thus maintaining it always in the conduction state. When the input voltage is low (below V_T), $Q2$ turns off. Since $Q1$ is always on, the output voltage is at about V_{DD}. When the input voltage is high (above V_T), $Q2$ turns on. Current flows from V_{DD} through the load resistor $Q1$ and into $Q2$. The geometry of the two MOS devices must be such that the resistance of $Q2$, when conducting, is much less than the resistance of $Q1$ to maintain the output Y at a voltage below V_T.

The NAND gate shown in Fig. 10-21(b) uses transistors in series. Inputs A and B must both be high for all transistors to conduct and cause the output to go low. If either input is low, the corresponding transistor is turned off and the output is high. Again, the series resistance formed by the two active MOS devices must be much less than the resistance of the load-resistor MOS. The NOR gate shown in Fig. 10-21(c) uses transistors in parallel. If either input is high, the corresponding transistor conducts and the output is low. If all inputs are low, all active transistors are off and the output is high.

10-8   COMPLEMENTARY MOS (CMOS)

Complementary MOS circuits take advantage of the fact that both n-channel and p-channel devices can be fabricated on the same substrate. CMOS circuits consist of both types of MOS devices interconnected to form logic functions. The basic circuit is the inverter, which consists of one

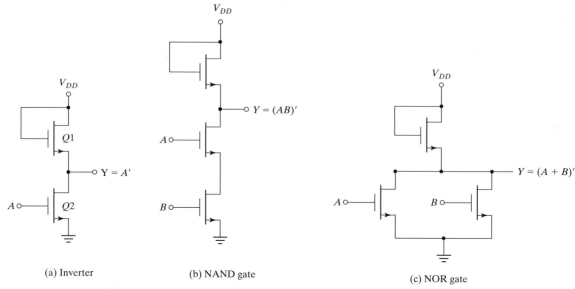

(a) Inverter   (b) NAND gate   (c) NOR gate

FIGURE 10-21
n-channel MOS Logic Circuits

p-channel transistor and one *n*-channel transistor, as shown in Fig. 10-22(a). The source terminal of the *p*-channel device is at V_{DD}, and the source terminal of the *n*-channel device is at ground. The value of V_{DD} may be anywhere from +3 to +18 V. The two voltage levels are 0 V for the low level and V_{DD} for the high level (typically, 5 V).

To understand the operation of the inverter, we must review the behavior of the MOS transistor from the previous section:

1. The *n*-channel MOS conducts when its gate-to-source voltage is positive.
2. The *p*-channel MOS conducts when its gate-to-source voltage is negative.
3. Either type of device is turned off if its gate-to-source voltage is zero.

Now consider the operation of the inverter. When the input is low, both gates are at zero potential. The input is at $-V_{DD}$ relative to the source of the *p*-channel device and at 0 V relative to the source of the *n*-channel device. The result is that the *p*-channel device is turned on and the *n*-channel device is turned off. Under these conditions, there is a low-impedance path from V_{DD} to the output and a very high-impedance path from output to ground. Therefore, the output voltage approaches the high level V_{DD} under normal loading conditions. When the input is high, both gates are at V_{DD} and the situation is reversed: The *p*-channel device is off and the *n*-channel device is on. The result is that the output approaches the low level of 0 V.

Two other CMOS basic gates are shown in Fig. 10-22. A two-input NAND gate consists of two *p*-type units in parallel and two *n*-type units in series, as shown in Fig. 10-22(b). If all inputs are high, both *p*-channel transistors turn off and both *n*-channel transistors turn on. The output has a low impedance to ground and produces a low state. If any input is low, the associated *n*-channel transistor is turned off and the associated *p*-channel transistor is turned on. The output is coupled to V_{DD} and goes to the high state. Multiple-input NAND gates may be formed by placing equal numbers of *p*-type and *n*-type transistors in parallel and series, respectively, in an arrangement similar to that shown in Fig. 10-22(b).

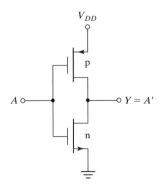

(a) Inverter

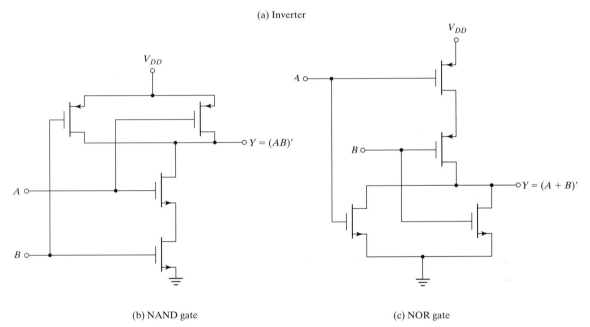

(b) NAND gate

(c) NOR gate

FIGURE 10-22
CMOS Logic Circuits

A two-input NOR gate consists of two *n*-type units in parallel and two *p*-type units in series, as shown in Fig. 10-22(c). When all inputs are low, both *p*-channel units are on and both *n*-channel units are off. The output is coupled to V_{DD} and goes to the high state. If any input is high, the associated *p*-channel transistor is turned off and the associated *n*-channel transistor turns on. This connects the output to ground, causing a low-level output.

MOS transistors can be considered as electronic switches that either conduct or are open. As an example, the CMOS inverter can be visualized as consisting of two switches as shown in Fig. 10-23(a). Applying a low voltage to the input causes the upper switch (*p*) to close supplying a high voltage to the output. Applying a high voltage to the input causes the lower switch (*n*) to close connecting the output to ground. Thus, the output V_{out} is the complement of the input V_{in}. Commercial applications often use other graphic symbols for the MOS transistors to emphasize the logical behavior of the switches. The arrows showing the direction of current flow are omitted.

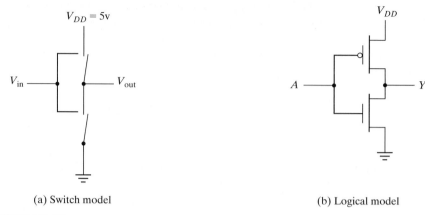

(a) Switch model   (b) Logical model

FIGURE 10-23
CMOS inverter

Instead, the gate input of the *p*-channel transistor is drawn with an inversion bubble on the gate terminal to show that it is enabled with a low voltage. The inverter circuit is redrawn in Fig. 10-23(b) using these symbols. A logic 0 in the input causes the upper transistor to conduct making the output logic 1. A logic 1 in the input enables the lower transistor, making the output logic 0.

CMOS Characteristics

When a CMOS logic circuit is in a static state, its power dissipation is very low. This is because there is always an off transistor in the path when the state of the circuit is not changing. As a result, a typical CMOS gate has a static power dissipation on the order of 0.01 mW. However, when the circuit is changing state at the rate of 1 MHz, the power dissipation increases to about 1 mW, and at 10 MHz to about 5 mW.

CMOS logic is usually specified for a single power supply operation over a voltage range from 3 to 18 V with a typical V_{DD} value of 5 V. Operating CMOS at a larger power supply voltage reduces the propagation delay time and improves the noise margin, but the power dissipation is increased. The propagation delay time with $V_{DD} = 5$ V ranges from 5 to 20 ns depending on the type used. The noise margin is usually about 40 percent of the power supply voltage. The fan-out of CMOS gates is about 30 when operated at a frequency of 1 MHz. The fan-out decreases with increase in frequency of operation.

There are several series of the CMOS digital logic family. The 74C series are pin and function compatible with TTL devices having the same number. For example, CMOS IC type 74C04 has six inverters with the same pin configuration as TTL type 7404. The high-speed CMOS 74HC series is an improvement of the 74C series with a tenfold increase in switching speed. The 74HCT series is electrically compatible with TTL ICs. This means that the circuit in this series can be connected to inputs and outputs of TTL ICs without the need of additional interfacing circuits. Newer versions of CMOS are the high-speed series 74VHC and its TTL compatible version 74VHCT.

The CMOS fabrication process is simpler than TTL and provides a greater packing densi-ty. This means that more circuits can be placed on a given area of silicon at a reduced cost per function. This property, together with it low power dissipation, good noise immunity, and rea-sonable propagation delay, makes CMOS the most popular standard as a digital logic family.

10-9   CMOS TRANSMISSION GATE CIRCUITS

A special CMOS circuit that is not available in the other digital logic families is the *transmis-sion gate*. The transmission gate is essentially an electronic switch that is controlled by an input logic level. It is used for simplifying the construction of various digital components when fabricated with CMOS technology.

Fig. 10-24(a) shows the basic circuit of the transmission gate. It consists of one *n*-channel and one *p*-channel MOS transistor connected in parallel.

The *n*-channel substrate is connected to ground and the *p*-channel substrate is connected to V_{DD}. When the *N* gate is at V_{DD} and the *P* gate is at ground, both transistors conduct and there is a closed path between input *X* and output *Y*. When the *N* gate is at ground and the *P* gate at V_{DD}, both transistors are off and there is an open circuit between *X* and *Y*. Fig. 10-24(b) shows the block diagram of the transmission gate. Note that the terminal of the *p*-channel gate is

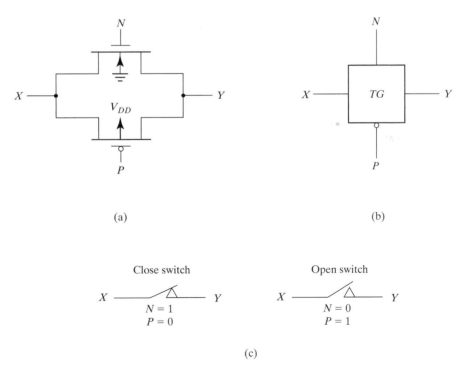

(a)

(b)

(c)

FIGURE 10-24
Transmission Gate (TG)

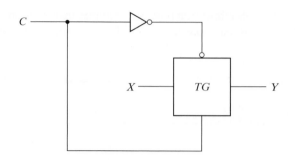

FIGURE 10-25
Bilateral Switch

marked with the negation symbol. Fig. 10-24(c) demonstrates the behavior of the switch in terms of positive-logic assignment with V_{DD} equivalent to logic-1 and ground equivalent to logic-0.

The transmission gate is usually connected to an inverter, as shown in Fig. 10-25. This type of arrangement is referred to as a *bilateral switch*. The control input C is connected directly to the n-channel gate and its inverse to the p-channel gate. When $C = 1$, the switch is closed, producing a path between X and Y. When $C = 0$, the switch is open, disconnecting the path between X and Y.

Various circuits can be constructed using the transmission gate. In order to demonstrate its usefulness as a component in the CMOS family, we will show three circuit examples.

The exclusive-OR gate can be constructed with two transmission gates and two inverters, as shown in Fig. 10-26. Input A controls the paths in the transmission gates and input B is connected to output Y through the gates. When input A is equal to 0, transmission gate $TG1$ is

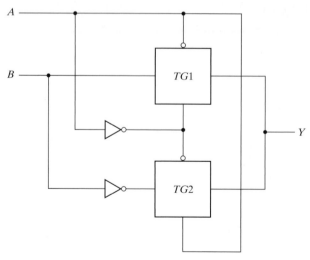

A	B	$TG1$	$TG2$	Y
0	0	close	open	0
0	1	close	open	1
1	0	open	close	1
1	1	open	close	0

FIGURE 10-26
Exclusive-OR Constructed with Transmission Gates

closed and output Y is equal to input B. When input A is equal to 1, $TG2$ is closed and output Y is equal to the complement of input B. This results in the exclusive-OR truth table, as indicated in the table of Fig. 10-26.

Another circuit that can be constructed with transmission gates is the multiplexer. A 4-to-1-line multiplexer implemented with transmission gates is shown in Fig. 10-27. The TG circuit provides a transmission path between its horizontal input and output lines when the two vertical control inputs have the value of 1 in the uncircled terminal and 0 in the circled terminal.

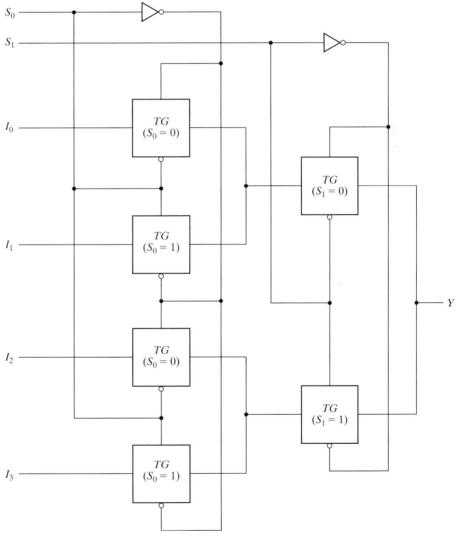

FIGURE 10-27
Multiplexer with Transmission Gates

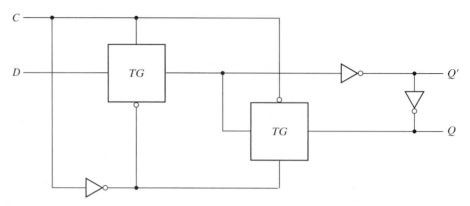

FIGURE 10-28
Gated *D* Latch with Transmission Gates

With an opposite polarity in the control inputs, the path disconnects and the circuit behaves like an open switch. The two selection inputs, S_1 and S_0, control the transmission path in the *TG* circuits. Inside each box is marked the condition for the transmission gate switch to be closed. Thus, if $S_0 = 0$ and $S_1 = 0$, there is a closed path from input I_0 to output Y through the two *TG*s marked with $S_0 = 0$ and $S_1 = 0$. The other three inputs are disconnected from the output by one of the other *TG* circuits.

The level-sensitive *D* flip-flop commonly referred to as gated *D* latch can be constructed with transmission gates, as shown in Fig. 10-28. The *C* input controls two transmission gates *TG*. When $C = 1$, the *TG* connected to input *D* has a closed path and the one connected to output *Q* has an open path. This produces an equivalent circuit from input *D* through two inverters to output *Q*. Thus, the output follows the data input as long as *C* remains active. When *C* switches to 0, the first *TG* disconnects input *D* from the circuit and the second *TG* produces a closed path between the two inverters at the output. Thus, the value that was present at input *D* at the time that *C* went from 1 to 0 is retained at the *Q* output.

A master-slave *D* flip-flop can be constructed with two circuits of the type shown in Fig. 10-28. The first circuit is the master and the second is the slave. Thus, a master–slave *D* flip-flop can be constructed with four transmission gates and six inverters.

10-10   SWITCH-LEVEL MODELING WITH HDL

CMOS is the dominant digital logic family used with integrated circuits. By definition, CMOS is a complementary connection of an NMOS and a PMOS transistor. MOS transistors can be considered as electronic switches that either conduct or are open. By specifying the connections among MOS switches, the designer can describe a digital circuit constructed with CMOS. This type of description is called switch-level modeling in Verilog HDL.

The two types of MOS switches are specified in Verilog HDL with the keywords **nmos** and **pmos**. They are instantiated by specifying the three terminals of the transistor as shown in Fig. 10-20.

```
nmos (drain, source, gate);
pmos (drain, source, gate);
```

Switches are considered as primitives so the use of an instance name is optional.

The connections to a power source (V_{DD}) and to ground must be specified when the MOS circuits are designed. Power and ground are defined with the keywords **supply1** and **supply0**. They are specified with the following statements:

```
supply1 PWR;
supply0 GRD;
```

Sources of type **supply1** are equivalent to V_{DD} and have a value of logic-1. Sources of type **supply0** are equivalent to ground connection and have a value of logic-0.

The description of the CMOS inverter of Fig. 10-22(a) is shown in HDL Example 10-1. The input, output, and the two supply sources are first declared. The module instantiates a PMOS and a NMOS transistor. The output Y is common to both transistors at their drain terminals. The input is also common to both transistors at their gate terminals. The source terminal of the PMOS transistor is connected to PWR and the source terminal of the NMOS transistor is connected to GRD.

The second module in Example 10-2 describes the 2-input CMOS NAND circuit of Fig. 10-22(b). There are two PMOS transistors connected in parallel with their source terminals connected to PWR. There are two NMOS transistors connected in series with a common terminal $W1$. The drain of the first NMOS is connected to the output and the source of the second NMOS is connected to GRD.

HDL Example 10-1

```
------------------------------------------
//CMOS inverter Fig. 10-22 (a)
module inverter (Y,A);
    input A;
    output Y;
    supply1  PWR;
    supply0  GRD;
    pmos (Y,PWR,A);        //(Drain,source,gate)
    nmos (Y,GRD,A);        //(Drain,source,gate)
endmodule
------------------------------------------
```

HDL Example 10-2

```
------------------------------------------
//CMOS 2-input NAND Fig. 10-22(b)
module NAND2 (Y,A,B);
    input A,B;
    output Y;
    supply1  PWR;
    supply0  GRD;
    wire W1;               //terminal between two nmos
    pmos (Y,PWR,A);        //source connected to Vdd
    pmos (Y,PWR,B);        // parallel connection
    nmos (Y,W1,A);         // serial connection
    nmos (W1,GRD,B);       // source connected to ground
endmodule
------------------------------------------
```

Transmission Gate

The transmission gate is instantiated in Verilog HDL with the keyword **cmos.** It has an output, input, and two control signals as shown in Fig. 10-24. It is referred to as a **cmos** switch. The relevant code is as follows:

```
cmos (output,input,ncontrol,pcontrol); //general description
cmos (Y,X,N,P);   //transmission gate of Fig. 10-24(b)
```

The ncontrol and pcontrol are normally the complement of each other. The cmos switch does not need power sources since V_{DD} and ground are connected to the substrates of the MOS transistors. Transmission gates are useful for building multiplexers and flip-flops with CMOS circuits.

HDL example 10-3 demonstrates the description of a circuit with **cmos** switches. The exclusive-OR circuit of Fig. 10-26 has two transmission gates and two inverters. The two inverters are instantiated with the module of a CMOS inverter. The two **cmos** switches are instantiated without an instance name since they are considered as primitives. A test module is included to test the circuit operation. Applying all possible combinations of the two inputs, the result of the simulator verifies the operation of the exclusive-OR circuit. The output of the simulation is as follows:

$$A = 0 \quad B = 0 \quad Y = 0$$
$$A = 0 \quad B = 1 \quad Y = 1$$
$$A = 1 \quad B = 0 \quad Y = 1$$
$$A = 1 \quad B = 1 \quad Y = 0$$

HDL Example 10-3

```
//XOR with CMOS switchs Fig. 10-25
module SXOR (A,B,Y);
   input A,B;
   output Y;
   wire Anot, Bnot;
//instantiate inverter
   inverter v1 (Anot,A);
   inverter v2 (Bnot,B);
//instantiate cmos switch
   cmos (Y,B,Anot,A);        //(output,input,ncontrol,pcontrol)
   cmos (Y,Bnot,A,Anot);
endmodule


//CMOS inverter Fig. 10-22(a)
module inverter (Y,A);
   input A;
   output Y;
   supply1  PWR;
   supply0  GRD;
   pmos (Y,PWR,A);          //(Drain,source,gate)
   nmos (Y,GRD,A);          //(Drain,source,gate)
endmodule


//Stimulus to test SXOR
module test_SXOR;
   reg A,B;
   wire Y;
//Instantiate SXOR
   SXOR X1 (A,B,Y);
//Apply truth table
   initial
     begin
          A=1'b0; B=1'b0;
        #5 A=1'b0; B=1'b1;
        #5 A=1'b1; B=1'b0;
        #5 A=1'b1; B=1'b1;
     end
//display results
   initial
     $monitor ("A =%b  B= %b  Y =%b",A,B,Y);
endmodule
```

PROBLEMS

10-1 The following are the specifications for the Schottky TTL 74S00 quadruple two-input NAND gates. Calculate the fan-out, power dissipation, propagation delay, and noise margin of the Schottky NAND gate.

Parameter	Name	Value
V_{CC}	Supply voltage	5 V
I_{CCH}	High-level supply current (four gates)	10 mA
I_{CCL}	Low-level supply current (four gates)	20 mA
V_{OH}	High-level output voltage (min)	2.7 V
V_{OL}	Low-level output voltage (max)	0.5 V
V_{IH}	High-level input voltage (min)	2 V
V_{IL}	Low-level input voltage (max)	0.8 V
I_{OH}	High-level output current (max)	1 mA
I_{OL}	Low-level output current (max)	20 mA
I_{IH}	High-level input current (max)	0.05 mA
I_{IL}	Low-level input current (max)	2 mA
t_{PLH}	Low-to-high delay	3 ns
t_{PHL}	High-to-low delay	3 ns

10-2 (a) Determine the high-level output voltage of the RTL gate for a fan-out of 5. (b) Determine the minimum input voltage required to drive an RTL transistor to saturation when $h_{FE} = 20$. (c) From the results in (a) and (b), determine the noise margin of the RTL gate when the input is high and the fan-out is 5.

10-3 Show that the output transistor of the DTL gate of Fig. 10-9 goes into saturation when all inputs are high. Assume that $h_{FE} = 20$.

10-4 Connect the output Y of the DTL gate shown in Fig. 10-9 to N inputs of other similar gates. Assume that the output transistor is saturated and its base current is 0.44 mA. Let $h_{FE} = 20$.

(a) Calculate the current in the 2 kΩ resistor.

(b) Calculate the current coming from each input connected to the gate.

(c) Calculate the total collector current in the output transistor as a function of N.

(d) Find the value of N that will keep the transistor in saturation.

(e) What is the fan-out of the gate?

10-5 Let all inputs in the open-collector TTL gate of Fig. 10-11 be in the high state of 3 V.

(a) Determine the voltages in the base, collector, and emitter of all transistors.

(b) Determine the minimum h_{FE} of $Q2$ that ensures that this transistor saturates.

(c) Calculate the base current of $Q3$.

(d) Assume that the minimum h_{FE} of $Q3$ is 6.18. What is the maximum current that can be tolerated in the collector to ensure saturation of $Q3$?

(e) What is the minimum value of R_L that can be tolerated to ensure saturation of $Q3$?

10-6 (a) Using the actual output transistors of two open-collector TTL gates, show (by means of a truth table) that when connected together to an external resistor and V_{CC}, the wired connection produces an AND function.

    (b) Prove that two open-collector TTL inverters, when connected together, produce the NOR function.

10-7 It was stated in Section 10-5 that totem-pole outputs should not be tied together to form wired logic. To see why this is prohibitive, connect two such circuits together and let the output of one gate be in the high state and the output of the other gate be in the low state. Show that the load current (which is the sum of the base and collector currents of the saturated transistor $Q4$ in Fig. 10-14) is about 32 mA. Compare this value with the recommended load current in the high state of 0.4 mA.

10-8 For the following conditions, list the transistors that are off and those that are conducting in the three-state TTL gate of Fig. 10-16(c). (For $Q1$ and $Q6$, it would be necessary to list the states in the base-emitter and base-collector junctions separately.)

    (a) When C is low and A is low.   (b) When C is low and A is high.

    (c) When C is high.

What is the state of the output in each case?

10-9 Calculate the emitter current I_E across R_E in the ECL gate of Fig. 10-17 when

    (a) At least one input is high at -0.8 V.

    (b) All inputs are low at -1.8 V.

    (c) Now assume that $I_C = I_E$. Calculate the voltage drop across the collector resistor in each case and show that it is about 1 V as required.

10-10 Calculate the noise margin of the ECL gate.

10-11 Using the NOR outputs of two ECL gates, show that when connected together to an external resistor and negative supply voltage, the wired connection produces an OR function.

10-12 The MOS transistor is bilateral, i.e., current may flow from source to drain or from drain to source. Using this property, derive a circuit that implements the Boolean function

$$Y = (AB + CD + AED + CEB)'$$

using six MOS transistors.

10-13 (a) Show the circuit of a four-input NAND gate using CMOS transistors. (b) Repeat for a four-input NOR gate.

10-14 Construct an exclusive-NOR circuit with two inverters and two transmission gates.

10-15 Construct an 8-to-1-line multiplexer using transmission gates and inverters.

10-16 Draw the logic diagram of a master-slave D flip-flop using transmission gates and inverters.

10-17 Write a test bench that will test the NAND circuit of HDL Example 10-2. The simulation should verify the truth table of the gate.

REFERENCES

1. TOCCI, R. J. and N. S. WIDMER. 2001. *Digital Systems Principles and Applications,* 8th ed. Upper Saddle River, NJ: Prentice Hall.

2. WESTE, N. E. and K. ESHRAGHIAN. 1993. *Principles of CMOS VLSI design: A System Perspective,* 2nd ed. Reading, MA: Addison-Wesley.

3. WAKERLY, J. F. 2000. *Digital Design: Principles and Practices*, 3rd ed. Upper Saddle River, NJ: Prentice Hall.

4. HODGES, D. A., and H. G. JACKSON. 1988. *Analysis and Design of Digital Integrated Circuits,* 2nd ed. New York: McGraw-Hill.

5. 1988. *The TTL Logic Data Book.* Dallas: Texas Instruments.

6. 1994. *CMOS Logic Data Book.* Dallas: Texas Intruments.

7. CILETTI, M. D. 1999. *Modeling, Synthesis, and Rapid Prototyping with Verilog HDL.* Upper Saddle River, NJ: Prentice Hall.

11 Laboratory Experiments

11-0 INTRODUCTION TO EXPERIMENTS

This chapter presents 18 laboratory experiments in digital circuits and logic design. They provide hands-on experience for the student using this book. The digital circuits can be constructed by using standard integrated circuits (ICs) mounted on breadboards that are easily assembled in the laboratory. The experiments are ordered according to the material presented in the book. The last section consists of a number of supplements with suggestions for using Verilog HDL to simulate and test the digital circuits presented in the experiments.

A logic breadboard suitable for performing the experiments must have the following equipment:

1. LED (light-emitting diode) indicator lamps.
2. Toggle switches to provide logic-1 and -0 signals.
3. Pulsers with pushbuttons and debounce circuits to generate single pulses.
4. A clock-pulse generator with at least two frequencies—a low frequency of about one pulse per second to observe slow changes in digital signals and a higher frequency for observing waveforms in an oscilloscope.
5. A power supply of 5 V.
6. Socket strips for mounting the ICs.
7. Solid hookup wire and a pair of wire strippers for cutting the wires.

Digital logic trainers that include the required equipment are available from several manufacturers. A digital logic trainer contains LED lamps, toggle switches, pulsers, a variable clock, power supply, and IC socket strips. Some experiments may require additional switches, lamps, or IC socket strips. Extended breadboards with more solderless sockets and plug-in switches and lamps may be needed.

Additional equipment required are a dual-trace oscilloscope (for Experiments 1, 2, 8, and 15), a logic probe to be used for debugging, and a number of ICs. The ICs required for the experiments are of the TTL or CMOS series 7400.

The integrated circuits to be used in the experiments can be classified as small-scale integration (SSI) or medium-scale integration (MSI) circuits. SSI circuits contain individual gates or flip-flops, and MSI circuits perform specific digital functions. The eight SSI gate ICs needed for the experiments are shown in Fig. 11-1. They include two-input NAND, NOR, AND, OR, and XOR gates, inverters, and three-input and four-input NAND gates. The pin assignment for the gates is indicated in the diagram. The pins are numbered from 1 to 14. Pin number 14 is marked V_{CC}, and pin number 7 is marked *GND* (ground). These are the supply terminals, which must be connected to a power supply of 5 V for proper operation. Each IC is recognized by its identification number; for example, the two-input NAND gates are found inside the IC whose number is 7400.

Detailed descriptions of the MSI circuits can be found in data books published by the manufacturers. The best way to acquire experience with commercial MSI circuits is to study their description in a data book that provides complete information on the internal, external, and electrical characteristics of the integrated circuits. Various semiconductor companies publish data books for the 7400 series. The MSI circuits that are needed for the experiments are introduced and explained when they are used for the first time. The operation of the circuit is explained by referring to similar circuits in previous chapters. The information given in this chapter about the MSI circuits should be sufficient for performing the experiments adequately. Nevertheless, a reference to a data book will always be preferable, as it gives more detailed description of the circuits.

We will now demonstrate the method of presentation of MSI circuits adopted here. This will be done by means of a specific example that introduces the ripple counter IC, type 7493. This IC is used in Experiment 1 and in subsequent experiments to generate a sequence of binary numbers for verifying the operation of combinational circuits.

The information about the 7493 IC that is found in a data book is shown in Figs. 11-2(a) and (b). Part (a) shows a diagram of the internal logic circuit and its connection to external pins. All inputs and outputs are given symbolic letters and assigned to pin numbers. Part (b) shows the physical layout of the IC with its 14-pin assignment to signal names. Some of the pins are not used by the circuit and are marked as *NC* (no connection). The IC is inserted into a socket, and wires are connected to the various pins through the socket terminals. When drawing schematic diagrams in this chapter, we will show the IC in a block diagram form as in Fig. 11-2(c). The IC number 7493 is written inside the block. All input terminals are placed on the left of the block and all output terminals on the right. The letter symbols of the signals, such as *A*, *R*1, and *QA*, are written inside the block, and the corresponding pin numbers, such as 14, 2 , and 12, are written along the external lines. V_{CC} and *GND* are the power terminals connected to pins 5 and 10. The size of the block may vary to accommodate all input and output terminals. Inputs or outputs may sometimes be placed on the top or the bottom of the block for convenience.

The operation of the circuit is similar to the ripple counter shown in Fig. 6-8(a) with an asynchronous clear to each flip-flop. When inputs *R*1 or *R*2 or both are equal to logic 0 (ground), all asynchronous clears are equal to 1 and are disabled. To clear all four flip-flops to 0, the output of the NAND gate must be equal to 0. This is accomplished by having both inputs *R*1 and *R*2 at logic-1 (about 5 V). Note that the *J* and *K* inputs show no connections. It is characteristic of TTL circuits that an input terminal with no external connections has the effect of producing a signal equivalent to logic-1. Also note that output *QA* is not connected to input *B* internally.

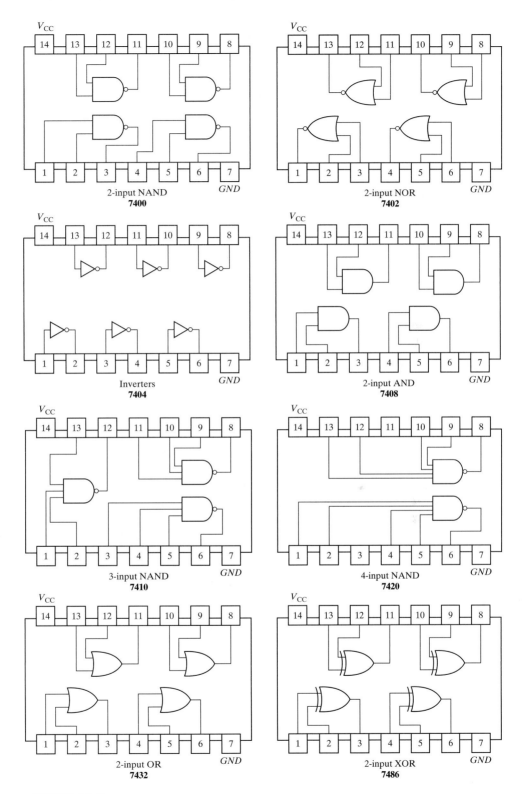

FIGURE 11-1
Digital Gates in IC Packages with Identification Numbers and Pin Assignments

439

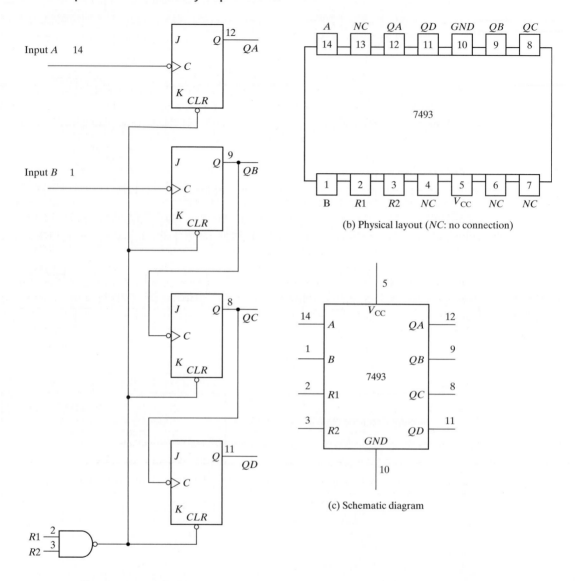

Input A   14

Input B   1

R1 2
R2 3

(a) Internal circuit diagram

A   NC   QA   QD   GND   QB   QC
14   13   12   11   10   9   8

7493

1   2   3   4   5   6   7
B   R1   R2   NC V_{CC} NC   NC

(b) Physical layout (NC: no connection)

(c) Schematic diagram

FIGURE 11-2
IC Type 7493 Ripple Counter

The 7493 IC can operate as a three-bit counter using input B and flip-flops QB, QC, and QD. It can operate as a four-bit counter using input A if output QA is connected to input B. Therefore, to operate the circuit as a four-bit counter, it is necessary to have an external connection between pin 12 and pin 1. The reset inputs, R1 and R2, at pins 2 and 3, respectively, must be grounded. Pins 5 and 10 must be connected to a 5 V power supply. The input pulses must be applied to input A at pin 14;, and the four flip-flop outputs of the counter are taken from QA, QB, QC, and QD, at pins 12, 9, 8, and 11, respectively, with QA being the least significant bit.

Figure 11-2(c) demonstrates the way that all MSI circuits will be symbolized graphically in this chapter. Only a block diagram similar to the one shown in this figure will be shown for each IC. The letter symbols for the inputs and outputs in the IC block diagram will be according to the symbols used in the data book. The operation of the circuit will be explained with reference to logic diagrams from previous chapters. The operation of the circuit will be specified by means of a truth table or a function table.

Other possible graphic symbols for the ICs are presented in Chapter 12. These are standard graphic symbols approved by the Institute of Electrical and Electronics Engineers and are given in IEEE standard 91-1984. The standard graphic symbols for SSI gates have rectangular shapes, as shown in Fig. 12-1. The standard graphic symbol for the 7493 IC is shown in Fig. 12-13. This symbol can be substituted in place of the one shown in Fig. 11-2(c). The standard graphic symbols of the other ICs that are needed to run the experiments are presented in Chapter 12. They can be used for drawing schematic diagrams of the logic circuits if the standard symbols are preferred.

Table 11-1 lists the ICs that are needed for the experiments together with the figure numbers where they are presented in this chapter. In addition, the table lists the figure numbers in Chapter 12 where the equivalent standard graphic symbols are drawn.

The rest of the chapter contains 19 sections. The first 18 sections present 18 hardware experiments requiring the use of digital integrated circuits. Section 11-19 outlines HDL simulation experiments requiring a Verilog HDL compiler and simulator.

Table 11-1
Integrated Circuits Required for the Experiments

		Graphic Symbol	
IC Number	**Description**	**In Chap. 11**	**In Chap. 12**
	Various gates	Fig. 11-1	Fig. 12-1
7447	BCD-to-seven-segment decoder	Fig. 11-8	
7474	Dual *D*-type flip-flops	Fig. 11-13	Fig. 12-9(b)
7476	Dual *JK*-type flip-flops	Fig. 11-12	Fig. 12-9(a)
7483	4-bit binary adder	Fig. 11-10	Fig. 12-2
7493	4-bit ripple counter	Fig. 11-2	Fig. 12-13
74151	8 × 1 multiplexer	Fig. 11-9	Fig. 12-7(a)
74155	3 × 8 decoder	Fig. 11-7	Fig. 12-6
74157	Quadruple 2 × 1 multiplexers	Fig. 11-17	Fig. 12-7(b)
74161	4-bit synchronous counter	Fig. 11-15	Fig. 12-14
74189	16 × 4 random-access memory	Fig. 11-18	Fig. 12-15
74194	Bidirectional shift register	Fig. 11-19	Fig. 12-12
74195	4-bit shift register	Fig. 11-16	Fig. 12-11
7730	Seven-segment LED display	Fig. 11-8	
72555	Timer (same as 555)	Fig. 11-21	

11-1   BINARY AND DECIMAL NUMBERS

This experiment demonstrates the count sequence of binary numbers and the binary-coded decimal (BCD) representation. It serves as an introduction to the breadboard used in the laboratory and acquaints the student with the cathode-ray oscilloscope. Reference material from the text that may be useful to know while performing the experiment can be found in Section 1-2, on binary numbers, and Section 1-7, on BCD numbers.

Binary Count

IC type 7493 consists of four flip-flops, as shown in Fig. 11-2. They can be connected to count in binary or in BCD. Connect the IC to operate as a 4-bit binary counter by wiring the external terminals, as shown in Fig. 11-3. This is done by connecting a wire from pin 12 (output QA) to pin 1 (input B). Input A at pin 14 is connected to a pulser that provides single pulses. The two reset inputs, $R1$ and $R2$, are connected to ground. The four outputs go to four indicator lamps with the low-order bit of the counter from QA connected to the rightmost indicator lamp. Do not forget to supply 5 V and ground to the IC. All connections should be made with the power supply in the off position.

Turn the power on and observe the four indicator lamps. The 4-bit number in the output is incremented by one for every pulse generated in the push-button pulser. The count goes to binary 15 and then back to 0. Disconnect the input of the counter at pin 14 from the pulser and connect it to a clock generator that produces a train of pulses at a low frequency of about one pulse per second. This will provide an automatic binary count. Note that the binary counter will be used in subsequent experiments to provide the input binary signals for testing combinational circuits.

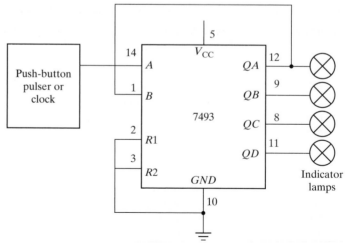

FIGURE 11-3
Binary Counter

Oscilloscope Display

Increase the frequency of the clock to 10 kHz or higher and connect its output to an oscilloscope. Observe the clock output on the oscilloscope and sketch its waveform. Using a dual-trace oscilloscope, connect the output of QA to one channel and the output of the clock to the second channel. Note that the output of QA is complemented every time the clock pulse goes through a negative transition from 1 to 0. Also, note that the clock frequency at the output of the first flip-flop is one-half that of the input clock frequency. Each flip-flop in turn divides its incoming frequency by 2. The four-bit counter divides the incoming frequency by 16 at output QD. Obtain a timing diagram showing the time relationship of the clock and the four outputs of the counter. Make sure that you include at least 16 clock cycles. The way to proceed with a dual-trace oscilloscope is as follows. First, observe the clock pulses and QA and record their timing waveforms. Then repeat by observing and recording the waveforms of QA together with QB, followed by the waveforms of QB with QC and then QC with QD. Your final result should be a diagram showing the time relationship of the clock and the four outputs in one composite diagram having at least 16 clock cycles.

BCD Count

The BCD representation uses the binary numbers from 0000 to 1001 to represent the coded decimal digits from 0 to 9. IC type 7493 can be operated as a BCD counter by making the external connections shown in Fig. 11-4. Outputs QB and QD are connected to the two reset inputs, $R1$ and $R2$. When both $R1$ and $R2$ are equal to 1, all four cells in the counter clear to 0 irrespective of the input pulse. The counter starts from 0, and every input pulse increments it by 1

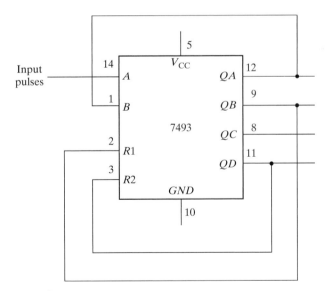

FIGURE 11-4
BCD Counter

until it reaches the count of 1001. The next pulse changes the ouput to 1010, making QB and QD equal to 1. This momentary output cannot be sustained, because the four cells immediately clear to 0, with the result that the output goes to 0000. Thus, the pulse after the count of 1001 changes the output to 0000, producing a BCD count.

Connect the IC to operate as a BCD counter. Connect the input to a pulser and the four outputs to indicator lamps. Verify that the count goes from 0000 to 1001.

Disconnect the input from the pulser and connect it to a clock generator. Observe the clock waveform and the four outputs on the oscilloscope. Obtain an accurate timing diagram showing the time relationship between the clock and the four outputs. Make sure to include at least ten clock cycles in the oscilloscope display and in the composite timing diagram.

Output Pattern

When the count pulses into the BCD counter are continuous, the counter keeps repeating the sequence from 0000 to 1001 and back to 0000. This means that each bit in the four outputs produces a fixed pattern of 1's and 0's, which is repeated every 10 pulses. These patterns can be predicted from the list of the binary numbers from 0000 to 1001. The list will show that output QA, being the least significant bit, produces a pattern of alternate 1's and 0's. Output QD, being the most significant bit, produces a pattern of eight 0's followed by two 1's. Obtain the pattern for the other two outputs and then check all four patterns on the oscilloscope. This is done with a dual-trace oscilloscope by displaying the clock pulses in one channel and one of the output waveforms in the other channel. The pattern of 1's and 0's for the corresponding output is obtained by observing the output levels at the vertical positions where the pulses change from 1 to 0.

Other Counts

IC type 7493 can be connected to count from 0 to a variety of final counts. This is done by connecting one or two outputs to the reset inputs, $R1$ and $R2$. Thus, if $R1$ is connected to QA instead of QB in Fig. 11-4, the resulting count will be from 0000 to 1000, which is 1 less than 1001 ($QD = 1$ and $QA = 1$).

Utilizing your knowledge of how $R1$ and $R2$ affect the final count, connect the 7493 IC to count from 0000 to the following final counts:

(a) 0101

(b) 0111

(c) 1011

Connect each circuit and verify its count sequence by applying pulses from the pulser and observing the output count in the indicator lamps. If the initial count starts with a value greater than the final count, keep applying input pulses until the output clears to 0.

11-2   DIGITAL LOGIC GATES

In this experiment, you will investigate the logic behavior of various IC gates:

7400 Quadruple 2-input NAND gates

7402 Quadruple 2-input NOR gates

7404 Hex inverters

7408 Quadruple 2-input AND gates

7432 Quadruple 2-input OR gates

7486 Quadruple 2-input XOR gates

The pin assignments to the various gates are shown in Fig. 11-1. "Quadruple" means that there are four gates within the package. The digital logic gates and their characteristics are discussed in Section 2-8. NAND implementation is discussed in Section 3-6.

Truth Tables

Use one gate from each IC listed above and obtain the truth table of the gate. The truth table is obtained by connecting the inputs of the gate to switches and the output to an indicator lamp. Compare your results with the truth tables listed in Fig. 2-5.

Waveforms

For each gate listed above, obtain the input-output waveform relationship of the gate. The waveforms are to be observed in the oscilloscope. Use the two low-order outputs of a binary counter (Fig. 11-3) to provide the inputs to the gate. As an example, the circuit and waveforms for the NAND gate are illustrated in Fig. 11-5. The oscilloscope display will repeat this waveform, but you should record only the non-repetitive portion.

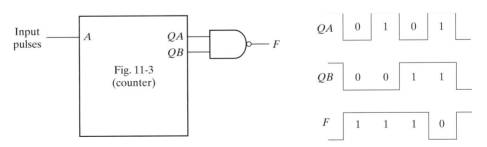

FIGURE 11-5
Waveforms for NAND Gate

Propagation Delay

Connect all six inverters inside the 7404 IC in cascade. The output will be the same as the input except that it will be delayed by the time it takes the signal to propagate through all six inverters. Apply clock pulses to the input of the first inverter. Using the oscilloscope, determine the delay from the input to the output of the sixth inverter during the upswing and again during the downswing of the pulse. This is done with a dual-trace oscilloscope by applying the input clock pulses to one of the channels and the output of the sixth inverter to the second channel. Set the time-base knob to the lowest time-per-division setting. The rise or fall time of the two pulses should appear on the screen. Divide the total delay by 6 to obtain an average propagation delay per inverter.

Universal NAND Gate

Using a single 7400 IC, connect a circuit that produces

(a) an inverter
(b) a 2-input AND
(c) a 2-input OR
(d) a 2-input NOR
(e) a 2-input XOR (See Fig. 3-32)

In each case, verify your circuit by checking its truth table.

NAND Circuit

Using a single 7400 IC, construct a circuit with NAND gates that implements the Boolean function

$$F = AB + CD$$

1. Draw the circuit diagram.
2. Obtain the truth table for F as a function of the four inputs.
3. Connect the circuit and verify the truth table.
4. Record the patterns of 1's and 0's for F as inputs A, B, C, and D go from binary 0 to binary 15.
5. Connect the four outputs of the binary counter shown in Fig. 11-3 to the four inputs of the NAND circuit. Connect the input clock pulses from the counter to one channel and output F to the other channel of a dual-trace oscilloscope. Observe and record the 1's and 0's pattern of F after each clock pulse and compare it to the pattern recorded in Step 4.

11-3   SIMPLIFICATION OF BOOLEAN FUNCTIONS

This experiment demonstrates the relationship between a Boolean function and the corresponding logic diagram. The Boolean functions are simplified by using the map method, as discussed in Chapter 3. The logic diagrams are to be drawn using NAND gates, as explained in Section 3-6.

The gate ICs to be used for the logic diagrams must be those from Fig. 11-1 that contain the following NAND gates:

7400 2-input NAND

7404 Inverter (1-input NAND);

7410 3-input NAND

7420 4-input NAND

If an input to a NAND gate is not used, it should not be left open, but, instead, should be connected to another input that is used. For example, if the circuit needs an inverter and there is an extra two-input gate available in a 7400 IC, then both inputs of the gate are to be connected together to form a single input for an inverter.

Logic Diagram

This part of the experiment starts with a given logic diagram from which we proceed to apply simplification procedures to reduce the number of gates and possibly the number of ICs. The logic diagram shown in Fig. 11-6 requires two ICs, a 7400 and a 7410. Note that the inverters for inputs x, y, and z are obtained from the remaining three gates in the 7400 IC. If the inverters were taken from a 7404 IC, the circuit would have required three ICs. Also note that in drawing SSI circuits, the gates are not enclosed in blocks as is done with MSI circuits.

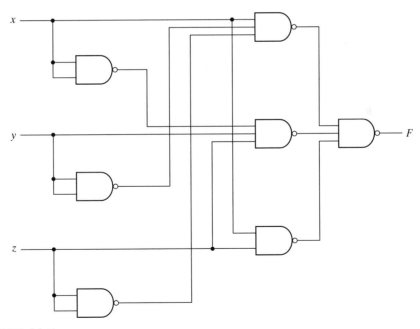

FIGURE 11-6
Logic Diagram for Experiment 3

Assign pin numbers to all inputs and outputs of the gates and connect the circuit with the x, y, and z inputs going to three switches and the output F to an indicator lamp. Test the circuit by obtaining its truth table.

Obtain the Boolean function of the circuit and simplify it using the map method. Construct the simplified circuit without disconnecting the original circuit. Test both circuits by applying identical inputs to both and observing the separate outputs. Show that for each of the eight possible input combinations, the two circuits have identical outputs. This will prove that the simplified circuit behaves exactly as the original circuit.

Boolean Functions

Given the two Boolean functions in sum of minterms:

$$F_1(A, B, C, D) = (0, 1, 4, 5, 8, 9, 10, 12, 13)$$

$$F_2(A, B, C, D) = (3, 5, 7, 8, 10, 11, 13, 15)$$

simplify the two functions by means of maps. Obtain a composite logic diagram with four inputs, A, B, C, and D, and two outputs, F_1 and F_2. Implement the two functions together using a minimum number of NAND ICs. Do not duplicate the same gate if the corresponding term is needed for both functions. Use any extra gates in existing ICs for inverters when possible. Connect the circuit and check its operation. The truth table for F_1 and F_2 obtained from the circuit should conform with the minterms listed.

Complement

Plot the following Boolean function in a map:

$$F = A'D + BD + B'C + AB'D$$

Combine the 1's in the map to obtain the simplified function for F in sum of products. Then combine the 0's in the map to obtain the simplified function for F' also in sum of products. Implement both F and F' using NAND gates and connect the two circuits to the same input switches, but to separate output indicator lamps. Obtain the truth table of each circuit in the laboratory and show that they are the complements of each other.

11-4   COMBINATIONAL CIRCUITS

In this experiment, you will design, construct, and test four combinational logic circuits. The first two circuits are to be constructed with NAND gates, the third with XOR gates, and the fourth with a decoder and NAND gates. Reference to a parity generator can be found in Section 3-8. Implementation with a decoder is discussed in Section 4-8.

Design Example

Design a combinational circuit with four inputs—A, B, C, and D—and one output, F. F is to be equal to 1 when $A = 1$ provided that $B = 0$, or when $B = 1$ provided that either C or D is also equal to 1. Otherwise, the output is to be equal to 0.

1. Obtain the truth table of the circuit.
2. Simplify the output function.
3. Draw the logic diagram of the circuit using NAND gates with a minimum number of ICs.
4. Construct the circuit and test it for proper operation by verifying the given conditions.

Majority Logic

A majority logic is a digital circuit whose output is equal to 1 if the majority of the inputs are 1's. The output is 0 otherwise. Design and test a three-input majority circuit using NAND gates with a minimum number of ICs.

Parity Generator

Design, construct, and test a circuit that generates an even parity bit from four message bits. Use XOR gates. Adding one more XOR gate, expand the circuit so it generates an odd parity bit also.

Decoder Implementation

A combinational circuit has three inputs—x, y, and z—and three outputs—F_1, F_2, and F_3. The simplified Boolean functions for the circuit are

$$F_1 = xz + x'y'z'$$
$$F_2 = x'y + xy'z'$$
$$F_3 = xy + x'y'z$$

Implement and test the combinational circuit using a 74155 decoder IC and external NAND gates.

The block diagram of the decoder and its truth table are shown in Fig. 11-7. The 74155 can be connected as a dual 2 × 4 decoder or as a single 3 × 8 decoder. When a 3 × 8 decoder is desired, inputs $C1$ and $C2$ must be connected together as well as inputs $G1$ and $G2$, as shown in the block diagram. The function of the circuit is similar to the one shown in Fig. 4-18. G is the enable input and must be equal to 0 for proper operation. The eight outputs are labeled with symbols given in the data book. The 74155 uses NAND gates, with the result that the selected output goes to 0 while all other outputs remain at 1. The implementation with the decoder is as shown in Fig. 4-21, except that the OR gates must be replaced with external NAND gates when the 74155 is used.

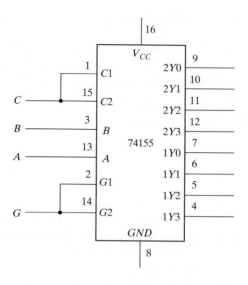

Truth table

Inputs				Outputs							
G	C	B	A	2Y0	2Y1	2Y2	2Y3	1Y0	1Y1	1Y2	1Y3
1	X	X	X	1	1	1	1	1	1	1	1
0	0	0	0	0	1	1	1	1	1	1	1
0	0	0	1	1	0	1	1	1	1	1	1
0	0	1	0	1	1	0	1	1	1	1	1
0	0	1	1	1	1	1	0	1	1	1	1
0	1	0	0	1	1	1	1	0	1	1	1
0	1	0	1	1	1	1	1	1	0	1	1
0	1	1	0	1	1	1	1	1	1	0	1
0	1	1	1	1	1	1	1	1	1	1	0

FIGURE 11-7
IC Type 74155 Connected as a 3 × 8 Decoder

11-5   CODE CONVERTERS

The conversion from one binary code to another is common in digital systems. In this experiment, you will design and construct three combinational-circuit converters. Code conversion is discussed in Section 4-3.

Gray Code to Binary

Design a combinational circuit with four inputs and four outputs that converts a four-bit Gray code number (Table 1-6) into the equivalent four-bit binary number. Implement the circuit with exclusive-OR gates. (This can be done with one 7486 IC.) Connect the circuit to four switches and four indicator lamps and check for proper operation.

9's Complementer

Design a combinational circuit with four input lines that represent a decimal digit in BCD and four output lines that generate the 9's complement of the input digit. Provide a fifth output that detects an error in the input BCD number. This output should be equal to logic-1 when the four inputs have one of the unused combinations of the BCD code. Use any of the gates listed in Fig. 11-1, but minimize the total number of ICs used.

Seven-Segment Display

A seven-segment indicator is used for displaying any one of the decimal digits 0 through 9. Usually, the decimal digit is available in BCD. A BCD-to-seven-segment decoder accepts a decimal digit in BCD and generates the corresponding seven-segment code. This is shown pictorially in Problem 4-9.

Fig. 11-8 shows the connections necessary between the decoder and the display. The 7447 IC is a BCD-to-seven-segment decoder/driver. It has four inputs for the BCD digit. Input D is the most significant and input A the least significant. The 4-bit BCD digit is converted to a seven-segment code with outputs a through g. The outputs of the 7447 are applied to the inputs of the 7730 (or equivalent) seven-segment display. This IC contains the seven LED (light-emitting diode) segments on top of the package. The input at pin 14 is the common anode (CA) for all the LEDs. A 47-Ω resistor to V_{CC} is needed in order to supply the proper current to the selected LED segments. Other equivalent seven-segment display ICs may have additional anode terminals and may require different resistor values.

Construct the circuit shown in Fig. 11-8. Apply the 4-bit BCD digits through four switches and observe the decimal display from 0 to 9. Inputs 1010 through 1111 have no meaning in BCD.

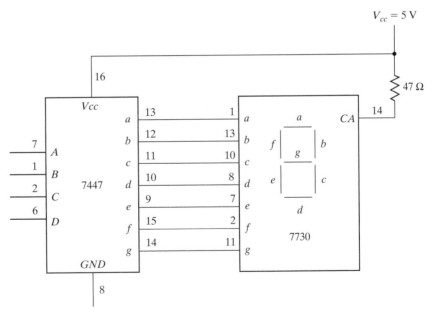

FIGURE 11-8
BCD-to-Seven-Segment Decoder (7447) and Seven-Segment Display (7730)

Depending on the decoder, these values may cause either a blank or a meaningless pattern to be displayed. Observe and record the output displayed patterns of the six unused input combinations.

11-6   DESIGN WITH MULTIPLEXERS

In this experiment, you will design a combinational circuit and implement it with multiplexers, as explained in Section 4-10. The multiplexer to be used is IC type 74151, shown in Fig. 11-9. The internal construction of the 74151 is similar to the diagram shown in Fig. 4-25

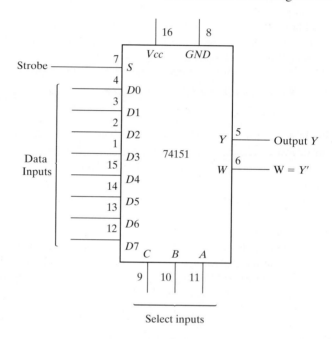

Function table

Strobe	Select			Output
S	C	B	A	Y
1	X	X	X	0
0	0	0	0	D0
0	0	0	1	D1
0	0	1	0	D2
0	0	1	1	D3
0	1	0	0	D4
0	1	0	1	D5
0	1	1	0	D6
0	1	1	1	D7

FIGURE 11-9
IC Type 74151 8 × 1 Multiplexer

except that there are eight inputs instead of four. The eight inputs are designated $D0$ through $D7$. The three selection lines—C, B, and A—select the particular input to be multiplexed and applied to the output. A strobe control S acts as an enable signal. The function table specifies the value of output Y as a function of the selection lines. Output W is the complement of Y. For proper operation, the strobe input S must be connected to ground.

Design Specifications

A small corporation has 10 shares of stock, and each share entitles its owner to one vote at a stockholder's meeting. The 10 shares of stock are owned by four people as follows:

Mr. W: 1 share

Mr. X: 2 shares

Mr. Y: 3 shares

Mrs. Z: 4 shares

Each of these persons has a switch to close when voting yes and to open when voting no for his or her shares.

It is necessary to design a circuit that displays the total number of shares that vote yes for each measure. Use a seven-segment display and a decoder, as shown in Fig. 11-8, to display the required number. If all shares vote no for a measure, the display should be blank. (Note that binary input 15 into the 7447 blanks all seven segments.) If 10 shares vote yes for a measure, the display should show 0. Otherwise, the display shows a decimal number equal to the number of shares that vote yes. Use four 74151 multiplexers to design the combinational circuit that converts the inputs from the stock owners' switches into the BCD digit for the 7447. Do not use 5 V for logic-1. Use the output of an inverter whose input is grounded.

11-7   ADDERS AND SUBTRACTORS

In this experiment, you will construct and test various adder and subtractor circuits. The subtractor circuit is then used for comparing the relative magnitude of two numbers. Adders are discussed in Section 4-3. Subtraction with 2's complement is explained in Section 1-6. A 4-bit parallel adder-subtractor is shown in Fig. 4-13, and the comparison of two numbers is explained in Section 4-7.

Half-Adder

Design, construct, and test a half-adder circuit using one XOR gate and two NAND gates.

Full-Adder

Design, construct, and test a full-adder circuit using two ICs, 7486, and 7400.

Parallel Adder

IC type 7483 is a 4-bit binary parallel adder. The pin assignment is shown in Fig. 11-10. The two 4-bit input binary numbers are $A1$ through $A4$ and $B1$ through $B4$. The 4-bit sum is obtained from $S1$ through $S4$. $C0$ is the input carry and $C4$ the output carry.

Test the 4-bit binary adder 7483 by connecting the power supply and ground terminals. Then connect the four A inputs to a fixed binary number such as 1001 and the B inputs and the input carry to five toggle switches. The five outputs are applied to indicator lamps. Perform the addition of a few binary numbers and check that the output sum and output carry give the proper values. Show that when the input carry is equal to 1, it adds 1 to the output sum.

Adder-Subtractor

The subtraction of two binary numbers can be done by taking the 2's complement of the subtrahend and adding it to the minuend. The 2's complement can be obtained by taking the 1's complement and adding 1. To perform $A - B$, we complement the four bits of B, add them to the four bits of A, and add 1 through the input carry. This is done as shown in Fig. 11-11. The four XOR gates complement the bits of B when the mode select $M = 1$ (because $x \oplus 1 = x'$) and leave the bits of B unchanged when $M = 0$ (because $x \oplus 0 = x$). Thus, when the mode select M is equal to 1, the input carry $C0$ is equal to 1 and the sum output is A plus the 2's complement of B. When M is equal to 0, the input carry is equal to 0 and the sum generates $A + B$.

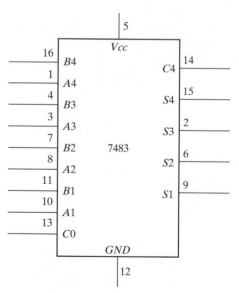

FIGURE 11-10
IC Type 7483 4-Bit Binary Adder

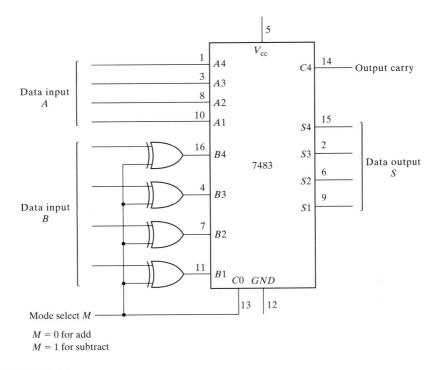

FIGURE 11-11
4-Bit Adder–Subtractor

Connect the adder-subtractor circuit and test it for proper operation. Connect the four A inputs to a fixed binary number 1001 and the B inputs to switches. Perform the following operations and record the values of the output sum and the output carry $C4$:

$$9 + 5 \qquad 9 - 5$$
$$9 + 9 \qquad 9 - 9$$
$$9 + 15 \qquad 9 - 15$$

Show that during addition, the output carry is equal to 1 when the sum exceeds 15. Also show that when $A \geq B$, the subtraction operation gives the correct answer, $A - B$, and the output carry $C4$ is equal to 1. But when $A < B$, the subtraction gives the 2's complement of $B - A$ and the output carry is equal to 0.

Magnitude Comparator

The comparison of two numbers is an operation that determines whether one number is greater than, equal to, or less than the other number. Two numbers, A and B, can be compared by first subtracting $A - B$ as done in Fig. 11-11. If the output in S is equal to zero, we know that $A = B$. The output carry from $C4$ determines the relative magnitude: when $C4 = 1$, we have $A \geq B$; when $C4 = 0$, we have $A < B$; and when $C4 = 1$ and $S \neq 0$, we have $A > B$.

It is necessary to supplement the subtractor circuit of Fig. 11-11 to provide the comparison logic. This is done with a combinational circuit that has five inputs, $S1$ through $S4$ and $C4$, and three outputs designated by x, y, and z, so that

$$x = 1 \qquad \text{if } A = B \qquad (S = 0000)$$
$$y = 1 \qquad \text{if } A < B \qquad (C4 = 0)$$
$$z = 1 \qquad \text{if } A > B \qquad (C4 = 1 \text{ and } S \neq 0000)$$

The combinational circuit can be implemented with the two ICs, 7404 and 7408.

Construct the comparator circuit and test its operation. Use at least two sets of numbers for A and B to check each of the outputs x, y, and z.

11-8   FLIP-FLOPS

In this experiment, you will construct, test and investigate the operation of various latches and flip-flops. The internal construction of latches and flip-flops can be found in Sections 5-2 and 5-3.

SR Latch

Construct an SR latch with two cross-coupled NAND gates. Connect the two inputs to switches and the two outputs to indicator lamps. Set the two switches to logic-1, and then momentarily turn each switch separately to the logic-0 position and back to 1. Obtain the function table of the circuit.

D Latch

Construct a D latch with four NAND gates (only one 7400 IC) and verify its function table.

Master–Slave Flip-Flop

Connect a master–slave D flip-flop using two D latches and an inverter. Connect the D input to a switch and the clock input to a pulser. Connect the output of the master latch to one indicator lamp and the output of the slave latch to another indicator lamp. Set the value of the input to the complement value of the output. Press the pushbutton in the pulser and then release it to produce a single pulse. Observe that the master changes when the pulse goes positive and the slave follows the change when the pulse goes negative. Repeat a few times while observing the two indicator lamps. Explain the transfer sequence from input to master and from master to slave.

Disconnect the clock input from the pulser and connect it to a clock generator. Connect the complement output of the flip-flop to the D input. This causes the flip-flop to complement with each clock pulse. Using a dual-trace oscilloscope, observe the waveforms of the clock and the master and slave outputs. Verify that the delay between the master and the slave outputs is equal to the positive half of the clock cycle. Obtain a timing diagram showing the relationship between the clock waveform and the master and slave outputs.

Edge-Triggered Flip-Flop

Construct a D-type positive-edge-triggered flip-flop using six NAND gates. Connect the clock input to a pulser, the D input to a toggle switch, and the output Q to an indicator lamp. Set the value of D to the complement value of Q. Show that the flip-flop output changes only in response to a positive transition of the clock pulse. Verify that the output does not change when the clock input is logic-1, when the clock goes through a negative transition, or when it is logic-0. Continue changing the D input to correspond to the complement of the Q output at all times.

Disconnect the input from the pulser and connect it to the clock generator. Connect the complement output Q' to the D input. This causes the output to complement with each positive transition of the clock pulse. Using a dual-trace oscilloscope, observe and record the timing relationship between the input clock and output Q. Show that the output changes in response to a positive edge transition.

IC Flip-Flops

IC type 7476 consists of two JK master-slave flip-flops with preset and clear. The pin assignment for each flip-flop is shown in Fig. 11-12. The function table specifies the circuit operation. The first three entries in the table specify the operation of the asynchronous preset and clear

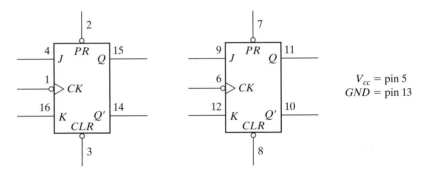

Function table

	Inputs					Outputs	
Preset	Clear	Clock	J	K		Q	Q'
0	1	X	X	X		1	0
1	0	X	X	X		0	1
0	0	X	X	X		1	1
1	1	⊓	0	0		No change	
1	1	⊓	0	1		0	1
1	1	⊓	1	0		1	0
1	1	⊓	1	1		Toggle	

FIGURE 11-12
IC Type 7476 Dual JK Master–Slave Flip-Flops

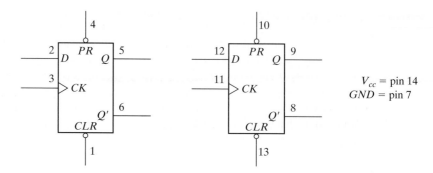

Function table

	Inputs			Outputs	
Preset	Clear	Clock	D	Q	Q'
0	1	X	X	1	0
1	0	X	X	0	1
0	0	X	X	1	1
1	1	↑	0	0	1
1	1	↑	1	1	0
1	1	0	X	No change	

FIGURE 11-13
IC Type 7474 Dual D Positive–Edge-Triggered Flip-Flops

inputs. These inputs behave like a NAND SR latch and are independent of the clock or the J and K inputs (the X's indicate don't-care conditions). The last four entries in the function table specify the clock operation with both the preset and clear inputs maintained at logic-1. The clock value is shown as a single pulse. The positive transition of the pulse changes the master flip-flop, and the negative transition changes the slave flip-flop as well as the output of the circuit. With $J = K = 0$, the output does not change. The flip-flop toggles or complements when $J = K = 1$. Investigate the operation of one 7476 flip-flop and verify its function table.

IC type 7474 consists of two D positive-edge-triggered flip-flops with preset and clear. The pin assignment is shown in Fig. 11-13. The function table specifies the preset and clear operations and the clock operation. The clock is shown with an upward arrow to indicate that it is a positive-edge-triggered flip-flop. Investigate the operation of one of the flip-flops and verify its function table.

11-9   SEQUENTIAL CIRCUITS

In this experiment, you will design, construct, and test three synchronous sequential circuits. Use IC type 7476 (Fig. 11-12) or 7474 (Fig. 11-13). Choose any gate type that will minimize the total number of ICs. The design of synchronous sequential circuits is covered in Section 5-7.

Up-Down Counter with Enable

Design, construct, and test a 2-bit counter that counts up or down. An enable input E determines whether the counter is on or off. If $E = 0$, the counter is disabled and remains at its present count even though clock pulses are applied to the flip-flops. If $E = 1$, the counter is enabled and a second input, x, determines the count direction. If $x = 1$, the circuit counts up with the sequence 00, 01, 10, 11, and the count repeats. If $x = 0$, the circuit counts down with the sequence 11, 10, 01, 00, and the count repeats. Do not use E to disable the clock. Design the sequential circuit with E and x as inputs.

State Diagram

Design, construct and test a sequential circuit whose state diagram is shown in Fig. 11-14. Designate the two flip-flops as A and B, the input as x, and the output as y.

Connect the output of the least significant flip-flop B to the input x and predict the sequence of states and output that will occur with the application of clock pulses. Verify the state transition and output by testing the circuit.

Design of Counter

Design, construct, and test a counter that goes through the following sequence of binary states: 0, 1, 2, 3, 6, 7, 10, 11, 12, 13, 14, 15, and back to 0 to repeat. Note that binary states 4, 5, 8, and 9 are not used. The counter must be self-starting; that is, if the circuit starts from any one of the four invalid states, the count pulses must transfer the circuit to one of the valid states to continue the count correctly.

Check the circuit operation for the required count sequence. Verify that the counter is self-starting. This is done by initializing the circuit to each unused state by means of the preset and clear inputs and then applying pulses to see whether the counter reaches one of the valid states.

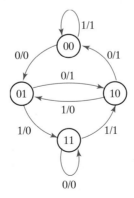

FIGURE 11-14
State Diagram for Experiment 9

11-10   COUNTERS

In this experiment, you will construct and test various ripple and synchronous counter circuits. Ripple counters are discussed in Section 6-3 and synchronous counters are covered in Section 6-4.

Ripple Counter

Construct a 4-bit binary ripple counter using two 7476 ICs (Fig. 11-12). Connect all asynchronous clear and preset inputs to logic-1. Connect the count-pulse input to a pulser and check the counter for proper operation.

Modify the counter so it will count down instead of up. Check that each input pulse decrements the counter by 1.

Synchronous Counter

Construct a synchronous 4-bit binary counter and check its operation. Use two 7476 ICs and one 7408 IC.

Decimal Counter

Design a synchronous BCD counter that counts from 0000 to 1001. Use two 7476 ICs and one 7408 IC. Test the counter for the proper sequence. Determine whether it is self-starting. This is done by initializing the counter to each of the six unused states by means of the preset and clear inputs. The application of pulses must transfer the counter to one of the valid states if the counter is self-starting.

Binary Counter with Parallel Load

IC type 74161 is a 4-bit synchronous binary counter with parallel load and asynchronous clear. The internal logic is similar to the circuit shown in Fig. 6-14. The pin assignment to the inputs and outputs is shown in Fig. 11-15. When the load signal is enabled, the four data inputs are transferred into four internal flip-flops, QA through QD, with QD being the most significant bit. There are two count-enable inputs called P and T. Both must be equal to 1 for the counter to operate. The function table is similar to Table 6-6 with one exception: the load input in the 74161 is enabled when equal to 0. To load the input data, the clear input must be equal to 1 and the load input must be equal to 0. The two count inputs have don't-care conditions and may be equal to either 1 or 0. The internal flip-flops trigger on the positive transition of the clock pulse. The circuit functions as a counter when the load input is equal to 1 and both count inputs P and T are equal to 1. If either P or T goes to 0, the output does not change. The carry-out output is equal to 1 when all four data outputs are equal to 1. Perform an experiment to verify the operation of the 74161 IC according to the function table.

Show how the 74161 IC together with a 2-input NAND gate can be made to operate as a synchronous BCD counter that counts from 0000 to 1001. Do not use the clear input. Use the NAND gate to detect the count of 1001, which then causes all 0's to be loaded into the counter.

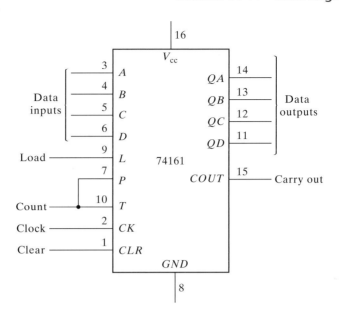

Function table

Clear	Clock	Load	Count	Function
0	X	X	X	Clear outputs to 0
1	↑	0	X	Load input data
1	↑	1	1	Count to next binary value
1	↑	1	0	No change in output

FIGURE 11-15
IC Type 74161 Binary Counter with Parallel Load

11-11   SHIFT REGISTERS

In this experiment, you will investigate the operation of shift registers. The IC to be used is the 74195 shift register with parallel load. Shift registers are explained in Section 6-2.

IC Shift Register

IC type 74195 is a 4-bit shift register with parallel load and asynchronous clear. The pin assignment to the inputs and outputs is shown in Fig. 11-16. The single control line labeled SH/LD (shift/load) determines the synchronous operation of the register. When $SH/LD = 0$, the control input is in the load mode and the four data inputs are transferred into the four internal flip-flops, QA through QD. When $SH/LD = 1$, the control input is in the shift mode and the information in the register is shifted right from QA toward QD. The serial input into QA during

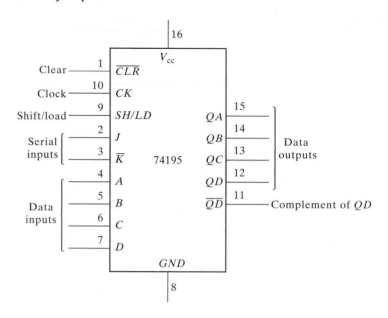

FIGURE 11-16
IC Type 74195 Shift Register with Parallel Load

Function table

Clear	Shift/ load	Clock	J	$\overline{K}$	Serial input	Function
0	X	X	X	X	X	Asynchronous clear
1	X	0	X	X	X	No change in output
1	0	↑	X	X	X	Load input data
1	1	↑	0	0	0	Shift from QA toward QD, $QA = 0$
1	1	↑	1	1	1	Shift from QA toward QD, $QA = 1$

the shift is determined from the J and $\overline{K}$ inputs. The two inputs behave like the J and the complement of K of a JK flip-flop. When both J and $\overline{K}$ are equal to 0, flip-flop QA is cleared to 0 after the shift. If both inputs are equal to 1, QA is set to 1 after the shift. The other two conditions for the J and $\overline{K}$ inputs provide a complement or no change in the output of flip-flop QA after the shift.

The function table for the 74195 shows the mode of operation of the register. When the clear input goes to 0, the four flip-flops clear to 0 asynchronously, that is, without the need of a clock. Synchronous operations are affected by a positive transition of the clock. To load the input data, the SH/LD must be equal to 0 and a positive clock-pulse transition must occur. To shift right, the SH/LD must be equal to 1. The J and $\bar{K}$ inputs must be connected together to form the serial input.

Perform an experiment that will verify the operation of the 74195 IC. Show that it performs all the operations listed in the function table. Include in your function table the two conditions for $J\bar{K} = 01$ and 10.

Ring Counter

A ring counter is a circular shift register with the signal from the serial output QD going into the serial input. Connect the J and $\bar{K}$ input together to form the serial input. Use the load condition to preset the ring counter to an initial value of 1000. Rotate the single bit with the shift condition and check the state of the register after each clock pulse.

A switch-tail ring counter uses the complement output of QD for the serial input. Preset the switch-tail ring counter to 0000 and predict the sequence of states that will result from shifting. Verify your prediction by observing the state sequence after each shift.

Feedback Shift Register

A feedback shift register is a shift register whose serial input is connected to some function of selected register outputs. Connect a feedback shift register whose serial input is the exclusive-OR of outputs QC and QD. Predict the sequence of states of the register starting from state 1000. Verify your prediction by observing the state sequence after each clock pulse.

Bidirectional Shift Register

The 74195 IC can shift only right from QA toward QD. It is possible to convert the register to a bidirectional shift register by using the load mode to obtain a shift left operation (from QD toward QA). This is accomplished by connecting the output of each flip-flop to the input of the flip-flop on its left and using the load mode of the SH/LD input as a shift-left control. Input D becomes the serial input for the shift-left operation.

Connect the 74195 as a bidirectional shift register (without parallel load). Connect the serial input for shift right to a toggle switch. Construct the shift left as a ring counter by connecting the serial output QA to the serial input D. Clear the register and then check its operation by shifting a single 1 from the serial input switch. Shift right three more times and insert 0's from the serial input switch. Then rotate left with the shift-left (load) control. The single 1 should remain visible while shifting.

Bidirectional Shift Register with Parallel Load

The 74195 IC can be converted to a bidirectional shift register with parallel load in conjunction with a multiplexer circuit. We will use IC type 74157 for this purpose. This is a quadruple 2-to-1-line multiplexers whose internal logic is shown in Fig. 4-26. The pin assignment to the inputs and outputs of the 74157 is shown in Fig. 11-17. Note that the enable input is called a strobe in the 74157.

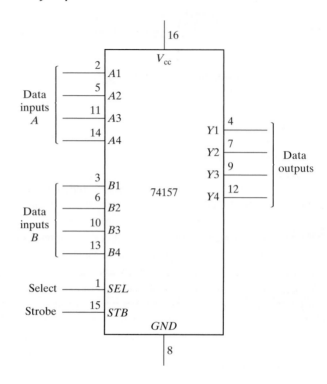

Function table

Strobe	Select	Data outputs Y
1	X	All 0's
0	0	Select data inputs A
0	1	Select data inputs B

FIGURE 11-17
IC Type 74157 Quadruple 2 × 1 Multiplexers

Construct a bidirectional shift register with parallel load using the 74195 register and the 74157 multiplexer. The circuit should be able to perform the following operations:

1. Asynchronous clear
2. Shift right
3. Shift left
4. Parallel load
5. Synchronous clear.

Derive a table for the five operations as a function of the clear, clock, and SH/LD inputs of the 74195 and the strobe and select inputs of the 74157. Connect the circuit and verify your function table. Use the parallel-load condition to provide an initial value into the register and connect the serial outputs to the serial inputs of both shifts in order not to lose the binary information while shifting.

11-12   SERIAL ADDITION

In this experiment, you will construct and test a serial adder-subtractor circuit. Serial addition of two binary numbers can be done by means of shift registers and a full adder, as explained in Section 6-2.

Serial Adder

Starting from the diagram of Fig. 6-6, design and construct a 4-bit serial adder using the following ICs: 74195 (two), 7408, 7486, and 7476. Provide a facility for register B to accept parallel data from four toggle switches and connect its serial input to ground so that 0's are shifted into register B during the addition. Provide a toggle switch to clear the registers and the flip-flop. Another switch will be needed to specify whether register B is to accept parallel data or is to be shifted during the addition.

Testing the Adder

To test your serial adder, perform the binary addition $5 + 6 + 15 = 26$. This is done by first clearing the registers and the carry flip-flop. Parallel load the binary value 0101 into register B. Apply four pulses to add B to A serially and check that the result in A is 0101. (Note that clock pulses for the 7476 must be as shown in Fig. 11-12.) Parallel load 0110 into B and add it to A serially. Check that A has the proper sum. Parallel load 1111 into B and add to A. Check that the value in A is 1010 and that the carry flip-flop is set.

Clear the registers and flip-flop and try a few other numbers to verify that your serial adder is functioning properly.

Serial Adder–Subtractor

If we follow the procedure used in Section 6-2 for the design of a serial subtractor (that subtracts $A - B$), we will find that the output difference is the same as the output sum, but that the input to the J and K of the borrow flip-flop needs the complement of QD (available in the 74195). Using the other two XOR gates from the 7486, convert the serial adder to a serial adder–subtractor with a mode control M. When $M = 0$, the circuit adds $A + B$. When $M = 1$, the circuit subtracts $A - B$ and the flip-flop holds the borrow instead of the carry.

Test the adder part of the circuit by repeating the operations recommended above to ensure that the modification did not change the operation. Test the serial subtractor part by performing the operations $15 - 4 - 5 - 13 = -7$. Binary 15 can be transferred to register A by first clearing it to 0 and adding 15 from B. Check the intermediate results during the subtraction. Note that -7 will appear as the 2's complement of 7 with a borrow of 1 in the flip-flop.

11-13   MEMORY UNIT

In this experiment, you will investigate the behavior of a random-access memory (RAM) unit and its storage capability. The RAM will be used to simulate a read-only memory (ROM). The ROM simulator will then be used to implement combinational circuits, as explained in Section 7-5. The memory unit is discussed in Sections 7-2 and 7-3.

IC RAM

IC type 74189 is a 16×4 random-access memory. The internal logic is similar to the circuit shown in Fig. 7-6 for a 4×4 RAM. The pin assignment to the inputs and outputs is shown in

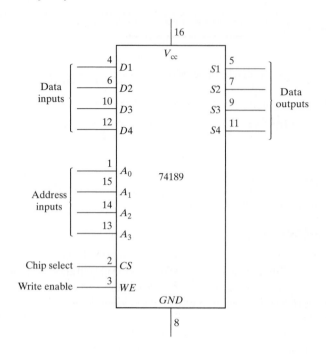

Function table

CS	WE	Operation	Data outputs
0	0	Write	High impedance
0	1	Read	Complement of selected word
1	X	Disable	High impedance

FIGURE 11-18
IC Type 74189 16 × 4 RAM

Fig. 11-18. The four address inputs select one of 16 words in the memory. The least significant bit of the address is A and the most significant is A_3. The chip select (CS) input must be equal to 0 to enable the memory. If CS is equal to 1, the memory is disabled and all four outputs are in a high impedance state. The write enable (WE) input determines the type of operation as indicated in the function table. The write operation is performed when $WE = 0$. This is a transfer of the binary number from the data inputs into the selected word in memory. The read operation is performed when $WE = 1$. This transfers the complement value stored in the selected word into the output data lines. The memory has three-state outputs to facilitate memory expansion.

Testing the RAM

Since the outputs of the 74189 produce the complement values, we need to insert four inverters to change the outputs to their normal value. The RAM can be tested after making the following connections: Connect the address inputs to a binary counter using the 7493 IC (shown in Fig. 11-3). Connect the four data inputs to toggle switches and the data outputs to four 7404 inverters. Provide four indicator lamps for the address and four more for the outputs of the inverters. Connect input *CS* to ground and *WE* to a toggle switch (or a pulser that provides a negative pulse). Store a few words into the memory and then read them to verify that the write and read operations are functioning properly. You must be careful when using the *WE* switch. Always leave the *WE* input in the read mode, unless you want to write into memory. The proper way to write is first to set the address in the counter and the inputs in the four toggle switches. To store the word in memory, flip the *WE* switch to the write position and then return it to the read position. Be careful not to change the address or the inputs when *WE* is in the write mode.

ROM Simulator

A ROM simulator is obtained from a RAM when operated in the read mode only. The pattern of 1's and 0's is first entered into the simulating RAM by placing the unit momentarily in the write mode. Simulation is achieved by placing the unit in the read mode and taking the address lines as inputs for the ROM. The ROM can then be used to implement any combinational circuit.

Implement a combinational circuit using the ROM simulator that converts a 4-bit binary number to its equivalent Gray code as defined in Table 1-6. This is done as follows. Obtain the truth table of the code converter. Store the truth table into the 74189 memory by setting the address inputs to the binary value and the data inputs to the corresponding Gray code value. After all 16 entries of the table are written in memory, the ROM simulator is set by connecting the *WE* line to logic-1 permanently. Check the code converter by applying the inputs to the address lines and verifying the correct outputs in the data output lines.

Memory Expansion

Expand the memory unit to a 32 × 4 RAM using two 74189 ICs. Use the *CS* inputs to select between the two ICs. Note that since the data outputs are three-stated you can tie pairs of terminals together to obtain a logic OR operation between the two ICs. Test your circuit by using it as a ROM simulator that adds a 3-bit number to a 2-bit number to produce a 4-bit sum. For example, if the input of the ROM is 10110, then the output is calculated to be $101 + 10 = 0111$. (The first three bits of the input represent 5, the last two bits represent 2, and the output sum is binary 7.) Use the counter to provide four bits of the address and a switch for the fifth bit of the address.

11-14   LAMP HANDBALL

In this experiment, you will construct an electronic game of handball using a single light to simulate the moving ball. This project demonstrates the application of a bidirectional shift register with parallel load. It also shows the operation of the asynchronous inputs of flip-flops. We will first introduce an IC that is needed for this experiment and then present the logic diagram of the simulated lamp handball game.

IC Type 74194

This is a 4-bit bidirectional shift register with parallel load. The internal logic is similar to Fig. 6-7. The pin assignment to the inputs and outputs is shown in Fig. 11-19. The two mode-control inputs determine the type of operation as specified in the function table.

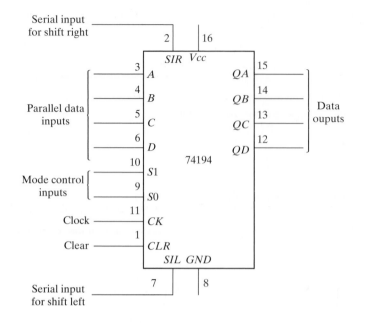

FIGURE 11-19
IC Type 74194 Bidirectional Shift Register with Parallel Load

Logic Diagram

The logic diagram of the electronic lamp handball is shown in Fig. 11-20. It consists of two 74194 ICs, a dual D flip-flop 7474 IC, and three gate ICs: 7400, 7404, and 7408. The ball is simulated by a moving light that is shifted left or right through the bidirectional shift register. The rate at which the light moves is determined by the frequency of the clock. The circuit is first initialized with the *reset* switch. The *start* switch starts the game by placing the ball (an indicator lamp) at the extreme right. The player must press the pulser push button to start the

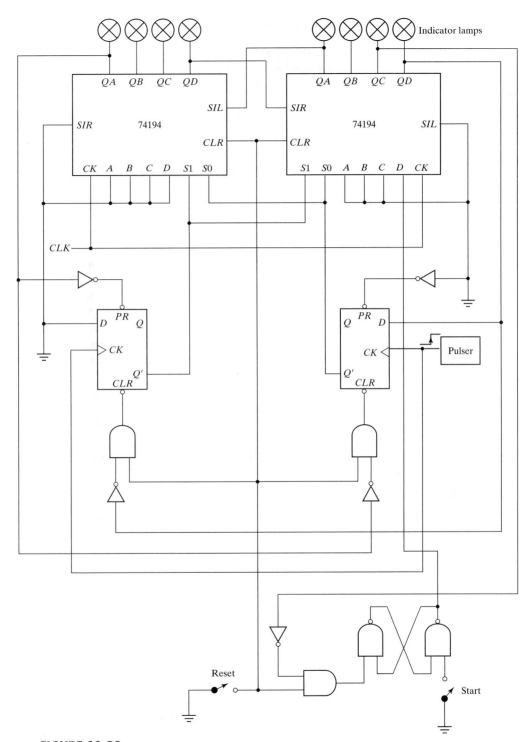

FIGURE 11-20
Lamp Handball Logic Diagram

469

ball moving to the left. The single light shifts to the left until it reaches the leftmost position (the wall), at which time the ball returns to the player by reversing the direction of shift of the moving light. When the light is again at the rightmost position, the player must press the pulser again to reverse the direction of shift. If the player presses the pulser too soon or too late, the ball disappears and the light goes off. The game can be restarted by turning the start switch on and then off. The start switch must be open (logic-1) during the game.

Circuit Analysis

Prior to connecting the circuit, analyze the logic diagram to ensure that you understand how the circuit operates. In particular, try to answer the following questions:

1. What is the function of the reset switch?

2. Explain how the light in the rightmost position comes on when the start switch is grounded. Why is it necessary to place the start switch in the logic-1 position before the game starts?

3. What happens to the two mode-control inputs, $S1$ and $S0$, once the ball is set in motion?

4. What happens to the mode-control inputs and to the ball if the pulser is pressed while the ball is moving to the left? What happens if it is moving to the right but has not reached the rightmost position yet?

5. Suppose that the ball returned to the rightmost position, but the pulser has not been pressed yet; what is the state of the mode-control inputs if the pulser is pressed? What happens if it is not pressed?

Playing the Game

Wire the circuit of Fig. 11-20. Test the circuit for proper operation by playing the game. Note that the pulser must provide a positive-edge transition and that both the reset and start switches must be open (be in the logic-1 state) during the game. Start with a low clock rate and increase the clock frequency to make the handball game more challenging.

Counting the Number of Losses

Design a circuit that keeps score of the number of times the player loses while playing the game. Use a BCD-to-seven-segment decoder and a seven-segment display as in Fig. 11-8 to display the count from 0 through 9. Counting is done with a decimal counter using either the 7493 as a ripple decimal counter or the 74161 and a NAND gate as a synchronous decimal counter. The display should show 0 when the circuit is reset. Every time the ball disappears and the light goes off, the display should increase by 1. If the light stays on during the play, the number in the display should not change. The final design should be an automatic scoring circuit, with the decimal display incremented automatically each time the player loses when the light disappears.

Lamp Ping-Pong TM

Modify the circuit of Fig. 11-20 so as to obtain a lamp Ping-Pong game. Two players can participate in this game, with each player having his own pulser. The player with the right pulser returns the ball when in the extreme right position, and the player with the left pulser returns the ball when in the extreme left position. The only modification required for the Ping-Pong game is a second pulser and a change of few wires.

With a second start circuit, the game can be made to start (serve) by either one of the two players. This addition is optional.

11-15   CLOCK-PULSE GENERATOR

In this experiment, you will use an IC timer unit and connect it to produce clock pulses at a given frequency. The circuit requires the connection of two external resistors and two external capacitors. The cathode-ray oscilloscope is used to observe the waveforms and measure the frequency.

IC Timer

IC type 72555 (or 555) is a precision timer circuit whose internal logic is shown in Fig. 11-21. (The resistors, R_A and R_B, and the two capacitors are not part of the IC.) It consists of two voltage comparators, a flip-flop, and an internal transistor. The voltage division from $V_{CC} = 5$ V through the three internal resistors to ground produce $\frac{2}{3}$ and $\frac{1}{3}$ of V_{CC} (3.3 V and 1.7 V) into the fixed inputs of the comparators. When the threshold input at pin 6 goes above 3.3 V, the upper comparator resets the flip-flop and the output goes low to about 0 V. When the trigger input at pin 2 goes below 1.7 V, the lower comparator sets the flip-flop and the output goes high to about 5 V. When the output is low, Q' is high and the base-emitter junction of the transistor is forward-biased. When the output is high, Q' is low and the transistor is cut off (see Section 10-2). The timer circuit is capable of producing accurate time delays controlled by an external RC circuit. In this experiment the IC timer will be operated in the astable mode to produce clock pulses.

Circuit Operation

Fig. 11-21 shows the external connections for the astable operation. The capacitor C charges through resistors R_A and R_B when the transistor is cut off and discharges through R_B when the transistor is forward-biased and conducting. When the charging voltage across capacitor C reaches 3.3 V, the threshold input at pin 6 causes the flip-flop to reset and the transistor turns on. When the discharging voltage reaches 1.7 V, the trigger input at pin 2 causes the flip-flop to set and the transistor turns off. Thus, the output continually alternates between two voltage levels at the output of the flip-flop. The output remains high for a duration equal to the charge time. This duration is determined from the equation

$$t_H = 0.693(R_A + R_B)C$$

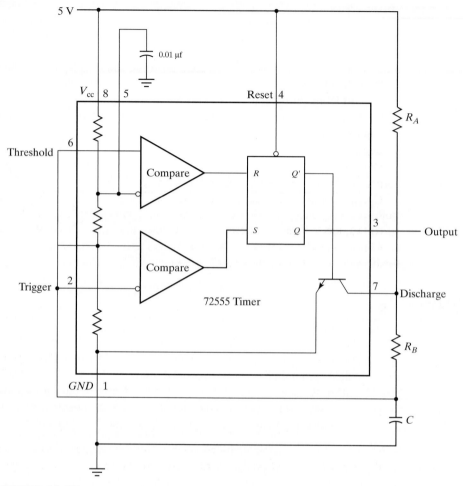

FIGURE 11-21
IC Type 72555 Timer Connected as a Clock-Pulse Generator

The output remains low for a duration equal to the discharge time. This duration is determined from the equation

$$t_L = 0.693R_BC$$

Clock-Pulse Generator

Starting with a capacitor C of 0.001 μF, calculate values for R_A and R_B to produce clock pulses, as shown in Fig. 11-22. The pulse width is 1 μs in the low level, and it is repeating at a frequency rate of 100 kHz (every 10 μs). Connect the circuit and check the output in the oscilloscope.

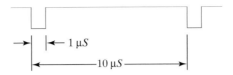

FIGURE 11-22
Output Waveform for Clock Generator

Observe the output across the capacitor C and record its two levels to verify that they are between the trigger and threshold values.

Observe the waveform in the collector of the transistor at pin 7 and record all pertinent information. Explain the waveform by analyzing the circuit action.

Connect a variable resistor (potentiometer) in series with R_A to produce a variable-frequency pulse generator. The low-level duration remains at 1 μs. The frequency should range from 20 to 100 kHz.

Change the low-level pulses to high-level pulses with a 7404 inverter. This will produce positive pulses of 1 μs with a variable-frequency range.

11-16   PARALLEL ADDER AND ACCUMULATOR

In this experiment, you will construct a 4-bit parallel adder whose sum can be loaded into a register. The numbers to be added will be stored in a random-access memory. A set of binary numbers will be selected from memory and their sum will be accumulated in the register.

Block Diagram

Use the RAM circuit from the memory experiment of Section 11-13, a 4-bit parallel adder, a 4-bit shift register with parallel load, a carry flip-flop, and a multiplexer to construct the circuit. The block diagram and the ICs to be used are shown in Fig. 11-23. Information can be written into RAM from data in four switches or from the 4-bit data available in the outputs of the register. The selection is done by means of a multiplexer. The data in RAM can be added to the contents of the register and the sum transferred back to the register.

Control of Register

Provide toggle switches to control the 74194 register and the 7476 carry flip-flop as follows:

(a) A LOAD condition to transfer the sum to the register and the output carry to the flip-flop upon application of a clock pulse.

(b) A SHIFT condition to shift the register right with the carry from the carry flip-flop transferred into the leftmost position of the register upon application of a clock pulse. The value in the carry flip-flop should not change during the shift.

(c) A NO-CHANGE condition that leaves the contents of the register and flip-flop unchanged even when clock pulses are applied.

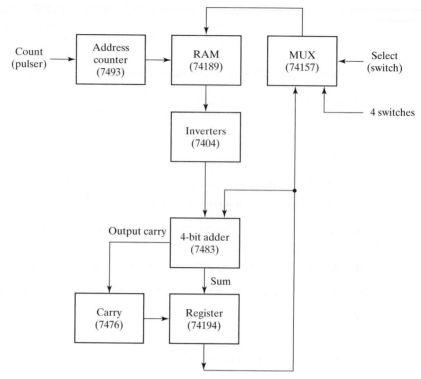

FIGURE 11-23
Block Diagram of a Parallel Adder for Experiment 16

Carry Circuit

In order to conform with the above specifications, it is necessary to provide a circuit between the output carry from the adder and the J and K inputs of the 7476 flip-flop so that the output carry is transferred into the flip-flop (whether it is equal to 0 or 1) only when the LOAD condition is activated and a pulse is applied to the clock input of the flip-flop. The carry flip-flop should not change if the LOAD condition is disabled or the SHIFT condition is enabled.

Detailed Circuit

Draw a detailed diagram showing all the wiring between the ICs. Connect the circuit and provide indicator lamps for the outputs of the register and carry flip-flop and for the address and output data of the RAM.

Checking the Circuit

Store the following numbers in RAM and then add them to the register one at a time. Start with a cleared register and flip-flop. Predict the values in the output of the register and carry after each addition and verify your results:

$$0110 + 1110 + 1101 + 0101 + 0011$$

Circuit Operation

Clear the register and the carry flip-flop to zero and store the following 4-bit numbers in RAM in the indicated addresses:

Address	Content
0	0110
3	1110
6	1101
9	0101
12	0011

Now perform the following four operations:

1. Add the contents of address 0 to the contents of the register using the LOAD condition.
2. Store the sum from the register into RAM at address 1.
3. Shift right the contents of the register and carry with the SHIFT condition.
4. Store the shifted contents of the register at address 2 of RAM.

Check that the contents of the first three locations in RAM are as follows:

Address	Content
0	0110
1	0110
2	0011

Repeat the above four operations for each of the other four binary numbers stored in RAM. Use addresses 4, 7, 10, and 13 to store the sum from the register in step 2. Use addresses 5, 8, 11, and 14 to store the shifted value from the register in step 4. Predict what the contents of RAM at addresses 0 through 14 would be and check to verify your results.

11-17   BINARY MULTIPLIER

In this experiment, you will design and construct a circuit that multiplies two 4-bit unsigned numbers to produce an 8-bit product. An algorithm for multiplying two binary numbers is presented in Section 8-6.

Block Diagram

The block diagram of the binary multiplier with the recommended ICs to be used is shown in Fig. 11-24(a). The multiplicand B is available from four switches instead of a register. The multiplier Q is obtained from another set of four switches. The product is displayed with eight indicator lamps. Counter P is initialized to 0 and then incremented after each partial product is formed. When the counter reaches the count of four, output P_c becomes 1 and the multiplication operation terminates.

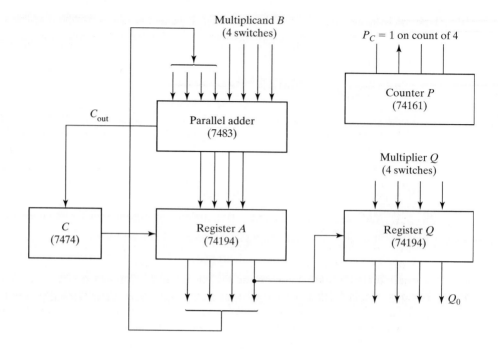

(a) Datapath block program

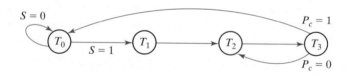

T_1: $A \leftarrow 0, C \leftarrow 0, P \leftarrow 0, Q \leftarrow$ Multiplier
T_2: $P \leftarrow P + 1$
T_2Q_0: $A \leftarrow A + B, C \leftarrow C_{out}$
T_3:   Shift right $CAQ, C \leftarrow 0$

(b) Control state diagram

FIGURE 11-24
Binary Multiplier Circuit

Control of Registers

The ASM chart for the binary multiplier in Fig. 8-14 shows that the three registers and the carry flip-flop are controlled with signals T_1, T_2, and T_3. An additional control signal that depends on Q_1 loads the sum into register A and the output carry into flip-flop C. Q_0 is the least significant bit of register Q. The control-state diagram and the operations to be performed in each state are listed in Fig. 11-24(b). T_2Q_0 is generated with an AND gate whose inputs are T_2 and Q_0. Note that carry flip-flop C can be cleared to 0 with every clock pulse, except when the output carry is transferred to it.

Multiplication Example

Before connecting the circuit, make sure that you understand the operation of the multiplier. To do this, construct a table similar to the one shown in Table 8-4, but with $B = 1111$ for the multiplicand and $Q = 1011$ for the multiplier. Along each comment listed on the left side of the table, specify which one of the state variables—T_1 or T_2 or T_3—is enabled in each case. (The states should start with T_1 and then repeat T_2 and T_3 four times.)

Datapath Design

Draw a detailed diagram of the datapath part of the multiplier, showing all IC pin connections. Generate the control signals—T_1, T_2, and T_3—with three switches and use them to provide the required control operations for the various registers. Connect the circuit and check that each component is functioning properly. With the three control variables at 0, set the multiplicand switches to 1111 and the multiplier switches to 1011. Sequence the control variables manually by means of the control switches as specified by the state diagram of Fig. 11-24(b). Apply a single pulse while in each control state and observe the outputs of registers A and Q and the values in C and P_c. Compare with the numbers in your numerical example to verify that the circuit is functioning properly. Note that IC type 74161 has master–slave flip-flops. To operate it manually, it is necessary that the single clock pulse be a negative pulse.

Design of Control

Design the control circuit specified by the state diagram. You can use any method of control implementation discussed in Section 8-7.

Choose the method that minimizes the number of ICs. Verify the operation of the control circuit prior to its connection to the data processor.

Checking the Multiplier

Connect the outputs of the control circuit to the data processor and verify the total circuit operation by repeating the steps of multiplying 1111 by 1011. The single clock pulses should now sequence the control states as well (remove the manual switches). The start signal S can be generated with a switch that is on while the control is in state T_0.

Generate the start signal S with a pulser or any other short pulse and operate the multiplier with continuous clock pulses from a clock generator. Pressing the S pulser should initiate the multiplication operation and upon completion, the product should be displayed in the A and Q registers. Note that the multiplication will be repeated as long as signal S is enabled. Make sure that S goes back to 0, then set the switches to two other four-bit numbers and press S again. The new product should appear at the outputs. Repeat the multiplication of a few numbers to verify the operation of the circuit.

11-18   ASYNCHRONOUS SEQUENTIAL CIRCUITS

In this experiment, you will analyze and design asynchronous sequential circuits. These type of circuits are presented in Chapter 9.

Analysis Example

The analysis of asynchronous sequential circuits with SR latches is outlined in Section 9-3. Analyze the circuit of Fig. P9-9 (shown with Problem 9-9) by deriving the transition table and output map of the circuit. From the transition table and output map, determine: (a) what happens to output Q when input x_1 is a 1 irrespective of the value of input x_2; (b) what happens to output Q when input x_2 is a 1 and x_1 is equal to 0; and (c) what happens to output Q when both inputs go back to 0?

Connect the circuit and show that it operates according to the way you analyzed it.

Design Example

The circuit of a positive-edge-triggered D-type flip-flop is shown in Fig. 5-10. The circuit of a negative-edge T-type flip-flop is shown in Fig. 9-46. Using the six-step procedure recommended in Section 9-8, design, construct, and test a D-type flip-flop that triggers on both the positive and negative transitions of the clock. The circuit has two inputs—D and C—and a single output, Q. The value of D at the time C changes from 0 to 1 becomes the flip-flop output, Q. The output remains unchanged irrespective of the value of D as long as C remains at 1. On the next clock transition, the output is again updated to the value of D when C changes from 1 to 0. The output then remains unchanged as long as C remains at 0.

11-19   VERILOG HDL SIMULATION EXPERIMENTS

Some of the hardware experiments outlined in this chapter can be supplemented by a corresponding software procedure using the Verilog Hardware Description Language (HDL). A Verilog compiler and simulator is necessary for this supplement. The following are suggestions for simulating and testing some of the circuits used in the laboratory experiments.

Supplement to Experiment 2 (Section 11-2)

The various logic gates and their propagation delays were introduced in the hardware experiment. In Section 3-9, a simple circuit with gate delays was investigated. As an introduction to the laboratory Verilog program, compile the circuit described in HDL Example 3-3 and then run the simulator to verify the waveforms shown in Fig. 3-38.

Assign the following delays to the Exclusive-OR circuit shown in Fig. 3-32(a): 10 ns for an inverter, 20 ns for an AND gate, and 30 ns for an OR gate. The input of the circuit goes from $xy = 00$ to $xy = 01$.

(a) Determine the signals at the output of each gate from $t = 0$ to $t = 50$ ns.
(b) Write the HDL description of the circuit including the delays.
(c) Write a stimulus module (similar to HDL Example 3-3) and simulate the circuit to verify the answer in part (a).

Supplement to Experiment 4 (Section 11-4)

The operation of a combinational circuit is verified by checking the output and comparing it with the circuit truth table. HDL Example 4-10 (Section 4-11) demonstrates the procedure for obtaining the truth table of a combinational circuit by simulating it. In order to get acquainted with this procedure, compile and simulate HDL Example 4-10 and check the output truth table.

In Experiment 4, you designed a majority logic circuit. Write the HDL gate-level description of the majority logic circuit together with a stimulus for displaying the truth table. Compile and simulate the circuit and check the output response.

Supplement to Experiment 5 (Section 11-5)

This experiment deals with code conversion. A BCD-to-excess3 converter was designed in Section 4-3. Use the result of the design to check it with an HDL simulator.

(a) Write an HDL gate-level description of the circuit shown in Fig. 4-4.

(b) Write a dataflow description using the Boolean expressions listed in Fig. 4-3.

(c) Write an HDL behavioral description of a BCD-to-excess-3 converter.

(d) Write a test bench to simulate and test the BCD-to-excess-3 converter circuit in order to verify the truth table. Check all three circuits.

Supplement to Experiment 7 (Section 11-7)

A 4-bit adder-subtractor is developed in this experiment. An adder-subtractor circuit is also developed in Section 4-4.

(a) Write the HDL behavioral description of the 7483 4-bit adder.

(b) Write a behavioral description of the adder-subtractor circuit shown in Fig. 11-11.

(c) Write the HDL hierarchical description of the 4-bit adder-subtractor shown in Fig. 4-13 (including V). This can be done by instantiating a modified version of the 4-bit adder described in HDL Example 4-2 (Section 4-11).

(d) Write an HDL test bench to simulate and test the circuits of part (c). Check and verify the values that cause an overflow with $V = 1$.

Supplement to Experiment 8 (Section 11-8)

The edge-triggered D flip-flop 7474 is shown in Fig. 11-13. The flip-flop has asynchronous preset and clear inputs.

(a) Write an HDL behavioral description of the 7474 D flip-flop using only the Q output. (Note that when Preset $= 0$, Q goes to 1, and when Preset $= 1$ and Clear $= 0$, Q goes to 0. Thus, Preset takes precedence over Clear.)

(b) Write an HDL behavioral description of the 7474 D flip-flop using both outputs. Label the second output Q_not and note that this is not always the complement of Q. (When Preset $=$ Clear $= 0$, both Q and Q_not go to 1.)

Supplement to Experiment 9 (Section 11-9)

In the hardware experiment, you are asked to design and test a sequential circuit whose state diagram is given by Fig. 11-14. This is a Mealy model sequential circuit similar to the one described in HDL Example 5-5 (Section 5-5).

(a) Write the HDL description of the state diagram of Fig. 11-14.

(b) Write the HDL structural description of the sequential circuit obtained from the design (This is similar to HDL Example 5-7, in Section 5-5).

(c) Fig. 11-24(b) (Section 11-17) shows a control state diagram. Write the HDL description of the state diagram using the one-hot binary assignment (see Table 5-9 in Section 5-6) and three outputs, T_1, T_2, and T_3.

Supplement to Experiment 10 (Section 11-10)

The synchronous counter with parallel load IC type 74161 is shown in Fig. 11-15. This is similar to the one described in HDL Example 6-3 (Section 6-6) with two exceptions. The load input is enabled when equal to 0, and there are two inputs (P and T) that control the count. Write the HDL description of the 74161 IC.

Supplement to Experiment 11 (Section 11-11)

A bidirectional shift register with parallel load is designed in the experiment by using the 74195 and 74157 IC types.

(a) Write the HDL description of the 74195 shift register. Assume that inputs J and K (bar) are connected together to form the serial input.

(b) Write the HDL description of the 74157 multiplexer.

(c) Obtain the HDL description of the 4-bit bidirectional shift register that has been designed in this experiment. (1) Write the structural description by instantiating the two ICs and specifying their interconnection, and (2) write the behavioral description of the circuit using the function table that is derived in this design experiment.

Supplement to Experiment 13 (Section 11-13)

This experiment investigates the operation of a random-access memory (RAM). The way a memory is described in HDL is explained in Section 7-2 in conjunction with HDL Example 7-1.

(a) Write the HDL description of IC type 74189 RAM shown in Fig. 11-18.

(b) Test the operation of the memory by writing a stimulus program that stores binary 3 in address 0 and binary 1 in address 14. Then read the stored numbers from the two addresses to check if the numbers were stored correctly.

Supplement to Experiment 14 (Section 11-14)

Write the HDL behavioral description of the 74194 bidirectional shift register with parallel load shown in Fig. 11-19.

Supplement to Experiment 16 (Section 11-16)

A parallel adder with an accumulator register and a memory unit is shown in the block diagram of Fig. 11-23. Write the structural description of the circuit specified by the block diagram. The HDL structural description of this circuit can be obtained by instantiating the various components. An example of a structural description of a design can be found in HDL Example 8-4 in Section 8-5. First, it is necessary to write the behavioral description of each component. Use counter 74161 instead of 7493, and substitute the *D* flip-flop 7474 instead of the *JK* flip-flop 7476. The block diagram of the various components can be found from the list in Table 11-1.

Supplement to Experiment 17 (Section 11-17)

The block diagram of a 4-bit binary multiplier is shown in Fig. 11-24. The multiplier can be described in two ways: (1) using the register transfer level statements listed in part (b) of the figure or (2) using the block diagram shown in part (a) of the figure. The description of the multiplier in terms of the register transfer level (RTL) format is carried out in HDL Example 8-5 (Section 8-7). In this experiment we will use the integrated circuit components specified in the block diagram to write the HDL structural description of the binary multiplier. The structural description is obtained by using the module description of each component and then instantiating them to show how they are interconnected. (See Section 8-5 for an example.) The HDL descriptions of the components may be available from the solutions to previous experiments. 7483 is described with a solution to Experiment 7(a), 7474 with Experiment 8(a), 74161 with Experiment 10, 74194 with Experiment 14, and the description of the control is available from a solution to Experiment 9(c).

12

Standard
Graphic Symbols

12-1 RECTANGULAR-SHAPE SYMBOLS

Digital components such as gates, decoders, multiplexers, and registers are available commercially in integrated circuits and are classified as SSI or MSI circuits. Standard graphic symbols have been developed for these and other components so that the user can recognize each function from the unique graphic symbol assigned to it. This standard, known as ANSI/IEEE Std. 91–1984, has been approved by industry, government, and professional organizations and is consistent with international standards.

The standard uses a rectangular-shape outline to represent each particular logic function. Within the outline, there is a general qualifying symbol denoting the logical operation performed by the unit. For example, the general qualifying symbol for a multiplexer is MUX. The size of the outline is arbitrary and can be either a square or a rectangular shape with an arbitrary length-width ratio. Input lines are placed on the left and output lines are placed on the right. If the direction of signal flow is reversed, it must be indicated by arrows.

The rectangular-shape graphic symbols for SSI gates are shown in Fig. 12-1. The qualifying symbol for the AND gate is the ampersand (&). The OR gate has the qualifying symbol that designates greater than or equal to 1, indicating that at least one input must be active for the output to be active. The symbol for the buffer gate is 1, showing that only one input is present. The exclusive-OR symbol designates the fact that only one input must be active for the output to be active. The inclusion of the logic negation small circle in the output converts the gates to their complement values. Although the rectangular-shape symbols for the gates are recommended, the standard also recognizes the distinctive-shape symbols for the gates shown in Fig. 2-5.

An example of an MSI standard graphic symbol is the 4-bit parallel adder shown in Fig. 12-2. The qualifying symbol for an adder is the Greek letter Σ. The preferred letters for the arithmetic operands are P and Q. The bit-grouping symbols in the two types of inputs and the sum output

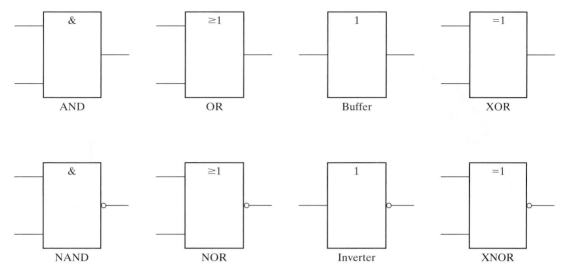

FIGURE 12-1
Rectangular-Shape Graphic Symbols for Gates

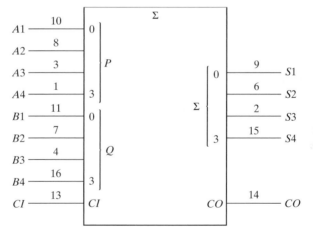

FIGURE 12-2
Standard Graphic Symbol for a 4-Bit Parallel Adder, IC Type 7483

are the decimal equivalents of the weights of the bits to the power of 2. Thus, the input labeled 3 corresponds to the value of $2^3 = 8$. The input carry is designated by CI and the output carry by CO. When the digital component represented by the outline is also a commercial integrated circuit, it is customary to write the IC pin number along each input and output. Thus, IC type 7483 is a 4-bit adder with look-ahead carry. It is enclosed in a package with 16 pins. The pin numbers for the nine inputs and five outputs are shown in Fig. 12-2. The other two pins are for the power supply.

Before introducing the graphic symbols of other components, it is necessary to review some terminology. As mentioned in Section 2-7, a positive-logic system defines the more positive of two signal levels (designated by H) as logic-1 and the more negative signal level (designated by L) as logic-0. Negative logic assumes the opposite assignment. A third alternative is to employ a mixed-logic convention, where the signals are considered entirely in terms of their H and L values. At any point in the circuit, the user is allowed to define the logic polarity by assigning logic-1 to either the H or L signal. The mixed-logic notation uses a small right-angle-triangle graphic symbol to designate a negative-logic polarity at any input or output terminal. (See Fig. 2-10(f).)

Integrated-circuit manufacturers specify the operation of integrated circuits in terms of H and L signals. When an input or output is considered in terms of positive logic, it is defined as *active-high*. When it is considered in terms of negative logic, it is defined as *active-low*. Active-low inputs or outputs are recognized by the presence of the small-triangle polarity-indicator symbol. When positive logic is used exclusively throughout the entire system, the small-triangle polarity symbol is equivalent to the small circle that designates negation. In this book, we have assumed positive logic throughout and employed the small circle when drawing logic diagrams. When an input or output line does not include the small circle, we define it to be active if it is logic-1. An input or output that includes the small-circle symbol is considered active if it is in the logic-0 state. However, we will use the small-triangle polarity symbol to indicate active-low assignment in all drawings that represent standard diagrams. This will conform with integrated-circuit data books, where the polarity symbol is usually employed. Note that the bottom four gates in Fig. 12-1 could have been drawn with a small triangle in the output lines instead of a small circle.

Another example of a graphic symbol for an MSI circuit is shown in Fig. 12-3. This is a 2-to-4-line decoder representing one-half of IC type 74155. Inputs are on the left and outputs on the right. The identifying symbol X/Y indicates that the circuit converts from code X to code Y. Data inputs A and B are assigned binary weights 1 and 2 equivalent to 2^0 and 2^1, respectively. The outputs are assigned numbers from 0 to 3, corresponding to outputs D_0 through D_3, respectively. The decoder has one active-low input E_1 and one active-high input E_2. These two inputs go through an internal AND gate to enable the decoder. The output of the AND gate is labeled EN (enable) and is activated when E_1 is at a low-level state and E_2 at a high-level state.

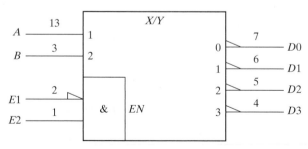

FIGURE 12-3

Standard Graphic Symbol for a 2-to-4-Line Decoder (one-half of IC type 74155)

12-2   QUALIFYING SYMBOLS

The IEEE standard graphic symbols for logic functions provides a list of qualifying symbols to be used in conjunction with the outline. A qualifying symbol is added to the basic outline to designate the overall logic characteristics of the element or the physical characteristics of an input or output. Table 12-1 lists some of the general qualifying symbols specified in the standard. A general qualifying symbol defines the basic function performed by the device represented in the diagram. It is placed near the top center position of the rectangular-shape outline. The general qualifying symbols for the gates, decoder, and adder were shown in previous diagrams. The other symbols are self-explanatory and will be used later in diagrams representing the corresponding digital elements.

Table 12-1
General Qualifying Symbols

Symbol	Description
&	AND gate or function
≥ 1	OR gate or function
1	Buffer gate or inverter
$=1$	Exclusive-OR gate or function
2k	Even function or even parity element
$2k + 1$	Odd function or odd parity element
X/Y	Coder, decoder, or code converter
MUX	Multiplexer
DMUX	Demultiplexer
Σ	Adder
Π	Multiplier
COMP	Magnitude comparator
ALU	Arithmetic logic unit
SRG	Shift register
CTR	Counter
RCTR	Ripple counter
ROM	Read-only memory
RAM	Random-access memory

Some of the qualifying symbols associated with inputs and outputs are shown in Fig. 12-4. Symbols associated with inputs are placed on the left side of the column labeled *symbol*. Symbols associated with outputs are placed on the right side of the column. The active-low input or output symbol is the polarity indicator. As mentioned previously, it is equivalent to the logic negation when positive logic is assumed. The dynamic input is associated with the clock input in flip-flop circuits. It indicates that the input is active on a transition from a low-to-high-level signal. The three-state output has a third high-impedance state, which has no logic significance. When the circuit is enabled, the output is in the normal 0 or 1 logic state, but when the circuit is disabled, the three-state output is in a high-impedance state. This state is equivalent to an open circuit.

The open-collector output has one state that exhibits a high-impedance condition. An externally connected resistor is sometimes required in order to produce the proper logic level.

Symbol	Description

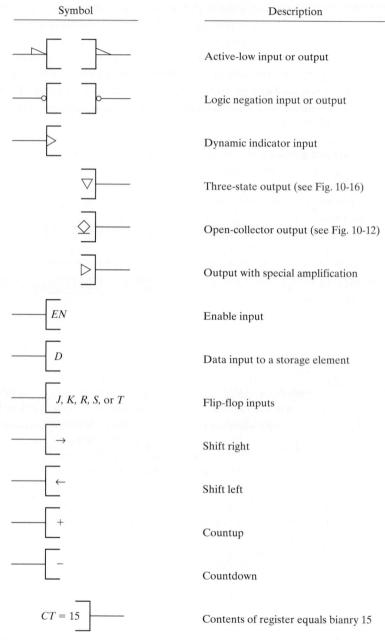

Active-low input or output

Logic negation input or output

Dynamic indicator input

Three-state output (see Fig. 10-16)

Open-collector output (see Fig. 10-12)

Output with special amplification

Enable input

Data input to a storage element

Flip-flop inputs

Shift right

Shift left

Countup

Countdown

Contents of register equals bianry 15

FIGURE 12-4
Qualifying Symbols Associated with Inputs and Outputs

The diamond-shape symbol may have a bar on top (for high type) or on the bottom (for low type). The high or low type specifies the logic level when the output is not in the high-impedance state. For example, TTL-type integrated circuits have special outputs called open-collector outputs. These outputs are recognized by a diamond-shape symbol with a bar under it. This indicates that the output can be either in a high-impedance state or in a low-level state. When used as part of a distribution function, two or more open-collector NAND gates when connected to a common resistor perform a positive-logic AND function or a negative-logic OR function.

The output with special amplification is used in gates that provide special driving capabilities. Such gates are employed in components such as clock drivers or bus-oriented transmitters. The *EN* symbol designates an enable input. It has the effect of enabling all outputs when it is active. When the input marked with *EN* is inactive, all outputs are disabled. The symbols for flip-flop inputs have the usual meaning. The *D* input is also associated with other storage elements such as memory input.

The symbols for shift right and shift left are arrows pointing to the right or the left, respectively. The symbols for count-up and count-down counters are the plus and minus symbols, respectively. An output designated by $CT = 15$ will be active when the contents of the register reach the binary count of 15. When nonstandard information is shown inside the outline, it is enclosed in square brackets [like this].

12-3   DEPENDENCY NOTATION

The most important aspect of the standard logic symbols is the dependency notation. Dependency notation is used to provide the means of denoting the relationship between different inputs or outputs without actually showing all the elements and interconnections between them. We will first demonstrate the dependency notation with an example of the AND dependency and then define all the other symbols associated with this notation.

The AND dependency is represented with the letter *G* followed by a number. Any input or output in a diagram that is labeled with the number associated with *G* is considered to be ANDed with it. For example, if one input in the diagram has the label *G* 1 and another input is labeled with the number 1, then the two inputs labeled *G* 1 and 1 are considered to be ANDed together internally.

An example of AND dependency is shown in Fig. 12-5. In (a), we have a portion of a graphic symbol with two AND dependency labels, *G* 1 and *G* 2. There are two inputs labeled with the number 1 and one input labeled with the number 2. The equivalent interpretation is shown in part (b) of the figure. Input *X* associated with *G* 1 is considered to be ANDed with inputs *A* and *B*, which are labeled with a 1. Similarly, input *Y* is ANDed with input *C* to conform with the dependency between *G* 2 and 2.

The standard defines 10 other dependencies. Each dependency is denoted by a letter symbol (except *EN*). The letter appears at the input or output and is followed by a number. Each

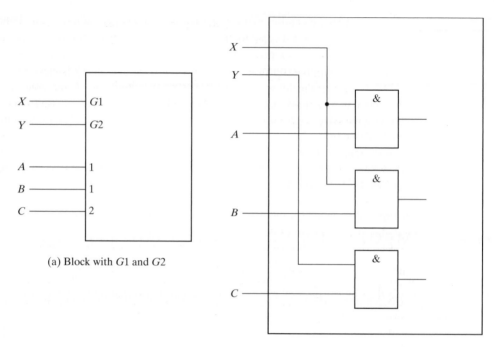

(a) Block with $G1$ and $G2$

(b) Equivalent interpretation

FIGURE 12-5
Example of G (AND) Dependency

input or output affected by that dependency is labeled with that same number. The 11 dependencies and their corresponding letter designation are as follows:

G Denotes an AND (gate) relationship

V Denotes an OR relationship

N Denotes a negate (exclusive-OR) relationship

EN Specifies an enable action

C Identifies a control dependency

S Specifies a setting action

R Specifies a resetting action

M Identifies a mode dependency

A Identifies an address dependency

Z Indicates an internal interconnection

X Indicates a controlled transmission

The V and N dependencies are used to denote the Boolean relationships of OR and exclusive-OR similar to the G that denotes the Boolean AND. The EN dependency is similar to the qualifying symbol EN except that a number follows it (for example, $EN\,2$). Only the outputs marked with that number are disabled when the input associated with EN is active.

The control dependency C is used to identify a clock input in a sequential element and to indicate which input is controlled by it. The set S and reset R dependencies are used to specify internal logic states of an SR flip-flop. The C, S, and R dependencies are explained in Section 12-5 in conjunction with the flip-flop circuit. The mode M dependency is used to identify inputs that select the mode of operation of the unit. The mode dependency is presented in Section 12-6 in conjunction with registers and counters. The address A dependency is used to identify the address input of a memory. It is introduced in Section 12-8 in conjunction with the memory unit.

The Z dependency is used to indicate interconnections inside the unit. It signifies the existence of internal logic connections between inputs, outputs, internal inputs, and internal outputs, in any combination. The X dependency is used to indicate the controlled transmission path in a CMOS transmission gate.

12-4   SYMBOLS FOR COMBINATIONAL ELEMENTS

The examples in this section and the rest of this chapter illustrate the use of the standard in representing various digital components with graphic symbols. The examples demonstrate actual commercial integrated circuits with the pin numbers included in the inputs and outputs. Most of the ICs presented in this chapter are included with the suggested experiments outlined in Chapter 11.

The graphic symbols for the adder and decoder were shown in Section 12-2. IC type 74155 can be connected as a 3 $\times$ 8 decoder, as shown in Fig. 12-6. (The truth table of this decoder is shown in Fig. 11-7.) There are two C and two G inputs in the IC. Each pair must be connected together as shown in the diagram. The enable input is active when in the low-level state. The outputs are all active-low. The inputs are assigned binary weights 1, 2, and 4, equivalent to 2^0, 2^1 and 2^2, respectively. The outputs are assigned numbers from 0 to 7. The sum of the weights of the inputs determines the output that is active. Thus, if the two input lines with weights 1 and 4 are activated, the total weight is $1 + 4 = 5$ and output 5 is activated. Of course, the EN input must be activated for any output to be active.

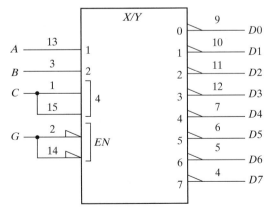

FIGURE 12-6
IC Type 74155 Connected as a 3 $\times$ 8 Decoder

The decoder is a special case of a more general component referred to as a *coder*. A coder is a device that receives an input binary code on a number of inputs and produces a different binary code on a number of outputs. Instead of using the qualifying symbol X/Y, the coder can be specified by the code name. For example, the 3-to-8-line decoder of Fig. 12-6 can be symbolized with the name *BIN/OCT* since the circuit converts a 3-bit binary number into 8 octal values, 0 through 7.

Before showing the graphic symbol for the multiplexer, it is necessary to show a variation of the AND dependency. The AND dependency is sometimes represented by a shorthand notation like $G\frac{0}{7}$. This symbol stands for eight AND dependency symbols from 0 to 7 as follows:

$$G0, G1, G2, G3, G4, G5, G6, G7$$

At any given time, only one out of the eight AND gates can be active. The active AND gate is determined from the inputs associated with the G symbol. These inputs are marked with weights equal to the powers of 2. For the eight AND gates just listed, the weights are 0, 1, and 2, corresponding to the numbers 2^0, 2^1, and 2^2, respectively. The AND gate that is active at any given time is determined from the sum of the weights of the active inputs. Thus, if inputs 0 and 2 are active, then the AND gate that is active has the number $2^0 + 2^2 = 5$. This makes $G5$ active and the other seven AND gates inactive.

The standard graphic symbol for a 8 × 1 multiplexer is shown in Fig. 12-7(a). The qualifying symbol MUX identifies the device as a multiplexer. The symbols inside the block are part

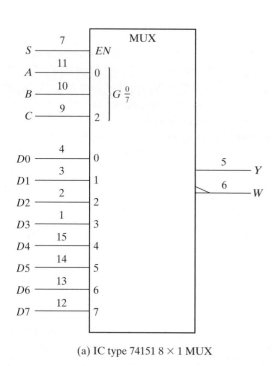

(a) IC type 74151 8 × 1 MUX

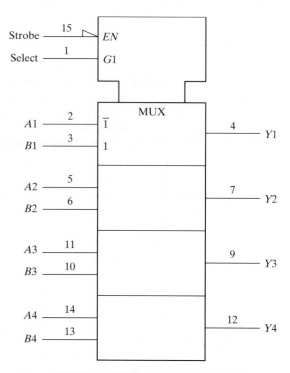

(b) IC type 74157 quadruple 2 × 1 MUX

FIGURE 12-7
Graphic Symbols for Multiplexers

of the standard notation, but the symbols marked outside are user-defined symbols. The function table of the 741551 IC can be found in Fig. 11-9. The AND dependency is marked with G_7^0 and is associated with the inputs enclosed in brackets. These inputs have weights of 0, 1, and 2. They are actually what we have called the selection inputs. The eight data inputs are marked with numbers from 0 to 7. The net weight of the active inputs associated with the G symbol specifies the number in the data input that is active. For example, if selection inputs $CBA = 110$, then inputs 1 and 2 associated with G are active. This gives a numerical value for the AND dependency of $2^2 + 2^1 = 6$, which makes $G6$ active. Since $G6$ is ANDed with data input number 6, it makes this input active. Thus, the output will be equal to data input D_6 provided that the enable input is active.

Fig.12-7(b) represents the quadruple 2×1 multiplexer IC type 74157 whose function table is listed in Fig. 11-17. The enable and selection inputs are common to all four multiplexers. This is indicated in the standard notation by the indented box at the top of the diagram, which represents a *common control block*. The inputs to a common control block control all lower sections of the diagram. The common enable input EN is active when in the low-level state. The AND dependency, $G1$, determines which input is active in each multiplexer section. When $G1 = 0$, the A inputs marked with $\overline{1}$ are active. When $G1 = 1$, the B inputs marked with 1 are active. The active inputs are applied to the corresponding outputs if EN is active. Note that the input symbols $\overline{1}$ and 1 are marked in the upper section only instead of repeating them in each section.

12-5   SYMBOLS FOR FLIP-FLOPS

The standard graphic symbols for different types of flip-flops are shown in Fig. 12-8. A flip-flop is represented by a rectangular-shaped block with inputs on the left and outputs on the right. One output designates the normal state of the flip-flop and the other output with a small-circle negation symbol (or polarity indicator) designates the complement output. The graphic symbols distinguish between three types of flip-flops: the D latch, whose internal construction is shown in Fig. 6-5; the master-slave flip-flop, shown in Fig. 6-9; and the edge-triggered flip-flop, introduced in Fig. 6-12. The graphic symbol for the D latch or D flip-flop has inputs D and C indicated inside the block. The graphic symbol for the JK flip-flop has inputs J, K, and C inside. The notation $C1$, $1D$, $1J$, and $1K$ are examples of control dependency. The input in $C1$ controls input $1D$ in a D flip-flop and inputs $1J$ and $1K$ in a JK flip-flop.

The D latch has no other symbols besides the $1D$ and $C1$ inputs. The edge-triggered flip-flop has an arrowhead-shaped symbol in front of the control dependency $C1$ to designate a dynamic input. The dynamic indicator symbol denotes that the flip-flop responds to the positive-edge transition of the input clock pulses. A small circle outside the block along the dynamic indicator designates a negative-edge transition for triggering the flip-flop. The master–slave is considered to be a pulse-triggered flip-flop and is indicated as such with an upside-down L symbol in front of the outputs. This is to show that the output signal changes on the falling edge of the pulse. Note that the master–slave flip-flop is drawn without the dynamic indicator.

Flip-flops available in integrated-circuit packages provide special inputs for setting and resetting the flip-flop asynchronously. These inputs are usually called direct set and direct reset. They affect the output on the negative level of the signal without the need of a clock. The graphic symbol of a master–slave JK flip-flop with direct set and reset is shown in Fig. 12-9(a).

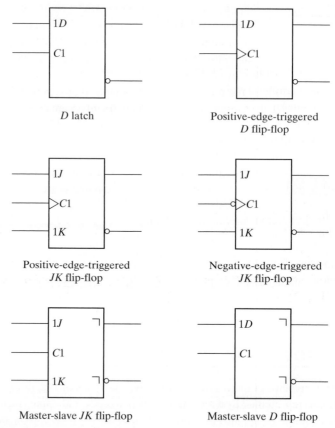

D latch

Positive-edge-triggered
D flip-flop

Positive-edge-triggered
JK flip-flop

Negative-edge-triggered
JK flip-flop

Master-slave JK flip-flop

Master-slave D flip-flop

FIGURE 12-8
Standard Graphic Symbols for Flip-Flops

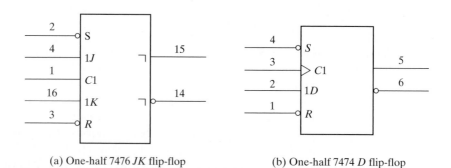

(a) One-half 7476 JK flip-flop

(b) One-half 7474 D flip-flop

FIGURE 12-9
IC Flip-Flops with Direct Set and Reset

The notations $C1$, $1J$, and $1K$ represent control dependency, showing that the clock input at $C1$ controls inputs $1J$ and $1K$. S and R have no 1 in front of the letters and, therefore, they are not controlled by the clock at $C1$. The S and R inputs have a small circle along the input lines to indicate that they are active when in the logic-0 level. The function table for the 7476 flip-flop is shown in Fig. 11-12.

The graphic symbol for a positive-edge-triggered D flip-flop with direct set and reset is shown in Fig. 12-9(b). The positive-edge transition of the clock at input $C1$ controls input $1D$. The S and R inputs are independent of the clock. This is IC type 7474, whose function table is listed in Fig. 11-13.

12-6 SYMBOLS FOR REGISTERS

The standard graphic symbol for a register is equivalent to the symbol used for a group of flip-flops with a common clock input. Fig. 12-10 shows the standard graphic symbol of IC type 74175, consisting of four D flip-flops with common clock and clear inputs. The clock input $C1$ and the clear input R appear in the common control block. The inputs to the common control block are connected to each of the elements in the lower sections of the diagram. The notation $C1$ is the control dependency that controls all the $1D$ inputs. Thus, each flip-flop is triggered

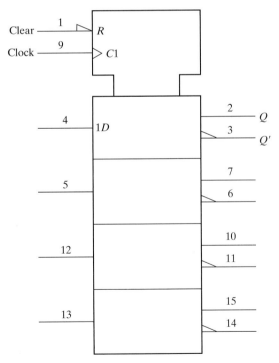

FIGURE 12-10
Graphic Symbol for a 4-Bit Register, IC Type 74175

by the common clock input. The dynamic input symbol associated with $C1$ indicates that the flip-flops are triggered on the positive edge of the input clock. The common R input resets all flip-flops when its input is at a low-level state. The $1D$ symbol is placed only once in the upper section instead of repeating it in each section. The complement outputs of the flip-flops in this diagram are marked with the polarity symbol rather than the negation symbol.

The standard graphic symbol for a shift register with parallel load is shown in Fig. 12-11. This is IC type 74195, whose function table can be found in Fig. 11-16. The qualifying symbol for a shift register is SRG followed by a number that designates the number of stages. Thus, $SRG4$ denotes a 4-bit shift register. The common control block has two mode dependencies, $M1$ and $M2$, for the shift and load operations, respectively. Note that the IC has a single input labeled SH/LD (shift/load), which is split into two lines to show the two modes. $M1$ is active when the SH/LD input is high and $M2$ is active when the SH/LD input is low. $M2$ is recognized as active-low from the polarity indicator along its input line. Note the convention in this symbology: we must recognize that a single input actually exists in pin 9, but it is split into two parts in order to assign to it the two modes, $M1$ and $M2$. The control dependency $C3$ is for the clock input. The dynamic symbol along the $C3$ input indicates that the flip-flops trigger on the positive edge of the clock. The symbol $/1 \rightarrow$ following $C3$ indicates that the register shifts to the right or in the downward direction when mode $M1$ is active.

The four sections below the common control block represent the four flip-flops. Flip-flop QA has three inputs: two are associated with the serial (shift) operation and one with the parallel

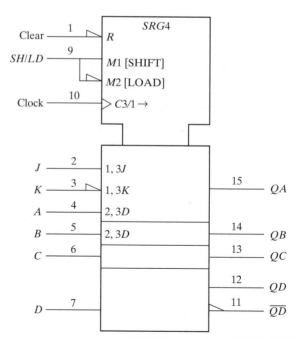

FIGURE 12-11
Graphic Symbol for a Shift Register with Parallel Load, IC Type 74195

(load) operation. The serial input label 1, 3 J indicates that the J input of flip-flop QA is active when $M1$ (shift) is active and $C3$ goes through a positive clock transition. The other serial input with label 1, 3 K has a polarity symbol in its input line corresponding to the complement of input K in a JK flip-flop. The third input of QA and the inputs of the other flip-flops are for the parallel input data. Each input is denoted by the label 2, 3 D. The 2 is for $M2$ (load), and 3 is for the clock $C3$. If the input in pin number 9 is in the low level, $M1$ is active. and a positive transition of the clock at $C3$ causes a parallel transfer from the four inputs, A through D, into the four flip-flops, QA through QD. Note that the parallel input is labeled only in the first and second sections. It is assumed to be in the other two sections below.

Fig. 12-12 shows the graphic symbol for the bidirectional shift register with parallel load, IC type 74194. The function table for this IC is listed in Fig. 11-19. The common control block shows an R input for resetting all flip-flops to 0 asynchronously. The mode select has two inputs and the mode dependency M may take binary values from 0 to 3. This is indicated by the symbol $M\frac{0}{3}$, which stands for $M0, M1, M2, M3$, and is similar to the notation for the G dependency in multiplexers. The symbol associated with the clock is

$$C4/1 \rightarrow \quad /2 \leftarrow$$

$C4$ is the control dependency for the clock. The $/1 \rightarrow$ symbol indicates that the register shifts right (down in this case) when the mode is $M1$ $(S_1 S_0 = 01)$. The $/2 \leftarrow$ symbol indicates that the register shifts left (up in this case) when the mode is M_2 $(S_1 S_0 = 10)$. The right and left directions are obtained when the page is turned 90 degrees counterclockwise.

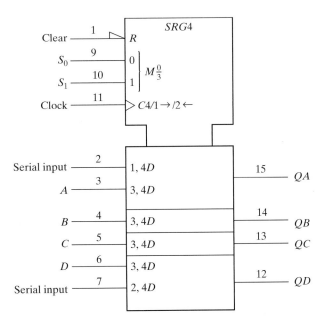

FIGURE 12-12

Graphic Symbol for a Bidirectional Shift Register with Parallel Load, IC Type 74194

The sections below the common control block represent the four flip-flops. The first flip-flop has a serial input for shift right, denoted by $1, 4D$ (mode $M1$, clock $C4$, input D). The last flip-flop has a serial input for shift left, denoted by $2, 4D$ (mode $M2$, clock $C4$, input D). All four flip-flops have a parallel input denoted by the label $3, 4D$ (mode $M3$, clock $C4$, input D). Thus, $M3$ $(S_1 S_0 = 11)$ is for parallel load. The remaining mode $M0$ $(S_1 S_0 = 00)$ has no effect on the outputs because it is not included in the input labels.

12-7   SYMBOLS FOR COUNTERS

The standard graphic symbol of a binary ripple counter is shown in Fig. 12-13. The qualifying symbol for a ripple counter is $RCTR$. The designation $DIV2$ stands for the divide-by-2 circuit that is obtained from the single flip-flop QA. The $DIV8$ designation is for the divide-by-8 counter obtained from the other three flip-flops. The diagram represents IC type 7493, whose internal circuit diagram is shown in Fig. 11-2. The common control block has an internal AND gate, with inputs $R1$ and $R2$. When both of these inputs are equal to 1, the content of the counter goes to zero. This is indicated by the symbol $CT = 0$. Since the count input does not go to the clock inputs of all flip-flops, it has no $C1$ label and, instead, the symbol $+$ is used to indicate a count-up operation. The dynamic symbol next to the $+$ together with the polarity symbol along the input line signify that the count is affected with a negative-edge transition of the input signal. The bit grouping from 0 to 2 in the output represents values for the weights to the power of 2. Thus, 0 represents the value of $2^0 = 1$ and 2 represents the value $2^2 = 4$.

The standard graphic symbol for the 4-bit counter with parallel load, IC type 74161, is shown in Fig. 12-14. The qualifying symbol for a synchronous counter is CTR followed by the symbol $DIV16$ (divide by 16), which gives the cycle length of the counter. There is a single

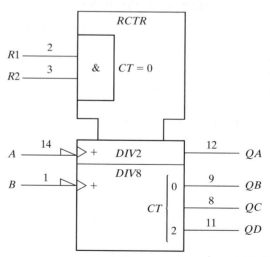

FIGURE 12-13
Graphic Symbol for Ripple Counter, IC Type 7493

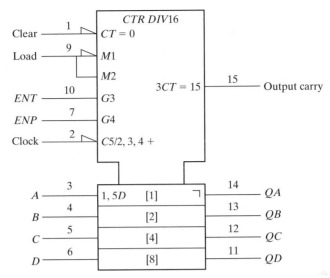

FIGURE 12-14
Graphic Symbol for 4-Bit Binary Counter with Parallel Load, IC Type 74161

load input at pin 9 that is split into the two modes, $M1$ and $M2$. $M1$ is active when the load input at pin 9 is low and $M2$ is active when the load input at pin 9 is high. $M1$ is recognized as active-low from the polarity indicator along its input line. The count-enable inputs use the G dependencies. $G3$ is associated with the T input and $G4$ with the P input of the count enable. The label associated with the clock is

$$C5/2, 3, 4 \ +$$

This means that the circuit counts up (the + symbol) when $M2$, $G3$, and $G4$ are active (load = 1, $ENT = 1$, and $ENP = 1$) and the clock in $C5$ goes through a positive transition. This condition is specified in the function table of the 74161 listed in Fig. 11-15. The parallel inputs have the label $1, 5D$, meaning that the D inputs are active when $M1$ is active (load = 0) and the clock goes through a positive transition. The output carry is designated by the label

$$3CT = 15$$

This is interpreted to mean that the output carry is active (equal to 1) if $G3$ is active ($ENT = 1$) and the content (CT) of the counter is 15 (binary 1111). Note that the outputs have an inverted L symbol, indicating that all the flip-flops are of the master–slave type. The polarity symbol in the $C5$ input designates an inverted pulse for the input clock. This means that the master is triggered on the negative transition of the clock pulse and the slave changes state on the positive transition. Thus, the output changes on the positive transition of the clock pulse. It should be noted that IC type 74LS161 (low-power Schottky version) has positive-edge-triggered flip-flops.

12-8   SYMBOL FOR RAM

The standard graphic symbol for the random-access memory (RAM) 74189 is shown in Fig. 12-15. The numbers 16×4 that follow the qualifying symbol RAM designate the number of words and the number of bits per word. The common control block is shown with four address lines and two control inputs. Each bit of the word is shown in a separate section with an input and output data line. The address dependency A is used to identify the address inputs of the memory. Data inputs and outputs affected by the address are labeled with the letter A. The bit grouping from 0 through 3 provides the binary address that ranges from $A0$ through $A15$. The inverted triangle signifies three-state outputs. The polarity symbol specifies the inversion of the outputs.

The operation of the memory is specified by means of the dependency notation. The RAM graphic symbol uses four dependencies: A (address), G (AND), EN (enable), and C (control). Input $G1$ is to be considered ANDed with $1EN$ and $1C2$ because $G1$ has a 1 after the letter G and the other two have a 1 in their label. The EN dependency is used to identify an enable input that controls the data outputs. The dependency $C2$ controls the inputs as indicated by the $2D$ label. Thus, for a write operation, we have the $G1$ and $1C2$ dependency ($CS = 0$), the $C2$ and $2D$ dependency ($WE = 0$), and the A dependency, which specifies the binary address in the four address inputs. For a read operation, we have the $G1$ and $1EN$ dependencies ($CS = 0, WE = 1$) and the A dependency for the outputs. The interpretation of these dependencies results in the operation of the memory as listed in the function table of Fig. 11-18.

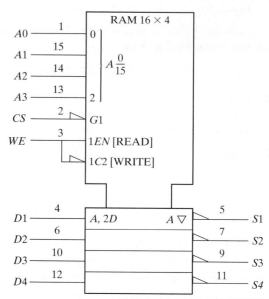

FIGURE 12-15
Graphic Symbol for 16×4 RAM, IC Type 74189

PROBLEMS

12-1 Figure 11-1 shows various small-scale integration circuits with pin assignment. Using this information, draw the rectangular-shaped graphic symbols for the 7400, 7404, and 7486 ICs.

12-2 Define the following in your own words:

(a) Positive and negative logic.   (b) Active-high and active-low.

(c) Polarity indicator.   (d) Dynamic indicator.

(e) Dependency notation.

12-3 Show an example of a graphic symbol that has the three Boolean dependencies—G, V, and N. Draw the equivalent interpretation.

12-4 Draw the graphic symbol of a BCD-to-decimal decoder. This is similar to a decoder with 4 inputs and 10 outputs.

12-5 Draw the graphic symbol for a binary-to-octal decoder with three enable inputs, $E1$, $E2$, and $E3$. The circuit is enabled if $E1 = 1$, $E2 = 0$, and $E3 = 0$ (assuming positive logic).

12-6 Draw the graphic symbol of dual 4-to-1-line multiplexers with common selection inputs and a separate enable input for each multiplexer.

12-7 Draw the graphic symbol for the following flip-flops:

(a) Negative-edge-triggered D flip-flop.   (b) Master–slave RS flip-flop.

(c) Positive-edge-triggered T flip-flop.

12-8 Explain the function of the common control block when used with the standard graphic symbols.

12-9 Draw the graphic symbol of a 4-bit register with parallel load using the label $M1$ for the load input and $C2$ for the clock.

12-10 Explain all the symbols used in the standard graphic diagram of Fig. 12-12.

12-11 Draw the graphic symbol of an up–down synchronous binary counter with mode input (for up or down) and count-enable input with G dependency. Show the output carries for the up count and the down count.

12-12 Draw the graphic symbol of a 256×1 RAM. Include the symbol for three-state outputs.

REFERENCES

1. 1984. *IEEE Standard Graphic Symbols for Logic Functions* (ANSI/IEEE Std. 91-1984). New York: Institute of Electrical and Electronics Engineers.

2. KAMPEL, I. 1985. *A Practical Introduction to the New Logic Symbols.* Boston: Butterworth.

3. MANN, F. A. 1984. *Explanation of New Logic Symbols.* Dallas: Texas Instruments.

4. 1985. *The TTL Data Book,* Volume 1. Dallas: Texas Instruments.

ANSWERS TO SELECTED PROBLEMS

CHAPTER 1

1-2   **(a)**   32,768   **(b)**   67,108,864   **(c)**   6,871,947,674

1-4 $(4310)_5 = 580$ $(198)_{12} = 260$

1-5   **(a)**   6   **(b)**   8   **(c)**   11

1-6   8

1-7   22.3125 (all three)

1-9   64276 octal

1-12   **(a)**   10000 and 110111   **(b)**   62 and 958

1-19   **(a)**   010627   **(b)**   009025   **(c)**   990975   **(d)**   989373

1-23

6	3	1	1	Decimal
0	0	0	0	0
0	0	0	1	1
0	0	1	1	2
0	1	0	0	3
0	1	1	0	4 (*or* 0101)
0	1	1	1	5
1	0	0	0	6
1	0	1	0	7 (*or* 1001)
1	0	1	1	8
1	1	0	0	9

1-28   Jane Doe

1-30 $62 + 32 = 94$ printing characters

1-31   bit 6 from the right

1-32   **(a)** 897   **(b)** 564   **(c)** 871   **(d)** 2,199

CHAPTER 2

2-2   **(a)** x **(b)** x **(c)** y **(d)** 0

2-3   **(a)** B **(b)** $z(x + y)$ **(c)** $x'y'$ **(d)** $x(w + y)$ **(e)** 0

2-4   **(a)** $AB + C'$ **(b)** $x + y + z$ **(c)** B **(d)** $A'(B + C'D)$

2-6   **(a)** $xy + x'y'$

2-8 $F(x, y, z) = \Sigma(1, 4, 5, 6, 7)$

2-9   **(a)** 10001100   **(c)** 00100011   **(d)** 01010010

2-11   **(b)** $(x' + y')' + (x + y)' + (y + z')'$

2-12 $T_1 = A'(B' + C')$
       $T_2 = A + BC = T_1'$

2-14   **(a)** $\Sigma(3, 5, 6, 7) = \Pi(0, 1, 2, 4)$

2-15   **(c)** $F = y'z + y(w + x)$

2-16 $\Sigma(1, 3, 5, 7, 9, 11, 13, 15) = \Pi(0, 2, 4, 6, 8, 10, 12, 14)$

2-19   **(a)** $AB + BC = (A + C)B$ **(b)** $x' + y + z'$

CHAPTER 3

3-1   **(a)** $xy + x'z'$ **(b)** $C' + A'B$ **(c)** $a' + bc$ **(d)** $xy + xz + yz$

3-2   **(a)** $x'y' + xz$ **(b)** $y + x'z$

3-3   **(a)** $xy + x'z'$ **(b)** $x' + yz$ **(c)** $C' + A'B$

3-4   **(a)** y **(b)** $BCD + A'BD'$ **(c)** $ABD + ABC + CD$ **(d)** $wx + w'x'y$

3-5   **(a)** $xz' + w'y'z + wxy$ **(d)** $BD + B'D' + A'B$ or $BD + B'D' + A'D'$

3-6   **(a)** $B'D' + A'BD + ABC'$ **(b)** $xy' + x'z + wx'y$

3-7   **(a)** $x'y + z$ **(c)** $AC + B'D' + A'BD + B'C$ (or CD)

3-8   **(a)** $F(x, y, z) = \Sigma(3, 5, 6, 7)$ **(b)** $F(A, B, C, D) = \Sigma(1, 3, 5, 9, 12, 13, 14)$

3-9   **(a)** Essential: xz and $x'z'$; Nonessential: $w'x$ and $w'z'$
       (b) $F = B'D' + AC + A'BD + (CD$ **or** $B'C)$

3-10   **(c)** $F = BC' + AC + A'B'D$
       Essential: BC', AC
       Nonessential: AB, $A'B'D$, $B'CD$, $A'C'D$

3-11   **(a)** $F = A'B'D' + AD'E + B'C'D'$

3-12   **(b)** $F = (A + D')(B' + D')$

3-13   **(a)** $F = xy + z' = (x + z')(y + z')$

3-15   **(b)** $F = B'D' + CD' + ABC'D = \Sigma(0, 2, 6, 8, 10, 13, 14)$

3-17 $F' = BD + BC + AC$

3-19   **(a)** $F = (w + z')(x' + z')(w' + x' + y')$

3-30 $F = (A \oplus B)(C \oplus D)$

3-35   Line 1: Dash not allowed, use underscore: Exmpl_3.
                      Needs semicolon at the end(;).

           Line 2: inputs should be input (no s at the end).
                      Last comma (,) change to semicolon (;).

           Line 3: No capitals in "Output", change to "output".

           Line 4: "A" cannot be output (defined as input).
                      "D" cannot be input (defined as output).

           Line 5: Too many entries for the not gate (only two allowed).

           Line 6: OR must be in lowercase: change to "or".

           Line 7: Remove semicolon (no semicolon after endmodule).

CHAPTER 4

4-1   **(a)** $F_1 = A + B'C + BD' + B'D$
                    $F_2 = A'B + D$

4-2 $F = ABC + A'D$
           $G = ABC + A'D'$

4-3   **(b)**   1024 rows and 14 columns

4-4 $F = x'y' + x'z'$

4-6 $F = xy + xz + yz$

4-7 $w = A \qquad x = A \oplus B \qquad y = x \oplus C \qquad z = y \oplus D$

4-8 $w = AB + AC'D'$

4-10   Inputs: A, B, C, D;   Outputs: w, x, y, z
           $z = D$
           $y = C \oplus D$
           $x = B \oplus (C + D)$
           $w = A \oplus (B + C + D)$

4-12   **(b)** $D = x \oplus y \oplus z$
                      $B = x'y + x'z + yz$

4-13

	Sum	C	V
(a)	1101	0	1
(b)	0001	1	1
(c)	0100	1	0
(d)	1011	0	1
(e)	1111	0	0

4-14   60 ns

4-18
$w = A'B'C'$
$x = B \oplus C$
$y = C$
$z = D'$

4-22
$w = AB + ACD$
$x = B'C' + B'D' + BCD$
$y = C'D + CD'$
$z = D'$

4-28
$F_1 = \Sigma(0, 5, 7)$
$F_2 = \Sigma(2, 3, 4)$
$F_3 = \Sigma(1, 6, 7)$

4-29
$x = D_0'D_1'$
$y = D_0'D_1 + D_0'D_2'$

4-34 $F(A, B, C, D) = \Sigma(1, 6, 7, 9, 10, 11, 12)$

4-35
When $AB = 00$, $F = D$
When $AB = 01$, $F = (C + D)'$
When $AB = 10$, $F = CD$
When $AB = 11$, $F = 1$

4-39

```
module Compare (A,B,Y);
input [3:0] A,B; //4-bit data inputs.
output [5:0] Y;  //6-bit comparator ouput.
reg [5:0] Y;     //EQ,NE,GT,LT,GE,LE
always @ (A or B)
      if (A==B)     Y = 6'b100011; //EQ,GE,LE
 else if (A < B)    Y = 6'b010101; //NE,LT,LE
      else          Y = 6'b011010; //NE,GT,GE
endmodule
```

4-42   (c)

```
module Convrt_bhv (BCD, EXS3);
input [4:1] BCD;
output [4:1] EXS3;
reg [4:1] EXS3;
   always @ (BCD)
      EXS3 = BCD + 4'b0011;
endmodule
```

CHAPTER 5

5-4   **(b)** $PQ' + NQ$

5-7 $S = x \oplus y \oplus Q$
$Q(t + 1) = xy + xQ + yQ$

5-8   A counter with a repeated sequence of 00, 01, 10

5-9   **(a)** $A(t + 1) = xA' + AB$
$B(t + 1) = xB' + A'B$

5-10   **(c)** $A(t + 1) = xB + x'A + yA + y'A'B'$
$B(t + 1) = xA'B' + x'A'B + yA'B'$

5-11   Present state: 00 00 01 00 01 11 00 01 11 10 00 01 11 10 10
Input: 0 1 0 1 1 0 1 1 1 0 1 1 1 1 0
Output: 0 0 1 0 0 1 0 0 0 1 0 0 0 0 1
Next state: 00 01 00 01 11 00 01 11 10 00 01 11 10 10 00

5-12

Present state	Next state 0	1	Output 0	1
a	f	b	0	0
b	d	a	0	0
d	g	a	1	0
f	f	b	1	1
g	g	d	0	1

5-13   **(a)**   State: $a\,f\,b\,c\,e\,d\,g\,h\,g\,g\,h\,a$
Input: 0 1 1 1 0 0 1 0 0 1 1
Output: 0 1 0 0 0 1 1 1 0 1 0

(b)   State: $a\,f\,b\,a\,b\,d\,g\,d\,g\,g\,d\,a$
Input: 0 1 1 1 0 0 1 0 0 1 1
Output: 0 1 0 0 0 1 1 1 0 1 0

5-15 $D_Q = Q'J + QK'$

5-16 $D_A = Ax' + Bx$
$D_B = A'x + Bx'$

5-18 $J_A = K_A = (Bx + B'x')E$
$J_B = K_B = E$

5-19   **(a)** $D_A = A'B'x$
$D_B = A + C'x' + BCx$
$D_C = Cx' + Ax + A'B'x'$
$y = A'x$

5-23   **(a)**   RegA = 125,   RegB = 125

(b)   RegA = 125,   RegB = 30

5-26 $Q(t + 1) = JQ' + K'Q$
When $Q = 0, Q(t + 1) = J$
When $Q = 1, Q(t + 1) = K'$

```
always @ (posedge CLK)
    if (Q==0) Q = J;
    else Q = ~K;
```

5-30 Two flip-flops E and Q with CLK.
AND gate with inputs A and B goes to the D input of E.
OR gate with inputs E and C goes to the D input of Q.
If the statements use blocking assignment with the symbol (=), then flip-flop Q should be pictured with its D input connected not to C + E, but to C + AB (one AND gate and one OR gate).

CHAPTER 6

6-4 1110; 0111; 1011; 1101; 0110; 1011

6-8 $A = 0010, 0001, 1000, 1100.$ Carry $= 1, 1, 1, 0$

6-9 **(b)** $J_Q = x'y; K_Q = (x' + y)'$

6-14 **(a)** 4; **(b)** 9; **(c)** 10

6-15 50 ns; 20 MHz

6-16 $1010 \rightarrow 1011 \rightarrow 0100$
$1100 \rightarrow 1101 \rightarrow 0100$
$1110 \rightarrow 1111 \rightarrow 0000$

6-17 $D_{A0} = A_0 \oplus E$
$D_{A1} = A_1 \oplus (A_0 E)$
$D_{A2} = A_2 \oplus (A_1 A_0 E)$
$D_{A3} = A_3 \oplus (A_2 A_1 A_0 E)$

6-19 **(b)** $D_{Q1} = Q_1'$
$D_{Q2} = Q_2 Q_1' + Q_8' Q_2' Q_1$
$D_{Q4} = Q_4 Q_1' + Q_4 Q_2' + Q_4' Q_2 Q_1$
$D_{Q8} = Q_8 Q_1' + Q_4 Q_2 Q_1$

6-21 $J_{A0} = LI_0 + L'C$
$K_{A0} = LI_0' + L'C$

6-24 $T_A = A \oplus B$
$T_B = B \oplus C$
$T_C = AC + A'C'$ (not self-starting)
$\quad = AC + A'B'C$ (self-starting)

6-26 Use a 2-bit counter

6-28 $D_A = A \oplus B$
$D_B = AB' + C$
$D_C = A'B'C'$

6-34

```
module Shiftreg (SI,SO,CLK);
   input SI,CLK;
   output SO;
   reg [3:0] Q;
   assign SO = Q[0];
   always @ (posedge CLK)
     Q = {SI,Q[3:1]};
endmodule
```

6-36   **(a)**

```
module updown (Up,Down,Load,IN,OUT,CLK);
   input Up,Down,Load,CLK;
   input [3:0] IN;
   output [3:0] OUT;
   reg [3:0] OUT;
   always @ (posedge CLK)
     if (Load) OUT = IN;
     else if (Up) OUT = OUT + 4'b0001;
     else if(Down)OUT = OUT -  4'b0001;
     else OUT = OUT;
endmodule
```

CHAPTER 7

7-2   **(a)** 2^{13} **(b)** 2^{31} **(c)** 2^{26} **(d)** 2^{21}

7-3   Address: 10 1101 0011 = 2D3 (hex)
Data: 0000 1101 0111 1011 = 0E7B (hex)

7-7   **(a)** 7×128 decoders, 256 AND gates   **(b)** $x = 46; y = 112$

7-8   **(a)** 8 chips   **(b)** 18; 15   **(c)** 3×8 decoder

7-10   0001 1011 1011 1

7-11   101 110 011 001 010

7-12   **(a)** 0101 1010;   **(b)** 1100 0110;   **(c)** 1111 0100

7-13   **(a)** 6   **(b)** 7   **(c)** 7

7-14   **(a)** 0101010

7-16   24 pins

7-18   **(a)** 256×8 **(b)** 512×5 **(c)** 1024×4 **(d)** 32×7

7-20   Product terms: yz', xz', $x'y'z$, xy', $x'y$, z

7-24 $A = yz' + xz' + x'y'z$
$B = x'y' + xy + yz$
$C = A + xyz$
$D = z + x'y$

CHAPTER 8

8-1   **(a)**   The transfer and increment occur at the same clock edge. After the transfer, the content of R2 is one more than the content of R1.
    (b)   Decrement the content of R3 by one.
    (c)   If (T1 = 1), transfer content of R1 to R0. If (T1 = 0 and T2 = 1), transfer content of R2 to R0.

8-7   ASM chart:
T0: Initial state: if (S = 1) then (RA ← Input A, RB ← Input B, go to T1).
T1: RA ← RA + (2's complement of RB), Borrow ← (complement of carry), go to T2.
T2: If (Borrow=0) then go to T0. If (Borrow=1) then RA ← (2's complement of RA), go to T0.

8-8   T0: AR ← input data, BR ← input data.
T1: if (AR [15]) = 1 (sign bit negative) then CR ← AR(shifted right, sign extension).
else if (AR = 0) then (CR ← 0).
else (positive non-zero) then (Overflow ← BR([15] ⊕ [14]), CR ← BR(shifted left).

8-9 $D_{T0} = T_2 + S'T_0$
$D_{T1} = ST_0 + (A_3A_4)'T_1$
$D_{T2} = A_3A_4T_1$

8-11 $D_A = A'B + Ax$
$D_B = A'B'x + A'By + xy$

8-14   ASM chart:
T0: (initial state) If S = 0 go back to state T0,
    If (S = 1) then BR ← multiplicand, AR ← multiplier, PR ← 0, go to T1.
T1: (check AR for zero) Z = 1 if AR = 0,
    if (Z = 1) then go back to T0 (done)
    If (Z = 0) then go to T2.
T2: PR ← PR + BR, AR ← AR − 1, go to T1.

8-15 $(2^n - 1)(2^n - 1) < (2^{2n} - 1)$ for $n \geq 1$

8-16   **(a)**   The maximum product size is 32 bits available in registers A and Q.
    (b)   P counter must have 5 bits to load 16 (binary 10000) initially.
    (c)   Z (zero) detection is generated with a 5-input NOR gate.

8-18 $2(n + 1)t$

8-19   MUX1: 0, 1, 1, Z'
MUX2: S, 0, 1, 0

8-21   **(a)** $E = 1$ **(b)** $E = 0$

8-22   A = 0110, B = 0010, C = 0000.

A * B = 1100	A | B = 0110	A && C = 0
A + B = 1000	A ∧ B = 0100	| A = 1
A − B = 0100	&A = 0	A < B = 0
~C = 1111	~| C = 1	A > B = 1
A & B = 0010	A || B = 1	A != B = 1

8-28

```
//Declare all inputs, outputs, and registers
    assign Z = ~|AR; //Z = 1 if AR = 0
    always @ (posedge CLK or negedge Clr)
        if (~Clr) pstate = T0;
        else pstate <= nstate;
    always @ (S or Z or pstate)
        case (pstate)
            T0: if (S) nstate = T1;
                else  nstate = T0;
            T1: if (Z) nstate = T0;
                else  nstate = T2;
            T2:     nstate = T1;
        endcase
    always @ (posedge CLK)
        case (pstate)
            T0: if (S)
                    begin
                      AR <= Ain;
                      BR <= Bin;
                      PR <= 0;
                    end
            T2:   begin
                      PR <= PR + BR;
                      AR <= AR - 8'b1;
                    end
        endcase
```

CHAPTER 9

9-2   Sequence of Y_1Y_2: 00, 00, 01, 11, 11, 01, 00.

9-3   **(d)**   When the input is 01, the output is 0. When the input is 10, the output is 1. Whenever the input assumes one of the other two combinations, the output retains its previous value.

9-4   **(c)**

	00	01	11	10
a	ⓐ, 0	b, 1	c, 1	d, 0
b	a, 0	ⓑ, 1	c, 1	ⓑ, 0
c	ⓒ, 1	b, 1	ⓒ, 1	d, 0
d	c, 1	b, 1	c, 1	ⓓ, 1

9-5   **(c)** $Y_1 = x_1'x_2 + x_2y_1$
$Y_2 = x_2 + x_1y_2$
$z = x_1x_2y_1' + x_1y_2'$

9-10 $S = x_2x_2'$
$R = x_1'x_2$

9-13   **(b)**   Two possible transition tables:

	00	01	11	10
a	ⓐ, 0	$b, -$	$-, -$	$e, -$
b	ⓑ, 1	ⓑ, 1	$-, -$	$d, -$
d	$a, -$	ⓓ, 1	$-, -$	ⓓ, 1
e	ⓔ, 1	$d, -$	$-, -$	ⓔ, 1

	00	01	11	10
a	ⓐ, 0	$b, -$	$-, -$	$b, -$
b	$c, -$	ⓑ, 1	$-, -$	ⓑ, 0
c	ⓒ, 1	$d, -$	$-, -$	$d, -$
d	$a, -$	ⓓ, 1	$-, -$	ⓓ, 1

9-18   3a: $(a, b)(c, d)(e, f, g, h)$
3b: $(a, e, f)(b, j)(c, d)(g, h)(k)$

9-20   Add states g and h to binary assignment.

	00	01	11	10
0	a	g	b	f
1	c	h	d	e

9-22 $F = A'D' + AC'D' + A'BC + A'CD'$

9-23 $Y = (x_1 + x_2')(x_2 + x_3)(x_1 + x_3)$

CHAPTER 10

10-1   Fan-out = 10; power dissipation = 18.75 mW; propagation delay = 3 ns; noise margin = 0.3 V

10-2   **(a)**   1.058 V   **(b)**   0.82 V   **(c)**   0.238 V

10-3 $I_B = 0.44$ mA, $I_{CS} = 2.4$ mA

10-4   **(a)**   2.4 mA   **(b)**   0.82 mA   **(c)**   2.4 + 0.82N   **(d)**   7.8   **(e)**   7

10-5   **(b)**   3.53   **(c)**   2.585 mA   **(d)**   16 mA   **(e)**   300 Ω

10-9   **(a)**   4.62 mA   **(b)**   4 mA

10-10   0.3 V

INDEX

License Agreement

SynaptiCAD

TestBencher Pro - DataSheet Pro - WaveFormer Pro - Timing Diagrammer Pro - VeriLogger Pro

Software License Agreement

- Read Before Use -

Please read and understand this license.

Note: Throughout this agreement, the word Software refers to the software product that you have licensed from SynaptiCAD.

You have purchased a license to use one of the following products: **TestBencher Pro, DataSheet Pro, WaveFormer Pro**, **VeriLogger Pro**, or **Timing Diagrammer Pro** software. The software is owned and remains the property of SynaptiCAD, is protected by international copyrights, and is transferred to the original purchaser and any subsequent owner of the Software media for their use only on the license terms set forth below. Opening the packaging for **TestBencher Pro, DataSheet Pro, WaveFormer Pro, VeriLogger Pro,** or **Timing Diagrammer Pro** and/or using either **TestBencher Pro, DataSheet Pro, WaveFormer Pro, VeriLogger Pro**, or **Timing Diagrammer Pro** indicates your acceptance of these terms. If you do not agree to all of the terms and conditions, return the unopened Software and manuals immediately for a full refund.

Use of the Software

- **SynaptiCAD** grants the original purchaser ("Licensee") the limited rights to possess and use the Software and User's Manual ("Software") for its intended purpose. Licensee agrees that the Software will be used solely for Licensee's internal purposes and that the Software will be installed on a single computer only. If the Software is installed on a networked system, or on a computer connected to a file server or other system that physically allows shared access to the Software, Licensee agrees to provide technical or procedural methods to prevent use of the Software by more than one user.

- One machine-readable copy of the Software may be made for BACKUP PURPOSES ONLY, and the copy shall display all proprietary notices, and be labeled externally to show that the backup copy is the property of SynaptiCAD, and that use is subject to this License.

- Use of the Software by any department, agency or other entity of the U.S. Federal Government is limited by the terms of the below "Rider for Governmental Entity Users."

- Licensee may transfer its rights under this License, provided that the party to whom such rights are transferred agrees to the terms and conditions of this License, and written notice is provided to SynaptiCAD. Upon such transfer, Licensee must transfer or destroy all copies of the Software.

- Except as expressly provided in this License, Licensee may not modify, reverse engineer, decompile, disassemble, distribute, sublicense, sell, rent, lease, give or in any other way transfer, by any means or in any medium, including telecommunications, the Software. Licensee will use its best efforts and take all reasonable steps to protect the Software from unauthorized use, copying or dissemination, and will maintain all proprietary notices intact.

LIMITED WARRANTY SynaptiCAD warrants the Software media to be free of defects in workmanship for a period of ninety days from the purchase. During this period, SynaptiCAD will replace at no cost any such media returned to SynaptiCAD, postage prepaid. This service is SynaptiCAD's sole liability under this warranty.

DISCLAIMER LICENSE FEES FOR THE SOFTWARE DO NOT INCLUDE ANY CONSIDERATION FOR ASSUMPTION OF RISK BY SYNAPTICAD, AND SYNAPTICAD DISCLAIMS ANY AND ALL LIABILITY FOR INCIDENTAL OR CONSEQUENTIAL DAMAGES ARISING OUT OF THE USE OR OPERATION OR INABILITY TO USE THE SOFTWARE, EVEN IF ANY OF THESE PARTIES HAVE BEEN ADVISED OF THE POSSIBILITIES OF SUCH DAMAGES. FURTHERMORE, LICENSEE INDEMNIFIES AND AGREES TO HOLD SYNAPTICAD HARMLESS FROM SUCH CLAIMS. THE ENTIRE RISK AS TO THE RESULTS AND PERFORMANCE OF THE SOFTWARE IS ASSUMED BY THE LICENSEE. THE WARRANTIES EXPRESSED IN THIS LICENSE ARE THE ONLY WARRANTIES MADE BY SYNAPTICAD AND ARE IN LIEU OF ALL OTHER WARRANTIES, EXPRESSED OR IMPLIED, INCLUDING BUT NOT LIMITED TO IMPLIED WARRANTIES OF MERCHANTABILITY AND OF FITNESS FOR A PAR-

TICULAR PURPOSE. THIS WARRANTY GIVES YOU SPECIFIED LEGAL RIGHTS, AND YOU MAY ALSO HAVE OTHER RIGHTS WHICH VARY FROM JURISDICTION TO JURISDICTION. SOME JURISDICTIONS DO NOT ALLOW THE EXCLUSION OR LIMITATION OF WARRANTIES, SO THE ABOVE LIMITATIONS OR EXCLUSIONS MAY NOT APPLY TO YOU.

Term

- This license is effective as of the time Licensee receives the Software, and shall continue in effect until Licensee ceases all use of the Software and returns or destroys all copies thereof, or until automatically terminated upon failure of Licensee to comply with any of the terms of this License.

General

- This License is the complete and exclusive statement of the parties' agreement. Should any provision of this license be held to be invalid by any court of competent jurisdiction, that provision will be enforced to the extent permissible, and the remainder of the License shall nonetheless remain in full force and effect. This License shall be controlled by the laws of the State of Virginia, and the United States of America.

Rider For U.S. Governmental Entity Users

This is a rider to **TestBencher Pro/ DataSheet Pro/ VeriLogger Pro/ WaveFormer Pro/ Timing Diagrammer Pro** SOFTWARE LICENSE AGREEMENT ("License") and shall take precedence over the License where a conflict occurs.

1. The Software was: developed at private expense (no portion was developed with government funds) and is a trade secret of SynaptiCAD and its licensor for all purposes of the Freedom of Information Act; is "commercial computer software" subject to limited utilization as provided in any contract between the vendor and the government entity; and in all respects is proprietary data belonging solely to SynaptiCAD and its licensor.

2. For units of the DoD, the Software is sold only with "Restricted Rights" as that term is defined in the DoD Supplement to DFAR 252.227-7013 (b)(3)(ii), and use, duplication or disclosure is subject to restrictions set forth in subparagraph (c)(1)(ii) of the Rights in Technical Data and Computer Software clause at 252.227-7013. Manufacturer: SynaptiCAD, PO Box 10608, Blacksburg, Va 24062-0608 USA.

3. If the Software was acquired under a GSA Schedule, the Government has agreed to refrain from changing or removing any insignia or lettering from the Software or Documentation or from producing copies of manuals or disks (except for backup purposes) and: (1) Title to and ownership of the Software and Documentation and any reproductions thereof shall remain with SynaptiCAD and its licensor; (2) use of the Software shall be limited to the facility for which it is acquired; and (3) if the use of the Software is discontinued at the original installation location and the Government wishes to use it at another location, it may do so by giving prior written notice to SynaptiCAD, specifying the new location site and class of computer.

4. Government personnel using the Software, other than under the DoD contract or GSA Schedule, are hereby on notice that use of the Software is subject to restrictions that are the same or similar to those specified above.